P9-DFL-022

Praise for

Elizabeth
A Biography of Britain's Queen

"One of the most pleasurable sections of Sarah Bradford's *Elizabeth: A Biography of Britain's Queen* consists of the early pages, where we are invited to imagine what it was like to be such a child, reared in simultaneous global fame and drastic seclusion, at a time when the monarchy, though reduced to chiefly ceremonial functions, still wore traces of prehistoric mystery and grandeur. Winston Churchill, who met Elizabeth for the first time when she was two and a half years old, presciently told his wife, 'She has an air of authority and reflectiveness astonishing in an infant.' On the much mooted relationship between Elizabeth and Mrs. Thatcher, Bradford is succinct: both women were 'highly professional and dedicated to their jobs,' but they came from different worlds . . . Bradford makes a sympathetic case for Charles, along the lines of his own possibly overabundant testimony: a sensitive child abused by a bullying father and distant, preoccupied mother was further hampered in his development by the isolating singularity of his position."

—JOHN UPDIKE, *The New Yorker*

"This new biography should find a place on your tea table. Bradford's extensive research . . . adds up to a portrait of a remarkable woman. Starting with a modest education, and given her strong preference for outdoor activities versus reading, the queen still comes across as an intelligent and capable executive."

—KIMBERLY B. MARLOWE, *The Seattle Times*

"Insightful . . . As queen of a people famous for emotional reserve, the frosty Elizabeth may represent the best, and worst, of the British character."

—CLARE MCHUGH, *People*

continued...

"[Bradford] is an intelligent and benign observer of her heroine's career and family's disasters. She gives a particularly sympathetic picture of the fate of Princess Margaret, an intelligent and lively girl who was refused her chance of happiness with Group Capt. Peter Townsend, a divorced man, by a stuffy palace staff, a reactionary archbishop and a conservative government, and who thereafter led a life of increasing frivolity and desperation. She also provides a persuasive picture of the route by which Elizabeth's children came to have such disastrous marriages."

—ALAN RYAN, *The Boston Sunday Globe*

"The secrets of the queen, her dysfunctional family—and even her dysfunctional pets—lay bared. Now, the world knows that her husband, Prince Philip, has committed adultery with 'a princess, a duchess, two or perhaps three countesses, two peeresses and a few untitled ladies.' Lady Bangor is a serious biographer . . . who has created a fascinatingly complex portrait of the queen and her court."

—AMY GAMERMAN, *The Wall Street Journal*

"With its evenhanded blend of public spectacle and intimate detail, Sarah Bradford's new biography, *Elizabeth*, is rumored to have nettled the Queen when published in Britain recently, but it is really the book she deserves. It's all here, the public occasions and ceremonies, the baffling indirections of court diplomacy, the knots and ravels of an intense family life. The book offers myriad fascinating examples of the fragility of the royal world. To read this book is to understand a great deal of the human dilemma."

—MARTHA DUFFY, *Time*

"This is not a spiteful book. On the contrary, Bradford . . . clearly admires her principle subject. But, where previous Elizabethan biographers have tended to be uncritical, she has produced an admirably objective, intelligent and highly absorbing portrait of the queen and her generally dysfunctional family."

—RAY MOSELEY, *Chicago Tribune*

SARAH BRADFORD

Elizabeth

A BIOGRAPHY OF BRITAIN'S QUEEN

Revised edition with
new Postscript

RIVERHEAD BOOKS, NEW YORK

Riverhead Books
Published by The Berkley Publishing Group
A division of Penguin Putnam Inc.
375 Hudson Street
New York, New York 10014

Copyright © 1996 by Sarah Bradford
Cover design by Michael Ian Kaye
Cover photograph by Cecil Beaton

All rights reserved. This book, or parts thereof, may not
be reproduced in any form without permission.

First published in Great Britain in 1996 by William Heinemann, London
First Farrar, Straus & Giroux hardcover edition published in 1996
First Riverhead trade paperback edition: May 1997

Visit our website at
www.penguinputnam.com

The Library of Congress Cataloging-in-Publication Data

Bradford, Sarah.
    Elizabeth : a biography of Britain's queen / Sarah Bradford.—
  1st Riverhead trade pbk. ed.
      p.   cm.
    Originally published: New York : Farrar, Straus & Giroux, 1996.
    Includes bibliographical references and index.
    ISBN 1-57322-600-9
    1. Elizabeth   II. Queen of Great Britain, 1926–   . 2. Great
  Britain—History—Elizabeth II, 1952—   . 3. Queens—Great Britain—
  Biography. I. Title.
  [DA590.B69   1997]
  941.085'092—dc20
  [B]   96-42966
                                                       CIP

Printed in the United States of America

10 9 8 7 6 5 4

For William

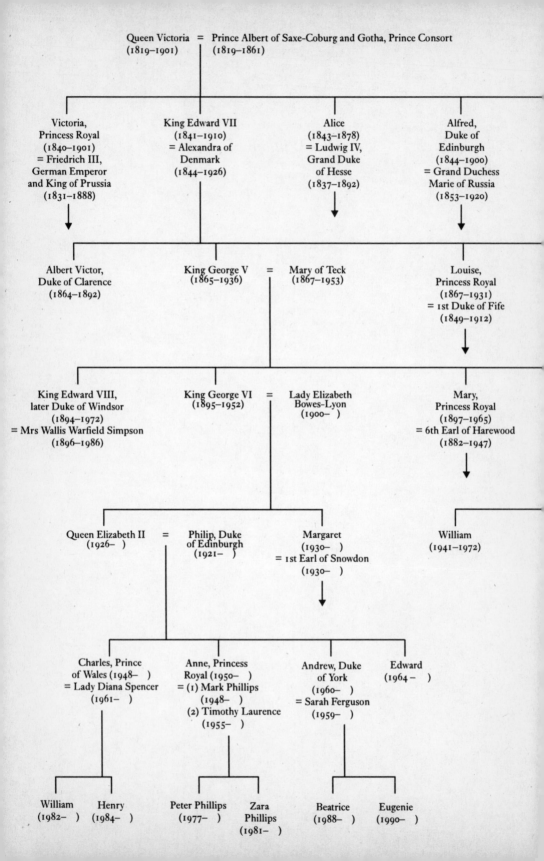

Queen Victoria = Prince Albert of Saxe-Coburg and Gotha, Prince Consort
(1819–1901)   (1819–1861)

Victoria,
Princess Royal
(1840–1901)
= Friedrich III,
German Emperor
and King of Prussia
(1831–1888)

King Edward VII
(1841–1910)
= Alexandra of
Denmark
(1844–1926)

Alice
(1843–1878)
= Ludwig IV,
Grand Duke
of Hesse
(1837–1892)

Alfred,
Duke of
Edinburgh
(1844–1900)
= Grand Duchess
Marie of Russia
(1853–1920)

Albert Victor,
Duke of Clarence
(1864–1892)

King George V
(1865–1936)

= Mary of Teck
(1867–1953)

Louise,
Princess Royal
(1867–1931)
= 1st Duke of Fife
(1849–1912)

King Edward VIII,
later Duke of Windsor
(1894–1972)
= Mrs Wallis Warfield Simpson
(1896–1986)

King George VI
(1895–1952)

= Lady Elizabeth
Bowes-Lyon
(1900–)

Mary,
Princess Royal
(1897–1965)
= 6th Earl of Harewood
(1882–1947)

Queen Elizabeth II
(1926–)

= Philip, Duke
of Edinburgh
(1921–)

Margaret
(1930–)
= 1st Earl of Snowdon
(1930–)

William
(1941–1972)

Charles, Prince
of Wales (1948–)
= Lady Diana Spencer
(1961–)

Anne, Princess
Royal (1950–)
= (1) Mark Phillips
(1948–)
(2) Timothy Laurence
(1955–)

Andrew, Duke
of York
(1960–)
= Sarah Ferguson
(1959–)

Edward
(1964 –)

William
(1982–)

Henry
(1984–)

Peter Phillips
(1977–)

Zara
Phillips
(1981–)

Beatrice
(1988–)

Eugenie
(1990–)

The House of Windsor

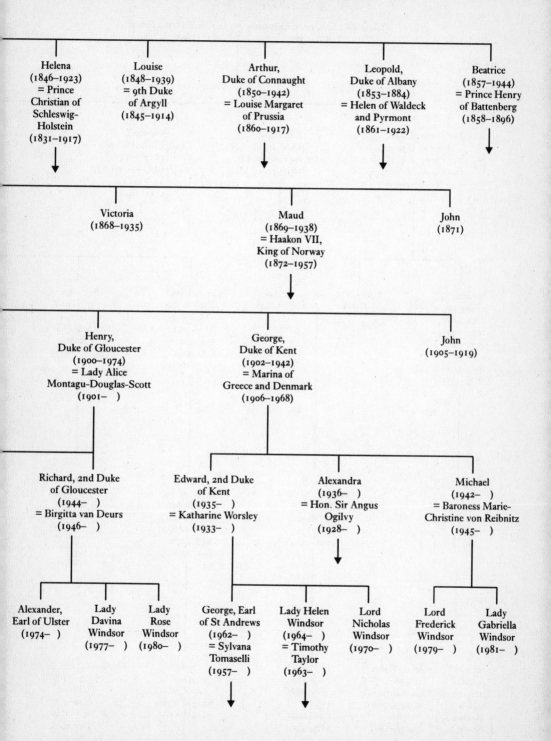

Helena
(1846–1923)
= Prince
Christian of
Schleswig-
Holstein
(1831–1917)

Louise
(1848–1939)
= 9th Duke
of Argyll
(1845–1914)

Arthur,
Duke of Connaught
(1850–1942)
= Louise Margaret
of Prussia
(1860–1917)

Leopold,
Duke of Albany
(1853–1884)
= Helen of Waldeck
and Pyrmont
(1861–1922)

Beatrice
(1857–1944)
= Prince Henry
of Battenberg
(1858–1896)

Victoria
(1868–1935)

Maud
(1869–1938)
= Haakon VII,
King of Norway
(1872–1957)

John
(1871)

Henry,
Duke of Gloucester
(1900–1974)
= Lady Alice
Montagu-Douglas-Scott
(1901–)

George,
Duke of Kent
(1902–1942)
= Marina of
Greece and Denmark
(1906–1968)

John
(1905–1919)

Richard, 2nd Duke
of Gloucester
(1944–)
= Birgitta van Deurs
(1946–)

Edward, 2nd Duke
of Kent
(1935–)
= Katharine Worsley
(1933–)

Alexandra
(1936–)
= Hon. Sir Angus
Ogilvy
(1928–)

Michael
(1942–)
= Baroness Marie-
Christine von Reibnitz
(1945–)

Alexander,
Earl of Ulster
(1974–)

Lady
Davina
Windsor
(1977–)

Lady
Rose
Windsor
(1980–)

George, Earl
of St Andrews
(1962–)
= Sylvana
Tomaselli
(1957–)

Lady Helen
Windsor
(1964–)
= Timothy
Taylor
(1963–)

Lord
Nicholas
Windsor
(1970–)

Lord
Frederick
Windsor
(1979–)

Lady
Gabriella
Windsor
(1981–)

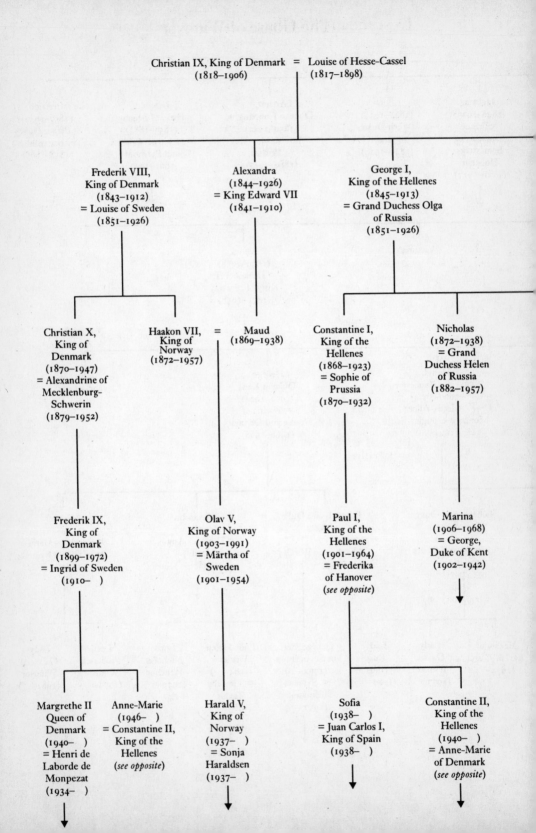

Christian IX, King of Denmark = Louise of Hesse-Cassel
(1818–1906)   (1817–1898)

Frederik VIII,
King of Denmark
(1843–1912)
= Louise of Sweden
(1851–1926)

Alexandra
(1844–1926)
= King Edward VII
(1841–1910)

George I,
King of the Hellenes
(1845–1913)
= Grand Duchess Olga
of Russia
(1851–1926)

Christian X,
King of
Denmark
(1870–1947)
= Alexandrine of
Mecklenburg-
Schwerin
(1879–1952)

Haakon VII,
King of
Norway
(1872–1957)

= Maud
(1869–1938)

Constantine I,
King of the
Hellenes
(1868–1923)
= Sophie of
Prussia
(1870–1932)

Nicholas
(1872–1938)
= Grand
Duchess Helen
of Russia
(1882–1957)

Frederik IX,
King of
Denmark
(1899–1972)
= Ingrid of Sweden
(1910–)

Olav V,
King of Norway
(1903–1991)
= Märtha of
Sweden
(1901–1954)

Paul I,
King of the
Hellenes
(1901–1964)
= Frederika
of Hanover
(*see opposite*)

Marina
(1906–1968)
= George,
Duke of Kent
(1902–1942)

Margrethe II
Queen of
Denmark
(1940–)
= Henri de
Laborde de
Monpezat
(1934–)

Anne-Marie
(1946–)
= Constantine II,
King of the
Hellenes
(*see opposite*)

Harald V,
King of
Norway
(1937–)
= Sonja
Haraldsen
(1937–)

Sofia
(1938–)
= Juan Carlos I,
King of Spain
(1938–)

Constantine II,
King of the
Hellenes
(1940–)
= Anne-Marie
of Denmark
(*see opposite*)

Descendants of Christian IX of Denmark

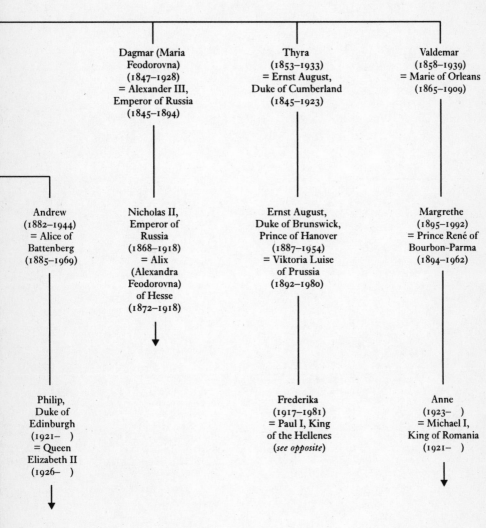

Dagmar (Maria
Feodorovna)
(1847–1928)
= Alexander III,
Emperor of Russia
(1845–1894)

Thyra
(1853–1933)
= Ernst August,
Duke of Cumberland
(1845–1923)

Valdemar
(1858–1939)
= Marie of Orleans
(1865–1909)

Andrew
(1882–1944)
= Alice of
Battenberg
(1885–1969)

Nicholas II,
Emperor of
Russia
(1868–1918)
= Alix
(Alexandra
Feodorovna)
of Hesse
(1872–1918)

Ernst August,
Duke of Brunswick,
Prince of Hanover
(1887–1954)
= Viktoria Luise
of Prussia
(1892–1980)

Margrethe
(1895–1992)
= Prince René of
Bourbon-Parma
(1894–1962)

Philip,
Duke of
Edinburgh
(1921–   )
= Queen
Elizabeth II
(1926–   )

Frederika
(1917–1981)
= Paul I, King
of the Hellenes
(*see opposite*)

Anne
(1923–   )
= Michael I,
King of Romania
(1921–   )

Contents

List of Illustrations ix

1 Destiny 1
2 Princess in an Ivory Tower 26
3 Heiress 58
4 Windsor War 86
5 A Princely Marriage 111
6 The Edinburghs 133
7 Sovereign Lady 167
8 Dark Princess 193
9 'The World's Sweetheart' 215
10 Tweed and Diamonds 243
11 Mountbatten-Windsor 264
12 Advise, Consult and Warn 294
13 Head of the Family 325
14 Daylight upon Magic 353
15 Extended Family 392
16 Grim Fairy-Tales 429
17 Family at War 464
18 Elizabeth R 494
Epilogue 524
Postscript 529

Acknowledgements 533
Sources 536
Select Bibliography 549
Index 553

List of Illustrations

First black and white plate section

Queen Victoria and her York great-grandchildren at Osborne, 1900.
   (Hulton Deutsch)
Elizabeth's christening, 29 May 1926. *(Camera Press)*
Elizabeth aged 23 months with 'Allah' Knight. *(Hulton Deutsch)*
The young Elizabeth congratulates the winner at a horse show.
   (Hulton Deutsch)
The first corgi: Elizabeth and friend, July 1936. *(Hulton Deutsch)*
Wallis Warfield Simpson in 1936. *(Hulton Deutsch)*
Edward as Prince of Wales, August 1932. *(Hulton Deutsch)*
Beside the swimming-pool at Fort Belvedere. *(Weidenfeld & Nicolson
   Archives)*
Sir Alan 'Tommy' Lascelles, January 1948. *(Hulton Deutsch)*
Returning from their first trip on the London Underground:
   Elizabeth with Lady Helen Graham, and Margaret with Marion
   Crawford, May 1939. *(Camera Press)*
The first meeting: Elizabeth and Philip at Dartmouth Royal Naval
   College, July 1939. *(Hulton Deutsch)*
Second Subaltern Elizabeth Alexandra Mary Windsor, April 1945.
   (Hulton Deutsch)
'Us four' at Royal Lodge, Windsor, 8 July 1946. *(Hulton Deutsch)*
Elizabeth and Margaret in deck games with officers on board HMS
   Vanguard, February 1947. *(Popperfoto)*
Stag night at the Dorchester: Philip and Mountbatten joking with
   fellow naval officers, 19 November 1947. *(Hulton Deutsch)*
Elizabeth and Philip pose for their wedding photograph in the
   Throne Room at Buckingham Palace, 20 November 1947. *(Camera
   Press)*
Honeymoon at Broadlands. *(Hulton Deutsch)*

Elizabeth with Harry S. Truman in Washington, 3 November 1951.
  (Popperfoto)
Elizabeth with Prince Charles Philip Arthur George, 21 December
  1948. *(Cecil Beaton/Hulton Deutsch)*
Elizabeth at London airport, greeted by Winston Churchill, Clement
  Attlee, Anthony Eden and Lord Woolton, 7 February 1952.
  (Hulton Deutsch)

Second black and white plate section

Coronation Day, 2 June 1953. *(Cecil Beaton/Victoria & Albert
  Museum, London)*
Peter Townsend with Margaret, Elizabeth and the royal party at
  Badminton in 1953. *(Hulton Deutsch)*
Margaret and Tony Armstrong-Jones pose for an engagement
  photograph at the Royal Lodge, Windsor, February 1960. *(Hulton
  Deutsch)*
Elizabeth with Anne and Charles in the early 1950s. *(Camera Press)*
Self-portrait by Baron Henry Stirling Nahum, *c*. 1956. *(Camera Press)*
Philip with his Private Secretary, Commander Michael Parker, at
  Gibraltar airport, 6 February 1957. *(Mirror Syndication
  International)*
'Bobo' – Margaret MacDonald. *(Hulton Deutsch)*
Lord Plunket, February 1955. *(Popperfoto)*
Lt. Col. the Hon. Martin Charteris, November 1961. *(Camera Press)*
Elizabeth with her Private Secretary, Sir Michael Adeane, arriving at
  the King Edward VII Hospital, 18 October 1963. *(Hulton Deutsch)*
Lady Susan Hussey. *(Tim Graham)*
Robin Janvrin and Sir Robert Fellowes, *c*. 1992. *(Photographers
  International Ltd)*
David George Coke Patrick Ogilvy, 13th Earl of Airlie. *(Tim Graham)*
Philip, Elizabeth, Andrew, Edward, Anne and Charles at Balmoral in
  1972. *(Patrick Lichfield/Camera Press)*
Anne and Captain Mark Phillips in the Corridor at Windsor Castle,
  November 1973. *(Norman Parkinson/Camera Press)*
Queen Elizabeth the Queen Mother, the Duke and Duchess of
  Gloucester, the Duke and Duchess of Windsor and Elizabeth, at
  the unveiling of a memorial plaque to Queen Mary, 7 June 1967.
  (Popperfoto)

A trio of Mountbattens. *(Mirror Syndication International)*

The Prince and Princess of Wales on honeymoon at Balmoral in 1981. *(Tim Graham)*

The Prince of Wales and Camilla Parker Bowles in 1975. *(Rex Features)*

Colour plate section

Elizabeth on a walkabout during the Jubilee summer of 1977. *(Hulton Deutsch)*

Elizabeth being carried by the islanders of Tuvalu during her tour of the South Pacific in 1982. *(Hulton Deutsch)*

Elizabeth with her racing manager and old friend, Lord Porchester, at the Derby, June 1985. *(Tim Graham)*

State banquet during the 1989 Commonwealth Conference in Kuala Lumpar, Malaysia. *(Tim Graham)*

Elizabeth and President Ronald Reagan on her state visit, March 1983. *(Hulton Deutsch)*

Elizabeth and Philip with President Nelson Mandela in Capetown, 20 March 1995. *(Tim Graham)*

Balmoral Castle, Aberdeenshire, Scotland. *(Tim Graham)*

Sandringham House, Norfolk, England. *(Tim Graham)*

Windsor Castle ablaze, 30 November 1992. *(Tim Graham)*

Elizabeth reviews the wreckage of her childhood home. *(Tim Graham)*.

Elizabeth and Philip with their senior grandchildren. *(Karsh of Ottawa/Camera Press)*

Elizabeth and her Prime Ministers. *(Tim Graham)*

Charles, Diana, Sarah and Andrew on a skiing holiday in 1987. *(Hulton Deutsch)*

Diana at the Serpentine Gallery, 29 June 1994. *(Camera Press)*

Elizabeth with the Queen Mother and Margaret watching the fly-past during the VE Day Commemoration, 8 May 1995. *(Camera Press)*

Elizabeth on her way to Edinburgh by Intercity, June 1991. *(BBC Picture Archive)*

Elizabeth aged sixty-nine in 1995. *(Camera Press)*

I

Destiny

'In a way I didn't have an apprenticeship, my father died much too young – It was all very sudden, kind of taking on and making the best job you can. It's a question of just maturing into what you're doing and accepting that here you are and it's your fate. I think continuity is very important. It is a job for life.'

Elizabeth II on television, EIIR

On a bitterly cold early February afternoon in 1952 a British Overseas Airways Corporation Argonaut aircraft taxied to a halt at London's Heathrow Airport. A reception line of members of the royal family and the British Government, among them the unmistakable figure of Winston Churchill, stood waiting on the tarmac. All were dressed in black mourning for the late King; despite the cold wind the men were hatless in honour of their new Queen. Aboard the aircraft a slim, young woman of twenty-five, her skin lightly tanned by the African sun, looked out of the window. Behind the line of men in dark overcoats ranged up to greet her loomed the black bulk of the ancient royal Daimlers. 'Oh,' she said, a momentary gleam of grim humour lighting her seriousness, 'I see they've brought the hearses.' She had waited to the last moment before donning a black coat and hat, as if to put off for as long as she could the moment of formal acknowledgement that her father was dead and that what private life she had had was forever over. As she stepped out to greet the members of her administration, she became an icon with a dual role: executive woman and symbol of her country first, wife and mother second. She had accepted her destiny.

Princess Elizabeth Alexandra Mary of York was just ten years and eight months old on Thursday, 10 December 1936, when she realised

that she would almost certainly be Queen of Great Britain. Tension
had been building up over the dark December days as her mother lay
ill with influenza in her third-floor bedroom and her father hurried in
and out of the house, a haunted look on his face, the muscles in his
cheek twitching with nerves. Outside the house, No. 145 Piccadilly,
silent crowds gathered waiting to hear if and when Elizabeth's father,
Prince Albert, Duke of York, would succeed his older brother, King
Edward VIII, Elizabeth's 'Uncle David', as King of Great Britain,
Emperor of India, King of the Dominions of Australia, Canada, South
Africa and New Zealand and titular head of the great British Empire
on which the sun never set.

Elizabeth learned the truth from a servant; everyone else was too
traumatised to think of keeping her informed of what was seen as one
of the most disgraceful and dangerous episodes in the history of the
royal family: her uncle had that morning abdicated his throne to
marry an American divorcée; her father, second son of the late King
George V, would be King in his place. As her father's eldest child,
Elizabeth was first in line to succeed him. Even at the age of ten, she
knew that this was not an occasion for celebration from either her own
personal point of view or that of her family, the House of Windsor.
She had seen her father's distress at the prospect of becoming King
and she had already had personal experience of the glass wall which
divides royalty from the rest of mankind. According to one source,
from that day she prayed nightly for the birth of a brother to supersede
her in the royal succession. She was already sufficiently trained in the
long history of her family and the British monarchy to know that a
voluntary abdication was without precedent. Two of her ancestors,
Charles I and James II, had been forced off the throne, but their
bloodline, even if abruptly diverted, had returned with their descendants. Legitimacy of descent was the basis of the dynastic right by
which her family held the British throne. It was the key to her own
extraordinary destiny. Elizabeth knew that this was a turning-point in
her life. Where any ordinary child would have headed the daily diary
she kept simply with the date, when Elizabeth sat down to write up
her swimming lesson notes for 10 December 1936, she headed her
entry 'Abdication Day'.

A complex web of bloodlines on her father's side traced Elizabeth's
descent back to the Saxon Kings of Wessex, who had emerged supreme
over the various Germanic tribes, invaders of the province of Roman
Britain after the departure of the imperial troops in the mid-fifth

century AD. The early Kings had claimed descent from Woden, the Saxon God of War, as justification for their right to rule; later, when they converted to Christianity, they sanctified their claims as the Lord's Anointed, Christ's deputies on earth. Elizabeth's most famous Saxon ancestor, Alfred the Great, was confirmed in Rome at the age of five by Pope Leo IV in 853 AD; and for some seven hundred years the Kings of England acknowledged papal supremacy. Except for the brief Cromwellian interregnum between 1649 and 1660, the descendants of Egbert, King of Wessex (802–39), have reigned continuously in Britain for nearly twelve hundred years. A succession of dynasties had followed the Saxons – Normans, Plantagenets, Tudors, Stuarts and finally, in 1714, Princess Elizabeth's own immediate ancestors, the Hanoverians. They were thoroughly German, but a thin bloodline of legitimacy took them back to another Elizabeth who was both Tudor and Stuart, James I's daughter, the Winter Queen.

By then the British people as represented (though not yet in any real democratic sense) by Parliament had laid down the limits of royal power. Power lay with the people in Parliament; the British monarchy was constitutional and Protestant. The third Hanoverian king, George III, had surrendered a large part of Crown property in return for an annual allowance from Parliament, the Civil List, an arrangement which definitively put his descendants in the hands of their subjects. Although the kings' powers sounded almost unlimited – they were supreme governors of the Church of England and heads of the armed forces, enjoying the right to appoint prime ministers and dissolve Parliaments – in actual fact all executive power was exercised by what was politely termed 'His (or Her) Majesty's Government'. For all the high-sounding titles of the royal household, many of them dating from the days when kings or queens held the real power of decision over their subjects' lives, the monarchs were in fact only very important cogs in a complicated machinery of government, control of which was increasingly slipping into democratic hands. Since all the most glamorous and valuable parts of their inheritance, the royal collections and the royal palaces, were now inalienable, the British royal family were in essence hereditary heads of state, dependent in the last instance on the will of their subjects to sustain them in that position.

The reality of their situation had taken some time to sink in. The first two Hanoverian kings had made no attempt to endear themselves to the population at large; George I spoke no English at all while George II spoke it badly. George III, who contrived to lose the

American colonies, was the first British monarch of the Hanoverian dynasty to be regarded with any affection by his people. He was simple and approachable, an engaging man with a taste and a talent for art and music, who formed one of the great royal collections, but his later life and reign were overshadowed by a terrible and agonising rare genetic disease, porphyria, which induced unpredictable and increasingly prolonged bouts of insanity. George III led an admirably domestic life with his Queen Charlotte, the first of his dynasty to do so, but as a role model for the royal family it was short-lived. Mistresses, bastards and extravagance characterised the lives of most of his sons. George IV, who had inherited his father's taste and was responsible for improving Windsor Castle, secretly married a Catholic, Mrs Fitzherbert, and subsequently a German princess, Caroline, from whom he later parted amidst resounding scandal. Caricatures of George IV exceeded in violence anything subsequently produced on the royal family; two of the most vicious artists had to be bought off. His brother, William IV, nicknamed 'Silly Billy', after forty years living with a common-law wife, married at the last moment in the hope of producing an heir, but perhaps fortunately for the subsequent history of the British monarchy, he failed.

His niece, Victoria, Elizabeth's great-great-grandmother, daughter of his younger brother, Edward, Duke of Kent (who had hastily dropped his French mistress and married a Saxe-Coburg princess for the same reason), had scarcely a drop of English blood in her veins. She was even younger than Elizabeth, only eighteen when she succeeded to the throne on her uncle William's death in 1837; by the time she died more than sixty-four years later, her large family, dynastic skills and powerful personality had made her 'the grandmother of Europe'. She was to be a role model for the young Elizabeth when she became Queen; Victoria's solemn promise on the morning of her accession, 'I will be good,' could have been echoed by her great-great-granddaughter. Victoria, like Elizabeth, was small but had exceptional self-possession and natural dignity to compensate for it. In Victoria's case (but not Elizabeth's), the self-possession was a mask concealing a temperament so highly-strung that her husband, Prince Albert (another Saxe-Coburg), confided that he sometimes feared for her sanity, suspecting that she might have inherited the madness of her grandfather George III (in fact, Victoria was a carrier of another genetic disease, haemophilia). Victoria was a passionate and demanding wife — she must, one royal historian told Harold Nicolson, official biographer to George V, 'have been great fun in bed'. Victoria liked sex but disliked childbirth and pregnancy; none the less, in twenty-two years of marriage she produced nine children, all of whom survived to adulthood. All marriage partners were carefully vetted for them by their mother, producing a raft of grandchildren including the German Kaiser, Wilhelm II.

When Albert died, presumably of typhoid, at Windsor Castle on 14 December 1861, Victoria withdrew into the deepest mourning. She was shy and disliked 'Society' with a capital 'S'; after Albert's death she appeared as little as she could in public, refusing even to perform state duties like the formal opening of Parliament. She spent as much time as she could in the Highlands at Balmoral, the holiday home that she and Albert had built, retreating to ever more remote lodges in the hills, where she spent hours painting watercolours or writing up her journals. Her reclusive life made her unpopular; she was seen not to be performing her public duties and rumours of her close relationship with her Scottish servant, John Brown, spread through society. In June 1867 the Cabinet went so far as to warn Victoria about it and in fashionable drawing-rooms the Queen was referred to as 'Mrs Brown'. There has never been any evidence that the Queen married John Brown; her strong sense of royalty made it very unlikely that she would do so. Brown was, however, allowed latitude with the Queen that no one else in her family or household would ever have been given. One of her Private Secretaries told his wife of seeing the Queen get up from the table after dinner and, with the utmost unconcern, step gracefully over the prostrate figure of John Brown, lying dead drunk on the floor behind her chair. Rumours of even more intimate behaviour, with Brown being seen entering the Queen's bedroom at night, circulated among the aristocratic families of the Queen's ladies-in-waiting, and, according to the Queen's doctor, she left instructions that a photograph of Brown should be placed in her hand when she was laid in her coffin. After her death, her son, Edward VII, who had detested Brown, destroyed several statues of him, and when her grandson succeeded as George V he had the last remaining statue, which had stood outside Brown's house at Balmoral, removed to an obscure position in the woods.

Victoria was exceptionally free from class or racial prejudice for a woman of her time. She was indulgent not only to Brown and his fellow Highlanders at Balmoral but also to her Indian servant, Abdul Karim, known as 'the Munshi', for whom she built a house at Balmoral in the style of an Indian bungalow to make him feel at home. She was deeply concerned when her son, the Prince of Wales, reported from India the snobbish treatment of Indians by British military and colonial officials. At a time when anti-Semitism was widespread in English society, the Queen preferred Benjamin Disraeli to any of her aristocratic Prime Ministers (with the exception of Lord Melbourne, the father-figure of her youth). Although prudish and dictatorial, she was also kind and humane. When the daughter of one of her German princely relations was seduced and made pregnant by a footman, Queen Victoria alone supported her. She hated snobbish behaviour and particularly the macho bullyboy attitudes – 'so-called manliness' she termed it – to be found in British educational establishments. When her son Prince Arthur was sent to the Royal Military Academy at Woolwich, the Queen 'dreaded him becoming harsh and stuck up; she distrusted the regular type of young officer'.[1] Despite her secluded life, Victoria's views on political and social questions usually coincided with those of the mass of her subjects. The high aristocrat, Lord Salisbury, who served as her Foreign Secretary and Prime Minister, used her as his sounding-board for public opinion: 'I have always felt', he wrote, 'that when I knew what the Queen thought, I knew pretty certainly what view her subjects would take, and especially the middle class of her subjects.'[2]

That the Queen was neither snobbish nor particularly sympathetic towards the aristocratic point of view did not, however, imply that she did not have a strong sense of her own position. To her, royalty was a caste apart. 'In our position which is so totally different from other people's,' she advised her eldest daughter, the Crown Princess of Germany, 'one ought not to be left alone, without a Child or a Relation.' There is a story, possibly apocryphal, of a royal doctor congratulating Queen Victoria on the birth of the Prince of Wales – 'a fine boy, ma'am,' he said. 'Prince, you mean,' was the weak but frosty reply. To Victoria and her royal relations, the world was simply divided into two groups, royalty and non-royalty. An observer of the court of her grandson, George V, told Harold Nicolson that in his opinion royalties never saw any difference or gradation between non-royalties, and that to them the Duke of Devonshire was much the same as any other commoner.

The members of a caste, according to the dictionary, are socially equal, have the same religious rites, generally follow the same occupation or profession, and have no social intercourse with those of another caste. Victoria's son and heir, Edward VII, certainly regarded kingship as a profession. When pressure was put on him by Germany and Italy to restore diplomatic relations with Serbia after the assassination in 1903 of the King and Queen, Edward claimed that British public opinion was too outraged to accept it, adding:

> I have another, and, so to say, a personal reason. My profession is to be King. King Alexander was also by profession a King. I cannot be indifferent to the assassination of a member of my profession . . . We should be obliged to shut up our businesses if we, the kings, were to consider the assassination of kings as of no consequence at all . . .[3]

Another feature of a profession or caste, which, like royalty, depends so greatly on ritual and ceremonial as its distinguishing features, is an obsession with outward form. The males of the House of Windsor since the reign of George IV have been fanatical on the subject of clothes. Even Queen Victoria, who herself wore a simple black dress and widow's cap after the death of Albert, was aware of its importance in sending signals to the public at large: '. . . it gives also the one outward sign from which people in general can and often do judge upon the *inward* state of mind and feeling of a person,' she wrote to Edward, aged ten; 'for this they all see, while the other they cannot see. On that account it is of some importance particularly in persons of high rank.'

Edward took his mother's advice very much to heart. At a public drawing-room at Buckingham Palace, he raged out loud at the Prime Minister, the absent-minded Lord Salisbury, who appeared in an odd mixture of clothing, having dressed in a hurry without the help of his valet. 'Here is Europe in a turmoil,' he shouted, 'twenty ambassadors and ministers looking on – what will they think – what *can* they think of a Prime Minister who can't put on his clothes?' A good deal of the battleground between Edward's son, George V, and George's own heir, Edward, Prince of Wales, later Edward VIII and Duke of Windsor, raged over the latter's innovations in dress. To George V, his son's thickly knotted ties, Fair Isle sweaters, trouser turn-ups and fondness for dinner jackets as opposed to tails, were the outward sign of his inner rejection of traditional values. Elizabeth's father, George VI, though more conservatively dressed than his brother, was intensely interested in clothes, spent hours with his tailors, suggested to the royal couturier Norman Hartnell that he design crinolines copied from

Winterhalter portraits to create a new image for Queen Elizabeth, and in the last week of his life spent time writing a long letter to the Chancellor of the Order of the Garter describing his own design for special boots and trousers to be worn with the Order. Elizabeth herself, although not really interested in clothes, has inherited the family sharp eye for correct detail in dress and decorations. 'How dull the royal family is,' the sharp-tongued Margot Asquith complained of George V's court, 'only interested in buttons and things.'

By the end of her reign in 1901 Victoria had immeasurably raised the status of the British monarchy in the public eye. The virtuous domestic image of her life with Albert had blotted out the memory of the disreputable sons of George III, her 'wicked uncles', with their extravagance, their mistresses and illegitimate children, and the scandal of George IV's divorce from his wife, Queen Caroline. Victoria had taken great care over her children's marriages and all but two had been successful. Prince Alfred, Duke of Edinburgh, had made a grand marriage with the Tsar's daughter, the Grand Duchess Marie, but the two did not get on; he died of cancer probably aggravated by addiction to alcohol, while she became so anti-British that she refused to allow their beautiful daughter, Marie, to contemplate marriage with Victoria's grandson, George, preferring to marry her off to a dull Hohenzollern who succeeded to the doubtful throne of Romania. Princess Louise married a commoner (i.e. a non-royal), the Marquis of Lorne, heir to the dukedom of Argyll, but their marriage ended in separation.

Victoria's principal problem, one which had become a family tradition since the arrival of the Hanoverians, was with the Prince of Wales. The position of the male heir to the throne, who, because of his status, cannot take an ordinary office job and yet has to wait until his parent dies before he can take on the work he is destined for, is a particularly difficult one. Just because he is the heir, his parents' expectations of him are high and it is difficult for him to win their approval. At the same time as he has virtually nothing meaningful to occupy his time, he is fawned on and flattered by everyone and invariably lands in trouble, usually sexual. Victoria's eldest son, the future Edward VII, Prince Albert Edward (known as 'Bertie' in the family), was no exception to the rule. His parents were in a chronic state of disappointment with him since childhood; he fell short of the academic standards they expected of him and showed a notable lack of enthusiasm for the rigorous educational programme they set up for him. Moreover, as he grew up it became obvious to them that he was a dedicated sensualist; his first sexual exploit with an actress when he was a young officer stationed at the Curragh in Dublin finished him irrevocably in his parents' eyes. Victoria, quite unfairly, blamed the distress this episode caused for Albert's death some months later. She married off the Prince as soon as possible to Princess Alexandra of Denmark.

Alexandra was beautiful, chic, empty-headed, affectionate, spoiled and strong-willed; like the twentieth-century Lady Diana Spencer, her beauty, charm and elegance made her an instant hit with the British public. She too had a strong affinity with children and the sick, adored birds and animals and kept her figure lithe with gymnastics. Increasing deafness made her withdraw from social life, but she retained her beauty until old age with carefully enamelled make-up, wigs which she cheerfully admitted to wearing, and hats with veils which helped to conceal her age. Bertie's marriage to Alexandra did not stop him indulging in a succession of mistresses, usually the wives of his friends but also, famously, the actress Lillie Langtry. His wife endured these serial affairs with great dignity; unlike the present Princess of Wales, she never made a scene, even generously allowing her husband's last mistress, the Hon. Mrs George Keppel, to visit him when he was dying. The British public was not so forbearing on her behalf and Bertie was once hissed at Ascot racecourse by the crowd, angry at one of his more public infidelities. There were scandals; on one occasion he had to take the witness stand in a divorce case, while the Tranby Croft affair involved cheating at baccarat at a house where he happened to be spending the weekend. His appetite for eating equalled his taste for women; he devoured huge quantities of food at short intervals preceded and followed by innumerable large cigars. At Sandringham, the country estate which he acquired in 1866 and where his mother fondly hoped he would lead a quiet life far from the temptations of London, he held enormous shooting-parties for his friends during which hundreds of pheasants would be killed in a day. He enjoyed racing and breeding racehorses, two of which won the Derby, and had the family passion for clothes. His Marlborough House set of friends (named after his London residence) – sporting 'swells' as they were called, dandies and court jesters – was a conspicuously alternative court to the hushed atmosphere and impenetrable respectability of his mother's household.

Yet on his mother's death in January 1901, Edward, to everyone's surprise, proved to be a successful King. He did not give up women (although more or less limiting himself to one permanent mistress, Alice Keppel), eating or racing, but he showed extraordinary dexterity in diplomacy, using his personal influence to establish the Entente Cordiale between England and France. His one – important – failure was with his nephew, the Kaiser, who had adored his grandmother, Queen Victoria, but detested his uncle Edward. The loathing was mutual, the animosity both personal and political. On Kaiser Wilhelm II's side there was envy of Edward's great international prestige, of the size of the British Empire and of the power of the British Navy. Edward could not forgive Wilhelm for his brutal treatment of his mother, Victoria (Edward's sister), and disliked his boorish behaviour on his English visits. Some people thought that the First World War might not have broken out had Edward VII still been alive, but, given his antipathy towards his German nephew, this must be an overestimate of his power to prevent it.

When Edward died in May 1910, a kind fate had already removed from the scene his eldest son, the Duke of Clarence, known as 'Eddy', a thoroughly unsatisfactory young man who would have been a disaster as king. Eddy was born prematurely at seven months and as he grew up it became obvious that, although amiable, he was stupid and indolent and interested only in polo and sex. A combination of naïveté and lust led to his being unwittingly involved in a major scandal, the Cleveland Street case. This concerned a homosexual brothel in which the male prostitutes were telegraph boys whose clients included members of Prince Eddy's father's own household. Prince Eddy, apparently, had visited the place in the hope of seeing 'poses plastiques', tableaux of naked women, the Victorian equivalent of a strip show. The case was hushed up with difficulty and probably gave rise to later rumours that the serial killer of prostitutes, 'Jack the Ripper', was in fact the Duke of Clarence. Prince Eddy proceeded to annoy his family by falling in love with a princess, Hélène of France, whose Catholic religion put her out of bounds as a marriage prospect. He was then steered in the direction of a more suitable girl, Princess May of Teck, who was to become the future Queen Mary and Elizabeth's grandmother.

Princess May, christened Victoria Mary but always known as 'May', was a shy, responsible girl, small but statuesque, with a fine complexion, blue eyes and blonde hair, neither pretty nor plain, with slightly canine looks as she grew older which persisted in her descendants, notably George VI and his daughter, Princess Elizabeth. She was emotionally inhibited and suffered from an inferiority complex derived from the consciousness that within the extremely status-conscious circle of European royalty she was considered insufficiently royal. Although her mother, Princess Mary Adelaide, as a granddaughter of George III through her father, Adolphus, Duke of Cambridge, was a first cousin of Queen Victoria, her father, Prince Franz, Duke of Teck, was the son of Duke Alexander of Württemberg by his morganatic marriage to the Hungarian countess, Claudine Rhèdey, an aristocrat but not a royal, whose family came from Szent-György in Transylvania and who died dramatically, trampled to death, when her horse threw her in front of a cavalry charge at a military review. Beyond that, Princess May was always embarrassed by her parents. Her mother was a complete extrovert who revelled in rich food (her weight at the age of twenty-four was computed by the American Ambassador to the Court of St James's to be 250lb). At dancing classes Princess May would be mortified to see her enormous mother occupying not one but two of the gilded chairs provided for spectators. She was equally embarrassed by the public rows which her father would regularly create at some imagined slight. Franz of Teck with his dark good looks had also brought with him a dubious heritage. He was liable to sudden fits of rage which, allied to the splenetic Hanoverian temperament, were to produce the 'gnashes' of his grandson, George VI, and the temper of his great-great-grandson, Charles, Prince of Wales. Teck and Mary Adelaide were virtually penniless, but both were irresponsibly extravagant; their consequent chronic poverty was induced by their fixed conviction that they should live in a style to which their birth entitled them. At one point the Tecks were obliged to resort to the time-honoured practice of aristocratic and not-so-aristocratic English debtors – living abroad. They retreated to Florence for some years before returning to England to be supported, to some extent, by Mary Adelaide's cousin, Queen Victoria. For their conscientious daughter, some of the humiliation this caused her came from the utter obliviousness her parents showed to their shortcomings. Opening a church fete in Kensington, Princess Mary Adelaide referred cheerfully to 'Mr Barker [a prominent local shopkeeper] to whom we owe so much'.

Queen Victoria, a perceptive judge of human nature, was quite unworried by May's lack of money and her 'tainted' blood, approving of her after a ten-day inspection at Balmoral in November 1891 as 'a superior girl – quiet and reserved *till* you know her well – ... & so sensible and unfrivolous'. May was duly betrothed to the future King

of England in the unpromising form of Prince Eddy. Shortly before
their wedding, however, Eddy went down with influenza while
shooting at Sandringham, and died of pneumonia on 14 January 1892,
his delirious shouts of 'Hélène, Hélène,' echoing in the ears of his
disconsolate fiancée. Eddy's death sent a shock-wave through the royal
family; a match was soon arranged between Princess May and Eddy's
younger brother, Prince George. They were engaged on 3 May 1893
and married two months later. May, Queen Victoria noted, 'had never
been in love with Eddy'. People thought her marriage to Prince
George merely one of convenience, but in fact it was based on deep
love and a similarity of character and tastes. 'People only said I
married you out of pity and sympathy,' Prince George wrote to her
later, 'that shows how little the world really knows what it is talking
about.'

Prince George, who succeeded his father as King George V, was
short and slight, with the fair hair and slightly prominent china-blue
eyes characteristic of the Hanoverians. He sported a trim naval officer's
beard and, having spent most of his formative years in the Navy, his
spiritual home, he had acquired its mannerisms and outlook, a fondness
for sharp expletives – 'damn fool' being his favourite – and salty wardroom jokes. Every day, morning and evening, he would tap the
barometer to check the weather and a large part of the daily diary
which he kept in his straggling, uneducated hand would be dedicated
to a description of the weather. He was talkative, even garrulous, and
had the reputation of never allowing his government ministers a word
in when they came to see him. He was, according to his biographer,
fundamentally a limited man, but extraordinarily loyal, straightforward
and honest. He had no illusions about his own intellectual capacities,
but a strong sense of his position and duties as a monarch. Like all
royalty, he did not like being told what he did not wish to hear. The
outspoken Sir Frederick 'Fritz' Ponsonby, who as Edward VII's
Assistant Private Secretary had made the King bellow with rage at his
unwanted advice, had much the same effect upon George V, of whom
he wrote: 'The King hated all insincerity and flattery, but after a time
he got so accustomed to people agreeing with him that he resented the
candid friend business . . .'

George's hatred of change was almost pathological; he wanted
everything to remain as it had been in the days of his childhood and,
when he became King, he saw to it that his court reverted to the
simpler ways and even the exact customs of his grandmother Victoria.

This adherence to the old demonstrated itself in small things such as his attachment to ancient hairbrushes, which he would have re-bristled over and over again rather than acquire new ones. His short temper would explode if a housemaid happened to move a piece of furniture from its accustomed place. At the traditional 'ghillies' ball' held at Balmoral for the staff, he refused to dance because he thought dancing had never been elegant since bustles went out of fashion. When, after the First World War, Queen Mary, as Princess May became known on her husband's accession, attempted to shorten her skirts in line with prevailing fashion, the result was an explosion of such proportions that she never tried to update her style again, remaining like a fly in amber as a relic of pre-war days. The post-war world was to him an abomination. 'He disapproved of Soviet Russia, painted fingernails, women who smoked in public, cocktails, frivolous hats, American jazz and the growing habit of going away for weekends,' his eldest son recalled.[4]

Curiously, for a man so fundamentally kind and even sentimental (the death of a sparrow would bring a tear to his eye), George V was a repressive, even tyrannical husband and father. His own childhood had been exceptionally happy; he had had a strong bond with his beautiful, adoring, childlike mother, worshipped his father while being more than a little afraid of him, and was devoted to his siblings, the unfortunate Prince Eddy and his three sisters, Maud, Louise and Victoria, who were collectively, if unflatteringly, known as 'the Hags'. In fact, Princess May had found it hard to fit in with the close family she had married into, nor did George's relations treat her kindly. Alexandra was a demanding and possessive mother, who did not welcome a rival for her son's affections. Shortly before their engagement, Alexandra wrote anxiously to her son of 'the bond of love between us – that of Mother & child – which *nothing* can ever diminish or render less binding – *& nothing & nobody* can or shall ever come between me & my darling Georgie boy'. Princess May had been made to feel a poor relation at her parents-in-law's glittering court, where she was criticised for being dull and boring. Her sharp-tongued sisters-in-law, particularly Princess Louise, Duchess of Fife, and Princess Victoria, liked to remind her of her morganatic blood. 'Poor May, with her Württemberg hands,' they would sigh audibly.

Unfortunately, just as they had been temperamentally incapable of expressing their love for each other except by letter, George V and Queen Mary found the same difficulties in showing their affection for their children. They were anxious but unsuccessful parents. Mabell, Countess of Airlie, Queen Mary's friend and lady-in-waiting, a close observer of the family relationships from 1902, denied that they were stern and unloving. 'Remembering them in my early days at Sandringham,' she wrote, 'before their family was even complete, I believe they were more conscientious and more truly devoted to their children than the majority of parents in that era. The tragedy was that neither had any understanding of a child's mind ... they did not succeed in making their children happy.'[5]

The couple had six children: Prince Edward, always known in the family as 'David', born in 1894; Prince Albert (Elizabeth's father), born eighteen months later in December 1895 and always known as 'Bertie'; Princess Mary, born in 1897; Prince Henry, born in 1900; Prince George, born in 1902; and lastly, Prince John, born in 1905. This last child seems to have been born with some form of brain damage; he developed epileptic fits when he was four and seems to have suffered from mental retardation. His condition later worsened so that he had to be separated from the rest of the family in 1917 and lived for two years at Wolferton Farm at Sandringham in the care of the family nanny, Lalla Bill, before dying there in 1919.

The children were brought up at physically extremely close quarters with their parents, particularly at York Cottage, their father's favourite home, a hideous cramped suburban villa in the grounds of the vast Sandringham House. Even after he became King, George V continued to live there, crammed in with his growing family, their attendant nurses and tutors, plus the royal household with equerries and ladies-in-waiting, valets and dressers. 'The congestion at York Cottage', a courtier recalled, 'had to be seen to be believed.' Even today when it operates as the estate office it is difficult to imagine how they could have functioned in such a confined space. Yet the children lived apart from their parents behind a green baize door and when they were small saw their parents for an hour a day at tea-time, an occasion spoiled by their sadistic nurse, who pinched David's arm as they went into the room, causing him to bawl and his father to demand that he be ejected. The same nurse deliberately upset Bertie's digestion by feeding him in a particularly springy carriage. When she collapsed with a nervous breakdown, Princess May was amazed to discover that she had not had a day off in three years and it was only then that the story of her ill-treatment of the children was revealed. Princess May's eldest son later described their childhood as 'buttoned up' and Lady

Airlie testified that she never saw them run but always solemnly shepherded by nurse or tutors. When they were naughty, they were summoned to their father's study, known as 'the Library' although there were no books in it, only the albums containing Prince George's famous stamp collection and glass-fronted cases displaying his prized collection of shotguns. 'For seventeen years', Harold Nicolson remarked of his subject as Duke of York, 'he did nothing but kill animals and stick in stamps.'

Prince George deliberately terrorised his children; as he told Lord Derby: 'I was frightened of my father and I'm damn well going to see that my children are frightened of me.' He did this not only because he modelled everything as far as he could on the days of his own childhood (even to the extent of employing his old tutor, the ingratiating but unlovable Canon Dalton), but also because he was rightly afraid that royal princes would have no one else to criticise them. As they grew up so his treatment of them worsened. He would pick on his eldest son at the slightest opportunity, usually for some sartorial fault, and shout, 'Get it out,' to his stammering second son, Bertie. George V also had the unattractive, and to his friends embarrassing, habit of making derogatory remarks about his sons. Talking about Bertie's stammer to Lord Halifax, he complained about how '"tiresome it was to everybody" ... He [George V] thought the best way of dealing with it was by mimicking him and laughing at him, and he always did this.'[6] Margot Asquith, outspoken wife of the Liberal Prime Minister, bravely told him that if he went on being so 'horrible' to his children, he would drive them to drink. 'He was always trying to mess up their social lives,' Loelia Ponsonby, Sir Frederick Ponsonby's daughter, recalled. 'He would find out if they were having a picnic on the river or whatever and put a stop to it.'[7] His secret fear, perhaps based on his memory of Prince Eddy's 'scrapes', was that his sons might fall into the hands of some designing woman, something which his tyrannical behaviour would conversely make more likely. A photograph of his youngest son, Prince George, at a fancy-dress ball with two sisters, leaders of the 'Bright Young Things', sitting at his feet clad only in silver-sequinned bathing costumes, caused an explosion that reverberated around Buckingham Palace. Queen Mary was too frightened of her husband to protect her children from his bullying; besides, she had an exaggerated respect for the greatness of his position. 'I always remember', she said, 'that as well as their father he is also their King.'

'The House of Hanover, like ducks, produce bad parents,' the Royal

Librarian, Sir Owen Morshead, told Harold Nicolson; 'they trample on their young . . .'[8] All the children of George V and Queen Mary suffered to some degree as a result of this harsh treatment. David, the Prince of Wales, had a nervous habit of twitching at his tie and fiddling with his cuffs; as a child he was practically anorexic, obsessively keen on exercise and difficult over food, possessed by the spectre of being overweight like his greedy grandfather, Edward VII. Prince Albert developed a crippling stammer at the age of seven and would fly into furious rages, later famously known as his 'gnashes'. Prince George went wild after leaving the Navy, into which he had been forced by his father, and plunged into night-life, sometimes louche; there were rumours of bisexuality and for a brief period he became addicted to drugs. All of them showed signs of nervous tension and sometimes smoked and drank too much. Princess Mary, being female, was not subjected to the same treatment by her father, but she was kept under strict control, not allowed to wear ultra-fashionable clothes and was despatched to do charity work with her mother instead of enjoying the frivolous social life of her contemporaries. Like her mother, she was emotionally intensely inhibited. Her son, the Earl of Harewood, wrote that she was conditioned to communicate only on as uncontroversial a level as possible. He believed it to be the result of an upbringing which discouraged direct discussion or any display of emotion. 'We did not talk of love and affection and what we meant to each other, but rather of duty and behaviour and what we ought to do.'[9] The pattern of royal family relationships was already being set.

But if in his private life he was an unsuccessful father, in his public role George V was an extremely successful King. Although initially he had suffered from comparison with his father, he showed a sure touch and his grandmother's ability to be in tune with the feelings of his subjects. 'I am not a clever man,' he once said, 'but if I had not picked up something from all the brains I've met, I would be an idiot.'[10] During the First World War he had set an example of austerity, giving up alcohol and keeping to a strictly limited diet while his two elder sons took part in the fighting. The Prince of Wales served in France as an officer in the Grenadier Guards (although, much to his chagrin, he was kept as far away as possible from active involvement), while Prince Albert was present as a naval midshipman at the Battle of Jutland. In 1917, in response to the anti-German feeling in the country, King George reinvented the British monarchy, changing its name and shedding dangerous continental royal connections. Although no one seems to have known precisely what the family name of the royal house was in 1917 (possibilities ranged from Saxe-Coburg to Wettin and the unacceptable Wipper), it was indubitably German. At the suggestion of his Private Secretary, Lord Stamfordham, George V lighted upon an inspired choice: from now on his family would be known as the House of Windsor, subtly connecting them in the public mind with the ancient castle which, perhaps as much as any other building, was the symbol of the historic British monarchy. At the same time he ordered a wholesale renaming of royal relations living in England – Battenbergs became Mountbattens with such native-sounding titles as Marquess of Milford Haven, and Queen Mary's Teck relations took the name Cambridge. 'I may be uninspiring,' George V remarked in response to H. G. Wells's reference to an 'alien and uninspiring Court', 'but I'm damned if I'm an alien.'

In that same year, 1917, he showed exactly how far he was prepared to go to preserve his dynasty and his throne. After the Russian revolution he refused to send a British warship to rescue the Tsar, his first cousin, and his family, a decision which may well have sealed their fate. When another first cousin, Queen Marie of Romania, daughter of the Grand Duchess Marie, came to England in 1919, she was told that cousin 'Georgie' as a 'strictly constitutional monarch' had been obliged to shun her mother and her Romanov relatives. Queen Marie, or 'Missy' as she was known in the family, had almost been engaged to George and knew him well. She sensed his fear 'of what Russia's blood-curdling example might instigate in quiet, steady England'. 'Everybody', she wrote, 'seemed to tread lightly, carefully, so as not to awake sleeping forces which would be difficult to control . . .' That year the King and the Prince of Wales attended a review of demobilised soldiers in Hyde Park when the men surged towards him asking bitterly, 'Where was the England fit for heroes to live in?' (a reference to the Prime Minister Lloyd George's wartime promise). 'Those men were in a funny mood,' he remarked pensively to his son as they rode back to Buckingham Palace.

George V and his advisers were well aware that the support of the British people could no longer be taken for granted. Events abroad had helped wonderfully to concentrate their minds. The social, ideological and political pressures generated by the Great War, a conflict affecting masses on the military and home fronts, had raised social expectations, toppled dynasties and changed the face of Europe. At the end of the war in 1918 the three great imperial thrones of continental Europe –

Austrian, German and Russian – had fallen, the throne of Greece seemed insecure, in Holland a strong republican movement threatened the future of the House of Orange, and in Germany all the royal relations of King George and Queen Mary had lost their positions. One event above all others had shaken the old European establishment to its foundations – the deposition and murder by the Bolsheviks of Tsar Nicholas II and his family. Even in Britain the spectre of Bolshevism and the class war seemed to hover over the Albert Hall in November 1918 when the Labour Party held an election rally, in the course of which the leader of the Transport Workers Union declared that he would like to see the Red Flag flying over Buckingham Palace and cheers were given for the Bolsheviks and Trotsky. Successive expansions of the franchise towards universal suffrage since 1885 had destroyed the exclusive property base of electoral power. Even before the war ended the more perspicacious royal advisers were looking into a democratic future: 'The Monarchy and its cost will have to be justified in the future in the eyes of a war-torn and hungry proletariat, endowed with a huge preponderance of voting-power,' Lord Esher, Edward VII's *éminence grise*, warned the King's Private Secretary, Lord Stamfordham.

The selling of the image of the 'family firm', as Princess Elizabeth's father later called it, was to be the major royal preoccupation of the post-war years. Both the two elder Princes had active parts to play in this campaign. The Prince of Wales was sent abroad on a series of world tours to carry the message to the Empire and to foreign heads of state that the British monarchy was alive and well in the twentieth century and represented by a handsome, blond prince in his mid-twenties, gifted with an exceptional crowd-pleasing charm. Elizabeth's father, Prince Albert, Duke of York, worked on the domestic front as President of the Industrial Welfare Association, an organisation directed at improving industrial relations through social welfare, canteens, hygiene and safety improvements. He was also actively involved in the Duke of York's camps, an idealistic and original attempt to improve understanding between the social classes. These were annual holiday camps to which the Duke of York personally invited 200 boys from public schools and 200 factory apprentices to join together for a week's games, concerts and other activities ending with the 'Duke's Day', which he would always attend, celebrated with a bonfire and the community singing of 'Under the Spreading Chestnut Tree'. The first camp was held in August 1921; they continued with increasing popularity and success until the outbreak of war in 1939.

Emotionally and psychologically Prince Albert's life had not been easy either in childhood or adolescence. As a child he had been forced by his father to wear iron splints on his legs to prevent his developing knock-knees; he was shy, stammered badly and hated lessons. A left-hander, he was forced to learn to write with his right. After a limited private education with a tutor, he was sent as a cadet to Osborne Naval College, where he was bullied and where some masters regarded him as an idiot because his stammer often prevented him from answering questions in class. After Osborne he just scraped into the Royal Naval College at Dartmouth, then joined the Navy, which he loved. But, after repeated illnesses finally diagnosed as an ulcer, he was invalided out and spent a miserable time kicking his heels at a desk job at the Admiralty. It was, however, during this period living with his parents at Buckingham Palace that he really got to know and understand his father and to sense the real affection which the King had revealed in his letters to him while he was away but which he kept well hidden beneath a gruff, hectoring manner when they were together.

In character and outlook he was the closest to his father of all the four sons. In the last year of the war he was seconded to the nascent Royal Air Force (RAF), where, despite his fear of flying, he passed his tests as a pilot. As his father once admitted, 'Bertie has more guts than the rest of them put together.' On the plus side he was, like many left-handed people, a fine athlete, a first-class shot and a good tennis player. He suffered from a fear of heights and of being the focus of attention of large crowds, which, on top of his stammer, made a nightmare of the public life he had to undertake as the King's son. He was shy and his stammer was a terrible handicap; it was not so much a stutter but a complete full stop in the middle of what he was saying and seemed to come upon him for no particular reason. He struggled against it with determination and, after treatment by an expert, mastered it so that later in life it was no more than a slight hesitation. He suffered from comparison with his elder brother, whose easy charm and boyish good looks made him the darling of the crowds. Although he was still close to his brother and looked up to him, he had naturally developed an inferiority complex where David was concerned, which remained with him all his life. The Prince of Wales was idolised to an extent to which no royal prince has been before or since. The press dubbed him 'Prince Charming'. Bertie remained in his shadow, humbly accepting that in most people's view he was very much second best. It had always been so. While the pair of them were at Dartmouth Royal Naval College, one of their tutors had written that the comparison of Bertie with his brother was like 'an ugly duckling and a cock pheasant'. But Bertie had a simple, kindly nature and people who knew him and his elder brother well compared their qualities rather differently. 'One is a gentleman,' said the Duke of Rutland, 'the other isn't.'

In June 1920 something happened which changed Prince Albert's life. At a London ball he fell in love with Lady Elizabeth Bowes-Lyon and determined to marry her. Elizabeth Bowes-Lyon, an aristocratic Scots girl whose family, like his, could trace descent back to King Robert the Bruce, was not quite twenty at the time. Born on 4 August 1900, she was the fourth daughter and ninth child of the Earl and Countess of Strathmore. The Bowes-Lyons's principal seat, Glamis, was the oldest inhabited dwelling in Britain and the setting used by Shakespeare for the murder of Duncan in *Macbeth*. Their violent coat of arms depicting two lions rampant and six crossbows recalled the days when the Thanes of Glamis employed a private army and a hangman (a bare white-walled room in the castle is still called 'the Hangman's Chamber'). The castle had its retinue of ghosts – a Grey Lady, a tongueless woman, a vampire servant and members of the rival Ogilvy clan who had died of starvation bricked up in the castle walls; there was an indelible bloodstain on the floor of Duncan's Hall where the King was supposedly murdered by a Thane of Glamis. A monster, reportedly a member of the family, hairy and deformed, had been locked in a secret chamber, where he survived for 100 years. Sir Walter Scott stayed at Glamis in 1792, aged twenty-two, and was duly frightened. 'When I heard door after door shut, after my conductor had retired, I began to consider myself as too far from the living, and somewhat too close to the dead,' he wrote. The Bowes-Lyons spent only the late summer and early autumn at Glamis; they owned another castle, Streatlam in County Durham, which they occasionally visited, but their principal home was St Paul's Walden Bury, a charming red-brick, early Georgian house in Hertfordshire, where Elizabeth spent most of her childhood. They also had a huge town house in St James's Square in London, which they used during the social 'Season'.

Elizabeth's childhood, unlike Prince Albert's, was an exceptionally happy one. 'I have nothing but wonderfully happy memories of childhood days at home,' she wrote, 'fun, kindness & a marvellous sense of security.'[11] This sense of security came partly from membership of a large clan, but particularly from her closeness to her mother and her brother, David, who was two years younger than herself. Her mother, Nina Cecilia Strathmore, always known as Cecilia, was a key influence in the life of Elizabeth, who inherited many of her qualities. A woman with an enormous zest for life and a gift for gardening and music, she believed that culture and the arts rather than academic qualifications were important for a girl's education. She herself taught Elizabeth to read and gave her her first music, dancing and drawing lessons. She also instilled in her the strong Christian principles she had inherited from her clergyman father, the Revd Charles Cavendish-Bentinck. Attendance at chapel, when the ladies of the household wore special crocheted lace caps, was an important part of life at Glamis.

Elizabeth's father inherited the Strathmore title and its attendant castles when she was only four and she grew up accustomed to a style of life which a friend described as 'feudal, almost royal'. The Bowes-Lyons were a sporting, military family, their politics were conservative and their style old-fashioned. Elizabeth's father, Lord Strathmore, had an absolute passion for cricket (it was probably because he was too busy with cricket and shooting at Glamis that he did not return to England to register Elizabeth's birth until six weeks after it had occurred and incurred a fine for lateness). A quiet, courteous, religious man, he was extremely conscientious about the responsibilities of his position, serving as Lord Lieutenant of the County of Angus for a large part of his life, taking care of his estates (he was an acknowledged expert on forestry) and his tenants. 'His sense of duty was developed to a high degree,' wrote one of his daughter's biographers, 'a characteristic he perpetually instilled in his children . . .'[12] Elizabeth's brothers, many of whom served in the famous Scottish regiment, the Black Watch, were excellent shots. Elizabeth herself was a keen and expert angler and learned how to handle a rifle from the stalkers at Glamis. She absorbed her social skills from her mother, who entertained effortlessly and with pleasure at all their various houses. Elizabeth hated formal schooling and preferred mixing with her mother's guests from Glamis to St James's Square, where she would meet grown-ups like the former Prime Minister, Lord Rosebery, and with the small army of servants and tenants who formed the Bowes-Lyon retinue. But with her charm and enjoyment of life and people, she inherited the fortitude of a long line of Scottish ancestors, the stamina, dismissal of physical weakness and refusal to complain for which she has become famous into her long old age. There was strength, toughness and an iron determination beneath the sweetness, as many people, not least of them Wallis Simpson, were to find out.

Elizabeth grew up saturated with the history of her Scottish home and developed a romantic passion for the Stuart family for whom her ancestors had fought. She showed an actress's poise at an early age; at seven she liked to take period costumes out of chests at Glamis and sweep through the Great Hall in crimson velvet and lace in the role of the Winter Queen, announcing, 'I am Princess Elizabeth.' Her acting ability was to stand her in good stead when, thirty years later, she was suddenly called upon to become Queen. She was just fourteen when the First World War broke out, an experience which quickly matured her. Four of her brothers enlisted for France; Fergus was killed at the Battle of Loos, while Michael was severely wounded, and captured and interned in a German prisoner-of-war camp. Glamis was turned into a convalescent hospital for wounded soldiers. Elizabeth, as the only unmarried daughter, helped her mother run the castle and entertain the men. In 1918 her mother was seriously ill and Elizabeth had sole responsibility for its management; she was just eighteen when the war ended, leaving her with intensely patriotic and strong anti-German feelings. She was never one to forgive or forget.

As a debutante immediately after the war, Elizabeth was an immediate success, as much for her personality as for her looks. She was small, dark-haired, with a beautiful complexion, blue eyes and a winning smile. She was witty, an excellent mimic and had the particular charm of being able to make each person feel that she was concentrating only on them. According to Lady Airlie, her radiant vitality, gaiety, kindness and sincerity made her irresistible to men. She was flirtatious and loved men; naturally they responded and she had a string of admirers. Utterly careless of fashion, she wore her hair with an unbecoming fringe which was well out of date and she dressed 'picturesquely, unfashionably' in her own distinctive style. She could certainly not be described as a 'flapper'. 'Lady Elizabeth was very unlike the cocktail-drinking chain-smoking girls who came to be regarded as typical of the 1920s,' Lady Airlie wrote. Supremely confident, Elizabeth never made any attempt to be anything but herself.

In September 1920 Prince Albert came over from Balmoral to stay at Glamis, escaping from the stifling dullness of the Balmoral house-party, which included, as usual, the King's great friend, Cosmo Lang, Archbishop of Canterbury, and Sister Agnes Keyser, the sharp-tongued foundress of the King Edward VII Hospital for Officers, whose speciality was repeating poisonous gossip about his sons' activities to the King. At Glamis he found a cheerful house-party, shooting during the day, dinner-parties and songs around the piano at night. There was also a good deal of competition from other young men. One of Elizabeth's admirers recalled: 'I was madly in love with her. Everything at Glamis was beautiful, perfect. Being there was like living in a Van Dyck picture . . . the magic gripped us all. I fell *madly* in love. They all did.'[13]

In the spring of 1921 Prince Albert proposed to her, but Elizabeth turned him down. Both Mabell Airlie, who had been backing the match and acting as confidante to both sides, and Lady Strathmore were upset on seeing him 'so disconsolate'. 'I like him so much,' Cecilia Strathmore told Mabell, adding percipiently, 'and he is a man who will be made or marred by his wife.' But, having set his heart on marrying Elizabeth, Prince Albert pursued her with dogged determination. Like his daughter Elizabeth just under twenty years later, he had fallen in love at once and for ever. He was at Glamis again in the autumn of 1921; in 1922 Elizabeth was among his sister's bridesmaids when she married Viscount Lascelles and that autumn he returned to Glamis. A fellow guest, the rich American socialite and diarist Henry 'Chips' Channon, later recalled the atmosphere there:

> The then Duke of York, afterwards King, used to come into my bedroom in the evening, and we would talk of the Glamis monster and the admittedly sinister atmosphere in the castle and of the other ghosts . . . One rainy afternoon, we were sitting about and I pretended that I could read cards, and I told Elizabeth Lyon's fortune and predicted a great and glamorous royal future. She laughed, for it was obvious that the Duke of York was much in love with her . . . I remember the pipers playing in the candlelit dining-room, and the whole castle heavy with atmosphere, sinister, lugubrious, in spite of the gay young party . . .'[14]

Elizabeth, even if she laughed it off, was beginning to feel the strain. Her mother noticed that she was 'really worried . . . I think she was torn between her longing to make Bertie happy and her reluctance to take on the responsibilities which this marriage must bring.' A false rumour that she was about to become engaged to the Prince of Wales, published in the *Daily News* on 5 January 1923, seems to have brought matters to a head, at least as far as Prince Albert was concerned. He told his parents that he intended to renew his proposal to Elizabeth for the last time. 'You'll be a lucky fellow if she accepts you,' his father replied, already captivated by Elizabeth's charm. Walking in the woods with Elizabeth at St Paul's Walden Bury on the weekend of 13 January, he proposed to her and this time she accepted him. A telegram was immediately despatched to Sandringham with the cryptic message, 'All Right. Bertie.' To Mabell Airlie, Prince Albert wrote thanking her for her help in persuading Elizabeth to give up her freedom, calling their engagement 'the wonderful happening in my life' and 'my dream which has at last been realized'.

People were surprised that the radiant, popular Lady Elizabeth had accepted the shy distinctly unglamorous Duke of York. There were malicious rumours that she would have preferred his brother, the Prince of Wales, who could have made her Queen, but there had never been any sign that he was interested in her; he was still in love with Freda Dudley Ward and, indeed, extremely keen that Elizabeth should marry Bertie. In fact, Elizabeth confided to Lady Airlie that the reason she hesitated in accepting his proposal was her reluctance to become a member of the royal family and step into the gilded cage. For someone who moved in Elizabeth's circles, a royal marriage was not necessarily a glittering prospect. The Bowes-Lyons were never courtiers; royalty held no special fascination for them and they tended to despise royal toadies. 'As far as I can see,' Elizabeth's mother was heard to remark, 'some people have to be fed royalty like sea-lions fish.' Some years later the Archbishop of Canterbury's chaplain, Dr Alan Campbell Don, who knew her family well, wrote after meeting the Yorks at luncheon: 'One cannot but be sorry for the little lady hedged about with the restrictions and penalties of royalty – what a fate for a daughter of Glamis.' Elizabeth was close enough to the royal family to understand what marrying one of them entailed, as the dying Duke of Buccleuch warned his daughter Alice when she told him she was thinking of getting engaged to the Duke of Gloucester: 'If you marry Harry, you become a servant of the Country.'

In the opinion of her friends Elizabeth certainly loved Bertie. She could have married virtually anyone she liked, but she chose him. As a woman of her class and time she perceived marriage as her destiny; she undoubtedly saw Bertie as good husband material. He was madly in love with her, they shared the same views and beliefs, he fitted in well with her family life. She was a strong woman; he was vulnerable and she could protect him, he was shy and she could bring him out. Physically he was an attractive man with a lean athletic figure, a good sportsman and a superb dancer, always immaculately dressed. Above all, although he lacked the flashing charm of his elder brother, he was sensitive to women and appreciative of them.

Even Queen Mary, guardian of the royal proprieties, approved of Elizabeth. Only once did Elizabeth slip up; in the first flush of excitement over her engagement she allowed a newspaper reporter into her house for an interview. Her royal parents-in-law were not amused. King George regarded almost all journals except *The Times* as 'those filthy rags of newspapers'. Queen Mary made it plain to Elizabeth that royalty did not do such things. Not only stiff upper lips but sealed ones were the order of the day. The lesson was not lost upon Elizabeth.

Bertie and Elizabeth were married on 26 April 1923 at Westminster Abbey, the ancient church in which they would be crowned King and Queen just over fourteen years later. It was not a lavish occasion; the King had decreed that 'the arrangements should be of as simple a character as possible and that no unnecessary expense shall be incurred'. The Duke of York was not, after all, the heir to the throne. *The Times*, voice of the establishment, reminded the public that a more significant marriage ceremony remained to be enacted: 'There is but one wedding to which [the public] look forward with still deeper interest – the wedding which will give a Wife to the Heir to the Throne, and, in the course of nature, a future Queen to England and to the British peoples.'

The marriage of Elizabeth and Bertie turned out to be supremely happy and successful. The writer and politician Alfred Duff Cooper saw them at the theatre in London at Christmas 1925, some four months before Princess Elizabeth was born. He described them to his wife, Lady Diana, as 'such a sweet little couple and so fond of one another. They reminded me of us, sitting together in the box having private jokes, and in the interval they slipped out, and I found them standing together in a dark corner of the passage talking happily as we might.' The birth of their first child was all that they needed to complete their happiness, although no one at the time could have had the remotest conception of how important a role that child would have to play.

2

Princess
in an Ivory Tower

'It has often seemed to me that in those days we lived in an ivory tower, removed from the real world . . . Looking back on it, it often seems to me as though while we were there the season was always spring.'

Marion Crawford, *The Little Princesses*

Princess Elizabeth Alexandra Mary of York was not born in one of her royal grandparents' palaces, nor even, as most babies were in those days, in her parents' home, but in the Strathmores' London house, 17 Bruton Street, in Mayfair, then the smartest residential quarter of the capital. The house has since disappeared, victim to the commercial redevelopment which has overtaken the area, and only a plaque marks the birthplace of the future Queen. In 1926 No. 17 was typical of the five-storeyed eighteenth-century town houses which aristocratic families like the Strathmores used as their London pieds-à-terre, not so much as a home but simply as somewhere to which they migrated for the social Season and the sittings of the Houses of Parliament. Elizabeth was born there because her parents refused to live in the house which King George V and Queen Mary had designated for them, White Lodge, a vast Palladian mansion in Richmond Park on the outskirts of London. Queen Mary had spent much of her childhood there; her eldest son, David, had been born there in June 1894 and it had hardly changed since. The Yorks complained constantly about the discomfort, the dilapidation, the eleven servants needed to run it and its remoteness from central London. Lord Lee of Fareham, who took the house on after the Yorks left, was astounded by the primitive conditions in which they had been expected to live. There was practically no central heating and the vast rooms were desperately cold, the electric lighting was inadequate and the wiring unsafe. The drains were suspect; there was only one lavatory on the whole ground floor of the huge house and that appeared to be about one hundred years old. Not surprisingly, the Duchess of York had decided to have her baby in the familiar comfort of her parents' London home.

It was a difficult birth at a difficult time. Elizabeth was a breech baby, her mother tiny and small-boned; the birth was a Caesarean, performed at 2.40 a.m. on 21 April 1926, just twelve days before the country was engulfed by the General Strike, which many observers saw as the onset of class struggle and even revolution. The King had been particularly apprehensive about the imminent strike. He sympathised with the miners, whose reaction to a proposed reduction in their wages precipitated the crisis. At Newmarket races earlier that month he had had a sharp exchange with Lord Durham, a leading coal-owner, telling him that he was sorry for the miners. When Durham angrily retorted that they were 'a damned lot of revolutionaries', the King told him, 'Try living on their wages before you judge them.' Against this grim background, Princess Elizabeth's birth registered as a happy dip on the graph of subversive incidents presented weekly to the Cabinet by Wyndham Childs, head of Special Branch.

As a sign of her membership of the royal family, a Government minister, the Home Secretary, Sir William Joynson-Hicks, waited in the next room while the Duchess of York went through long, difficult hours of labour before the baby was born. This antiquated royal custom was supposedly designed to prevent the repetition of a rumoured changeling being brought in in a warming-pan and substituted for the royal baby in 1688, but it was in fact an even more ancient relic of the days when kings performed every important function in public, or rather in the presence of privileged courtiers. This applied even to the most private functions; the original task of the court official entitled the Groom of the Stool had been literally that, to wipe the royal bottom.

In any case, as far as Elizabeth was concerned, precautions against changelings seemed particularly unnecessary. She was third in the line of succession to the throne, while her uncle, the Prince of Wales, was still expected to marry and have children. Even if he did not, her mother was only twenty-five and could presumably produce a boy who would supersede her. The Duchess of York had wanted a girl and the royal grandparents were delighted with their first female grandchild (they already had two male grandchildren, George and Gerald Lascelles, sons of Princess Mary, the Princess Royal). 'The baby is a little darling,' Queen Mary wrote after visiting Bruton Street that afternoon, 'with a lovely complexion and pretty fair hair.'

She was named Elizabeth Alexandra Mary after her mother, her grandmother and her great-grandmother, Queen Alexandra, who had died in November the previous year, aged eighty. Her father had particularly wanted his daughter to be called after her mother; the fact that it had also been the name of a reigning queen, the formidable Elizabeth I, seemed to him irrelevant. Another possibility, Victoria, was dismissed. 'I have heard from Bertie about the names,' George V, whose approval had first to be given, reported to Queen Mary. 'He mentions Elizabeth, Alexandra, Mary, I quite approve and will tell him so, he says nothing about Victoria. I hardly think that necessary.' Victoria, the indomitable, strong-willed matriarch, who had shaped the royal family for the twentieth century, was, however, to be a powerful role model for Elizabeth and it would not be long before comparisons began to be drawn between them.

Elizabeth was christened in the private chapel in Buckingham Palace (later destroyed by a bomb during the Second World War) on 29 May, just over two weeks after the General Strike had ended. There were strong echoes of Victoria about the ceremony: the gold, lily-shaped font used for her children's christenings was brought up from Windsor Castle for the occasion and the baby wore a heavy satin and Honiton lace christening robe which had been made for Victoria's eldest daughter and used by all subsequent royal children. Victoria's last surviving son, the Duke of Connaught, was among her godparents; her other godparents were the King and Queen, her aunt, the Princess Royal, her maternal aunt, Lady Elphinstone, and her grandmother, Lady Strathmore. She cried so much that her nurse dosed her with dill water, an old-fashioned remedy, to the amusement of her uncle, the Prince of Wales. It was the last time that Elizabeth ever made a public scene.

She had been born into a traditional world of wealth and privilege which had continued practically unchanged since her own parents' childhood. Although the British aristocracy that underpinned the hereditary monarchy had been perceptibly in decline over the last forty years, the process had been gradual. The way of life of Princess Elizabeth's parents and grandparents was still based on a hierarchy of servants, butlers and footmen, housekeepers and housemaids, chefs, cooks and kitchenmaids, chauffeurs and 'odd-job' men. For the first four years of her life Elizabeth was an only child and, as for all upper-

and middle-class children of her time, her world was the nursery. For the first years of her life the one constant was her nurse Clara Knight, nicknamed 'Allah' (pronounced 'Ah-la'), who had also been her mother's nurse. Allah, a countrywoman born near the Strathmores' home in Hertfordshire, was one of the classic, now extinct breed of English nannies so highly prized that they were exported to rich and aristocratic European and American families. Nannies were never seen out of uniform except in their nightgowns and were utterly devoted to their 'babies', remaining spinsters all their lives although given the courtesy title of 'Mrs'. Nannies ruled their children's lives, supervising their meals, their clothes and all their waking hours. Good nannies like Allah provided stability and a protective cocoon, ensuring that life was disciplined and lived according to the clock. They were obsessed by 'potty training' and 'bowel regularity', which meant that the child would be put on the pot and be expected to 'go' at a certain hour every morning immediately after breakfast. Every morning and afternoon at a certain hour, Elizabeth would be wheeled out in her gleaming, highly sprung perambulator to take the air on the triangular stretch of grass adjoining Hamilton Place behind her home, its privacy protected by iron railings through which the public would watch this ritual. Such regimentation suited Elizabeth, who grew up to be disciplined, punctual, responsible and orderly.

In January 1927, when she was only nine months old, her parents were sent on an official tour of Australia and New Zealand, which, in the days before air travel, took them six months. 'I felt very much leaving on Thursday,' her mother wrote, 'and the baby was so sweet, playing with the buttons on Bertie's uniform it quite broke me up.' 'Sweet' was the sickly adjective most people seem to have used about Elizabeth, who spent the period of her parents' absence with doting grandparents, particularly George V. 'Your sweet little daughter has four teeth now which is quite good for eleven months,' he wrote to the Duchess of York in March (never having bothered to notice such things in his own children). Elizabeth was a good, quiet child with, one visitor remarked, 'the sweetest air of complete serenity'. Her parents returned on 27 June, loaded with no less than three tons of toys and letters for 'Princess Betty'. That day, Elizabeth, aged a year and two months, saw them for the first time for six months and on the same day too she was held up for public inspection by cheering crowds on the same centre balcony at Buckingham Palace which was to be the stage for so many public appearances during her lifetime. She had

been separated from her parents for almost half her life, a royal pattern
which was to be imposed on her own young children when she became
Queen.

On their return the Yorks moved into 145 Piccadilly, the house in
which Elizabeth was to spend the next ten years of her life. This house
too would disappear, this time as a result of a direct hit by a German
bomb during the Second World War. In 1927 it was a plain, stone-
fronted five-storeyed house on the north side of Piccadilly looking
south over the trees of Green Park to the grey bulk of Buckingham
Palace. No. 145 was bigger than Bruton Street; apart from the usual
reception rooms, it had a ballroom, library and conservatory, twenty-
five bedrooms and an electric lift. The Yorks' staff included a butler,
Mr Ainslie, an under-butler, two footmen, a housekeeper, Mrs Evans,
and the cook, Mrs Macdonald. There was also a steward's room boy,
whose duty it was to serve the meals to the senior servants, three
kitchenmaids, a dresser for the Duchess, a valet for the Duke, an 'odd-
job' man, a night-watchman, an RAF orderly and a Boy Scout to
operate the telephone. Elizabeth moved into a nursery floor at the top
of the house with Allah Knight, and the nursery maid, a young Scots
girl, named Margaret MacDonald, known as 'Bobo', who would remain
one of the people closest to Elizabeth for more than sixty years. Here
Elizabeth lived her serene, orderly life, her toys carefully arranged in
glass-fronted cabinets, her toy ponies in a row in the passage outside
the nursery. At night she folded her clothes on a chair with her shoes
lined up neatly underneath. Lady Airlie's present to her for her third
Christmas was a dustpan and brush, not something which most
children would regard with enthusiasm. A sickly contemporary
description shows her as a good little girl, unquestioningly obeying the
rules:

> And so, when Princess Elizabeth's nurse, descending to the morning
> room or the drawing room, says in her quiet tones, 'I think it is bed
> time now, Elizabeth,' there are no poutings or protests, just a few last
> joyous skips and impromptu dance steps, a few last minute laughs at
> Mummy's delicious bed time jokes, and then Princess Elizabeth's hand
> slips into her nurse's hand, and the two go off gaily together across the
> deep chestnut pile of the hall carpet to the accommodating lift, which
> in two seconds has whisked them up to the familiar dear domain which
> is theirs to hold and to share.[1]

A more perceptive observer, Winston Churchill, met Elizabeth for the first time at Balmoral in September 1928 when she was two and a half years old. '[She] is a character,' he told his wife, Clementine. 'She has an air of authority and reflectiveness astonishing in an infant.'[2]

The 'infant' was already the subject of intense public attention. Aged only three she made the cover of *Time* as a fashion setter; children all over the world were dressed in yellow instead of the usual pink or blue when it was revealed that yellow was the predominant colour in her clothes and the decoration of her nursery. Her parents were taken aback by the universal passion for Elizabeth. In the autumn of 1928 the Duchess of York, who was in Edinburgh on an official visit without her daughter, reported to Queen Mary:

> I fear it has been a very great disappointment to the people . . . The
> Moderator mentioned in his welcoming address 'our dear Princess
> Elizabeth' . . . It almost frightens me that the people should love her so
> much. I suppose that it is a good thing, and I hope that she will be
> worthy of it, poor little darling.

In the first ten years of her life Elizabeth learned what it meant to be royal; she saw a good deal of her grandparents, the King and Queen, and had first-hand experience of the extreme deference with which everyone treated her grandfather. In March 1929, when George V was sent to recuperate at Bognor Regis after his near-fatal illness, Elizabeth went there to cheer him up. According to Lady Airlie, the King would really play with her, a thing which he had never done with his own children. When they got back to London, Elizabeth and her grandfather would wave at each other across the intervening Green Park; he called her Lilibet, imitating her own attempts at saying her name. The name stuck. She was Lilibet to her family from then on. Elizabeth was the King's favourite grandchild. A visitor to Sandringham in 1928, when Elizabeth was one year and nine months old, described them together:

> She perched on a little chair between the King and me; and the King
> gave her biscuits to eat and to feed his little dog with, the King
> chortling with little jokes with her – she just struggling with a few
> words, 'Grandpa' and 'Granny' and to everyone's amusement has just
> achieved addressing the very grand-looking Countess of Airlie as
> 'Airlie'. After a game of bricks on the floor with the young equerry

Lord Claud Hamilton, she was fetched by her nurse, and made a
perfectly sweet little curtsey to the King and Queen and then to the
company as she departed.[3]

Elizabeth was certainly privileged as far as her grandfather was
concerned. Her first cousin, George Lascelles (later Earl of Harewood),
regarded him with 'awe'. 'I don't think he cared very much for
children,' he wrote. 'The possibility of getting something wrong was,
where my grandfather was concerned, raised to heights of extreme
probability . . .' The Lascelles boys irritated him and he frequently
shouted at them, either for being nervous of his parrot, Charlotte,
which always sat at the breakfast table with him, or sneezing. 'No
amount of assurance that I had hay fever could stop the shouts of "Get
that damn child away from me", which made a rather strong
impression on an awakening imagination,' Lascelles recalled. In contrast George V liked Elizabeth to sit next to him at breakfast when
they were at Sandringham, and on Sunday afternoons he would take
her round the gardens and to visit the Stud and show her his favourite
horses, Scuttle and Limelight. It seems probable that Elizabeth's love
of horses, racing and breeding racehorses was influenced by her
grandfather's interest in them. He also gave her her first pony, a
Shetland called Peggy, for her fourth birthday in April 1930 at Easter,
which was always spent at Windsor with her grandparents; Queen
Mary gave her a building set, the blocks made from fifty different
woods from different parts of the Empire. It was a typical present
from Queen Mary, whose ruling passion was the British monarchy and
who was always intent on instilling into her granddaughter a sense of
family, its significance and its responsibilities.

She was four years and four months old when her sister, Margaret
Rose, was born at Glamis on 21 August 1930. This time the fact that
the new baby was not a boy caused disappointment. The Prince of
Wales was thirty-six and still showing no signs of marrying and
fathering an heir. It had taken the Yorks three years to produce
Elizabeth; and four more had passed before the arrival of their second
child. There were rumours about the Duke's fertility (he had suffered
a severe case of mumps while a cadet at Osborne which could well
have affected him) and the odds on the Duchess of York giving birth
to a son were narrowing, despite the fact that she was still only thirty.
The arrival of a second daughter focused world attention even more
firmly on Elizabeth as the probable heir to the British throne. A

waxwork figure of her on her pony was set up in Madame Tussaud's; chocolates, china and hospital wards were named after her; her face appeared on a six-cent stamp in Newfoundland; a popular song was composed in her honour; and a slice carved out of Antarctica around longitude 80° was called Princess Elizabeth Land. Her father was beginning to draw comparisons between her and Queen Victoria. In conversation with Osbert Sitwell he made an oblique reference to the possibility of Elizabeth's following in her great-great-grandmother's footsteps. 'From the first moment of talking,' he told Sitwell, 'she showed so much character that it was impossible not to wonder that history would not repeat itself.'[4]

The arrival of Margaret Rose in the royal nursery meant that Allah Knight's attention was switched exclusively to the new baby, while her assistant, Bobo MacDonald, looked after Princess Elizabeth. Born in the Black Isle, north of Inverness, she was the daughter of a railway worker and was brought up in the railway company's house beside the line. She was twenty-two when she joined the Yorks' household at the time of Elizabeth's birth and was allowed by Allah to hold the baby Princess when she was six weeks old. Bobo looked after Elizabeth first as her nursemaid and then as her dresser when she grew up. The forthright, red-haired Scots girl became the one person whom Elizabeth trusted absolutely outside her immediate family and had considerable influence over her, encouraging her to follow her own thrifty principles. As a child, Elizabeth kept a large box in which wrapping paper from Christmas or birthday presents would be put away neatly smoothed, the gift ribbon rolled up for future use; when she became Queen, she was famous for carefully turning off the lights in her palaces to save electricity. Bobo's sister, Ruby MacDonald, replaced her as nursemaid and later became as attached to Margaret as Bobo was to Elizabeth.

Elizabeth now had an additional responsibility, as she saw it, in her sister, who was to prove more of a handful than the toy dogs and ponies and was to remain so all her life. Margaret was an entirely opposite character to Elizabeth. She was extrovert, capricious, attention-seeking, imaginative and naughty. One of her governesses said that she was the most difficult child she had ever had to teach. 'Princess Elizabeth was always charming and unselfish,' one of her mother's friends wrote, 'Princess Margaret naughty but amusing. I remember one day when Princess Margaret was about 5 or 6 and we were all visiting the mausoleum at Frogmore, her confiding to me as we looked at the tombs together: "I have found out something – DOG and GOD are the same word changed round" . . . she obviously felt she had made a horrific discovery.'[5] Another governess, Marion Crawford, known as 'Crawfie', who arrived when Margaret was two, called her a 'born comic'. Both the children bit their nails and had sibling scraps, usually when forced to wear hats which they hated: they would snap the elastic under each other's chins with shrill cries of 'You brute!' and 'You beast!'

'Of the two children', Crawfie wrote, 'Lilibet was the one with the temper, but it was under control. Margaret was often naughty but she had a gay, bouncing way with her which was hard to deal with. She would often defy me with a sidelong look, make a scene, kiss and be friends and all forgiven and forgotten. Lilibet took longer to recover, but she always had the more dignity of the two.'

Elizabeth was maternally protective of her sister and would never hear a word of criticism of her. Even when Margaret had done something particularly exasperating, Elizabeth would simply say, 'Oh, Margaret!' In return, Margaret gave Elizabeth her total loyalty; at times Margaret's behaviour might cause strain, sometimes even when they were grown up she would lose her temper with her sister, even when that sister became the Queen, but the underlying family feeling was always there. The relationship established in the nursery was to continue into their adult lives, with Elizabeth as the responsible elder sister and Margaret as the naughty girl who was always getting into scrapes.

Elizabeth's strongest relationship within her family was with her father, whom she resembled more closely in character. She inherited his shyness, his seriousness and the dedicated professionalism with which he tackled everything he undertook. Like him, and like her grandmother, Queen Mary, she did not find it easy to express her emotions ('She bottles things up,' a friend later said of her). Elizabeth took after her father in being reserved and quiet about her feelings, but, according to Crawfie, 'if you once gained her love and affection you had it for ever, but she never gave it easily'. They understood one another at a deep personal level, although she was more intelligent than he was. 'The Duke was immensely proud of her,' Crawfie wrote. 'He had a way of looking at her that was touching.' His relationship with his younger daughter was completely different. 'Margaret brought delight into his life,' Crawfie said. 'She was a plaything. She was warm and demonstrative, made to be cuddled and played with. At one time he would be almost embarrassed, yet at the same time most touched and pleased, when she wound her arms round his neck, nestled against him and cuddled and caressed him. He was not a demonstrative man.' The Duchess provided the 'fun' element in family life; she was the initiator of games, charades, sing-songs round the piano, always as the life and soul of the party oiling the social wheels, skimming happily over the surface.

The sisters were always close, welded together by their parents in a close-knit family quartet, 'us four' as their father called it. He was desperately determined that his younger daughter should not suffer the discrimination which he had experienced in comparison with his elder brother, the acknowledged heir to the throne ('You will never know the difference eighteen months could make,' he once told Mrs Baldwin, the Prime Minister's wife, bitterly referring to his childhood and adolescence). As far as possible, the four-year difference between the two children was to be ignored and, from the moment the youngest was out of baby clothes, the two would be dressed the same with dresses, shoes and hats in identical colours. This apparently was considered perfectly normal for upper-class families at the time, but it struck even the assimilated Chips Channon as odd when he saw the two princesses still dressed the same at the Thanksgiving Service for the end of the Second World War in 1945, when Elizabeth was nineteen and Margaret not yet fifteen. Their father would over-compensate for what he saw as the inferiority of Margaret's position as the younger sister relative to the royal heiress by spoiling her, thus storing up trouble for the future.

The Great Depression following on the Stock Market crash of 1929 had made little impact on Elizabeth's sheltered world. When Britain went off the Gold Standard in September 1931, the King ordered a 50 per cent cut on the money he received from the Government on the Civil List. The Prince of Wales, who had already sold his horses to concentrate on golf but now had other expensive hobbies, was furious when telephoned by his father in a Biarritz night-club where he was dancing with his mistress, Viscountess Furness, to be ordered to give up £10,000 a year. The Duke of York, whose own Civil List allowance was to be curtailed, decided to give up hunting. 'It has come as a great shock to me that with the economy cuts I have had to make my hunting should have been one of the things I must do without,' he wrote to Ronald Tree, Master of the Pytchley Hunt. 'And I must sell my horses too. This is the worst part of it all and the parting will be terrible.'

From Elizabeth's point of view, it was, however, an improvement. Instead of renting expensive houses in the shires for the hunting season as her father had been in the habit of doing, George V gave him in September 1931 the Royal Lodge in Windsor Great Park, originally built for George IV by the architect, Sir Jeffrey Wyatville, in the fashionable Gothic style. By the time the Yorks saw it, it was dilapidated and inconvenient. Most of George IV's house had been pulled down by his successor, William IV, who left only the great saloon and chapel and added an octagonal pavilion. Subsequent tenants had partitioned off the great saloon, spoiling its proportions. The Yorks took out the partitions to make a large drawing-room and added two wings on either side, with two bedrooms for themselves on the ground floor of one wing. Characteristically, the Duke's was an austere room, neat and tidy like a sailor's cabin, furnished with a hard bed, a simple dressing-table and one bookcase on which was laid out a few personal mementoes, while his wife's was decorated in her favourite grey-blue, the large bed in blue silk with lemon pleating, and furniture and cupboards of white apple wood.

The Yorks now had a country house and their lives followed the traditional aristocratic pattern. On Fridays the family left 145 Piccadilly to spend the weekend at the Royal Lodge, where the Duke of York developed his passion for gardening, helped by his wife and children; both the children had their own plot to cultivate. In 1932 the people of Wales presented Elizabeth with a miniature cottage, known as the 'Y Bwthyn Bach', 'The Little House', fully equipped down to the last vacuum cleaner, in which she and Margaret Rose could play, Marie-Antoinette-like, at being housewives. The cycle of their lives was now settled: weekends in the country, Easter with the King and Queen at Windsor Castle, August and September with their grandparents in Scotland, either with the Strathmores at Glamis or at Balmoral (later at Birkhall, a house on the Balmoral estate), Christmas and the New Year at Sandringham.

Consciously or unconsciously, the picture of the Yorks as the Happy Family with which every household in the land could identify was being built up. Newspaper and magazine photographs showed the family on the lawn at the Royal Lodge, the Duchess sitting smiling as Elizabeth played with the dogs (Labradors at this early stage), as the Duke of York, with Princess Margaret in his arms, proudly looks on. This was an innovation; royal photographs since the days of Queen Victoria had depicted serried ranks of unsmiling royals seated on chairs, with attendant sedate children dressed in sailor suits, or, if they were still 'toddlers', in skirts and petticoats. No one could imagine a scene in which King George V and Queen Mary sat on the ground playing with children and dogs. Deliberately or not, these domestic shots were a counterpoint to the off-duty pictures of the Prince of Wales, night-clubbing in tails or with an informal group round the swimming-pool at Fort Belvedere, the miniature castle not far from the Royal Lodge that was his weekend retreat. A famous photograph of a swimming party at 'the Fort', as it was known, showed his mistress Thelma Furness, sultry and sexy-looking in a bathing dress, sitting on the ground in front of the Duchess of York, fully clothed, wearing strings of pearls and seated on a bench. The clash between the two lifestyles was only too evident.

The Happy Family image was a reflection of the reality. Elizabeth saw a good deal more of her parents than most children of her age and class, certainly more than the children of the international smart set who were left behind as their parents visited each other's houses for weekends or holidayed in Venice and the South of France in summer and at ski resorts such as Kitzbuhel in winter. The Yorks never went abroad except on duty. Although they spent the occasional weekends away with friends like Mrs Ronnie Greville at Polesden Lacey, on most occasions the children went too, and for both parents their home was also their official base. The Duchess of York taught Elizabeth to read, much as her mother had taught her, reading Bible stories aloud on Sunday mornings and 'the right sort of books' on winter evenings. They would sing songs around the piano after tea and then start on fairy stories – *Alice*, *Black Beauty*, *Peter Pan* – and 'anything about horses and dogs'.

In the spring of 1932 Miss Crawford joined the Yorks' household as Elizabeth's governess. Marion Crawford was a tall, slim, twenty-three-year-old Scots girl, independent-minded and ambitious, who had trained at Moray House in Edinburgh teaching underprivileged children. When she joined the Yorks, her intention was to return there to train as a child psychologist when her job with Elizabeth was over. Like Bobo, Crawfie came through personal recommendation. She had taught one of the Duchess of York's nieces, but in the Duke's eyes her principal qualification as governess to his daughter was her walking ability (she regularly walked six miles a day to teach her private pupils). Crawfie never returned to Moray House or to child psychology; she was to remain with Elizabeth and Margaret for sixteen years.

Three years later she published a book about her experiences in the royal household, *The Little Princesses*, which today seems tame and sugary, but in the buttoned-up early 1950s was as sensational as Andrew Morton's *Diana: Her True Story* was to be in the 1990s. As the first royal employee to publish an intimate account of their family life, traitor Crawfie would become a non-person as far as the royal family was concerned.

Crawfie's account is not entirely to be trusted. There was undoubtedly some beefing up of the manuscript to suit her publishers. Certain remarks and conversations are pure fantasy which could charitably be put down to memory lapses after the passage of years. The characters are cardboard and superficially observed and the style is that of a women's magazine, but the book does have value as a portrait drawn by an intelligent observer who came from outside and who had no longer, in the royal context, any reason to colour her picture rose. Yet Crawfie's portrayal of life with the Yorks, though sometimes mawkish, was a happy one. She fell for her employers, particularly the Duchess, and their family: 'The Duke and Duchess were so young, and so much in love. They took great delight in each other and in their children.'

Crawfie first saw Elizabeth sitting up in bed driving an imaginary horse with a pair of toy reins. When asked if she usually drove in bed, Elizabeth replied seriously, 'I mostly go once or twice round the park before I go to sleep. It exercises my horses.' She and Margaret had a collection of over thirty toy horses, each one of which would be solemnly unsaddled before they went to bed. In Hamilton Gardens or at the Royal Lodge, her favourite games involved horses. Elizabeth and her cousin, Margaret Elphinstone, would pretend to draw Margaret sitting in a miniature cart, or Elizabeth would harness up Crawfie as a drayhorse delivering goods on a round, as she saw them doing from the windows of No. 145. She groomed, fed and watered her toy ponies, keeping the necessary brushes and pails lined up in the corridor outside her nursery. At Royal Lodge she was already being taught to ride her own pony; it was the beginning of a lifelong passion for horses. There was nothing unusual about this at her age, but most girls end their love-affair with the horse at puberty; only relatively few, like Elizabeth, never do. Perhaps her interest lasted because it was technical and practical as well as passionate: she was to become an acknowledged expert on the breeding and form of racehorses. Dogs were equally important to her. Nineteen thirty-three was the Year of the Corgi, when her father bought the first of the long line of the short-legged and short-tempered Welsh breed that was to become inseparable from Elizabeth's domestic image. This animal, whose pedigree name was Rozavel Golden Eagle but who was always known as Dookie, was not popular among the royal household, being all too prone to snap at ankles or proffered hands, but the Yorks none the less bought another one named Jane and founded a dynasty. Elizabeth had an unusual rapport with animals, particularly dogs; in some ways she seemed more interested in them than she was in human beings. Like her father, who was an expert on wildlife and game, she was a country person at heart. She told Crawfie that when she grew up she would marry a farmer so that she could have 'lots of cows, horses and dogs and children'.

At their first meeting Crawfie had been struck by the 'long comprehensive look' the child gave her. The six-year-old Elizabeth already had a sharp and critical eye ('She never misses a thing,' her friends and courtiers would later say of her). 'How do you do? Why have you no hair?' was her opening remark to her new governess who sported a short haircut known as an 'Eton crop'. Aged four and a half at a children's fancy-dress party given by her mother's friend Lady Plunket, at Londonderry House, Elizabeth spotted a baby dressed as a fairy. 'What a pretty baby, what's her name?' she asked the child's nurse. 'Raine, Your Royal Highness,' she replied. 'What a *funny, funny* name,' said Elizabeth. The fairy baby was Raine McCorquodale, Barbara Cartland's daughter, later to become distantly connected to Elizabeth as the stepmother of her daughter-in-law, Diana, Princess of Wales.[6]

Crawfie found Elizabeth almost too self-disciplined, her passion for orderliness amounting almost to an obsession. She would sort the coffee sugar crystals given her by her parents as a treat after luncheon into sizes, while Margaret simply gulped them down. After Crawfie once told her sententiously, 'Nothing is impossible if you try hard enough', Elizabeth took her at her word and went on trying night after night to place her shoes exactly parallel under her chair, with her clothes carefully folded on it, even getting out of bed later to try and reach perfection. Order, ritual and attention to detail were already an important part of her life.

Education was not at a premium in the York family. As Crawfie recalled:

No one ever had employers who interfered so little. I had the feeling that the Duke and Duchess, most happy in their own married life, were not over concerned with the higher education of their daughters. They

wanted most for them a really happy childhood, with lots of pleasant
memories stored up against the days that might come out and, later,
happy marriages.

In other words, what was good enough for the children's mother was
good enough for them. Prince Albert, with miserable memories of his
own schoolroom days, was anxious for his daughters to be happy above
everything else. The education of women was not considered important
in royal and aristocratic circles, where it was regarded merely as a
necessary tool for those unfortunates who would have to earn their
living and irrelevant to the needs of girls whose destiny was marriage.
Queen Mary seems to have been the only member of the family who
was concerned that the girls should be well educated. She remonstrated
with her daughter-in-law over the fact that the children's education
was confined to their governess. 'I don't know what she meant,' the
Duchess of York told a friend. 'After all I and my sisters only had
governesses and we all married well – one of us *very* well . . .'

King George V's only stipulation was that his granddaughters
should be taught good handwriting. 'For goodness' sake,' he told
Crawfie, 'teach Margaret and Lilibet to write a decent hand, that's all
I ask you. None of my children could write properly. They all do it
exactly the same way. I like a hand with some character in it.' It was
typical of the King to hold up his sons as a bad example. In fact, the
handwriting of his three eldest sons closely resembled his own, an
untidy, illiterate-looking scrawl, often with misspelt words; only Prince
George, the youngest, wrote with an elegant individual style. Royal
children have only their own parents as role models in everything and
handwriting was no exception; just as King George's children copied
his hand, so Elizabeth's handwriting was to turn out so like her
mother's that their signatures are almost indistinguishable.

Queen Mary, however, was not so easy to please. For her, the goal
of the children's education was to make them aware of their royal
history and the nature of the British monarchy and Empire. To
Crawfie's curriculum, which included the singing, dancing, music and
drawing considered accomplishments suited to the education of a
young lady since well before the days of Jane Austen, Queen Mary
insisted on adding subjects that she considered essential for royal
children. 'Her Majesty felt that genealogies, historical and dynastic,
were very interesting to children and, for these children, really
important,' Crawfie recorded. The Queen also suggested that the

children should be taught the physical geography of the Dominions and India as a follow-up to the interest in the Empire which she hoped she had inspired in Elizabeth with her present of the blocks of wood. It may have been due to her insistence that Crawfie's efforts were supplemented by a French governess, Mrs Montaudon-Smith, always known as 'Monty', while Crawfie added her own touch of current affairs to the curriculum by taking out a subscription to *The Children's Newspaper*, a carefully edited publication, and *Punch*. Queen Mary's presents to the children were generally educational, classic authors such as Robert Louis Stevenson, Jane Austen and Kipling, while she took it upon herself to take them on cultural expeditions, 'instructive amusements' as she called them, every Monday, either to a museum or to places like the Tower of London and the Royal Mint.

Queen Mary did not hesitate to comment on the children's progress in letters dictated to her ladies-in-waiting and despatched to Crawfie. Some of her remarks would have been considered interfering by their mother had she seen them. 'Is arithmetic more valuable than history to them?' she queried; 'they will never do their own household books . . .' 'Shouldn't they get a more intellectual indoor game than Racing Demon?' 'I am distressed by their late and fluctuating bedtime,' she wrote. 'Princess Margaret's character is more complicated and difficult but . . . her general outlook and attitude to life may improve.'[7]

The children were in awe of their grandmother, finding her strict and intimidating. They were unable to penetrate, as perhaps only Prince George and her close friends like Lady Airlie could, the Queen's formidable shyness and reserve to discover the kind, gentle, even lighthearted personality within. The Queen's determination to make the children sensible of their position and her emphasis on how to behave did not endear her to them. On one occasion when she took Elizabeth to a concert at the Queen's Hall, the child fidgeted so much that her grandmother asked her if she would not prefer to go home. 'Oh, no, Granny,' Elizabeth said, 'we can't leave before the end. Think of all the people who'll be waiting to see us outside.' Some people might have thought this showed unusual thoughtfulness on Elizabeth's part. Queen Mary regarded it as vulgar, undignified and distinctly unroyal to pay attention to such things. The child might be getting swollen-headed. Elizabeth was sent home in disgrace. Yet in some ways Elizabeth and her grandmother were alike. The writer and traveller Augustus Hare, meeting the then Duchess of York in 1899, wrote of her 'dignified simplicity and single-mindedness' and 'the high

sense of duty by which her naturally merry, genial nature is pervaded'.[8]
She liked hard work and found it difficult to condone laziness,
untidiness and waste.

Queen Mary's influence on her eldest granddaughter should not be
underestimated. Queen Mary regarded herself, and was looked on by
the rest of the family, as the guardian of the royal flame. Lady Airlie
went so far as to say that her sense of the duty of a monarch was so
strong that she approved of Catherine the Great 'on the grounds that
she loved her kingdom to the extent that she would go to any lengths
for it even commit terrible crimes'. She was the repository of all
knowledge about the family and on how royalty should behave. When
the young Elizabeth herself became Queen, she would say things like
'Grannie always told me I would have to stand a lot', and part of her
apparent reluctance to smile in public came from her grandmother's
inculcation of the rule that real royalty did not smile in public. Lord
Harewood recalled 'the awe and near-reverence with which Queen
Mary was generally treated. Even my mother seemed to approach her
wearing metaphorical kid gloves.' When Queen Mary came to visit, all
the women members of the York family would greet her with the
regulation curtsey and kiss her hand and both cheeks, repeating the
process when she departed.

Crawfie's expeditions, unlike Queen Mary's, were intended to bring
the children into contact with 'the real world'. Elizabeth's cage was
gilded, its bars invisible, but they were none the less there. 'Other
children always had an enormous fascination, like mystic beings from
a distant world,' Crawfie wrote, 'and the little girls used to smile shyly
at those they liked the look of. They would so have loved to speak to
them and make friends, but this was never encouraged.' She began to
take them on forays into the 'ordinary world' only to be frustrated by
popular interest in them. On one rather sad occasion she took them by
underground to Tottenham Court Road station to the YWCA in Great
Russell Street, where Elizabeth, unused to serving herself, left her pot
of tea behind on the canteen counter and was bawled out by the
woman behind it: 'If you want it, you must come and fetch it yourself.'
They were soon recognised (two immaculately dressed children accompanied by a governess and a detective could hardly fade into the
background of the YWCA canteen), the detective called up a car to
save them from the gathering crowd and the modest adventure into
the outside world was over. From then on Princess Elizabeth's closest

view of ordinary life came from the top of a London bus and even that was cut short when the IRA began a terrorism campaign.

The children's life was by no means as isolated as Crawfie made out as far as other children were concerned, although the circle of their friends was certainly exclusive. There were frequent children's parties at No. 145 attended by upper-class children such as the Beaumonts (who lived next door at No. 144), the Mountbatten and Elphinstone cousins, the sons of the Yorks' great friends, the Plunkets, Myra Wernher, Elizabeth Lambart, Alathea Fitzalan-Howard, May Cambridge, and the children of courtiers such as the Hardinges and the Leghs. Elizabeth had a particular friend named Sonia Graham-Hodgson, daughter of a distinguished Harley Street radiologist. Exquisitely dressed in party dresses by Allah, the Princesses would go out to other children's parties, which the nannies enjoyed more than the children did.

Ordinarily, Elizabeth's day would start with a visit to her parents' bedroom after breakfast, then a morning of half-hour lessons with a break for elevenses and recreation in Hamilton Gardens, followed by reading before lunch, which the girls would usually eat with their parents when at home. Singing, dancing, music or drawing lessons took place in the afternoon, followed by tea, when, in the days before he became besotted with Wallis Simpson, Uncle David would often join them (his home, York House in St James's Palace, being only a short walk from No. 145) and stay for the card games they played after tea – Snap, Happy Families, Racing Demon or Rummy. Then it would be bathtime attended by their mother and father and riotous games like pillow fights in the nursery until Allah called time for bed. 'Then, arm in arm, the young parents would go downstairs, heated and dishevelled and frequently rather damp. The children called to them as they went, until the final door closed, "Goodnight Mummy, Goodnight Papa!"'

Elizabeth was of course unaware of the problems which Uncle David was already causing his family. The likelihood of the Prince of Wales marrying a suitable girl now seemed increasingly remote. He had only once a long time ago shown any romantic interest in a single woman, Lady Rosemary Leveson-Gower, but the King and Queen had disapproved of her parentage, and the Prince had not persisted with it. Since his first sexual awakening with a young French girl in France during the First World War, his attention had been focused exclusively on married women. He was a man crippled by the high expectations of

him as Prince of Wales, with a sense of inferiority in the face of his
great heritage which made him shrink from any responsibility. He
preferred experienced women who would make no serious demands
upon him and would mother him, direct him and, as Wallis Simpson
was to do, dominate him. His relationship with his father was, in the
Hanoverian tradition, conducted on the basis of mutual suspicion and
hostility. He was traumatised by the experience of the First World
War which no one of his generation could forget, at odds with his
heritage and with everything that his father represented. He rebelled
against his father's court and its traditions, worshipping the modern
world represented by America as offering a better, more liberated
future. The qualities of courage and humanity which he had shown in
the trenches during the war became subsumed by a frantic need to
ward off boredom and a sense of his own worthlessness through sex,
alcohol, jazz, night-clubs and golf. 'I feel such a bloody little shit,' he
had written despairingly to one of his aides in 1919. Looking, as royalty
always do, for a role model in the past, he would question his great-
uncle, the Duke of Connaught, about Edward VII's sexual exploits as
Prince of Wales, disregarding the old Duke's warnings that 'they
wouldn't stand for it nowadays'.

In inner court circles the Prince's behaviour was by now causing the
greatest disquiet. The golden-hearted charmer 'full of fun and rags
with everyone', as one of his entourage described him, whose abundant
vitality had enchanted them all in the early 1920s, had turned into a
difficult, obstinate charge whose impulses they could not control and
whose lapses they struggled to conceal. By the mid-1920s his woman-
ising, drinking and selfishly irresponsible behaviour shocked his closest
aides. For Sir Alan 'Tommy' Lascelles, his Private Secretary, the
crunch had come when he had been with the Prince in Africa in
November 1928. An urgent telegram from the Prime Minister arrived
for the Prince informing him of his father's dangerous illness and
requesting his immediate return. The Prince had refused to take it
seriously and carried on with his plans for the seduction of a woman
married to a local government official. For Lascelles, this particular
episode was the last straw; he resigned and joined George V's
household, vowing never to serve the Prince again (only to find, to his
chagrin, that he was faced with the Prince as King a few years later).
The Prince was already showing that penchant for American married
women which led to his involvement with Wallis Simpson. Since early
1930 Thelma Furness, born Morgan, wife of the shipping magnate,

Viscount Furness, had been his mistress, a fact of which the court, always well-informed, was well aware. The Yorks (although not George V and Queen Mary) had liked the good-natured Thelma, but when she was replaced by her friend, Wallis Simpson, in 1933, the situation became increasingly threatening.

Elizabeth saw less of her other two uncles, Prince Henry, Duke of Gloucester, and Prince George, Duke of Kent. The two brothers were entirely different. Prince Henry, 'Harry' in the family, was tall, a typical Hanoverian in looks, pink-faced, with bright blue protuberant eyes. Like his two elder brothers, he was no intellectual; he was a huntin'-shootin'-and-fishin' squire with a passion for practical jokes such as stitching mustard plasters into the trouser seats of pompous guests' evening clothes. He enjoyed military life as an officer in a cavalry regiment, loved riding, although he was accident-prone, and mess dinners, when his braying laugh would be heard over the after-dinner port. He was popular with his fellow-officers and men, less so with senior officers who were apt to regard him as a liability and a buffoon. His conversation tended to be on Wodehousian lines: 'Done any good judgin' lately?' he enquired of an Irish judge seated next to him at dinner. As a royal, he had a distinct drawback in being tone-deaf and, according to his elder brother, unable even to recognise the national anthem unless everybody stood up.

Surprisingly, however, he shared with his younger brother, Prince George, their mother's interest in antiques. Prince Henry collected *netsuke*, miniature elephants, sporting prints, pictures and books. But while Queen Mary's taste was limited by her passion for the family – to her a second-rate portrait of some German princely relation was more desirable than a work by a great artist – Prince George was a genuine connoisseur, the most discerning royal collector since George IV, and was seriously interested in interior decoration, a characteristic inherited from his maternal grandfather, Franz of Teck. His father's determination to make a naval officer out of him had been a mistake. For once Queen Mary had tried to argue with the King, pointing out that George, with his sensitive, aesthetic tastes, was not suited to naval life. She was, of course, overruled. Prince George went to Dartmouth Naval College just as David and Bertie had done and was absolutely miserable there. Subsequently, life on board ship was a nightmare of home-sickness and sea-sickness until finally the King gave in; Prince George became a civil servant, working first for the Foreign Office, then for the Home Office in the unlikely role of Inspector of Factories.

Once back on dry land, Prince George threw himself with enthusiasm into London night-life. He moved into York House with David and the two of them became inseparable. Apart from his brother, Prince George's closest friends tended to be cultivated homosexuals like Prince Paul of Yugoslavia and Chips Channon. There were rumours about a 'boy in Paris' to whom Prince George had written compromising letters and of a liaison with Noël Coward. But Prince George was also actively interested in women; among his mistresses were the black singer Florence Mills and a string of society girls, notably Lois Sturt and Poppy Baring. He went through a brief period of drug addiction in the late 1920s after a trip to Kenya with his brother David when an American lover, Kiki Whitney Preston, introduced him to cocaine and morphine. He was saved by David, who sent him to a country house staffed by nurses to wean him from his addiction. Tall, dark, with sensual good looks, Prince George was also extremely good company.

Prince George's rackety bachelor life officially came to an end in August 1934 when he proposed to his friend Prince Paul of Yugoslavia's sister-in-law, Princess Marina of Greece. Princess Marina was a cousin, the daughter of Prince Nicholas of the royal house of Greece, descendants of Queen Alexandra's favourite brother, Willy. On her mother's side her blood was purple rather than merely blue: she was descended from the Russian imperial family, the Romanovs. Princess Marina was the perfect choice for an aesthete like Prince George, exquisitely beautiful, tall, dark, slim, with the exotic cheekbones of her Russian imperial ancestry. She was chic and sophisticated, having run a boutique in Paris and lived a peripatetic international life since 1922, when the royal family were – not for the first or last time – expelled from Greece. She and Prince George shared the same taste in people, which was not at all the same as the mainstream royal family represented by the Yorks. Their friends were amusing and talented, men like Cecil Beaton and Noël Coward; Prince Paul and his wife, Marina's sister, Olga, and her other sister Elizabeth, 'Woolly', married to Count Carl zu Toerring-Jettenbach; and a string of princely German and Greek relations, including the family of the young Prince Philip of Greece, Princess Elizabeth's future husband.

Princess Marina's chic beauty made her an instant hit with the British public. 'Don't let them change you,' an admirer shouted as she drove with Prince George from Victoria Station, where she had arrived from her home in September 1934. 'It's all so lovely and happy that I can hardly believe it,' Prince George wrote to Prince Paul. 'Everyone is so delighted with her – the crowd especially – 'cos when she arrived at Victoria Station they expected a dowdy princess – such as unfortunately my family are but when they saw this lovely chic creature – they could hardly believe it . . ."⁹

Prince George and Princess Marina were married on 29 November at Westminster Abbey; Elizabeth and her cousin, Lady Mary Cambridge (granddaughter of Queen Mary's brother, Adolphus, Marquess of Cambridge), were the two bridesmaids. Among the guests in the Abbey, sitting in some of the best seats, were Mr and Mrs Ernest Simpson. The increasing prominence of Mrs Simpson in the Prince of Wales's life was a source of hidden anxiety to the royal family. At the eve-of-wedding party given by the King and Queen, Wallis had stood out in a violet lamé dress with vivid green sash to match the emerald and diamond jewellery given her by the besotted Prince. To the King's concealed rage, the Prince of Wales introduced her to his parents. George V later told his Private Secretary, Clive Wigram, of his 'fury' that the Prince had 'smuggled Mrs Simpson into the Palace' and then had the effrontery to introduce her to him and the Queen. 'That woman in my own house,' he had thundered. By the autumn of 1934 the royal family had no illusions about the Prince of Wales's obsession with Wallis, a chic, amusing, twice-married American from Baltimore. Prince George, his brother's constant companion until his marriage to Princess Marina, was their principal source of information. 'Since Mrs Simpson had entered his [the Prince of Wales's] life,' he told a friend, 'neither he nor his brothers had ever seen him as in days gone by.'¹⁰ By the spring of 1935 the fact that the heir to the throne had a married mistress whom he loaded with expensive jewellery was well known in the United States and Canada, where the Hearst Press gave the affair headline treatment, including the pair's skiing holiday to Kitzbuhel in February and their trips to Vienna and Budapest. In Britain, however, the newspapers kept their collective mouths shut; the Prince's passion for Wallis was known only to his family and the small closed circle of London society.

The nine-year-old Princess Elizabeth was completely unaware of all this, although she had, according to Crawfie, met Mrs Simpson once when Uncle David had brought her over to tea at Royal Lodge. The famous 'long, cool stare' may well have been trained on Uncle David's chatty American friend and she may have picked up the vibrations of dislike emanating from her mother. She may well have wondered why Uncle David was no longer a regular visitor at tea-time, but her parents' policy was the rigid convention in 'polite society' when '*pas devant les enfants*' would be hissed whenever any indelicate subject raised its head. She certainly would not have read anything about her uncle and his mistress in *Punch* or *The Children's Newspaper*.

Superficially all seemed well in the family for the huge celebrations of her grandfather's twenty-five years on the throne, the Silver Jubilee. On 6 May 1935 Elizabeth, dressed in pink like her sister, left Buckingham Palace to drive with her parents in an open carriage to St Paul's Cathedral for a Thanksgiving Service. It was her first real experience of the pomp and glamour of a royal occasion. Cheering crowds lined the streets, some people fainting in the heat, unusual for early May. The Yorks formed part of a huge procession headed by the Speaker of the House of Commons in his magnificent gilded state coach, then carriages with the Dominion Prime Ministers and the Prime Minister of Great Britain, Ramsay MacDonald, the Lord Chancellor in his vast wig, the royal aunts and cousins, Elizabeth's Uncle George, now Duke of Kent, with his glamorous wife, and Uncle Henry, Duke of Gloucester. Troops of the Household Cavalry in glittering cuirasses and helmets topped by flowing horsehair tails, red and blue uniforms, skin-tight breeches and high black boots, swords held erect, trotted between the royal carriages. At the end of the procession, raising the loudest cheer, came her grandparents, Queen Mary in silver and diamonds, glittering, as one person described it, like the slopes of the Eiger.

There was a great outpouring of love for the simple old King, which surprised him most of all. Returning flattered but puzzled from a hugely successful tour of the poorest streets of London's East End, he told his old friend, the Archbishop of Canterbury, 'But I cannot understand. I am quite an ordinary sort of fellow.' To which the Archbishop somewhat unflatteringly replied, 'Yes, Sir, that is just it.' Twenty-five years earlier, on the King's accession, Lloyd George, Chancellor of the Exchequer in Asquith's Government, had diagnosed the secret of the King's appeal: 'The King is a very jolly chap but thank God there's not much in his head. They're simple, very very ordinary people, and perhaps on the whole that's how it should be.'[11] In a special broadcast from Buckingham Palace the King expressed his feelings: 'I can only say to you, my very very dear people, that the Queen and I thank you from the depths of our hearts for all the loyalty and – may I say so? – the love, with which this day and always you have surrounded us.'

Foreign observers underlined the paternal image that George V publicly represented (in contrast to his private performance of that role). The *Deutsche Allgemeine Zeitung* hailed the King as 'father of the nation', while the French Ambassador, René Corbin, reported to his minister that George V had become during the course of his reign 'not only the King, but the Father of his peoples and to the loyalty has come to add the warmth of love. That is the secret of the personal and living emotion which today fills the heart of this Kingdom and Empire.' He could not, he said, but be struck by 'the cohesion and power which the family of the British Democracies draw from their attachment to the Crown, considered at the same time as a paternal force and the symbol of unity'.[12] For Elizabeth, the Empire and the monarchy which she had learned about in the schoolroom took on reality during those days of celebration of her grandfather's Silver Jubilee, when the royal family seemed borne on a huge wave of love and excitement. She was too young to have known the times when things did not seem quite so secure; when, after the assassination of his cousin, the Tsar, and the discontent of traumatised troops returning from the Great War, followed by the General Strike, her grandfather had been haunted by the fear of revolution and had realised that he was going to have to work to keep his throne. In that, he had been eminently successful.

King George's apotheosis came as his life was nearing its end. That winter his doctor, Lord Dawson of Penn, told the Prime Minister, Stanley Baldwin, that the old King was 'packing up his luggage and getting ready to depart'. The family Christmas at Sandringham was overshadowed by the weakness of the King and by a certain awkwardness in the atmosphere. The Kents were there, with their new baby, Prince Edward, born in October, and the Gloucesters, Uncle Harry and his new wife, the former Lady Alice Montagu-Douglas-Scott, whom he had married in November (Elizabeth and Margaret had been bridesmaids, dressed by Norman Hartnell in Kate Greenaway dresses with the skirts specially shortened on the King's orders because 'I want to see their pretty little knees'). The King, whose favourite sister, Princess Victoria (a sharp spinster detested for her interference by her royal nephews), had died in December, looked thin and bent. He slept badly and frequently needed oxygen to help him breathe at night. The prospects for the future of the monarchy weighed on him; that year he had openly expressed doubts about his eldest son as his successor. 'I pray to God that nothing will come between Bertie and Lilibet and the throne,' he told his friend and confidant Cosmo Lang, Archbishop of

Canterbury. 'After I'm gone, the boy will ruin himself within six months,' he predicted. The Prince of Wales was even more bored and restless than usual and kept slipping off to telephone Wallis Simpson.

The year 1936 opened badly for everyone. While the Princesses remained at Sandringham, their parents returned to Royal Lodge, where the Duchess developed influenza and then pneumonia. At Sandringham Elizabeth worried about the change in her grandfather, who would fall asleep at meals. On 16 January he stayed in bed; Queen Mary, alarmed, summoned the Duke of York to return to Sandringham. On Saturday, 18 January, the shooting-party invited by the King left with Elizabeth and Margaret. Everyone remarked on how unhappy Elizabeth looked. Two days later King George V died just before midnight on 20 January (hastened on his way by a lethal injection of morphine and cocaine). Crawfie returned early from her Christmas holiday to look after the children. 'Don't let all this depress them more than is absolutely necessary, Crawfie,' the Duchess of York had written to her. 'They are so young.' It seems odd that Princess Elizabeth should have been so shielded from the death of her beloved grandfather, but avoiding excessive emotion was a royal family tradition. None the less, with her innate sense of appropriateness, the troubled little girl asked, 'Oh, Crawfie, ought we to play?'

Even at that age Elizabeth was made aware that the public face of royal life was a series of staged tableaux. On 27 January, dressed in black with a black velvet beret on her head, she was taken to see the lying-in-state of her grandfather in the sombre great Westminster Hall with its vaulted wooden roof. Silent people filed past the purple catafalque on which the coffin lay, the crown and sceptre glittering on top. Elizabeth was struck by the stillness of her father and his three brothers, who, dressed in uniform, stood vigil at the four corners of the coffin. 'Uncle David was there', she later told Crawfie, 'and he never moved at all . . . not even an eyelid.' The following day, dressed in the same new black coat and beret, she stood clutching her mother's hand as her grandfather's coffin was lowered into the family vault beneath St George's Chapel, Windsor. 'The British monarchy has never before stood so high in the world's estimation,' the Archbishop of Canterbury's chaplain, Dr Don, wrote in his diary in tribute to the late King. 'King George is mourned by myriads outside the British Empire.'[13]

The new reign had begun with a sinister sign. As the gun carriage bearing George V's coffin rumbled towards Westminster Hall, the jewelled Maltese cross on the imperial crown had broken loose and tumbled into the gutter. 'A most terrible omen,' Harold Nicolson MP noted in his diary. 'Christ, what's going to happen next?' the new King, Edward VIII, walking behind the coffin was heard to exclaim. 'That', another MP, Walter Elliot, remarked to a fellow MP beside him, 'will be the motto of the new reign.' While his father lay dying, Edward, in a gesture which was widely seen as symbolic of his determination to turn his back on the old ways, had ordered the clocks at Sandringham to be put back thirty minutes in line with Greenwich Mean Time. ('Sandringham Time' had been instituted by Edward VII as a means of gaining extra daylight for his shooting-parties and of countering Queen Alexandra's chronic unpunctuality.) At the proclamation of the new King in the courtyard of St James's Palace Wallis Simpson could clearly be seen seated at a window with Edward standing beside her watching the ceremony. Uncle David was now King Edward VIII and proceeded to fulfil his father's prediction in just under a year: 1936 was to go down in history as the Year of Three Kings.

The death of George V made an enormous difference in the Yorks' life which the ten-year-old Elizabeth cannot have failed to sense. Her parents were devastated, not only by natural family grief but by a sense of spiritual exile. 'Though outwardly one's life goes on the same, yet everything is different – especially spiritually and mentally,' the Duchess wrote to George V's doctor, Lord Dawson. 'I mind things I don't like more than before.' Among the things the Duchess minded was the predominance at the new court of 'Queen Wallis', as Chips Channon immediately dubbed her. From being the King's favourite daughter-in-law and, as far as Bertie was concerned, the closest to him of all his sons, the Yorks were no longer welcome. Wallis returned their dislike of her with good measure, joking about Bertie's dullness and his wife's dowdiness and ample figure. In private she and the King now referred to the Duchess as 'Cookie'. Under Wallis's direction the new King was busy sacking his father's old servants; Bertie was not consulted. He was, however, asked to do a review of how economies might be made at Sandringham, although he apparently did not know that his brother was planning to sell the family home. Through the King's Principal Private Secretary, Sir Alexander 'Alec' Hardinge, whose wife Helen was an old friend of the Duchess, the Yorks learned of his personal staff's unhappiness, of his hours spent closeted with Mrs Simpson while his private secretaries and other officials waited outside, of the government despatch boxes containing state papers taken to Fort Belvedere and returned unopened or with the ring marks of cocktail glasses on them.

To the public, however, Edward was still their idol. In July Elizabeth went to watch Uncle David present the Colours at the annual military ceremony. Her father and Uncle David were on horseback, but while she, her grandmother, uncles and aunts sat in the Royal pavilion, the 'new court', Wallis and her friends, sat in a separate stand. As the King rode off after the ceremony a lunatic pushed through the crowd with a gun in his hand; the police knocked the man's arm and the revolver skidded harmlessly under the horse's hooves. At the time Edward believed it to be an assassination attempt, but with cool courage he rode on without flinching and, as a result, his popularity with the public rose to new heights. At the end of the month the King took his mistress on a cruise on a yacht, the soon to be notorious *Nahlin*. Photographs of the King in shorts bathing with Wallis appeared all over the world, but not in Britain. The royal family at home were wretched, but kept up appearances. When the King visited Queen Mary on his return to England, she simply asked him whether he had found it 'warm in the Adriatic'.

So far, despite the King's obvious infatuation, Queen Mary had refrained from raising the subject with him. She told Lady Airlie:

I have not liked to talk to David about his affair with Mrs Simpson, in the first place because I don't want to give the impression of interfering in his private life, and also because he is the most obstinate of all my sons. To oppose him over doing anything is only to make him more determined to do it. At present he is utterly infatuated, but my great hope is that violent infatuations usually wear off . . .[14]

In any case, personal discussions were not the rule in the royal family, as Lord Harewood attested. 'I think they [his parents] found it as hard to talk in a serious yet personal vein to us as we did to them,' he wrote. Talking about the family at the time of the Abdication, he said:

People kept much more private and much more quiet about things like that and were much more able to bottle up their feelings. I think the whole of my mother's family tended to bottle up their feelings very much. To the point of being a fault . . . it was a tradition not to discuss anything awkward . . . But that went much wider than just that family. It was general in a way that we find difficult to realise now.[15]

Loelia Ponsonby described her mother as taking it as axiomatic that 'Reserve is one of the Cardinal Virtues synonymous with Decency' and that, as a result, when she, Loelia, grew up she was unable to articulate her feelings. These strict codes of behaviour were to survive within the royal family and the royal household long after they had been abandoned elsewhere and, indeed, were to shape Elizabeth's own attitudes when she had to face similar family crises in the course of her reign.

The Yorks were at Birkhall as usual in August, but this year the hostess at Balmoral was not Queen Mary but Wallis Simpson, occupying the Queen's suite; the Duchess of York had a distinctly frosty exchange with Wallis at a Balmoral dinner-party. Elizabeth remained at Birkhall, an eighteenth-century house on the Balmoral estate which was still lit by oil lamps, and went out for tea and games with their near neighbours, the Hardinges, children of Sir Alec Hardinge (later an active participant in the campaign to dissuade the King from marrying Wallis). As a gesture of defiance to the new regime and to underline their loyalty to the old traditions, the Yorks invited Archbishop Lang, a guest of the late King's at Balmoral for the past twenty-five years but definitely persona non grata with the new King, to stay. The Duke of York was unhappy and anxious that September, in despair about his brother's behaviour. On the 23rd he and the Duchess had been asked to deputise for the King at the opening of the new Aberdeen Infirmary; the King had cried off on the grounds that he was still in mourning for his father, but the real reason for his refusal to attend was made only too clear when he was seen, thinly disguised by driving goggles, meeting Wallis at Aberdeen station just as the Yorks were engaged in the opening ceremony. The resulting photographs outraged not just the royal family but the Scottish public. For the Duke of York, the most hurtful aspect of it all was the way his brother excluded him from any consultation over the major changes he intended to make on the Balmoral estate. 'David only told me what he had done when it was all over,' he complained to Queen Mary, 'which I might say made me rather sad . . . I never saw him alone for an instant.'

Elizabeth and her family were at Glamis for the last week of their holiday in mid-October. She and Margaret Rose, as her sister was still

called, were always happy there. 'Margaret Rose says that the Castle is
alive,' the Duchess wrote to Osbert Sitwell, 'I believe she is right.' On
18 October the Duke was in his element, out partridge-shooting with
his father-in-law and seven brothers-in-law at Colliedrum. It was the
last day for many months that he would enjoy peace of mind. On the
19th he took the night train for London with his family, only to be told
on arrival by Alec Hardinge that on the 27th Mrs Simpson would be
petitioning for a divorce from her husband and that the King had
refused the Prime Minister's appeal to prevent the divorce from going
forward. Hardinge warned the Duke of York that the affair might end
with his brother's abdication. Prince Albert was 'appalled and tried
not to believe what he had been told'.

The Yorks remained on the sidelines as the situation worsened;
Prince Albert made repeated attempts to talk to his brother, but the
King either fobbed him off or refused to talk about the matter, until
on the morning of 17 November he summoned Bertie to the Palace to
tell him what he had told the Prime Minister and Queen Mary the
previous evening: that he intended to marry Mrs Simpson, with or
without the Government's approval, and that, if necessary, he was
prepared to abdicate in order to do so. 'Oh,' Bertie replied, 'that's a
dreadful thing to hear. None of us wants that, I least of all.' Three
days later, on Edward's return from Wales where, shocked by the
numbers of unemployed, he had uttered the famous words 'Something
must be done ...', he told his brother George that he was going to
marry Wallis and that she would be 'Queen of England ... and
Empress of India, the whole bag of tricks'. That evening, at Chips
Channon's dinner-party, the King was euphoric, triumphantly in love.
Wallis wore on her finger their 'engagement ring', a magnificent
emerald which had once belonged to the Great Mogul and had cost
the King a cool quarter of a million pounds.

But, as the rest of the royal family saw it, it was David's duty to his
country and to the Empire to put the public interest before his private
passion. Not only was divorce widely regarded as taboo at the time
(and particularly so in royal circles where it would be many years
before a divorced person would be permitted to set foot in the Royal
Enclosure at Ascot), but there was a supra-national dimension to the
question. Since 1931 the Statute of Westminster had granted autonomy
to the self-governing Dominions of Canada, Australia, New Zealand,
South Africa, Newfoundland and the Irish Free State. The Crown was
'the symbol of the free association of the members of the British

Commonwealth of Nations ... united by common allegiance to the Crown', and the King was individually sovereign of each of those countries. As King he was Supreme Governor of the Church, which still did not recognise divorce; it was unthinkable to his family that he could contemplate marriage to a twice-divorced woman. As King, however, he was also above the law, and there would have been nothing to prevent him from marrying Wallis in secret. This he was honourably determined not to do and, as it began to dawn upon him that the people might not be willing to accept Wallis as Queen, he contemplated a morganatic marriage by which she would be his wife, but not Queen, nor would any children she might have succeed to the throne. But to do this would require parliamentary legislation and, therefore, the consent of the Government to an alteration to the royal succession and title, and not only of the British Government but of the Commonwealth Governments as well. Once he had asked Government's advice as to the marriage, he was constitutionally bound to take it or provoke a crisis of the first magnitude. The Government's answer, after consultation with the Prime Ministers of the Dominions, was against the marriage. The King was therefore faced with the unpalatable choice of losing his throne or losing Wallis. For a moment, urged on by Wallis, who had fled abroad to escape public hostility, he thought he could keep both by appealing to the people over the head of the Government.

On the morning of 3 December the story broke in the national press. This sensational development was unwittingly caused by the innocent remarks about the King's private life made by the Bishop of Bradford, Dr Blunt (known thereafter as 'the Blunt instrument'). The Bishop, like the vast majority of the British public, had never heard of Mrs Simpson; he was simply commenting on the King's failure to attend church and take communion, which as Supreme Governor it was his duty to do. First reported in the *Yorkshire Post* on 2 December the Bishop's remarks were interpreted as a reference to the King's affair with Wallis. The wall of silence was breached and the nation informed that their idolised King proposed to marry a twice-divorced American. Most were appalled. After a lecture by Harold Nicolson in Islington, the presiding vicar asked the audience to stand and sing the national anthem. Only about ten out of four hundred did so. The vicar told Nicolson that he never thought he would have lived to see the day when his congregation refused to sing 'God Save the King'. Romantics like Winston Churchill and right-wing fanatics like Sir Oswald Mosley supported the King against the Government.

Over the weekend of 4–6 December the King dithered, incommunicado at the Fort, talking only to his chosen advisers and refusing to see or talk to Bertie. Officially, Elizabeth was supposed to know nothing, although the story was in all the newspapers and *Punch* (if she was allowed to see it) carried a cartoon of Baldwin putting 'The Choice' to the King with the Abdication document laid out between them and the caption, 'The Throne is Greater than the Man'. Over that weekend at the Royal Lodge, with her mother in bed with influenza again, she must have noticed her father's preoccupation. Prince Paul of Yugoslavia and his wife came to tea, after which Paul told Chips Channon that 'the Duke of York is miserable, does not want the throne and is imploring his brother to stay'.

On the evening of Monday, 7 December, the King called Bertie to the Fort and told him that he intended to abdicate; that night the Duke returned to London with his family. On the night of the 8th, worn out by family discussions and appalled by the burden which faced him, Bertie broke down and sobbed on his mother's shoulder. By Thursday, 10 December, it was all over; that morning the King signed the Instrument of Abdication in the presence of his three brothers and the lawyers who were to hammer out the financial arrangements between the past and future Kings. Prince Albert returned to No. 145 to find a large crowd 'cheering madly'. 'I was overwhelmed,' he wrote simply in his diary. At 1.52 p.m. the following day, Friday, 11 December 1936, he was formally proclaimed King George VI of Great Britain, Ireland and the Dominions beyond the Seas. That night, after a farewell family dinner-party, the former Edward VIII, now HRH Prince Edward of Windsor, made his famous Abdication broadcast: 'I have found it impossible to carry the heavy burden of responsibility and to discharge my duties as King as I would wish to do without the help and support of the woman I love ...' Later he said goodbye to his mother, sister and brothers and left England in a naval destroyer. From that moment he became a non-person as far as the royal family was concerned, an unmentionable skeleton in the family cupboard. Elizabeth was never to hear her parents mention him in her presence.

Whether they talked about him or not, the sense of shock and shame in the family was palpable. Lord Harewood recalled a 'hangdog' expedition to London from Yorkshire to witness the proclamation of

the new King at St James's Palace. 'We all felt miserable,' Queen
Mary wrote in her diary that day, after watching the ceremony from
Marlborough House with the King and her two granddaughters. Her
niece, the Duchess of Beaufort, later told her biographer, James Pope-
Hennessy, that the Abdication was the worst experience of Queen
Mary's life. The new King wrote apologetically to the Prime Minister:
'I hope that time will be allowed me to make amends for what has
happened.' Then he with the Queen, their children and Queen Mary
left for Christmas at Sandringham on 22 December. For Elizabeth, it
can hardly have been a happy Christmas in the big house full of
memories of her beloved grandfather. Queen Mary retired to her
room, ill with the shock and strain of the last months; the new Queen
was still recovering from a serious bout of 'flu and the King seemed on
the verge of a nervous breakdown. The cause of all this unhappiness
was Uncle David's irresponsibility. The Abdication had been a
traumatic experience for the royal family which was never to be
forgotten. There can have been no doubt in Elizabeth's mind that the
Duke of Windsor, as he had now become, had let the side down.

3

Heiress

'I thought it all *very, very* wonderful and I expect the Abbey did too. The arches and beams at the top were covered with a sort of haze of wonder as Papa was crowned . . .'

HRH Princess Elizabeth, 'The Coronation Diary,
12 May 1937'

On 17 February Elizabeth and the nursery retinue moved from No. 145 Piccadilly, her home for ten years, to Buckingham Palace. It was a short distance but a huge step in a life which could never be 'normal' again. No. 145 had faced directly on to a street along which ordinary people, cars, buses and horse-drawn carts passed on their daily business. Buckingham Palace, the official headquarters of the British monarchy, stood aloof, a huge stone pile with a vast forecourt distancing it from the public. Beyond the railings and visible from all points of the compass, Queen Victoria sat enthroned on a huge and elaborate monument of white marble, a constant presence and reminder of the past, while beyond her the wide Mall designed as a ceremonial approach to the Palace stretched down to Admiralty Arch, another memorial to his mother erected by Edward VII.

Everything at Buckingham Palace was on a monumental scale. Successive royal ancestors of Elizabeth had added to the original Buckingham House, bought by George III in 1762 for his nineteen-year-old Queen, Charlotte. George IV had begun to remodel the house and turn it into a palace on his accession in 1820. His favourite architect, John Nash, created a new façade on the western front overlooking the gardens and another on the east with wings on either side. Inside, at first-floor level, he designed a magnificent series of state rooms. On the death of George IV in 1830 Nash lost his job, having vastly exceeded the original estimates while the Palace was not even ready for occupation. The next monarch but one, Queen Victoria, became the first sovereign actually to live at Buckingham Palace, moving in on 13 July 1837, just over one hundred years before her great-great-granddaughter came to live there. The Palace became considerably more pompous under Victoria and Edward VII; the golden Bath stone of Nash's building was hidden behind a massive new grey east front, which is the public face of Buckingham Palace.

The huge house, like the American White House, is not just a home for the family but also an administrative centre and a theatre for state entertainments. Some three hundred people work there; it has its own post office and a postman who delivers letters to the various offices. It takes two men a week to wind and service something in the region of three hundred palace clocks; there are two thousand electric lightbulbs regularly needing replacing. Crawfie discovered the Vermin Man and his grisly contraption, the 'sticky-trap'. This was a piece of cardboard with a lump of aniseed in the middle surrounded by a sea of treacle; the mouse, lured by the smell of the aniseed, became stuck in the treacle trying to reach it and was then despatched by the Vermin Man. Crawfie, less accustomed to the place than Elizabeth, felt uncomfortable there. The wind moaned in the chimneys and the family apartments were separated from each other by interminable corridors. Electric light had only recently been installed and switches had been placed in odd and inconvenient places – Crawfie's bedroom light could be turned on or off only by a switch outside in the passage some two yards from her door. Behind the gilt of the state apartments parts of the Palace were dilapidated. When the housemaid came to draw Crawfie's curtains, the whole thing, pelmet and all, collapsed on the floor. When the King showed his daughters the schoolroom on the top floor facing the Mall, unhappy memories of his own schooldays there overwhelmed him. Taking one look at the gloomy room, its windows barred by the heavy stone balustrades outside, he turned away, closed the door and said, 'No, that won't do.'

None the less, Buckingham Palace seemed like home to the King; he had lived there for thirteen years before his marriage. Characteristically, Edward VIII had never liked it. To him the building had a dank, musty smell and, as he wrote in his memoirs, he never lost the feeling of not belonging there. No doubt the ghost of his father lingered, a disapproving shadow to his eldest son but a comforting memory to George VI and his family. Absolute quiet had reigned in the Palace while George V and Queen Mary lived there, an oasis of nineteenth-

century calm in twentieth-century London; the arrival of the new
family brought the place to life. For Elizabeth too the Palace was
familiar territory. The children were excited by the move and enjoyed
rearranging their stable of toy horses in the long corridor outside their
rooms. They liked racing down the passages to visit their parents.
'People need bicycles in this place,' Elizabeth remarked; Margaret used
to ride her tricycle down the corridors. The King had their rocking-
horses placed outside his study so that he could hear the children
playing on them. After the dreary square of grass behind No. 145 the
huge Palace gardens, including a large lake inhabited by ducks, were a
delight. Another favourite place was a small hill at the end of the
garden, from which they could look down on the everyday world
outside as they had at No. 145. There were always crowds outside the
Palace, gazing up as though expecting something to happen. From
behind the lace curtains the Princesses stared back, just as fascinated.
The fact that from now on there would always be crowds looking at
them as if they were rare beasts (which, in a sense, they were) was
something that they had come to accept as normal.

The King and Queen occupied the pink and gold Belgian suite on
the ground floor while the apartments that had been George V's and
Queen Mary's were redecorated. When Queen Mary had moved out
to Marlborough House after her husband's death, she had thriftily
taken the silk wall coverings from two of her sitting-rooms, the 'Green
Tea Room' and the 'Boudoir', with her. They had to be replaced at a
cost of £550 to the public purse. All the walls were repapered and the
gilding on the mouldings touched up. New baths were installed in both
the King's and the Queen's bathrooms. The King chose to use as his
bedroom his father's dressing-room, perhaps because it was a good
deal smaller than the King's official bedroom but also perhaps because
it reminded him so much of his father and his father's evening ritual
of dressing for dinner when he used to like having his family round
him. The Princesses' rooms were on the second floor above. Elizabeth
now had a sitting-room of her own and a room adjoining. There was a
room for Crawfie, another for Bobo, a day nursery and a night nursery,
over which Allah Knight still reigned, and two bathrooms, neither of
them what would nowadays be called *en suite*. The Queen, like her
mother, had taste and a touch for creating a welcoming atmosphere
wherever she lived. When Lady Airlie, who as Queen Mary's lady-in-
waiting had known the Palace well, visited them there shortly after
they moved in, she remarked on how cosy and homely the atmosphere

was. The King smiled proudly, 'Elizabeth can make a home wherever she is.'

The public side of their life was at that time the most important. Elizabeth watched as her father and mother acted out their parts in the pageant of monarchy, a role which Edward VIII had found so irksome, although he had possessed the gifts to do it supremely well. Monarchy is superb theatre or a meaningless charade, whichever way you like to look at it. The new King and Queen, trained in the extreme formality of the court of George V and Queen Mary, understood that the Duke and Duchess of York had to be seen to be transformed into King George VI and Queen Elizabeth. A young couturier, Norman Hartnell, was brought in to glamorise the Queen's wardrobe. Her figure was not suited to the skinny chic that Wallis and her contemporaries wore; she was not prepared to confine herself to the strict dieting which society women underwent in order to look good in clinging crepe by Mainbocher or Patou. Chips Channon was to describe her as looking 'bosomy' at the Coronation and rumours circulated that she was pregnant. Queen Mary with her unchanging style provided an outstanding example of how to be regal without being fashionable. Her Edwardian dresses, long-skirted, in soft colours and fabrics, often edged with fox furs, her toque hats and, above all, the ease with which she wore staggering amounts of jewellery without looking either overloaded or vulgar, had become established in the public eye. At the Silver Jubilee Channon, no mean judge of style, had noted: 'Suddenly she has become the best-dressed woman in the world.' The new King, who had an unerring eye for clothes, found the perfect answer for his wife in the romantic Winterhalter portraits of Victoria and Albert and various Saxe-Coburg relations lining the walls of the Marble Hall. 'His Majesty made it clear in his quiet way', Hartnell wrote, 'that I should attempt to capture this picturesque grace in the dresses I was to design for the Queen. Thus it is to the King and Winterhalter that are owed the fine praises I later received for the regal renaissance of the romantic crinoline.'[1] He designed two crinoline evening dresses for the Queen to wear at banquets for state visits; one, in silver tissue over silver gauze with a deep collar of silver lace sewn with diamonds, he described as 'the first great dress I designed for any member of the Royal Family'. Later Cecil Beaton, the outstanding image-maker of his age, was called in to photograph the Queen wearing that same dress. Seeing her now he found it 'inexplicable that before I could have felt it was dreary and dowdy to have the Yorks on the throne . . . [I took] many more lovely pictures that should be very romantic of the fairy Queen in her ponderous palace.'[2]

State occasions at the 'ponderous palace' were very grand. Harold Nicolson attended the first dinner-party there in March 1937 and was impressed by the splendour. Tall footmen with powdered hair stood motionless on each fourth step of Nash's Grand Staircase, leading up to the drawing-rooms of the state apartments. The dining-table glittered with gold candelabra and scarlet tulips with the fabulous Windsor gold services massed in tiers along the walls. There were state visits by the Kings of the Belgians and Romania and by President Coty of France, on which occasion Elizabeth made a short speech of welcome in French to the President. Then there were the courts at which debutantes and recently married ladies were 'presented' to the King and Queen. They were occasions of the utmost formality when the King and Queen wore crowns and sat on thrones while the women in full evening dress with five-foot trains, three ostrich feathers in their hair and a white tulle veil hanging down behind, curtseyed to them in turn as their names were called out by the Lord Chamberlain. The men wore knee breeches and silk stockings; officials of the household, ambassadors and privy counsellors were in their uniforms, glittering with gold braid, orders and decorations. The Princesses stared down from the windows at the guests arriving in their plumes and jewels – 'a fly's eye view,' Elizabeth called it. Their favourite was Princess Marina, always beautiful and exquisitely dressed. Garden-parties which they now attended with their parents were less amusing. Wearing childish smocked silk frocks with matching knickers, white socks and the hated straw hats, they walked with their parents through the 3,000 guests in the Palace gardens. Once Crawfie overheard Elizabeth instruct her sister on how to behave. 'If you do see someone with a funny hat, Margaret, you must *not* point at it and laugh. And you must *not* be in too much of a hurry to get through the crowds to the tea table. That's not polite either.'

From the age of ten, Elizabeth was becoming accustomed to the extraordinary pomp and ceremony surrounding her parents, so that to her it appeared a normal part of life. This included the swarm of household and staff with medieval-sounding names: the Lord Chamberlain, the Keeper of the Privy Purse, the Mistress of the Robes, the Yeomen of the Silver and Gold and of the China and Glass pantry, the Pages of the Chambers, the Pages of the Backstairs and of the Presence (all adult men, not boys as their titles would suggest), some four hundred servants headed by the Palace Steward, plus the equerries, ladies-in-waiting, Ladies of the Bedchamber and Women of the Bedchamber, the King's and the Queen's Private Secretaries and their staff, the Crown Equerry in charge of the grooms and coachmen looking after the seventy-five horses and state carriages in the Royal Mews.

The King and Queen were already training Elizabeth for the day when she would be at the head of this vast establishment. Since she had become the obvious heir to the throne they were taking her education more seriously. 'I have started my daughter on Latin,' the Duchess of York had told Osbert Sitwell in January 1935. Elizabeth was often there when her parents entertained diplomats to lunch; on one such occasion in 1937, Sir Miles Lampson, British envoy to Cairo, was amused to see the King fiddling with the knobs of his recently acquired television set, unable to make it work. 'Long before most children do,' Crawfie wrote, 'Lilibet took an interest in politics, and knew quite a bit about what was going on in the world outside . . . The King would also talk to his elder daughter more seriously than most fathers do to so young a child . . . It was as if he spoke to an equal.'

Her parents were anxious that she and her sister should as far as possible feel that they were ordinary children and a part of the world beyond the Palace walls. The result was the formation of the 1st Buckingham Palace Company of Girl Guides (at Elizabeth's insistence two Brownies were added to the Palace Company, so that Margaret, too young to be a full-fledged Guide, should not feel left out). The idea was that it should be a substitute for going out to school, so that the Princesses should meet and play with and compete with other children on an equal basis. As an exercise in democracy it was somewhat limited. 'They were all duke's daughters and Mountbattens – it wasn't at all democratic,' one former member said. The other girls were expected to curtsey to the Princesses; the first meeting, Crawfie recalled, was spoilt by the attendant nannies and governesses, while the children wore their best party frocks and white gloves. Some of the more pampered children were shown up in a game which involved taking off their shoes and piling them in a heap in the middle of the floor, then finding them, putting them back on and racing to see who could get back to the starting line first. 'This never went very well,' Crawfie wrote, 'as quite half the children did not know their own shoes! Lilibet and Margaret told me this with scorn. There was never any nonsense of that kind in *their* nursery.'

The Guides met every Wednesday evening at five o'clock at the Palace. Patricia Mountbatten, eldest daughter of the King's cousin, Lord Louis Mountbatten, was the leader of Kingfisher patrol with Elizabeth as her second in command. 'She was really efficient,' Countess Mountbatten recalled, 'very organised, and very responsible, keen and enthusiastic. She told me years later that she was rather frightened of me. I was terribly taken aback.' Guide activities took place in the palace gardens with George V's summerhouse as head-quarters, or at the Palace swimming-pool. Elizabeth apparently enjoyed it, but some of the less practically minded and co-ordinated girls dreaded the prospect of Wednesdays and 'those awful team games'. Elizabeth Cavendish 'used to feel positively sick' at the thought as did Diana Legh, daughter of Sir Piers 'Joey' Legh, the Master of the Household. 'You used to have to tie a certain knot round your middle and then be hauled to safety off a rock by your team. And whenever it came to me to throw the rope out to a drowning person it always stuck half way and I used to lose it for the whole side.' The captain was an alarming lady who used to marshal the girls and tell them what to do; Crawfie apparently used to act as second in command and a buffer between the tough captain and the more nervous girls. 'She was charming, always fun and nice,' one remembered. 'I liked her and the Princesses certainly did.' The expeditions they enjoyed the most were in Windsor Great Park, where they went on treks, dragging camping equipment in a trek cart; then they would camp, build fires and cook sausages on sticks and 'dampers', an Australian version of sausage-rolls.[3] That was the closest the Princesses got to ordinary life. Even on their first seaside holiday near Eastbourne detectives had to accompany them on beach picnics to keep the crowds away, and when taken as a great treat to have tea in a hotel, it would have to be held in a private room upstairs.

As soon as they had moved into Buckingham Palace their parents' Coronation loomed. The date, 12 May 1937, had originally been set for the Coronation of Edward VIII; arrangements were so far advanced that it could not now be put off, although thousands of Edward mugs and cups had to be scrapped and King George VI and Queen Elizabeth souvenirs hastily manufactured in their place. Dressmakers came and went at the Palace. The King sat in his study, practising his new signature. He had always signed himself 'Albert'; now he had become 'George, R.I.', King-Emperor like his father. He had chosen to call himself George to emphasise the continuity which had so nearly been dangerously broken with the brief reign of Edward VIII. He also practised wearing the heavy crown which he would wear on Coronation Day, an event which he was not looking forward to. Any public ceremonial occasion is a nightmare for a stammerer; not only would he be the star player, but also there was no way in which the ancient rite could be changed to avoid words which were difficult for him. Bets were laid in the City that he would not be up to the occasion; there were rumours about the state of his physical and mental health, even that he was an epileptic. The Archbishop of Canterbury and the Earl Marshal, the Duke of Norfolk, had come to the conclusion that the actual ceremony could be filmed but not televised. The Archbishop was said to fear that people might disrespectfully watch it in pubs; in any case at that time transmissions could be seen only within a twenty-five-mile radius from the Crystal Palace transmitter. The real reason, however, as the Archbishop noted privately in his papers, was that television offered no possibility of censorship should the King break down during the ceremony. The King practised dutifully with his therapist, Lionel Logue. With Logue's help and the Queen's encouragement, he had gone a long way towards mastering his stammer, but the pauses were still painfully noticeable and he dreaded broadcasting above all things. For him, the post-Coronation broadcast would be much more of an ordeal than the ceremony itself.

Elizabeth had been thoroughly prepared for the day by Queen Mary, who had provided a colour panorama of George IV's Coronation to instruct her granddaughters in the full symbolism of the event and the curious-sounding names of all the participating officials. The Princesses could be sure that, whatever happened, their slim, elegant father would cut a better figure in satin breeches, silk stockings and ermine robes than the excessively corpulent George IV. When the day came, Elizabeth kept an account of it specially for her parents, written in pencil on lined paper bound with pink silk ribbon with the title 'The Coronation, 12 May 1937. To Mummy and Papa. In Memory of Their Coronation, From Lilibet By Herself.' The day started extremely early; while Their Majesties were woken at three in the morning by the testing of loudspeakers outside the Palace, the Marine band chose to kick off at dawn.

At 5 o'clock in the morning I was woken up by the band of the Royal Marines striking up just outside my window [Elizabeth wrote]. I leapt out of bed and so did Bobo. We put on dressing-gowns and shoes and

Bobo made me put on an eiderdown as it was so cold and we crouched
in the window looking onto a cold, misty morning. There were already
some people in the stands and all the time people were coming to them
in a stream . . . Every now and then we were hopping in and out of bed
looking at the bands and the soldiers. At six o'clock Bobo got up and
instead of getting up at my usual time I jumped out of bed at half-past
seven . . .[4]

She and Margaret were, as usual, dressed identically in cream
Nottingham lace long dresses with gold bows and purple velvet ermine-
trimmed cloaks, with double strings of small real pearls round their
necks and, on their heads, gilt coronets in a simple medieval style
chosen for them by their father. They wore silver pumps. 'What do
you think of my slippers?' Elizabeth asked Crawfie, lifting her skirt to
reveal that Allah had dressed her, as always, in short white socks. The
two Princesses drove to Westminster Abbey in a horse-drawn carriage.
'At first it was very jolty but we soon got used to it,' Elizabeth wrote.
There Elizabeth sat next to Queen Mary, who had deliberately broken
with the royal tradition that the widows of kings do not attend the
coronation of their successors in a public show of support for the new
regime ('Grannie looked too beautiful in a gold dress patterned with
gold flowers,' Elizabeth thought). On her bosom glittered the Garter
Star, which she had coolly written to her eldest son asking him to loan
her for the occasion, which had, after all, originally been designed as
his own Coronation. A specially built-up seat had been provided for
Margaret to enable her to look out of the high windows. Her sister
was, as always, maternally concerned about her behaviour. 'I do hope
she won't disgrace us by falling asleep in the middle,' she told Crawfie
anxiously. 'After all, she is *very* young for a Coronation, isn't she?' In
the end, Margaret behaved impeccably. 'She was wonderful,' Elizabeth
reported afterwards. 'I only had to nudge her once or twice when she
played with the prayer books too loudly.'

The King, to everyone's and his own relief, played his part to
perfection. Others did not. Despite the transcendental exultation which
he felt as he, like his predecessors in a line stretching back to Alfred
the Great, became one of the Lord's Anointed, his sharp eye noted the
failings of prelates and aristocrats who muffed their roles. When the
King knelt for the great moment of taking the coronation oath, the two
bishops, his official 'supporters' who were supposed to hold the Order
of Service for him to read, failed him. 'When this great moment came

neither Bishop could find the words,' he recorded later. 'So the Archbishop held his book down for me to read, but horror of horrors his thumb covered the words of the Oath.' The Duke of Portland, whose official task it was to carry the Queen's crown, and the Marquess of Salisbury, who was bearing the King's crown, both succeeded in entangling the Garter chains they were wearing in the tassels of the cushions on which the crowns rested as they presented them to the Archbishop to be placed on the altar. 'My Lord Great Chamberlain [the Earl of Ancaster] was supposed to dress me,' the King noted, 'but I found his hands fumbled & shook so I had to fix the sword myself. As it was he nearly put the hilt of the sword under my chin trying to attach it to the belt.' The King, whose practical mind had tried to foresee every difficulty, had taken the precaution of having a marker put on the crown so that it would be placed on his head the right way round. Now he discovered that some officious person had removed it. 'The Dean and the Archbishop had been juggling with it so much that I never did know whether it was right or not,' he wrote. As the final straw, when he rose to move towards his throne from the ancient Coronation Chair first used in 1307 and containing the Stone of Scone traditionally supposed to be the stone of Joseph of Arimathea's vision brought from the Holy Land, a clumsy bishop trod on his robe. 'I was brought up all standing, owing to one of the Bishops treading on my robe. I had to tell him to get off it pretty sharply as I nearly fell down.'[5]

The appearance of the Queen, 'dignified, and smiling', reminded everyone of the two ghosts at the occasion. Prince Charming, whose Coronation this should have been, became the first British monarch to listen in to the Coronation of his successor, from the rented French château where he sat with Wallis Simpson, whom he had hoped would be his Queen. Winston Churchill, a fervent supporter of King Edward VIII, had never really wanted Queen Wallis. Now he was convinced. 'You were right,' he whispered to his wife. 'I see now the "other one" wouldn't have done.'

'Papa [was] looking very beautiful in a crimson robe and the Cap of State,' the eleven-year-old Elizabeth had thought at the beginning of the service, the high point of which, her father's crowning, had passed in a 'haze of wonder'. 'What struck me as being rather odd', she wrote, 'was that Grannie did not remember much of her own Coronation. I should have thought it would have stayed in her mind for ever.' By the end, however, she was finding the service 'rather boring as it was all prayers.

Grannie and I were looking to see how many more pages to the end, and we turned one more and it said "Finis". We both smiled at each other . . .' If she thought that she would one day be playing the central role in the ceremony unfolding below her, she did not mention it.

After the Coronation the King seemed to grow in confidence, as if the ancient ceremony had confirmed to him that he really was the King. Crawfie thought he actually appeared taller, while Chaplain Don, witnessing a public ceremony a month later, was 'much struck by the King's demeanour – he has found himself and is growing in stature as the months go by – it is as though the charisma of the Coronation had effected a deepening and enlightening of the inner man . . .' The Queen, not having been brought up in the royal family and with Queen Mary as a hard act to follow, had to learn the part.

'To fulfil the task she had set herself, meant study, planning and tremendous concentration,' said a friend who knew her well both as Duchess of York and as Queen, 'and perhaps the discipline of such a training has curtailed a good deal of spontaneity and must inevitably lead to some artificiality.'6

She invented herself and her own image as Queen. Like Queen Mary, she never changed her style to suit current fashion; with the help of Hartnell, she impressed it on the public mind – the crinolines, the draped misty blue crepe, the triple row of huge real pearls, the off-the-face hat, and always the high heels to increase her stature. She invented her own version of the obligatory royal wave, a twirling, wrist-driven gesture which became her trademark; she had the self-confidence to break the royal tradition and smile. She perfected the art of keeping the royal distance between herself and the rest of the world without seeming to do so; she was so successful that not one of her old friends accused her of being stand-offish, although a study of her correspondence as Duchess of York and Queen reveals a marked difference. Her warmth sometimes led her old friends to overstep the mark. When they did so, the King pounced. Replying to a letter from Walter Monckton, a much-appreciated go-between where the Duke of Windsor was concerned, he gently reminded him that real familiarity was *lèse-majesté*: 'I gave the Queen your "love and duty", the King wrote, 'at which she was both surprised and pleased. I wonder if you did not mean "loyal duty"!! Anyhow it made us laugh . . .'7

As a natural actress, she certainly gave the impression that she was thoroughly enjoying herself, much to Wallis Simpson's disgust. 'Really David,' she wrote, 'the pleased expression on the Duchess of York's [she could not bring herself to call Elizabeth the Queen] face is funny to see. How she is loving it all.'[8] Harold Nicolson, attending a grand dinner at Buckingham Palace, was full of admiration for the way the new Queen handled herself:

> The Queen . . . wears upon her face a faint smile indicative of how much she would have liked her dinner-party were it not for the fact that she was Queen of England. Nothing could exceed the charm or dignity which she displays, and I cannot help feeling what a mess poor Mrs Simpson would have made of such an occasion . . .'[9]

The Abdication, although never mentioned by the family, was neither forgiven nor forgotten. The new Queen echoed Queen Mary's outrage and backed up her blacklisting of those people whom they considered the ringleaders of the pro-Wallis and Edward clique. Prominent among them was the brilliant, American-born hostess Emerald Cunard, who had made the running at the court of Queen Wallis (Noël Coward was heard to scream on receiving yet another invitation from Lady Cunard: 'I am sick to *death* of having "quiet suppers" with the King and Mrs Simpson!'). While the King told Prince George that neither he nor Marina must see Lady Cunard again, Queen Mary wrote to Prince Paul of Yugoslavia, George's brother-in-law and a man who owed Emerald Cunard many favours, asking that they too ostracise her. When the celebrated hostess Lady Londonderry sent her in advance the guest list for a post-Coronation ball, the Queen replied thanking her for her 'thoughtfulness in writing to ask about certain people being invited to the party on Wednesday', and adding that Lady Cunard was the only person that they did not want to meet just at that moment.[10]

Uncle David married Wallis, who had reverted to her maiden name of Warfield for the occasion, at the Château de Candé in France on 3 June 1937. His family were not amused by the fact that he had chosen, perhaps with some subconsciously Freudian gesture of defiance against his father, the late King's birthday as the date of his marriage. Not one member of the Duke of Windsor's family and only seven English friends attended the wedding of the man who only six months earlier had been the idolised King-Emperor. The King had forbidden his brothers to go to the wedding and Lord Louis Mountbatten, once the bridegroom's great friend, had thought it politic to decline.

The King and his brother were by now barely on speaking terms, the relationship having gone downhill with astonishing rapidity since the night of their emotional farewell in December. George VI had subsequently discovered that the Duke had lied to him over the amount of money at his disposal and that he had something like £1 million salted away as savings on his income from the Duchy of Cornwall, money which by rights should have gone with the Crown. The King's temper was not improved on finding that part of the interest on this sum which should have been his had been made over to Wallis. A bitter family quarrel ensued. The King had promised as part of the Abdication arrangement that the Duke should be paid an allowance of £25,000 on the Civil List, but after the revelation of the huge proportions of the Duke's nest-egg, both Churchill and Neville Chamberlain, the Chancellor of the Exchequer, usually on opposing sides, advised the King to pay the sum himself in order to avoid a parliamentary discussion of the subject. 'The moment this [the Duke's £1 million savings] is disclosed,' Churchill wrote to Chamberlain, 'the Labour Party could hardly help drawing the moral of the very large savings which it is possible for Royal persons to make, and to argue that the existing Civil List should be reduced.' Chamberlain, for once, agreed, thus avoiding, as he told his sister Ida, 'a discussion which would thoroughly discredit the Duke himself but would not fail to give another jolt to the Monarchy'. The King, therefore, reluctantly agreed to pay the allowance out of his private purse. He had also to buy out the Duke's interests in Balmoral and Sandringham, which, being family as opposed to Crown property, Edward had inherited as eldest son. After much wrangling the total valuation of the properties was settled at £289,853; this, invested in War Loan, produced £10,144 per annum which was paid to foreign residents tax free. The King would top this up with a further £11,000 a year, an allowance which would cease on his death.

Windsor supporters charged him with treating his brother meanly, but it is significant that when the King's official biographer, Sir John Wheeler-Bennett, saw the papers concerning the affair, he told the diarist Robert Bruce Lockhart 'how, as Duke of Windsor, Edward was inveterately greedy of money and made great demands on his brother, King George VI – demands which the King fulfilled at considerable sacrifice to himself . . . how insistent the Duke was on his demands and how little gratitude he showed when his extravagance was paid for by the King'. Wheeler-Bennett's book was published in 1958, but none of this information appeared in it. Elizabeth II, with the reputation of the royal family to consider, no doubt preferred it to remain out of the public domain. In August 1949 Churchill told Lord Beaverbrook that the Duke of Windsor had a tax-free 'income of £100,000 a year from England [something like £4–5 million in today's money], the charge on the royal estates [Sandringham and Balmoral] and so on . . .'[11] The Duke himself, as he admitted, saw money as his insurance against revolution. 'I belong to a profession that has been losing ground for centuries.' What he failed to add was that Wallis's ideas of the standard of living befitting an ex-King cost a great deal of money. When Queen Mary's biographer, James Pope-Hennessy, visited them at their French country home, Le Moulin des Tuileries, in the late 1950s, he found that 'Every conceivable luxury and creature comfort is brought, called on, conscripted, to produce a perfection of sybaritic living.'

The King had to fund these expensive family arrangements out of his private income, the money, rumoured to be close on £1 million, which George V had settled on each of his sons and the sums which as King he received from the Duchy of Lancaster. 'George VI didn't have a bean,' a courtier declared with cheerful exaggeration. While this might not have been strictly true, the sums which he had had to hand over to his brother, and would have to continue to provide on an annual basis, made a large hole in both his capital and his income. It seems to be at this moment that George VI came to an agreement with Chamberlain, who had succeeded Baldwin as Prime Minister after the Coronation, not to pay tax on his private income; the justification for this concession presumably being that the cost of paying off the Duke of Windsor was to be borne by him personally and not, as originally promised, by the public through the Civil List. The fiscal arrangement between the King and the Government was kept secret and remained so as far as the public and even the politicians were concerned until more than fifty years later, when Elizabeth agreed to rescind it in the face of popular outcry.

It was to be well over a year before the details of the handing-over of Balmoral and Sandringham were settled; at one point Edward threatened not to allow the King to use them. There was a nasty scene over George V's fabulous stamp collection, which was, however, discovered to be Crown and not private property. An unbridgeable gulf was created by the King's refusal to allow Wallis to take the title of Royal Highness on her marriage to the Duke, a decision seen by the Windsors and by many experts as both illegal and unfair. The King to his dying day refused to reconsider it, arguing that her becoming a Royal Highness would 'make nonsense of the Abdication' when the people of the Dominions had specifically rejected the suggestion that she should become either Queen or a member of the royal family. In any case, he argued firmly, as King he was the 'fount of honour', the source of all ennoblement, and that was that. The Duke of Windsor was deeply affronted by this public snubbing of his wife; he never forgave his brother, and more particularly he never forgave his brother's wife, or his mother, both of whom he blamed for the decision.

Elizabeth would have known of her uncle's marriage, but she would have remained unaware of the details of the post-Abdication family quarrels until she came to the throne. They were to remain firmly under official wraps until revealed by the Windsors' historian, Michael Bloch, in the 1980s. Nor was she at the time aware of the extent to which her father was haunted by his brother. While the family was staying at Balmoral in October 1937, Sir Ronald Lindsay, the British Ambassador in Washington, arrived at the Castle for high-level discussions about the Duke of Windsor's proposed visit to the United States. He found the King, the Queen and Tommy Lascelles, the King's Private Secretary, obsessed with the Duke's behaviour: 'he was trying to stage a come-back, and his friends and advisers were semi-Nazis,' they told the Ambassador. Lindsay's private comment in a letter to his wife was:

> It interested me to notice that really the King does not yet feel safe on his throne, and up to a point he is like the medieval monarch who has a hated rival claimant living in exile . . . in some ways the situation operates on the King just as it must have done on his medieval ancestors – uneasiness as to what is coming next – sensitiveness – suspicion . . .[12]

The Queen was fiercely protective of her vulnerable husband; since she had become Duchess of York in 1923, she had regarded her principal role as being to support him. 'She brought all her qualities into play to help [him] through all his public life, to overcome his difficulties and to bring out his best qualities,' a friend said. The Duke of Windsor was the principal threat to her husband's peace of mind at that moment and she was determined that he should be kept at bay. She felt even more strongly about this than either her husband or

Chamberlain, who had initially insisted that payment of an allowance to the Duke should be contingent on his returning to England only with the Government's consent. Walter Monckton, who was involved in the negotiations, wrote:

> I think the Queen felt quite plainly that it was undesirable to give the
> Duke of Windsor any effective sphere of work . . . she naturally
> thought that she must be on her guard because the Duke of Windsor
> . . . was an attractive, vital creature who might be the rallying point for
> any who might be critical of the new King who was less superficially
> endowed with the arts and graces that please.[13]

After the outbreak of the Second World War, when it became essential to remove the Duke from German-dominated Europe, she lobbied the Government to keep him as far away as possible. In one letter, which has since disappeared, she went so far as to say that if the Duke returned, the King would have a nervous breakdown.

Her uncle remained a problem for the future as far as Elizabeth was concerned. She and Margaret always looked forward to the annual holiday at Balmoral. 'It was the chief landmark in their calendar,' Crawfie wrote. Of all the royal homes, Balmoral was the one at which the spirit of her great-great-grandmother was most in evidence. Victoria and Albert had fallen in love with the area known as Deeside on their first visit there, mainly because it reminded them of Albert's native Thuringia. Between 1852 and 1859 they had built their own castle in a scaled-down version of the Scottish baronial style on the banks of the River Dee, where the dark brown water rushes constantly over boulders. The Dee valley itself is peaceful with green fields fringed by dark pinewoods and silver birch trees. Victoria created the Riverside Walk upriver from the castle, which is punctuated at intervals by graceful white-painted miniature suspension bridges. She also bought the Ballochbuie Forest of Native Caledonian Pines with its wild cats, mounds of heather and blueberries and strange ant-heaps. Heather-covered hills surround the valley; up on the moors the air is fresh and there are views of the North Cairngorms with patches of permanent snow gleaming on the mountain-tops. The whole place is dominated by the brooding, purple hill of Lochnagar, with its dark upland lake.

Victoria's influence still reigns over the interior of the castle. Although Queen Mary banished the ginger paint which had covered much of the panelling in Victoria's day, the walls were still hung with beige on white flocked trellis paper with the old Queen's cypher 'VRI'. Upstairs the bedroom furnishings remained more or less the same. Tartan reigned over the linoleum, rugs, curtains, the old-fashioned bedroom china of jug, basin, soap-dish on the washhand stand, dishes and pin boxes on the dressing-tables. The tartan and thistle chintzes made for the queen were still in use. The castle featured innumerable oil paintings and prints of Highland scenes and wildlife by Victoria and Albert's favourite artist, Sir Edwin Landseer. Antlers protruded from every available space not occupied by Landseers or by solemn portraits of bearded ghillies who had served the family in the past. In the front hall a full-sized marble statue of Prince Albert, creator and presiding spirit of the place, stood wearing a slightly pained expression. Outside, the gardens were dotted with statues placed there by Victoria: a life-size bronze boar, a chamois poised on a rock over a fountain and, of course, ones of Victoria and Albert themselves, a Jubilee present to the Queen from the Balmoral tenantry. One figure was not quite so obvious: the statue of John Brown, erected by the Queen in front of the elegant house she had built for him, had been discreetly relegated by her grandson, George V, to an obscure situation in the woods.

Balmoral was, and is, essentially a holiday home for the royal family. The family always spent most of August (arriving in time for the opening of the grouse-shooting season on the 'Glorious Twelfth'), all of September and the early part of October at Balmoral. They left with a sense of great regret: 'soon we must leave this peaceful place and return to London,' the Queen wrote to Duff Cooper at the beginning of October. 'It is so lovely now, the birches are turning from silver to gold, the air is cold & the sun shines, so that I am sorry to go.' The King was in his element out 'on the hill' stalking or spending the day on the grouse moor – he was an expert shot. The Queen had been taught to shoot by her brothers, but preferred fishing quietly beside the Dee to the discomforts of days out on the moors, scratched by the heather and deafened by the guns. For the children there would be picnics, often at the Glassalt Shiel, a simple granite double-bowed and gabled lodge built by Victoria at the head of the peat-brown Loch Muick beside a rushing burn in a wood of pines and larches where there was always the fresh wind-borne smell of pine. At the castle tea was an occasion with shrimps, hot sausage-rolls and Scottish speciali- ties – scones, baps and bannocks – laid out on a table in the drawing- room. At night, after dinner, which almost inevitably featured roast grouse, the King's seven pipers wearing the Balmoral tartan would march playing their bagpipes through the hall and twice round the dining-room table, watched from above by the Princesses in their dressing-gowns. Elizabeth had friends of her own age there, children of courtiers who spent their holidays in houses on the Balmoral estate. In the years before the war they started their own magazine, *The Snapdragon*, edited by Winifred Hardinge, daughter of Alec, sub-edited by Joey Legh's daughter, Diana, and handwritten on lined paper stapled together. Elizabeth was a contributor; one issue contained a piece by her, significantly describing her experiences looking out of the window of Buckingham Palace when they were changing the guard. Circulation was extremely limited and *The Snapdragon*'s existence was curtailed by the outbreak of the war; it was Elizabeth's first and only experiment in journalism.

The King had not been able to enjoy a trouble-free holiday at Balmoral. Apart from the routine work with his private secretaries on the red despatch boxes of state papers, which pursued him wherever he was, he also had to cope with the traditional visit from the Prime Minister. Chamberlain, a striking figure with a shock of white hair and dark eyebrows over piercing eyes and a curving beak of a nose, was an abrasive politician with strongly held views and a disdainful way of dealing with opponents. He had the self-confidence of his great Birmingham political dynasty and was perhaps too convinced of the rightness of his own views. He had few friends, but those he had appreciated his integrity and his unlikely passion for birds, trees, flowers and Shakespeare. Like the Queen, he was a passionate angler. Both the King and the Queen came to be fond of Chamberlain, who put himself out to charm them both and flattered himself, as he boasted to his sister, Ida, that he had succeeded. He had shot with the King and fished with the Queen, picnicked with the family on Loch Muick, and driven with them and their millionaire neighbour, J. Pierpont Morgan, to the toy-like pink castle of Abergeldie downriver from Balmoral, where the Queen had dived under the fruit nets and 'thoroughly enjoyed' the gooseberries. Disapproving of the conduct of King Edward VIII, he had gone out of his way to help his successor. The King had personal and financial reasons for feeling grateful to Chamberlain and, being himself a novice in politics and foreign affairs, had come increasingly to rely on his judgement.

At Balmoral that autumn of 1937, the King and the Prime Minister (after discussing the Duke of Windsor) had turned their attention to foreign affairs, a subject of which the King had almost no experience. From November 1936 until the late summer of 1937 the British Government and people had been absorbed first by the trauma of Abdication and then with the euphoria of the Coronation. While Edward VIII had been still on the throne in March 1936 Hitler had marched into the Rhineland; the democratic countries had reacted with no more than feeble protests (Edward VIII claimed that he had played his part in damping down the British Government's reaction). Since then Germany had signed agreements with both Italy and Japan and actively backed the fascist side in the Spanish Civil War. In November 1937 Lord Halifax, a friend of both the King and Chamberlain, was to undertake a so-called 'private' visit to Germany which would include a meeting with Hitler at Berchtesgaden. The meeting between the lofty, patrician Halifax, wearing the classic English gentleman's uniform of bowler hat and impeccably rolled umbrella, with the small, unmistakably plebeian dictator in what Halifax would have regarded as a quaint pantomime outfit would have been comical had it not resulted in a disastrous misunderstanding which led to Munich and ultimately to war. Halifax looked on the Nazi leaders like Hitler and Goering as essentially harmless figures of fun; Hitler saw Halifax as a specimen of a race whose will to fight had been in decline since the age of Sir Francis Drake and which would certainly not stand in the way of his European ambitions. Less than four months later, as Chamberlain pursued his policy of courting the Italian fascist leader Mussolini, Hitler annexed Austria, began to stir up trouble in Czechoslovakia and, early in May 1938, undertook a state visit to Rome, which mobilised all the resources of Cinecittà to produce a full-blown exhibition of militaristic pomp.

None of this would have meant very much to Elizabeth; European *realpolitik* at this stage concerned her only because the King and Queen's first overseas state visit had been planned against the lowering background of the fascist alliances as a demonstration of the solidarity of the two democracies, Britain and France. The imminent departure of her parents for Paris on 28 June was completely overshadowed for her by the sudden death of her beloved grandmother, Cecilia Strathmore, at Glamis five days earlier. Elizabeth's expression of emotion was unusual for her, so much so that Crawfie reported to a friend: 'Princess Margaret is too young to realise what has happened but Princess Elizabeth has felt it deeply.' Like her father, and even more her grandfather and grandmother, she bottled up her human emotions.

Whereas the death of a sparrow would bring tears to George V's eyes and the death of a dog prompt long letters of condolence from his granddaughter, the loss of a beloved human being aroused more complicated feelings which they were constitutionally unable to put into words. 'Only once', Crawfie reported on the death of Lord Strathmore aged eighty-nine six years later, 'did she [Elizabeth] walk right into my arms, thinking of nothing but that for the moment she had to have a little comforting. That was when she came into my room, very white and wide-eyed. "Oh, Crawfie, Grandfather Strathmore is dead," she said and burst into tears.' Lord Strathmore, Crawfie wrote, 'was a most gentle and humorous person . . . a countryman through and through. He timed all his movements by country things – the coming of the migrants, the wild geese on the river, the rising of the sap.' Somewhat eccentrically, he ate plum pudding every day of his life. Both Elizabeth and Margaret adored him.

The Queen was devastated by her mother's death, as she told Neville Chamberlain:

> I have been dreading this moment ever since I was a little child and now that it has come, one can hardly believe it. She was a true 'Rock of Defence' for us, her children, & Thank God, her influence and wonderful example will remain with us all our lives.
>
> She had a good perspective of life – everything was given its *true* importance. She had a young spirit, great courage and unending sympathy whenever or wherever it was needed, & such a heavenly sense of humour. We all used to laugh together and have such fun. You must forgive me for writing to you like this, but you have been such a kind friend and counsellor to us during the last year . . .[14]

Publicly, however, the Queen kept the proverbial stiff upper lip. The state visit went ahead on 19 July with a new wardrobe designed by Hartnell in white, the alternative royal mourning colour. It was a resounding success. At the gala night given in their honour at the Paris Opéra Winston Churchill, with Diana Cooper, Venetia Stanley and the Duchess of Rutland, watched the King and Queen ascend the staircase, the Queen glittering in diamonds and a white Winterhalter-style crinoline. 'I felt proud of my nation,' the duchess wrote. 'The French went mad about the King and Queen. Winston was like a schoolboy he was so delighted . . .' At Versailles at a review of 50,000 troops of the French army, an emotional Churchill spoke of the French

army as 'the bulwark of European freedom'. Less than two years later
that bulwark would have crumbled and Hitler himself would be driving
as a conqueror down the Champs-Elysées.

Hitler disturbed the royal peace less than two months later. The
family were at Balmoral as usual, having arrived there in the royal
yacht, the *Victoria & Albert*, cruising up the east coast of England so
that the King could stop off to visit the Duke of York's camp at
Southwold on the Suffolk coast. On 14 September, warned by
Chamberlain that intelligence reports indicated that Hitler intended to
attack Czechoslovakia that month, the King took the night train back
to London to find that his sixty-nine-year-old Prime Minister had
boarded a plane for the first time in his life and flown to Germany to
meet Hitler at Berchtesgaden. As war fever mounted, trenches were
dug in Hyde Park and the King was fitted with a gas mask;
Chamberlain made his famously dispirited broadcast ('How horrible,
fantastic, incredible, it is that we should be digging trenches and trying
on gas masks here because of a quarrel in a far-away country between
people of whom we know nothing'). Hitler then apparently drew back
from the brink; Chamberlain flew to Munich to sign the 'piece of
paper' which he triumphantly flourished to cheering crowds at the
airport on his return. The King was delighted; he had wanted to go to
Heston in person to welcome the Prime Minister, but had to content
himself with appearing beside him on the balcony at Buckingham
Palace. 'Yesterday was a great day,' he told Queen Mary, but as
Chamberlain proudly informed the public outside No. 10 Downing
Street that he had brought back 'peace with honour', Hitler was
preparing to invade the Sudetenland. Within five months Czechoslovakia would cease to exist as an independent nation. While most people
from the American President, Franklin Delano Roosevelt, to the
former Kaiser agreed with the King's support for Chamberlain's
efforts to preserve peace, Winston Churchill warned, 'this is only the
beginning of the reckoning'. Elizabeth, now fiercely anti-Hitler, was
disappointed that there would be no war and was reproved by Allah
for saying so. 'You don't know what war is,' Allah told her, and gave
the children a lecture on the casualties of the Great War.

The threat of another European conflict hung in the air by the early
summer of 1939 when the King and Queen set out across the Atlantic
for the most important state visit they were ever to make, 'the tour
that made us,' as the Queen later described it. They were to visit first
Canada and then the United States, the latter as the personal guests of

President Roosevelt. The American visit was a brave gesture; although the Duke of Windsor's planned trip there had ended in fiasco and had had to be cancelled in the face of American outrage over his visit to Nazi Germany, there were still many Americans who regarded the Duke as the rightful King and had no high opinion of George VI or his Queen, as a widely publicised article in *Scribner's* bluntly put it:

> If a public relations counsel had the power to choose from scratch
> which British personalities he would drop into the American scene for
> the greatest British profit, they would not have been King George and
> Queen Elizabeth. The important fact about the United States is that a
> large part of the country still believes that Edward, Duke of Windsor,
> is the rightful owner of the British throne, and that King George VI is
> a colorless, weak personality largely on probation in the public mind of
> Great Britain, as well as for the United States . . .
> As for Queen Elizabeth, by Park Avenue standards, she appears to
> be far too plump of figure, too dowdy in dress, to meet American
> specifications of a reigning Queen. The living contrasts of Queen Mary
> (as regal as a woman can be) and the Duchess of Windsor (chic and
> charmingly American) certainly does not help Elizabeth . . .

The personal success or lack of it of the King and Queen in the United States, the author warned, 'will be the difference between success and failure of British–American relations during the next critical international period you expect to face during the next few years'.

In the event, the royal visit was a public relations triumph. The American press, with very few isolationist exceptions, was enthusiastic about the couple, while on a personal level the King established a friendly relationship with the President and even succeeded in impressing Eleanor Roosevelt with his knowledge of social welfare. 'The British sovereigns have conquered Washington,' Arthur Krock wrote in the *New York Times*, 'where they have not put a foot wrong and where they have left a better impression than even their most optimistic advisers could have expected.' The President praised them to his cousin as 'very delightful and understanding people who know a great deal not only about foreign affairs in general but also about social legislation'.

On 22 June 1939 the Princesses, accompanied by Allah and Crawfie, boarded a destroyer at Southampton to meet their parents' ship, the *Empress of Britain*, in mid-Channel. There was a joyful reunion as

Margaret held her mother's hand and boasted how much thinner she had got – 'not like a football like I used to be'. 'All the time', Crawfie wrote, 'the King could hardly take his eyes off Lilibet.' There was a jolly luncheon in the liner's dining-room during which the King threw balloons out of the portholes and Crawfie felt weak at the knees after a champagne cocktail. The seventy-eight miles of track from Southampton to Waterloo were lined with people cheering and waving flags; once they arrived, 50,000 people crowded the Mall in front of Buckingham Palace waving handkerchiefs and even umbrellas, singing 'God Save the King', 'Land of Hope and Glory' and 'For He's a Jolly Good Fellow', and shouting 'We Want the King' and 'We Want the Queen', until the royal family came out on the balcony. It was, according to the *Daily Mirror*, 'the greatest of all homecomings, the greatest royal day since the Coronation'. In the two years which had passed since she had last stood on that balcony with her parents, it was apparent to Princess Elizabeth that 'Mummy' and 'Papa' had established themselves as firmly in the people's affection as ever her grandparents had. All, it seemed, she would have to do would be to follow their example.

She had recently turned thirteen years old. Within a month of that day on the Palace balcony she was to have a meeting with destiny in the form of a young naval cadet, Prince Philip of Greece. She owed this meeting to the Prince's uncle, Louis Francis Albert Victor, born a Prince of Battenberg in 1900 but re-named Mountbatten with the rest of his clan and given the courtesy title of Lord in 1917. Always inexplicably known to family and friends as 'Dickie', Lord Louis, as a great-grandchild of Queen Victoria, was her father's cousin. Like most of the royal family he was of German origin, a descendant on both sides of the princely house of Hesse (albeit 'tainted' in the eyes of purists by strains of illegitimacy and a morganatic marriage). His ruling passion was the genealogy of his family with its web-like veins of royal connections to the Windsors, the Wittelsbachs, the Romanovs, Habsburgs and Hohenzollerns. Lord Louis, as he was known to the public, had been at Cambridge with Elizabeth's father, but had dropped the less interesting second son to go on a world tour with his brother, the Prince of Wales. It would not be unfair to say that Dickie stuck to the Prince of Wales like glue until the Abdication, when he returned to his former allegiance to the new King George VI. George VI was amused by him, saw through him to a certain extent, but liked his naval jokes, shared his passion for uniforms and decorations, and admired his undoubted qualities of leadership and initiative. The Queen, however, did not share his affection for his cousin. She disliked what she, in her straightforward way, saw as his eye for the main chance and tendency to change sides when it suited him; she did not sympathise with the 'fast' lifestyle which he and his wife, the fabulously rich Edwina Ashley, pursued. Later she disapproved even more of their 'champagne socialist' views. Mountbatten had looks, charm, brains and a twin ambition – to advance his family to an unassailable position and to avenge the insult to his father, Prince Louis of Battenberg, who had been sacked from his post as First Sea Lord in the autumn of 1914 simply because of his German blood.

Mountbatten was to use the royal connection for all it was worth; even he, however, perhaps did not realise at the outset that the Great Leap Forward would come through his nephew, Prince Philip of Greece, then aged eighteen, a cadet in his first year at Dartmouth Royal Naval College. Prince Philip was, by blood at least, more royal than his uncle and more closely linked to the British royal family. Born in 1921, he was the son of Mountbatten's elder sister, Princess Alice, and Prince Andrew of Greece. On his mother's side he was a direct descendant of Queen Victoria; through his father he was, like his first cousin, Princess Marina, descended not only from the Greek/Danish royal family but also from the Russian imperial family, his grandfather, George I of the Hellenes (Queen Alexandra's brother 'Willy'), having married the Grand Duchess Olga, granddaughter of Tsar Nicholas I. Prince Philip's father was one of their seven children. Prince Philip was the youngest child and only son of Prince Andrew and Princess Alice; he had four sisters and was seven years younger than the youngest of them.

Life had been difficult and rootless for him almost from the start. Born in 1921 on the kitchen table of the family villa, Mon Repos, in Corfu, he was a refugee less than a year later when George V sent a British warship to rescue his family from the latest Greek coup (his father, Prince Andrew, was almost shot by the leaders and probably would have been had it not been for British intervention). The Greek royal family had never been rich in royal terms; as nominal rulers of one of the poorest countries in Europe and occupants of probably the most insecure throne, they had had neither time nor opportunity to accumulate valuable possessions. In 1922 Philip was a more or less penniless refugee in Paris, where his family settled in St Cloud, supported by Prince Andrew's brother, Prince George, who had had the good fortune to marry a woman who was not only a Bonaparte but also the granddaughter of Louis Blanc, founder of the Monte Carlo casino. It was not exactly a lonely life; there were other houses on the St Cloud estate beside the big, ugly villa in which Prince Philip's family lived and Paris was full of royal cousins, both Russian and Greek, refugees from the various regimes. Prince Philip himself lived in an extremely cosmopolitan, virtually all-female household consisting of his Greek father, his German mother, his four sisters (who thought of themselves as Greeks), a Greek lady-in-waiting, a French governess, a much-loved English nanny, Mrs Nicholas, an Italian butler and a French cook. It was an explosive mixture; 'there were always terrible rows among the staff,' Prince Philip's sister, Sophie, recalled. Perhaps in revolt against the preponderance of women in his family and household, he grew up an aggressively male little boy, described by his first headmaster as 'rugged' and 'boisterous'. Photographs of the time show a blond little boy with a fierce, independent expression, but, perhaps as a result of Nanny's influence, he was apparently 'always remarkably polite'.

Prince Philip's parents were in many ways an ill-assorted couple. His father, Prince Andrew, was described by his youngest daughter as 'delightful, extrovert, with a colossal sense of humour, very amusing'. Prince Philip, who got on extremely well with his father when he was around, which was increasingly rarely, inherited his father's forehead and the shape of his head, and his mother's fine nose and lips and the narrow Mountbatten eyes. Princess Alice had been very deaf from childhood, but she had learned to lip-read in several languages. She was very strict with her children; Prince Philip's relationship with her was good if not superficially affectionate. She was as courageous and independent-minded as he was. While living in German-occuped Athens during the Second World War (when she lost over 40lb living off flour mixed with warm water), she saved the lives of two Jews, a mother and daughter. They had two rooms at the top of Prince George's house where she lived and when the Germans came to look for them, Princess Alice pretended to be not only deaf but half-witted, so they went away.

Princess Alice did not play a part in her son's adolescence. When Philip was only ten, a very vulnerable age, his world began to crumble round him, not for the first or the last time. His mother had a breakdown, apparently caused by the menopause, and was sent for treatment to Vienna and Berlin and subsequently to a Swiss clinic.

The house at St Cloud was given up and Prince Philip's father went off to live in the South of France. By 1931 all his sisters had married German aristocrats: Princess Sophie, the youngest, known as 'Tiny', married Prince Christopher of Hesse at the age of sixteen in 1930; his three other sisters all married in 1931 – Margarita to Prince Godfrey of Hohenlohe-Langenburg, Theodora, known as 'Dolla', to Berthold, Margrave of Baden and Cecile to George Donatus, Prince of Hesse and the Rhine. Prince Philip was sent to the preparatory school in England, Cheam, to which he was later to despatch Prince Charles. Cheam was followed by a brief two terms in Germany at the school founded by Kurt Hahn at Schloss Salem, home of Philip's sister, Dolla, and her husband Berthold, later to become better known after its transition to Scotland as Gordonstoun. Hahn, a German Jew, was arrested after the Nazis came to power in 1933 and, after the intervention of highly placed British friends, he fled to Britain, where he founded Gordonstoun. In 1934 Philip was sent to school there, a formative experience which he was also to insist his sons must share.

As a teenager, despite being a member of a large extended family, Philip was very much on his own. Friends at Gordonstoun remember there always being uncertainty as to where he should spend his holidays. He was fond of his third sister Cecile's husband, George Donatus of Hesse, and spent most of his holidays with them at Wolfsgarten or in Darmstadt, but this haven came to a tragic end when Cecile and George were killed in an air crash in 1937 en route for the London wedding of George's younger brother, Prince Ludwig, to an English girl, Margaret Geddes. In London Philip stayed at Kensington Palace with his Mountbatten grandmother, the Dowager Marchioness of Milford Haven. 'He was very independent,' his sister said, 'he and his grandmother had frightful tussles of will.' His Mountbatten cousins remember on one occasion seeing Philip race up the stairs at Kensington Palace and stopping at the top to stick his tongue out at her. He also stayed in the country with his mother's brother George, Marquess of Milford Haven, and his exotic lesbian Russian wife, Nadejda. In 1938, the year after Cecile's death, George Milford Haven died of cancer, leaving Prince Philip in the occasional care of his younger brother, Lord Louis.

At this point in Prince Philip's career, Lord Louis did not represent the 'surrogate father' he is often made out to be. He was only beginning to take an interest in his nephew, who seems to have first visited Adsdean, the Mountbattens' country house, in the spring of 1938, accompanied by his cousin, David Milford Haven. 'Philip was here all last week doing his entrance exams for the Navy,' Mountbatten wrote to his wife in terms which suggest this was his first prolonged encounter with his nephew at close quarters. 'He had his meals with us and he really is killingly funny. I like him very much.'[15] According to Mountbatten's official biographer, the decision that Philip should join the Navy and not, as he had first chosen, the Air Force, was Mountbatten's. It was as a result of this decision that when in July 1939 the King, the Queen and the two Princesses, accompanied by Mountbatten, made an official visit to the Royal Naval College at Dartmouth on the *Victoria & Albert*, his nephew, Elizabeth's cousin, was a cadet there. 'Philip accompanied us and dined on board,' Mountbatten noted briefly in his diary on 22 July 1939, and on the 23rd: 'Philip came back aboard V and A for tea and was a great success with the children.' Just how much of a success Philip was, Crawfie, with the benefit of hindsight, was only too willing to elaborate.

Philip was extremely handsome; tall with Nordic good looks, bleached blond hair and fine features. He was confident and, Crawfie thought, a bit of a show-off and 'rather off-hand in his manner'. The crucial meeting took place at the Captain's House at Dartmouth; two of the boys had developed mumps and, therefore, Philip seems to have been the only cadet with whom the Princesses were allowed to come into contact. He joined them playing with a clockwork train on the nursery floor, but, not surprisingly, soon got bored with the childish amusement and suggested going to the tennis courts and jumping over the nets instead. 'I thought he showed off a good deal,' Crawfie wrote, 'but the little girls were much impressed. Lilibet said, "How good he is, Crawfie. How high he can jump." She never took her eyes off him the whole time.' Philip was quite polite, but did not pay her any special attention, spending most of his time teasing 'plump little Margaret'. He joined them on the yacht for lunch and again the next day for lunch and tea, when he devoured platefuls of shrimps and a banana split before the girls' admiring eyes. The King, busy reliving old experiences at Dartmouth and comparing records in the College punishment books with the Rear Admiral commanding Yachts, seems not to have noticed anything until Philip brought himself to his attention by being the last of the small boats to turn back as the *Victoria & Albert* left harbour. 'Damn young fool!' he is said to have roared, as the boy, rowing furiously, faded in the yacht's wake. Beside him on the bridge, Uncle Dickie was perhaps making a mental note.

There was, after all, only five years' difference between his nephew and the future Queen. Elizabeth, as her father's official biographer was authorised by her to confirm, had fallen in love with her future husband at their first meeting.

4

Windsor War

'She says that she would like to make Windsor her home, since all the happiest memories of childhood are associated with the castle . . .'

Queen Elizabeth II in a reported conversation

The countdown to the Second World War had already begun by the time the royal family left for Balmoral on 6 August buoyed up by confident assurances from Chamberlain that Hitler understood that 'Britain meant business' and would not risk a major war over Danzig, the latest crisis he had precipitated. On 16 March, speaking from the ancient Hradschin Castle in Prague, Hitler had dissolved what remained of the Czech state and announced a German Protectorate over Bohemia and Moravia; the city of Memel was next, surrendered by the Lithuanian Government on 21 March. On the same day Ribbentrop, the German Foreign Minister, had reopened negotiations aimed at forcing the Polish Government to cede the port of Danzig and ten days later Chamberlain had given the Polish Government the public guarantee that would lead to Britain's eventual declaration of war on Germany. Chamberlain, convinced that he had frightened Hitler off, went for his usual salmon-fishing holiday early in August.

At Balmoral the King lunched with the boys at the Duke of York's camp beside the Dee and took them for strenuous climbs up Lochnagar. On 9 August he broke his holiday for a visit of inspection to the Reserve Fleet at Weymouth, after which he wrote confidently to Queen Mary, 'I feel sure it will be a deterrent factor in Hitler's mind to start a war.' He should, perhaps, have remembered that a similar display by the Grand Fleet, which he had witnessed in July 1914, had not prevented the outbreak of the First World War a few weeks later. On 22 August news that Germany and Russia had signed the Nazi–Soviet

Pact destroyed the peace at Balmoral. The King, informed by Chamberlain on the 23rd that Parliament was to meet the next day, immediately took the train for London, leaving the Queen and the Princesses behind.

'Who is this Hitler spoiling everything?' Margaret reportedly asked Crawfie. At Buckingham Palace her father spoke of the German dictator in much the same terms, complaining to Sir Miles Lampson about Hitler's disruption of his sporting holiday much as his father had at the outbreak of the previous war. 'He had never had so many grouse up there as this year. He had got 1,600 brace in six days and had been much looking forward to this week's shoot. It was utterly damnable that the villain Hitler had upset everything,' Lampson reported on 29 August. 'HM thought that there would now be peace and that this time Hitler's bluff would be called.'[1] Within five days all hope of peace was gone. On 1 September German troops crossed the Polish border; from eleven o'clock on the morning of Sunday, 3 September, no answer having been received to their ultimatum, Great Britain and France were at war with Germany. On that day the King began a diary, sitting at the same desk at which his father had sat only twenty-five years before writing in his own diary, 'Please God, protect dear Bertie's life.' The King's mind went back to that moment when he, like so many other young men, had cheered the news of war with Germany. No one was cheering in 1939.

> At the outbreak of War at midnight of Aug 4th–5th 1914, I was a midshipman, keeping the middle watch on the bridge of HMS 'Collingwood' at sea, somewhere in the North Sea. I was 18 years of age.
>
> In the Grand Fleet everyone was pleased that it had come at last. We had been trained in the belief that War between Germany & this country had to come one day, & when it did come we thought we were prepared for it. We were not prepared for what we found a modern war really was, & those of us who had been through the Great War never wanted another.[2]

At Balmoral the Princesses were in limbo, their mother having hurried south on the 28th to join the King in London. The castle was closed, Crawfie summoned back from holiday and the children moved into Birkhall. They remained there until Christmas, cheered up by a regular evening telephone call from their parents, who were spending the weekdays at Buckingham Palace and sleeping nights at Windsor Castle. They worried about their parents and missed them. 'Do you think the Germans will come and get them?' Margaret asked. The war touched Elizabeth deeply for the first time when on 14 October a German submarine penetrated the defences of the northern naval base at Scapa Flow and sank the battleship *Royal Oak* with the loss of more than 800 lives. 'We were continually studying *Jane's Fighting Ships*,' Crawfie wrote, 'and the little girls took a personal interest in every one of them. Lilibet jumped horrified from her chair, her eyes blazing with anger. "Crawfie, it can't be! All those nice sailors."' They vented their rage against the Germans by throwing cushions at the wireless when William Joyce, 'Lord Haw-Haw', gave his anti-British broadcasts. Six months later they shocked their mother by their bloodthirsty delight at the success of a British bombing raid on the island of Sylt.

It was still the period of the phoney war, when, for the French and British allies at least, nothing much happened. At Birkhall life continued on an even keel. Crawfie gave them lessons and Mrs Montaudon-Smith taught them French; they learned to sing French duets together as a surprise for their parents. There were sewing-parties for war work every Thursday afternoon with tea organised by Allah, attended by the crofters and the wives of the local farmers and estate employees. Later, evacuee mothers from Glasgow joined in; the King had lent them Craigowan House on the Balmoral estate, but not all of them appreciated the peace of the Highlands, complaining about the quiet. At these sewing-parties the Princesses handed round tea and played records on an ancient gramophone with six scarves stuffed down the horn to muffle its raucous tone. Margaret's favourite was Beniamino Gigli singing 'Your tiny hand is frozen', which, according to Crawfie, described the temperature inside Birkhall only too accurately. The situation was considered safe enough for them to join their parents for the traditional Christmas at Sandringham, even though, situated as it was on the coast of the North Sea, it was not that far away from Germany. It was to be the last Sandringham holiday for a long time; the Big House was far too uneconomical to be used in wartime and the next few Christmases would be spent in the security of Windsor.

That Christmas their father, dressed in the uniform of Admiral of the Fleet (he had resolved that as long as the war lasted he would no longer wear civilian clothes) and sitting in front of two huge microphones, delivered the live broadcast which was always such an ordeal for him. His hesitations were evident, and at one point he went back, as his therapist Logue had trained him to do, and began a phrase again, but his carefully chosen words about the uncertainties that the new year was likely to bring made it the most memorable he ever gave and he ended with a quotation which seemed to his listeners to epitomise the uncertainties of the future:

'I said to the man who stood at the Gate of the Year, "Give me a light that I may tread safely into the unknown." And he replied, "Go out into the darkness, and put your hand into the Hand of God. That shall be better than light, and safer than a known way."'
  May that Almighty Hand guide and uphold us all.

Elizabeth felt almost guilty at enjoying Christmas with her family so much in the aftermath of the *Royal Oak* tragedy. 'Perhaps we were too happy,' she wrote to Crawfie. 'I kept thinking of those sailors and what Christmas must have been like in their homes.' The war could touch her only through the medium of the wireless and the newspapers. They were protected, cocooned, kept in the country out of harm's way, first staying at Sandringham until February, then going straight to the Royal Lodge at Windsor, where Crawfie joined them once again. There they remained until 'that man' rampaged westwards through Europe in the spring and early summer of 1940. On 9 April German forces occupied Denmark and attacked Norway; by the end of the month King Haakon, or 'Uncle Charles' as he was known in the British royal family, was on his way to Britain in a British warship. The Allied, principally British, Expeditionary Force sent to protect Norway had been an evident failure and in an historic debate on the conduct of that campaign on 8 May Conservatives and Opposition joined forces to defeat the Government. Since the Labour Party refused to serve in a national government led by Chamberlain, the Prime Minister had no alternative but to offer his resignation to the King and was replaced by Winston Churchill, who had entered the Cabinet the previous September. The King was reluctant both to see Chamberlain go and to see Churchill succeed him. He would have preferred Lord Halifax, the Foreign Secretary, whom he knew and trusted, but Churchill was the man of the hour. Initially the family remained loyal to Chamberlain and suspicious of Churchill, who had not only been Chamberlain's principal opponent over Munich but also a leading supporter of Edward VIII during the Abdication crisis. Queen Mary even went so far as to write to her lady-in-waiting, Lady Cynthia Colville, whose son Jock had been Chamberlain's Private Secretary, saying that she hoped he would remain with Chamberlain 'and not go on with the new Prime Minister'. The King told Chamberlain at his farewell audience on 10 May that he thought he had been 'grossly unfairly treated', while the Queen wrote personally to tell him

> how deeply I regretted your ceasing to be our Prime Minister. I can never tell you in words how much we owe you. During these last desperate & unhappy years, you have been a great comfort and support to us both . . . These last few days have been so terrible in every way . . . it is hard to sit here and think of all those splendid young men being sacrificed to Hitler. You did all in your power to stave off such agony, & you were right . . .

The two Princesses had listened to his farewell broadcast on 11 May with real emotion. 'I *cried*, Mummy,' Princess Elizabeth told her mother.[3]

Events moved quickly and menacingly through May and June 1940. Royal refugees began to arrive at Buckingham Palace; King Haakon's appearance at the end of April was followed on 13 May by that of Queen Wilhelmina of the Netherlands, who had just managed to evade a parachute force sent to capture her. On 11 May Hitler had launched a concerted attack on Holland, Belgium and the Netherlands on a front stretching from the North Sea to the Moselle. On 13 and 14 May seven German divisions crossed the Meuse and drove westwards, outflanking both the French main defences on the Maginot Line and the British Expeditionary Force. On 15 May the French Premier, Paul Reynaud, telephoned Churchill with the stunning news that 'the war was lost' and the road to Paris open to the Germans. On 31 May, as the last British and French troops who could escape were still being ferried across the Channel from Dunkirk, the King told Hugh Dalton, Minister of Economic Warfare, that the date for Hitler's invasion of Britain was, according to the latest information, 1 August.

On 12 May the Queen had telephoned the Royal Lodge telling Crawfie to take the children to the safety of Windsor Castle – 'at least for the rest of the week'. They were to remain there for five years. Lord Hailsham wrote to Churchill of his fears that the Germans would make the royal family, and the Princesses in particular, their target. 'I observe that the Nazis both in Norway and in Holland made a desperate effort to capture the royal family,' the former Lord Chancellor told Churchill on 19 June 1940; 'no doubt they will do the same in this country if they can; and in the British Empire it would be a more serious matter because the Crown is the principal link between us and the Dominions.' Strangely, Hailsham seemed to think that it would not matter all that much if the King were captured since the Regency Act of 1937 would enable the Government to put the royal power into commission in that event. 'But so far as the little Princesses are concerned, the same observation does not apply,' he wrote, 'and I suggest that the time has come . . . that they should be sent to Canada . . . if the Nazis got hold of their Persons they would be able to bring tremendous pressure to bear on the King and Queen to accept intimidation by threatening death and even worse things.'[4] The King flatly refused to agree to the suggestion (although many British children, mainly of the upper classes, were being sent to the United States and Canada for their safety), and Churchill concurred, minuting on 18 July, 'I strongly deprecate any stampede from this country at the present time.' Queen Mary, much against her will, was evacuated from Marlborough House and sent down to Gloucestershire to spend the war at Badminton with her niece, the former Lady Mary Cambridge, now Duchess of Beaufort. Despite her sojourns at Sandringham and Balmoral, Queen Mary was emphatically not a country person. 'So *that's* what hay looks like!' she remarked on being driven past a harvested field.

Some not particularly stringent precautions were, however, taken to protect the royal family. An air-raid shelter had been prepared at Buckingham Palace since the Munich scare in September 1938, but it was simply a former housemaids' sitting-room in the basement equipped with Victorian buttoned upholstered settees, armchairs and ornate tables, and provided with pails of sand and a hand pump for dousing fires. Since June the King, Queen and members of the household had been having shooting practice in the Palace garden; while a special unit was formed for their protection consisting of a company of Coldstream Guardsmen and two troops of armoured cars from the 12th Lancers and the Northamptonshire Yeomanry, named the Coates Mission after its commanding officer, Major Jimmy Coates. Its duties were to guard the family in London, Windsor and at Sandringham, and, in the event of a German invasion, to escort them to one of three large country houses well away from the Channel coast: Madresfield, near Malvern, Pitchford House in Shropshire and Newby

Hall in Yorkshire. On one occasion when King Haakon asked for a demonstration of the reaction if the Palace was attacked by parachutists as had happened in Holland, the Coates Mission did not distinguish itself. The King pressed the alarm signal with no result. The officer of the guard telephoned the duty police sergeant and was informed there was no attack; it was only when alerted by an equerry that a party of Guardsmen appeared and proceeded to thrash the Palace shrubbery 'as if they were beaters on a shoot rather than men engaged in the pursuit of a dangerous enemy'. The King did not seriously contemplate the possibility of protecting Windsor against parachute attack until 13 October 1940, when he invited the Commander-in-Chief Home Forces, Alan Brooke, to lunch to discuss the subject. By then the invasion scare was over.

The danger was none the less real, not so much from invasion but from bombing. After the Battle of Britain effectively ended the threat of invasion, the Blitz began. On the night of 7–8 September 1940 more than 200 German bombers attacked London; by dawn on the morning of the 8th more than 400 Londoners had been killed and 1,357 seriously injured. On the 9th a bomb fell on the north side of the Palace but did not explode; the King, as yet unused to bombs, continued working in his study directly above it. Fortunately he was not there when it did explode in the early hours of the next morning breaking the windows on all floors on that side of the Palace, including his study, and demolishing his newly built swimming-pool. For security, the King and Queen then moved to apartments facing the inner courtyard, and they were in the King's sitting-room there on the morning of 13 September, having driven up from Windsor through an air raid, when the Germans made a direct attack on the Palace. 'The King & I saw 2 of the bombs drop quite close to us in the quadrangle. They screamed past the window and exploded with a tremendous boom and crash about 15 yards away,' the Queen wrote to Osbert Sitwell. 'We both thought we were dead, & nipped quickly into the passage, where we found our two pages crouching on the floor. They rose at once & we then descended quickly to the basement, pretending really that it was nothing.' '6 bombs had been dropped,' the King recorded in his diary. 'The aircraft was seen coming down the Mall below the clouds having dived through the clouds & had dropped 2 bombs in the forecourt, 2 in the quadrangle, 1 in the Chapel & the other in the garden. There is no doubt it was a direct attack on the Palace.' The King knew quite well that the Germans would like him dead and that they thought they had the perfect substitute in his discontented brother. Through intelligence sources he knew of the overtures made to the Windsors while they were in Lisbon that summer and of the Nazis' abortive plot to kidnap the Duke before he left Portugal to take up the only job he had been offered by the British Government, Governor of the Bahamas (ironically referred to by the Windsors as 'Elba').

Although the King and Queen slept at Windsor, their presence in the Palace throughout the war was a brave gesture. There were official suggestions that the King and Queen should occupy various citadels in central London with protected basements designed to withstand a direct hit by a 500lb bomb. One of these was Curzon House, which had the advantage, unlike Buckingham Palace, of being difficult to identify from the air. 'I have an Air Mosaic of London taken from 13,000 feet,' an official told the King's Principal Private Secretary, Hardinge, 'and I have difficulty in recognising the building at all whereas the Palace, of course, is a landmark . . .'[5] The King, however, merely instructed the Office of Works to strengthen the existing Buckingham Palace shelter. The fact that the King and Queen shared the dangers faced by the people of London was of immense propaganda value to them; as the Queen famously remarked after the Buckingham Palace bombing: 'Now I feel I can look the East End in the face.' The shy, stammering King showed that he was brave and had the common touch. As he was visiting a shattered street in the aftermath of a bombing raid, someone called out, 'Thank God for a good King!' George VI replied, 'Thank God for a good people!' The war, and the Blitz in particular, created a bond between George VI and his people which was never to be broken. On Sunday, 13 October, Elizabeth did her bit for the family war effort by making her first broadcast, addressed to 'the children of the Empire', from Windsor Castle. Crawfie thought it was full of the 'rather sweet human touches' which the Queen liked to put in, but Jock Colville, now Churchill's Secretary, listening in with Churchill's daughter, Diana Sandys, was 'embarrassed by the sloppy sentiment she was made to express', although he thought 'her voice was most impressive and, if the monarchy survives, Queen Elizabeth II should be a most successful radio Queen'.

At Windsor, Elizabeth could feel the vibrations of the bombs hitting London shake the chalk hill on which the Castle stood. One clear moonlit night in November 1940 wave upon wave of bombers roared directly over the Castle en route to obliterate most of the city of Coventry and bring a new verb into the German language, '*Coventri-*

eren', meaning 'to obliterate'. Windsor, the home of her adolescence, came to have a special place in her heart, which was why, when it was severely damaged by fire in 1992, it seemed like a direct blow by a malignant fate against herself as much as against the monarchy.

While Buckingham Palace is majestic and dull, Windsor is romantic, beautiful, historic. Its great bulk rising above the flat surrounding countryside is a potent symbol of past power and historical continuity. Almost every English king or queen has added to the Castle since William I, the Conqueror, built a wooden castle on the chalk bluff above the River Thames and moved from the old Saxon kings' hunting lodge two miles away by the river. By the time Henry III died in 1272, the broad outlines of the Castle were fixed. They were, to quote the historian of Windsor, 'a castle on a hill, a round tower on a mound, two wards with walls and towers round them, all for power and prestige; and to the south of the hill two parks, one large and one small, for pleasure. For the next seven hundred years all that was to be done was to fill and re-fill this outline.'[6] The Castle changed as each monarch sought to reaffirm his or her personal image of the monarchy. Edward III founded the chivalric Order of the Garter to bind the most powerful nobility personally closer to him and created St George's Chapel as the theatre for the Order's ceremony. As personal power passed from sovereign to people, the Castle and the monarch who resided there became a symbol of the nation; in 1824 the Chancellor of the Exchequer justified the huge expense of the re-medievalising of Windsor as an expression of the power and prestige of the nation which had recently triumphed in the Napoleonic Wars.

If Buckingham Palace is corporate headquarters, Windsor Castle is a village. Among the huge medieval walls and towers later accretions huddle like swallows' nests under eaves: houses, offices, workshops and gardens dating from the sixteenth to the twentieth centuries. The Castle covers thirteen acres and contains over 1,000 rooms for the royal family and over 350 people who live and work there: the staff and the royal household, the gardeners, policemen, firemen, carpenters, plumbers and archivists, the Dean and his ecclesiastical circle centring on St George's Chapel, canons, vergers and choristers; the Military Knights and retired courtiers and their families with their grace-and-favour houses, all of them like a colony of bees in their cells round the central figure of the sovereign. From the age of thirteen Elizabeth lived with this weight of tradition around her, the huge castle with its army of servants, quaint-sounding officials and colonies of royal pensioners, seeming just a part of normal life to a teenager whose only real communication with the outside world came through the media.

Windsor during the war was dark, the chandeliers taken down, the state apartments muffled in dustsheets, the windows blacked out at night (a job which, one old man grumbled to Crawfie, took all night to complete). By the autumn of 1941 fuel economies were in force. There was virtually no central heating, only log fires, which were allowed in the sitting-rooms, but not in the bedrooms. The number of boilers in operation was reduced so that on certain days of the week there was no hot water supply to some of the residential areas and hot water had to be fetched from the Great Kitchen as it had in the days of the early Georges. Baths were painted with a red or black line at the five-inch level above which water was not supposed to go and notices hung in every bathroom enjoining fuel economy. Only one electric lightbulb was allowed in each bedroom. In the Great Park the land was ploughed up for cereals, gardens were dug up and cultivated in the Dig for Victory campaign, carriage horses pulled agricultural machinery, and the King was photographed with the champion porker from his herd of Large White Pigs, fed entirely on swill from the Castle kitchens, an inspiration to the numerous Pig Clubs which sprang up throughout the country. As part of the war effort the Princesses collected tinfoil, rolled bandages and knitted socks for the forces (a trial for Elizabeth who was not a skilled knitter) and contributed from their pocket money to the Red Cross, the Girl Guides and the Air Ambulance Fund.

In 1940 Elizabeth was fourteen and Margaret ten, but the floor which they occupied in the Augusta Tower was still known as 'the nursery' and Allah Knight was still very much in charge. The 'royal nursery' consisted of five rooms: the 'day nursery', the schoolroom, Elizabeth's bedroom, Margaret's bedroom and Allah Knight's bed-room. Bobo's room was on the floor above, while Crawfie slept on the top floor of the Victorian Tower. Mrs Knight ruled the nursery floor as she had at No. 145. Meals were served in the nursery brought up by the nursery footman, Cyril Dickman, from the Great Kitchen at least. five minutes' walk away. The girls were called by Bobo for breakfast at 9 sharp – 'it had to be on time, I might tell you,' the footman recalled. By 9.30 they had to be in the schoolroom before being let off, usually to ride in the Park, from 11 to 12. Lunch was at 1 p.m., then back to the schoolroom for lessons from 2 until 4.30, when there was a properly laid-up tea with sandwiches and cakes. From five o'clock until 7.30 there was free time, often spent with the

Girl Guides, and at 7.30 supper, sausage and mash being one of their favourite dishes. At 9 p.m. the nursery footman took the dogs out for a walk.

Elizabeth's strong sense of history was enhanced by her daily experience of living at Windsor. Crawfie shuddered at such gruesome relics as the shirt that Charles I was executed in or the bullet extracted from Nelson's heart ('Though interesting, I personally found them somewhat sinister things to share a shelter with,' she wrote), but Elizabeth was fascinated by the historical and personal connotations of the Castle. It was, among other things, the burial place of her ancestors; she had seen her grandfather's coffin lowered into the family vault beneath St George's Chapel. For the past year she had taken twice-weekly history lessons from the Vice-Provost of Eton, Henry Marten, joint author of Warner and Marten's school textbook, *History of England*. Marten was an eccentric figure with curious mannerisms; he kept lumps of sugar in his pocket and munched them at intervals when not taking bites at his handkerchief. He never looked directly at Elizabeth but over her head as if he were taking a class, and sometimes absentmindedly addressed her, the way he did the Eton boys, as 'Gentlemen'. He kept a pet raven in his study at Eton which occasionally nipped his ear. During the war he came up to the Castle to tutor the Princess, arriving in a dog-cart with a Gladstone bag loaded with books, which weighed a ton, according to the footman deputed to carry it, just as if Queen Victoria (whom he greatly admired, passing his enthusiasm for her on to Elizabeth) was still alive. Marten taught her Walter Bagehot on the British constitution, the bible of the British monarchy, which even George V and George VI (who were neither of them scholastically inclined) mastered word for word. He was, as one of his pupils, Lord Home, described him, a racy and enthusiastic teacher to whom history and historical personalities were very much alive. Elizabeth was also fascinated by the stories of Queen Victoria told her by Victoria's granddaughter, Princess Marie Louise. Reminiscing one Christmas at Windsor about conversations with the old Queen, Princess Marie Louise stopped and said to Elizabeth that it must be boring for her to hear old people talking about things that happened long ago. 'But, Cousin Louie,' Elizabeth said, 'it's *history* and therefore so thrilling . . .'

From 1942 Antoinette de Bellaigue joined the Princesses' intimate circle. A Belgian aristocrat who had escaped from Belgium just before the German invasion, she had been introduced to the Queen by the

Hardinges and asked to join the household to teach the Princesses French. Antoinette de Bellaigue, 'Toni' to the Princesses, was able to give them a more cosmopolitan education than either Crawfie or Mrs Montaudon-Smith had been capable of providing. Her idea was to give them, in their isolated, somewhat narrow life, an idea of European culture and civilisation through French language and literature. At Sir Henry Marten's suggestion, she gave them lessons in continental history; he would set essays on the topics Mme de Bellaigue had taught them, which they would have to return to him written in French. Marten emphasised to her that dates were not important in themselves; the point about education was to teach a person to appraise a situation from all sides and develop their judgement. 'Elizabeth II has always had from the beginning a positive good judgement,' Mme de Bellaigue told the royal biographer, Elizabeth Longford. 'She had an instinct for the right thing. She was her simple self, *très naturelle*. And there was always a strong sense of duty mixed with *joie de vivre* in her character.' Mme de Bellaigue remained a lifelong friend of Elizabeth's; her son, Sir Geoffrey de Bellaigue, worked for the Queen at Windsor as Director of the Royal Collection and Surveyor of the Queen's Works of Art.

None the less, apart from Elizabeth's sessions with Sir Henry, hers was an essentially old-fashioned, somewhat limited education and Margaret's even more so (later in life she often complained about how bitter she felt at being comparatively uneducated). There were dancing classes on Saturday mornings given by the famous Miss Vacani, who taught all the upper-class children in London, and drawing lessons on Thursday afternoons with Elizabeth's friend, Alathea Fitzalan-Howard, and the two Hardinge girls, Elizabeth and Winifred. Both Elizabeth and Margaret went for twice-weekly riding lessons which included jumping, while Elizabeth had progressed to the difficult but elegant art of riding side-saddle. They still had a Guide company and Elizabeth had become a patrol leader, but the novelty was wearing off; 'we're always teaching them things and do not learn anything new,' she complained.

The King and Queen were grooming Elizabeth for her future position. When important visitors came to lunch at Buckingham Palace, Elizabeth would be there, urged on by her mother to speak to her neighbour, usually some important ambassador or war leader. Eleanor Roosevelt, invited by the Queen to observe the part played by British women in the war effort, came to stay at Buckingham Palace in

October 1942 and met the sixteen-year-old Elizabeth at family tea. The President's wife, no mean judge of character, was impressed, writing that she was 'quite serious and with a great deal of character and personality. She asked me a number of questions about life in the United States and they were serious questions.'[7]

There were outings such as a day at Elstree where Noël Coward's war film, *In Which We Serve*, was in production. Mountbatten masterminded the party, taking his younger daughter, Pamela, along with the royal family. A rocking stage was set up for the deck scenes on board HMS *Torrin*, based on Mountbatten's ship, HMS *Kelly*, sunk under him in the Battle of Crete. It was all too realistic for most of the party, particularly for the two youngest, Pamela and Margaret. 'It was a toss-up who was going to be sick first,' Lady Pamela recalled. 'It was too awful, worse than the real sea.' On another more formal occasion, Elizabeth accompanied her mother to a poetry-reading in aid of the Free French organised by the Queen's friend Osbert Sitwell, which ended with a display of 'tired and emotional' behaviour by one of the poets, Lady Dorothy Wellesley. According to Edith Sitwell:

> Lady Peel (Beatrice Lillie) tried to enfold her in a ju-jitsu grip and hold her down to her seat, Stephen Spender . . . seeing her wander outside, tried to knock her down and sit on her face, Raymond Mortimer . . . induced her to take his arm and go into Bond Street where she promptly sat down on the pavement, banging her stick and using frightful language about A the Queen and B Me . . . she smacked Harold Nicolson.

Writing to thank Osbert Sitwell for a book he had sent her for her birthday, Elizabeth politely told him how much she had enjoyed the 'Poets Reading'.

Nineteen forty-two, the year of Elizabeth's sixteenth birthday, was also the year of her confirmation on 1 March, officiated by her grandfather's old friend, Cosmo Lang, Archbishop of Canterbury, who had also christened her. Queen Mary came up from her wartime home at Badminton for the ceremony. There was no doubt which of the two Princesses she preferred. 'Lilibet much grown, very pretty eyes and complexion, pretty figure. Margaret very short, intelligent face but not really pretty.' Lady Airlie made the by now commonplace comparison with Queen Victoria. 'The carriage of her head was unequalled, and there was about her that indescribable something which Queen Victoria had.' She also formally registered under the wartime youth service scheme at the local Labour Exchange at 11 a.m. on Saturday, 25 April 1942, and was given a registration card, E. D. 431.[8] In honour of her sixteenth birthday she was made Colonel of the Grenadier Guards in place of her great-great-uncle, the Duke of Connaught, who had died that year. This meant a great deal to her; as she told Osbert Sitwell, one of the birthday presents she had particularly appreciated was from the Grenadiers: 'the Regiment gave me a Colonel's Colour for my birthday'. A parade was held in the morning for inspection by Elizabeth. 'It was a bit frightening inspecting a Regiment for the first time,' she wrote to a friend, 'but it was not as bad as I expected it to be.' (Harold Nicolson later noted her enthusiasm for her regiment: 'Princess Elizabeth a clear nice girl with a most lovely skin, very keen about the Grenadiers.') In the afternoon there was a 'a very good entertainment' organised by the King with all his favourite radio stars, Jack Warner, Vera Lynn and Tommy Handley, who put on a special performance of his show *ITMA*.

On 25 August 1942 the royal family were at Balmoral when news came that the Duke of Kent had been killed. Ironically, the King and the Duke of Gloucester had been eating a picnic lunch out shooting on the moors in vile weather, low mist, rain and a chill east wind, just as, not far to the north-east, an RAF Sunderland flying boat with the Duke of Kent on board en route for Iceland, flying 700 feet too low in dense mist known locally as 'haar', hit the top of a hill and burst into a fireball, killing all on board. The King was devastated. 'He died on Active Service,' he wrote in his diary, as if to justify and make some meaning out of his brother's death, but, as with so many wartime aeroplane accidents, it had been unnecessary, due to pilot error and disorientation in bad visibility. He found it hard to restrain his tears at the family funeral four days later in St George's Chapel. The Duchess of Kent was left a widow at thirty-five with three children, the youngest, Prince Michael of Kent, a baby of only seven weeks. 'It was a great shock to the two little girls,' Crawfie wrote (Elizabeth, now sixteen, could hardly be accurately described as such). 'It was the second uncle they had lost completely, for though the first, Uncle David, was not dead, they did not see him any more. The Royal Conspiracy of silence had closed about him as it did about so many other uncomfortable things.'

Despite the horrors of the war, life within the comforting walls of Windsor Castle was far from unpleasant. Apart from the familiar courtiers such as the King's equerry, his old naval friend, Sir Harold Campbell, the Master of the Household, Joey Legh, and the Private Secretaries Hardinge and Lascelles, there was the eccentric artist Gerald Kelly, an old Etonian Irishman of charm and talent, and brother-in-law of the satanist Aleister Crowley. Kelly had been commissioned in 1938 to execute the official Coronation portraits of the King and Queen and, on the outbreak of war, had moved down to Windsor with the paintings to continue his work. He remained there throughout the war despite mildly humorous complaints by the King as to the length of his stay.

During the war there was always the training battalion of the Grenadiers stationed at Windsor, and it was the job of the 300-strong No. 1 Company, known as the Castle Company, to guard the royal family. Young officers of the Castle Company, such as Mark Bonham Carter and Hugh Euston, used to lunch regularly with the Princesses and their governesses, Crawfie and Monty. 'There was a very happy atmosphere when one lunched,' one officer remembered. 'Princess Elizabeth was reserved but charming . . . her sister was very forward.' The young officers used to accompany the Princesses and their friends on picnics in Windsor Great Park and there would occasionally be small dances of around one hundred people. At weekends when the King and Queen were there, there were often childish games like sardines played all over the Castle. The Queen was the life and soul of these occasions; once when Eleanor Roosevelt was staying there after the war, she was amused by after-dinner charades with the Queen prancing round wearing a false beard while Churchill sat grumpily frowning in an armchair. At Christmas there was always a pantomime in which the Princesses took part, scripted by a local schoolmaster with a supporting cast of local schoolchildren. Sometimes even the Guardsmen appeared on stage with the King directing operations. Pantomime posters were put up in the empty frames from which ancestral portraits had been removed for safe-keeping with ludicrous effects: Mother Goose appearing in a vast heavy gilt frame labelled Henrietta Maria, or Dick Whittington and his cat as Charles I. A friend and contemporary of Elizabeth's who lived near the Castle described life there as having 'a happy family atmosphere'; contrasting it with her own family relationships which were difficult, she said, 'it was really what a family should be . . . they were very, very devoted'.

This cherished childhood lived in such close tandem with a sister four years younger than herself meant that Elizabeth was, as a friend said, 'relatively young [for her age]', while Margaret was precocious for hers.

> The thing about her was that she was shy . . . didn't find things easy naturally and there was always this stark comparison between her and Princess Margaret. The King used to look at Princess Margaret in sort of amazement that he had produced this object who found everything so easy and was a pretty little thing. Princess Elizabeth was much more Hanoverian, much more conscientious, much more solid; her face lit up when she smiled but looked rather dead when she didn't – which remains the case today.

'The King spoiled Princess Margaret dreadfully,' the daughter of one of his courtiers said. 'She was his pet . . . she was always allowed to stay up to dinner at the age of 13 and to grow up too quickly. The courtiers didn't like her much – they found her amusing but . . . She used to keep her parents and everyone waiting for dinner because she wanted to listen to the end of a programme on the radio. I remember my father despairing of her.' Crawfie, sensibly, worried about the effect this was having on Elizabeth and asked friends, 'Could you this year only ask Princess Elizabeth to your party? We really are trying to separate them a bit because Princess Margaret does draw all the attention and Princess Elizabeth lets her do that.' Elizabeth herself used to say, 'Oh, it's so much easier when Margaret's there – everybody laughs at what Margaret says . . .' Her mother also had the same effect of silencing Elizabeth. 'I noticed that, when the Queen was present, her daughter made no conversational effort and relapsed into silence,' Cecil Beaton wrote after one royal photographic session.

One thing, however, no teacher could provide the Princess with and that was the experience of ordinary life and people. She was still noticeably shy. Crawfie recorded that the Princess seemed not to like camping out and sleeping in tents with the Guides, which Princess Margaret still enjoyed, divining the reason: 'She was getting older, and had been brought up so much alone, I could understand why she did not want to undress before a lot of other children and spend the night with them.' Despite her registration at the Labour Exchange at the age of sixteen, the King had been reluctant to allow his precious daughter to venture into the outside world, an attitude which caused her increasing frustration. 'I ought to do as other girls do,' she said. Although as heir presumptive she was considered old enough at eighteen to be appointed a Counsellor of State, the King was not prepared to allow her to do any kind of war work beyond the Castle walls. Brought up as she had been in an innocent world surrounded with love and kindness, she was horrified when presented with the distressing facts of real life. In 1944 while her father was in Italy on a visit to the Eighth Army, her duty as Counsellor in his absence included signing the reprieve of a murderer. Her attitude was characteristic, one of puzzlement and at the same time a belief in a rational solution. 'What makes people do such terrible things?' she asked. 'One ought to know. There should be some way to help them. I have so much to learn about people!'

Although he had made her a Counsellor of State at eighteen, the King rejected repeated suggestions from various quarters that she should be created Princess of Wales on the grounds that the title specifically denoted the wife of the Prince of Wales. He and Churchill agreed that the best way of quashing speculation in the press was to issue an official announcement on 12 February 1944 'that the King does not contemplate any change in the style and title of Princess Elizabeth on her approaching 18th birthday'. Princess Elizabeth she was to remain until she became Elizabeth II.[9]

Elizabeth and her friends used to joke about the young Guards officers, calling those they particularly liked their 'flirts'. Hugh Euston, heir to the Duke of Grafton, was the favourite. He was favoured too by the King, who certainly saw him as a possible husband for his daughter. Hugh Euston was fond of Elizabeth – they remain friends to this day – but the job of royal consort (as opposed to being a free, rich, landed aristocrat in charge of his own destiny) did not appeal to him. 'I think Hugh Euston got a bit worried that he was going to be pushed into it,' a friend said. 'I think he got himself posted somewhere else but I think that at the back of her [Elizabeth's] mind there was always Prince Philip.'

Elizabeth had never forgotten her meeting with the blond Viking Prince at Dartmouth in July 1939. Since then royal gossips had been connecting her name with Prince Philip's. Chips Channon, who loved to move in royal circles, noted in his diary after a visit to Athens in January 1941 that the subject was openly discussed among the Greek royal family. After a confidential conversation with Prince Philip's aunt, Princess Nicholas of Greece, mother of Princess Marina, he met Prince Philip at a cocktail party 'looking extraordinarily handsome'. 'He is to be our Prince Consort,' Channon noted, 'and that is why he is serving in our Navy.' Behind the scenes, Philip's relations were already envisaging a sensational marriage for the young Prince and were to continue their manoeuvres during the war years. Elizabeth, at any rate, was innocently unaware of their expectations. As early as September 1942 in a letter to Crawfie she dropped a hint that she had been discussing Philip with her friends and that he was 'the one'. Philip arrived with his cousin David Milford Haven for Christmas and New Year 1943–4 – 'we laughed a great deal,' Elizabeth wrote. Margaret was more exuberant: 'Philip came!' she wrote. He and Milford Haven 'went mad and we danced and danced and danced . . . the best night of all'.[10]

Philip had had a tough, often uncomfortable war. At first, from January 1940, he had been kept out of harm's way on various undramatic postings around the Indian Ocean on an elderly battleship, HMS *Ramillies*, as a midshipman based in Colombo escorting Australian transports to the Mediterranean until the Italians invaded Greece in the autumn of 1940. From January 1941 he joined the battleship *Valiant* at Alexandria and was plunged into action. His first experience of war had come on 28 March off Cape Matapan in the southern Peloponnese when his battle squadron under Admiral Cunningham had sunk several Italian warships. Life had been difficult and dangerous off Crete towards the end of May when several ships in his squadron were destroyed by German fire and *Valiant* itself narrowly escaped being bombed and sunk by a Dornier. Several miles away the following day, his uncle had his destroyer, the *Kelly*, sunk under him; when he finally got ashore in Egypt, one of the first people to greet him was his nephew, impeccable in white ducks and sporting a golden beard and moustache, highly amused at his uncle's dishevelled appearance. In June 1942 Philip, at twenty-one one of the youngest first lieutenants in the Royal Navy, was posted back to Britain as a second in command on the destroyer *Wallace*. It was then that he met a young Australian, Michael Parker, who was to become his close friend and boon companion. Parker was first lieutenant on his fellow ship, *Lauderdale*, and both were on a tough but unglamorous assignment, convoy duty up and down the east coast of Britain from Rosyth on the Firth of Forth south to Sheerness at the mouth of the Thames Estuary, an area known as 'E-boat Alley'.

In 1944, the year of Elizabeth's eighteenth birthday, Mountbatten, in collusion with Philip's cousin King George of Greece, made not just one but two moves to advance Philip's cause. In March King George boldly raised the subject of an engagement with his cousin, George VI, only to meet with a firm rebuff. 'We both think she is far too young for that now,' George VI told Queen Mary. 'I like Philip. He is intelligent, has a good sense of humour & thinks about things in the right way . . . We are going to tell George that P. had better not think any more about it for the present.' Mountbatten returned to the charge in August with the idea that Prince Philip should change his Greek nationality for British citizenship as a first step and, having discussed the matter with George VI, flew to Cairo on 23 August to put the idea to the Greek King and to Philip, who happened to be in Alexandria then with his ship. Even before Mountbatten arrived in Cairo, George VI had fired off a warning shot across his bows. 'I have been thinking the matter over since our talk,' the King wrote to him on 10 August, 'and I have come to the conclusion that we are going too fast.' Mountbatten, he said firmly, should confine his talks with George of Greece to the question of citizenship. Mountbatten took the hint; 'Family hold back' was to be the policy for the present. 'Philip entirely understood that the proposal [British citizenship] was not connected with any question of marrying Lilibet,' he wrote to his mother, Philip's grandmother, on 28 August, '. . . though there is no doubt that he would very much like to one of these days.' Six months later he warned his sister, Philip's mother, not to raise the subject with the King and Queen, 'the best hopes are to let it happen – if it will – without parents interfering. The young people appear genuinely devoted and I think after the war it is very likely to occur.'[11]

Philip himself did not entirely welcome his uncle Mountbatten's activities on his behalf nor his too obvious enthusiasm for the match. 'Please, I beg of you,' he wrote, 'not too much advice in an affair of the heart or I shall be forced to do the wooing by proxy.' He was too determined to be his own man to want to feel that he was being pushed, or being seen to be pushed, into anything, let alone this particular marriage. He also very much disliked gossip about the machinations of the Greek royal family over it. But he was often on leave in Britain during his spell on 'E-boat Alley' in 1942 and 1943, staying with his cousin Princess Marina at her house, Coppins, at Iver in Buckinghamshire, a convenient distance from Windsor. Princess Marina and her first cousin were very close; she regarded him in a sense as her protégé. 'She very much encouraged the marriage,' one observer said. The ubiquitous Chips Channon, visiting Princess Marina in the autumn of 1944, noted the number of times he found the signature 'Philip' in the visitors' book. 'As I signed the visitors' book I noticed "Philip" written constantly. It is at Coppins that he sees Princess Elizabeth, I think she will marry him.' Already in February that year, after gossiping with Lord and Lady Iveagh who had had tea with the King and Queen at Buckingham Palace, he had recorded his belief that the marriage would take place.

In January 1944 Queen Mary, an altogether more reliable source, had confided to her old friend Lady Airlie that Elizabeth and Philip had

> been in love for the past eighteen months. In fact longer, I think . . .
> But the King and Queen feel that she is too young to be engaged yet.
> They want her to see more of the world before committing herself, and
> to meet more men. After all she's only nineteen, and one is very
> impressionable at that age.

Mabell Airlie, an incurable romantic who had played Cupid to 'Prince Bertie's' romance with Elizabeth Bowes-Lyon, objected. She herself had fallen in love at nineteen and it had lasted until her husband's death. 'Yes, it does happen sometimes [Queen Mary agreed] and Elizabeth seems to be that kind of girl. She would always know her own mind. There's something very steadfast and determined in her – like her father.'

The last full year of the war, 1944, had been a great strain, particularly during the summer when the anxious days of the Allied invasion of Normandy coincided with the arrival of Hitler's new weapon, the V1 flying bomb. More than 100 people were killed when the Guards' chapel just yards from Buckingham Palace took a direct hit during the Sunday morning service on 18 June. It was the only time during the war, Crawfie wrote, that she saw the Queen really shaken; everyone's nerves were on edge, as the Queen wrote to Osbert Sitwell at the time of D-Day in June 1944:

> It has been an exhausting few months with the anxiety over our
> invasion of France lying heavily on the head & mind, and now these
> great battles raging, & so many precious people killed, makes the days
> long & worrying . . . Now we have to fight a new attack on London . . .
> On Sunday in Church I weakly let a tear leave my eye thinking of the
> sorrows of so many good & brave people, & feeling unhappy for them,
> & as I did so, I felt a small hand in mine & the anxious blue eye of
> Margaret Rose wondering what was the matter. I remembered with a

dreadful pang that I did exactly the same thing to my mother, when I
was just about Margaret's age. I remembered so vividly looking up at
my mother in church & seeing the tears on her cheeks, & wondering
how to comfort her . . . she had then had 4 sons in the army . . . I could
not bear to think that my daughter should have to go through all this in
another 25 years . . .[12]

Among the 'precious people' killed in Normandy was a friend of the
Queen's, the artist Rex Whistler.

It was not until the spring of 1945, just before her nineteenth
birthday, that Elizabeth was at last allowed 'out' to join the Auxiliary
Territorial Service, always known as the ATS, as No. 230873 Second
Subaltern Elizabeth Alexandra Mary Windsor. Much as she adored
her father, Elizabeth found his protectiveness frustrating. It was as if
he could not bear her out of his sight, as if he wanted to preserve their
happy family life in aspic, prolonging her childhood for as long as he
could. Most of Elizabeth's friends and contemporaries were working –
as drivers, canteen helpers, secretaries. She longed to go out and
acquire a skill as they had, to 'do her bit' for the war effort. At last she
had been allowed to enrol on an NCO's cadre course for the ATS and
she was determined to start on time even though she was just
recovering from a bad attack of mumps. She spent a good deal of time
the day before the course started on Friday, 23 March, polishing the
buttons on her new uniform. Ugly and unflattering as it was – a khaki
cloth-belted tunic and skirt worn with khaki stockings and regulation
flat heavy brown shoes – she cherished it as a symbol of freedom and
an adventure into the outside world. For some time past, Junior
Commandant Violet Wellesley (known as 'Auntie Vi' to her subordinates, as Elizabeth was to discover) had been coming over to Windsor
to teach Elizabeth to drive in preparation for the course, which was
intended to make her not only an expert driver but also capable of
maintaining the various vehicles she would have to drive. On the
morning of the 23rd, Elizabeth, buttons gleaming, presented herself to
her father for inspection. Margaret was envious and 'madly cross';
once again, as Elizabeth used to complain to Crawfie, 'Margaret always
wants what I've got.'

At Camberley the eleven women who had been told by the
Commandant that they had had 'the honour to be picked to attend a
Cadre Course with HRH the Princess Elizabeth for three weeks'
awaited her arrival with as much eagerness and curiosity as she must

have felt herself. It was the first time in history, they had been told, that a woman member of the royal family had ever attended a course with 'other people' and they were under strict instructions for security reasons not to reveal the identity of the new subaltern on the course. Elizabeth had led such a secluded life since the beginning of the war that no one was sure quite what she looked like. 'Quite striking,' one girl noted in the diary she kept of the course, 'short pretty brown crisp curly hair. Lovely grey-blue eyes, and an extremely charming smile, *and* she uses lipstick!'[13] Both as Princess and as Queen, Elizabeth was and is fascinated by 'ordinary people'. Her own world was peopled by royalty, courtiers and servants; these three weeks in 1945 would, she hoped, give her her first chance to mix with people of her own age who did not come into those categories.

But at first she found it difficult to get in touch with the other women. While they slept in dormitory huts, she went back every evening to spend the night at Windsor. At lectures protocol was observed: she sat in the middle of the front row flanked by two sergeants, with the lower ranks behind. She was 'whisked away' by the officers between each lecture and lunched in the officers' mess. 'We are all rather sore,' Corporal Eileen Heron wrote, 'at this rate no one except Patsy Young (a sergeant) who sits next to her will ever speak to her.' It was to be the story of Elizabeth's life, always being 'whisked away' as soon as she had the chance to talk to 'ordinary people'. She did what she could to escape the imposed segregation. 'She is very interested in us,' Eileen Heron wrote. 'When anyone is asked a question she turns round to have a good look at the person concerned. It is her only opportunity to attach names to the right people.' Although a 15cwt Bedford staff car had been sent to Windsor to be set up on blocks in a courtyard for her first lesson, the second half of the Practical Mechanics lesson at Camberley provided her first occasion for embarrassment. Shown how to handle a spanner and asked if she had ever held one before, she 'looked slightly surprised, giggled slightly and said "No! Never."'

Elizabeth's second day was not much of an improvement:

> Standing Orders and Map-reading after break with Elizabeth. She was rather bored with Standing Orders – they're not much to do with her anyway, except to know what her driver should do. Mechanics in the afternoon – lecture on Oil . . . She was whisked off by the officers in the interval again – however, the Second thinks she will be a bit freer

from officers in a few days time. They seem to be breaking her in very
gently. We are told that the Queen wishes her to do Drill.

By the third day, however, the press discovered the not very closely
guarded secret. 'IT'S OUT!! There are awful libels in the Daily Mail
today about all the things she isn't doing,' a shocked Eileen Heron
wrote. Elizabeth was beginning to detach herself from her praetorian
guard of officers and talk to her fellow cadets (although the Company
Sergeant Major sat watchfully at a distance). She had found out their
names 'to give to Mummy' and said that she had spent the previous
evening explaining the ignition system at length to her father. 'These
cups of tea are getting a nice chatty institution,' Corporal Heron wrote.
'She talks much more now she is used to us, and is not a bit shy.'
There was a great fuss when Elizabeth's aunt, the Princess Royal,
came for an inspection. Elizabeth said her aunt had written to her and
asked her if she would be there during the inspection. 'I don't know
where else she thought I'd be,' she commented. Afterwards she told
her colleagues how funny it seemed for her to be at the receiving
instead of the inspecting end and that she would never forget the hard
work everybody had to put in for inspections. There was still more
spit, polish and panic on 9 April when the King, Queen and Margaret
came. 'The Queen, we felt, was especially interested in US,' Eileen
Heron wrote, 'and looked at us critically to see what sort of girls her
daughter was associating with.' Margaret watched Elizabeth closely all
the time and pounced on an opportunity to show off, spotting a case of
weak compression when her sister had not. 'It's missing,' said Margaret. 'How do you know?' said Elizabeth. 'Why shouldn't I know?'
Margaret replied cheekily, poking one of her sister's buttons. 'I imagine
Margaret has been haunting their chauffeurs lately,' Eileen Heron
commented. The course ended on 16 April 1945; Elizabeth confided to
her colleagues how sorry she was that it was over and 'says she will
feel quite lost next week, especially as she does not know yet what is
going to happen to her as a result of the course. She would *love* to join
H.Q. Crawley Rise, as a junior officer . . .' On 27 July 1945 she was
given the rank of junior commander. 'I've never worked so hard in my
life,' Elizabeth told a friend. 'Everything I learnt was brand new to me
– all the oddities of the insides of a car, and all the intricacies of map-
reading. But I enjoyed it all very much and found it a great experience.'
Fifty years later during the celebrations of VE (Victory in Europe)
Day in 1995, Elizabeth recalled how much confidence her ATS training

had given her. All her life she was to take pride in being a fast, skilful driver. (On one occasion at Balmoral her skill saved her life and those of her passengers when she was driving along a hill track and a soldier from the regiment on protection duty came round a blind corner on the wrong side of the road.) Being an expert driver and familiar with the workings of the combustion engine, however, were not to be essential parts of Elizabeth's future. This pioneering expedition into unfamiliar territory outside the Castle walls lasted only a few months as the King, of course, had known it would. As head of the armed forces and the confidant of Churchill at their weekly lunches, he knew perfectly well that, when Elizabeth had started in the ATS, the end of the war could not be far off.

VE Day came at last on 8 May 1945. During the celebrations Elizabeth, wearing her ATS uniform, and Margaret slipped out of the Palace with young Guards' officer friends, including Henry Porchester and John Wills. Porchester recalled:

> We went down Birdcage Walk, up Whitehall, up Piccadilly, into the
> Ritz Hotel and back to Hyde Park Corner down to the Palace.
> Everyone was very jolly, linking arms in the streets, and singing 'Run,
> Rabbit, Run', 'Hang out the Washing on the Siegfried Line', 'Roll
> out the Barrel', that sort of thing all night . . . We stood outside the
> Palace. They'd tipped off the King and Queen that at a certain time
> we were going to be in the crowd outside Buckingham Palace and
> everyone started to shout 'We want the King, we want the King'. At
> last they came out on the balcony and we were mixed up in the crowd,
> no one noticed, no one recognised Princess Elizabeth or Princess
> Margaret.[14]

'Poor darlings, they have never had any fun yet,' the King wrote in his diary. By 'fun' the King meant the kind of social life which he and his wife had enjoyed in the 1920s, the non-stop dancing, either at lavish private balls, or to Ambrose at the Embassy Club. He and the Queen intended to see that their daughter met suitable young men at enjoyable parties which they would give for her. This, however, was not the kind of life which Elizabeth felt she had missed out on. Unlike her mother, always the life and soul of parties, and her sparkling younger sister, Elizabeth did not really enjoy them. She had no small talk and used to lie in the bath before dressing for a ball wondering what on earth she was going to talk about. 'She was a shy girl who didn't find social life easy,' a friend at the time remembered. 'I don't think she particularly enjoyed being a young girl, all that sort of stuff . . . She quite enjoyed it once she could get going but it didn't come absolutely naturally to her, she hadn't the temperament and needed confidence.'

There was another reason why Elizabeth was not particularly interested in parties. She was not, like most girls of nineteen, looking for a man of her dreams. She had already found him and, just like her father when he fell for Lady Elizabeth Bowes-Lyon, she would not consider anyone else. On the night of 15 August 1945, VJ Day, there was a dinner-party at Buckingham Palace to celebrate the ending of the war with Japan. The King, Queen and Princesses made their appearance on the balcony and then the two girls, as they had on VE Day, went out with a party of young Guardsmen to join the celebrations on the street and to shout for their parents to come out again on the balcony. But, as she cheered the final ending of the Second World War, Elizabeth's thoughts were in the Far East where First Lieutenant Prince Philip of Greece, RN, was on duty aboard the destroyer HMS *Whelp*. On 2 September 1945 *Whelp* with Philip aboard escorted the USS *Missouri* into Tokyo Bay for the signature by the Japanese of the formal instrument of surrender. By the end of the year Philip and his ship were heading home. That Christmas Allah Knight died of meningitis at Sandringham. Elizabeth's prolonged girlhood was over.

5

A Princely Marriage

'A princely marriage is the brilliant edition of a universal fact,
and, as such, it rivets mankind.'

Walter Bagehot, *The English Constitution*

Elizabeth was now nineteen. As a mark of her transition from
childhood, she was given her own suite of rooms at Buckingham
Palace, with two ladies-in-waiting, Lady Mary Strachey and the
Hon. Mrs Vicary Gibbs, and a full programme of public engagements. She also had her own housemaid and a footman, Cyril
Dickman, who had been the nursery footman at Windsor and would
be, as Palace Steward, the head of her domestic staff when she
became Queen. Bobo remained with her as her dresser; Crawfie and
Antoinette de Bellaigue were also still in the background, emphasising
the continuity of the secure nursery and schoolroom life she had
always known. She was now allowed to choose her own clothes and
the decoration of her rooms, but since she was not particularly
interested in either, these things tended to be decided by her mother
and Bobo, although Norman Hartnell provided guidance over her first
'grown-up' dresses. The result was that her bedroom was decorated
in her mother's favourite colours, pink and beige, with flowered
chintzes and white-painted furniture, while her clothes followed her
mother's taste and were often more suited to a thirty year old than a
girl of nineteen. One object, however, showed that in one most
important matter she was determined to make her own choice.
Prominent on her desk stood a photograph of Prince Philip of Greece,
his Viking features concealed behind a bushy beard which he had
acquired on the Pacific Station.

Philip was twenty-five when he returned to England on 20 March
1946. As a handsome, experienced naval officer, Philip was intensely

attractive to women. Apart from his physical appeal, he was good company. 'He was very amusing, gay, full of life and energy and he was a tease,' his cousin said. Even before he had first met Elizabeth at Dartmouth in 1939 there had been girls in his life. He had enjoyed a relationship with a beautiful young Canadian debutante, Osla Benning, in the summer of 1939 and almost become engaged to her, but rumour had it that the ever-vigilant Mountbatten, with other prospects in mind, had put a stop to it. When Philip and Mike Parker had been based together in Australia on the Pacific Station during the last year of the war, there had always been 'armfuls of girls' on their nights out ashore, according to Parker. News of their escapades had reached the ears of senior courtiers at the Palace. One confided his doubts about the likelihood of the future Prince Consort's remaining faithful in the light of his behaviour in Australia; but, like most courtiers, he would not report this kind of thing to his employers. There had never, apparently, been anything serious; he was too cool emotionally to fall in love. 'Philip [and his uncle, Louis Mountbatten] are cold, Germanic Battenbergs,' a relation said of him. He was dominant, masculine, but not a romantic. 'He's 150 per cent male and that's his trouble really,' a contemporary said of him. Typically he was always dismissive when later questioned by biographers about his romance with Elizabeth, as if talking about such things was not what a real man would do:

> I went to the theatre with them [the royal family] once, something like
> that. And then during the war, if I was here I'd call in and have a meal.
> I once or twice spent Christmas at Windsor, because I'd nowhere
> particular to go. I thought not all that much about it, I think. We used
> to correspond occasionally . . .'

Philip has remained an enigma to his biographers. He is a man who arouses strong, often opposite reactions. He is intelligent, practical and competent, a man for solving problems, for change and movement and ideas which are not always well thought out. He bottles up his feelings and can explode without warning; he is impatient, restless, driven. He can be a bully, even cruel, but he can be warm and kind to people he knows are in trouble. He can be courteous (his manners towards his mother-in-law are impeccable), but he can also be arrogant, rude and overbearing – particularly towards politicians, a breed he holds in almost universal contempt. On many occasions when his wife became

Queen, he would embarrass her by holding forth on subjects with which he was not totally acquainted in front of professionals who were, and he would speak to political guests at Windsor or Buckingham Palace in a manner which most hosts (and guests) would find intolerable. He is an action man who likes to think his own way through problems, someone who likes to challenge established ways and notions.

The key to his character is that he has had to be self-reliant and independent since the age of ten. Since the family broke up at St Cloud in 1930, he had had nowhere that he could call home, just a succession of relatives' houses, schools, ships. By 1946 he was virtually an orphan. His father, Prince Andrew, had died on 3 December 1944 in Monte Carlo, which was then in occupied France, while Philip was at sea. Philip had therefore been unable even to attend his funeral; after the war he and Mike Parker travelled to Monaco to collect from the Prince's mistress all that he had left to bequeath to his son, a pair of hairbrushes and cuff-links and some trunks full of old suits. At his grandmother's home in Kensington Palace, he kept trunks described by his valet as 'donkey's years old' crammed with junk from childhood and schooldays – even baby clothes – as if he wanted to be able to cling on to some tangible identity in his rootless life. His mother was still in Athens, where she founded an order of nuns and where his cousin, George of Greece, had obtained his throne back as a result of a plebiscite in 1946 and was now installed as King George II of the Hellenes. The remainder of his family, his three surviving sisters, were all living in Germany, fortunately for them in the Allied Zone. His sister Princess Sophie, widowed when her husband, Prince Christopher of Hesse, was killed in Italy during the war, was about to marry again, to Prince George of Hanover. Philip borrowed a Canadian army vehicle and dashed across war-ravaged Europe to turn up unexpectedly in time for the wedding at Salem in May 1946.

He was not only virtually homeless but also practically penniless with only his naval pay to live on, just enough to run a black MG sports car. On his return to England he went to a naval training establishment at Corsham near Bath called HMS *Royal Arthur*; whenever he had leave, he would dash up to London and beg a bed at the Mountbattens' house at 16 Chester Street while they were spending the weekend at Broadlands. On Saturday nights he would be out till the early hours. The Mountbatten servants loved him: 'He was so considerate, so anxious to avoid giving trouble to people who, after all, were paid to look after the family, that we all thought the world of him and looked forward to his visits,' wrote John Dean, then butler at Chester Street and later Prince Philip's valet.[2]

Philip was very short of clothes, often arriving in London with only a razor and without even a clean shirt. At night after he had gone to bed, John Dean would wash and iron his shirt for him and mend his socks. 'He was very easy to look after, and never asked for things like that to be done for him, but I liked him so much that I did it anyway.' Dean noticed that whenever he did bring a weekend bag, it always contained a small photograph of Elizabeth in a battered leather frame.

Philip's independence of spirit and his refusal to kow-tow to anyone were qualities which particularly appealed to Elizabeth, surrounded as she was by the deference of courtiers, servants – anybody, in fact, with whom she came into contact outside her own family. They were not, however, qualities which endeared him to courtiers. Opposition to the idea of her marriage with Philip came not so much from within her own family as from the older courtiers, Tommy Lascelles, now the King's Private Secretary and therefore the most influential man at court, and Joey Legh, and also from the King's old friends, Lords Eldon, Stanley and Salisbury, and the Queen's brother, David Bowes-Lyon. 'They were bloody to him,' one of Elizabeth's ladies recalled. They would have preferred the Princess to marry someone with a high position of his own, who would have slipped easily into court circles – a rich, sporting, English duke rather than a penniless foreign prince. The Greek royal family were regarded as being very much at the bottom of the royal heap; frequently without a job and, by royal standards, without the means to support themselves. Princess Marina's pride in her breeding and her closeness to her own family, to her sisters and Prince Philip, came not just from a sense of superior bloodlines but also a touch of 'poor relation' feeling. She is alleged to have referred to the Queen and her sister-in-law, the Duchess of Gloucester, as 'those common little Scottish girls'. Some people at court were suspicious of the Mountbatten connection, regarding Uncle Dickie as 'too pushy' and 'a German'. At the end of the Second World War the British as a whole, always xenophobic, were understandably anti-German. Moreover, Mountbatten and his wife were regarded by the British establishment, including the Queen, as either dangerously or ludicrously left-wing, whichever way you liked to look at it. 'My father, you see,' Countess Mountbatten said, 'was always regarded as much too progressive from the point of view of the old-fashioned brigade ... dangerous ideas you know ... they thought now here's his nephew who's going to have the same ideas and we're jolly well going to keep him in his place. The old brigade really thought, I think, he could be a dangerous influence.'[3]

Tommy Lascelles probably summed up early court reactions to Prince Philip when he told a friend, 'They felt he was rough, ill-mannered, uneducated and would probably not be faithful.' What Lascelles meant by 'rough and ill-mannered' was that Prince Philip was 'cocky', i.e. showed insufficient respect for courtiers such as himself; by 'uneducated', that he had not been to one of the acceptable English public schools, namely Eton or Harrow (although Lascelles himself had gone to Marlborough and not to Eton). Lascelles typified 'the men with moustaches', as Princess Margaret called the senior courtiers. 'Tall and aristocratic of bearing, with a long face and long thin hands and feet, his manner was at the outset austere,' Sir John Wheeler-Bennett wrote of him. His intimate circle of friends appreciated 'the delightful and unusual workings of his mind', his shrewd judgement and his dry, often caustic wit, but to most people he was the 'aloof, austere, jealous guardian of the royal prerogative; a man who had the reputation not only of not suffering fools gladly, but of rarely enduring their presence in the same room'.[4] He had the intimidating ability to maintain a total silence if he had nothing particular to say and was given to issuing discouraging dicta such as 'I prefer books to men', and, at the outset of the First World War, 'Thank God I'm an Englishman.' As a first cousin of Lord Harewood he was related to the royal family by marriage, while his wife was the daughter of one of the Viceroys of India. Wheeler-Bennett's view of Philip was that he had 'great shrewdness and charm, but is a German Junker at bottom. Laughs too loudly at bad jokes; talks too loud; airs his opinions too much.' To Philip, the Lascelles he met at Buckingham Palace in 1946 appeared cold, snobbish and pedantic, a 'stuffed shirt'. He was, in short, just the type of man to make Philip's sensitive hackles rise. 'The effect of his childhood upon his character', a relation said, 'definitely must have made him feel that he wasn't going to be pushed around by the world – he'd have felt he'd have to stand up for himself because there weren't that many people around to do it.'

Elizabeth was probably unaware of the hostility towards Philip on the part of some of the courtiers and her father's friends, but if she had been it would have made no difference. She was in love with him and wanted to marry him, and when he proposed to her at Balmoral in the late summer of 1946 she accepted. It does not seem to have been any formal kind of proposal. Prince Philip himself described it to his biographer in his usual offhand way: 'I suppose one thing led to another. It was sort of fixed up. That's what really happened.' 'Lilibet's engagement keeps meandering on for ages,' Margaret reported to Crawfie. Nothing was to be official because the King wanted it that way. Although he liked Philip, with his naval background and ward-room sense of humour so like his own, and thought him, as a princely relation, a suitable husband for the Princess, he could hardly believe that his daughter had fallen definitively in love with and was deter-mined to marry the man she had met when she was only thirteen. It was with difficulty that he faced the wrench of parting from her and breaking up the family quartet – 'us four', as he called it – which was so close to his heart. In return for his agreement, the King exacted a promise from his daughter that nothing official should be announced for a year until after her twenty-first birthday and the family's return from their forthcoming official tour of South Africa early the following year. He was torn, he later told her, between fear that she should think him hard-hearted and his longing for one last tour together. 'I was so anxious for you to come to South Africa as you knew,' he told her. 'Our family, us four, the "Royal Family" must remain together . . .'

In fact, the King's options as to a suitable husband for his daughter were limited. She was the heir to the throne and under the terms of the Act of Settlement could not marry a Catholic, which removed most Europeans from the running except the Protestant Germans, who were ruled out because of the recent war. The two 'suitable' English candidates in terms of position and money, the heirs to the dukedoms of Grafton and Rutland, both became engaged to other girls in 1946. In choosing Philip, who, despite his German blood, was by nationality a Greek, one of Britain's wartime allies, Elizabeth, as usual, had done the right thing. Philip might have been poor, but he had a good war record, having been 'mentioned in despatches' for the battle off Cape Matapan, and he was royal, which meant that he understood the constraints and responsibilities of royalty as no outsider ever really can. Prince Philip put it bluntly: 'After all, if you spend ten minutes thinking about it – and a lot of these people spent a great deal more time thinking about it – how many obviously eligible young men, other than people living in this country, were available?'

Some of the more romantic-minded in royal circles thought that if Elizabeth and Philip were in love, they should show it more. They were thought almost too keen to take part in all the social activities, never showing lover-like tendencies to want to be alone with each other. The two of them had the same attitude towards displays of emotion, regarding them as somehow 'phoney'. Elizabeth had always been emotionally aloof and undemonstrative, only, as Crawfie revealed, showing her feelings when deeply moved. Partly this was temperamental, partly training and the influence of her grandmother, Queen Mary. The old 'stiff-upper-lip' attitudes of the British ruling class were even more marked when it came to royalty. At a deep level, however, the couple understood each other; her calm, controlled temperament was the perfect foil for his hyperactive, sometimes cantankerous nature; as was his penchant for positive action for her more conservative approach.

Philip was none the less sensitive to hints of it being an arranged marriage. He very much disliked gossip about the behind-the-scenes machinations of the Greek royal family on his behalf and, once again, he felt obliged to tell his uncle Mountbatten to back off. Before he left for India in March 1947 Mountbatten had been very much to the fore. According to his official biographer, Philip Ziegler, he took much credit for the match between his nephew and the heir to the throne and showed himself keenly interested in every detail of the wedding and the future household. 'I am not being rude, but it is apparent that you like the idea of being the General Manager of this little show,' Philip wrote on 29 January 1947, 'and I am rather afraid that she might not take to the idea quite as docilely as I do. It is true that I know what is good for me, but don't forget that she has not had you as Uncle *loco parentis*, counsellor and friend as long as I have . . .'[5] This letter may have been intended to warn his uncle not to be too bossy when the King, Queen, Philip and Elizabeth went to dinner with the Mountbattens, their daughter Patricia and her husband, John Brabourne, at 16 Chester Street two nights before the royal family set off for their South African tour.

On 1 February 1947 the family sailed from Portsmouth in the Royal Navy's latest battleship, HMS *Vanguard*. The tour had been planned for a year with, as its twin purpose, the object of helping the King's friend Field Marshal Jan Smuts against the Nationalist Party in the forthcoming election and to give the King, exhausted by the strains of war and in poor health, the chance of a prolonged holiday with his family. When the time to leave came, however, Britain was in the grip of a fuel crisis after the worst winter of the century. On 29 January Big Ben struck once and then ground, symbolically, to a halt; at Windsor the Thames froze over. A financial crisis as severe as the weather loomed; the King did not want to leave his country at such a time and later offered to return, but the Prime Minister, Clement Attlee, told him that to cut short his visit would magnify the crisis in international eyes. It was not an auspicious start; the weather in the Channel was atrocious, so bad that when the French battleship *Richelieu* (which His Majesty's Navy had tried to sink at Oran in 1940) took up station off the French coast and attempted to fire a salute in his honour, it signally failed to produce more than a puff of white smoke and the King was unreasonably annoyed. As the *Vanguard* sailed southwards across the Equator and the sun shone, the Princesses relaxed and played deck games with the ships' officers. Elizabeth wrote regularly to Philip and occasionally to Crawfie as she and Margaret were in the habit of doing when they were away or when Crawfie was on holiday. Among the naval officers on *Vanguard* she told Crawfie, there were 'one or two "smashers"'. Also in the party was another 'smasher', the King's handsome equerry, ex-Battle of Britain ace, Group Captain Peter Townsend, with whom Margaret was to have a sensational romance.

The South African tour made a tremendous impression on Elizabeth. Not only was it her first-ever trip outside the British Isles, but it was her first experience of the British Commonwealth and Empire which was to play such a large part in her life and reign. The South African part of the visit was tense; the Boer-supported Nationalist Party remained aloof and unforgiving of the British, their press hostile. *Die Burger* commented disapprovingly on the mingling of 'Europeans and non-Europeans' in the crowds and mocked the King's pronunciation of an Afrikaans sentence at the opening of Parliament. (The royal visit did not prevent the victory of the Nationalist Party the following year and the subsequent foundation of an apartheid regime in South Africa.) The King, according to local (non-Nationalist) reports, became restless at the intense security designed to keep him away from his African subjects. He was 'tired to death at being ordered about and sleuthed by Afrikander policemen wherever they moved', and on one occasion, when he thought he was out of earshot, remarked to the Queen, 'We've shaken off the Gestapo at last.' One incident showed the extent of the King's irritation at the way he was being 'driven' on his visit to his South African kingdom and, equally, Elizabeth's awareness and her attempts at damage limitation. At the state banquet in Pretoria, an official forgot to switch off the microphone following Smuts's introductory speech. Smuts invited the King to follow him, whereupon the King replied crossly: 'I'll speak when I've had my coffee and the waiters have left the room'.

Smuts urged him, 'They're waiting for you now in England, Sir.'

The King, mutinously, 'Well, let them wait. I have said I will speak when the waiters have left the room.'

Elizabeth (intervening anxiously), 'Can't we be heard?'

Alerted by his daughter's intervention, the King relented, stood up and made his speech. 'Well, I suppose I may now have my coffee,' he said as he sat down.[6]

Tension led to a sad, unpleasant incident at Benoni on the Rand, when the King, claustrophobic and unnerved by the crowds pressing in on the car, began to get in a rage, shouting at the driver. The Queen attempted to soothe him and the two Princesses were trying to make light of things when a man broke from the crowd and raced after the car; clutching something in one hand, he grabbed the car with the other. The Queen, fearing some kind of attack, beat him with her parasol while the attendant policemen leapt on him and roughed him up. It turned out that the man had been clutching not a weapon but a ten-shilling note as a birthday present for Elizabeth. The King, appalled, sent to ask if the man was all right and even apologised for his own behaviour to the equerry who had been present, Group Captain Peter Townsend. 'I'm sorry about today,' he said, 'I was very tired . . .'[7]

Once beyond the confines of South Africa the tour became more relaxed in atmosphere and the King schoolboyish in his relief at escaping the strict regimentation and often hostile scrutiny to which he had been subjected in his 'Kingdom'. In southern Rhodesia before setting out for a picnic he teased the Governor's ADC: 'Do ADCs always wear ties for picnics?' he said, giving it a sharp tug; later, at the picnic, when handed an enormous tomato, he remarked, 'What am I to do with this – throw it at you?' With his usual sharp eye for details of dress and decoration he told off the Governor for wearing one of his stars in the wrong place and his miniature medals overlapping the

wrong way. The Governor looked down his nose for a minute or two
before replying coolly, 'That's funny, Sir, because they are on the same
way as yours.' 'Oh,' said the King, 'of course I always look at mine in
the mirror.'[8] The family climbed to visit Cecil Rhodes's grave in the
Matopos hills. Characteristically, the Queen wore her usual high-heeled
shoes and when even she realised that she could not make it wearing
them, dutiful Elizabeth handed over her more sensible pair and made
the climb in stockinged feet. On his return from this solemn occasion
the King shouted 'Off parade at last' and threw his hat at the ceiling,
which was caught by the ADC and returned to him; he then threw it
on to the floor and the Queen kicked it into the dining-room. The King
then seized the gong and went round the house beating it before trying
to hang it round one official's neck, saying, 'I'm sure you'd like another
one of these!' He then opened the door of the ladies' lavatory and,
seeing a fur hanging on a peg, said, 'My God, some woman has left her
beard in here.' Even sixteen-year-old Margaret did not fail to note the
difference between South Africa and the British-ruled territories where
black Africans were concerned. Writing from Durban, where the family
had enjoyed the spectacle of a Zulu dance, she noted after a visit to
Basutoland how much happier the people were there than in South
Africa – 'though one mustn't say so too loudly'.

Back in South Africa again, four days before she embarked on
Vanguard for the return voyage to England, Elizabeth marked her
twenty-first birthday with a speech of dedication broadcast 'to all the
peoples of the British Commonwealth and Empire': 'I should like to
make that dedication now. It is very simple. I declare before you all
that my whole life, whether it be long or short, shall be devoted to
your service and the service of our great imperial family to which we
all belong . . .' The vow of service was heartfelt and one to which
Elizabeth was to maintain a lifelong devotion. Within a few years the
reign of apartheid would begin and South Africa would defiantly leave
the Commonwealth. It would be forty-eight years, during which
Elizabeth would be resolute in her support of the black cause, before
she would return to visit a free South Africa as head of the
Commonwealth.

Back in England, the King could no longer hold out against his
daughter's engagement. While the family was still in South Africa
there had been protracted discussions about Prince Philip's naturalisation as a British subject and controversy as to what his new name
would be. The family name of the Danish royal house from which his

father was descended, Schleswig-Holstein-Sonderburg-Glucksburg, was not only an absolute mouthful but also, by sounding utterly foreign, would defeat the object of his naturalisation. The College of Heralds, in a moment of non-inspiration, suggested 'Oldcastle' as a direct translation of another family name, Oldenburg. In the end, the Home Secretary, James Chuter Ede, sensibly suggested that since Philip's father's names represented such a tongue-twister, the simple solution would be for him to take his mother's name, Battenberg, for which the anglicised form of Mountbatten already existed. On 18 March Prince Philip of Greece became simply Lieutenant Philip Mountbatten, RN. It was only later that it was discovered that the whole process had been entirely unnecessary since, as a descendant of the Electress Sophia, he was and always had been, *de facto*, a British subject.[9] On 10 July 1947 the engagement announcement was issued by Buckingham Palace:

> It is with the greatest pleasure that The King and Queen announce the betrothal of their dearly beloved daughter The Princess Elizabeth to Lieutenant Philip Mountbatten, RN, son of the late Prince Andrew of Greece and Princess Andrew (Princess Alice of Battenberg), to which union The King has gladly given his consent.

Even if the more intractable Old Guard were still antipathetic towards Philip, the King and Queen were delighted with their prospective son-in-law. 'We feel very happy about it, as he is a very nice person, & they have known each other for some years which is a great comfort,' the Queen wrote to Osbert Sitwell. 'Everyone has been so kind about the announcement, & having minded so much about Mr Molotov's "no's", I think that people feel like a moment of rejoicing over a young lady's "yes"!'[10] At the royal garden-party held to celebrate the engagement Mabell Airlie liked the fact that Philip, defiantly self-confident, wore a shabby old uniform and hadn't tried to impress by getting a new one.

Elizabeth's engagement in July and her wedding on a dark November day provided a touch of romance against a bleak backdrop. It was, as Churchill said, 'a flash of colour on the hard road we have to travel'. People were delighted to watch the nice, sensible, pretty girl whom they had seen grow up enjoy her romance with the handsome naval lieutenant in his well-worn uniform. Nineteen forty-seven, the eleventh year of the King-Emperor's reign, was the moment of truth for post-war Britain. The hard winter had precipitated a fuel crisis in February, unemployment rose and production fell. There was a serious financial crisis that summer; the dollar credits upon which the British Government had been surviving were almost exhausted and on 20 August the Chancellor of the Exchequer, Hugh Dalton, suspended the convertibility of the pound, a serious blow to Britain's international credibility. Suspension of the convertibility of the pound brought home the unpleasant truth that Britain was no longer a world power and could no longer afford her Empire. War had hastened imperial disintegration already evident before 1939; post-war ideology, coupled with the common-sense realisation that Britain no longer possessed the necessary resources in men and money, escalated the process. The Victory Parade over which the King had presided in June 1946 had been the swan song of his Empire. In 1947 George VI had gloomily surveyed a plantation of trees in Windsor Great Park, each tree representing a colony of his Empire. 'This is Singapore,' he said, pointing to one. 'There is Malaya . . . Hong Kong is over there. Burma too over there. They have all been lost to the Empire Plantation. The time may soon come when we shall have to cut out the Indian tree – and I wonder how many more . . .' On 15 August, with the independence of India presided over by Mountbatten, the last Viceroy, the King lost the 'jewel' in his imperial crown and the imperial 'I' (Imperator) in his title bestowed by Disraeli on his great-grandmother not quite seventy years earlier. He was no longer King-Emperor.

However keenly the King felt the loss of his patrimony in private, in public he accepted it with a good grace. He got on extremely well with the Labour Government, particularly with Ernest Bevin, the Foreign Secretary, whose bulldog patriotism and earthy sense of humour he admired. The court economised; there were few entertainments, as Queen Mary complained to Hugh Gaitskell, then Minister for Fuel and Power, at a dinner for the Shah of Iran. 'They don't do enough of this sort of thing nowadays.' The Cold War had broken out in Europe and over all hung the threat of the atomic bomb.

There were certain parallels between the position of the monarchy after the Second World War and the situation in 1918. Britain had achieved a hollow victory in both long drawn-out wars and at immense cost in blood and money. The country had turned against Churchill, representing the *ancien régime* of the aristocratic ruling class, and towards Socialism and a Labour Government under Attlee in the landslide election of 1945. The landed aristocracy, former pillars of the throne, a class to which Elizabeth's father belonged in spirit and her mother by birth, was in terminal decline burdened by the heavy taxation necessary to pay for the establishment of the Welfare State. The King did at times feel threatened as he saw his fellow monarchs abroad defeated by Communism, while at home the large country estates of his youth were disappearing. 'Everything is going now,' he told Vita Sackville-West in 1948, on hearing that her family home, Knole, had been taken over by the National Trust. 'Before long I shall also have to go.' After a visit by King Michael of Romania, who had been recently exiled from his country, the King, according to Vita's son, Ben Nicolson, visiting Windsor as Assistant Surveyor of the King's Pictures, was 'worried much by the prospects of a Republic', mirroring his father's fears in 1918.[11]

Elizabeth was aware that her father felt he would have to tread carefully, especially when it came to financial negotiations with the Government. Now, as in 1918, the cost of the monarchy had to be seen to be justified. Mountbatten acted as a channel of communication with the ruling Labour Party. The MP and journalist Tom Driberg warned him that there was considerable feeling in the Labour Party against lavish allowances for the Prince on his marriage, or undue extravagance over the ceremony itself. Mountbatten promised to pass on the information. He wrote to Driberg from India in July:

> You can rest assured that he [Philip] thoroughly understands this problem and indeed he spoke to me about it when I was home in May. I am sure he is entirely on the side of cutting down the display of the wedding, and his own personal feelings are against receiving any civil list for the very reasons which you give. I have, however, persuaded him that it is essential he should take something. [Philip had virtually no money beyond his pay; his] tiny little two-seater made a big hole in his private fortune, and except when travelling on an officer's warrant he usually goes Third-class by train . . . as a future Prince Consort, however, I think you will agree that Third-class travel would be regarded as a stunt and a sixpenny tip to a porter as stingey . . . It really amounts to this: you have either got to give up the Monarchy or give the wretched people who have to carry out the functions of the Crown enough money to be able to do it with the same dignity at least as the Prime Minister or Lord Mayor of London is afforded.[12]

Despite refusing the King's request to declare a public holiday for his daughter's wedding, thought inappropriate at a time of strikes and

low productivity, the Labour Government responded sympathetically
to his proposals for financial provision for her and her husband,
suggesting an annuity of £50,000 for the Princess upon her marriage
(later whittled down to £40,000 by the House of Commons), 90 per
cent of which was to be tax-free, and £10,000 for her husband. In
return, the King handed over to the Treasury £100,000 savings made
on the Civil List during the war years' economies (as George V had
done in the First World War) to contribute towards the cost of these
annuities. Even in the afterglow of the wedding the debate on the
allowances for Elizabeth and Philip caused resentment, as John Gordon
of the *Express* informed his master, Lord Beaverbrook:

> The Princess Elizabeth money debate has caused a lot of talk . . . a
> large number of people think the King made a mistake in asking for so
> much at such a time . . . Many think that the Royal Family is very well
> looked after & that they could afford to keep the heir out of the Duchy
> [of Cornwall] funds . . . until she comes to the throne. I am surprised
> that the King made the mistake because up to now he has stepped
> gently and very wisely. The marriage itself has been extremely popular.
> The only criticism is that the young couple are going after too many
> big and expensive houses . . .[13]

The King was as sensitive to the need to suppress his German
connections as his father had been in 1917. None of the royal German
relations were to be invited to the wedding, not even Philip's three
sisters who had German husbands. Anti-German feeling in Britain in
the immediate post-war period ran too high for the King to risk the
embarrassment of underlining how many of his and the bridegroom's
relations were actually Germans. One opinion poll taken at the time of
the engagement produced a disapproval rating of 32 per cent against
the marriage on the grounds that Philip was 'a foreigner'. Princess
Marina's sister, Elizabeth, was not invited either; her husband, Count
Carl zu Toerring-Jettenbach, was regarded as a Nazi sympathiser. Her
other sister, Princess Olga, married to Prince Paul of Yugoslavia, was
another enforced absentee. Churchill had condemned the unfortunate
Prince Paul (or 'Palsy', as he contemptuously referred to him) as a
treacherous collaborator for his part in the pact between Germany and
Yugoslavia in 1941. The King and Queen remained friendly towards
Prince Paul, and had visited him secretly during their South African
tour, but it was still thought impolitic to court a row by bringing him

and Princess Olga out of exile to attend the wedding. Most embarrassing of all was the Eton-educated Duke of Saxe-Coburg and Gotha, a grandson of Queen Victoria through his father, Leopold, Duke of Albany, and brother of Princess Alice, who was married to Queen Mary's brother, the Earl of Athlone. The Duke of Coburg had enthusiastically embraced the Hitler regime to the extent of becoming a Nazi *gauleiter* and had had his estates confiscated after the war. Prince Philipp of Hesse, another descendant of Queen Victoria, who had acted as a go-between for Hitler and Mussolini, had been arrested by the Americans for Nazi activities.

One family absentee caused a good deal of comment. The bride's uncle, the Duke of Windsor, was not invited to his niece's wedding, the first great royal occasion since the Coronation of George VI. This was a clear indication of how family attitudes had not softened over the ten years since the Abdication. The Duke of Windsor had occasionally visited London to stay with his mother at Marlborough House, but his pleas to Queen Mary to receive his wife had still fallen on deaf ears and, although he was on reasonably cordial terms with the King, the Queen refused to see him. 'You could always tell when the Duke was coming to Buckingham Palace,' Joey Legh, Master of the King's Household and one of the ex-King's closest friends before the advent of Wallis, recalled. 'There was a tense atmosphere and the Queen would disappear. I begged her to give him just a cup of tea, but she wouldn't.'[14] Another family absentee was the Princess Royal, who allegedly stayed away in protest against her brother's non-invitation, giving ill-health as the reason, although she was seen to attend a public function two days later.

At this time a separate event marked the end of an era in the royal family's life: on 16 September 1947 Crawfie and Major George Buthlay were married in Dunfermline Abbey. George Buthlay, who came from Aberdeen (the nearest big town to Balmoral), was fifteen years her senior and had previously married and divorced. He and Crawfie had known each other for some time. Now that Elizabeth was engaged to be married and Margaret, at seventeen, was of an age to leave the schoolroom, the devoted Crawfie felt she could at last lead her own life after sixteen years' royal service. Even so, she had found it difficult to break the news that she was going. She had consulted Queen Mary while the family were away in South Africa. Queen Mary's reaction was, as Crawfie wrote, a typical one: '"My dear child. You can't leave them!"' The royal family do not like change; they do not like trusted

servants to depart and they find it difficult to accept that their
employees' personal interests can come before their own; the closer
the person is to them – a Crawfie or a favourite lady-in-waiting – the
more difficult it is for them to accept it. Crawfie tried to put her case
to Queen Mary in terms of the fact that Lilibet and Margaret were no
longer in need of her. '"I don't see how they could manage without
you," Queen Mary replied. "I don't think they could spare you just
now."' In the royal tradition of non-communication, however, Queen
Mary did not pass on Crawfie's news, or, if she did, the Queen put on
a good show of being totally surprised when Crawfie requested to see
her on 'a very urgent and important matter of a personal nature'.
When Crawfie showed her the photograph of Buthlay, there was a long
silence, interrupted by the governess's explanation that she had wanted
to get married at the start of the war and had not done so, 'Because I
felt I had a duty to Their Majesties, and considered it would be unfair
of me to leave the Princesses when they most needed me'. '"Why
Crawfie," the Queen said gently, "that was a great sacrifice you
made."' None the less, she followed this up by saying, '"Does this
mean you are going to leave us? You must see that it would not be at
all convenient just now. A change at this stage for Margaret is not at
all desirable."' The Queen said not a word about Elizabeth's intended
engagement (close as Crawfie was to the family, she was not officially
told until Elizabeth showed her her engagement ring made up of stones
belonging to Philip's mother, on the eve of the official announcement
in July). Margaret returned to the schoolroom after the South Africa
trip as if nothing had changed, arriving for lessons carrying the same
pencil box she had used as a small child, full of very small pencils
pared down to the last stub and erasers down to the last rub, an
economy both the girls had always practised. Although even while the
Princesses had been in South Africa the popular newspapers had
featured opinion polls asking readers what they thought of Princess
Elizabeth's marriage to Prince Philip of Greece, and on a visit to a
factory the girls had shouted at Elizabeth, 'Where's Philip?', within
the Palace the family had played their cards close to their chest, as
usual. No one, beyond 'us four', had been told.

'Suddenly that look of strain we had all been conscious of disappeared from Lilibet's eyes,' Crawfie wrote. Once the engagement
became official the royal machine got under way again to provide the
glamour that had been missing from the public stage since 1939. The
royal dressmaker, Norman Hartnell, designed a fairy-princess dress in

ivory silk satin garlanded with white roses of York in raised pearls, entwined with ears of corn embroidered in crystal and interspersed with embroidered star flowers and orange blossom, tulle on satin and satin on tulle. Wedding presents came from all over the world, ranging from the magnificent – a thoroughbred filly from the Aga Khan and a hunting lodge from the people of Kenya – to the prosaic – hundreds of pairs of nylon stockings (a rare commodity in those days of clothes rationing and austerity); even a turkey from a lady in Brooklyn sent to Princess Elizabeth 'because she lives in England and they have nothing to eat in England'. Among the 1,500 presents on display at St James's Palace was a woven cotton tray-cloth made specially by Gandhi at Mountbatten's suggestion, misidentified by Queen Mary, who was not in any way favourably disposed towards the Mahatma, as a loin-cloth. 'Such an indelicate gift . . . what a horrible thing,' she exclaimed. Philip attempted to silence her comments by loud praise of Gandhi, but Queen Mary merely pursed her lips and moved on in disapproving silence. On her next visit to the display Princess Margaret nipped on ahead and managed to hide the offending object behind some other presents. Otherwise, Queen Mary was in her element; the marriage of her favourite granddaughter involving as it did two members of the 'Old Family', as she liked to call the Hanoverians to distinguish them from Albert's more lowly Saxe-Coburg-Gotha line, was precisely the dynastic alliance she had hoped for. She amused herself by working out tables of their relationship: third cousins through Queen Victoria, second cousins once removed through King Christian IX of Denmark, fourth cousins once removed through collateral descendants of George III.

Despite the absence of the Germans there was a respectable gathering of royalty, many of them relations: the King and Queen of Denmark, the Kings of Norway, Romania and Iraq, the Queen of the Hellenes, the Princess Regent and Prince Bernhard of the Netherlands, the Prince Regent of Belgium, the ex-King and Queen of Yugoslavia, the Pretender to the Spanish throne, the Count of Barcelona and his wife, Prince Jean and Princess Elisabeth of Luxembourg, ex-Queen Victoria Eugenia of Spain, and ex-Queen Helen of Romania. It was a 'week of gaieties such as the court had not seen for years', Queen Mary's lady-in-waiting wrote. 'There were parties at St James's Palace to view the wedding presents, a Royal dinner-party for all the foreign Royalties, and an evening party at Buckingham Palace which seemed after the years of austerity like a scene out of a fairy tale.' It was the

first post-war royal get-together on a grand scale, although the same
cast (again without the German relations) had assembled the previous
year for the wedding in Romsey of Mountbatten's eldest daughter,
Patricia, to his former ADC, John, Lord Brabourne. 'Saw many old
friends,' Queen Mary recorded in her diary two nights before the
wedding. 'I stood from 9.30 till 12.15 a.m.!!! Not bad for 80.' She did
not mention the only untoward incident; perhaps she was not aware of
it: according to Sir John Colville, 'an Indian Rajah became uncontrol-
lably drunk and assaulted the Duke of Devonshire (who was sober)'.
At least, she could reflect, the dynasty showed every sign of surviving
not only Hitler but the Socialists. At this party the King led the conga,
a dance in which everyone present formed a chain by holding on to the
waist of the person in front; the chain then snaked through the Palace
corridors with such riotous enthusiasm that Princess Juliana's tiara fell
off and had to be retrieved and stuck on again.

One of the King's most cherished wedding presents to his daughter
and future son-in-law was to bestow upon them his favourite Order,
the Garter. Typically, he ensured his daughter's precedence by giving
it to her a week before he gave it to Philip. At the same time he
carefully chose titles for 'Lieutenant Mountbatten', tactfully referring
to each part of the United Kingdom except Northern Ireland (possibly
because relations with Eire, soon to become the Republic of Ireland,
were at a delicate stage). Philip Mountbatten, RN, became a Royal
Highness and, in ascending order, Baron Greenwich, Earl of Merioneth and Duke of Edinburgh. From 21 November he was to be
known as His Royal Highness Prince Philip, Duke of Edinburgh, and
Elizabeth as Her Royal Highness The Princess Elizabeth, Duchess of
Edinburgh. Philip was to rank as a British prince, signing himself
'Philip' and not 'Edinburgh'.[15] The titles were only gazetted on the
morning of the wedding with the announcement of the Garter which
Philip had been given the previous day. The King's desire to keep it
all secret meant that it was too late for the printing of the order of
service for the wedding. For all his high-sounding titles, the bridegroom's name appeared on these simply as 'Lieutenant Philip Mountbatten, RN'.

Prince Philip and his best man and cousin, David Milford Haven,
spent the night before his wedding at the Kensington Palace apartments of his grandmother, the Marchioness of Milford Haven, where
his mother, Princess Alice, was also staying. 'Their rooms were
astonishingly poor and humble – floors scrubbed boards with worn

rugs,' John Dean noted. A riotous stag-night party was held at the Dorchester Hotel. It was very much a naval officers' night out, masterminded with his usual efficiency by Mountbatten (now no longer Viceroy but Governor-General of the newly independent India), who had understandably felt unable to miss his nephew's wedding. The occasion was slightly marred by the first of the Prince's run-ins with the press, although this was handled with aplomb by Mountbatten who persuaded the photographers to hand over their cameras for the guests to take photographs of them. The flashbulbs were then ripped out of the cameras and smashed, effectively ending the photographers' night out. At 7 a.m. on the wedding morning, Dean brought Philip his tea and found him in great form, cheerful and in no way nervous. He breakfasted as usual on toast and coffee, then dressed in his ordinary naval uniform, his concession to his new status being the insignia of Knight Companion of the Order of the Garter. His ceremonial sword had belonged to his grandfather, Prince Louis of Battenberg, a touch which must have pleased his uncle Mountbatten (and may well have been suggested by him). Philip was ready too soon, but resisted the temptation to have a cigarette; he gave up smoking from the day of his wedding to please Elizabeth, a non-smoker. He did, however, have a gin and tonic with Milford Haven before leaving for the Abbey at 11 a.m. Among the small crowd waiting to wave him goodbye was Miss Pye, nicknamed 'pie-crust' by Philip, his grandmother's maid for fifty years, and the Palace sweep and other retainers. He shook hands with all of them and even ordered coffee for the shivering band of press reporters assigned to watch him leave.

Elizabeth's wedding morning, 20 November, began with the ritual cup of tea brought to her in bed by Bobo and the familiar sound of the pipers on the Palace terrace. Hartnell's team arrived at 9 a.m.; it took an hour and ten minutes to finally fit the dress and 15ft train. There were last-minute panics as the tiara given her by Queen Mary snapped as it was being fitted and had to be hastily repaired. The Princess wanted to wear the double string of pearls given her by her parents; they were still with the wedding presents at St James's Palace and an agitated Jock Colville, Elizabeth's new Private Secretary, was sent to struggle through the crowds on foot to retrieve them. Finally the bouquet could not be found until a frantic search revealed it in a cold cupboard. At 11.15 Elizabeth set out for Westminster Abbey with her father beside her in the huge Irish state coach. The continuity of her girlhood had been emphasised by Bobo and the early morning cup of tea; Cyril, her footman over the last ten years, stood on the carriage behind her. She had personally invited Cyril to the wedding, but his immediate boss, the Serjeant Footman, had vetoed it: 'No, you're on duty and you've got to go on the carriage.' Ahead of them and behind them trotted the Household Cavalry with bobbing plumes and gleaming boots and cuirasses; it was the first time they had been permitted to wear full ceremonial dress for six years. Inside the Abbey, the women guests all wore long dresses, long gloves and hats, which rather belied the celebrating Archbishop of York's claim in his address that the marriage was 'in all essentials exactly the same as it would be for any cottager who might be married this afternoon in some small country church in a remote village in the dales'. During the signing of the Register, both the King and Queen Mary were deeply moved and on the verge of tears, the King even going so far as to tell the Archbishop: 'It is a far more moving thing to give your daughter away than to be married yourself.'[16]

Back at the Palace after the ceremony, at the wedding breakfast, bunches of white heather and myrtle from the trees that had provided Queen Victoria's wedding bouquet, sent down from Balmoral, decorated the table. The speeches were relatively short on the orders of the King and Queen, who remembered suffering from long-winded relations on their own wedding day. Elizabeth's going away outfit was a 'love-in-a-mist crepe dress with blue velvet cloth travelling coat, blue felt bonnet trimmed with ostrich pompom and curved quills in two tones of blue'. Her parents and family lined the staircase pelting them with rose petals before, despite the freezing weather, the newly married couple drove off in an open carriage so that the waiting crowds could see them to Waterloo Station. With them, snuggled under rugs next to hot-water bottles, went the Princess's favourite corgi, Susan; while in attendance were, apart from the inevitable detective, the two familiar figures from Windsor nursery days, Bobo and Cyril. At Waterloo, the red carpet extended from the point at which the carriage stopped right to the train; Susan stole the show by tumbling out first in a shower of rose petals. The Princess, John Dean noted, had fifteen pieces of luggage; the Duke in comparison one big case and one small one.

The honeymoon had been tactfully divided between two locations – his and hers: the first part was to be spent at Broadlands, the Mountbattens' handsome Palladian-style house beside the River Test in Hampshire, the second at Birkhall, familiar to Princess Elizabeth as the family holiday home at Balmoral before the war. The *Express*, loyally pursuing its proprietor's long-standing vendetta against Mountbatten, alleged that Mountbatten had been having difficulty getting licences to repair the roof and some of the rooms at Broadlands, but as soon as the authorities learned that Princess Elizabeth was to spend her honeymoon there, the licences were mysteriously forthcoming. The first night at Broadlands was, as honeymoon first nights often are, somewhat chaotic. Everything was unfamiliar. The Broadlands staff, in the absence of the Mountbattens in India, was disorganised, the Buckingham Palace party either elated by wedding celebrations or, in the case of the newly weds, utterly exhausted. The telephone never stopped ringing until the Princess's staff managed to get on to the Palace and tell them to get the Post Office virtually to cut them off. Once they ventured outside the house, public interest made it impossible for them to be alone. Snoopers hid in the trees and long grass and when the newly weds went for Sunday morning service to nearby Romsey Abbey, people climbed over tombstones to peer through the windows; some of them carried chairs, ladders, even a sideboard, to give them a better view and afterwards there was a queue of people waiting for the chance to sit in the seats the honeymooners had sat in. A week later, Elizabeth and Philip returned briefly to London to lunch with the King and Queen before taking the train to Scotland for two weeks at Birkhall, cosy with huge log fires and surrounded by deep snow. Elizabeth, always considerate of her staff, was concerned to see that Bobo and Cyril should have the opportunity to get out and see their friends. 'As soon as we've finished dinner, off you all go,' she would say.

While on honeymoon, she received from the King one of the most touching letters a father could have written to his newly married daughter. Her wedding day had been for him one of extreme and mixed emotions. A poignant photograph taken just as the 'Edinburghs' turned away to leave after the balcony appearance at Buckingham Palace in front of the crowds shows them in brief consultation, absorbed in each other to the exclusion of the King, who watches them from the background, the position which he knows he must now occupy in his beloved daughter's life.

I was so proud of you & thrilled at having you so close to me on our long walk in Westminster Abbey [he wrote], but when I handed your hand to the Archbishop I felt that I had lost something very precious.

You were so calm & composed during the Service & said your words with such conviction, that I knew everything was all right . . .

I have watched you grow up all these years with pride under the skilful direction of Mummy, who, as you know is the most marvellous person in the World in my eyes, & I can, I know, always count on you, & now Philip, to help us in our work. Your leaving us has left a great blank in our lives but do remember that your old home is still yours & do come back to it as much & as often as possible. I can see that you are sublimely happy with Philip which is right but don't forget us is the wish of

Your ever loving & devoted
Papa.

In marrying Philip and escaping from the cocooning folds and crystallised childhood of 'us four', Elizabeth had made the first step towards taking control of her own life.

6

The Edinburghs

'The Edinburghs . . . looked divine. She wore a very high tiara and the Garter – he was in the dark blue Windsor uniform, also with the Garter. They looked characters out of a fairy-tale . . .'

Chips Channon describing a ball at Windsor, 18 June 1949

Both as a wife and the heir to the throne, Elizabeth continued to do what was expected of her. Within three months she was pregnant. Even Tommy Lascelles had come round to Philip: '. . . such a nice young man,' he confided to Harold Nicolson, 'such a sense of duty – not a fool in any way – so much in love poor boy – and after all put the heir to the throne in the family way all according to plan'.[1]

The marriage was a success on every level; physically, mentally and temperamentally the couple were compatible. Elizabeth was physically passionate and very much in love with her husband. Philip found her sexually attractive and was equally, although perhaps more coolly, in love. And importantly, for a man like Philip, he loved and respected her. Theirs was a traditional marriage, Elizabeth was used to a household in which the man came first. She had not yet acquired the authority which she was to have when she became Queen, and Philip was a particularly dominant male. There were times when he would tell her publicly, in his typically naval impatient way, not to be 'such a bloody fool'. On one occasion, driving down late to Goodwood House with Mountbatten, he drove even faster than his usual hair-raising speed, causing his wife to draw in her breath. 'Do that once more,' he told her, 'and I'll put you out!' When they arrived, Mountbatten said to the Princess that Philip had been driving much too fast and why hadn't she told him so. 'But didn't you hear him?' she said. 'He said he'd put me out.' Yet he was also supportive, determined to help her in every way he could and never to let her down. 'At home he was very attentive and protective,' John Dean wrote. 'If he had been out during the day he would always go straight to her room when he returned.' This period when they lived as a newly married couple with, in a short space of time, two children was probably the happiest of their lives.

For the first year they had no home of their own. Sunninghill Park, a large house in Windsor Great Park, which the King had designated for them (and which was later to be the site of the young Yorks' controversial house), burnt down. Their main London home was to be Clarence House overlooking the Mall next to St James's Palace, but when the couple visited it in October 1947, they had found it dreadfully dilapidated. It had originally been built in 1825–30 for Queen Victoria's uncle, William IV, when Duke of Clarence; its last royal occupant had been the Duke of Connaught, Victoria's favourite son, who had died in 1942 aged ninety-one. During the war the building had been used by the Red Cross and, when the Princess saw it, it was used as offices for the Central Chancery of the Orders of Knighthood and as a Building Maintenance Depot by the Ministry of Works. Practically no modernisation had been carried out during the Duke of Connaught's time or since. According to the report prepared for submission to the Treasury by the Ministry of Works, much of the decoration was 'in very bad taste', 'bathroom facilities' were 'totally inadequate', a proper electric lighting system had never been installed and the only lighting that existed was by means of surface wiring on cleats installed for the Red Cross as a temporary measure during the war. There was not one single modern bathroom, only an antique copper bathtub hidden in a cupboard in one of the bedrooms. The only central heating was provided by a couple of hot-water radiators in the stair halls. The roofs had leaked due to bomb damage to nearby buildings during the war and made the plaster ceilings on the upper floors so unsafe as to need replacing.[2] Elizabeth, according to an official of the Ministry of Works who accompanied them round the house on this occasion, did not seem at all concerned by the condition of the building, but took 'a very intelligent interest in the building plans'. Her main concern was for the comfort of her staff, the official noted. There were eleven servants' bedrooms. 'Her Royal Highness commented that she would be lucky if she got as many servants.' Philip remarked that the burning down of Sunninghill had been lucky for them in one way because the house was so isolated that 'they would never have been able to keep a single maid there'.[3]

They were both anxious to know when the work would start and the house be ready, but things were complicated by the fact that the money – an estimated £50,000 – would have to be voted by Parliament. The money was voted through, but there was, understandably, a good deal of complaining by the general public and the trades unions that the money should not be spent on one young couple but on providing desperately needed public housing. Any kind of building work was a difficult and sensitive subject in post-war Britain. Philip wanted a cinema installed in the basement of Clarence House and was prepared to pay for it himself. The Kinematograph Renters Society stepped in with an offer to provide a complete cinema as a wedding present, but the Ministry of Works pointed out if a private individual living in the Westminster area were to apply to Westminster Council for a licence for similar work, the application would undoubtedly be turned down and the applicant advised to defer the project for the time being. It continued to be a sensitive subject for the next two years as in normal circumstances only essential building work was being allowed and cinema owners were not being permitted either to build new cinemas or to carry out major restoration work. In the end it was allowed on the grounds that it was a gift from the Kinematograph Renters Society and would cost only £1,500, but the Ministry remained nervous about the embarrassment that might be caused if the news got out in the press.[4] The Minister of Works came under considerable fire in Parliament and in the newspapers over the cost of refurbishing Clarence House and figures for it were grossly exaggerated. It finally cost £28,000 over and above the original £50,000 voted by Parliament and part of the excess was paid by the Privy Purse and from the Princess's Wedding Fund.[5] In the end it was not until May 1949, eighteen months after their wedding, that they were to move into Clarence House.

On their return from honeymoon they were lent Clock House in Kensington Palace by Elizabeth's great-aunt and uncle, the Earl and Countess of Athlone, who were on a visit to South Africa in 1948, but within three months the Athlones returned and Clarence House, plagued by construction problems and industrial disputes, was still very far from ready. The young couple were forced to move in with their in-laws at Buckingham Palace, back to Elizabeth's former apartments in which Philip, now at work all day at the Admiralty as operations officer 'pushing ships around', was given a bedroom and a sitting-room. It was hardly the ideal start and the couple were to remain as guests of the King and Queen at Buckingham Palace, Windsor, Balmoral and Sandringham for a year.

Neither Philip nor his valet, John Dean, enjoyed the formality of the huge household. Dean discovered that Bobo, whom he had first met at the start of the royal honeymoon, was already an important personage at the Palace. She was, he said, 'a small, smart, rather peremptory Scotswoman', who, when he told her his name was Dean but he was always known as John, replied firmly, 'Well, to me you will always be "Mr Dean". We have to keep a certain standing in the house.' Dean recalled:

> All twenty-one years of her service in the Royal Household
> seemed to be imprinted on her face and stature, but she was
> quite friendly when thawed. I greatly enjoyed her company. She
> was a lovely dancer and very good fun, with a nice sense of
> humour, but even when we were staying in some village, and
> were out socially in the local pub, she always addressed me as
> 'Mr Dean'. She always referred to Princess Elizabeth as 'My
> Little Lady'.

In private and to the Princess's face, Bobo would call her Lilibet.

Hierarchical distinctions were strictly observed at the Palace, reaching a height of formality at lunch in the Steward's Room, where thirty or forty of the senior staff sat down at a long wooden table in strict order of precedence. As Philip's valet, Dean found himself quite low down, with the King's two valets, Thomas Jerram and James MacDonald, a brusher (of the royal suits) and the Pages of the Presence all above him. Before the meal the men stood behind their chairs with the women seated waiting for the Palace Steward, Mr Ainslie, to say Grace. Then they sat down to be served by waitresses and 'Steward's Room Boys', after which Ainslie banged on the table for silence and said 'leaving Grace' followed by a toast to the King and Queen drunk in water. The men remained seated until the Queen's dressers rose, led by the head dresser, Miss Willox, and then trooped out still in order of their precedence in the household.

For all the rigid protocol, Dean was struck by the 'immense loyalty' which prevailed among the staff despite unrealistic scales of pay and unacceptable hours. There was very little jealousy or juggling for power precisely because everything was done by precedent and strict order of seniority, and promotions when they occurred were handled on that basis. The Civil Service union had secured recognition at the Palace in 1946, but its influence was weak because of the resistance of the older staff.

In return the staff were extremely well treated and there was a great sense of community fostered by the Buckingham Palace Social Club, which held weekly dances, whist drives and social gatherings. By the standards of austerity in Britain outside the Palace walls, life was good for the staff. John Gibson, a boy from the back streets of loyalist Belfast who joined as a kitchen porter in 1946 and later became a footman in the Edinburghs' household, found the Palace surprisingly shabby and old-fashioned. The carpets in the corridors were worn and in the freezing winter of 1947 the only heating came from coal fires. John Dean described his room there as 'extremely old-fashioned', furnished only with a plain iron bedstead, a dressing-table and armchair, a washhand stand with jug and basin and a bathroom down the corridor. He was, however, looked after by an elderly chambermaid who called him 'Sir'.

Elizabeth now had her own household and access to Foreign Office telegrams, which arrived in boxes specially made for her. Her first Private Secretary was Jock Colville, who had served as Private Secretary first to Chamberlain and then to Churchill. In the spring of 1947 he was invited by Tommy Lascelles to become Elizabeth's Private Secretary. There was no interviewing, no overt headhunting for jobs like these. Colville was a member of the magic circle of courtiers and aristocrats, known at court almost since his birth as the son of Lady Cynthia Colville and the grandson of the Marquess of Crewe. His training had been in the Foreign Office, traditionally regarded as a seed-bed for royal officials. Colville knew enough about court life not to want to become a permanent part of it; spurred on by Churchill, who pronounced 'it is your duty to accept', he joined on the basis of a two-year secondment, which meant that he could return to his diplomatic career. The Princess's ladies-in-waiting included Lady Margaret 'Meg' Egerton, whom Colville later married, recruited in the same apparently informal way after the shy Princess had stayed with her family in March 1946 for a race meeting. Prince Philip's Private Secretary was quite definitely his own personal choice and as unlike the aristocratic courtier model as he could find, Commander Michael Parker, RN. After their return from honeymoon their joint household expanded, to be headed by General Sir Frederick Browning as Comptroller from January 1948. Always known as 'Boy', Browning, married to the writer Daphne du Maurier, was a dashing war hero and a survivor of the disaster at Arnhem. He was exceptionally handsome (the society photographer, Baron, said that he was the best-looking man he had ever photographed) and wore his clothes with style. A member of his staff described him as 'delightful, boyish, very short fuse, a great disciplinarian but very kind and greatly loved by the Household and particularly by the domestic staff'. 'He was an outstanding man,' another said, 'a natural gentleman.' He had been recommended to Philip by Mountbatten, whose Chief of Staff he had been on his South-East Asia Command. 'Boy has drive, energy, enthusiasm, efficiency and invokes the highest sense of loyalty and affection in his subordinates,' he wrote. 'His judgement in all matters that he understands is absolutely sound, and he would sooner die than let his boss down . . . he is not a "yes man" or even a courtier and never will be. He will fearlessly say what he thinks is right . . . Frankly, Philip, I do not think you can do better.'[7]

Some people thought that Browning had been put into the household as a restraining influence on Philip and Mike Parker, but, although he was considerably older than both, the three of them managed to maintain a boyish camaraderie. He was occasionally shocked by Philip's unconventional ways. When Philip visited the Brownings at their home, Menabilly, both Boy and Daphne, told by the man they had brought in to act as his valet that 'those buggers at the Palace had forgotten to pack the Duke's pyjamas', were surprised when Philip rejected the loan of a pair – 'Never wear the things.' James MacDonald, George VI's former valet, later confessed to one of Browning's staff how embarrassed he was when he went in to see Philip in the morning and found him naked in bed with the Princess (who always wore a silk nightgown). Queen Elizabeth had been used to knock considerately on the door to let him know when he could come in and the King would by then always be wearing a dressing-gown. 'Prince Philip didn't care at all,' said MacDonald. Boy was shocked too, later on, when Philip used to give his children swimming lessons in the Palace pool naked. But there were jokes, as on one occasion when at a film premiere line-up Elizabeth Taylor, then married to Michael Wilding and pregnant, displayed a prominent cleavage: 'Hop in,' Philip advised Browning out of the corner of his mouth as they passed.

In May 1948 Elizabeth undertook her first official tour abroad with Philip visiting Paris for four days over the hottest Whitsun weekend of the century. The Parisians were taken by surprise at the quality of her French accent (polished by Antoinette de Bellaigue) and of her speech, the work of Colville, no mean writer as his later books were to show, delivered with a cool, clear precision despite the constant clicking of cameras and deafening ringing of nearby church bells. They were also taken aback by the twenty-two-year-old Princess's beauty when seen in the flesh, the startling blue eyes and the clear skin which effaced the rather heavy jaw emphasised by photography. Philip too, although far more photogenic than his wife, was in real life, as Harold Nicolson commented, much better looking than in his photographs; a teenage girl who saw him at the time went so far as to call him 'a dream of beauty'. Chips Channon, seeing the couple at a ball a year later, described them as 'that glamorous couple, the Edinburghs ... they looked divine'. The trip was in some

senses an echo of her parents' triumphal visit to Paris only ten
years before when they equally had taken the city by storm. This
time Communism, not Fascism, was the threat behind this
expression of Anglo-French solidarity. The Cold War had set in
in earnest; this was the year of the Russian blockade of Berlin
and the Allied air-lift which eventually forced the Soviets to back
down. They drove to lunch in the Grand Trianon at Versailles,
where the fountains played, shimmering in the heat; the table-
cloths were specially woven for the occasion with the couple's
initials entwined with roses. They travelled down the Seine to be
greeted by Charles de Gaulle's brother at a heated, crowded
reception at the Hôtel de Lauzun, attended a banquet and a
reception at the British Embassy (at which the Princess glittered
in a diamond tiara and necklace given her by the Nizam of
Hyderabad as a wedding present), went to Fontainebleau,
lunched at Barbizon and visited Vaux-le-Vicomte. Their last
night was spent at the Opéra, where Elizabeth's mother had
scored her triumph in Hartnell's white crinoline in the summer
of 1938, and they were enthusiastically cheered as they stood
floodlit at the top of the steps waving to the crowds. 'In four
hectic days,' Colville wrote, 'Princess Elizabeth had conquered
Paris.'

Behind the glittering façade, however, concealed from the
public, neither Elizabeth nor Philip was feeling well. She was
several months pregnant and the heat, the constant standing and
being on parade had had their effect on her. Philip had a bad
stomach upset, so much so that Elizabeth tried to persuade him
to cancel his engagements, but he insisted on going on, looking
green and not in the best of tempers. There was one particularly
distressing evening which had been designed as a private treat
for the young couple. As Colville told Elizabeth Longford:

We went to a most select three-star restaurant [the Tour
d'Argent], the French had been turned out, so we found a table,
just a party of us all alone in this vast restaurant. Prince Philip
spotted a round hole in a table just opposite us, through which
the lens of a camera was poking. He was naturally in a frightful
rage. We went on to a night-club, again the French all turned

out. One of the most appalling evenings I have ever spent.
Everybody dressed up to the nines – nobody in either place –
except the lens.[8]

Philip's dislike of media intrusion was growing; his reaction to it
was one aspect of his temperament which his wife found
uncomfortable.

According to Colville, public enthusiasm for Elizabeth was just
as high in Britain as it had been in Paris as she travelled through
the United Kingdom, sometimes with Philip but often without
him as he was still a serving naval officer. (It was now agreed that
the Edinburghs should take on as many as possible of the King
and Queen's engagements.) Even Colville, often acerbic in his
comments on contemporaries, dipped his pen in sugar when
describing her effect on the public: 'Quite mysteriously, a visit
by a young princess with beautiful blue eyes and a superb natural
complexion brought gleams of radiant sunshine into the dingiest
streets of the dreariest cities. Princes who do their duty are
respected; beautiful Princesses have an in-built advantage over
their male counterparts.'[9]

The imminent birth of Elizabeth's first child was preceded by
a flurry of questions as to protocol and precedent. In August
Lascelles wrote to the Home Secretary, James Chuter Ede,
confirming that the King wanted him to be in attendance at the
birth, but by 4 November George VI had changed his mind
because of suggestions from the Dominions that their representatives also should be invited, which, in his view, would give the
custom a constitutional significance which it never had. Ede and
Attlee then told the King on 5 November 'that it would be
advisable for Your Majesty to put an end to the practice now',
and an announcement was made that day.[10] There was considerable fuss over both the name and title of the soon-to-be-born
child. Under the terms of George V's Letters Patent of 30
November 1917, only the children of the sovereign, the children
of the sons of the sovereign, and the eldest living son of the
eldest son of the Prince of Wales were to be styled Royal
Highnesses. No provision had been made for the heir to the
throne being a daughter and so new Letters Patent would have to

be issued. As Lascelles told the King on 9 October, 'As things stand at present, Princess Elizabeth's son would be "Earl of Merioneth", her daughter "Lady X Mountbatten" . . .' Letters Patent were hastily issued to the effect that Elizabeth's children 'shall have and at all times hold and enjoy the style, title or attribute of Royal Highness and the titular dignity of Prince or Princess prefixed to their respective Christian names'. One matter, however, Elizabeth's surname, was glossed over and was to cause considerable controversy in the future. According to the King's Assistant Private Secretary, Edward Ford, 'the effect of the Proclamation by George V of 17 July 1917 was that all descendants in the male line of Queen Victoria, other than female descendants who may marry or have married, shall bear the name of Windsor but Princess Elizabeth having married no longer has the name of Windsor, but is in fact Mountbatten'.[11]

On 14 November 1948 at 9.14 p.m. Elizabeth's first child, a 7lb 6oz boy, HRH Prince Charles Philip Arthur George, was born at Buckingham Palace. The baby's father, who had become impatient waiting for his appearance, was on the squash court with Mike Parker when Tommy Lascelles, moving at an unaccustomedly rapid pace, came in to announce the birth. No name had yet been chosen for the child, but genealogists had already worked out that he was fifth in descent from Queen Victoria, thirty-second from William the Conqueror and thirty-ninth from Alfred the Great. He was the most Scottish prince since Charles I and the most English since Edward VI. He was descended on both sides from the Electress Sophia through whom the Hanoverian House of Windsor's title to the throne was established under the Act of Settlement in 1701; his Scottish ancestry included Robert the Bruce and Mary Queen of Scots, while through his maternal grandmother his Welsh bloodline could be traced back to Owen Glendower, and, again through her, to the most ancient Irish names including the Ui Neill high kings. Her ancestry also included the granddaughter of a plumber, John Walsh. From every point of view, the baby was truly a prince of the United Kingdom.

Elizabeth was enchanted with her son, particularly his hands – 'fine, with long fingers, – quite unlike mine and certainly unlike his father's,' she wrote; (they were unkindly later described by a journalist as 'like sausages'). 'It will be interesting to see what they become' (later Charles was to display an aptitude for the cello). Queen Mary immediately set herself the task of finding out which of his immediate ancestors the child most resembled. Poring over old photograph albums of Queen Victoria, she decided that he looked like Prince Albert (when he grew up, however, Charles would resemble his Mountbatten rather than his Saxe-Coburg ancestors). For the child's christening Queen Mary gave him, with her usual sense of dynastic propriety, a silver gilt cup and cover which George III had given to a godson in 1780 – 'so that I gave a present from my great grandfather to my great grandson 168 years later,' she recorded in her diary.

History does not, record her reaction to the new Prince's parents' choice of his first name. Charles, the favoured name of the Stuart dynasty, has been a particularly unfortunate one for British monarchs. Charles I lost his throne and his head; his son, Charles II, regained his crown only after a chequered career in exile. His great-nephew, Charles Edward Stuart, 'Bonnie Prince Charlie', the hero of the 1745 uprising who regarded himself as Charles III, died a virtually penniless, bloated drunk in exile. Elizabeth and Philip, however, were only too happy to depart from the predictable procession of Georges and Edwards favoured by the Hanoverians. As they proudly told friends, they chose the name simply because they liked it. They were determined that nobody should know it in advance and their staff remembered the 'glee' with which they announced it. 'Prince Philip would want to fly in the face of tradition,' one commented. Boy Browning's reaction was 'Charles – bad news . . .'

Prince Charles was christened on 15 December in the White and Gold Music Room at Buckingham Palace; among his godparents were the King, Queen Mary, the King of Norway, Prince George of Greece, the Dowager Marchioness of Milford Haven, Patricia Brabourne and Elizabeth's uncle, David Bowes-Lyon. Elizabeth had sent handwritten notes to her senior staff inviting them to the celebration and among the thirty guests were Mr Ainslie, the Palace Steward, Mrs Ferguson, the Palace housekeeper, Jerram, the King's valet, Miss Willox, the Queen's dresser, John Dean and, of course, Bobo and Ruby MacDonald. The Edinburghs' own staff from the country house in Surrey which they had rented, Windlesham Moor, were also there, including Mr King, the Steward, and Mrs Barnes, the cook, who baked the cake. To mark the occasion, Elizabeth had asked for the mothers of every other British child born on 14 November to be sent food parcels.

Elizabeth's delight in her new baby was overshadowed by concern for her father, whose health had been undermined by the anxieties of the war and the crisis years which followed. 'As a result of the stress he was under the King used to stay up too late and smoked too many cigarettes,' Alec Hardinge told his son. The King had left for the South African tour in January 1947 a deeply tired and anxious man. The break from the Palace had not really revitalised him; the programme had been punishing and he had lost 17lb by the time he returned. By January 1948 he was suffering from cramp in his legs, the early symptoms of Buerger's disease (arteriosclerosis resulting from smoking) which was restricting the flow of blood to his lower legs and feet. By August he was in discomfort most of the time; his secretaries noted that he would kick his leg against the desk in an attempt to restore circulation. On 12 November, two days before Prince Charles's birth, his surgeon, Professor Learmonth, came up with an alarming diagnosis: the King had a condition of early arteriosclerosis with a danger of gangrene developing and even the possibility of his right leg requiring amputation. News of this was kept from Elizabeth until after the birth of her child when two days later the King reluctantly agreed to announce the cancellation of his projected tour of Australia and New Zealand.

Nicotine addiction had been a family curse from Edward VII onwards. Smoking had played a major part in Edward's death and that of his son, George V. Even Queen Mary smoked; her present to her son Bertie on his eighteenth birthday had been a cigarette case. George VI was only fifty-four, but his life was already endangered. He was too ill to go to Sandringham for Christmas, which the family spent in London, and on 12 March 1949 Learmonth performed a lumbar sympathectomy in a specially fitted-up operating theatre at the Palace. 'I am not in the least worried,' the King said as he went under the anaesthetic, but his family were. 'He is so ill, poor boy, so ill,' Queen Mary told Harold Nicolson on the day of the operation 'in such a sad voice'. The Queen, usually calm in the face of illness, was reported to be 'frantic', but the operation was a success and seemed to give the King a new lease of life. He was in noticeably good form during Ascot week that summer and even danced at the ball given in honour of Waterloo Day, 18 June, at which the Queen looked magnificent in a white satin semi-crinoline and the splendid rubies left her by her friend the famous hostess Mrs Ronnie Greville, while the glamour of the Edinburghs, according to Chips Channon, eclipsed them all.

The Edinburghs were indeed radiantly happy. They had a baby son and now, with the move to Clarence House in June 1949, a home of their own. For Philip, it was the first real home he had had since the departure from St Cloud when he was ten years old. He and Elizabeth had taken a good deal of care over the planning and decoration of Clarence House and the arranging of their wedding presents, which had been stored in the Orangery at Windsor. They consulted their staff about the design of their workplaces and the staff quarters were, in John Dean's opinion, 'as near ideal as could possibly be imagined'.

Elizabeth and Philip had separate but communicating bed-rooms in the manner of all upper-class couples at the time. Elizabeth's was pink and blue with a draped canopy hanging from a crown. Philip's room was panelled in light wood with red furnishings and an adjoining bathroom lined with photographs of the ships he had served in. Their dressing-tables were placed a few feet from the communicating door so that they could talk to each other as they dressed. Elizabeth's sitting-room was painted aquamarine blue, a colour fancifully described by the editor of *Country Life* as 'catching the sensation of an early morning in September, when the sky is of a pale cloudless blue but the sun is still veiled by a thin haze and the lawn is silvered with dew'.[12] No less than three photographs of Philip stood on her Chippendale working desk. Philip's study, panelled in white Canadian maple, another wedding present, featured three large portraits by Laszlo of his parents and his grandfather, Prince Louis of

Battenberg. The general impression of the main reception rooms with their Nash ceilings and eighteenth-century furniture was light, pleasant and conventional. The pictures throughout the house were chosen by Philip. Elizabeth had taken part in all the discussions and even helped mix the soft green paint for the dining-room walls. She was extremely practical by nature and when someone complained about the smell of paint in the room she said, 'Put a bucket of hay in there and that'll take it away.' But Philip was the dominant influence here and at Windlesham Moor. He was mad on gadgets and had installed every kind of modern machinery in the kitchens and laundry-rooms. According to Dean, he loved 'home-making' and often brought back from Ideal Home Exhibitions newly invented objects like electric mixers which had been designed as labour-saving devices for servantless couples.

Prince Charles's nursery had white walls with a pale blue line on the ceiling mouldings, and white chintz curtains and covers with black line-drawings of nursery-rhyme figures on them. There was a glass-fronted cabinet for his toys, many of which – toy soldiers, mice, horses and teddy bears – had belonged to his mother. His hairbrush, silver rattle and perambulator were the same as his mother had used during the reign of Allah Knight at No. 145 Piccadilly. He had two Scottish nurses – Helen Lightbody, given the courtesy title of 'Mrs' as Allah Knight had been, passed on to Elizabeth from the Gloucesters' nursery and her junior, the nurserymaid, Miss Mabel Anderson, who was to become a key figure in his life. Before the move to Clarence House, Prince Charles had spent all his time at Windlesham Moor, Surrey, where the country air was considered healthier for him, seeing his parents only at weekends. In those days, upper-class babies saw a great deal more of their nannies than their parents and Elizabeth, although fond of him, was not particularly maternal.

Windlesham Moor, which the couple rented from a Mrs Warwick Bryant, was a two-storey, whitewashed house with four reception-rooms, five main bedrooms and staff quarters, far from cramped by most people's standards but for the royal couple probably the smallest house they had ever lived in. Philip in particular enjoyed it. 'I believe that in those early days the Duke was uneasy in the atmosphere of the Palace with its formalities,' Dean wrote, 'and that this heightened his pleasure in having a country home that was so different.' The couple would motor to Windsor to ride in the Great Park and on Sundays join the King and Queen at the Royal Lodge to attend the private chapel in the grounds. Windlesham had fifty acres and a garden famous for its azaleas and rhododendrons, but unlike her parents, Elizabeth was uninterested in gardens. In order to get her to admire his handiwork, Huggett, the head gardener, an ex-Guardsman, had to appeal to her sense of duty. 'Ma'am, from one Grenadier to another, I think you ought to come round the garden after church,' he told her. On Sundays Philip would get the servants and the household out for a game of cricket on the pitch he had converted from the tennis courts and local teams would be invited along to play. No mean bowler himself, he was outshone as an all-rounder by Mike Parker.

Philip was very weight conscious – even today he has a remarkable figure for a man of his age. At Buckingham Palace he used to come back and have a game of squash followed by a swim in the pool and on weekends at Windlesham he piled on the sweaters and went for runs, coming back so exhausted that he would have to lie down, much to Elizabeth's amusement. 'I think Prince Philip is mad, John,' she used to remark to Dean. Otherwise he was not vain about his appearance, although worrying about his hair which was already thinning and had to be combed just right to cover the bald spot at the back. He used lotion from Topper's of Bond Street, who also cut his hair. He shaved with a Gillette razor, as they were then called, refusing to use an electric one. He had a sentimental attachment to things which had belonged to his father; the ivory handle of his shaving brush had been Prince Andrew's, as had the gold signet ring which he always wore with his plain gold wedding ring. His shoes came from Lobb and his hats from Lock in St James's, both traditional suppliers to the royal family, but on the whole his lack of interest in clothes was the despair of his valet. Although he did care about his uniforms, of which he had three, when he was first married he had only one grey lounge suit, evening clothes and a shooting suit; otherwise he wore a blazer and flannels. 'He is difficult to dress,' Dean wrote, 'because he's not interested in clothes and is set on his own ideas – he wears suede shoes with evening dress and he simply cannot tie a tie.' When his father's trunks turned up from France, he had Prince Andrew's old suits altered – one was a blue lounge suit, moth-eaten and darned, but he insisted on wearing it. Although Philip was, according to Dean, by nature 'pleasant and courteous to servants', he tended to be outspoken 'in naval fashion' with Dean, who was inclined to take offence. On one occasion he called Dean a 'stupid clot' and they were not on speaking terms for several days. Often when Philip and his valet were having an argument in the dressing-room, Elizabeth would say, 'Listen to them, Bobo, they're just like Papa and Jerram. Only sometimes I think they're worse.'

Perhaps because of his early experiences of having no money of his own, Philip was careful with it. Thrift seems to be a royal characteristic. In those days the women of the family used to send their stockings to Harrods to be repaired. On the other hand, they were generous tippers. When Elizabeth and Philip went to stay, as they often did in the first years of their marriage, with the Brabournes in their two converted farm cottages in the village street at Mersham-le-Hatch in Ashford, Kent, the butler and cook would get £3 each, graduating down to £1 for the most junior member of staff – while a visit to the Duke of Beaufort's vast house, Badminton in Gloucestershire, could cost them £20 in tips. Beyond tipping and church collections, when Bobo and Dean would dole out the requisite amount – half a crown for the 'family' churches at Sandringham, Windsor and Balmoral, a more ostentatious £1 for 'strange' ones – the royals never carried money or dealt in cash. Shopping would be charged to accounts which would be settled by Boy Browning and the Clerk Comptroller at Clarence House, ex-naval Petty Officer Leslie Treby.

Both Elizabeth and Philip had simple tastes in food and drink. Like her mother, Elizabeth has a weakness for chocolate, but she has always been abstemious as far as alcohol is concerned and in those days never drank anything but orange juice with her meals, barely touching a glass of wine when dining out. Philip would have a glass of beer with lunch, a gin and tonic in the evening.

Although the food was simple, the standards of service at Clarence House were as high as they would have been at Buckingham Palace or any great house.

In return for all this cherishing, Elizabeth took a great interest in her staff. There had almost been a family row between the Edinburghs and the Athlones over Bennett, the Athlones' butler, who had worked for them at Clock House. 'Through Bobo they pinched Bennett,' a courtier said, 'on one condition, that whenever Lord Athlone was going out on some official function, Bennett would go and put his uniform out and help him dress. He was absolutely wonderful, he not only did flowers beautifully but on tour he always kept staff happy and arranged outings for them.' Bennett stayed with Elizabeth when she became Queen, becoming Page of the Presence, the top staff job. Like her grandfather, George V, Elizabeth disliked change, particularly in personnel, but the apparently limitless pool of domestic servants which had existed before the Second World War had drastically shrunk and even Ainslie, the Palace Steward, found himself at a disadvantage at the Labour Exchange when competing for staff in pay and conditions. Although Dean described staff conditions at Clarence House as 'wonderful', people who had not been brought up 'in service' found the rates of pay and severe restrictions on personal freedom unattractive (time off was one half-day a week and every second Sunday, with additional free time during the day and when the royals were not in residence) and there was a high turnover among junior servants. Elizabeth, Dean said, was a 'considerate employer'; she insisted on the very best medical attention for her staff and if anyone left she wanted to know the reason why. On one occasion she was 'quite put out' when a kitchenmaid left without her being told about it. When there were dinner-parties and a cinema show afterwards, the staff were always invited to join the guests. On occasions when she had to dress up for some important function, she liked to give the wives of the employees a chance to see her close-up and they would line the stairs as she left. But, brought up as she was, she still had very little notion how the other half lived. 'It's fun to dress up sometimes, isn't it?' she would remark as she swept through the hall in satin and diamonds, to a woman whose idea of an evening out was beans and toast in a café. While Elizabeth took an intense interest in the personnel and liked to be informed about what was going on in her household, Philip liked to be in charge. 'As at all our homes,' Dean wrote, 'the Duke took a great interest in the way the place was run.' On nights when he dined at home, the menu book would be sent up — 'if there were alterations or suggestions to be made, they were usually written by the Duke'.

Elizabeth was still used to having things decided for her, either by her parents or her husband. Before the move to Clarence House, she had lived in her parents' households just as she always had. According to Crawfie, even though marriage had given her a bloom and self-assurance she had not had before, in the early months back at Buckingham Palace 'Lilibet continued her childhood's habit, and always went down to the Queen to ask, "Shall I do this?" or "Do you approve of that?" Gradually she became more self-reliant,' Crawfie went on, 'and in this her husband has been a great help to her. I think he has brought her more in touch with the outside world, and a more natural and unconventional life than court life can ever be . . .' Elizabeth's existence revolved around Philip. Crawfie describes her as standing at four-thirty every afternoon at the window of her room in Buckingham Palace, waiting 'to see the tall, lean figure coming past the fountain in the centre of the road outside the Palace, or to see his small sports car turn in at the Palace gates. Usually a [good] deal too fast . . .'

In that year, 1949, when Elizabeth and Philip moved out of the Palace and into Clarence House, Crawfie was to become a non-person at the Palace. She had definitely retired from royal service at the end of 1948, her reward being the lifetime tenure of Nottingham Cottage at Kensington Palace, given her by the King. Nottingham Cottage is one of the most attractive houses in the 'KP' complex and today is occupied by one of the more important figures in the Palace hierarchy, Princess Margaret's Private Secretary. It was Crawfie's first home, described by her as a dream of 'seasoned red brick . . . with roses round the door . . . snapdragons, lavender and scented white Mrs Simpkins carnations . . . in the little square garden'. As a mark of her appreciation, Queen Mary had filled the house with Victorian furniture and flower prints. On 1 January 1949 she had received a letter from the Queen expressing her gratitude for her 'devotion and love' for Lilibet and Margaret.

By March, however, the Queen had got wind of a suggestion that Crawfie was to write a book about the Princesses and wrote to tell her how worried she was at the idea. Worry became reality when in October the Queen's friend Nancy, Lady Astor, sent her a copy of the manuscript of Crawfie's book, which was to be published in the American *Ladies Home Journal*, and which she had obtained through her friends, the magazine's editors, Bruce and Beatrice Gould. On 19 October the Queen replied with a six-page letter to Lady Astor telling her that the whole thing had been 'a great shock for us' and that she thought 'our late and completely trusted governess' had 'gone off her head' because she had promised in writing that she would not publish any story about their daughters.[13] Her Private Secretary, Major Thomas Harvey, followed this up with a further letter to Nancy Astor enclosing the Queen's comments on Crawfie's manuscript and asking for 'specific passages which cause particular offence' to be removed from the American publication. The Queen, Harvey wrote, was 'shocked and distressed' that a person who had held a position of trust in her house should break a time-honoured tradition by writing and publishing personal reminiscences. 'Such a thing is utterly alien to the spirit and custom of Their Majesties' households and staff and great regret is felt by all those who care for the sanctity of their family life at this unhappy breach of decency and good taste...'[14] The list of the cuts requested by the Queen seems to have been lost. The American edition did, however, contain an account of Wallis Simpson's visit to the Yorks at the Royal Lodge, which was later omitted from the British edition.

The Goulds were taken aback by the royal reaction, unable to see why the Queen should object so much to such a sympathetic portrayal of her family. 'I realize,' Bruce Gould wrote to Nancy Astor, 'that the whole idea of royalty is a kind of conspiratorial ballet which depends upon everyone's unquestioning acceptance of the agreed-upon steps.' Even though Crawfie had broken with

tradition, he argued, *The Little Princesses* represented a propaganda bonus for the family. The Queen, however, had learned
her lessons from Queen Mary. Later she was even to cover up
for the Duke of Windsor in an effort to keep the family myth
intact. No light, however roseate, was to be cast upon the magic.
Crawfie represented a dangerous example which could be followed. Nancy Astor went to see the Queen and found her 'deeply
distressed' by Crawfie's behaviour. 'She thinks she must have
gone queer,' Lady Astor told the Goulds, 'for it was not too long
ago that they [the family] saw her, and they felt she was not quite
her old self.' Nancy saw the Queen's point: 'Imagine if your
Confidential Secretary did a thing like this! It's small wonder
they are shocked, but I believe it's more the hurt – someone they
loved and trusted and who gave her written word!'[15] 'Doing a
Crawfie' entered the royal language. It meant betrayal by 'telling'
or 'sneaking' just as 'doing an Uncle Dickie' meant pulling a
sharp stroke, like loaning the family a trusted servant while
Mountbatten was abroad and thus getting them to pay the wages.

Crawfie's story is a tragic one. For sixteen years she had
devoted herself to Elizabeth and Margaret. She had loved them
and been loved by them in return. 'They [the royal family] did
love her – they loved her very much. That's why they were so
hurt,' a lady-in-waiting who was at Clarence House at the time
said. Her marriage to George Buthlay which should have provided her with security and a fairy-tale ending was not the haven
she had dreamed of. She was thirty-eight when she married
Buthlay, an age which in those days was considered too old to
bear your first child. Within months of her leaving, her treasured
relationship with the royal family had begun to turn sour under
the pressure of her husband's demands. 'She was besotted with
him,' a member of the household said. Buthlay, they say, tried to
capitalise on the royal connection, boasting of it in his business
transactions, and attempting to use his wife to persuade the royal
family to switch their account from Coutts to Drummonds, the
bank for which he worked. Crawfie, perhaps at his prompting,
annoyed the family by asking to be made a lady-in-waiting. 'He
put her up to it,' a courtier said. 'He was a terrible man, always
trying to feather his nest – writing to companies and mentioning

his Palace connections.' Crawfie seems to have brooded over the fact that she had been made a Commander of the Royal Victorian Order, which is in the sovereign's personal gift, and not the more elevated Dame. When asked why she had not been given it, a courtier opined, 'Jealousy in the Household, possibly an element of snobbishness, some of them were awful to her.' Whether Crawfie, prodded by her husband, felt resentful over this or not, the grant of Nottingham Cottage for her lifetime, or £100 (around £10,000 in today's money) per annum in lieu if she did not wish to live there, was not ungenerous.

Money certainly seems to have been the spur for the 'great betrayal'. Crawfie got $6,500 tax free from the *Ladies Home Journal*. The world rights were sold by Curtis Publishing to Newnes for £30,000 with a special tax-avoiding deal for Crawfie. Publication in Britain began in *Woman's Own* in March 1950. John Gordon, scourge of the royal family (and the Mountbattens) during the late 1940s, 1950s and 1960s as editor and chief columnist of the *Sunday Express*, tracked his fellow Scot. He had wanted to buy the rights to serialise *The Little Princesses*, but had already laid out £25,000 on the Duke of Windsor's story. According to Gordon, Crawfie's problem had been how to capitalise on *The Little Princesses* and subsequent books using her insider knowledge while avoiding the swingeing British tax system then in force. Newnes had got round this by signing her up as social editor of *Woman's Own* on a lifetime's contract at an agreed yearly sum which was to include any future books. Having taken Newnes's shilling, Crawfie found herself on a treadmill of royal biography. There were articles on 'Princess Elizabeth in Malta' and a profile of Princess Margaret for *Look*, in which she portrayed the King as telling her ' "You know I see a lot of you in Princess Margaret, Crawfie." ' [16] Gordon was in the market for Crawfie's services, but Buthlay's demands had proved a sticking point. 'We could have put her under contract if we had agreed to take her husband in our office staff in Aberdeen at about £500 a year,' Gordon wrote to his employer, Lord Beaverbrook. 'But I couldn't agree to that. He is a very difficult fellow and would have been most troublesome to us.' [17]

Crawfie fled from Nottingham Cottage in the autumn of 1950,

as Gordon reported to Beaverbrook. 'As you assumed,' he wrote, 'I was the author of the paragraph in Hardcastle about Crawfie's departure from Kensington Palace. I printed it as part of the pressure on her to do some more writing about the Palace. Persuasion is difficult at the moment because she has been brought to the edge of a nervous breakdown by all the trouble, but she will bend in good time.' Gordon's willingness to exploit, even to increase, Crawfie's misery for his own ends hardly qualified him to blame the Palace for 'freezing her out'. 'They put the black hand on her,' he wrote. 'The neighbours all living on palace charity were afraid even to be seen speaking to her. So she decided to pack up and go . . . If once this story comes to be written,' he continued optimistically, 'it will rock the Palace. If one could only quote some of the Queen's letters which I have read (bad spelling and all) it would beat Windsor's [the Duke's story then being serialised in the *Express*].'[18]

Gordon had an eye on the possibility of exploiting those letters and others from the two Princesses and Queen Mary. By 1954 he managed to come to an agreement with Crawfie over them, but he was warned off by Beaverbrook's lawyers, who advised that an injunction could be sought against their purchase or publication. Having failed to sell the letters to Beaverbrook in 1954 (most of them were returned to the Royal Archives before she died, the remainder being dealt with by her solicitor according to her instructions), poor Crawfie saw her journalistic career come to an abrupt end in the summer of 1955. As part of her agreement with Newnes, Crawfie had been responsible for a sugary weekly column on royal events for *Woman's Own*, trading on her position as a former royal insider. This proved to be her downfall. 'The bearing and dignity of the Queen at the Trooping of [*sic*] the Colour ceremony . . . last week caused admiration among the spectators,' she wrote in a column dated 16 June 1955. But that year the ceremony had been cancelled because of a rail strike. She also conjured up for her readers a sparkling description of Royal Ascot: 'Ascot this year had an enthusiasm about it never seen there before.' Unfortunately for Crawfie, that too had been postponed for the same reason. As Robert Lacey, one of Elizabeth's early biographers, put it, 'her column created a sensation she did not intend. She concluded her career as a writer more rapidly than as a governess.' Crawfie lived for more than thirty years in retirement in Aberdeen, embittered by her experiences and disillusioned with her marriage. Buthlay predeceased her, leaving instructions in his will which excluded her from the ceremony of dispersing his ashes. Virtually friendless except for her family solicitors, Crawfie lived until 11 February 1988. There were no flowers from the royal family – from the Queen Mother, Lilibet or Margaret – at her funeral.

There were changes in Elizabeth's household in 1949. Her Private Secretary, Jock Colville, left to return to his diplomatic career and a posting in Lisbon, taking with him his wife, the former Meg Egerton, who was replaced as lady-in-waiting by her sister, Lady Alice. Colville was succeeded by the man who was to become her longest-serving Private Secretary, Colonel the Hon. Martin Charteris. 'Choosing me was an act of pure nepotism,' Charteris said later. 'I knew Jock Colville . . . and my wife was friends with Alan Lascelles . . . There was no vetting, no security clearance, no board interviews . . . In fact, years afterwards when it was too late it was realised that I had never signed an Official Secrets document.'[19] Charteris, as he frankly admitted, fell in love with his employer at his first interview with her in November 1949. 'There', he said, 'was this really pretty woman, bright blue eyes, blue dress, brooch with huge sapphires. She was so young, beautiful, dutiful, the most impressive of women.' Even before he saw her, he had been impressed by her business-like manner. Arriving early for an 11.30 appointment, he had been received by Boy Browning, who rang through to her at 11.25. 'Martin Charteris is here to see you, Ma'am. Shall I bring him in?' There was a crisp reply, 'Yes. At half-past eleven.' They got on, he recalled, 'really well', but then he heard nothing more, so eventually he rang up Colville to ask whether he had got the job or not. 'Of course they're expecting you,' said Colville. 'You start work on 1 January.'

Just as news of Crawfie's 'betrayal' came in the autumn of 1949, Elizabeth's life was taking a new direction, offering her a means of escape into the real world. The shadow of her father's ill-health seemed to have lifted and, as a result, Philip was going back to sea. He still regarded himself as a working naval officer more than a royal consort. He helped Elizabeth in her public duties, suggesting phrases for speeches and coaching her to lower the high girlish tone of her voice. He helped his shy wife rather as the Queen helped the King, giving her confidence and taking the lead in potentially awkward situations. 'She was marvellous at doing her duties,' one of her ladies-in-waiting said, 'but she found social things difficult. She was especially shy with people of her own class and she was outshone by Princess Margaret. She really was agonisingly shy.' When it came to social and even public occasions Elizabeth still felt herself very much in the shadow of her mother, whose social graces were celebrated. On whistlestop train tours where groups of people would be waiting for her to wave to them, she would say, 'Mummy would have loved this, she'd be so much better at it . . .' Even in her early years as Queen on world tours she would still sometimes feel outshone by her confident, glamorous husband and aware of his effect on the female section of the public. When she attended women's lunches without him, she would confide with clear-sighted modesty, 'I know they'd rather see Philip.'

Philip loved Clarence House and enjoyed running his own 'tight ship' there, but he still hoped for his own command and longed to go back to sea. In October 1949 he was posted as first lieutenant and second-in-command to HMS *Chequers*, leader of the first Mediterranean destroyer flotilla based in Malta. Also there was his uncle Mountbatten in command of the First Cruiser Squadron, having made the strange transition from Viceroy and then the first Governor-General of an independent India back to serving naval officer. Although promoted to Vice-Admiral he was not even second-in-command of the Mediterranean Fleet, then one of the most powerful naval forces afloat. When in port, Philip spent a lot of time with his uncle and aunt at the Villa Guardamangia. According to his uncle, their initial reunion was not easy. Prince Philip was 'very busy showing his independence' and did so with some brusqueness. Mountbatten was hurt. 'The trouble about not having a real son of one's own but only a couple of nephews and a son-in-law is that however much one may like them they will never feel the same way about the older generation if one isn't their real father,' he complained to his beloved daughter Patricia, 'not that I blame them tho' it makes me feel a bit sad at times.' As time passed, however, their relationship got back to normal. 'Philip is right back on 1946 terms with us and we've had a heart to heart in which he admitted he was fighting shy of coming under my dominating influence and patronage.'[20]

On 20 November Elizabeth flew out to join her husband and, after spending a few courtesy nights at the Governor's residence, moved in with the Mountbattens. Mountbatten, who seemed never to tire of the excitement of having royal relations, was enchanted to have the heir to the throne actually staying in his house. He was, perhaps, a little in love with her. 'I don't think I need to tell you how fond I've become of her,' he told Patricia. 'Lilibet is quite enchanting and I've lost whatever of my heart is left to spare entirely to her. She dances quite divinely and always wants a Samba when we dance together and has said some very nice remarks about my dancing.' He was anxious to know what she really thought of him since Philip had told him 'she used *not* to like me' and commissioned Patricia to find out. Elizabeth's original opinion of Mountbatten may well have been influenced by her mother's reservations about him, but in Malta, getting to know him better, she became fond of him. He was good company and easy to talk to and there was a distinct shortage of royal uncles since the Duke of Kent had died and the Duke of Windsor had become a skeleton in the family cupboard. She found it easier to communicate with older adults than with most people of her own age unless she knew them really well. Then there was polo, which involved horses, her real passion. Philip became bitten by the polo bug in Malta under the influence of his uncle. Elizabeth used to sit beside Mountbatten at polo matches watching her husband play. Significantly while Mountbatten pointed out the players to her – 'There's so and so playing' – Elizabeth, recognising the horse rather than the man, would correct him: 'No, it can't be so and so because it's Grayling.' Elizabeth's entourage remained suspicious of him. One lady was despatched to Malta with strict instructions from Browning, who knew his old chief well: 'Remember you've got Dickie – he'd always rather

do something under the table than above.' Further, he told her
to make sure that 'Princess Elizabeth wasn't bossed about by
Dickie'.

At Guardamangia Elizabeth gazed wide-eyed out of a window,
fascinated by the experience of seeing people living in caves. It
was all a long way away from Buckingham Palace and Clarence
House. The few months in Malta were to be the only period in
which Elizabeth could lead a near-normal life as a naval wife out
of the public eye despite the inevitable presence of her detective.
Mike Parker was there too – 'He and Prince Philip were like boys
together,' a courtier said. 'He [Parker] jollied things up.' There
was swimming, dancing, picnics, expeditions by boat to the
beaches and coves round the island and to Gozo. She could even
go shopping and out to the hairdresser and enjoy in-jokes with
the other naval wives. She was happy and pregnant, apparently
not missing her son, at home in London with his grandparents
and his nannies. He spent Christmas with them at Sandringham;
it was perhaps the beginning of his lifelong devotion to his
grandmother. The King too doted on him, writing to his daughter
in the terms that his own father had used about her when they
had left her in 1927: 'He is too sweet for words stumping around
the room.' She returned home on 28 December, but flew out
again to join Philip on 28 March 1950. Her twenty-fourth
birthday was on 21 April 1950. Peter Howes, Mountbatten's Flag
Captain, organised a group of young officers into an impromptu
choir. At 8.45 a.m. her telephone rang. When she answered, she
heard a spirited rendering of 'Happy Birthday' accompanied by
some of the band of HMS *Liverpool*. According to Mountbatten
who heard it from Bobo, 'Lilibet was wildly excited and kept
saying, "Oh! Thank you, thank you! That was sweet but who are
you?"' This was followed by the second verse rendered by the
Officers' Glee Club and a bagpipe refrain. 'Lilibet first went
white, then quite red, and ended up with tears in her eyes.'
'She's so sweet and attractive,' he added, 'at times I think she
likes me too but she's too reserved to give any indication.'[21]

Elizabeth flew back to England to await the arrival of her baby.
Leaving Malta on 9 May the plane had to turn back and land at
Nice because of severe thunderstorms and the royal party spent

the night at the Negresco before going on to London the next day. It was a particularly happy time for her as she told a friend:

> Both Philip and I are very thrilled about the new baby and we only hope that Charles will take kindly to it. He has only seen Fortune Euston's baby at close quarters and he then tried to pull her toes off and poke her eyes out, all of which she took very kindly, having a brother of 2 who presumably did the same.

Philip's naval career was progressing; he had been told that he was to be promoted to lieutenant commander and would get command of his own ship. 'Philip will be remaining in the Mediterranean for some time as he has just got command of a ship which has been his goal ever since he returned to naval duties and not unnaturally he is very thrilled about it,' Elizabeth wrote.

Before taking up his command, Philip followed his wife to England, arriving on 27 July in good time for the birth at 11.50 a.m. on 15 August 1950 of Princess Anne Elizabeth Alice Louise at Clarence House. For Prince Charles, the return of his father closely followed by the appearance of a new baby must have been something of a shock. A photograph of the time shows him peering into the cradle with a slightly puzzled air. He was almost two years old and had not seen his father for nearly a year, his mother only at intervals. Now the appearance of a new sister as the focus of everyone's attention must have been very confusing; only his loving grandparents and his unchanging nursery retinue provided stability. His father left again for Malta on 1 September and in December his mother went out to join him. At Christmas Prince Charles and his new sister went as usual with their grandparents to Sandringham.

Philip's first command was a frigate, HMS *Magpie*. Reports of his effect upon *Magpie*'s crew were various. Philip was fiercely competitive; his ship had to be the best at everything, on manoeuvres and even at the annual regatta where she won six out of ten events with the captain rowing stroke in one of the winning races. The crew called him 'Dukey' – presumably not to his face. Some of them liked him, or said they did: 'He worked us like

hell, but treated us like gentlemen.' Some did not; one said he'd
rather die than serve in that ship again, while another described
him as 'stamping about like a —— tiger'. With *Magpie* he went
on several official jaunts, and that December, with *Magpie* acting
as escort, he took Elizabeth on board HMS *Surprise* to Greece to
visit his royal relations, his cousin King Paul and his wife, Queen
Frederika, a Hanover to whom he was related by marriage. They
visited Rome officially in April 1951. The Embassy gave a very
grand party to celebrate Elizabeth's birthday on the 21st, which
she did not enjoy because all she really wanted to do was go and
dine in a Roman restaurant. 'She wouldn't speak to Philip for
quite a few days. I mean he could have thought of it, couldn't
he?' one of the party said. The sophisticated Romans criticised
Elizabeth for her unfashionable clothes, criticisms which were
widely reported in the American media. Elizabeth, who had led
such a sheltered, grand but unsophisticated existence, found the
glamorous Romans in their couture clothes and fantastic jewellery
unfamiliar and intimidating. The undisguised enthusiasm of one
Roman princess for Philip made her giggle, but she was shocked
by the utter disregard of Lent in the capital of Catholic Christen-
dom. At a period when self-denial was supposed to be the order
of the day and even weddings were not celebrated, the Roman
aristocracy gave endless parties at which they danced the night
away. 'It was a growing-up process for her,' one of her entourage
said. At home there were the inevitable protests against the heir
to the throne being received by the Pope. It was her first
experience of press criticism, made perhaps all the more painful
by the easy triumph of the Paris visit two years earlier.

Since June 1950, before the birth of Princess Anne, Elizabeth
had been extending her experience of public affairs by reading
Cabinet papers and memoranda.[22] Now her brief period of
freedom was almost over. Her father was dying, although neither
he nor his family were yet aware of it. 'The King walked with
death,' Churchill was to say of him. The possibility of a fatal
thrombosis was always there. At the opening of the Festival of
Britain Exhibition in May 1951 he looked extremely ill; after the
investiture of his brother, the Duke of Gloucester, as Great
Master of the Order of the Bath, he had a temperature and,

feeling as if he had 'flu, retired to bed. The doctors diagnosed a small area of 'catarrhal inflammation' on the left lung. The King, relieved, wrote to Queen Mary that the condition had been on his lung for only a few days at the most 'so it should resolve itself with treatment'. He took a Whitsun break at Balmoral with the Queen and Princess Margaret. The Queen, always oblivious to ill-health in herself and those round her, did not appear particularly concerned about her husband, but one of her ladies-in-waiting listened to his continual coughing with foreboding. The King felt very tired; the outbreak of the Korean War in the summer of 1950 had worried him deeply, and in December fears that the Americans might be going to deploy the atomic bomb there sent Prime Minister Clement Attlee on a flying visit to Truman. 'The incessant worries & crises through which we have to live have got me down properly,' he wrote to a friend. He placed as much reliance on homeopathy as he did on his clinical doctors, principally on Sir John Weir whom he had made one of his official physicians on his accession in 1937. The entire royal family was interested in homeopathy; Weir treated not only the King but also the Queen, Queen Mary and the Duchess of Gloucester. The King was his keenest patient; he even named one of his racehorses, Hypericum, after a homeopathic remedy. Elizabeth and, later, Prince Charles were also firm believers in the benefits of homeopathy.

In July the Edinburghs returned from Malta for good. It was by now obvious that the King would need their support in carrying out public duties, including a state visit to Canada and the United States planned for that autumn. They were due to leave on 25 September on the liner *Empress of Britain*, but the plan was abruptly cancelled when, after tests on the King in London on 7 September, a tumour showed up on the tomography and an immediate bronchoscopy was arranged for the 15th. The bronchoscopy confirmed the doctors' worst fears: the tumour was malignant. No one mentioned the word cancer except Churchill's doctor, Lord Moran, who, reading between the lines of the doctors' bulletin, warned Churchill. The King was told only that he had a blockage in one of his bronchial tubes which would necessitate the removal of his left lung, but his family knew the

truth. They spent an agonising three hours waiting at Buckingham Palace while the surgeon, Mr Clement Price Thomas,
operated. At one moment it was thought that he might have to
cut the nerves of the larynx, which would mean the King could
never speak above a whisper. The operation was apparently
successful. The King recovered consciousness and at 5 p.m. the
doctors issued a cautious bulletin to the crowd of 5,000 who had
been waiting silently outside. Privately in medical circles the
long-term prognosis for the King's survival was gloomy. Lord
Moran's opinion was 'even if the King recovers he can scarcely
live more than a year'.

As Elizabeth left Malta, Edwina Mountbatten had remarked,
'They're putting the bird back in its cage.' She had just been
learning to enjoy life outside the cage, but now her father's illness
hung like a cloud over her and Philip. At any moment she could
be precipitated on to the throne and all chance of a relatively
normal life for either of them would be ended. She flew to
Canada with Philip on 8 October to begin the postponed state
visit, the first time a member of the royal family had flown the
Atlantic. Martin Charteris travelled with, beneath his bunk, the
necessary accession documents, the sword of Damocles hanging
over his employer. Elizabeth was already being shown state
papers, and at home she read the daily parliamentary reports. In
Canada she read the airmail *Times* each day, concerned to keep
herself abreast of current affairs. For thirty-five days they
traversed the American continent, crossing it twice, a distance of
some 10,000 miles in Canada alone. Again Elizabeth was following
in her parents' footsteps on their gruelling but triumphant tour
in 1939. That was part of the problem. For the first time after all
her ecstatically received tours in the United Kingdom, the
Princess encountered newspaper criticism first hand. With memories of the radiantly smiling Queen still fresh – her visit had
been only twelve years before – the Canadian press was less
enchanted by her often straight-faced daughter. 'Why doesn't
she smile more?' they asked. When Martin Charteris pleaded
with Elizabeth to oblige them, she replied, 'Look Martin, my
jaws are aching.' 'We had rather a rough time,' he recalled. Philip
caused offence in some quarters by referring to Canada as 'a good

investment', an unfortunate choice of phrase which to some people had a distinctly exploitative colonialist ring. He always wrote his own speeches; this was not the last time he was to fall into a verbal trap of his own making which a trained courtier would have avoided. There were moments of enjoyment; one memorable photograph of the Canadian tour showed them, relaxed and smiling, whirling arm in arm through a square dance. Elizabeth was wearing the de rigueur full swirling skirt; Philip was in check shirt and jeans, hastily bought for them by Bobo and John Dean.

In Washington they stayed at Blair House as the White House was being repainted. 'Truman was like an uncle and loved her,' Charteris recalled. He took the couple up to the top floor, where his deaf old mother-in-law, Mrs Wallace, was bedridden, and yelled at her, 'Mother! I've brought Princess Elizabeth to see you!' In the last general election, which had taken place in Britain on 25 October during the course of the tour, Churchill had been returned to power. Confused, the old lady told Elizabeth, 'I'm so glad your father's been re-elected.' Elizabeth presented the President with gifts from her father, a rare pair of blue john (fluorite) and ormolu candlesticks by Matthew Boulton and an eighteenth-century carved gilt landscape mirror with a flower painting set above. It was on the grand scale – 6ft 8in high and 4ft 7in across – and was accompanied by a personal letter from the King to the President written on 20 September (three days before his operation), asking him to accept the presents 'for the White House to mark the occasion of its restoration'. 'We've just had a visit from a lovely young lady and her personable husband,' the President replied in his down-home style. 'They went to the hearts of all the citizens of the United States . . . As one father to another we can be very proud of our daughters. You have the better of me – because you have two!'

Prince Charles had had his third birthday on 14 November while his parents were absent yet again. The King was well enough to attend his grandson's birthday party and a charming photograph, which was to be one of his daughter's favourites, shows them sitting side by side on a brocade sofa at Buckingham Palace, the King smiling down at his grandson while a neatly dressed Prince Charles, his hair gleaming and immaculately combed by Nanny Lightbody for the occasion, looks intent on telling his grandfather something. This was to be Prince Charles's first and only recollection of his grandfather. Like his mother, Prince Charles appeared solemn in most of his photographs. In one family shot taken that summer, he is shown looking warily, even apprehensively, at the camera, his eyes squinting against the sun, while an extrovert Princess Anne, not yet a year old, cheekily pushes her father's chin with her hand.

The King sent the royal train to Liverpool to meet Elizabeth and Philip who had returned by sea. When he met them, his appearance was not reassuring. 'The King looked awful,' Charteris recalled. The nation, less well-informed, took the publication of the King's photograph with his grandson as proof of his recovery and on 2 December a day of National Thanksgiving was celebrated in churches all over the country. The King was only fifty-six, but his public life was virtually over, a fact underlined by his deputing to Elizabeth and Philip the state visit to Australia and New Zealand which he had been so anxious to undertake but had had to postpone because of his illness in November 1948. He created them both Privy Counsellors on 4 December. Christmas was celebrated as usual at Sandringham with the entire inner circle of the royal family, except the Harewoods, present. It had been a less taxing time than usual for the King since, because of his extreme weakness, the Christmas broadcast, which he always dreaded and which ruined the first part of Christmas Day for him, had been pre-recorded so that for once he did not have to deliver it live. None the less, in the family photograph he looked gaunt, a shadow compared with the hearty bucolic form of his brother, the Duke of Gloucester, standing behind him. Next to him, Queen Mary also looked frail; she would survive him by barely a year. Princess Anne sat happily centre-stage on his knee, while Prince Charles stood beside his grandmother, who encircled him with a comforting arm.

Both the Queen and the King wanted to believe that he was better. He enjoyed himself out shooting, but he also did his duty writing personal letters to Truman and Eisenhower, intended to help Churchill on his forthcoming visit to Washington. He was planning to leave for South Africa with the Queen on 10 March to convalesce at Botha House, the Prime Minister's official country residence, which had been offered him by Dr Malan, the Nationalist Party leader who had replaced the King's friend, Field Marshal Smuts. On 29 January he went up to London for a consultation with his doctors, who pronounced themselves 'very well satisfied' with their patient. Only nine days before, however, Lascelles had become sufficiently concerned about the fragility of the King's health that he had sent Churchill in the United States a warning telegram. On 30 January the King, the Queen, the Edinburghs and Margaret, with Peter Townsend in attendance and other friends, went to a performance of *South Pacific* at the Drury Lane Theatre. It was a family get-together to celebrate the doctors' favourable report and a send-off for the Princess and the Duke who were to fly off for their antipodean state visit the next morning. Photographed sitting together, the King's face was so finely drawn as to resemble a death mask, although he looked not old but youthful; both his daughters looked much as they had in the Crawfie days of 'The Little Princesses'. It was as though the family, on the verge of dissolution, had gone back in time. The next day, 31 January, he took the unusual step of going as far as Heathrow Airport to see his daughter off to Kenya, the first stage of her journey. He stood hatless in the cold wind, his eyes with the straining, glaring look they took on in moments of emotion. In his heart of hearts he knew that he was, in Churchill's phrase, 'walking with death' and that there was always a possibility he might not see his beloved daughter again. Churchill, who was with him at the airport, described him as 'gay and even jaunty; [he] drank a glass of champagne. I think', he added, 'he knew he had not long to live.' Bobo told Dean that he had said, 'Look after the Princess for me, Bobo,' and that she had never before seen him so upset at parting from her.

He died, suddenly and without warning, of a thrombosis in his sleep at Sandringham, just six days later, in the early hours of 6 February 1952. His daughter became Queen in Kenya as she sat on the platform of the Treetops Hotel in the branches of a giant wild fig tree watching and photographing the animals at the salt-lick. On guard at the foot of the tree stood a famous 'white hunter', Jim Corbett, armed with a heavy-calibre rifle, ostensibly to protect the Princess from wild elephants but also, unknown to her, from possible attack by the Mau-Mau terrorists who might be in the area. Unconscious that her father had died, she and Philip returned to Sagana Lodge, their wedding present from the people of Kenya, to prepare for their journey down to Mombasa to embark on the SS *Gothic* for New Zealand and Australia. No news came from Buckingham Palace nor even from the BBC. Sir Edward Ford, the King's Assistant Private Secretary, believes that the Palace telegram announcing the King's death which had been despatched to Kenya was never sent because the telegraphist took the agreed code 'Hyde Park Corner' as the address and not the message, while at the BBC the men in charge had decided that only the distinguished broadcaster John Snagge had a voice of sufficient dignity for such an announcement but couldn't find him. Michael Parker was alerted by telephone as to what had happened by Martin Charteris, who had heard the news from a journalist at the Outspan Hotel where he had gone to lunch. Parker crept around outside the house to attract the attention of Philip and beckoned him out on to the lawn. The news struck Philip like a thunderbolt; it was a moment he had been dreading – the end of his independent life. 'He looked as if you'd dropped half the world on him,' Parker recalled. 'I never felt so sorry for anyone in all my life.' It was 2.45 p.m. local time, 11.45 a.m. in London, when he told his twenty-five-year-old wife that she had become Queen of Great Britain, her Dominions and her possessions beyond the seas. Martin Charteris, who had dashed up from the Outspan Hotel immediately after telephoning the news to Parker, found the new Queen 'very composed, absolute master of her fate'. She was sitting at her desk, drafting papers, letters of apology for the cancellation of the tour, a slight flush on her face the only sign of emotion. 'What are you going to call yourself?' he asked. 'My own name, of course – what else?' she replied.

7

Sovereign Lady

'I never imagined that anyone could grasp their destiny with such safe hands.'

Lord Charteris of Amisfield

Sitting in a bucking Dakota on the flight from Nanyuki to Entebbe, the first leg of her journey home, the new Queen looked down on the white cone of Mount Kilimanjaro and bush fires raging on the surrounding plains. Beside her, Martin Charteris was explaining what she would have to expect when she got home, the protocol and the ritual to be observed on the accession of a new sovereign. It was, after all, an occasion which he had rehearsed privately ever since their Canadian journey. Elizabeth was wearing a light-coloured cotton dress; all the mourning clothes with which nowadays she always travelled in case of just such an eventuality as this were waiting for her at Entebbe, having been flown up from Mombasa where her staff had already loaded everything on to the *Gothic*. The last time Charteris had seen her before the news of the King's death, she had been 'wearing blue jeans with windblown hair and looking wonderful', talking excitedly about rhinoceros. Now there was this composed young woman asking about the Accession Council.

To the other people travelling with her on the plane she appeared calm, although John Dean saw her get up once or twice and return to her seat looking as if she had been crying. It was mid-afternoon when they arrived at Heathrow; as the engines died, the Duke of Gloucester and the Mountbattens came aboard and with them Philip's Extra Equerry, Squadron Leader 'Peter' Beresford Horsley, with a note from Queen Mary for the new Queen. On the tarmac Churchill was the first to greet Elizabeth, but seemed so overcome with emotion that he could not speak. Instead of her own car from Clarence House, one of the

sepulchral black Rolls-Royces from the Palace stood waiting for her, a
reminder of her new status. When Elizabeth arrived at what had been
her home, Clarence House, she found Tommy Lascelles waiting with
a bundle of papers. The first document she signed as Queen was
hardly a decorous one; it related to an army buggery case.

Half an hour later Queen Mary came round in a limousine from
nearby Marlborough House. Queen Mary was an expert on the niceties
of royal protocol and the deference due to the head of the House of
Windsor. Just as she had always made a point of curtseying to her son,
the King, on leaving the dining-room with the ladies at Balmoral and
Sandringham, so now she made formal obeisance to his daughter. 'Her
old Grannie and subject must be the first to kiss Her hand,' she said.
Elizabeth was 'absolutely horrified', according to one observer. She
had managed publicly to conceal her grief at the loss of her father
whom she had so deeply loved and admired; the appearance of his
mother, her grandmother, on such a formal mission was something of
an ordeal, symbolising as it did the loneliness of her new position in
which 'family' had to take second place to 'Family'.

The transition was abrupt and shocking; a violent, aching wrenching
of old roots, the sudden disappearance of her beloved father. Even
within the family the adjustment would not be an easy one. Elizabeth
was now the Queen and head of the family; her husband was now her
subject, her mother and sister in limbo. The formal meeting of her
Accession Council held in nearby St James's Palace on the following
morning, 8 February, was an additional strain. One of those present
remembered 'a slight figure dressed in deep mourning, entered the
great room alone, and, with strong but perfectly controlled emotion,
went through the exacting task the Constitution prescribed'. After
reading her formal Declaration of Sovereignty to the assembled Privy
Council, which involved mentioning her father's name twice, she said
simply, 'My heart is too full for me to say more to you today than that
I shall always work as my father did.' Philip stepped forward and led
her out; in the back of the car she finally broke down and sobbed.
Outside from the ramparts of St James's Palace the Garter King of
Arms dressed in the playing-card costume that was a relic of the
Tudor court, proclaimed her accession: 'Queen Elizabeth the Second,
by the grace of God Queen of this Realm and of all Her other Realms
and Territories, Head of the Commonwealth, Defender of the
Faith . . .'

That afternoon they drove down to Sandringham, where her father's body lay and her mother and sister were waiting, numb with shock and grief. It was as if their world had come to an end. The King had been the centre of their universe; now he was suddenly gone and their world had shifted on its axis, its focal point the new Queen. Both were stunned. 'Mummy and Margaret have the biggest grief to bear for their future must seem very blank, while I have a job and a family to think of,' Elizabeth wrote. Forty years later an old friend recalled the Queen Mother's overwhelming grief: 'She was absolutely heartbroken, for a few months I thought she wasn't going to pull herself together. I'm sure she thinks about him a great deal now, still misses him.' 'The Queen minded so terribly that she became unapproachable as she still is [on a personal level],' a courtier's daughter said, 'and she lived completely in her own little world and also resented and was terribly jealous of her daughter becoming Queen so that at one blow not only did she lose the King but the whole of the happiest and gayest family life of anyone one knows all fell to pieces at the same time.'

It took Queen Elizabeth several months before she could bring herself even to answer letters of condolence from personal friends. She told Osbert Sitwell:

It is very difficult to realise that the King has left us. He was so much better, & so full of plans and ideas for the future, and I really thought he was going to have some years perhaps less anguished than the last fifteen. I think that those years after the war were terribly anxious & frustrating and it was all very hard & grinding work, and I longed for him to have some peace of mind. He was so young to die, and was becoming so wise in kingship. He was so kind too, and had a sort of natural nobility of thought & life, which sometimes made me ashamed of my narrower & more feminine point of view. Such sorrow is a very strange experience – it really changes one's whole life, whether for better or worse I don't know yet . . .[1]

Queen Elizabeth, however, was a woman of inner strength and considerable resources. On 17 February she issued a statement to the people. She would be called 'Queen Elizabeth the Queen Mother' and she commended to them 'our dear daughter; give her your loyalty and devotion; in the great and lonely station to which she has been called she will need your protection and love'. She seemed uncertain about what her own future role would be: 'My only wish now is that I may be allowed to continue the work we sought to do together . . .' In the event she found consolation in her native country, Scotland. Staying with her friends the Vyners, near Ullapool on the coast of Caithness, she came upon the ultimate retreat, a dilapidated castle standing in a bleak landscape by the sea. She bought it, renaming it the Castle of Mey. In Scotland she found the peace to recuperate and to comfort herself reading, as she wrote to Edith Sitwell thanking her for sending her an anthology of poems:

> I started to read it, sitting by the river, and it was a day when one felt engulfed by great black clouds of unhappiness and misery, and I found a sort of peace stealing round my heart as I read such lovely poems and heavenly words.
>   I found a hope in George Herbert's poem, 'Who could have thought my shrivel'd heart, could have recovered greennesse. It was gone quite underground', and I thought how small and selfish is sorrow. But it bangs one about until one is quite senseless, and I can never thank you enough for giving me such a delicious book wherein I found so much beauty and hope, quite suddenly one day by the river.[2]

For Elizabeth, the huge reversal in position between herself and her mother posed problems. Apart from her grief at the loss of her husband, the Queen Mother could not help feeling jealous of her daughter, who had suddenly become the focus of all the attention and the possessor of the power that had recently been hers. From now on Elizabeth would always have to undertake a careful balancing act, conscious of the need, even though she was now the Queen, not to upstage her mother in public. At public functions such as premieres, she would try to ensure that they went in together, and on more intimate occasions such as tea at Sandringham when she had lent her mother the house, sensitive to any appearance of usurping her mother's position as hostess, she would leap guiltily away from the teapot which she had been about to pour when she saw the Queen Mother approaching. The situation was particularly delicate at Windsor that Easter of 1952:

> It was the first time they had lived under the same roof since the King died [a courtier said], and there was an awkwardness about precedence, the Queen not wanting to go in front of her mother and the Queen Mother being used to going first. According to Lascelles, the Queen Mother couldn't bear it – she was so young to be widowed and it

wasn't likely she'd marry again and she minded the change of position although the Queen did everything possible to ease the situation.

The Queen Mother's strength, her capacity for enjoying life and the great reservoir of affection which she had built up with the people at large would carry her through. She had always swept the awkward things of life under the carpet, regally ignoring anything nasty which reared its head. This gliding approach protected her, but it also encouraged a tendency in her family not to face up to difficulties and this was to have dangerous consequences. 'Queen Elizabeth is an [emotional] ostrich,' a courtier said.

Things would not, however, be easy for her daughter Margaret, the spoiled darling of her father, the centre of attention at all the parties at Windsor, Balmoral and Buckingham Palace. Unlike her mother and sister, she had never had any role to play apart from exercising her talent to amuse and often (if you were a courtier's wife) to infuriate. As the sparkling leader of society she already had the air and reputation of an *enfant terrible*. Some people thought that she would have liked to have been Queen. For Margaret, the death of her father meant expulsion from a childhood paradise. 'The King's death', a friend said, 'was a terrible thing for Princess Margaret, she worshipped him and it was also the first time anything really ghastly had happened to her.' Her grief was heartbreaking – the unsympathetic John Gordon reported that she had had to be given bromide for four days to calm her. To Nancy Astor, she wrote a touching letter about her father in response to her condolence:

> You know what a truly wonderful person he was, the very heart and centre of our family and no one could have had a more loving and thoughtful father.
> We were such a happy family and we will have such lovely memories of him to remember when the grief of his loss has lessened. He was so kind and brave all his life.
> We are thanking God for His words of comfort that make us sure he is with Him, safe and happy and perhaps closer to us than he has ever been.[3]

The psychological turmoil in Princess Margaret's inner life and affections in the wake of her father's death was to have serious consequences in her sister's Coronation year.

Elizabeth, as she had said, was borne along by her public duties and the incredible wave of universal public sorrow and tributes to her father. 'He was a grand man,' President Truman wrote in his diary, 'worth a pair of his brother Ed.' Some people were surprised, even shocked, by the outpourings of grief. The writer James Pope-Hennessy described it as 'press hysteria ... this national obsession'. The journalist James Cameron, who had travelled with the King on his South African tour, shared Cape brandy with him and witnessed his last, lonely evening swim in the Indian Ocean, expressed the general feeling when he wrote:

> While the King lived we spoke of him as this, and as that, endowing
> him with all the remote virtues of an infallible man; such men do not
> die. But the King died; and we found somehow a different thing: that
> we loved him ... the sudden shadow fell momentarily across the heart
> of every man; loyal men and cynics, the rich and the dispossessed,
> reactionaries and radicals.[4]

Etched into the public consciousness was the photograph of three queens, Queen Mary, Queen Elizabeth the Queen Mother and the new sovereign, three grieving black-veiled figures waiting for the arrival of the late King's coffin from Sandringham on 11 February 1952. It had travelled the same route as his father's had in 1936: from the little church at Sandringham to Wolferton station, then by train to London and on the same gun carriage through the streets to the lying-in-state at Westminster Hall, where 300,000 people filed by in respect during the three days before the funeral on 16 February.

On the morning of the funeral at Windsor, Elizabeth walked immediately behind her father's coffin, causing a certain amount of disappointment to Mountbatten, who, having ascertained that his father, Prince Louis of Battenberg, had walked immediately behind the coffin of Edward VII, had applied for the position himself and had to be dissuaded by the Earl Marshal, the Duke of Norfolk. Elizabeth had been expected to ride in a carriage in the funeral procession, but, in view of her decision, the Earl Marshal told Mountbatten, 'I am sure that on reflection you will not press for what you have asked, namely, that you should walk, and be in fact the only individual, apart from the Sovereign's Standard [bearer], to be between the Queen and her father.'[5] Behind her walked the King's surviving brothers, the Dukes of Windsor and Gloucester, the former looking, according to one observer, 'positively jaunty' as he followed his younger brother's body.

There had been a faint gesture of reconciliation. The Duke of Windsor, who had been in New York at the time of his brother's death and had humiliatingly learned of it from news reporters, had travelled in the *Queen Mary* to attend the funeral, leaving his wife behind. On his arrival on 13 February he had been entertained at tea by Elizabeth, Philip and the Queen Mother. This surprised him, as he told the Duchess: 'Officially and on the surface my treatment within the family has been entirely correct and dignified. But gosh they move slowly within these Palace confines & the intrigues and manoeuvrings backstage must be filling books . . .'[6] 'Now that the door has been opened a crack try and get your foot in, in the hope of making it even wider in the future,' the Duchess instructed him. He was to try and make his peace with the Queen Mother. 'I am sure you can win her over to a more friendly attitude,' she continued with unwarranted optimism.[7] The Queen Mother had no illusions about the Windsors' feelings towards her; she now had an additional reason for her unforgiving stance: she blamed them as the principal cause of her husband's early death. Had he not been forced by the Abdication to take up the burden of kingship under such exceptionally difficult circumstances, she felt, he would still be alive. Queen Mary, gliding over the emotional surface as was her wont, took it that there had been a reconciliation. 'Of course, David rushed over at once, nice of him but a bit disturbing,' she wrote to her brother and sister-in-law, the Athlones. 'However he saw E [the Queen Mother] and the girls. He had not seen them since 1936, so that feud is over, a great relief to me.'[8]

The thaw, however, was more apparent than real, much of it due to the tactful behaviour of the Duke, who, on his wife's strict instructions, never mentioned her. He did succeed in obtaining a private interview with the Queen Mother, who was pleasant but non-committal. 'Cookie [the Windsors' uncomplimentary nickname for her ever since she was Duchess of York] listened without comment & closed on the note that it was nice to be able to talk about Bertie with somebody who had known him so well.' The Duke was not deceived. 'Cookie was sugar,' he wrote to his wife, '. . . and M[ountbatten] and other relations and the Court officials correct and friendly on the surface. But gee the crust is hard & only granite below.' His own feelings towards his family were hardly warm; he was extremely angry at the decision, which he hoped to persuade the Palace to reverse, to cut off the

£10,000 a year the King had been paying him. He had recently bought a country house, the Moulin des Tuileries, in France, and, as very rich men so easily do, was feeling poor. 'It's hell to be even this much dependent on these ice-veined bitches, important for WE [their private pet name for themselves based on their initials] as it is,' he wrote to the Duchess.[9]

He did not include the new Queen under this uncomplimentary heading; both he and Wallis referred to her as 'the girl' (formerly they had nicknamed her 'Shirley Temple' after the child star, and her parents consequently 'Mr and Mrs Temple'). 'Clarence House was informal & friendly. Brave New World, full of self-confidence & seem to take the job in their stride.' Mountbatten, however, was not forgiven for his desertion and his failure to turn up at Candé for the wedding in 1937. '*Mountbatten*,' he wrote, 'one can't pin much on him but he's very bossy & never stops talking. All are suspicious & watching his influence on Philip.'[10] The Duke never understood the reasons for his family's attitude towards him, or realised that Elizabeth, as one of her courtiers put it, 'disapproved of Uncle David'. Moreover, she had no time to spare for his problems. In the days between her return from Kenya and her father's funeral she received a deputation led by Churchill from the House of Commons, the Prime Minister of New Zealand, the High Commissioners of Commonwealth countries, ministers, ambassadors and foreign ministers, and entertained to lunch the royal relations assembled for the funeral who were staying at Buckingham Palace. On one evening alone she received the President of the French Republic at 6.30 p.m., the President of the Turkish Republic at 6.45 and the President of the Praesidium of Yugoslavia at 7.

Elizabeth was enjoying her new responsibilities; to Jock Colville, now once again Churchill's Private Secretary, she seemed 'at ease and self-possessed'. The public – and the politicians – seized on the accession of this twenty-six-year-old woman as the dawning of a new 'Elizabethan age', a promise of a future for Britain struggling in post-war trauma, feeling both in its pride and in its purse the effects of the contraction of empire and the growing realisation that Britain was no longer a great power. Elizabeth was surrounded by love and affection; as Churchill had put it in his moving Address of Sympathy on the King's death in the House of Commons on 11 February 1952:

A fair and youthful figure, Princess, wife and mother, is the heir to all our traditions and glories never greater than in her father's days, and to all our perplexities and dangers never greater in peacetime than now. She is also heir to all our united strength and loyalty.

She comes to the Throne at a time when tormented mankind stands uncertainly poised between world catastrophe and a golden age. That it should be a golden age of art and letters, we can only hope – science and machinery have their tales to tell – but it is certain that if a true and lasting peace can be achieved, and if the nations will only let each other alone an immense and undreamed of prosperity with culture and leisure ever more widely spread can come, perhaps even easily and swiftly, to the masses of the people in every land.

Let us hope and pray that the accession to our ancient Throne of Queen Elizabeth the Second may be the signal for such a brightening salvation of the human scene.

At the late King's funeral at St George's Chapel, Windsor, among the wreaths was one whose message particularly touched Elizabeth. It was from Churchill and bore the same inscription as the Victoria Cross: 'For Valour'. As she watched her father's coffin lowered into the vault into which aged nine she had seen her grandfather's disappear,* she was particularly conscious of the continuity that her family represented and determined to carry on in the traditions which her father and grandfather had established, virtuous and dedicated, putting duty and service above all else.

The first and principal casualty of Elizabeth's accession to her father's throne and to the traditions which he represented was to be her husband. Philip's naval career came to an abrupt end. 'Prince Philip loved the sea and adored the Navy and was always on great form when he was serving,' John Dean observed. 'When he came home, finally, it must have been a terrific sacrifice ... I could tell from his mood that he hated leaving behind a life in which he was so thoroughly happy.' Not only had he been forced to give up the service in which he had spent most of his life, but also Clarence House, the first real home he had had and on which he had lavished such care and attention. Nobody wanted to move; Queen Elizabeth naturally clung to Buckingham Palace in which she had so recently lived with her husband and which held so many memories for her. Philip did not

---

* The King's premature death had left no time for a permanent resting-place to be prepared. After some seventeen years in the George III Vault, his coffin was interred in a vault in the new George VI Memorial Chapel on 31 March 1969.

want her to move into Clarence House, noting in a memo to Browning that (as in fact turned out) Prince Charles would one day need a house of his own while his grandmother could well live a very long time. He suggested that rather than leave Clarence House, he and his family should continue to live there, while using Buckingham Palace as an office. 'Prince Philip didn't want to go to Buckingham Palace,' one of the Queen's household said, 'but all the old codgers like Lascelles said "you must go".' Churchill backed them up; Buckingham Palace had always been the home of the monarch and would continue to be so.

Where Philip had once been so much in charge, his influence was now restricted to walking a pace behind his wife at public functions and organising as much of the private side of their lives as he was allowed to do. His predecessor as consort (he was never to be given the title, 'Prince Consort', which Victoria had conferred on Albert) had become long before his death in 1861 virtual ruler of England, as Disraeli once declared. The King had made Philip a Privy Counsellor, but Elizabeth had no intention of involving him in her official business as ruler. She would operate just as her father had, with access to state papers and reports of Cabinet meetings and parliamentary proceedings, supplemented by a weekly interview with the Prime Minister. Philip was relegated to carrying out official duties and the overseeing of the estates. He would have to carve out a role for himself. The imbalance between his position and hers and her anxiety to compensate for it were to influence the course of their and their children's lives.

The most wounding blow for Philip came only three days after the King's funeral. On 18 February 1952 an agitated Queen Mary sent for Jock Colville. Prince Ernst August of Hanover had returned from a family gathering at Broadlands and told her that Mountbatten had said to a party of royal guests 'that the House of Mountbatten now reigned'. Queen Mary had spent a sleepless night worrying over this and was greatly relieved when Colville assured her that he doubted if the Government would contemplate any such change. Colville informed Churchill, who immediately consulted the Cabinet that day. The Cabinet 'were strongly of the opinion that the family name of Windsor should be retained' and invited the Prime Minister 'to take a suitable opportunity of making their views known to Her Majesty'.[11] On the 20th they were informed by Churchill 'that it was the Queen's pleasure that she and their descendants should continue to bear the family name of Windsor', and the Lord Chancellor was deputed to prepare a draft proclamation on the lines of George V's 1917 pronouncement on the

Queen Victoria and her York great-grandchildren at Osborne, 1900.
From left to right: Prince Albert (Elizabeth's father), Princess Mary
(christened Victoria but always called Mary), Prince Edward
(later Edward VIII and Duke of Windsor), Prince Henry on the Queen's lap

Elizabeth's christening, 29 May 1926.
Back row (left to right): Prince Arthur, Duke of Connaught, George V,
Prince Albert, Duke of York, the Earl of Strathmore. Front row (left to right):
Lady Elphinstone, Queen Mary, the Duchess of York holding Elizabeth,
the Countess of Strathmore, Princess Mary (the Princess Royal)

'The long, cool stare': Elizabeth aged 23 months with 'Allah' Knight

'A lifelong passion for horses':
the young Elizabeth congratulates
the winner at a horse show

The first corgi: Elizabeth and friend
in the garden behind No. 145 Piccadilly
in July 1936, five months before
her uncle's abdication

The woman he loved: Wallis Warfield Simpson in 1936 (left)
'Uncle David': Edward as Prince of Wales
in the uniform of the Welsh Guards, August 1932 (right)

Beside the swimming-pool at Fort Belvedere. From left to right:
The Hon. Mrs Jock Gilmour, Lord Louis Mountbatten, the Duke of York,
Prince Gustav Adolf of Sweden, his wife, Princess Sybilla, Princess Ingrid
of Sweden, the Duchess of York (fully clothed and with hat and pearls) and,
seated in front of her, the Prince of Wales's current American mistress,
Lady Furness (born Thelma Vanderbilt)

Sir Alan 'Tommy' Lascelles,
Private Secretary to George VI
and Elizabeth, January 1948

Returning from their first trip on
the London Underground: Elizabeth
with Lady Helen Graham, her
mother's lady-in-waiting, and Margaret
with the famous Marion Crawford,
'Crawfie', May 1939

The first meeting: Elizabeth (front row, third from left) and Philip
(standing centre back row beside his uncle, Lord Mountbatten) at Dartmouth
Royal Naval College in July 1939 – the first photograph taken of them together

Second Subaltern Elizabeth Alexandra Mary Windsor
learns how to change a wheel, April 1945

'Us four' at the Royal Lodge, Windsor, 8 July 1946

Elizabeth (far left) and Margaret (running, far right) in deck games with officers
on board HMS *Vanguard* bound for South Africa, February 1947
Stag night at the Dorchester: Philip (centre) and Mountbatten (second from right)
joking with fellow naval officers, 19 November 1947

Elizabeth and Philip pose for their wedding photograph in the Throne Room
at Buckingham Palace, 20 November 1947, with the best man,
David Milford Haven, and bridesmaids including Margaret (on Philip's left)
and Lady Pamela Hicks (second from left). The pages are Prince William
of Gloucester (left) and Prince Michael of Kent (right)

Honeymoon at Broadlands

The Princess and the President: Elizabeth with Harry S. Truman
in Washington, 3 November 1951

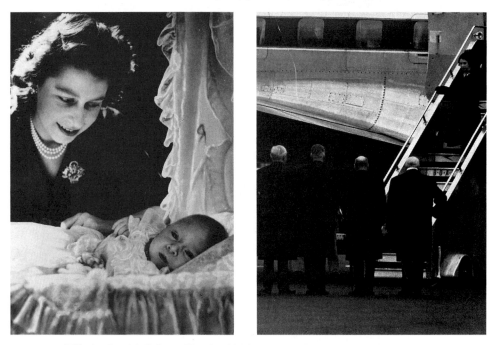

Elizabeth with Prince Charles Philip Arthur George, aged five weeks,
at Buckingham Palace, 21 December 1948 (left)
The new Queen: Elizabeth at London airport on her return from Nairobi
following George VI's death, to be greeted by (from right to left)
Winston Churchill, Clement Attlee, Anthony Eden and Lord Woolton, 7 February 1952
(right)

House of Windsor.[12] Philip subsequently had what a courtier described as 'a huge row' at Sandringham with the Lord Chancellor over it – 'He really minded about it' – and followed up with a 'strongly, but ably, worded memorandum' objecting to its intended declaration that the royal family remained the House of Windsor. According to Colville, this annoyed Churchill, who ordered Colville to attend no less than two meetings with the Lord Chancellor, the Lord Privy Seal, the Home Secretary and the Leader of the House of Commons, 'to draft a firm, negative answer', which was finalised and passed by Churchill on 12 March. Presumably because of the fierce behind-the-scenes row that the question had aroused, it was decided not to make it the subject of a public proclamation, but instead a declaration by the Queen to the Privy Council which would subsequently be published in the *London Gazette*.[13] On 7 April the Lord Chancellor produced a memorandum for the Cabinet which recorded the Queen's amended draft declaration. The message was unequivocal: 'I hereby declare My Will and Pleasure that I and My children shall be styled and known as the House and Family of Windsor, and that my descendants who marry and their descendants, shall bear the name of Windsor.'[14]

Why did Elizabeth deliver what amounted to a slap in the face to her husband? Mountbatten, whose tactlessness had brought on the whole affair, attributed it to his enemy Lord Beaverbrook's malign influence over Churchill, 'coupled with Winston's disenchantment with what I did in India'. Paranoia about Dickie Mountbatten's ambition was certainly rife. Just before the King's death, John Gordon reported to Beaverbrook that one of the Greek royal family had told him that the Mountbattens ('dangerous people') were 'determined to be the power behind the throne when Elizabeth succeeds', but thought they would not succeed as 'Elizabeth was developing into a strong-minded woman who would not be controlled by him'. Gordon reported suspicions that the Mountbattens were trying to get Philip pronounced King or King Consort.[15] But Philip himself, according to Arthur Christiansen, editor of the *Daily Express*, almost the only newspaper-man whom Philip knew and liked, 'sees through his uncle and fully realises how great are the Mountbatten ambitions'. Christiansen reported a conversation with Philip's sister, the Margravine of Baden, which showed his family to be just as resentful of Mountbatten's attempts to capture the throne as the Palace officials were.[16] None the less on this particular point, the question of the family name, Philip shared his uncle's views, although he seems to have been prepared to compromise on the name 'Edinburgh'. The Mountbatten side of the family later excused Elizabeth on the grounds that she was young and overborne by Churchill, and, as Edward Ford's letter of 1948 demonstrated, Mountbatten had a point. But the feeling within her own family, particularly where her grandmother and mother were concerned, was strongly against any change and she was probably moved as much by family piety as by anything else. She could hardly be expected to repeal the change made specifically by her grandfather or go against what would undoubtedly have been the feelings of her father. She was convinced by the Lord Chancellor's points in his memorandum of 7 April: 'It cannot be doubted that by His Proclamation of 1917 King George V intended that, so long as there was a member of His House to ascend the Throne, the name of the House should be Windsor . . .' And especially by the next point:

> Nor can it be questioned what was the wish of George VI. It may be
> assumed that He expected to be succeeded by a daughter, but it is
> certain that it was His wish that the name of the Royal House should in
> that event continue to be Windsor. When he conferred a dukedom
> upon HRH the Duke of Edinburgh he did not intend that the name of
> Edinburgh should supersede that of Windsor as the name of the Royal
> House . . . Permanence and continuity are valuable factors in the
> maintenance of a constitutional monarchy and the name of the Royal
> House should not be changed if change can be avoided.

Philip took it very hard. 'I'm nothing but a bloody amoeba,' he exploded. It was not an entirely appropriate simile for a man who had fathered two children by his wife; amoebas, as every schoolchild (but not, apparently, Philip) knows, are self-reproducing, but the sense was clear enough. He felt robbed of his identity and he was, perhaps, disconcerted by Elizabeth's new-found ease and self-confidence. 'I no longer feel anxious or worried,' she told a friend. 'I don't know what it is – but I have lost all my timidity somehow becoming the Sovereign and having to receive the Prime Minister . . .'[17] Philip had lost his dominant role and it unnerved him. As a relation said:

> I think psychologically it was a terrible blow, because [the] poor young
> man felt already that everybody was giving him a hard time and there
> he was being told that his own children couldn't take his name. It was
> really hurting and it took him a long time to get over that one. It was a
> mistake. I can understand her making it because I think she was

persuaded that it was her duty to do it . . . perhaps she was too young to see the implications of what it would do to somebody to say you can't give your children your name. I think it . . . for some time was quite a difficult situation [between them]. Of course she put it right later. By then the damage had been done . . . it's history now. But it's a pity because it did make for difficulties, obviously. I mean it's a psychological difficulty that's very difficult to get over . . .

The whole affair put a strain on the marriage which had not been there before.

Even before the declaration was made on 9 April there had been a further pin-prick to Philip's self-esteem. The consort's throne used by his mother-in-law as Queen Consort at the annual state opening of Parliament was taken out of the House of Lords and sent for storage at the country house of Lord Cholmondeley, the Lord Great Chamberlain, because it was (mistakenly) believed that only a female consort could occupy a throne and share the sovereign's canopy on that occasion. A male consort would only be allowed a 'chair of state' on a lower level. Philip could be forgiven for thinking that the fanatical attachment of Government and Palace to what they believed to be correct protocol was aimed at diminishing himself. He was particularly prickly with the Old Guard of Elizabeth's Palace household, headed by the to him stuffed-shirt figure of Tommy Lascelles, whom Elizabeth had inherited from her father as Private Secretary, and the charming but utterly conventional Joey Legh, Master of the Household, both of whom tended to look upon him as an interloper. Philip, said one of his staff, 'got very fed up with purple corridors and people telling him what he couldn't do'. It didn't help that, while the Queen's secretariat moved smoothly in to the offices which were already there, his own rooms had not been made ready. There was a noticeable gulf between the two offices. 'Tommy Lascelles was terrifying, he used to stare at you,' a young lady clerk who worked for Philip recalled. 'None of the women in the private secretaries' office were under forty-five, the young ones in Prince Philip's were regarded as if they were the Folies Bergère . . .' Things improved a year later when Lascelles retired and was succeeded by Michael Adeane, who worked well with Edward Ford and Martin Charteris, but, as they recall, Philip still believed in giving the private secretaries a hard time.

As a sop and in deference to his organisational ability, Elizabeth appointed him to chair the Coronation Commission. Discussions about the date of the ceremony had begun even before the King's funeral. A day in 1952 was ruled out for various reasons – the restoration of the Abbey would not be complete in time, but more importantly, as Churchill wrote to Robert Menzies, the Prime Minister of Australia, the seriousness of the economic situation made it 'vital that not a single working day should be unnecessarily lost in this year of crisis', or, as he put it more succinctly to Lascelles, 'Can't have Coronations with the bailiffs in the house.'[18] The Government at first favoured May 1953, but on mature consideration the Home Secretary advised the Cabinet that the choice to be offered Elizabeth should be narrowed down to between 29 May and 2 June in order to avoid a clash with Derby Day on 3 June, a sacred day in the horse-racing calendar. The Cabinet advised that on the whole Tuesday, 2 June, was the most suitable date. Elizabeth, already a fanatical devotee of the turf, quite understood; Tuesday was to be the day. Lascelles wrote to Colville on 10 April conveying the Queen's approval of 2 June. Colville then wrote to the Duke of Norfolk, who, as Earl Marshal, would be responsible for all the Coronation arrangements, a half-humorous letter which nevertheless showed the overwhelming importance attached to racing by the English establishment (Churchill himself was a keen racehorse owner). Tuesday, 2 June, he told the Duke, was the first day of the Epsom meeting and he didn't know if the Jockey Club (the supreme and exclusive ruling body of English racing) would consider it a good thing to have the Derby the following day or whether they would push the whole Epsom meeting and Ascot as well a week forward to avoid this contretemps. 'Incidentally,' Colville wrote, 'the reason why June 2 was chosen is that the possible dates were narrowed down to May 28th to June 6th. The Cabinet was opposed to two bank holidays in Whitsun week for production reasons; June 1, being a Monday, would entail a great deal of Sunday travel which would upset the Sabbatarians and June 2nd seems to be the first possible date which will upset nobody but the runners in the Rosebery Memorial Handicap!'[19] Apparently the grandees of the Jockey Club (who to a peer would be attending the Coronation) did not raise any objections and the date of 2 June was officially announced on 29 April together with the membership of the Coronation Commission.

The composition of the Coronation Commission, nominated by Elizabeth, reflected the importance which she – and the Government – placed on the Commonwealth. She had been the first British

sovereign to have been specifically entitled 'Head of the Commonwealth' at her accession, while the Royal Titles Act of 1953 stipulated
that she was separately Queen of each of the Commonwealth territories
which were not republics. She proposed the Duke of Edinburgh as
Chairman of the Committee with the Duke of Norfolk as Vice-
Chairman, and representatives of all Commonwealth Governments
present. Bernard Fitzalan-Howard, 16th Duke of Norfolk, hereditary
Earl Marshal of England, and, unusually, for a high aristocrat, a
Catholic by family tradition, was a bluff, conservative, sporting figure
who, in the words of one biographer, had 'failed to pass what in those
days was an undemanding entrance examination to Christ Church,
Oxford, particularly when the candidate was a duke'.[20] He had then
joined the army as an officer in the Royal Horse Guards, one of the
two cavalry regiments whose official duty is to guard the sovereign. He
was an enthusiastic racing man, having bought his first thoroughbred
on his twenty-first birthday, a steward of the Jockey Club, the Queen's
representative at Ascot race meetings, and president of the MCC
(Marylebone Cricket Club). As a duke since the age of eleven, he
viewed human beings with little unnecessary respect. 'If the bishops
don't learn to walk in step we'll be here all night,' he lectured them at
a Coronation rehearsal, and when asked if it were true that peers
carried sandwiches in their coronets during the service, he answered,
'Probably. They're capable of anything.' A few months before the
Coronation, a peer had nervously approached him saying that he was
afraid he might not receive an invitation because he had been divorced.
'Good God, man,' the Duke replied. 'This is a coronation not Royal
Ascot.' His training at marshalling troops and organising the tenants
of his large estates, plus his experience of past state occasions such as
the funerals of George V and the Coronation of George VI, had given
him immense expertise in mounting huge theatrical ceremonies which
required precise timing behind the pomp and splendour.

Philip, the moderniser, does not seem to have made much headway
against his Vice-Chairman. The first and most important decision
taken by the Committee, reported on 10 July 1952, for which Norfolk
was subsequently blamed, was that no television should be allowed
inside the Abbey for the service. A 'cinematographic film' was to be
made and television viewers would have to be satisfied with a later
showing of that. Their decision was approved by the Cabinet. Historians have believed that Elizabeth stepped in and overruled the
Government. A study of Cabinet papers and other contemporary

sources show the truth to have been rather different. In this, the first pitched battle of her reign between the traditionalists, those who wanted to preserve the 'mystique' and magic of royalty, and the modernisers, who wanted to let light in on the magic, Elizabeth sided with the traditionalists. In most situations her reactions were conservative; she may have felt that certain moments of the ceremony were so sacred that they should be private. Churchill's feeling was that live television would impose too much additional strain upon the Queen, but he was certainly influenced by a minute, dated 7 July 1952, from Colville saying that the Queen herself did not want it televised.[21]

When the decision was announced by the Commission on 20 October that no television cameras would be allowed to film east of the screen in Westminster Abbey, there was uproar. 'A very odd way of doing things,' commented the Chairman of the BBC, Sir Alexander Cadogan, who had not been consulted, adding shrewdly, 'I think that we can leave it to an enraged public opinion to bring pressure on the Government.' Next day he commented with satisfaction, 'The Press have started up well on the Coronation ban ... Everyone [i.e. the Government, the Palace and the Commission] has already got the wind up.'[22] 'Let the People see the Queen,' John Gordon demanded. A hasty retreat was beaten with Tommy Lascelles telling the BBC that there would be 'a compromise': television would be allowed into the Abbey to film the service but not the communion. The Palace 'compromise' was taken up by the Cabinet. The public would see, live, the recognition, the crowning and the homage, but would be excluded from the most private and sacred parts of the ceremony, the anointing, the communion prayers and the Queen's communion. The episode of televising the Coronation was a typical example of part misunderstanding, part cock-up, according to Edward Pickering's report to Beaverbrook:

> The chief opponent of television seems to have been the Queen herself. It was because of her known antipathy that the matter was never fully examined. Lack of technical understanding caused much of the confusion. The Cabinet, for example, were under the impression that it was necessary to have high-powered lamps trained on the Coronation chair; at no stage was the BBC consulted. Both the Cabinet and the Court were surprised by the public indignation caused by the decision.[23]

When she saw how much her people wanted to see her actually crowned and how outraged they were that they should be excluded from a spectacle confined only to high officials, peers and foreigners, Elizabeth became convinced that the ban was a mistake and sent Tommy Lascelles to the BBC to propose the 'compromise'. But she was certainly not the origin of the 'Let the People see the Queen' movement. For the first time the public had insisted on its rights to seats at the royal spectacle, a significant beginning to the later events of her reign.

Queen Mary was not there to see her favourite granddaughter crowned. According to her biographer, she never recovered from the shock of George VI's death. She had been too frail to attend his funeral, although she watched the procession pass her windows at Marlborough House. Clutching the hand of her old friend Mabell Airlie, and seeing in her mind's eye a little boy in a sailor suit, she had whispered only, 'There *he* goes.' At this intimation of mortality, she had drawn up a new will, going over the catalogues of her collections, tracing the particular family connections. She left everything (apart from a few boxes and candlesticks to the Duke of Windsor) to the new Queen, with 'not even a toque', as a friend remarked, for her loyal lady-in-waiting, Lady Cynthia Colville. She died at 10.15 on the evening of 24 March 1953, aged eighty-five. In the large crowd gathered outside Marlborough House, women were weeping. There was a sense almost that a national monument had disappeared, a connection with a happier time. 'A wave of emotion has swept over the land,' Chips Channon wrote, 'and there has not been a word of criticism of the grand old lady.'

Queen Mary's death hardly came as a shock to Elizabeth; she had been ailing since the end of February, suffering abdominal pains and telling her friends that she did not wish to go on living as an 'old crock'. But her death meant yet another gloomy ceremony at Westminster Hall and a funeral in St George's, Windsor, a sad reminder for Elizabeth of her father's only just over a year before. It meant the embarrassing presence of Uncle David, who had not been invited to the forthcoming Coronation.

The Duke had not been invited principally because Elizabeth did not want him there, as she told the Archbishop of Canterbury, Dr Fisher, during a meeting on 6 November 1952, at which it was agreed that it was 'a) altogether out of the question that the Duke should come, and b) it was wholly and entirely undesirable that the Duke should come', the Archbishop noted. 'It would create a very difficult situation for everybody, and if he had not the wit to see that for himself, then he ought to be told it. He is coming to England in December, and the Queen feels quite sure that he will raise the question. We agreed that if he did, he should be told not to come, and it looked as though the Queen would have to tell him. The Queen would be less willing than anyone to have him here.'[24] Fortunately for Elizabeth, Churchill took the same view and, when the Duke consulted him on 18 November as to whether he should not be invited, told him bluntly that it would be 'quite inappropriate for a King who had abdicated to be present as an official guest at the Coronation of one of his successors'.[25] The Duke apparently accepted this and issued a press statement on Churchill's advice. Elizabeth was not yet prepared to heal the family rift.

The Duke had arrived in England in response to a summons from his mother's doctor on 11 March, accompanied by his sister, the Princess Royal, disembarking from the *Queen Elizabeth* from New York. Not surprisingly he was in a rebellious frame of mind. His niece had refused to continue the £10,000 a year which he felt was rightfully owing to him; feeling poor he had contracted to write an extensive article on the Coronation at which he would not be present. He felt resentful at being parted from his wife, the more so, perhaps, since she was in the midst of a public and much gossiped-about affair with a homosexual playboy-about-New York, James Donoghue. 'What I think of having to make this ridiculous and costly trip instead of our being together in Palm Beach is nobody's business,' he wrote to his wife. 'Work [for the restoration of the allowance] on Cookie and Shirley [the Queen],' the Duchess commanded him. The whole family gathered at Marlborough House the morning after Queen Mary's death 'for archbishoply prayers and a last look at Mama', as the Duke put it. 'My sadness', he wrote, 'was mixed with incredulity that any mother could have been so hard and cruel towards her eldest son for so many years and yet so demanding at the end without relenting a scrap. I'm afraid the fluids in her veins have always been as icy cold as they now are in death.'[26] He had never been able, or even tried, to understand his mother's feelings over the Abdication. To her, it had been the Great Betrayal; to him, the Great Renunciation. To be fair to him, the royal family, with the exception of his sister, had not been exactly welcoming to him during his stay in England. He had stayed either with his friend Lord Dudley in the country or in Dudley's son's house in London;

only after their mother's death did his surviving brother, the Duke of Gloucester, invite him to stay at York House, St James's Palace, when he returned after a brief visit to France to London for the funeral. 'What strange things do happen for believe it or not I'm to be the "Unknown Soldier's" guest,' he told the Duchess. 'Maybe age has softened him a little like it has done to Mary [the Princess Royal].' No one else softened towards him; he was not amongst the twenty-eight royal guests invited to the dinner at Windsor Castle after the funeral on 31 March. Estrangement seemed once again total; the Duke no longer felt part of the royal family, as he put it, 'beyond Burke's Peerage and Who's Who'. His last letter to his wife, written on his return to London after the funeral, was bitter: 'What a smug, stinking lot my relations are and you've never seen such a seedy worn-out bunch of old hags most of them have become . . .'

Queen Mary had specifically asked in her will that if she should die before the Coronation, mourning for her should not be allowed to affect it. The Coronation was the occasion for a huge national party in which everybody participated, from village carnivals to London's East End street parties. Churchill was determined that people should enjoy themselves; food rationing was still in force, but he insisted that a bonus of an extra 1lb on the sugar ration should be issued to everyone – despite the dire warnings of the Ministry of Food that this would lead to a shortage. For Coronation week caterers would be allowed additional sugar and fat to make potato crisps, toffee apples and other treats, and organisers of street parties were to get rations over and above the catering scale. Eggs were to be decontrolled and sweets derationed and the traditional practice of roasting a whole ox was to be allowed under specific conditions. Rationing was certainly not in evidence at the Household Brigade's Coronation Ball at Hampton Court on 29 May. The whole palace was floodlit and the fountains surrounded by massed flowers; the men wore tailcoats and decorations and the women ballgowns and tiaras. 'We danced in the Great Hall and supped in the orangery,' Jock Colville wrote. 'A world that vanished in 1939 lived again for the night. The Queen, dancing with the Duke of Edinburgh, looked as beautiful as the people imagined her to be.'[27]

Elizabeth, like Victoria before her, was to be seen as 'the Nation's Hope', a heavy burden on the shoulders of a twenty-seven-year-old woman who had no real power to influence the future of her country but would remain a symbol for its well-being. Optimism was fragile and Britain's grasp on reality was uncertain. Despite the Government's earnest attempts to emphasise the Commonwealth, to most people it was a new-fangled term which had little significance. The recent ascent of Everest by New Zealander Edmund Hillary and Sherpa Tensing of Nepal was represented as a symbol of a new age and seen as an achievement of empire. 'Does not the lesson of Everest stand out clear?' asked the *Evening Standard* editorial on Coronation Day entitled 'Onward to Glory': 'while collectively and acting in unity the men of the Empire can conquer everything, singly they can conquer nothing? Long live the Queen! Long also may there live the Imperial unity which can make her reign one of peace and wondrous glory.' This was not precisely the message which the Government was spending over £2 million to get across. Britain could no longer rest on imperial laurels dreaming past dreams of glory; the future, it was then thought, lay with the Commonwealth and with Britain's ability to work and pay her way.

Elizabeth was a willing participant in the Government's plans. On coming of age she had dedicated herself to the Empire, which was now being transformed into the Commonwealth. On her accession she had been proclaimed head of the Commonwealth and she was determined that the symbolism of her Coronation day should include visible reference to the Commonwealth. When she had first called the royal couturier, Norman Hartnell, to the Palace the previous October to discuss the dress she should wear for the Coronation, she had simply specified that it should be in white satin and 'on the lines of my wedding dress'. When Hartnell came back to her with the idea that it should not be unrelieved white and produced prepared designs of embroidered emblems of the United Kingdom, Elizabeth thought it over and at a subsequent audience asked if he could embroider the dress with symbols of the Commonwealth countries; Ceylon's lotus flower, Australia's wattle, and Pakistan's wheat and jute were among those added to the traditional English rose, Scottish thistle and Welsh leek. As the Coronation date drew near she practised at the Palace, listening to records of her father's Coronation, sheets pinned to her shoulders to represent the robes she would wear, or sitting, just as her father had, with the heavy 5lb St Edward's Crown traditionally used for the actual crowning on her head. The ballroom at the Palace was marked out with posts and tapes to show her where she would have to go; she attended several rehearsals at the Abbey at which the Duchess of Norfolk, coached by the Earl Marshal, went through the ritual movements which Elizabeth herself would have to perform.

Coronation Day itself was a day of dreary drizzle, unusually cold for the time of year, but enlivened by the spirits of the spectators. From the Palace, Elizabeth could hear the cheers of the 30,000 crowd lining the Mall twelve deep as the news spread of the conquest of Everest. They were entertained by a series of processions going down the Mall towards the Abbey: the Lord Mayor of London in his elaborate coach; the junior members of the royal family in cars; foreign royalty including the cheerful, elephantine Queen Salote of Tonga, indomitable in an open carriage in the rain, dwarfing the frail Sultan of Kelantan who sat opposite her; Churchill, pink and baby-faced, leaning angrily out of his carriage window as a traffic jam developed at the narrow passage through Admiralty Arch at the foot of the Mall. Back at the Palace, Elizabeth seemed at ease, stopping on her way along the corridor to show the housemaids the details of her gown, before travelling with Philip by her side in the huge Gold State Coach, decorated with baroque palm fronds and garlands, and the door panels with classical scenes painted by Cipriani in 1761. She was wearing Queen Victoria's diadem on her head, with the St George's Cross and the other emblems of the United Kingdom glittering in plain diamonds. In her white dress and with a radiant, eager smile on her face as she waved to the crowds, she might have been a young bride on the way to the church, had it not been for her ermine and velvet cloak and train. Beside her Philip sat resplendent in the uniform of Admiral of the Fleet (the exalted rank to which with Field Marshal and Air Chief Marshal he had recently been promoted) with cocked hat, gold bullion epaulettes and Garter Star. The carriage was drawn by four pairs of the Windsor Greys in scarlet and gold harness with postillions in gold-braided red jackets astride the near-side horses and grooms and beefeaters (Yeomen Warders) walking beside it in their uniforms of scarlet and gold.

At 11 a.m. the coach drew up to the Abbey door. Elizabeth stepped out and went to her 'retiring room' to prepare for the ceremony. As the room had no windows, the Minister of Works, David Eccles, had had the happy idea of lightening it up with a *trompe l'oeil* mural by Roland Pym showing Victoria and Albert bowling along in an open carriage through a sunlit Windsor Great Park. Since nine o'clock that morning a series of elaborate processions had preceded her up the aisle to take up their stations, royalties, envoys and rulers of foreign states

attended by men with playing-card uniforms and extravagantly medieval-sounding titles. The procession of members of the royal family,
including the Harewoods, Mountbattens and Cambridges, was
attended by Rouge Dragon Pursuivant of Arms and Portcullis Pursui-
vant of Arms; the procession of Princes and Princesses of the Blood
Royal, their Royal Highnesses the Princess Royal, the Duchesses of
Gloucester and Kent and their children, Princess Alice, Countess of
Athlone, and her husband, brother of Queen Mary, Lady Patricia
Ramsay, daughter of the Duke of Connaught, and Princess Marie
Louise, was attended by Bluemantle Pursuivant of Arms and Rouge
Croix Pursuivant of Arms; and, finally the procession of Queen
Elizabeth the Queen Mother and Princess Margaret, the Lord Cham-
berlain of Her Majesty's Household, the Earl of Airlie and the Mistress
of the Robes, the Dowager Duchess of Northumberland, with Ladies
and Women of the Bedchamber, was attended by Somerset Herald,
Windsor Herald, Richmond Herald, Chester Herald, York Herald and
Lancaster Herald. Six minutes later the regalia to be used in the
ceremony was delivered to the peers who were to carry them: Saint
Edward's Staff to the Earl of Ancaster; the Sceptre with the Cross to
the Viscount Portal of Hungerford; the golden spurs to Lords Hastings
and Churston; the various swords of Justice, Mercy and State to the
Dukes of Buccleuch and Queensberry, the Earl of Home, the Duke of
Northumberland and the Marquess of Salisbury; the Rod with the
Dove to the Duke of Richmond and Gordon; the Orb to Earl Alexander
of Tunis; St Edward's Crown to the Lord High Steward; the Paten,
Chalice and Bible to the Bishops of London, Winchester and Norwich.

At 11.15 to the tune of the anthem 'I was glad when they said unto
me, We will go into the House of the Lord', Elizabeth entered the
Abbey through the west door, the focus of 7,500 people crowded
within its walls and of millions watching on television. Acclaimed by
the boys of Westminster School with shouts of 'Vivat Regina', she
walked slowly up the aisle preceded by a huge procession of church
dignitaries, the officers of the Orders of Knighthood, the Garter
Knights who were to hold the canopy above the Queen for her
anointing, the Lord Privy Seal, the Prime Ministers of the Commonwealth followed by Churchill, the Archbishop of York, the Lord
Chancellor, the Archbishop of Canterbury, both Archbishops preceded
by their episcopal crosses, a clutch of high officers of the College of
Heralds including Lyon King of Arms, Norfolk Herald Extraordinary,
and royal expert Dermot Morrah in his office as Somerset Herald

Extraordinary. Immediately after them walked the Duke of Edinburgh wearing his peer's robes and followed by a page carrying his coronet; he was flanked on his left by an official entitled the Harbinger with three Gentlemen-at-Arms and on his right by the Standard Bearer also with three Gentlemen-at-Arms, and followed by the officers of his household, dubbed 'the Duke's Beasts' – Boy Browning, Mike Parker and Peter Horsley. The peers and bishops carrying the regalia followed, with the traditional high court officials and the chief members of the College of Heralds, Norroy and Ulster King of Arms, Clarenceux King of Arms, Garter Principal King of Arms, the Earl Marshal, the Lord High Steward of Ireland, the High Constable of Scotland, the Great Steward of Scotland and the Lord High Constable of England. Behind them at last came Elizabeth, still wearing her diadem and her 'royal robe' of crimson velvet trimmed with ermine and bordered with gold lace, the huge train borne by her Mistress of the Robes, the Dowager Duchess of Devonshire, and her six maids of honour, all the daughters of dukes, earls or marquesses, and, with the exception of Lady Anne Coke and Lady Moyra Hamilton, with resoundingly double- and triple-barrelled names: Lady Jane Vane-Tempest-Stewart, Lady Mary Baillie-Hamilton, Lady Jane Heathcote-Drummond-Willoughby, Lady Rosemary Spencer-Churchill. Beside her walked the Bishops of Durham and Bath and Wells, her 'supporters' according to a tradition established at the Coronation of Richard I in 1189. Bringing up the rear were her ladies-in-waiting – under the title of Ladies of the Bedchamber and Women of the Bedchamber – and the officials of her household, including Lascelles, and, as her equerries, her Assistant Private Secretary, Michael Adeane, Peter Townsend, Lord (Patrick) Plunket, one of her favourites, and Viscount Althorp, father of the as-yet-unborn future Princess of Wales. Prince Charles himself, now aged four and a half, had been brought in by his nanny through a side door to sit between his grandmother, Queen Elizabeth, and Princess Margaret, 'Aunt Margot'. His mother had decided that he should wear ordinary clothes – a buttoned-up shirt and shorts – and not appear like some miniature royal puppet in coronet and ermine.

Then began the ceremony, which in its essentials had changed little over 1,200 years. Coronations had taken place at Westminster since Edward the Confessor built the great abbey church there in the eleventh century; it was rebuilt by Henry III on the same site in the thirteenth century. William the Conqueror's was the first Coronation to take place there on Christmas Day 1066; he deliberately chose the site to connect his crowning with Edward and the Saxon kings. The connection with Edward was maintained by his successors; the Coronation Chair in which the Queen would sit for her crowning is still known as St Edward's Chair, even though it was actually made in 1300 on the orders of Edward I to enclose the Stone of Scone, which he had captured from the Scots – it was used for the first time at the Coronation of his successor, Edward II. (In 1950 some Scottish Nationalist students had stolen the Stone of Scone, a potent symbol of England's subjection of Scotland, but it had since been returned.) The crown with which the Queen would be crowned is called St Edward's Crown, although it was in fact remade for the Coronation of Charles II in 1661. The Puritans who had decapitated Charles I sold the regalia; even the Saxon King Alfred's crown 'of goulde wyer worke set with slight stones and 2 little bells', which had been used for the crowning of English kings up till the time of Charles I, was sold for the value of its gold – £248 10s 6d. Only the eagle-headed ampulla, which holds the holy oil for the anointing, and the anointing spoon date from before the reign of Charles II.

The core of the ceremony remained the same as it had for centuries – the recognition by the assembled congregation of their sovereign, the administering of the Coronation oath, the anointing with holy oil, the investiture with the regalia and the actual crowning. As the Queen stood beside St Edward's Chair, the Archbishop turning to the four sides of the church asked, 'Sirs, I here present to you Queen Elizabeth, your undoubted Queen: wherefore all ye who are come this day to do your homage and service, Are you willing to do the same?' The congregation roared 'God Save Queen Elizabeth' as the trumpets sounded. Returning to her 'Chair of Estate', the Queen sat for the administration of the Coronation oath, promising to govern according to their respective laws and customs the peoples of the United Kingdom of Great Britain and Northern Ireland, Canada, Australia, New Zealand, the Union of South Africa, Pakistan and Ceylon, and of her possessions and the other territories to any of them belonging or pertaining. There was no mention either of Commonwealth or Empire. She also promised to the utmost of her power to maintain in the United Kingdom the 'Protestant reformed religion established by law'. Going to the altar and laying her hand on the Bible she swore, 'The things which I have here before promised, I will perform and keep. So help me God.' Then she kissed the Bible and signed the oath. While the choir sang Handel's 'Zadok the Priest', she sat in St Edward's

Chair, having taken off her crimson velvet royal robe, under a canopy held somewhat unsteadily by four Garter Knights while the Archbishop anointed her in the form of a cross on the palms of both hands, the breast and the crown of the head, intoning: 'As Solomon was anointed by Zadok the priest and Nathan the prophet, so be thou anointed, blessed and consecrated Queen over the peoples whom the Lord thy God hath given thee to govern.' The Knights removed the canopy and the Mistress of the Robes helped her put on a simple white dress and then a tunic and girdle of cloth of gold. There followed a good deal of dressing and undressing in robes, presentation of swords, spurs, armils, the orb, the sceptre and the ring, before the actual coronation with St Edward's Crown as she sat in St Edward's Chair.

At this moment all the peeresses, a forest of white-gloved arms and glittering jewels, placed their coronets on their heads in unison. Then Elizabeth took her place on a throne on a dais to receive the homage performed in person by the Archbishop, the Duke of Edinburgh, the Dukes of Gloucester and Kent, and the senior peer on behalf of his peers. Philip knelt before her and placing his hands between hers, vowed, 'I, Philip, Duke of Edinburgh, do become your liege man of life and limb, and of earthly worship; and faith and truth will I bear unto you, to live and die, against all manner of folks. So help me God.' Then he rose, touched her crown and kissed her left cheek – no mean feat when she had the bulky crown upon her head. When the homage was over, the drums beat and the trumpets sounded, while the congregation shouted 'God Save Queen Elizabeth, Long Live Queen Elizabeth, May the Queen live for ever'. Finally Elizabeth came down from her throne to the singing of the *Te Deum* and in St Edward's Chapel took off the royal robe of red velvet and replaced it with her previous robe of purple velvet, changed St Edward's Crown for the lighter but more impressive Imperial State Crown studded with, among other precious stones, the Black Prince's Ruby, Queen Elizabeth I's pearl earrings, the Stuart sapphire from Charles II's crown and part of the huge Cullinan diamond, and, carrying the sceptre in her right hand and the orb in her left, proceeded to the west door while choir and congregation sang the national anthem.

There had been a few mistakes during the ceremony just as there had been at her father's Coronation. Elizabeth had forgotten to curtsey at the agreed point, disappointing her Maids of Honour who had spent hours getting it right. Archbishop Fisher moved forward at the wrong moment, throwing the elaborate ceremonial out of kilter, and the Dean of Westminster had provided the wrong dish for the Queen's offering of a small bag of gold. 'A really vast thing,' the Archbishop complained. 'I could only just lift it . . . When I turned to the Queen it was so far across I could not get anywhere near her and she had to stretch into the middle with her little bag . . .' England's premier baron, Mowbray Segrave and Stourton, provided a touch of comic relief: 'He came down from his homage all over the place, bunching up his robe and, as the Queen said, with moth balls and pieces of ermine flying all over the place', while the Duchess of Norfolk noted that when he did his homage, 'he had filthy hands and he looked straight out of comic opera'.[28]

Elizabeth's ordeal was over. There had been one moment when she had seemed to feel the strain; at 12.20 p.m. just over an hour into the service as the sword of state was delivered to her, she was seen to pass her hand over her forehead and eyes and glance round to her right, as if, Tom Driberg, MP, who was observing the ceremony for *Picture Post*, thought, she was looking at her husband or perhaps her son. The moment passed; when she got up to lay the sword on the altar, she was calm and composed. Dressed in her white shift and gold tunic, bare-headed and looking very young, she might have been a vestal virgin. There was an element of sacrifice in the air, inherent in the ancient role of kingship which was emphasised by the elaborate ceremonial, the red and gold robes, the sparkle of jewels, the measured movements of the old men performing the ancient ritual. For Elizabeth personally, it was the dedication of a life to an idea; it was one for which she had been prepared since the day in May fifteen years before when she had seen her father go through the same experience of consecration and dedication. For her, as for him, the ceremony had a deep spiritual significance.

8

Dark Princess

'One of the functions of the royal family in the minds of the people is to be the continuing story of Peyton Place . . . And of course in that story there is always somebody who is not actually behaving as they should be . . . The dark princess, if you like . . . the archetypal princess [has] lovely golden hair, but her sister has black hair . . . And she is the subject of the moon, not of the sun . . .'

Lord Charteris of Amisfield, interviewed on *The Windsors*
TV series, 1994

Even before the Coronation Elizabeth had known that her sister was in love with a divorced man sixteen years her senior and that she herself might soon be confronted by a crisis which could cause a public sensation for the monarchy on the lines of 1936. Early in the new year Margaret and Group Captain Peter Townsend had informed her that they were in love and wished to marry. And it was on Coronation Day itself, just after Elizabeth, radiant and regal, had left the Abbey church, escorted by her husband, that Margaret, standing in the Abbey porch waiting for the carriage to take her back to Buckingham Palace, flicked a piece of fluff off Townsend's uniform, an affectionately possessive gesture which alerted the world to another sensational royal romance.

The Margaret–Townsend affair was the first example of the dangers of the family policy, initiated by Queen Elizabeth, of 'ostriching', of ignoring a potentially dangerous situation until it became explosive, of 'non-interference' and 'non-confrontation'. Queen Victoria would have taken a line of positive interference and prevention, forestalling any threat of danger to the monarchy. The romance was a time-bomb waiting to explode, but no action had been taken in time to defuse it. Despite the apparent closeness of her ties with her family, Elizabeth, occupied with her own romance and marriage, then living her separate happy life at Clarence House, had remained unaware until too late of her sister's developing love for her father's equerry. The Queen Mother closed her eyes to what was happening under her nose, and when Lascelles tried to warn her about it, she not only ignored it but was angry with him in the ancient royal tradition of 'Shoot the messenger'. Lascelles then did nothing more about it until forced to when the situation became public. When Elizabeth was told about it, her reaction was human and sympathetic. 'The Queen was always nice to Princess Margaret about Peter Townsend,' a friend said. 'She did her best to understand the situation but her own life was so uncompli- cated and had always been straightforward that she couldn't under- stand why Princess Margaret had to go and fall in love with a married man . . .' Elizabeth, for all the best human reasons – sympathy for her sister in her grief and loneliness after their father's death – took the line that her sister must be left to work out her own destiny, but in the end was blamed for precisely the opposite, for sacrificing her sister's happiness on the altar of the monarchy.

The late King himself had noticed the attraction between his daughter and his handsome equerry probably as early as late May or early June 1951, when he, the Queen and Margaret were on holiday at Balmoral, a break which was intended to be a period of recuperation for him after a recent bout of ill-health (which had proved to be the onset of lung cancer). Townsend quotes an incident on the moors at Balmoral when they returned for the traditional late summer holiday:

> One day after a picnic lunch with the guns, I stretched out in the heather to doze. Then, vaguely, I was aware that someone was covering me with a coat. I opened one eye to see Princess Margaret's lovely face, very close, looking into mine. Then I opened the other eye, and saw, behind her, the King leaning on his stick, with a certain look, typical of him: kind, half amused. I whispered, 'You know your father is watching us?' At which she laughed, straightened up and went to his side. Then she took his arm and walked away leaving me to my dreams.[1]

What those dreams were, Townsend did not specify, but earlier that year he had confessed to Margaret that he loved her and that his own marriage was in trouble. He did not admit this in his memoirs; according to him, nothing explicit happened between him and Mar- garet until the new year of 1953, when, in a moment of spontaneous combustion, they declared their love for each other.

The King had not taken the possibility of a romance seriously for various reasons; there were always clustered round Margaret a selection of younger and more suitable men – single, titled heirs to large fortunes and stately homes – who would be able to maintain her in the style to which she was accustomed. There had been 'Sunny', Marquess of Blandford, a man with the prominent eyes and lack of chin character-istic of the Spencer-Churchills, who, as heir to the Duke of Marlbor-ough, could have offered her Blenheim, a far grander palace than most of the royal homes. Margaret had flirted with him and told her parents that he would make an ideal husband, but Blandford became engaged to one of her friends, Susan Hornby, and married her in 1951. Margaret had her twenty-first birthday at Balmoral in August that year; her parents had high hopes that she would marry the most eligible of the young men around her, Johnny Dalkeith, heir to the Duke of Buccleuch, three huge estates and beautiful houses filled with fabulous furniture and paintings, including the only Leonardo da Vinci in private hands.[2] As one of her closest friends, Colin Tennant, son and heir of the millionaire Lord Glenconner, said later: 'If the King had lived, he would have made Princess Margaret marry Johnny Dalkeith. With his houses and his land, she would have had a virtual state of her own.' But after the King's death, Dalkeith became engaged to and married a beautiful model and ex-debutante, Jane McNeill.

The King would have thought it inconceivable that his daughter would contemplate a serious romance with a married member of his household and the possibility of allowing her to marry a divorced man, however innocent, would not have crossed his mind. He would not have been surprised that she was attracted by him; 'Princesses always fall in love with equerries,' one royal lady commented cynically. The combination of a handsome face, a uniform, propinquity and the lure of the unusual was a powerful aphrodisiac. In the circumstances, with Elizabeth happily married, he was simply glad that Margaret was amused and not lonely.

Ironically the situation had arisen because of an admirable desire on the King's part to widen the system by which royal equerries were chosen beyond the two senior services, the Army and the Navy, backed by personal connections. He wanted to honour the RAF, the service of which he had once been an unwilling member, which had saved the country in the Battle of Britain, but was still not represented at court. Group Captain Peter Townsend, a Battle of Britain hero who had led 'B' flight of Hurricanes in the famous No. 43 Squadron (known as

Kate Meyrick's Own after the owner of a famous London watering-hole, the 43), seemed the ideal choice. Townsend says that he first met Princess Margaret at Buckingham Palace in February 1944 on his way to his first audience with the King. The Princesses had been waiting on purpose to see their first Battle of Britain pilot close to – the heroes of 1940 were then on a par with film stars for glamour and, according to Margaret, as they spied on him coming in, Elizabeth said to her, 'Bad luck. He's married.' Margaret was thirteen, the same age as Elizabeth had been when she fell in love with Philip, and she developed an instant crush on the young pilot. 'He was very beautiful,' a (male) family friend admitted.

The King and Townsend hit it off immediately. 'The King did not try, or even need, to put me at my ease,' Townsend recalled; '. . . the humanity of the man and his striking simplicity came across warmly, unmistakably . . . sometimes he hesitated in his speech, and then I felt drawn towards him, to help him keep up the flow of words. I knew myself the agonies of a stammerer.' They were both shy and suffered from tension – Townsend's war experiences of exhaustion, fear and death had plunged him into a nervous breakdown at the age of twenty-six. He had made a typically hasty wartime marriage to the beautiful Rosemary Pawle, fathered a son and suffered a serious breakdown, which had resulted in three months' hospitalisation. He recovered, but the careless, reckless courage of 1940 had left him for ever:

> I knew in my bones that I should never again be the pilot I once had
> been [he wrote]. I had gone too far down the hill ever to get to the top
> again. In my thoughts and visions I saw myself crashing, over and over
> again, to a horrible death. I was convinced I was going to die . . .
> exactly the reverse to what I had felt during the herioc days of 1940,
> when I was convinced that I was going to live! The more I flew, and
> there could be no relenting, the more fear, stark, degrading fear,
> possessed me. Each time I took off, I felt sure it would be the last . . .[3]

The King came to regard Townsend with an almost paternal affection; the young equerry was to be the only non-member of the family who could calm him when he had one of his 'gnashes' and the appointment which had been intended only for three months lasted almost ten years.

Townsend came closer to the heart of the royal family than any other member of the royal household has ever done. What happened to him and his marriage and, indeed, to Margaret is an object lesson in the dangers of flying too close to the sun. Wiser insiders like Jock Colville, who knew what court life could do to you, refused to be drawn into it on more than a temporary basis. People from high aristocratic circles like the King's Master of the Household, Joey Legh, knew how to treat royalty and where to draw the line. Joking, laughing, even daring to tell the King what to do when he accidentally peppered a beater with shot, Legh always knew it was thus far and no further; doing his duty but writing loving letters to his wife whenever they were separated. Courtiers of the old school knew the strain court life imposed on wives and families and ensured as far as they could that it was never a question of divided loyalties.

Peter Townsend did not belong to the same social stratum as the other members of the household. His was a middle-class, backbone of the Empire, background. His father had been a colonial administrator in Burma and he had attended a middle-class public school, Hailey-bury, where once, as a fifteen-year-old schoolboy, he had seen a stammering Duke of York open a new dining-hall. He was naïve and vulnerable, sensitive, deeply religious, an idealist and a dreamer. He was extremely handsome with brown wavy hair, bright blue eyes, finely drawn features and a lean, slim figure. Opinions of him among courtiers and the royal family's friends were divided. The King's Assistant Private Secretary, Sir Edward Ford, has gone on record as saying that he regarded Townsend as a close friend. Margaret's aristocratic friends found him boring: 'Solemnity. Talk about mystical nonsense. Oh, boring fellow.' 'He was very holy, always quoting the Bible,' said another. There was jealousy and disapproval of his closeness to the royal family. 'He fell in love with the royal family, which is always a mistake,' said one courtier. 'The King and Queen made him into a sort of household pet . . . he was always around.'

Rosemary Townsend was beautiful, socially ambitious and attractive to men ('tiresomely flirtatious,' one lady-in-waiting said of her). Townsend rather unkindly recorded her first reaction to the news of his royal job: 'We're made.' As with many wartime marriages, time had proved that the couple had very little in common beyond a passing attraction. After two children and Townsend's breakdowns caused by battle trauma, the physical spark was no longer there. Left at home for hours at Adelaide Cottage, Windsor, a grace-and-favour house granted them by the King when it became obvious that Townsend's appointment had turned out to be long-term, Rosemary can hardly be blamed if her eyes wandered elsewhere for amusement. Townsend's three-month absence as equerry on the South African tour in 1947 did not help matters. While on tour he wearied members of the royal entourage with his dreams of emigrating and 'getting away from all this' to farm in the Transvaal. His wife greeted his plans with absolute horror. She had no wish whatsoever to drag herself and her children away from Windsor into the isolation of colonial life. She had a romance with a dashing Guards officer, who walked out on her when he found things getting too serious; by that time the Townsend marriage was in deep trouble. Courtiers noticed that he was spending more and more time with Margaret. One remembers being at Adelaide Cottage for the birthday party of one of the Townsends' sons. 'The telephone rang and it was someone saying, "Would Peter go riding with Princess Margaret?" It was a birthday party. He was not on duty. And he went. He was a double-crosser . . .' Rosemary, like several of the courtiers' daughters, had a crush on the King, who, always responsive to pretty women, showed a liking for her in return. 'She was a very good painter and she was always in the Palace copying pictures and flirting with the King. Queen Elizabeth didn't like it one bit.' The Queen, moreover, was particularly fond of Townsend. 'She loved having him around – he was a good-looking young man.' His presence was an essential part of their everyday amusements, partnering her and Margaret at canasta and gentling the King along; and, as the King became iller and more irritable, so Townsend's gift for calming him became more and more necessary.

The first rumours about Margaret and Townsend had begun in the foreign press after the Princess made her first solo tour representing her sister with Princess Alice, Countess of Athlone, at the Inauguration of Crown Princess Juliana as Queen of the Netherlands on 6 September 1948. Margaret, dressed in pink with a matching ostrich feather hat, did her duty admirably, according to her experienced royal cousin, Princess Alice, but at the celebratory ball afterwards she was reported to have been noticeably radiant when dancing with Townsend and leaning against him and taking his arm as they toured the Rijksmuseum the next day. A lady-in-waiting who accompanied the royal party, however, says that the reports were rubbish and that none of the entourage saw anything which could be thus interpreted. Similarly, she says, theories that the seeds of the romance started on the South African tour are unfounded: 'Princess Margaret actually sneaked on Peter for something he was supposed to do and hadn't done. It made

us very angry because we liked him and thought it was unfair.'
Courtiers, on the whole, are not very observant and are disinclined to
delve beneath the surface or pry into the private lives of their
employers. The notion that a married member of the household was
having a secret romance with the King's daughter was not something
which had yet crossed their collective minds.

Townsend in his memoirs dates the beginning of their close
friendship from his appointment as Deputy Master of the Household
in August 1950, when he was given his own green-carpeted private
office on the south side of Buckingham Palace. By then he spent even
more time away from his family and his marriage was merely a façade.
He and Margaret had long talks; she was aware of the emptiness of his
home life. He in turn came to realise that despite the crowds of young
men and the night-clubbing, the newspaper headlines which depicted
the Princess as leader of a 'Margaret Set', her life was equally, perhaps
even more, empty. '. . . already she is a public character, and I wonder
what will happen to her?' Chips Channon had mused on seeing her at
a Windsor Ball in 1949 when she was nineteen. 'There is already a
Marie-Antoinette aroma about her . . .' Margaret had no importance
and no status beyond that of her existence as princess and younger
sister, and with only a few minor official engagements to carry out, she
had nothing to do but play. She was quick and witty, a gifted mimic,
singer and piano-player, and loved dancing. With her gifts and her
capricious, prima-donna temperament, Margaret in another life might
have made a successful musical comedy star. She was also intelligent
and intellectually starved. Her education had ceased when Crawfie left,
a fact which later in life she came to resent. Crawfie had tried to
arrange for Margaret to take advanced history lessons with Sir Henry
Marten as Elizabeth had done, but nothing had come of it. 'Sir Henry
was far from well,' Crawfie had written, '[and] Margaret's social life
became more and more demanding.' When she remonstrated with the
Queen about Margaret's late nights, the Queen replied, 'We are only
young once, Crawfie. We want her to have a good time. With Lilibet
gone, it is lonely for her here . . .' 'As always they could not bring
themselves to cross her,' Crawfie commented.

She was very short – what is politely called petite (her grandmother,
Queen Mary, had earned her granddaughter's dislike by repeatedly
and tactlessly asking her, 'When are you going to grow?') – but equally
very slender, with her mother's complexion and cornflower blue eyes
– Margaret's were larger, her best feature. Otherwise she had no

family traits; people remarked on her Semitic looks, her full, sensuous lips and the contrast between her radiant pink and white complexion and her dark hair. At twenty, Margaret was lovely, outshining her elder sister in looks and ability to fascinate men. But Elizabeth, as usual, had everything Margaret wanted: a handsome husband with whom she was very much in love and two adorable small children. She was happy, busy and now had the all-important job of being Queen. 'Poor you,' Margaret had said at the time of Uncle David's abdication, when Elizabeth's fate had been borne in on them both. In her heart of hearts she did not mean it, however much she might protest to the contrary. Hers was a complex personality; she could be warm, generous and kind, or alternatively selfish and cruel. She was liked by the domestic staff but disliked by many of the courtiers, who thought her spoiled and arrogant, and particularly by their wives, who were not impressed when Margaret deliberately collared their husbands to dance with her, leaving them on the sidelines. As one courtier's wife said:

> She had everything and then she destroyed herself. Her nature was to make everything go wrong. Nice one day – nasty the next. She was the only one who would come up to you at a party and really talk to you – then the next day she'd cut you. She antagonised her friends with her tricks, being horrid to their wives. She'd come up to a man and get him to dance with her cutting out his wife . . . Then she'd be so tiresome in house parties – keeping people up too late and buggering up evenings.

To Townsend, however, she revealed her best, more serious side. She was the most intellectually and emotionally religious member of her family, even going so far as to attend post-confirmation classes. It was a shared interest between Townsend and herself. Looking back to those days he wrote of her:

> What ultimately made Princess Margaret so attractive and lovable was that behind the dazzling façade, the apparent self-assurance, you could find, if you looked for it, a rare softness and sincerity. She could make you bend double with laughing; she could also touch you deeply. I was but one among many to be so moved. There were dozens of others; their names were in the papers, which vied with each other, frantically and futilely, in their forecasts of the one whom she would marry. Yet I dare say that there was not one among them more touched by the Princess's *joie de vivre* than I, for in my present marital predicament, it gave me what I most lacked – joy. More, it created a sympathy between

us and I began to sense that, in her life too, there was something lacking.

Their feelings for each other were strengthened after the King's death. In her loneliness and grief, Margaret leant even more on him. 'Peter was always there for her, he was incredibly kind, sensitive, gentle and understanding,' a friend said. Other courtiers, however, took a dim view of the relationship, which Townsend always denied when tackled about it. Efforts were made to remove him from court: Boy Browning tried to get him a job at the Air Ministry, but Townsend refused to go. Rather than leave, he went to the Queen on her accession and begged her to give him another job on the grounds that his marriage was breaking down. He did not, at that time, tell her that he was in love with Margaret and wanted to marry her. He was made Comptroller of the Queen Mother's Household, a position which ensured his continuing proximity to Margaret. He had refused to be reconciled with Rosemary because of her adultery. Rejected, Rosemary had embarked on another affair, a serious one, with John de Laszlo, son of Philip de Laszlo whose portraits of royalty and grandees were to be found on the walls of every palace in Europe. When the new Queen, Philip and Margaret lunched with the Townsends at Adelaide Cottage in June 1952, divorce proceedings had already begun. Six months later Townsend won a decree nisi against his wife on the grounds of her adultery with de Laszlo. Two months later Rosemary married de Laszlo and dropped out of royal but not society circles; the de Laszlo marriage did not last and she subsequently married the Marquess Camden. To her credit, she maintained a rigorous silence over her first marriage. The divorce made a vital difference to the Townsend–Margaret romance; he was now legally free, the innocent party. In their new-found happiness, the pair seem to have been oblivious of the public sensation the news of their plans to marry would cause. Both of them afterwards claimed naïveté; it seems difficult in retrospect to accept this at face value. Townsend was, indeed, somewhat unworldly. Margaret was an intelligent twenty-three-year-old, but he was thirty-eight and should have known better than to embark on a serious romance with the young Princess without any apparent consideration for the consequences both for her and for her family in the circumstances of the time. Margaret was well-versed in her religion and aware of its attitude towards divorce. As a member of her family she knew all about the Abdication and the reasons behind it. The only reasonable interpretation of her behaviour is that, solipsistically, she regarded her love for Townsend and her desire to marry him as of overwhelming importance.

The timing was particularly unfortunate coming as it did in the run-up to the Coronation. None the less, Elizabeth's immediate reaction was sisterly when Margaret told her and her mother that she and Townsend were in love and planned to marry. 'If they were disconcerted as they had every reason to be,' Townsend later wrote, 'they did not flinch, but faced it with perfect calm and, it must be said, considerable charity.' The Queen Mother resorted to her usual behaviour in the face of something disagreeable, sweeping it under the carpet. As sovereign, however, the Queen was well aware of the difficult situation which she would face as monarch, head of the family and Supreme Governor of a Church which did not recognise divorce. She would necessarily have to become officially involved because, under the Royal Marriages Act of 1772, which applies to all descendants of George II (other than princesses marrying into a foreign family), as sovereign her permission would be essential before they could marry. Otherwise Princess Margaret could wait until she was twenty-five and then could marry within twelve months without the sovereign's consent provided Parliament had received written notice of her intention and that both Houses agreed. The Queen's reaction was to be sympathetic and play for time. 'Under the circumstances', she said, 'it isn't unreasonable for me to ask you to wait a year.'

Lascelles's reaction when he was informed by Townsend was absolutely lacking in charity. 'You must be either mad or bad or both,' he exclaimed. The extent of Townsend's naïveté was demonstrated by his surprise at Lascelles's hostility. 'He was a friend and I was asking for his help,' he later wrote disingenuously. Lascelles, intellectually and socially super-snobbish as he was, would certainly never have admitted Townsend to the narrow category of his friends. Having been through the trauma of the Abdication over a similar issue, he was appalled at the prospect of another public controversy involving the monarchy. It is hard to see what kind of help Townsend expected Lascelles, whose first duty was to the monarchy, to give. Townsend offered to resign, but Lascelles, rightly foreseeing that such a move would inevitably arouse speculation, told him to stay put. Lascelles then went to the Queen with the advice that Townsend should immediately be removed from his position at Clarence House and given an overseas appointment. Elizabeth, intensely human at heart, loving and protective of her sister and fond of Townsend, refused to take a tough line. She adopted the compromise solution of making him her equerry and transferring him from Clarence House back to Buckingham Palace. Lascelles then took it upon himself, according to one source, to tell people to cold-shoulder the couple. Elizabeth and Philip, however, remained friendly towards them. On the evening of the day on which Margaret had told her about their love affair, Elizabeth invited the couple to dine alone with herself and Philip. Philip got on perfectly well with Townsend, although the two men were completely dissimilar in character and could never have been described as soul-mates. He had known Townsend's elder brother, Michael, as captain of the destroyer *Chequers*, on which they had travelled to Greece; he occasionally played squash with Peter at Buckingham Palace or badminton and golf at Windsor. He treated Margaret as a somewhat tiresome younger sister; 'he has always been quite sharp with her,' a courtier said. On this occasion he behaved, according to Margaret, 'like a chum', although some of the bright remarks with which he attempted to lighten the atmosphere were distinctly unwelcome to the loving couple. The romance had come as a complete surprise to him, as it had to Elizabeth, and he was particularly annoyed when, later on, the newspapers fantasised about his ill will towards Townsend. 'What have I done? I haven't done anything,' he would exclaim angrily after reading some such report. He was, however, furious when, in the aftermath of 'the piece of fluff' incident, the papers were full of Townsend rather than the Queen and her Coronation.

The Margaret–Townsend affair, although far less disquieting in its implications than Edward VIII's determination to marry Mrs Simpson, touched a raw nerve in the British body politic, setting up Pavlovian reactions in every stratum of society. Among the leaders of the establishment, the principal courtiers and the politicians, the alarm bells rang loud and clear. 'We had to establish a new reign,' a courtier said. 'We simply couldn't afford another Edward/Mrs Simpson situation . . .' The parallels with 1936 were clearly there and in may ways it seemed a re-run of the Abdication. The British press, despite the stories in foreign newspapers, had hitherto failed to take up the story and did not do so until the 'piece of fluff' incident provoked comment that could no longer be ignored. Lascelles then realised that further concealment would be impossible and that the situation required immediate action. On 13 June, the day before the story was to break in the British newspapers, he drove down to Churchill's country house, Chartwell, to tell him of Princess Margaret's 'wish to marry the recently divorced Peter Townsend'. It was also a re-run of 1936 in the Churchill household. 'A pretty kettle of fish,' Colville commented, curiously using the same phrase Queen Mary had said to Baldwin when he had visited her to discuss the Abdication. Churchill's first reaction was also on the same lines: the course of true love must run smooth and why shouldn't the beautiful young Princess marry her handsome war hero? Mrs Churchill sharply pointed out to her husband that he was 'making the same mistake that he had made at the Abdication'. This time Churchill listened to his wife. He ordered the Attorney-General, Sir Lionel Heald, to prepare a report on the constitutional position and to take informal soundings among Commonwealth Prime Ministers as to their views on the marriage. It was decided in Cabinet that the Government could not approve the marriage – the Marquess of Salisbury, a high churchman and close friend of the late King, being particularly firm on the subject. In the meantime, Churchill promised Lascelles that at his next meeting with the Queen, he would urge Townsend's removal from court.

In the end the press precipitated Townsend's departure. On 14 June *The People* issued a floater under the banner headline '*The People* Speaks Out'. The British people, it said, should be aware that according to 'scandalous rumours' around the world the Princess was in love with a divorced man and wanted to marry him. They named him as Townsend. The story was of course, they said, tongue-in-cheek, 'utterly untrue' since it was 'quite unthinkable that a Royal Princess, third in line of succession to the throne, should even contemplate marriage with a man who has been through the divorce courts'. The fact that Townsend had been the innocent party in his divorce 'cannot alter the fact that a marriage between Princess Margaret and himself would fly in the face of Royal and Christian tradition'. *The People* succeeded in flushing the fox out of the Palace. Lascelles and the Queen's Press Secretary, Commander Richard Colville, warned Elizabeth that there would be endless speculation and that Townsend would have to go. Churchill backed them up, informing Elizabeth of the Cabinet's opposition to the marriage. No evidence has yet come to light as to whether or not he also told her that it was unlikely that they would approve it even after Margaret's twenty-fifth birthday. Margaret, according to her biographer, was not to know this. She and Townsend agreed together that they should separate for a while but that they still ultimately intended to marry. Margaret remains very bitter that Lascelles never told her that she would never get the Government's consent for her marriage even if she did wait until she was twenty-five. A fellow courtier's impression at the time was that Lascelles was 'very bored by the whole thing and didn't believe it would ever come off. The fact that Townsend was offered the choice of Singapore, Johannesburg or Brussels as air attaché shows he [Lascelles] didn't take the whole thing seriously...' Naturally, since he had two sons of school age in England, Townsend chose Brussels.

On 30 June the Queen Mother and Margaret left for a visit to southern Rhodesia scheduled to last sixteen days. According to Townsend, on the morning of her departure, 'The Princess was very calm for we felt certain of each other and, though it was hard to part, we were reassured by the promise, emanating from I know not where, but official, that my departure would be held over until her return on 17 July.' Churchill's orders, however, were that he was to leave Britain within seven days of his posting, two days before the Princess was due to return. Before he left, although the news had broken in the *Evening News*, Elizabeth made a special gesture of friendship towards Townsend by taking him with her as equerry on her post-Coronation visit to Belfast. 'I thought it was a most generous and admirable act on her part,' he recalled. 'She shook hands with me on the tarmac. It was the last time I saw her until many years later.'[4] Halfway through her Rhodesian tour, Margaret received the news that Townsend would be gone before she got back. The effect upon her was devastating. 'She collapsed as she does when things go terribly wrong. She was so upset that she wouldn't be able to see him when she got back. Officially, it was put out that she was ill but she just collapsed from emotional shock. The Queen Mother had to continue the tour without her,' a member of the party said.

The separation was to last two years instead of the one originally stipulated, but it certainly failed in its object to make Margaret forget Peter. She felt that he had been badly treated and she herself was, in a friend's words, 'utterly lost and lonely'. Elizabeth was happily married and too busy to have much time for her. For six months from 24 November 1953 until 10 May 1954 she was out of the country on her post-Coronation Commonwealth tour. 'Her mother', a friend said, 'was completely unapproachable and remote, she refused to believe it at all or discuss it with anyone so Princess Margaret could never consult her about it.' Being royal, she was automatically cut off from most ordinary relationships and interests that other people have, so Townsend in his banishment took on even more importance. 'They were real companions and soul-mates,' a friend said, while another felt 'dreadfully sorry for her because you couldn't see how they were ever going to get married and they were terribly in love'. They wrote to each other every day, 'long, long letters', a correspondence which no one made any attempt to prohibit. Margaret outwardly continued with her social life, but her inward emotions were made obvious to Elizabeth on one 'ghastly evening' at Balmoral on the occasion of Margaret's twenty-fourth birthday. The newspaper headlines were full of rumours of Colin Tennant's engagement to the Princess (she says that he proposed to her and she turned him down; he denies any proposal was ever made) and the estate was besieged by newsmen. As a result both Tennant and Margaret were in a state of nervous tension. The Queen Mother wanted the party to dress up and sing a specially composed song for Margaret's birthday as they had always done when the King was alive. 'The Queen thought it might end in trouble but she didn't like to spoil her mother's enjoyment', so they all dressed up as druids in sheets and sang this song. The result was just as Elizabeth had feared: the evening was a disaster. A friend recalled: 'The Queen Mother couldn't see what had upset Princess Margaret, the Queen knowing this would happen and unable to stop it, and Princess Margaret in tears, partly because it reminded her of the times when the King and Peter were there and partly because she had caught some of Colin Tennant's nervous tension . . .'

It was to be another year before the saga reached its climax. In February and March 1955 Margaret undertook a triumphant tour of the West Indies. 'She seemed inspired,' a friend said. Calypsos were composed in her honour and her welcome eclipsed even Elizabeth's on her Coronation tour the previous year. Then the day after she returned Townsend revived all the speculation by giving an interview to the *Daily Sketch* in Brussels. When asked whether he would marry Princess Margaret, he replied, 'Wait and see.' There was an absolute furore and Townsend claimed he had been misquoted. The newspaper's proprietor, however, was adamant that the initiative for the interview had come from the Group Captain. Friends of Margaret surmised that, in the wake of her sensational West Indian tour, he was staking his claim. August 21 would be Margaret's twenty-fifth birthday, when she would be free to marry without the consent of her sister (although the parliamentary hurdle remained).

At Sandringham, where the Queen Mother was hostess to Margaret and her friends early in August, there was great tension. Cecil Beaton had taken a series of birthday photographs of the Princess and much time was spent in choosing one to be sent to Peter. Margaret, a friend said, 'was very moody, sad and difficult', refusing to go to bed at night and doing the opposite of what her mother said. 'We felt sorry for Queen Elizabeth, she knew what was the matter and she didn't know how to cope with the situation and she was much too reserved to talk about it to anyone.' Margaret knew that the time for a decision would be approaching. In her view it had to be marriage or nothing; the family could not afford a scandal. 'So she rationalised her behaviour and said it would do no harm if she did marry him.' When friends warned her that marrying Townsend could harm the Queen's position, she replied that that was nonsense and any comparison with the Windsors made her furious. 'She has always despised them as completely beyond the pale,' a friend said.

The royal family, with Dominic Elliot as Margaret's ostensible escort, travelled north for their annual holiday, pursued by newsmen, an estimated three hundred of whom were around Balmoral on Sunday, 21 August, which they hoped might be a day of decision. Nothing happened either in public or in private. In September the action switched to London, where Peter Townsend had arrived en route to the Farnborough Air Show. To the consternation of the courtiers, he was making absolutely no attempt to keep a low profile, moving round the city in a chauffeur-driven red Daimler pursued by a posse of newsmen, who staked out houses of friends of Margaret's from which he put through private calls to the Princess at Balmoral. 'He thought everyone was being beastly and there was no reason why he shouldn't go to Balmoral,' a courtier said. 'He talked a lot about religion and was very intense and incredibly egocentric. "It was God's will that he should make this marriage . . ." He seemed to have no thought for Princess Margaret's difficulties or anything else.' One evening, when one of the go-betweens commissioned to put in the calls to Balmoral was late, he took the bit between his teeth and rang the castle himself. 'You should have seen the look on their faces when the page came in and said Group Captain Townsend was on the telephone for Princess Margaret,' one of those present said. Townsend then returned to Brussels with nothing resolved.

And at Balmoral nothing was discussed. The Queen Mother, when approached by Margaret for her advice, became so upset that the discussion had to be abandoned. Elizabeth, honest and honourable as always, was determined that no pressure should be put on Margaret and that she should be free to come to her own decision without being told by her sister what she owed to the monarchy or the Church. She therefore resolutely sidestepped Margaret's attempts to sound her out, although personally feeling that the marriage would not be a happy one as, in her view, Peter Townsend, like many people in the wake of a divorce and in a difficult emotional situation, was fantasising and not living in the real world. It was a pattern she was resolutely to adopt in future family crises. Margaret's anxiety to consult her family was an indication of the doubts she herself felt and of a natural desire to shift the weight of responsibility on to other shoulders. Elizabeth, even though she was now Queen and head of the family, enclosed in the familiar surroundings of Balmoral, shrank from taking up the dynastic position of 'the Monarch' and spelling out the position to her sister. She seemed, said one observer, not to have any idea of the seriousness of the situation and the intensity of public feeling. Her attitude was the same as that of any wise elder sister (or indeed mother, since Queen Elizabeth had abdicated the responsibility). She said that she wanted friends to ask the couple together so that they could see as much as possible of each other in normal surroundings before they decided. Margaret, however, was at last beginning to face up to the potential consequences of her decision. At the Glassalt Shiel, which of all places at Balmoral is the most haunted by the shade of Queen Victoria, she sat down and wrote 'Reasons why I shouldn't marry Peter: because it does harm to the Queen' and 'Reasons why I should marry Peter: because I couldn't live without him . . .'

Elizabeth's new Prime Minister, Churchill's successor, Anthony Eden, came to Balmoral after five months in office for his first visit as Prime Minister on 1 October. There was a good deal of speculation at the time that the question of Margaret's marriage was high on the agenda. It seems likely that Elizabeth raised the possibility with Eden and asked him to sound out his Cabinet's reaction as to the likelihood of parliamentary consent to it, although, as we have seen, Margaret had not yet had any discussions with her sister about it, nor had she come to a final decision. Eden later told friends that he was relieved that the Queen had not asked him for his opinion. He was in an embarrassing position since he too had been the innocent party in a divorce and in 1952 had remarried, to Clarissa Churchill, Winston's niece. Even after Eden left, there were no family discussions about the affair, although everyone knew that Townsend would be returning to London on 12 October for three weeks and, with Elizabeth's approval, would be seeing as much as possible of Margaret in social situations with mutual friends before they came to a decision. Elizabeth, according to Margaret, was 'very nice but refused to mention "it" at all' and after a last picnic on the day Margaret was to leave Balmoral, she deliberately took the dogs out for a walk in order to avoid the discussion which she knew Margaret wanted, arriving back just in time to say goodbye.

Margaret at any rate seems to have had no inkling of any difficulty with the Government as she took the night train south on 11 October. On the train she was chatting happily and showing her companions the huge photographs of Townsend which were featured on the front pages of every newspaper. 'Isn't he handsome?' she asked proudly and was quite put out when Princess Alexandra tactlessly said she thought he looked rather lined. They breakfasted at Clarence House and Townsend came round for tea that afternoon from the Abergavennys' flat in Lowndes Square, where he was staying, arriving just before the Queen Mother came down from the Castle of Mey. That evening they began a series of dinner-parties with friends. 'It was the oddest sensation going there [Clarence House] then,' a friend said. 'Outside there were crowds of people and nothing else was discussed anywhere, nothing else to read about in the newspapers, but inside there were no papers in evidence. One couldn't believe the peace and calm of that house where the tremendous drama was taking place.' Elizabeth remained at Balmoral. Hard though it may seem to believe, until that moment the royal family had not mentioned the situation to anyone, until Lord Salisbury advised Clarence House that some public statement must be made as the speculation was doing the royal family much harm. Queen Elizabeth and her Private Secretary, Oliver Dawnay, spent hours on the scrambler telephone between Clarence House and Buckingham Palace discussing the wording of a statement to be issued on 14 October by the Press Secretary, Commander Colville. The statement made a vain appeal to the press to leave the Princess alone and declared that 'no announcement concerning Princess Margaret's personal future was at present contemplated'. It was not enough to satisfy the press, who that day, Friday, 18 October, pursued the couple down to Allanbay, a handsome, late-Georgian house overlooking a lake near Binfield in Berkshire, which belonged to Margaret's first cousin, the Hon. Mrs John Wills. The Clarence House household complained that Townsend seemed to court the press rather than trying to avoid them as they advised him to. 'We were all amazed that the newspapers seemed to know where he was going to be before we did,' said one. Townsend simply refused to hide or to sneak out of side entrances as the courtiers would have preferred him to do.

While the couple spent a romantic weekend at Allanbay with policemen fending off the press, the Queen Mother was at Royal Lodge and Elizabeth still at Balmoral. The Queen Mother was by now deeply unhappy. She felt unable to communicate with Margaret, who refused to listen to her and contradicted everything she said, so that she felt the best thing she could do was to keep out of it as much as possible. She was suffering from a feeling of guilt that she should have tried to do more about the affair earlier and that it was now too late. The publicity had at last brought home to her, as it had to Elizabeth, the damage that the situation was doing to the family. Meanwhile Eden travelled up to Balmoral on 18 October to have his Tuesday audience with Elizabeth as far from the public eye as possible. The message he had to convey was the same as it had been in 1953: Lord Salisbury had threatened to resign if the Cabinet approved the marriage. Now that Margaret was twenty-five she was at liberty to marry Townsend if she chose, but the hard choice which Eden had to put to Elizabeth was that since the Government would not sanction the marriage, if she did insist on going ahead with it, he would have to introduce a parliamentary bill which would deprive her (and any children she might have) of the right of succession, and herself of her rights to function as a Counsellor of State and to her Civil List income (which would have been more than doubled from £6,000 to £15,000 if the marriage were approved by Parliament). Like the Windsors, the Townsends would probably be required to live abroad for the first few years. Eden further told Elizabeth that he thought the whole issue would damage the standing of the Crown.

On the surface and in the press it seemed a re-run of 1936. Margaret felt, as her Uncle David had about Wallis Simpson, that she could not live without Peter Townsend. The popular and left-wing press accused the establishment and the Church of hypocrisy. 'Go on, Marg, do what you want,' women shouted at the Princess when she visited the East End. The traditionalists regarded it as unthinkable that the Princess should marry a divorced man. But in essence it was all less important than the fuss made it seem. The Princess was not, as her Uncle David had been, head of state and of the Commonwealth, or Supreme

Governor of the Church of England. The resignation of the Marquess of Salisbury, although important to the Government, would not have provoked a constitutional crisis. Things had changed since the days when Lord Halifax would have to examine his conscience before sitting next to a divorced woman at dinner. True, divorcées were not invited into the Queen's palaces nor aboard her yacht; at Royal Ascot they were now allowed into the royal enclosure but not on to the royal lawn. Yet the Prime Minister and two other Cabinet ministers were divorced. The royal family was still, however, considered to be a special case. *The Times* spelled it out in 1955, just as it had in 1936:

> Now in the twentieth-century conception of the monarchy the Queen has come to be the symbol of every side of life of this society, its universal representative in whom her people see their better selves ideally reflected; and since part of their ideal is family life, the Queen's family has its own part in the reflection. If the marriage which is now being discussed comes to pass, it is inevitable that this reflection becomes distorted . . .

This was the moral straitjacket into which the royal family was to be confined, trapped by an image of its own creation.

The public discussion of their dilemma concentrated the couple's minds on the realities of their future. Townsend wrote of his meeting with Princess Margaret on the evening of 22 October: 'We were both exhausted, mentally, emotionally, physically. We felt mute and numbed at the centre of this maelstrom.' Margaret spent the following day with her sister and brother-in-law at Windsor. No one has revealed what was said at Windsor that day, but no doubt she would have been told of the Government's attitude. At one point, with Elizabeth, Philip, Margaret and her mother present, there was an awkward episode when the Queen Mother pathetically said that Margaret hadn't even thought where they were going to live, whereupon Philip said 'very sarcastically' that it was still possible even nowadays to buy a house and the Queen Mother left the room angrily slamming the door. Perhaps the surroundings reminded Margaret of her childhood and of her father and what he would have thought of her proposed marriage, and brought home to her what she would be giving up for love. She telephoned Townsend 'in great distress'. 'She did not say what had passed between herself and her sister and her brother-in-law,' he wrote, 'but doubtless the stern truth was dawning upon her.' It was dawning upon them both.

While the Windsors' marriage had been supported by a great deal of money, the Townsends would have to live on his pay, already stretched by the education of his two sons. For a Princess who had once said, 'I cannot imagine anything more wonderful than being who I am', the prospect of losing her royal status was unthinkable. Townsend knew that he could not ask her to step down from her life of spoiled luxury and be an ordinary housewife. Both of them must have realised that love was unlikely to survive the kind of mundaneness life held out for both of them under the circumstances. The final blow was that they would be expected to live abroad, just as the Windsors had. After a sleepless night, Margaret had made up her mind. Early the next morning Townsend telephoned to tell her that he thought they loved one another enough to make the sacrifice not to marry. It was a mutual decision.

On the evening after Margaret returned from Windsor, they sat down together to draft their statement of renunciation. When they had finished, 'For a few moments', Townsend wrote, 'we looked at each other; there was a wonderful tenderness in her eyes which reflected, I suppose, the look in mine. We had reached the end of the road.' By the 27th Margaret had taken the irrevocable step of officially informing the Archbishop of Canterbury, Dr Fisher, of their decision. The apprehensive prelate, expecting an awkward discussion, reached for a reference book. 'You can put away your books, Archbishop,' the Princess told him. 'I am not going to marry Peter Townsend.' They spent one final weekend together with Lord and Lady Rupert Nevill at their house near Uckfield in Sussex, which, Margaret later told friends, she had enjoyed more than any other of her life. All the difficult decisions had been made: 'They both knew that they loved each other more than anyone else in the world and they both felt they had made the right decision.' Early on the morning of Monday, 31 October, Townsend came to her room to say goodbye. Instead of feeling agonised, they had felt complete contentment. They returned separately to London and at six o'clock Townsend made a last visit to the Princess at Clarence House, where they drank to their past and to their separate futures. Townsend returned to Uckfield en route for Brussels. The statement they had agreed on was finally released at 7 p.m. that evening:

> I would like it to be known that I have decided not to marry Group Captain Peter Townsend. I have been aware that, subject to my

renouncing my rights of succession, it might have been possible for me to contract a civil marriage. But, mindful of the Church's teaching that Christian marriage is indissoluble, and conscious of my duty to the Commonwealth, I have resolved to put these considerations before any others.

I have reached this decision entirely alone, and in doing so I have been strengthened by the unfailing support and devotion of Group Captain Townsend. I am deeply grateful for the concern of all those who have constantly prayed for my happiness.

Margaret.

Margaret told a friend that she had been determined to underline the religious aspect of her renunciation and that Eden, because of his own divorce and remarriage (and, presumably, those of the other divorced members of the Cabinet), had tried to have it cut out. Ordinary people reacted differently. She received 6,000 letters from people telling her of their own romantic problems.

Amazingly, the royal family did not rally round Margaret on the night of her formal renunciation. She dined alone while her mother kept an official engagement at London University. The Queen Mother did not say goodnight to her daughter on her return. For some time they had barely been on speaking terms; for the Queen Mother, the Townsend affair had been as traumatic as the Abdication had for Queen Mary. Elizabeth telephoned for a brief conversation, after which Margaret returned to watching boxing on television. The King's death and his widow's subsequent withdrawal, Elizabeth's marriage and Margaret's romance had weakened the family bonds that had linked 'us four' so closely together.

Margaret's life has not been happy or successful; perhaps given her position and her personality it never would have been. It is by no means certain that if she had married Townsend, even keeping her royal position and income, she would have been happy. Marriage without position would have been a disaster. She is seen as a sacrificial victim of the image of the monarchy, forced by what some people saw as hypocrisy, others as right thinking, to make the cruel choice between love on the one hand, duty, security and regal comfort on the other. Resentment at the sacrifice she made in 1955 has rankled and has not helped to make her contented in her life. Principally she has blamed Lascelles for not telling her the marriage was impossible from the outset – at one moment, seeing him on the drive, she contemplated telling her chauffeur to run him over, but she curbed it and they lived in uneasy proximity in Kensington Palace until his death in 1981 aged ninety-four. Lascelles was only a scapegoat; if anyone was to blame, it was the couple themselves in the first instance and in the second Margaret's family, who could not bring themselves to be cruel to be kind. The Queen Mother had closed her eyes to the growing romance taking shape in her own house; since the death of her husband she had clung to the household in which, as far as she could be, she was happy. Townsend was necessary to her. Elizabeth, now the head of the family, was devoted to her mother and sister and could not bear to see them unhappy. She felt that she had inherited responsibility for them from her father. In the interests of the monarchy perhaps she should have pointed out, as Queen Victoria most certainly would have, that the marriage was impossible and sent Townsend away before the scandal became public and protracted. As a wise and kind human being she played for time, refusing to pressurise her sister, insisting that Margaret make her own decision. In the end the Princess was free to marry whomever she chose as long as she was prepared to sacrifice everything for love and take the consequences. When Elizabeth's Private Secretary, Martin Charteris, was asked on television if Margaret had been sacrificed on the altar of the establishment, he replied with a meaningful shrug, 'She sacrificed herself.' The end of the Townsend affair in 1955 had both public and private consequences. Unfairly, to a growing section of the people it linked the monarchy with a hypocritical establishment, while in private Elizabeth was made to feel still more responsibility for her sister. In her dealings with her sister's love affair, Elizabeth had failed to make the connection with the public dimension of the royal family's private life and was to make the same mistake again when it came to the lives of her own children.

9

'The World's Sweetheart'

'England now had three assets: her Queen "the world's sweet-heart", Winston Churchill, and her glorious historical past.'

Bernard Baruch in conversation with Jock Colville,
5 January 1953

On 24 November 1953, just over five months after millions of people worldwide had seen her crowned, Elizabeth set off on a six-month grand tour of the Commonwealth, her first step towards the fulfilment of the speech of dedication which she had made on her twenty-first birthday in 1947. For Elizabeth, her role as head of the Commonwealth was as important as her position as Queen of Great Britain. Where her parents had been Empire-minded, Elizabeth was Commonwealth-orientated and would remain steadfastly so, sometimes in conflict with the views of her British prime ministers. Since 1949 the sovereign of Great Britain had been designated as 'Head of the Commonwealth' and would be acknowledged as such in member countries, which, like India, were republics. In 1953 the Royal Titles Act had reflected the fact that the other members of the Commonwealth were full and equal members with the United Kingdom, so that Elizabeth as she was in Britain was equally queen of each of her separate realms, acting on the advice of her ministers there, and legislation on the royal title was to be enacted by each country's parliament.

Travelling with Philip on the SS *Gothic*, she covered some 43,000 miles in her six-month tour, beginning in Bermuda and going on via the Bahamas and Jamaica to Belize, then through the Panama Canal to Fiji and Tonga, where she renewed her acquaintance with the giant Queen Salote and the equally giant turtle, Tuimalila, which had been introduced to Captain Cook nearly 200 years before. At Christmas she was in New Zealand, hailed by the Maoris as 'The rare White Heron of the Single Flight'. Later on the *Gothic*, Elizabeth had the other members of the party in stitches as she did the *haka* in evening dress complete with grunts and exaggerated gestures. Wearing her Coronation dress she opened the parliaments of New Zealand, Australia and Ceylon. In Ceylon, after protracted intergovernmental discussions as to whether or not she should remove her shoes when entering the Sacred Shrine at the Temple of the Tooth at Kandy (where a tooth held to have belonged to the Buddha was exhibited), she visited the shrine – removing her shoes – and then witnessed the Royal Perahera, a procession of some 600 Kandyan chiefs with 125 'lavishly-caparisoned' elephants, 1,000 torchbearers and over 600 Kandyan dancers and drummers.[1] In New Zealand, according to the British High Commissioner's report, she was received with 'adulation' as was Philip, 'who also, in his own right, made a great and lasting impression'. The United Kingdom High Commissioner in Australia reported similar enthusiasm there. 'Neither at the time of the Coronation nor during the Queen's time in Australia did I ever hear or read any croaking nonsense that this would prove to have been the last Coronation,' he wrote.[2]

For Elizabeth, there was the 'smile' problem again, just as there had been in Canada on the whistlestop tours and motorcades. Lady Pamela Mountbatten, who was with her, recalled:

> What the Queen did find a strain was that as she was passing somebody
> it was the one moment in their life when they could see the Queen and
> therefore she must be smiling; but she couldn't maintain that smile for
> a motorcade which was lasting perhaps 45 minutes. You get a twitch.
> So there is a moment when you have to relax your muscles, and of
> course that one moment when you're not smiling disappoints people
> who have travelled miles to see you.

'Isn't she looking cross?' Elizabeth would hear people saying as she went past, often surreptitiously holding up her pearls to avoid having a white ring round her neck by the evening. People were unashamed in their curiosity, Lady Pamela remembered:

> She went through some awful ordeals – the Queen would be in her box
> looking at the race-course and the entire crowd between the box and
> the course would have their backs to the course, and would gaze at her
> with their racing-glasses. There is a strain after, say, the first 20

minutes. And the same at all civil balls and so on. People were so
fascinated to see what they might have thought of as a waxwork,
actually moving and speaking.[3]

On one occasion, an over-enthusiastic spectator pushed herself
between Elizabeth and her lady-in-waiting. 'I had to get out my hat
pin and poke the damned woman with it to get her out of the way,' the
lady said. Ladies-in-waiting on tour with the Queen have to keep just
behind her, an extra copy of her speech in their handbags, and to be
on hand to deal with the bouquets with which she is always being
presented. Then there is always the problem of the Queen and the
lavatory; the lady-in-waiting is responsible for gently persuading the
cloakroom attendant to allow the Queen to powder her nose in privacy
and then standing guard outside the door. On one occasion in
Philadelphia, the Hon. Mary Morrison had to wrestle outside the door
to the ladies' cloakroom with an FBI agent clad in a green satin evening
dress who was determined to carry out her mission of watching over
the Queen.

In Tobruk Elizabeth and Philip watched as the new royal yacht,
Britannia, came into harbour with Prince Charles, now aged five, and
Princess Anne, aged three, on board. It had been five months since
Elizabeth had seen her children, almost a repetition of her own
experience when her parents had gone on their tour of Australia and
New Zealand when she was just over a year old, yet the family
greetings in the true Windsor tradition were formal in public, a
handshake from Charles for his mother and no hugs until they were in
private. Elizabeth's absence was frequently to be repeated; with her
new role as head of the Commonwealth she was to be the most
travelled British monarch in history and possibly the most travelled
head of state in any age. *Britannia* had been designed to see that she
did it in style.

The question of a new royal yacht as a replacement for the ageing
Victoria & Albert, which had been launched in 1899, had first been
raised in June 1938 by Alfred Duff Cooper when First Lord of the
Admiralty in Chamberlain's Government.[4] The King had replied that
although he realised *Victoria & Albert* was out of date and deteriorating, he would not want construction of the new yacht to 'impede, or
interfere with,' the naval construction programme, 'either as regards
labour or finance'.[5] The Government agreed that it was an inopportune
moment to include £900,000 for a royal yacht in the already increased

defence estimates and with the outbreak of war the plan was dropped. After the war, Mountbatten while Fourth Sea Lord had come forward with the ingenious money-saving wheeze of buying second-hand from a Mr Arida the yacht *Grille*, which had been built for Hitler, but never used by him.[6] His Majesty replied not surprisingly that 'he would . . . greatly prefer to have a British-built yacht rather than one that had been built by the Germans for Hitler'.[7] Mountbatten therefore pursued the idea of constructing a new yacht, a typically imaginative and expensive gesture. The excuse for building such a magnificent ship at a time of austerity was that in time of war it would be converted for use as a hospital ship (it never was). Persuaded by Mountbatten's eloquence and also moved by the idea that to have such a yacht would help the ailing King in his convalescence, Attlee's Government had in June 1951 sanctioned its construction at John Brown's shipyard on the Clyde, but the King had died before work on the yacht began and it had finally been launched by Elizabeth in April 1953. 'My father felt most strongly, as I do, that a yacht was a necessity, and not a luxury for the head of our great British Commonwealth, between whose countries the sea is no barrier, but the natural highway,' she had said in her speech. *Britannia* was to be a source of great pleasure and prestige for her family, and, towards the end of the yacht's life as refits became more frequent and more expensive, equally a cause of embarrassment and public criticism. It was a Labour First Lord of the Admiralty, J. P. Thomas, who said of it, 'The country wants the Queen to have this yacht and they want it to be worthy of her and her family', but the overall cost of *Britannia* when completed was just over £2 million and even before the royal yacht had reached Tobruk, John Gordon had given it a tremendous 'hammering' in the *Sunday Express*, setting the pattern for the future.

Hugh Casson, who had just designed the decor for Philip's study and library at Buckingham Palace, had been invited by Philip to take a consultancy on the interior design of *Britannia*. The Queen, Sir Hugh wrote in his diary, had been anxious to keep down costs while at the same time incorporating a sense of tradition in the design, and much of the furniture from the previous royal yacht, the *Victoria & Albert*, had been used. 'The royal couple took a close interest in every aspect of the design,' he recalled. 'The Queen is a meticulous observer with very strong views; there was no question of showing her a drawing and her saying: "All right, that will do." She had definite views on everything from the door-handles to the shape of the lampshades.' For the reception-rooms, 'the overall idea was to give the impression of a country house at sea'.[8] Even when new, *Britannia* was stately and old-fashioned with tall mahogany double doors linking the anteroom with the drawing-room, Queen Victoria's satinwood desk against a wall and Hepplewhite chairs from the *Victoria & Albert* in the dining-room.

Elizabeth was to become immensely attached to the yacht, as indeed were all the family. Aboard the yacht she can enjoy greater privacy than anywhere else; uniquely, it combines the formality of Buckingham Palace and the holiday status of Balmoral and Sandringham. During state visits she can entertain in great style aboard the yacht, or, after a long and tiring day, come aboard and relax. Her apartments – and Philip's – are located on the top deck with access to a veranda sun deck, a lift connects them with the state rooms below, and two floors down are the offices of the private secretaries and the lady clerks. Elizabeth's and Philip's bedroom suites are built with floor levels 2 feet higher than the deck outside, consequently the windows are too high for passing ratings to look inside (as if they would dare). Officers and ratings are issued with soft-soled plimsolls so that the noise of their feet will not disturb the royals or sully the immaculate decking, and there is as little shouting of orders as possible. Here, as everywhere else, Bobo had pride of place after the Queen – the yacht crew nicknamed her the 'QE3' – 'It was more trouble getting Miss MacDonald on board than the Queen,' a member of the royal staff said – and woe betide any steward who failed to bring her her tray with champagne and glasses at the appointed hour. Her cabin was specially reserved just for her. Once, when Princess Alexandra's daughter, Marina Mowatt, used it, she was warned not to move anything in case Bobo noticed it. (Bobo's influence with Elizabeth was already predominant – on the 1953–4 Commonwealth tour, members of the household were warned 'for heaven's sake don't upset Bobo or you'll ruin HM's day'.)

Reunited, the family sailed back home via Gibraltar, where Philip is alleged to have thrown peanuts at photographers stationed in the apes' cages. Off the Needles, Churchill clambered aboard from a naval launch to greet his sovereign. Together they stood on the bridge of the royal yacht as it sailed up the Thames, with Churchill regaling Elizabeth and Philip with the river's history. 'One saw this dirty commercial river', Elizabeth recalled, 'and he was describing it as the silver thread which runs through the history of Britain. [He] saw things in a very romantic and glittering way.' Churchill's Address of

Welcome on her return was hyperbolic even by his high standards. 'I assign no limits', he said, 'to the reinforcement which this Royal journey may have brought to the health, the wisdom, the sanity and hopefulness of mankind.'[9]

Churchill's relationship with Elizabeth was tender and romantic. When her father died, Jock Colville had found the old man sitting alone with tears in his eyes, looking straight in front of him, unable to concentrate on his official papers, and had attempted to comfort him by saying how well he would get on with the new Queen. Churchill's only response had been that 'he did not know her and she was only a child'. A few weeks later, after Churchill had suffered an arterial spasm which could have been the precursor of a stroke, his doctor, Lord Moran, had consulted Colville and Salisbury about the possibility of persuading him to retire, or, as Salisbury suggested, to continue as Prime Minister in the House of Lords instead of the Commons. Moran, knowing Churchill's reverence for the monarchy, suggested that the Queen should do it, and was disconcerted when Lascelles told them to forget it. 'If she said her part, he would say charmingly: "It's very good of you, ma'am, to think of it" and then he would very politely brush it aside.' Churchill did not tend to take women seriously on an intellectual level; still less the inexperienced young Elizabeth, although he was moved by her attractiveness, her seriousness and her grasp of the responsibilities of her position. As he got to know her, he became more and more besotted with her; by 1955 when he was eighty-one and on the eve of retirement, Colville described him as being 'madly in love' with the Queen and the half-hour audiences as stretching to an hour and a half.

'Winston treated the Queen with extraordinary deference and courtesy,' a member of the household at the time recalled:

> On one occasion the film chosen for the Royal Command Film Performance was, I think, *Beau Brummel*, in which George III is depicted as very mad and George IV as a libertine. The Queen clearly complained to Winston the next day about seeing her ancestors thus portrayed. Winston was outraged. The old boy came out muttering, 'The Queen had an awful evening – this must not recur.' By the next evening the Home Secretary or the Permanent Under Secretary at the Home Office had been summoned and told that the Queen must not be subjected to such an experience again and that a selection committee must be set up to vet films for the Royal Command Performance. And who do you think was appointed to chair the selection committee? Only

Lord Radcliffe who chaired all the most important Commissions and Committees. This instant reaction to the Queen's complaint was typical of Winston.

At audiences their conversations ranged far and wide. 'Winston would come out saying, "She was asking me about my pig-sticking days on the North-West Frontier . . ."'

In the first year of their relationship as Queen and Prime Minister, Churchill took the initiative in inviting himself to Balmoral to acquaint himself better with Elizabeth. He spent from 1 to 3 October there. According to Colville, who accompanied him, the stay was a success:

> The Queen and Prince Philip, who had a very young party staying with them, may have been a little reluctant, but the visit went off well and was in the event enjoyed by both sides, although Winston (aged nearly seventy-eight and not having touched a gun for years) complained to me on the way home that he thought he should have been asked to shoot![10]

It was at Balmoral that Churchill had first met Elizabeth when she was two and a half years old and been impressed by her as 'a character'. In his thank-you letter to her his mind ranged back to the days when he had been a guest there not only of her father and grandfather but even of her great-grandfather, Edward VII. He commented favourably on Prince Charles: 'I was keenly impressed by the development of Prince Charles as a personality since I last saw him at Windsor. He is young to think so much.' He had enjoyed, he said, 'such good talks' with the Duke of Edinburgh about 'the Navy, Flying, Polo and Politics'. Shortly after he left Balmoral he was immensely flattered by Elizabeth's request that he should have a portrait bust sculpted by Oscar Nemon to be placed in Windsor Castle. Nemon wrote that Churchill said that the honour the Queen had done him had 'touched him more than if she had bestowed upon him the Order of the Garter! . . . he is deeply moved and is very proud to be immortalized in company with his great ancestor the first Duke of Marlborough.'[11] In fact Elizabeth, after careful enquiries to find out whether it would be accepted, went on to offer Churchill the Garter, which he had refused in the previous reign. Now that it was in the personal gift of the sovereign (Churchill had been offered it in 1945 when nominations for the Garter were still in government hands, but since 1946 George VI had succeeded in wresting it into the total control of the sovereign), he felt it would be discourteous to repeat his refusal, which had greatly disappointed the King, and although he would have preferred to remain 'Mr Churchill', he was attracted by the idea that the first Duke of Marlborough's father's name had been Sir Winston Churchill. And so, when Elizabeth had formally made the suggestion in April 1952, he accepted and was installed as a Knight at the Garter Ceremony on 14 June 1954.

To Elizabeth he was the towering war leader of her adolescence and her father's friend. Churchill more than any other single figure represented Britain's 'glorious historical past'. He had fought in one of the last cavalry charges ever made, at the Battle of Omdurman in 1898 when her great-great-grandmother was on the throne; he had served in Government under her grandfather and fought in the First World War, and he had been her father's Prime Minister during the Second. His huge grasp of world affairs, his fierce patriotism and his rolling periods of speech spiced with puckish humour fascinated her, and they shared a passion for racing. Churchill was there to commiserate with her when her horse, Aureole, was beaten by Pinza in the post-Coronation Derby; racing talk occupied a certain proportion of the weekly prime ministerial audiences. At Christmas Elizabeth wrote congratulating him on the success of his horse, Pol Roger, at Kempton Park. When Aureole won the Derby Trial Stakes at Lingfield on 16 May 1953, Churchill sent a congratulatory cable to which the Queen replied, 'Most grateful for your kind message of congratulations. Sorry you were not in closer attendance.'

At seventy-eight he was no longer the man he had once been; he was now rather deaf, had suffered a mild coronary in 1941 and his first stroke in 1949. His enormous stamina, indomitable spirit and enjoyment of power had borne him along, but he was now carrying the additional burden of the Foreign Office in the absence of Eden, who was undergoing surgery in Boston. Despite all this he had in no way changed his style of life; there were still huge cigars, pints of champagne and draughts of brandy over late-night after-dinner conversations which fascinated but wearied his colleagues. Fate caught up with him on 23 June 1953 during an official dinner in honour of the Italian Prime Minister, Alcide de Gasperi. Churchill rose to lead his male guests into the drawing-room to join the ladies, tottered and slumped into the nearest chair. Clutching the hand of his neighbour, Jane Clark, wife of the art historian Kenneth Clark, he muttered, 'I want a friend ... They put too much on me. Foreign Affairs ...', his voice trailed off. He could not walk and his speech was slurred; he had suffered a massive stroke. Somehow his son-in-law, Christopher Soames, married to his daughter, Mary, and Jock Colville managed to get rid of the guests and the waiters without anyone realising what had happened. Those who had noticed something wrong thought that the Prime Minister was drunk. He even managed to get through a Cabinet meeting the following morning without his ministers being aware of the seriousness of his condition – R. A. 'Rab' Butler only remarking that he was 'curiously and unexpectedly silent' and Harold Macmillan that he was 'very white' and 'spoke very little'. When Churchill did speak, however, by making a titanic effort, he managed to enunciate his words distinctly enough so that no one noticed anything wrong. He was determined not to give in or give up and, although his condition was worsening, the next day gave Colville 'strict orders not to let it be known that he was temporarily incapacitated and to ensure that the administration continued to function as if he were in full control'.

Colville, however, with his Palace training, knew that Elizabeth must be told. By Friday Churchill was almost completely paralysed and Moran told Colville that 'he did not think the Prime Minister could possibly live over the weekend'. 'It occurred to me rather forcibly', Colville recalled, 'that the accepted successor, Mr Anthony Eden, was at that moment on the operating table in Boston ... and that, if indeed Lord Moran were right and the Prime Minister were to die over the weekend, a very serious constitutional problem would present itself.'[12] It was and is a constitutional principle that the Queen's Government must be carried on and that the Queen has the right to choose whom she will invite to form a government in the event of a Prime Minister's death. In this case Eden, who lay incapacitated in hospital, had waited so long in the wings to take over from Churchill (who was wont to call him, to his annoyance, 'my Princess Elizabeth') that it would hardly be fair not to give him the chance to recover. In defiance of Churchill's order Colville rang Lascelles on the secret scrambler phone to tell him the truth, 'that the queen must be prepared, so shortly after her Coronation, to be faced with the necessity of appointing a new Prime Minister on Monday morning'. Together the two Private Secretaries cobbled together a plot which would, not for the last time, mean that Rab Butler, the obvious candidate for Prime Minister, would not be allowed to step into the breach. Instead, together with Lord Salisbury, he was to advise Elizabeth that a caretaker government should be formed, led by Salisbury, who would not take the title of Prime Minister but would act as head of the Government until Eden was well enough to take over. News of this extraordinarily unconstitutional conspiracy was to be kept secret within a small circle; Colville nobbled the Press Lords Camrose and Beaverbrook and with their help, and that of Churchill's friend Brendan Bracken, he succeeded in gagging Fleet Street so that not a word of Churchill's condition leaked out. An anodyne bulletin was issued to the press to the effect that the Prime Minister was tired and 'in need of a complete rest'.

Elizabeth acquiesced in this charade although Churchill remained unaware that she had been told that he might not last the weekend. On the day after she heard from Lascelles of his conversation with Colville she wrote Churchill a personal letter from Edinburgh, where she and Philip were on their post-Coronation tour of the United Kingdom. It is hardly surprising under the circumstances that the result was somewhat stilted. 'My dear Prime Minister, I am so sorry to hear from Tommy Lascelles that you have not been feeling too well these last few days,' she wrote. 'I do hope that it is not serious and that you will be quite recovered in a very short time.' Having skimmed over the surface of Churchill's health she resorted to the safer subject of the local weather. 'Our visit here is going well and Edinburgh is thrilled by all the pageantry,' she informed him. 'We have been lucky in having fine weather, but I fear that it is now raining after a thunderstorm . . .'[13] Churchill was, according to Moran, 'thrilled' by this letter. He replied immediately giving her some account of 'the circumstances in which he had been stricken down' and 'spoke of his plight as if it had happened to someone else'. He told her that he hoped he might soon be up and about and able to carry on his work until the autumn, when Eden would be well enough to take over.

Against all the odds and his doctors' predictions, Churchill survived, gradually regaining most of his faculties. By the last week in July he was well enough to move from his home at Chartwell to his official residence, Chequers, and on 2 August he drove over to Windsor to see Elizabeth. He had still not made up his mind to retire, telling her that he would make the decision in a month's time when he saw whether he would be fit enough to face Parliament and the annual Conservative Party Conference in October. Two weeks later Elizabeth sent him an invitation to spend the day with her at Doncaster races to watch Aureole run in the St Leger and go on to Balmoral afterwards. Ignoring the advice of his doctors and his wife, Churchill insisted on accepting the royal invitation and on 11 September he and Clementine travelled by train to Doncaster to watch the St Leger from the royal enclosure and then travelled on to Balmoral on the royal train. He accompanied Elizabeth to Crathie Church for Sunday service, last having been there with Edward VII forty-five years ago, long before she was born. There was a crowd waiting to give him unprecedented cheers. Elizabeth told a friend that she found the improvement he had made since she had last seen him at the beginning of August 'astonishing'.

Since the day of his stroke in June 1953, however, one question had been present both in his and Elizabeth's mind: when would he resign? Eden had returned home from Boston still extremely frail but clearly expectant; the unspoken question hung in the air whenever he was with Churchill. Churchill was determined to face the Conservative Party Conference the next month, where delegates watched like hawks during his major speech. The stroke was still a secret (though rumours about it were going the rounds), but Churchill's Margate performance convinced his audience that he was not finished yet. It had been thought that he would resign and hand over to Eden before the Queen's departure in November for the Commonwealth tour. Churchill's reluctance to relinquish the reins of power was to cloud the political horizon for the next two years. 'The Queen's going away from the country complicates things,' Colville told Moran. 'The PM [Churchill] says that if he is going to retire he will do so soon, so as to give the new PM time to settle in before the Queen leaves the country. But he won't.'[14] He did not. When Elizabeth left on 24 November 1953, Churchill was still her Prime Minister.

When she returned in May 1954, she might well have expected his resignation to be imminent. He had previously talked of waiting until she was back in the country in order to hand in his resignation; he had then told Eden he would go at the end of July, but he was still in No. 10 Downing Street for his eightieth birthday on 30 November 1954. Elizabeth sent him a present of silver coasters and a more personal gift underlining their shared passion for racing: the opportunity to take up a vacant subscription for a mare to be serviced by her prize-winning stallion, Aureole. 'I shall buy the most suitable mare I can find in the December sales and hope for the future,' her octogenarian Prime Minister replied.

Elizabeth was well aware of the general feeling, particularly among his Cabinet, that Churchill should go. Even supporters like Macmillan were exasperated. 'Churchill refuses to go and there is no likelihood of his changing his mind,' Macmillan noted in his diary in the second week in December. The crew were getting mutinous and Eden's relationship with the Prime Minister was more like that of Fletcher Christian with Captain Bligh. A Cabinet meeting was held on 22 December, ostensibly to discuss the date of the general election, but actually, as Macmillan admitted, 'to discuss how long Churchill should stay'. When a truculent Churchill growled that it was clear they wanted him out, nobody contradicted him. By the end of February it seemed he had almost made up his mind to go, planning a farewell dinner-party for Elizabeth on 4 April 1955, which was to be the eve of his resignation, as he wrote to tell Sir Michael Adeane, who had now replaced Lascelles as Elizabeth's Private Secretary. But he still kept his colleagues guessing. At a Buckingham Palace luncheon for the state visit of the Shah of Iran and Queen Soraya, Prince Charles and Princess Anne were brought in afterwards to meet the guests. Princess Anne was fascinated by the old Prime Minister, who sat slumped in a chair looking all too like the eightieth-birthday portrait by Graham Sutherland which he so much disliked. On 29 March Eden and his wife Clarissa were to give a dinner-party intended as a farewell honour for the Prime Minister, but on that same day he resolved to postpone his resignation yet again and at an audience with Elizabeth that evening told her that 'he thought of putting off his resignation. He had asked her if she minded and she said no!' But on the next day, moved by Eden's amiability at the previous night's dinner, he changed his mind again back to 5 April 1955 and on 31 March asked Adeane to inform Elizabeth that he would resign on that date as planned.

Elizabeth replied via Adeane, 'that though she recognised your wisdom in taking the decision which you had, she felt the greatest personal regrets and that she would especially miss the weekly audiences which she had found so instructive and, if one can say so of State matters, so entertaining'.[15] This was not mere resignation letter politeness; she meant it. Asked once which of her Prime Ministers did she enjoy audiences with most, she said, 'Winston, of course, because it was always such fun.' But when asked whether it had been like Lord Melbourne with the young Victoria, she replied, 'Not at all . . . He could be very stubborn . . .' Churchill, for his part, was described by one of the royal Private Secretaries as coming away from his audiences 'purring'. His reluctance to give up the pleasure of these weekly private talks as well as the reins of power was certainly a factor in the gloom with which he contemplated his resignation. The old man's romantic affection for Elizabeth nearly caused an embarrassing moment at his resignation audience with her on the day after the farewell Downing Street dinner.

It had been Colville's idea that since his service as Prime Minister had been so exceptional, it would be 'appropriate' if he were to be offered an exceptional honour by the Queen – a dukedom, just as his famous ancestor John Churchill had been made Duke of Marlborough for his services to the nation. The Palace reply was that no more dukedoms were ever going to be conferred except on royal personages. 'However, it did seem appropriate. Could I give the undertaking that the Prime Minister would refuse it?' When Colville took soundings with Churchill, he found him adamantly opposed to it – he wished to die in the House of Commons as Winston Churchill. 'I rushed to the telephone', Colville recalled, 'and rang up Sir Michael Adeane and said that he could safely tell the Queen the dukedom could be offered.' On the day, however, Colville had serious misgivings:

> I was greatly disturbed because as I saw the Prime Minister going off in his frock coat and his top hat and knowing as I did that he was madly in love with the Queen . . . I was rather alarmed that sentimental feelings might indeed make him accept at the last moment. In which case I knew that both the Queen and Sir Michael would be very angry with me for having given this pledge.
> When he returned from his audience the first thing I said to him as we sat in the Cabinet room was 'How did it go?' With tears in his eyes he said, 'Do you know, the most remarkable thing – she offered to make me a Duke.'
> With trepidation I asked what he had said. 'Well you know, I very nearly accepted, I was so moved by her beauty and charm and the kindness with which she made this offer, that for a moment I thought of accepting. But finally I remembered that I must die as I have always been – Winston Churchill. And so I asked her to forgive my not accepting it. And do you know, it's an odd thing, but she seemed almost relieved.'[16]

In a handwritten letter from Windsor Elizabeth told him sincerely how much she missed him and how neither his successor, Anthony Eden, nor any other of his successors, 'will ever, for me, be able to hold the place of my first Prime Minister, to whom both my husband and I owe so much and for whose wise guidance during the early years

of my reign I shall always be so profoundly grateful'. Churchill's reply
also illuminated his relationship with Elizabeth and the respect he had
grown to have for her:

> I have tried throughout to keep Your Majesty squarely confronted with
> the grave and complex problems of our time. Very soon after taking
> office as First Minister I realized the comprehension with which Your
> Majesty entered upon the august duties of a modern Sovereign and the
> store of knowledge which had already been gathered by an upbringing
> both wise and lively. This enabled Your Majesty to understand as it
> seemed by instinct the relationships and the balances of the British
> constitution so deeply cherished by the mass of the Nation and by the
> strongest and most stable forces in it. I became conscious of the Royal
> resolve to serve as well as rule, and indeed to rule by serving.

Lastly, he paid tribute to the effect of her 'sparkling presence' linking
and illuminating the structure of 'our new formed Commonwealth'.[17]

The Queen had not consulted anyone as to Churchill's successor.
Out of politeness she had asked Churchill at their farewell audience
whether he would like to recommend anyone, but he had replied that
he would leave it up to her to decide. In practice there was only one
choice, Anthony Eden, Churchill's long-acknowledged heir, who held
the unconstitutional title of 'Deputy Prime Minister' to which George
VI had objected as implying automatic succession and therefore
impinging on the royal prerogative of theoretical choice in the matter.
Eden was the brilliant star of the 1930s, when his resignation in protest
against Chamberlain's dealings with the dictators had won him the
admiration of Churchill and his followers. Extremely handsome, always
impeccably dressed, cultivated and intelligent, he had operated at the
top level in world affairs with only a six-year break since replacing
Halifax as Foreign Secretary in December 1940. Although only fifty-
eight when he succeeded to the premiership, he was past his prime,
his health permanently undermined by the slip of a surgeon's knife
during an operation for gallstones in April 1953. His relationship with
Elizabeth was distinctly warmer than it had been with her father and
her grandfather, both of whom he had served in government. 'When
he first took office', an aide said, 'he was very sensible that he was
following the towering figure of Churchill who had felt towards her as
if she were his granddaughter and spoke to her like that. He was very
conscious that the Queen might think him a lesser figure in that post

but the Queen treated him so well that he didn't feel like that . . . He always spoke of her with warm affection – he was very fond of her. He was sensitive to the Queen and consulted her on a wide range of subjects.' Both Eden and his Colonial Secretary, Alan Lennox-Boyd, were surprised by the extent of Elizabeth's interest in and knowledge of the Commonwealth even in those early days of her reign. 'When Lennox-Boyd was Colonial Secretary,' Professor Dilks recalled, 'he went to check with Eden to find out some question about the grazing rights of Somali tribesmen – Eden scoffed at the idea that the Queen might ask or even know about the question, but she did.'[18]

Elizabeth was learning to be, as her father before her had quickly had to learn, a professional. Where Edward VIII's brief reign had been marked by official 'boxes' returned unopened and ringed with telltale circular stains from cocktail glasses, George VI had been thorough in his work and used to enjoy catching out unwary ministers who might have skimped their official briefs. This was a game which his daughter too liked to play; she had caught out Churchill, who, in his later years, had been lazy about reading papers on certain subjects even when warned to do so by Jock Colville, who, as her former Private Secretary, was well aware of the Queen's working methods. Harold Wilson, her Prime Minister for two terms (1964–70 and 1974–6), was to be mortified when the same thing happened to him at his first audience.

Elizabeth was always well briefed. Not only did she see state papers delivered to her daily in leather-covered boxes whose colours denoted the different departments, but she also saw copies of minutes of Cabinet meetings and received a daily abstract of proceedings in Parliament. 'I was astonished', Harold Macmillan, her Prime Minister in 1960, was to note in his diary, 'at Her Majesty's grasp of all the details set out in various messages and telegrams.' 'He was struck', wrote royal biographer Robert Lacey, 'by her remarkable skill in not taking too much out of herself. She never reacted excessively. She never used a phrase carelessly. She would never give away an opinion early in the conversation, but would always ask first of all for his opinion and listen to it right through.' 'You couldn't have had a better person to work for,' one of her former private secretaries said. 'Prompt, great common sense, decisive. Didn't leave things in abeyance. If you asked a question you got the answer. If you left work for her it would always be ready next morning. Very open to suggestions but not by any means accepting them . . . And she was frightfully accessible – when problems came up she would never say – "Don't bother me now."' 'The Queen never reads a book,' said another, 'but when it comes to State Papers she is a very quick and absorbent reader – doesn't miss a thing. She impresses all the Prime Ministers.'

Elizabeth dislikes dictating letters, preferring her secretaries to draft letters for correction and discussion. She likes to scribble little notes, often humorous and always to the point, as for instance on the state visit of the King and Queen of Thailand: 'Please tell the band under no circumstances to play excerpts from "The King and I" . . .' 'No more hospitals – we've had quite enough this year . . .' On a biography of Prince Charles: 'Very gooey and sentimental but quite nice. There are 4 inaccuracies [listing the page numbers].'

In one area of her work Elizabeth did lack confidence and ability. 'She was not very good about speeches,' an aide said. 'Not a natural composer of them. Relied a good deal on Prince Philip. The draft would be put up by one of the private secretaries and then she would alter it, or rather Prince Philip would. Speeches by Committee don't turn out very original.' 'She's a very honest person, it's difficult to make her say something or quote something particular unless she really knows about it,' another said. 'For instance, if you suggested she should say "We are very pleased to be here in Hull today", she would cross out the "very".' Since she doesn't find speaking easy, Elizabeth always reads her speeches, which contributes even more to the general impression of lack of spontaneity which she gives. She just cannot memorise the words or improvise, any more than her mother does. Maybe it is inherited; there is a story, perhaps apocryphal, of Queen Mary going to the launch of the liner, the SS *Queen Mary*, and telling her lady-in-waiting beforehand, 'Oh, dear, I'm sure I'm not going to remember the name.'

In 1956 Elizabeth was thirty; still young, lovely and popular, an object of adulation across a world which still seemed largely unchanged since her father's day; but her uninterrupted four-year honeymoon with her people would soon be over. Eden had been in office less than a year when he initiated a disastrous post-imperial adventure which brought to the surface currents that had been troubling the British psyche since the 1930s, currents that erupted into a wave of criticism against Britain's institutions not excluding the monarchy. At the end of July 1956 Elizabeth was at Goodwood Races when a proclamation was brought to her in the Duke of Richmond's box authorising the calling up of army reserves. At a hastily summoned Privy Council meeting on the following day, 2 August, at Arundel Castle, home of her host, the Duke of Norfolk, she signed the document, the first public step towards a war with Egypt three months later.

On 13 June 1956 the last British troops had left the Suez Canal area, which they had garrisoned for over seventy years. Ten days later Colonel Gamal Abdel Nasser became President of Egypt and just over one month later, on 26 July, following the withdrawal of American and British finance for the Aswan Dam, he nationalised the Anglo-French-owned Suez Canal Company. Initial reaction in both Britain and France was furious. Eden, who had an inbuilt dislike of dictators in general, and of Nasser in particular, set the tone by declaring that 'Nasser had his thumb on Britain's windpipe', and both Britain and France drew up secret plans for an attack on Egypt, culminating in a tripartite agreement known as the Sèvres Treaty signed by Britain, France and Israel on 24 October. This secret agreement finalised a conspiracy between the three countries by which Israel would attack Egypt on 29 October. Britain and France would demand a ceasefire and temporary occupation of the Canal by their forces on the 30th, and in the event of either warring party refusing the ceasefire the allied forces would invade Egypt on the 31st. Duly on 29 October the Israelis attacked, on the 30th Britain and France issued their ultimatum, and Eden made a statement in the House of Commons revealing his plans. At a meeting of the United Nations Security Council in New York later that day, Britain and France enraged the United States and the Soviet Union by vetoing a US resolution calling on the Israelis to withdraw. The British then bombed Egyptian airfields, destroying the Egyptian air force; it was a successful military operation at great political cost.

In the House of Commons the fact that Britain had bombed a country with which it was not actually at war raised the political temperature to heights equalling those of May 1940 preceding the fall of Chamberlain. People were outraged by this and troubled by the open breach between Britain and the United States at the United Nations. The Commonwealth countries, which, like the United States, had not been granted the courtesy of prior consultation, were, in the words of Eden's biographer, in a state of 'anger, confusion and dismay'. Arab public opinion was naturally solidly behind Nasser, creating problems for Arab regimes friendly to Britain such as the Iraqi royal family. Eden's majority among the British who thought Nasser should be taught a lesson melted away in the face of the bungling of military planners who had not taken into account the time it would take to get the main force from their Cyprus bases to the Egyptian mainland. While they were still *en route*, the Israelis and the Egyptians agreed to a ceasefire, thus destroying the point of the expedition. A Gallup poll taken in November showed a majority in Britain were against the Suez action. By the time the British paratroops and the Anglo-French seaborne forces had landed on 5 and 6 November, a run on the pound had developed. Britain's gold and dollar reserves fell by 15 per cent that month, and the Americans, when appealed to for help, bluntly told the British that none would be forthcoming without a ceasefire. Isolated in Cabinet and in Parliament, Eden accepted the principle of a UN-brokered ceasefire. The Suez operation had become a fiasco. Even those in favour of it were disgusted by this apparently abject surrender with no objective achieved (beyond the destruction of the Egyptian air force). 'By stopping when they did,' Eden's biographer wrote, 'the British incurred the maximum of odium and the minimum of advantage.'

Eden was finished, physically and politically. He had been suffering since October from recurrent fevers, the legacy of the bungled bile duct operation. On 19 November his doctors advised a complete rest, preferably in a warm climate. Ian and Ann Fleming offered the Edens their Jamaica house, Goldeneye; on 23 November the exhausted Prime Minister and his wife flew out there to general astonishment and dismay. He returned in December to a notably cool reception from his party and the country. It was a sad end for a great career in Parliament and at the Foreign Office. On 20 December Eden, who had always dominated the House of Commons, was forced on the defensive over the issue of collusion with Israel over Suez and lied: 'there were no plans to get together to attack Egypt ... there was no foreknowledge that Israel would attack Egypt'. His final defiant declaration, 'I would be compelled ... if I had the same very disagreeable decisions to take again, to repeat them', offended everybody, both those who had supported the Suez operation but had disliked the bungling and the forced retreat and those who had opposed it. They were his last words in the House of Commons, where the mood was described not so much as hostile but, more fatally, as dismissive. Early in January his doctors told him that if he continued in office he was unlikely to survive; he decided to resign – in his wife's words, 'he wanted to stay alive'. On 8 January he drove down to Sandringham with his wife to see Elizabeth; they dined and spent the night there. Elizabeth expressed her personal sadness and offered him an earldom; it was agreed that he would come to Buckingham Palace the next day formally to hand over his seals of office and at 6 p.m. on 9 January he did so.

Eden's conversations with the Queen on 8 January at Sandringham have remained secret although he made a memorandum of them at the time and subsequently wrote two others. He was always extremely sensitive on the question of whether or not Elizabeth approved of the Suez operation. When Robert Lacey published an article in the *Sunday Times* implying that the Queen had been strongly opposed to the Suez operation but had been unable to prevent it, Lord Avon (as Eden had by then become) in January 1976 was 'dealing somewhat angrily with Martin Charteris' over it, and told Lacey in April 1976 that the Queen 'understood what we were doing very well'. He was most emphatic that she did not disapprove of the operation, although he was honest enough to admit that 'nor would I claim that she was pro-Suez', according to his biographer. He remembered her as being absolutely constitutional and impartial and, as Lacey conceded, it would have been quite improper for him to discuss or disclose any more than that. Lacey's subsequent biography of the Queen recounted the suspicion of 'at least one of his [Avon's] close colleagues' that he had not told the Queen the whole story of the Anglo–French–Israeli negotiations leading up to the Sèvres Treaty and had done so only after the event. Eden's comment was that Mountbatten, Lacey's source, was 'ga-ga [and] a congenital liar'.

The truth is that attitudes at the Palace had reflected the confusion and dismay felt by the nation at large. In the Queen's Private Office Sir Michael Adeane was in favour of armed intervention, while the Deputy and Assistant Private Secretaries, Martin Charteris and Edward Ford, were against it. Both Charteris and Ford were familiar with the Middle East and the Arab world; Charteris in particular having been head of military intelligence in Palestine in 1946, while Ford had had the doubtful honour of acting as tutor to Prince Farouk of Egypt and had fought in the North African campaign. Neither of them could view with equanimity the prospect of alienating the entire Arab world, as would inevitably result due to Britain's attacking the recently resurgent Arab nationalism symbolised by Nasser's Egypt in conjunction with the Israelis less than a decade after the Arab–Israeli war of 1948. Britain's oil interests lay with the Arabs, particularly Iraq, where the instability following Suez soon led to the overthrow of the pro-Western royal government. Then there was Mountbatten, who, in the words of one of the household, was 'always about' at the Palace.

He had been involved in the operation as one of the Chiefs of Staff, but was increasingly unhappy about it; he wrote two letters to Eden telling him so, one as early as August, although he never sent them. While he may not have had the courage to tell the Prime Minister that he thought he was wrong for fear of losing his job, he would have had no such inhibitions about letting Elizabeth and Philip know. According to one of the people close to her at the time, her private view of the Suez operation was that it was 'idiotic'.

It is highly unlikely that Eden actually told the Queen in advance about Britain's conspiracy with France and Israel over the attack on Egypt. Only Selwyn Lloyd, the Foreign Secretary, and two British representatives who actually signed the document were in on the secret of the Treaty (or Protocol) of Sèvres, and it was agreed at the time that there would be total official secrecy between the parties as to what had been agreed not only then but permanently. Eden did not reveal its existence to his Cabinet. Given the divergence of opinion among her own advisers and the lack of information which would have illustrated the risks Eden was actually taking, it is understandable that Elizabeth should have felt unable to exercise her constitutional right 'to advise, counsel and warn'. 'Being so inexperienced, the Queen probably didn't – which she would have nowadays – ask him if he had consulted the Commonwealth Prime Ministers first,' an aide said; 'as a result they all sided against Britain at the UN.'

Eden found her perfectly correct and in his utter public isolation at the end he also found her kind. According to his biographer, of all the letters which he received on his resignation, none meant more to him than a handwritten letter from the Queen. Tactfully she did not mention Suez, only her sadness at his resignation and his illness which was the cause of it:

You know already how very deeply I felt your resignation last week, and how much I sympathise in the tragic turn of fate which laid you low . . . There is no doubt that you took the only possible course after the doctors had given you their verdict, but one can only guess at what it must have cost you to do it. I want to thank you not only for the loyal and distinguished service you have given to me, first as Foreign Secretary and then as Prime Minister, but for the many years' work, both in and out of office, which you have devoted to the greatness and prosperity of our country.

Much has been said and written during the last week about your record in the House of Commons and as a Statesman; I am only

anxious that you should realize that that record, which has indeed been
written in tempestuous times, is highly valued and will never be
forgotten by your Sovereign.[19]

Eden replied that he was 'more grateful than I can express' for her
'generous words', touching briefly on the 'odious' decision to retire
and his disappointment at not getting the Americans to act in concert
with the British against Russian designs in the Middle East. He
continued:

> But it is not of all this, with which Your Majesty is only too familiar,
> that I want to write. It is rather to try to express what my Sovereign's
> understanding and encouragement has meant at a time of exceptional
> ordeal. It is the bare truth to say that I looked forward to my weekly
> audience, knowing that I should receive from Your Majesty a wise and
> impartial reaction to events, which was quite simply the voice of our
> land.
>   Years ago Baldwin told me that the post of Prime Minister was the
> most lonely in the world. That may be true in respect of colleagues.
> That I have not found it so is due to Your Majesty's unfailing
> sympathy and understanding . . . as I pursue health across the world I
> can never forget Your Majesty's kindness to me, and I count myself
> proud and happy to have served as your First Minister . . .

The aftershock of Suez, Eden's resignation and the manner of his
replacement were to have serious repercussions for Elizabeth, making
her for the first time the target of criticism more direct than any aimed
at a monarch since the wave of carping against what was seen as Queen
Victoria's selfish and self-imposed isolation in the 1870s. Eden himself
took no direct part in the choice of his successor; he believed
scrupulously in the Queen's right of choice in the matter, but his
suggestion that Lord Salisbury should take soundings from the Cabinet
led afterwards to accusations of an establishment 'fix'. Eden's resignation came as a total surprise to the Cabinet as a whole. Harold
Macmillan, then Chancellor of the Exchequer, one of the two principal
candidates, had been told personally by Eden that afternoon, in an
emotional meeting in which both had recalled their cathartic experience
of the Great War and their subsequent political careers. 'I can see him
now on that sad winter afternoon, still looking so youthful, so gay, so
debonair,' Macmillan recalled, ' – the representative of all that was
best in the youth that had served in the 1914–1918 War.' The

subsequent Cabinet meeting in which Eden announced his decision was short but emotional. Salisbury was almost in tears as he spoke of his lifelong friendship with Eden; both Butler and Macmillan said a few words, then left the Cabinet to deliberate the succession. 'It was all over,' Macmillan wrote, 'a dramatic end to an extraordinary and, in many ways, unique career. What seemed so dreadful was that he waited so long for the Premiership, and held it for so short a time.'[20]

Then began the ritual dance of the choice of the chieftain. The members of the Cabinet were called individually, 'like schoolboys to the headmaster's study', as most of them described the experience, to be interviewed by Salisbury, accompanied by the Lord Chancellor, Lord Kilmuir, in Salisbury's room at the Privy Council offices. Salisbury, who mispronounced his 'r's', was brief and to the point: 'Well, which is it?' he asked each one. 'Wab [Butler] or Hawold [Macmillan]?' The consensus of opinion was overwhelmingly for 'Hawold'; only one minister plumped for 'Wab'. Salisbury also consulted the Chief Whip, Edward Heath, the Party Chairman and the Chairman of the 1922 Committee, all of whom recommended Macmillan. Butler's equivocation over Suez had won him no friends; Heath's findings mirrored those of the Cabinet majority, that there was a lot of strong feeling in the party against Butler but not much against Macmillan. The following day Salisbury went to the Palace to tell Elizabeth the results of the soundings while Adeane consulted two influential Conservative peers, Lords Chandos and Waverley. Churchill arrived at the Palace; no one at court had at first thought to contact him nor had he wanted to be involved, having refused a call from Eden to come up to London from Chartwell. But his secretary, Anthony Montague-Browne, thought of appearances. 'I prompted Adeane,' he told Churchill's biographer. 'He *ought* to be seen to go to the Palace.' Churchill also recommended Macmillan, as he later told Butler: 'Well, old cock, you're not such a bad old thing. You looked after me when I was ill. But I told her to choose the older man. Harold's ten [he was actually eight] years older than you . . .'

And so, the sixty-two-year-old Harold Macmillan, calming his nerves by reading *Pride and Prejudice* as he waited at his official residence, No. 11 Downing Street, next door to the Prime Minister's at No. 10 and symbolically linked to it by the umbilical cord of an internal corridor, became the Queen's next Prime Minister. Elizabeth was brief but friendly as she received him at the Palace shortly after two o'clock on the afternoon of 10 January. She already knew him; as

Secretary of State for Defence, Foreign Secretary and Chancellor of the Exchequer in Churchill's and Eden's administrations, she had had occasion to see him several times on official business, but this, as Macmillan wrote in his diary, was the beginning of a quite different relationship. In other words, Elizabeth knew Macmillan superficially and by reputation; she was soon to know him intimately. Macmillan was a complex man; as a politician he was a curious mixture of idealism, histrionics, Machiavellian guile and ruthlessness. As a man he was inhibited, vulnerable, intelligent and highly cultivated, yet uncertain of himself and given to fits of depression – the 'Black Dog' which haunted Churchill. All this he concealed under an impeccably establishment exterior: the erect bearing and strict dress codes of an officer of the elite Brigade of Guards in which he had served during the First World War. He was a member of the exclusive White's Club in St James's, then the preserve of the land-owning aristocracy, and he was married to a daughter of one of England's grandest dukes, the Duke of Devonshire, owner of Chatsworth and numerous other houses and estates, including that ultimate symbol of privilege, a first-class Yorkshire grouse moor. His wife, Lady Dorothy's, reaction to the summons to the Palace typified that of the real grandee: 'What do *they* want?' The abiding image of Macmillan stamped on the public mind during the years of his premiership was of a figure in tweed plus-fours, shotgun clamped to shoulder or elegantly angled over his arm, grouse-shooting on some landowner's moor. The reality was very different; Macmillan was the grandson of a poor Scottish crofter and his grand relations by marriage tended to regard him as an earnest bore, certainly not as 'one of us'. In private life he was lonely and suffered from the constant humiliation of his wife's longstanding affair with a fellow Conservative MP, the witty and popular Robert 'Bob' Boothby, a fact which was well known in the circles in which they moved. This private loneliness, coupled with the isolation of his office 'at the top of the greasy pole', as Disraeli put it, made his relationship with Elizabeth particularly important to him on a personal level, even if he had not held the old-fashioned but strictly constitutional view of his position in relation to her. 'The Prime Minister is above all the Queen's First Minister,' he wrote in his memoirs. 'His supreme loyalty is to her.'

Macmillan's appointment was greeted by a wave of surprised disapproval from the general public, who had been led to believe by the newspapers that Butler would be the man. The implication was that Elizabeth had been persuaded by her father's old friend, 'Bobbety'

Salisbury, into appointing one of his own kind, the son-in-law of a duke, over the meritorious Butler. The truth was that there had been a perfectly proper consultation with the leading representatives of the Conservative Party; moreover, Salisbury did not, apparently, much care personally for Macmillan, but that was not how it appeared. If a Mr Salisbury had been the channel of communication by which the Queen had appointed a man whose wife was a plain Mrs, the theory is unlikely to have taken hold. Much was also made of Macmillan taking Heath to a celebratory dinner of champagne and oysters at the Turf Club, then the stamping-ground of racing bluebloods. In emphasising this they chose to ignore the fact that Macmillan's guest, Edward Heath, who as Chief Whip was there to discuss the formation of the new administration, was the son of a small businessman with his own building and decorating firm in Broadstairs, Kent. What they saw was a procession of peers to the Palace including two, Chandos and Waverley, who were not even in the Government; the conclusion was that Elizabeth, in the grip of the old aristocratic ruling class, had appointed the Prime Minister of their choice. Elizabeth has been accused of a 'miscalculation' in being seen to accept their recommendation and of naïveté in not realising the view which public opinion would take of this. To be fair, the fault lay rather in the old 'magic circle' system by which the Conservative leader emerged, which involved her in the appearance of a conspiracy when there was not, as there had been in the case of Eden, an obvious candidate. And it had been the outgoing Prime Minister, Eden himself, who had suggested that Salisbury head the consultation process. What is true, however, is that Elizabeth and her advisers in Downing Street and the Palace had not caught up with the deep change in British attitudes which was just beginning to emerge.

Suez was the catalyst for this change. It had an effect upon the British psyche as traumatic as the war in Vietnam had upon the Americans' view of themselves and their role in the world. In the words of Macmillan's biographer, the British people went to bed one night regarding themselves as belonging to a power of the first rank when Nasser nationalised the Suez Canal on 26 July 1956 and woke up to the reality of relegation to the second division, no longer capable of manipulating their global destinies in the imperial manner of the past. Nothing could ever be the same again; people were angry and bewildered and looking for scapegoats. Just to make things worse, the Hungarian uprising had taken place at the same time and been crushed without help from the West, preoccupied by an unnecessary post-imperial adventure. The cause of the disaster seemed to lie in outdated establishment attitudes orchestrated by men living in a past which was no longer relevant. Newsreel pictures of the time looked and sounded as if they might have been recorded in the 1930s; plummy-voiced commentators talked about 'our men' and 'giving Nasser a lesson'. Eden's reaction to Nasser was born out of his experiences in the 1930s and his reaction to Nasser and the Suez Canal in 1956 was Pavlovian, the same as it had been to Hitler and Munich a generation before. Elizabeth, whose image at the Coronation had so recently been linked with the traditional splendours of Britain's historic past, was bound to suffer when Suez revealed that the emperor had no clothes. The monarchy had become the symbol of the nation; in traumatised post-Suez Britain the question was bound to be raised whether that image was the right one. The manner of Macmillan's appointment and the outcome of the Townsend–Margaret affair, when the Queen's sister had been seen as a victim of outdated attitudes, reinforced the impression of a Britain ruled in its own interests by a traditional class with the monarchy as the gilded front for its corruption.

John Osborne, then billed by the newspapers as the Angry Young Man after the success of his play on working-class life, *Look Back in Anger*, used almost exactly the same words when he attacked the monarchy in October 1957 in an article actually written in the aftermath of Suez: 'My objection to the Royal symbol is that it is dead; it is a gold filling in a mouth full of decay.' He described royalty worship as a 'fatuous industry' sustained by empty minds and empty lives. 'When the mobs rush forward in the Mall,' he said, 'they are taking part in the last circus of a civilisation that has lost faith in itself and sold itself for a splendid triviality.' Malcolm Muggeridge, TV pundit and ex-editor of *Punch*, analysed the current passion for the royal family as 'the royal soap opera . . . a sort of substitute or ersatz religion'. Muggeridge's remarks (in an article for the *Saturday Evening Post*) were widely misrepresented in the British press as a personal attack on the royal family and Muggeridge was banned from the BBC, but neither his nor Osborne's criticisms were directed at Elizabeth herself. That task was undertaken by a young peer, the thirty-three-year-old Lord Altrincham, who found himself famous, or rather notorious, overnight after the publication in August 1957 of his periodical, the *National and English Review*, an issue devoted to articles

on the monarchy by such figures as Dermot Morrah, royal correspondent of *The Times* and Arundel Herald Extraordinary.

In his own introductory piece Altrincham turned a critical eye on
Elizabeth, although the main focus of his attack was upon her courtiers.
'The Queen's entourage', he wrote, 'are almost without exception the
"tweedy" sort' who had failed to live with the times. While the
monarchy had become 'popular' and multi-racial (by which he meant
in its relations with the Commonwealth), the royal household had
remained 'a tight little enclave of British ladies and gentlemen' who
might be 'shrewd, broad-minded and thoroughly suitable for positions
at Court', but the same could equally well be said of people from any
other background. In any case, said Altrincham, the fact that the
Queen's staff was so restricted, socially and ethnically, created an
unfortunate impression. On the social side it seemed 'utterly absurd'
to him that the presentation parties for debutantes which should have
been 'quietly discontinued in 1945' were still being held every year.
'Inevitably they made the monarchy seem to be identified with a
particular class.' When tackled by reporters, Altrincham spoke quite
plainly about certain officials of the Queen's household, specifically the
Lord Chamberlain, the Earl of Scarbrough, Sir Michael Adeane, and
the Master of the Horse, the Duke of Beaufort, describing them as
'not imaginative, a second-rate lot, simply lacking in gumption'.

The passages of Altrincham's article which caused the greatest
sensation were those which were interpreted and quoted as direct
criticism of Elizabeth, although Altrincham had intended them to
illustrate how her 'true character' was being misrepresented by her
advisers who made her behave and speak in a quite unnatural manner.
Their motivation was, he said, that they were afraid that the mystique
of monarchy would be threatened if her public words and actions
resembled those of a normal person of her age. Her speeches were
'prim little sermons' and her style of speaking 'a pain in the neck'.
'The personality conveyed by the utterances which are put into her
mouth is that of a priggish schoolgirl, captain of the hockey team, a
prefect and a recent candidate for confirmation.' Most people who had
not read the original article but only garbled newspaper versions took
this as a reference not to the content of the speeches but to Elizabeth's
voice, which is, like her mother's, high and girlish with a 'cut-glass
accent'. Altrincham compounded his sin by appearing to include the
revered Queen Mother in his strictures:

Like her mother she [the Queen] appears to be unable to string even a few sentences together without a written text. When she has lost the bloom of youth, the Queen's reputation will depend, far more than it does now, upon her personality. It will not then be enough for her to go through the motions; she will have to say things which people can remember and do things on her own initiative which will make people sit up and take notice. As yet there is little sign that such a personality is emerging . . .

Altrincham was publicly physically attacked in front of television cameras by a sixty-four-year-old empire loyalist, who was lying in wait for him as he came out of Broadcasting House. The borough of Altrincham in Cheshire from which his father, Edward Grigg, a distinguished civil servant, had taken his title, disowned him (as soon as he was legally allowed to in 1963, Altrincham repaid the compliment by giving up his peerage, becoming known as John Grigg). In the storm of abuse that descended upon his head, no one listened to Altrincham's reasons for writing what he did. They were in fact the same as had motivated Osborne and Muggeridge: dismay at the mindless adulation of the monarchy which had developed since the death of George VI and the crowning of his daughter.

Something uncomfortably akin to Japanese Shintoism was in the air [he later wrote]. After the Second World War the monarchy reverted to its prewar routines almost as though nothing had happened, and virtually no changes were introduced by the Queen when she succeeded her father in 1952. At the same time public attitudes towards the monarchy were marked by a degree of blandness and servility quite alien to the British tradition. There was much fatuous talk of a new Elizabethan age, though the age was, in fact, as unlike that of the first Elizabeth as the young Queen herself was unlike her illustrious predecessor. Britain seemed to be compensating for loss of power in the world by lapsing into a state of collective make-believe, in which the hieratic aspects of the monarchy were grossly exaggerated and the healthy habit of criticising office-holders was ceasing to apply to the monarch.[21]

Significantly, for all the indignant talk of horse-whipping and cries of 'bounder', a *Daily Mail* poll found that its younger readers between the ages of sixteen and thirty-four agreed with Altrincham and among all age groups a majority thought that the court circle should be widened. The image of the young Elizabeth as the prisoner of a circle of elderly men and outdated attitudes, reinforced by the myths surrounding Macmillan's appointment, was a powerful one. For the first time the spotlight was turned critically on all areas of Elizabeth's life, both public and private.

10

Tweed and Diamonds

'Poor young Altrincham ... saying that the Queen was dull
and surrounded by dull people and that she cared only for
horses and made platitudinous speeches, has got into a frightful
row ... Yet essentially what he said was true.'

Harold Nicolson, Diary, 7 August 1957[1]

Elizabeth was furious with Altrincham. Although personally the least
self-important of women, she had the same sense of the position of the
sovereign and the monarchy as any of her predecessors. She had, in
fact, been planning to dispense with the outdated ritual of debutante
presentation parties, but, according to one court source, 'she carried
on with them for one more year just to show that she wasn't going to
bow to Altrincham'.

The truth was that the guard was changing slowly but almost
imperceptibly at Buckingham Palace. Philip's charge towards modernisation had not made much headway even after the departure of
Lascelles in 1953 after the Coronation. Lascelles had unfortunately
crowned his career by causing Elizabeth unwittingly to offend the
Scots. When she visited her Scottish kingdom on her Coronation tour
in June 1953, Lascelles had advised her to wear day clothes for the
most solemn ceremony of all: the presentation of the Honours of
Scotland – crown, sceptre and sword – in St Giles's Cathedral. After
the huge pomp and ceremony in London, Elizabeth's simplicity was
taken not as a gesture to austerity and democracy but as a Sassenach
snub. Lascelles refused the customary peerage offered to a departing
Private Secretary and was annoyed when Churchill recommended him
for the Grand Cross of the Bath (with the title of 'Sir'). He lived on
for another thirty years, the repository of many secrets that he had
confided to his diary, snippets of which he would show to friends or

favoured historians. Even in his days at court he had unbuttoned with people he liked, such as Harold Nicolson. 'Assuredly Tommy is the most uncourtierly courtier,' Nicolson confided in *his* diary after a revealing conversation with Lascelles. Sections of Lascelles's diary have been published in expurgated volumes; the rest is embargoed at Windsor until some unspecified time in the next century. Lascelles became surprisingly mellow and relaxed on his release from court life, cultivating his literary tastes (his diary shows that he was a writer manqué); his portrait, commissioned by Elizabeth, shows him bearded, wearing a high-necked sweater and tweed jacket like the artist he felt that at heart he was and quite unlike the 'stuffed shirt' image of his courtier days.

Lascelles's replacement as Elizabeth's Private Secretary, Sir Michael Adeane, who was to serve the Queen for nearly twenty years from 1953 to 1972, could have been described as 'Palace-bred'. Born in 1910, he was the grandson of Lord Stamfordham, Assistant Private Secretary to Queen Victoria and Private Secretary to George V as Prince of Wales and as King. Stamfordham had not belonged to the high aristocracy, being born plain Arthur Bigge, the son of a Northumbrian parson, but he was perhaps the most influential Private Secretary of the century upon whom George V greatly depended and in whom he had confided since his youth. He relied on Stamfordham for advice on everything, even the name of his dynasty. It was at Stamfordham's suggestion that the name Windsor had been chosen in 1917. His grandson, Michael Adeane, had the establishment background characteristic of top household officials: Eton and Cambridge, then a commission in his father's regiment, the Coldstream Guards. After serving as an aide-de-camp to the Governor-General of Canada, Lord Tweedsmuir (the writer John Buchan), he had joined the royal household in 1937 as an Assistant Private Secretary to George VI until war broke out, when he had returned to his regiment. In 1945 he came back to his job at the Palace before succeeding Lascelles as Private Secretary. Adeane was the ideal royal official, intelligent, self-effacing and not without the sense of humour necessary to survive life at court. He certainly showed the self-control and calm temperament which enabled him to cope in the famous story of how one day, as he was hurrying out of Buckingham Palace on an urgent mission, he was accosted by a royal biographer with questions to ask. With impeccable courtesy he stood listening, showing merely the faintest sign of wanting to leave, but it was only after several minutes that he said, 'I do hope you'll forgive me, but I've just heard that my house is on fire. I wouldn't mind but as it's part of St James's Palace . . .'

Adeane was generally regarded as a 'safe pair of hands'; the Palace job fitted him like a glove and to Elizabeth he represented continuity, tradition and caution, qualities which she appreciated. Altrincham's naming of Adeane as among the 'second-rate lot . . . lacking in gumption' was unfair, on academic grounds alone – he had a First Class degree in History from Cambridge. 'Michael Adeane was highly civilised,' his artist friend, John Ward, RA, whom he introduced to the royal household, said. 'He drew and did watercolours. He was a very distinguished, shrewd man, who would face difficulties head on and never evade anything.' He was, however, more inclined to a cautious conservatism and old-fashioned attitudes than his colleagues in the Private Office. Alone among the Palace Secretaries he was a supporter of the Suez operation and he was more likely than the other two men in the Private Office to take the view that what was good enough in his grandfather's time was good enough for him.

The Hon. Martin Charteris (now Lord Charteris of Amisfield), educated at Eton and the Royal Military College at Sandhurst, the grandson of an earl and a duke, had the ideal background for the royal household, but lacked the blinkered approach and faint touch of pomposity that often went with it. Highly intelligent and cultivated, he had a puckish sense of humour and a quizzical approach to life which lightened the atmosphere in the Private Secretaries' Office. Charteris's charm concealed a nimble and far-seeing mind and his relaxed manner a consummate diplomatic ability and a steely resolve in defence of his Queen. He was and is one of the few courtiers who realised that openness is the best defence against prying and that an air of concealment only strengthens a journalist's determination to investigate. Equally, as a loyal friend and servant to Elizabeth, he was prepared to tell her things he thought she should know but about which others had not dared to approach her. He discovered a hidden talent for sculpture when Oscar Nemon was working on a portrait bust of the Queen and later in life became an honorary Fellow of the Royal Academy. He was devoted to Elizabeth and, as he freely admitted, had been a little in love with her since first meeting her on his appointment as her Private Secretary when she was Princess Elizabeth. 'There was definitely a twinkle in the Queen's relationship with Martin,' a courtier said.

His colleague, Edward Ford, once described himself as 'encircled by dog collars'. He was the son of a Dean of York, headmaster of Harrow, and grandson of a Bishop of Westminster, one of his uncles was Bishop of Pretoria and another was a monk. His own training was legal and military. Educated at Eton and New College, Oxford, he had trained as a lawyer before the war (as a pupil in the chambers of Ronald Armstrong-Jones, father of Princess Margaret's future husband), then fought in the Grenadier Guards. His introduction to the Palace came through Lascelles, whose only son he had tutored; he had worked as Assistant Private Secretary to George VI and continued in the same job under Elizabeth. Tall and dark with the leonine head of a nineteenth-century bishop, he, like Charteris, was worldly and had a lively sense of humour. Both of them, privately, thought some of Altrincham's strictures were 'the best thing that had happened to the Palace for years'.

The same could not be said of the Queen's Press Secretary, Commander Richard Colville, whom, like several other officials, she had inherited from her father. Colville, a relation of Jock, was described by Peter Townsend as 'a thin man, with a thin face, straight black hair, black-rimmed spectacles and dressed (invariably, it seemed) in formal black clothes'. He had 'distinguished himself gallantly' in the Navy during the Second World War and his attitude to journalists was that of the press-gang rather than the press officer. 'I am not', he informed a visiting Canadian newspaperman who asked to see round Buckingham Palace, 'what you North Americans would call a public relations man.' Born in 1907, he was already middle-aged by the time he was appointed Press Secretary in 1947 and remained there until 1968, as resolutely defensive of his Queen throughout the Swinging Sixties as he had been in his naval days. He had had absolutely no previous qualification for the job and was incapable of making any distinction between scandal-mongers and serious journalists. 'All were made to feel', George V's biographer, Kenneth Rose, wrote, 'that their questions were impertinent if not downright vulgar.' Colville was a protagonist of the siege mentality at Buckingham Palace which has caused so much friction between Palace officials, newspapermen and writers and which earned him a rebuke from the Press Council. 'Press inquiries', Rose wrote, 'were met at best with guarded courtesy, sometimes with impatient disdain, never with good humour.' He was prepared to answer questions about the Queen's public engagements but was reluctant to trespass on what he conceived to be her private life, telling the Press Council that in his view the Queen was 'entitled to expect that her family will attain the privacy at home which all other families are entitled to enjoy'. The Press Council replied that 'the private lives of public men and women, especially royal persons, have always been the subject of natural curiosity. That is one of the consequences of fame or eminence or sincere national affection. Everything therefore that touches the Crown is of public interest and concern.'[2] It was the beginning of a battle of views which was to rage with increasing vigour over the following years of Elizabeth's reign. Some people, not least Elizabeth herself, might feel that the pendulum was to swing too far away from Commander Colville's 'right to silence' as far as the private life of the royal family was concerned.

Not all the courtiers whom Elizabeth inherited from her father were elderly or even middle-aged. Patrick, 7th Baron Plunket, whom she had known since childhood, was only three years older than she was. His family had enjoyed a special relationship with her family; his parents, Terence 'Teddy' and Dorothé, had been close friends of her mother and father when they were still the Yorks. Terence Plunket, the 6th Baron, had been a handsome, amusing Anglo-Irish aristocrat, a good raconteur and a talented portraitist who specialised in caricatures of his friends; Dorothé, his wife, was half-American, the daughter of Cecil B. de Mille's leading lady, Fannie Ward, and 'Diamond Joe' Lewis, who had made a fortune (and lost most of it) in South Africa with Solly Joel and 'Babe' Barnato. The Plunkets were members of the international set; they were on their way in a private plane to a party to be given for them by William Randolph Hearst in California in the spring of 1938 when the plane crashed, killing them both. Patrick, the eldest of three brothers, was just fifteen, but he was old enough, after Eton and Cambridge, to enlist in the Irish Guards and pick up a wound in the 1939–45 war. King George VI had appointed him an equerry and the Queen made him her Deputy Master of the Household in 1954. Patrick Plunket was not at all 'tweedy'; like his parents, he was amusing and had taste and a gift for entertaining. He loved masterminding the grand occasions – the Queen's banquets and state receptions, the house-parties for Ascot week at Windsor – and with a wide circle of friends outside the hunting, shooting and racing people Elizabeth had been used to, he livened up the guest list. Rooms would be decorated with pyramids of delphinium spires or entire syringa trees, and the tables with Georgian silver he had hunted out of the strongrooms. Plunket was a connoisseur with a collector's eye for paintings and furniture; he was a trustee of the Wallace Collection and the National Art Collections Fund and played an important advisory role in transforming the bomb-damaged Royal Chapel (in which Elizabeth had been christened) into the Queen's Gallery, opened in 1962 to the public for exhibitions of works of art from the royal collections. Patrick Plunket was a genuine friend of Elizabeth's, an antidote to the horsey, 'tweedy' friends like the Rupert Nevills, who encouraged her more philistine and anti-intellectual tendencies.

The structure and titles of the officers and officials of Elizabeth's court remained the same as they had for her forebears, with the Lord Chamberlain (then the Earl of Scarbrough) at the head of the household, with, under him, the heads of the six departments. These include the Private Secretary, who deals with the Queen's official business; the Keeper of the Privy Purse (then Lord Tryon, whose name was made the object of much mirth during the debates on the Queen's Civil List in 1962), who acts as the Queen's treasurer; and the Comptroller in the Lord Chamberlain's Office, responsible for great royal occasions such as weddings and funerals, and more mundane affairs such as garden-parties, investitures and the organisation of state visits by foreign heads of state. Until 1987 the Lord Chamberlain's Office also controlled the royal collections of books, paintings, furniture and works of art with their respective Librarian and Surveyors. Within the scope of the Lord Chamberlain's Office are lords-in-waiting, gentlemen-at-arms, Yeomen of the Guard, the Royal Company of Archers, the Marshal of the Diplomatic Corps, the Secretary of the Central Chancery in charge of the various Orders, and exotic figures like the Queen's Bargemaster and the Royal Watermen; the Comptroller also supervises the annual upping of the Queen's swans. Other departments are those of the Master of the Household, with responsibility for domestic arrangements, staff, catering and entertaining, and the Crown Equerry, in charge of the Royal Mews, which includes horses, carriages, cars and attendant staff. Among the Lord Chamberlain's ceremonial duties is to attend the Queen on such occasions as state banquets when he has the unenviable task of walking backwards in front of her holding his white staff of office until she reaches her seat, and at the funeral of the sovereign he breaks this staff over the royal coffin before it is interred (this is easier than it sounds, made foolproof by the fact that the staff is constructed in two parts screwed together). The three so-called 'Great Officers of State' whose titles date back to the Middle Ages – the Lord Steward, the Master of the Horse and the Lord Great Chamberlain (whose office is hereditary and held by the Marquesses of Cholmondeley for alternate reigns) – are not required to do anything beyond occasional ceremonial duties.

The Mistress of the Robes (almost always a duchess – the Duchess of Devonshire in 1957) is the grandest of the Queen's Ladies. She has nothing to do with the Queen's clothes and her duties are largely honorary, being in charge of the rota of the ladies-in-waiting and attendance on state occasions and important state visits. Below her come the Ladies of the Bedchamber, usually the wives of peers who attend the Queen on important occasions and foreign tours but do not do the everyday work like the other ladies-in-waiting, the four Women of the Bedchamber. These are almost always titled and attend the Queen on public and semi-private occasions, make her private as opposed to official arrangements, deal with her private correspondence and letters written to her by children, and do her personal shopping for presents, etc. They work on fortnightly rotas and beyond perks like bed and board at the various royal palaces and residences (if they want it) get very little remuneration. They were and are recruited informally on the basis of private recommendation and personality; Elizabeth has to feel that they are the kind of person she feels at home with and can share jokes with.

Elizabeth's domestic staff has always been important to her; they are never to be referred to as servants. It was through her closeness to certain key figures such as Bobo and Bennett that she learned what really went on in the Palace and among the staff. Elizabeth liked to feel she was in charge. At Buckingham Palace, unlike Clarence House, she was the dominant figure. 'I always found from my very young days', a senior member of her staff recalled, 'that if anything was wrong it was far better to go and say so to her ... I always felt I could tell the Queen anything and she would be understanding ... quietly, perhaps she might have been a bit irritated but she was always very good if you told her the truth about it. I've known people to try and pull the wool over her eyes but she was quite cross when she found out that they weren't telling her exactly the gospel truth ...' Importance in the Palace domestic hierarchy depends on the proximity which a position brings them in relation to the Queen. Elizabeth was surrounded by familiar figures, such as Cyril Dickman, who had been nursery footman at Windsor during the war and was to rise steadily through the ranks of seniority to the top job of Palace Steward, and Ernest 'Bennie' Bennett, her butler at Clarence House, who became the Queen's Page, one of the Palace positions which brings its holder into close personal touch with the sovereign.

Elizabeth, as an executive woman at a high level, still felt compelled to do not only the job her father had done as sovereign but also the one her mother had done as royal hostess.

> She must have an iron constitution [a member of her staff said], considering the amount of official work, ceremonial stuff, she had to do. Obviously she had the Master of the Household to look after the running of it but she didn't go round with her eyes shut. In fact she was very quick at seeing anything or picking up on anything and she liked to know what was going to happen. For instance, before a big dinner or people coming, she was always very concerned about the arrangements . . . she always used to go around the vistors' rooms, see they're right, papers there, stationery, all the lamps lit, all that sort of thing. She'd be concerned whether they were going to have chocolates in their room and drinks in their room . . . she concerned herself with all that detail . . . She would look at the books in the rooms and if it was somebody she particularly knew their likes and dislikes she might think one of them was unsuitable or she'd say, 'Get it out of the library and put it there.' She always passed the menu every day. She would get the menu book up at breakfast time . . .

Bobo, of course, headed the list in terms of real power and influence and continued to do so until incapacitated by old age. Although officially termed the Queen's dresser (there are always two) and answerable to the Master of the Household, in practice Bobo regarded herself as answerable only to Elizabeth. She felt herself perfectly within her rights to ignore the dictates of successive Masters of the Household if they did not suit her – attempts to limit the tray service to which she was accustomed at Sandringham were doomed to failure. Even senior male members of the royal household like Boy Browning were frightened of her. 'I've heard her be quite acid to some Members of the Household,' a colleague said. Her power lay in her intense loyalty and absolute devotion to her 'Little Lady'. 'She adored the Queen and had a tremendous grip on the Queen's possessions,' a member of the household said. 'She was a no-nonsense Scot and jolly tough.' 'She had a great influence on the Queen,' a fellow staff member said. 'She was a formidable lady. I got on with her very well but I had to be careful in everything I said or did. Miss MacDonald to a great degree was the Queen's eyes and ears at the Palace and it didn't do you any good to fall foul of Miss MacDonald. If things went wrong Miss MacDonald would make more fuss than the Queen would. If you upset Miss MacDonald it was for life ...' Elizabeth's respect for Bobo's utter integrity as far as she was concerned, coupled with the habit of a lifetime since the nursery, meant that she would give in to Bobo. 'If the Queen said something and Miss MacDonald said something else – then it would probably go Bobo's way.' 'She was very protective of the Queen and she made sure that no one took any advantage and she would also guide the Queen on the track that she thought she should go with clothes or what she was going to do ... if the Queen was doing things she thought she shouldn't, she'd tell her she was wrong but she certainly didn't boss her about.' But Bobo, it was rumoured, was the one person at the Palace who could make Elizabeth cry.

One of Bobo's particular spheres of interest was dealing with the Queen's dressmakers. She would attend the sessions with Norman Hartnell and Hardy Amies, and later Ian Thomas and a tailor, John Anderson. Mr Rayne, who went to the Palace in a morning suit, designed her shoes; and, in those days, her milliners were Aage Thaarup, who was responsible for her much-criticised hats, and Simone Mirman. (Latterly her milliner has been Frederick Fox, a favourite with royal ladies.) All of them were kept strictly in their place, but Hardy Amies, who once made some unfortunate remark which was repeated to Bobo and interpreted by her as criticism, was a particular *bête noire*. He was never forgiven. Elizabeth loyally stuck by him, but there were battles which Bobo inevitably won. If she did not like a dress, it would be put away, perhaps only to be brought out forty years later after she retired. She would limit the dressmakers' power by not allowing them any influence over the accessories, be they shoes, hats or handbags. If one of them dared to make a suggestion, Bobo would say tartly, 'You know you're here for the clothes not the accessories.' She would never let Elizabeth have an expensive handbag because it offended her Scottish ideas of thrift.

Elizabeth has never been a fashion victim, but, one of her milliners said, 'She's interested in the way she looks, likes to have clothes that work, that are easy. She likes to be comfortable.' To her, clothes are props, a part of her job, which is why she likes clear colours that stand out, like cantaloupe or turquoise. 'I can't wear beige because people won't know who I am,' she will say. Black is never allowed, which is a pity because she looks fabulous in it, nor are dark colours because they

photograph as black. Elizabeth has very definite ideas as to what will
suit her – 'That's too chic for me,' she will say. When wide power
shoulders were fashionable, she would say, 'Oh, it's all right for Miss
[Joan] Collins but it's not really for me, is it?' She shortened her skirt
lengths in the 1960s, but always tried a dress out by sitting down in it
to see how far it rode up. Her yardstick is appropriateness, suiting the
dress to the occasion – she always has to look like the Queen. 'When
the Queen comes in it's an appearance,' one of her dressmakers said,
'so she knows that it's got to be a hat, that's politeness to her audience,
she's got to be dressed up. So at 10 o'clock in the morning the Queen
is dressed in afternoon clothes.' The unchanging image is in the Queen
Mary tradition; in this, as in so many other ways of being royal,
'Grannie' has been an influence. In the same way, her much-criticised
hairstyle never changes, partly because for continuity of image she has
to look the same for coins and stamps, partly because it has to be a
style which can be quickly adapted to hats for formal day occasions
and a tiara for evening, and partly because she likes to employ the
same personnel. (She has used only two hairdressers during her long
reign; the present one, Mr Charles Martyn, has worked for her since
1968.) She is intensely practical about clothes as about everything else
– when she gave a state banquet for the Reagans in California, Amies
had designed a dress with huge bows on the shoulders that looked
quite inappropriate with her long earrings and tiara. 'It was entirely
our fault,' Amies said, but the Queen said, 'Oh, don't go on about it. I
think it's a very pretty dress and I'm going to like it. Just take the
bows off . . .' However outspoken Bobo might have been, Elizabeth's
manners with her dressmakers are always 'impeccable'; she never says
she doesn't like something, just conveys by raising an eyebrow that
something is not quite right.

Although she is only 5ft 3in, she can wear with unselfconscious
assurance jewellery which on most women would look vulgar or
overdone. She carries herself with a natural dignity and she moves
well. 'The Queen has an aura,' one of her royal relations said. Yet
despite being the owner of one of the most fabulous jewellery
collections in the world, she is not particularly interested in it and
leaves the choice of what she wears to her dresser. She often forgets
what pieces she happens to have on – on one occasion Margaret
commented on a particularly pretty brooch her sister was wearing;
'Oh, do you think so?' Elizabeth said vaguely. '*I* gave it to you,' said
the Queen Mother. The image most people have of the Queen off-

duty is of a countrywoman wearing the inevitable headscarf tied under the chin in a style first fashionable in the early 1950s, riding in hacking jacket and jodhpurs or walking her dogs wearing a mackintosh and tweed or tartan skirt. On less strenuous occasions at home in the country the skirt would appear with the timeless twinset and pearls.

Basically, as Altrincham had diagnosed, the atmosphere at Elizabeth II's court was almost indistinguishable from that under George VI, reflecting what Lacey called 'the confined perspectives of her upbringing'. Elizabeth had been brought up in a male-dominated world and was content for it to remain that way. She preferred dealing with men; neither Elizabeth nor her mother or her sister makes any secret of their preference for the company and conversation of men over women. Her work, the political side in particular, meant that she came in contact almost exclusively with men. She was the dominant figure in a man's world; her position included being head of her armed forces. As the daughter and granddaughter of serving officers, as, however briefly, an officer herself, and as Colonel of the Grenadier Guards, she had a special understanding of that world too. 'The Palace ethos', a royal observer said, 'is that of a Guards regiment.'

None of the top household officials were women; women remained in their traditional sphere as Ladies of the Bedchamber or ladies-in-waiting or, on a lesser level, lady clerks. Educationally and temperamentally women were not considered to be up to the top jobs in the household, any more than they were in the political and business world of the day. Elizabeth chose her ladies from personal knowledge or recommendation, principally for their ability to get on with people. The Palace had to run without friction, which was one reason why the members tended to come from the same group or class, not to put too fine a point on it. Personal ambition for promotion or for money was out of place; sucking-up to the boss was frowned upon. For most courtiers it was an unbroken rule not to get too close to any particular member of the family. It was no coincidence that the top officials had public school and military backgrounds; it meant that they were used to a clearly defined hierarchy and a chain of command. The lady clerks and even the younger ladies-in-waiting were in awe of the Private Secretaries. Everyone knew their place and the system worked like clockwork. It had another – financial – advantage; everyone in the household, from top to bottom, worked for far less money than they would have earned outside. It was considered an honour to work for the Queen and, in return, there was a sense of community, of being looked after, of being part of a great national institution which was run on a personal basis with the rewards of grace-and-favour accommodation, free board and lodging. It was feudal but not oppressive with a comforting sense of continuity, like working for a great estate.

Altrincham had hit the nail on the head when he called Elizabeth's courtiers 'tweedy'; she is 'tweedy' herself. As a child she had told her riding master, Horace Smith, that she would like to be 'a lady living in the country, with lots of dogs and horses'. Breeding and training gundogs and thoroughbreds are her two private interests, both of which she approaches with her usual professionalism. She breeds labradors and spaniels at Sandringham and is very knowledgeable about gundogs. 'Because she's the Queen, people wouldn't quite believe how knowledgeable she is on them,' one of her Sandringham employees said. 'And she does understand them, she doesn't put up with any nonsense from them and if they are going to be a bit wayward she would deal with them on the spot, how they should be dealt with.' 'She doesn't have much time to train them but she has a terrific ability to take a dog off anyone . . . she could go to the kennels and take over a dog that was trained or part-trained and take it for a walk and the dog would stick to her like glue and this is strange, really, because whoever has handled them and fed them and trained the dog, it takes a bit to get them away from them . . .' She is also regarded as an expert 'picker-up', directing up to four dogs to retrieve wounded birds at a shoot, which requires knowledge of wind direction, natural cover, the way the birds are flying and where the wounded birds are likely to make for. She learned this on her own initiative; the King did not encourage her, feeling that it was not right that princesses should be working gun-dogs in the shooting field. When he wouldn't allow her to handle his labradors at Balmoral, she would just go ahead with her corgis; when she became Queen and inherited Sandringham, she came into her own. Elizabeth is competitive; she looks for excellence and likes to win. She was to improve the standard of the Sandringham gun-dogs so that over the years of her reign they were to win top dog prizes in the Game Fair International four times and achieved field trial champion status.

Elizabeth's real passion is for breeding and racing thoroughbreds, something which she inherited from her grandfather, George V, who named a bay filly Lilibet after her. 'No owner was keener or took a greater interest in his horses than he did . . . not only in racing . . . but even more in the breeding and welfare of the young stock,' the King's

Sandringham stud manager wrote. When George VI succeeded, he admitted to his father's stud manager that he knew 'nothing about breeding or anything else', but he took a great interest in his two strings of racehorses – 'the Hirelings', Big Game and Sun Chariot, which his racing manager, Charles Moore, leased from the National Stud and trained with Fred Darling at Beckhampton from 1940, and his own horses, divided between studs at Hampton Court, Sandringham and Wolferton (which is at Sandringham), which were trained at Newmarket by Cecil Boyd-Rochfort. During the war, the King used to give Elizabeth his trainers' reports to read and took her down to Beckhampton to see the horses, when Fred Darling noticed that it was Elizabeth who identified the horses for her father. It was on this occasion that she was allowed to pat Big Game and later she admitted that she did not wash her hand for some time afterwards because she felt it was such a privilege to have touched such a high-class colt.

In 1945 she attended her first royal Ascot and saw the royal colours win with her father's horse, Rising Light; and when the Aga Khan gave her a filly foal named Astrakhan as a wedding present, she registered her own racing colours – scarlet, purple hooped sleeves and black cap – in 1949. That summer she and her mother bought a steeplechaser, Monaveen, but after he was killed racing at Hurst Park on New Year's Day 1951, she never bought another jumper. By then her most successful racehorse, Aureole, had been born (on 14 April 1950) and named by Elizabeth. He was a colt of uncertain temperament and had the temerity to lash out at Her Majesty when she offered him an apple at Boyd-Rochfort's Freemason Lodge in the spring of 1952. He was, however, foremost in her thoughts on her Coronation Day. Just as she was about to leave Buckingham Palace for Westminster Abbey, a lady-in-waiting asked her if everything was all right. Elizabeth replied that everything was fine: Boyd-Rochfort had telephoned to tell her that Aureole had gone well in the final run-up of his preparation for the Derby. On that occasion he came second to Pinza, but after he won his final race, the King George VI and Queen Elizabeth Stakes, at Ascot in July 1954 an excited Elizabeth was seen running to the unsaddling enclosure to greet him, arriving in front of her racing manager. She was the leading winning owner in 1954, but for her racing, as for other areas of her life, things were going downhill. By 1956 the Royal Stud was in the doldrums and 1959 was its worst year since 1944.

Racing and the breeding of racehorses is a therapeutic alternative to the strain of her daily life (even on Sundays her Private Secretary is on hand and there is no day in the year on which she does not have to deal with her 'boxes'). For someone normally so isolated from everyday life, her racing world involves her closely with the people concerned, not so much the other owners but with the personnel at the studs and training establishments. She likes to know. 'Oh,' she might say, 'X, the stallion man, is feeling pretty low, his wife's giving him a hard time . . .' News from her racing establishments is a welcome relief from the often unrelieved diet of bad news which she gets in her working life. 'People don't realise that most of the time the Queen gets bad news,' her racing manager said. 'Our ambassador somewhere's died, or there's been an air crash and a lot of people killed, or bad news politically – all sorts of things. It all comes to her and so . . . when the horses run well, the right sexed foal has been born, it's a bit of an uplift to her and I think she gets a kick out of that . . . when we buy a horse we'll try and be on the telephone to her whilst it's being bought, so she gets the thrill of the thing – the horse we're interested in coming into the ring and then listening to the auctioneer . . .'[3] As in her working life, Elizabeth is a master of her subject: 'The wonderful thing about the Queen is that she knows the whole of racing and breeding and you don't have to explain anything to her. For instance, if she has a runner at Warwick, she will know it's a left-handed course, she knows the people on the ground itself, what that means, and she knows the runners . . .' When it came to breeding, which possibly interests Elizabeth more than just racing, her expertise, having started when she was still in her teens, was growing all the time. Her racing manager said:

> The Queen's knowledge of her own mares and the make and shape of the animal, what it should look like and what it shouldn't . . . all this sort of thing [is remarkable]. She would have been very good at stable management and she would have been a very good trainer if she'd been able to. She's very interested in stable management, stud management, the way the staff handle the horses, all those sorts of things . . .[4]

It was through a shared passion for racing that she got to know one of her oldest and closest friends, Lord Porchester, known as 'Porchy', who is just over two years older than she is. The friendship between Elizabeth and Porchy went back to 1944, when he was just twenty and

Coronation Day, 2 June 1953

The Princess and the Group Captain: Peter Townsend (standing extreme left)
with Margaret (plus her trademark cigarette holder), Elizabeth (in front
with camera) and the royal party watching the Olympic Horse Trials
at Badminton in the spring of 1953 (left)

'Blissful' couple: Margaret and Tony Armstrong-Jones pose for an
engagement photograph at the Royal Lodge, Windsor, February 1960 (right)

Young mother: Elizabeth with Anne and Charles in the early 1950s

Baron by Baron:
self-portrait by
Baron Henry
Stirling Nahum,
c. 1956

The parting of the ways:
Philip with his Private
Secretary and old friend,
Commander Michael Parker,
at Gibraltar airport before
Parker left for London to face
the music, 6 February 1957

'Bobo' – Margaret MacDonald,
Elizabeth's trusted dresser
and confidante

Lord Plunket, Elizabeth's childhood
friend and later Master of her
Household, February 1955

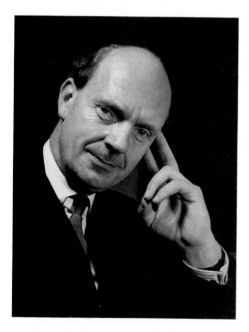

Lt. Col. the Hon. Martin Charteris
(later Lord Charteris of Amisfield),
then the Queen's Assistant Private
Secretary, at the time of her visit to
Ghana in November 1961

Elizabeth seen with her Private
Secretary, Sir Michael Adeane,
arriving at the King Edward VII
Hospital for her fateful visit to
Harold Macmillan, 18 October 1963

Lady Susan Hussey,
Woman of the Bedchamber
to Elizabeth and confidante
of Prince Charles

The Queen's men:
Robin Janvrin, then Assistant
Private Secretary, and
Sir Robert Fellowes, Private
Secretary, pictured in
Buckingham Palace courtyard,
c. 1992

David George Coke Patrick
Ogilvy, 13th Earl of Airlie,
Lord Chamberlain since 1984

Happy Family:
Philip, Elizabeth, Andrew,
Edward, Anne and Charles
photographed at Balmoral
in the year of Elizabeth and
Philip's silver wedding, 1972

The fairy-tale Princess
and her Soldier: Anne and
Captain Mark Phillips pose
for their engagement
photographs in the Corridor at
Windsor Castle, November
1973

Reconciliation? The first public appearance of the Duchess of Windsor
with the members of her husband's family – from left: Queen Elizabeth
the Queen Mother, the Duke and Duchess of Gloucester, the Duke and
Duchess of Windsor and Elizabeth, at the unveiling of
a memorial plaque to Queen Mary, 7 June 1967

A trio of Mountbattens: the Prince of Wales with his uncle and father
at a polo match about a year before Mountbatten's assassination in August 1979.
The body language is significant: the Prince points questioningly at himself,
his mentor's hand is placed in a fatherly manner on his shoulder,
while his father, arms crossed, stands somewhat apart, his attention fixed elsewhere

Love Story I:
The Prince and Princess
of Wales on honeymoon
at Balmoral, 1981

Love Story II:
The Prince of Wales and
Camilla Parker Bowles
in 1975

she seventeen. Porchester had joined the Royal Horse Guards, the 1st Household Cavalry Regiment, during the war. When he returned, his first ceremonial appearance was on the first Whitehall guard that took place after the war and then as part of the Sovereign's Escort riding beside the royal carriage to St Paul's for the Thanksgiving Service at the end of the war. From then on he and his brother officers were frequent guests at Buckingham Palace for evening parties or for dinners as escorts for the Princesses. The mutual bond was horses, or rather racehorses. Porchester had owned a racehorse since he was eighteen, a present from his father, which was also in training at Beckhampton with Fred Darling. Elizabeth, the King and Queen noticed, had developed an enthusiasm for racing which made Porchester an ideal companion for her and they encouraged the friendship.

Porchester, or the 7th Earl of Carnarvon as he has been since 1987, is not one of the chinless wonders whom Noël Coward noted contemptuously in Princess Margaret's circle. Half-American, he is the more serious son by his first wife of 'Porchy' Carnarvon, whose exploits in pursuit of women were legendary. Carnarvon is a man of good judgement, responsible, the chairman of a multitude of councils and charities, most of them concerned with the conservation of the countryside and sport, regional planning and local administration; he has served as a county councillor and alderman. He has been a Verderer of the New Forest, is High Steward of Winchester, an honorary fellow of Portsmouth Polytechnic and an honorary Doctor of Science of the University of Reading, an influential member of the Jockey Club, and a member of White's Club, the Portland (a London bridge club for experts who are not afraid of high stakes) and Hampshire Cricket Club. His grandfather was famous as the discoverer with Howard Carter of the tomb of Tutankhamun. For Elizabeth, one of his principal virtues was not just his knowledge of and enthusiasm for racing and breeding horses, or even as a loyal friend whom she can entirely trust, but also that her father liked him. They shared interests in shooting and the conservation of game and the lore of the countryside. Porchester was one of the few young men whom the King would invite out shooting with his own friends, all expert shots, such as the Queen's brother, David Bowes-Lyon, and Lord Eldon. Porchy had started shooting at a young age and was already very knowledgeable in those post-war years at Sandringham and Balmoral; the King would quite often put Porchy next to him in the line where all the birds were driven, which was a great honour. Porchester founded the Game

Research Association, a subject which fascinated the King, who summoned all the Sandringham keepers to a lecture on partridge rearing in the private cinema. 'He asked them all if there were any questions they'd like to ask afterwards,' Porchester remembered, 'and of course there was dead silence. I think the Norfolk keepers reckoned they knew enough about it without any research.'

At the first Ascot party at Windsor after the war, Porchester committed *lèse-majesté* and was still forgiven. Both the King and Porchester had had winners that day and were in a celebratory mood when the Duke of Beaufort (the Master of the Horse, one of Altrincham's 'second-rate lot') tapped the table and got up to say, 'With the King's permission I'd like to propose a toast to the first winner the King has had at Royal Ascot.' The King, who hated making impromptu speeches, got up and said, nervously and abruptly, 'Thank you, but someone else won a race today at Ascot and he can answer the toast for me', and sat down leaving young Porchester appalled at the prospect of addressing the assembled guests in the vast Waterloo Chamber on the King's behalf. Hardly knowing what he was saying, he ventured a topical joke – the name of one of the best-known jockeys of the day, "Charlie Smirke", a notoriously sharp rider, came into his mind. He blurted out, 'I don't suppose there are many people who have had a "Charlie Smirke" done on them by the Monarch.' There was a deathly silence. Then the King laughed and everyone else followed suit, but, as Porchester remembered, 'it was quite a nerve-racking moment'. As they left the room, Ulick Alexander, the Keeper of the Privy Purse, told Porchester, 'Well, I suppose you just got away with that.'[5]

Like her father, but unlike her mother and her sister, Elizabeth does not appreciate intellectuals and writers. Daphne du Maurier, staying at Balmoral during her husband's tenure as Comptroller of the Duke of Edinburgh's household, found Philip quick and easy to talk to but Elizabeth heavy-going. Elizabeth, bright and sure of herself when it came to her work – politics and world affairs – or her principal interest – horses (du Maurier described her face 'lighting up' when she spoke of them) – could not rise above the most banal small talk on literary subjects. It was not a world with which she was at all familiar. While her mother's friends included people like Duff Cooper, Osbert Sitwell and Kenneth Clark, Elizabeth's were almost entirely confined to Guards officers. As Princess Elizabeth, she had had as friends Mountbatten relations like Patricia Brabourne and her husband, with whom she and Philip had often stayed in the country, and her first cousin, formerly Jean Elphinstone, and her husband, John Wills. Non-family friends were people she had known since Windsor days, former members of the 'Bodyguard' as the young Guards officers stationed there were known, like Lord Rupert Nevill, son of the Marquess of Abergavenny, and his wife 'Micky', Hugh Euston (now Duke of Grafton) and, of course, Porchester.

That is in so far as she can have friends. Wallis Simpson, writing of the Prince of Wales's sadness at the approaching marriage of his hitherto inseparable companion, Prince George, diagnosed that par-ticularly royal loneliness. Even when Prince George and his brother were laughing and joking with their friends, she wrote in her memoirs, there was an 'invisible barrier' between the two Princes and the others. When Elizabeth became Queen, an invisible barrier went up, not because she wanted it to but simply because her position put her on a lonely plane of her own. Asked whether Elizabeth had a 'best friend', a cousin replied, 'I don't think she has ... I do count myself as a friend but ... there is no way one can get that close to somebody in that position. She is surprisingly outgoing to someone she feels she can trust. But then there can't be that many.' She has old friends but no best friends. 'I think of her as a very straightforward person in many ways who has to hold herself in much more than anybody else because whatever she says or does is noted and commented on or reported in perhaps a different way from which it was intended and she has to be very careful ...'

Fortunately for someone in her unique position, Elizabeth is essentially private and self-contained. It is her strength, enabling her to withstand the pressures of her job with an apparent ease which surprises people. She does not give of herself easily, in public or in private, performing her role with dignity and an economy of emotion which has made it possible for her to carry the burden that she does. She enjoys public occasions no more than her father did and a great deal less than her mother does. Public life is simply something which she has known was her duty ever since her childhood when she shocked her grandmother by whispering 'Grannie, we can't disappoint these people who've been waiting to see us.' Over the years it has become second nature, but it is still impeccably done; ambassadors come away entranced, prime ministers feel they have a confidante. There are limits, thresholds which are never crossed. As James Callaghan, her second Labour Prime Minister, said of her: 'there is friendliness but not friendship'. It has all been done at considerable cost to herself; she can rarely, if ever, let herself go with people. As one of her contemporaries who has known her since childhood said of her, 'She'd be a most wonderful friend if only she weren't the Queen.' Her gift for mimicry, sense of humour, the ready laugh that she shows in private have had to be repressed in public; the most she allows herself are dry one-liners which sometimes reveal an uncomfortably critical eye. 'You feel a tremendous inhibition there,' one woman politician said. 'I think there's tremendous warmth there when it's allowed to show itself,' a relation said, 'but it's terribly controlled.' 'She may look grumpy in photographs, but in fact she does smile a hell of a lot.' 'She's got a wonderful sense of humour – this is the one thing that never comes over to people when they see photographs looking rather glum. When she smiles the whole face comes to life. She loves a good laugh – I've seen the Queen laugh till the tears ran down her face about some ridiculous things.' 'The woman I see is full of jokes and fun and amusing and only too ready to laugh at anything – particularly herself,' one of her fashion advisers said. 'If only people could see her as she is.' 'She is very self-contained and is perfectly happy on her own with the dogs and her photograph albums,' a former aide says. 'She's not gregarious – she likes being alone reading her detective stories.' 'She's not a people person, she's a horse person, a dog person, likes being on her own,' another relation said. 'She finds it easier to relate to horses and dogs than people and has an extraordinary empathy with them.'

Elizabeth had to tread carefully between the conservative influences of her upbringing – consideration for the feelings of her mother and the people and way of life which she had inherited from the late King – and the modernising tendencies of her husband. The official attitude of the Palace towards Altrincham's criticism was dismissive. The Lord Chamberlain, the Earl of Scarbrough, titular head of the royal household, another of the trio named by Altrincham as 'second-rate and lacking in gumption', a sixty-one-year-old Yorkshire nobleman who was frequently the Queen's host for the Doncaster race meetings and one of her own appointees at her accession, went on record as saying he was not interested in Lord Altrincham's views. Nevertheless, he had the foresight to try and escape from one of his traditional responsibilities, that of censoring plays. With playwrights like John Osborne around, Scarbrough thought it was time to disassociate the Palace from this potentially controversial duty, but when he approached the Home Secretary, Rab Butler, in 1957 with a view to disembarrassing himself of the chore, he was told that the system worked perfectly well and it was not until 1968 under his successor, Lord Cobbold, that the Palace managed to lay down the burden.

The tedious and outdated circus of debutante presentation parties, which, Altrincham had rightly said, should have been quietly dropped in 1945, was abandoned after 1958. Presentation at court had been an essential part of social initiation in the days when, in Disraeli's phrase, 'the high aristocracy clustered round the throne'. It marked the year when a girl, usually at the age of seventeen, 'came out' of the schoolroom into society in search of a husband and was then duly invited to balls and the other events of the London 'Season'. After their marriage they were 'presented' again. By the 1950s presentation was no longer even a glamorous occasion but a snobbish survival; there were no ostrich feather head-dresses, jewels or satin dresses with trains of a specified length, it was simply an afternoon reception at which several hundred young women dressed in 'afternoon dresses', hats and white kid gloves to the elbow, filed past the Queen and the Duke of Edinburgh, dropping a curtsey as an official intoned their name, to the background of a military band playing dance music. There was no personal contact whatsoever as there was with investitures, when the Queen would happily stand for hours bestowing medals, knighthoods and a brief chat on worthy recipients who at least had earned their right to be there. In 1958 it was announced that the Queen would hold no more presentation parties but would increase the number of garden-parties at Buckingham Palace and Holyrood House in Edinburgh to widen the circle of people who could be presented to their sovereign. That year, as if in response to Altrincham's suggestion that some household officers should have Commonwealth backgrounds, an assistant press secretary was appointed from Canada, the intention being that someone from one of the Commonwealth countries should hold the appointment for at least two years. This did not, however, fulfil his concept of an ethnic mixture at the Palace; the appointees were always to be from the 'Old [i.e. white] Commonwealth'. Philip had been responsible for one innovation intended to increase access by the outside world to the Palace – informal lunches for half-a-dozen people to enable Elizabeth to meet a cross-section of her subjects. Early guests included the editor of *The Times*, the Bishop of London, the managing director of Wembley Stadium, the headmaster of Eton and the

Chairman of the National Coal Board, a selection that could hardly be called adventurous. Later in the reign the net would be spread wider to include actors, writers and sports personalities.

Some observers thought they noticed an immediate change in the most highlighted aspect of Altrincham's criticisms. The Queen's Christmas speech, Harold Nicolson noted, came over 'with a vigour unknown in pre-Altrincham days'. Great effort had, indeed, been put into this, Elizabeth's first televised Christmas broadcast. Boy Browning's wife, Daphne du Maurier, had prepared draft suggestions, but it does not seem that they were used. Just as the prospect of having to deliver live the post-luncheon radio talk had always ruined her father's Christmas lunch, so did this first live performance spoil Elizabeth's day. 'I hope your Christmas went off well – ours was upset by the television which was nerve-racking,' she told a courtier. Elizabeth is not a natural television performer. She has to an unusual degree the ability to appear (and is) utterly unselfconscious when in the focus of still or television cameras in her active life, but as soon as she is required to do a face-to-face broadcast to camera it is quite a different thing, as Michael Adeane was to explain to Macmillan's press officer in 1963: 'The Queen is gay and relaxed beforehand but in front of the cameras she freezes and there is nothing to be done about it.' Two years earlier, Adeane had confessed to Harold Nicolson that 'he would give his soul to find some reason for stopping the Christmas broadcast. He says it must always be the same and will become monotonous . . .'[6]

For Elizabeth, the constraints were compensated for by the fulfilment which she found in her job. Within the parameters of that job life was reasonably straightforward for a woman with her temperament and training. Never rebellious, she had accepted her lot without question. As she had gained in confidence and understanding, she had begun to enjoy the political side of her work. Rab Butler told Robert Lacey how much she enjoyed political gossip:

> She seemed fascinated by Parliament – who was rising, who falling.
> Like all clever women she was very interested in personalities and,
> apart from the national interest, she enjoyed evaluating to what degree
> the Government had suffered a setback or had scored points in political
> terms. She appeared totally to appreciate the personal ambition
> inspiring the political animal, and was fascinated by the length one
> would go to secure his own advantage at the expense of another . . .[7]

At a time when other women's lives were largely limited to finding husbands and looking after them, having children and caring for them, she was exceptional in the horizons and power which her job offered her.

Her womanhood had helped her in her public life, in her debut as 'the world's sweetheart' when people had been moved by her youth and her sex. Later people would judge her in her other private role as a woman and a mother treading a difficult line which other executive women have to tread between the demands of public life and the needs of private life. Her efforts to preserve some kind of a 'normal' life for her children would be doomed to failure; the essence of royalty is that it should be above the crowd, not of it. 'Normal' human beings will behave just as their contemporaries do, neither better nor worse. At the end of the 1950s Elizabeth can have had little conception of the increasingly fierce spotlight in which she and her family would have to live their lives in the future. As far as the press was concerned, the monarchy had enjoyed a charmed life for almost a century. The protracted Margaret–Townsend affair had for the first time allowed the press to have a thoroughly enjoyable time speculating over a royal scandal and romance and demonstrated how the private lives of the Windsors could fascinate a nation and sell a lot of newspapers. In July 1955 one of Elizabeth's advisers told Harold Nicolson that he thought the position had become 'very difficult since the press become more vulgar and more ravenous every week'. Altrincham's criticisms had been intended to be helpful, seeking to aid Elizabeth not to attack her, but, as Nicolson put it, 'his article saying that the monarchy was dull has had an Emperor's Clothes effect, and people are now critical when they hear her speeches and see her on the television. I fear we may be entering on one of those anti-monarchical phases which recur from time to time as in 1871 . . .'[8] As the nation moved into the most dramatic, non-violent social revolution in its history, the attention focused on Elizabeth and in a most unwelcome fashion on the most private area of her life, her marriage.

Mountbatten-Windsor

'The Queen's in a terrible state; there's a fellow called Jones in
the billiard room who wants to marry her sister, and Prince
Philip's in the library wanting to change the family name to
Mountbatten . . .'

Duke of Gloucester to Harold Macmillan, December 1959

At the moment when British paratroopers were descending from the
sky over the Canal Zone, Elizabeth's husband was on the royal yacht
Britannia off the eastern coast of Ceylon (as it then was). Accompanied
by Mike Parker, he was halfway through what was billed as a tour of
the outlying territories of the Commonwealth, many of them never
visited before by a member of the royal family. It had been prompted,
officially, by an invitation to open the 1956 Olympic Games in
Melbourne. Philip was escaping from the Palace. On that four-month
tour he could feel free to grow a naval-looking beard and indulge his
interest in painting (a talent inherited from his father), wildlife, and
science with a visit to the British scientific station in Antarctica. No
one seems to have questioned the cost of this expedition, which was as
much a personal quest for space as a public duty. For one tricky
moment it seemed as though *Britannia*, which was listed as a hospital
ship, might have to turn back and take part in the Suez expedition;
fortunately for Philip, the operation was called off before a decision
had to be taken. He had been away since October; by the time the tour
was over rumours that Elizabeth's marriage was in trouble had made
headlines across the world. 'Last week', *Time* reported on 18 February
1957, 'the [rumour] mongering winds were howling louder around
Buckingham Palace than they had since the day of Wallis Warfield
Simpson and Edward VIII.'

Like the piece of fluff which Princess Margaret had picked off Peter Townsend's uniform, the trigger for the reports was news of something apparently unrelated. Eileen Parker was suing her husband, Michael, for divorce. The Parker marriage had been in trouble for some time; like Townsend's, it had been a wartime decision taken in haste and repented at leisure. As in the case of the Townsends, the demands of Palace life had proved the last straw. When the story broke, Philip and Parker were approaching Gibraltar almost at the end of their tour. When they reached the island, Parker, accompanied by a lawyer and a contingent of the world's press, flew back to London. To save further embarrassment to his employer, he resigned; the Townsend experience only two years before had proved that divorce was still a dirty word as far as Palace circles were concerned. This was underlined by the Queen's Press Secretary, Commander Colville, who took the trouble to motor down to London airport to meet Parker in order to deliver an unwelcoming message. 'Hello, Parker,' he said, 'I've just come to let you know that from now on, you're on your own.'

Parker's sacrifice did not save the Duke from the repercussions. In fact it prompted a national wave of sentiment in his favour reminiscent of what *Time* called 'the emotional binge' over the outcome of the Townsend affair. 'Why', the *Daily Express* (owned by Lord Beaver-brook, always happy to pursue a long-standing vendetta against the royal family) demanded, 'should a broken marriage be a disqualification for royal service' when the twice-married Eden had until recently been the Queen's First Minister? Gossip columnists digging into Parker's past – and Philip's – came up with the Thursday Club organised by the top society photographer, Baron, who was inevitably described as 'court photographer'. The Thursday Club was an informal luncheon club, which met in an upstairs room at Wheeler's Restaurant in Old Compton Street; the restaurant's proprietor, Bernard Walsh, was one of its founder members. Members included journalists like Arthur Christiansen, editor of the *Daily Express*, and Frank Owen, editor of the *Daily Mail*; actors like James Robertson Justice, David Niven and Peter Ustinov; and humorists like Patrick Campbell and Larry Adler. Another member was Don Stewart, the left-wing scriptwriter exiled from Hollywood in the McCarthyite purges, who once lay down on the pavement beside a pigeon and asked it, 'Got any messages?' The brilliant Conservative politician Iain Macleod was a guest who later became a member, while other more shady people who appeared from time to time included Stephen Ward, later to become notorious during the Profumo scandal, and the spy Kim Philby. It was a typically all-male affair with no purpose beyond starting the weekend early. The members ate fish and drank Wheeler's house white wine and the atmosphere, according to one member, was of 'high spirits stimulated by the brilliance of the back chat', funny stories, barracking and dirty talk.

The animating spirit and original founder of the Thursday Club, Baron Henry Stirling Nahum (always known simply by his first name), was a colourful figure in London society. He was the descendant of Italian Jews from Tripoli who settled in Manchester, where they founded a business in the cotton trade. Baron and his twin brother, Jack, a barrister, had both achieved successful careers for themselves in London. Baron made his name in 1936 with a picture of Larry Adler, described by Peter Ustinov as 'the harmonica genius and infant prodigy'. Baron was an amusing, charming, swashbuckling figure who liked women, ballet and fast cars. He was something of a fantasist with a passion for royalty; his friend Peter Ustinov described him as 'an individualist with the seeds of Walter Mitty in his youthful soul'. He met Philip at Broadlands in 1947 when he was photographing the Mountbattens; Philip invited him to take his own wedding pictures and within a short time they were friends. Baron introduced Philip, his cousin David Milford Haven, and Parker to a social circle in London which was as far removed as it was possible to be from Philip's royal in-laws' 'tweedy' and ultra-respectable friends. He was an enthusiastic party-giver – his fancy-dress party on New Year's Eve at his studio in Brick Street, Mayfair, was an annual event – and was always surrounded by beautiful women. It was a world in which aristocrats met showgirls, a peculiarly 1950s London phenomenon, which ended with the Profumo scandal in 1963 (Stephen Ward was one of Baron's friends and made a drawing of him). Baron and his brother were 'passports to all sorts of people in London . . . they were lively lads at a very lively time'.

The Thursday Club did not confine itself to lunches. According to Larry Adler, a founder member with Baron, they gave Philip a Bachelor Night party at Baron's flat in the mews of Bruton Place – 'Boy, was he nervous . . . his face was white with fear'[2] – and there would be an annual dinner for Philip at Mike Parker's flat. There were a lot of schoolboyish high jinks – at a pre-wedding lunch for Guy Middleton, Philip and Milford Haven bet Baron that he couldn't take a photograph of the cuckoo coming out of the clock. Baron had his camera all set up when, just before the hour, Philip and Milford Haven threw smoke bombs into the fireplace and the room filled with smoke. Everybody's faces were black, the police were called, but it was hushed up. Pranks were one thing, sexual scandal quite another.

The Palace was not amused when gossip columnists linked Philip with Baron's girlfriend, the beautiful musical star Pat Kirkwood, whose legs Kenneth Tynan once described as 'the eighth wonder of the world'. Their first meeting took place in October 1948, when Elizabeth was heavily pregnant with Charles. According to Pat Kirkwood some forty years later, they met when Baron came to pick her up at the Hippodrome Theatre near Leicester Square, where she was playing in the musical *Starlight Roof*, bringing with him Philip and a naval equerry named 'Basher' Watkins. They had dinner at Les Ambassadeurs, an ultra-fashionable Mayfair restaurant and gambling club which frequently featured in Ian Fleming's James Bond books, and then went to the Milroy night-club, where Philip asked Pat Kirkwood to dance. Several couples, described by Kirkwood as 'courtiers', looked shocked. Philip pulled faces at them, but they reported back to the Palace. The King was outraged and Baron put in the royal doghouse.[3] Pat Kirkwood has always denied that she and Philip had an affair. Baron himself in his memoirs certainly gave the impression that his own feelings for Pat Kirkwood were unrequited: 'Several years of my life were wasted in blind devotion to the beautiful and glamorous Pat Kirkwood,' he wrote in *Baron by Baron*, published posthumously in 1957. There were rumours too of Philip's relations before his marriage with Hélène Cordet, who in the late 1950s ran a night-club called The Saddle Room in Hamilton Place, but the Duke's authorised biographer, Tim Heald, insists that the two of them were just childhood friends.

Philip's defence, then and always, against allegations of infidelity is the impossibility of escaping from his detectives. At a party with Prince Bernhard of the Netherlands, husband of Queen Juliana, he once got down on his knees and salaamed to him – 'You're a lucky guy,' he told him. 'Nobody recognises you – you can have as many girlfriends as you like. I have six security men behind me all the time . . .' Prince Bernhard, according to a witness, was not amused. The Duke's four-month absence and the Parker divorce gave the media pegs on which to hang their rumours. Joan Graham, London-based 'Mayfair Set Correspondent' of the Baltimore *Sun*, sent a report of 'whispers' that 'the Duke of Edinburgh had more than a passing interest in an unnamed woman and was meeting her regularly in the apartment of the court photographer'. The rest of the American press took up the story with 'REPORT QUEEN, DUKE IN RIFT OVER PARTY GIRL'. At the time the story created great excitement; Thursday Club luncheons were represented as orgies and the rumour went round that Mike Parker had been dropped specifically so that he could no longer lead the Duke astray. Through gritted teeth Michael Adeane's office denied that there was any rift between the Queen and her husband, and Elizabeth let it be known that she planned to fly that week to Lisbon to join Philip there two days before beginning a joint state visit. No fewer than 150 reporters were jostling each other on the tarmac at the Montijo Military Air Base near Lisbon when the Queen's plane arrived; they had worked out exactly how long the royal couple had spent apart – 124 days and five hours. Philip appeared at ease as he chatted with royal diplomats waiting to greet the Queen. In anticipation of the meeting he had shaved off the ginger beard he had grown during a six-week beard-growing contest on board *Britannia*; when he boarded the plane, he found the entire party, including his wife, wearing false ginger whiskers. Elizabeth emerged from the plane 'with a broad grin' and, after shaking hands with the assembled dignitaries, the couple drove off 'in dignified silence', according to the reporters, one of whom claimed to have spotted a 'tiny smudge of lipstick' on the ducal cheek – 'an all's well signal that spread to the four corners of the earth', *Time* announced.

Elizabeth was very much in love with her husband and it showed. Baron himself said when he first photographed her at the time of her marriage: 'She was a shy young woman, most friendly and eager to co-operate, but not always at ease in front of the camera. The only thing you could be quite certain of was her feelings toward Prince Philip. She was always so much gayer whenever he was in the room.'[4] Philip, on the other hand, was absolutely undemonstrative. Mike Parker, venturing to the edge of indulgence and friendship, used to plead with him to show Elizabeth a little more affection in public – 'put your arm round her or something' – only to be met with the fierce stare which Philip meted out to people when he considered they were being 'bloody fools'.

The Thursday Club provided Philip with the social outlet that he needed, to be able to enjoy himself with congenial people he could trust. It was all very like the wardroom atmosphere in the Navy.

Eventually he was prevented by media interest from enjoying even that; from the late 1950s he was no longer to be seen at the Thursday Club luncheons. Mike Parker had been important to him as a link with a happier period of his life as a naval officer and then as a companion in his more daring activities – flying and sailing, which also provided him with an escape from the earth-bound constraints of royal life. Philip loved sailing as much as Elizabeth disliked it; she never went with him to Cowes week, the high point of the sailing social calendar. Philip had learned to sail at Gordonstoun and Dartmouth, but had taken it up for pleasure only since his marriage when the Island Sailing Club had given him a Dragon-class yacht as a wedding present. For years he sailed this boat, which he named *Bluebottle*, in the Cowes week races, crewed by his colourful sailing companion, 'drinking, yarning and singing chum', Uffa Fox. Fox, a builder and sailor of small boats, and Philip became a feature of the Cowes week regatta; with Fox the Prince sailed *Coweslip*, a Flying Fifteen, one of Fox's designs, given him by the people of Cowes, and *Bloodhound*, a pre-war twelve-metre designed for ocean-racing. Philip was intensely competitive; people who sailed with him had to have nerves as cool as he had. 'He would have been a wonderful helmsman if only he'd had more time to do it,' a sailing friend said. 'He was as cool as a cucumber – at Cowes he would get into a schmozzle of yachts crowding round a buoy in roaring water and he'd sail into the melee and come straight through without touching anyone.'

At Cowes he enjoyed the after-race life as much as he was allowed to. He joined a spoof club known as the Imperial Poona Yacht Club, originally founded by Oxford undergraduates as a take-off of colonial bores. He is on the membership list as the 'Maharaja of Cooch Parwani', which loosely translates as 'the Maharaja of Not-a-Lot', and when Buz Mosbacher, an American member, skippered his boat to victory in the America's Cup, the Prince sent him a telegram: 'Poona is proud of you. Cooch Parwani.' Like the Thursday Club, the Poona Yacht Club is a wardroom, let-your-hair-down experience in the course of which grown-up yachtsmen with serious sailing credentials behave like boys. The Duke enjoyed it, feeling safe in the company of men who would not talk to the press, of whom he was becoming increasingly wary. 'He wasn't able to go to the Poona or things like that if there were women there in case the media made up rumours,' a friend said. 'There were always rumours . . .'

The four months 'alone' on *Britannia* represented a watershed in

Prince Philip's life. Significantly it was at that point that Baron went out of his life, swiftly, as we have seen, to be followed by Parker. Philip had invited Baron to join him in Australia for the Olympic Games and Baron had decided that, in order to make himself more mobile for the tour, he would have an operation to ease his arthritic hips, the result of a bad car crash in 1922. The operation went tragically wrong and he died suddenly in hospital on 5 September 1956 aged forty-nine. His death caused a sensation at the time. 'Lordly by name and lordly by nature he dared to cut a dash,' his friend, the journalist Donald Edgar, wrote in a two-part obituary entitled 'The Man Who Knew Everybody'. 'Baron was a gambler,' Peter Ustinov wrote, 'and it sometimes seemed to me as I watched him at work and at play that for him the whole of existence was a pastime with a score.'[5] Curiously, when after Baron's death Parker visited his studio to find a replacement photographer for the tour, he rejected the star pupil, Antony Armstrong-Jones, as 'too bohemian'. Parker's enforced departure left a large hole in Philip's life; they had been companions in arms and 'mates' in a real sense for so long. Parker had provided a breath of fresh air in the stuffy corridors of the Palace, contributing to the light-hearted tone of Philip's staff there. He was genial, relaxed and good company. He had kept Philip company whenever needed, even learning to fly with him under Peter Horsley's tuition. 'Prince Philip was a very good pilot – went solo very quickly,' Horsley said. 'Parker was a terrible pilot – took it as a joke.' Other people at the Palace were less sorry about the disappearance of Baron and Parker, both of whom were considered responsible for leading Philip astray.

Boy Browning collapsed with a nervous breakdown in July 1957 and finally had to retire from his position as treasurer to the Duke of Edinburgh in 1959. He was highly strung and frequently in bad health; according to friends, he blamed himself for some of the disaster at Arnhem. He was under the emotional stress of having a serious affair with a woman in London while remaining devoted to Daphne du Maurier and, as a result of his difficulties, he drank too much. He had kept his personal problems to himself; when Margaret Forster's excellent but grim biography of Daphne came out, Elizabeth wrote to his family saying how surprised she had been to read that he had such a sad life. Browning, like the rest of Elizabeth's male senior household, was a little in love with her. 'You could always tell when he was going in to see her,' a Clarence House aide said. 'He'd give his shoes an extra polish and check himself out in the mirror.' And, despite the differences in their personalities and background, he had been extremely fond of Philip – 'saying farewell to him affected me much more than I expected,' he wrote.

For a hyperactive and intelligent man such as Philip, the role of royal consort was not an easy one. As Prince Albert had complained in January 1854:

> A very considerable section of the nation had never given itself the trouble to consider what really is the position of the husband of the Queen Regnant. When I first came over here, I was met by this want of knowledge and unwillingness to give a thought to the position of this luckless personage. Peel cut down my income, Wellington refused me my rank, the Royal family cried out against the Foreign interloper, the Whigs in office were only inclined to concede me just as much space as I could stand upon.[6]

One hundred years later Philip had found himself very much in the same position; his anguished exclamation – 'I'm nothing but a bloody amoeba' – expressed much the same feelings as his predecessor. He had had to create his own 'space to stand upon'.

He has no constitutional role other than as a Privy Counsellor. He sees no state papers. He has apparently never wanted, nor has he been given, the title of 'Prince Consort' which Victoria bestowed upon Albert. 'He never wanted to get involved with the business of state,' an aide said. 'He was always going to hoe his own furrow.' He saw his most important role, according to Parker, as 'looking after the Queen in first place, second and third'. He had to do this without subsuming his entire personality into the role of consort, something which, as a natural leader, he would have found impossible. The strong sense of duty and service inculcated at Gordonstoun and in the Royal Navy carried him along. Philip being the man he was, the prospect of inventing a role for himself did not daunt him. 'He saw it as a challenge,' an aide said. 'He always supported the Queen 100 per cent and he took over the things the King had done like running the estates.' 'The fifties was a very fertile time for him,' a colleague said. 'He started to set out his own agenda and by '56 he was really sorting things out.' He also took on the headship of various organisations concerned with the areas which particularly interested him – science and technology (as Patron of the Industrial Society and President of the British Association for the Advancement of Science), young people and sport (President of the National Playing Fields Association and Patron of the Outward Bound Trust, President of the Central Council of Physical Education, the Amateur Athletics Board and the Commonwealth Games Federation, and of the Royal Yachting Association), all of which he undertook in the 1950s. In response to an idea of his old headmaster, Kurt Hahn, he set up the Duke of Edinburgh's Award Scheme designed to stretch the mental and physical capacities of youngsters. Besides all this there were endless visits of inspection; 'in the early days he had very dreary engagements, gas works, that sort of thing,' an employee said.

In some situations (increasingly so where the media was concerned) his sharp intelligence and restless, often abrasive, personality made things more difficult for him than they would have been for a less driven man. This is the conclusion one of his authorised biographers, Tim Heald, came to at the end of a period of close observation of his subject:

> Still he puzzles me. Real humility sits uneasily alongside apparent
> arrogance; energy and optimism co-exist with sudden douches of cold
> water; real kindnesses are mingled with inexplicable snubs; certainty
> and uncertainty, sensitivity and insensitivity, walk hand in hand. He is
> gregarious, he is a loner; he loves argument, he cannot bear to lose one.
> On the one hand he will make a detour of thousands of miles to console
> the victims of a hurricane; on the other, he once got into such a bate
> with an equerry who failed to take shotgun lessons that he stopped the
> car and ordered him out. These apparent inconsistencies certainly
> make him intriguing; but they also make him exasperating. He is
> energetic, mercurial, quixotic, and ultimately impossible to pin down –
> partly on purpose . . .[7]

Given the ducal temperament, it is open to doubt whether he would have had an ultimately successful career in the Navy. Despite his intelligence and ability (he has a sharper brain than either his uncle Mountbatten or his son the Prince of Wales), his dislike of being ordered about by pompous officials would certainly have brought him into collision with superior gold braid on his way to the top. He has a naturally rebellious temperament; even his sense of duty gives way under the stress of irritation with officialdom. On one occasion, when he was flying his aircraft to Australia, a refuelling stop was planned in one of the Gulf States. When the Foreign Office liaison officer discovered that the Duke intended merely to stop, refuel and fly on, he pointed out to the Palace that several local rulers important to Britain's interests in the area would be deeply offended if the Queen's husband did not meet them as he passed through. Philip was forced to conform, but he never forgave the official concerned and when, at the end of the official's career in the diplomatic service, Elizabeth wanted to honour him personally, her husband objected. 'X is the biggest shit even the Foreign Office has ever produced,' he exploded (the man in question got his honour none the less). Exasperation, his biographer concluded, is a keynote in his character. Never one to suffer fools gladly and with a bullshit detector finely tuned, he would pounce on the slightest example of stupidity, incompetence or humbug leaving officials, politicians and self-satisfied businessmen dismayed in his wake. On one occasion the mayor of a local town was proudly showing him round a new housing development carefully zoned according to price. 'And that', the mayor pointed, 'is the lower income area.' 'Oh, you mean the ghetto,' said the Duke.

Philip's abrasiveness with the media and his sensitivity to what newspapers say about him have not helped the royal family. Criticism is met with anger, kind words ignored. In the early days Mike Parker used to call up his fellow Thursday Club member Arthur Christiansen for advice about his master's bad relations with the press (and was continuing to do so as late as 1963). 'Usually, of course, when it was too late for advice to have had any effect,' Christiansen commented.[8] As early as 1955 during the Margaret–Townsend furore, one of Elizabeth's Private Secretaries admitted to Harold Nicolson that 'the Duke is beginning to get journalists on his nerves . . . and that [the Palace] is always afraid of some outburst'.[9] The bad blood between Philip and the press had begun with his eve-of-wedding party, and continued through such episodes as the pelting of cameramen with nuts in Gibraltar, 'mistakenly' turning a hosepipe on reporters at the Chelsea Flower Show, and telling a climbing photographer that he hoped he would break his neck. Even his friendship with Christiansen did not prevent him referring publicly to the *Daily Express* as 'a bloody awful newspaper'. To be fair to Philip, John Gordon of the *Sunday Express* was frequently provocative and went to considerable lengths to discover things that might be discreditable to the royal family and particularly to the Mountbattens and Philip. In 1961 he reported to Beaverbrook that he was in hot water with the Duke of Edinburgh because he had found out that the Duke was the only civilian helicopter pilot who was allowed to fly over the house tops of London. 'The safety rule applied to all others is that helicopters must not leave the line of the river'; it was breached by Philip every time he flew his helicopter in and out of Buckingham Palace. He also claimed that the 'purple band' (exclusion of all other aircraft from the route of the royal plane) was unofficially applied to Philip's helicopter flights, disrupting other air services.[10]

Elizabeth did what she could to mitigate the difficulties of her husband's position. Many men might have resented being permanently publicly relegated to second place. Even in the midst of her family, Elizabeth is still the Queen, the 'Lord's anointed'. She comes into the room last and if her husband happened to be late and enter the room after her, he would apologise. While some men would find this a problem, for Philip, born into a royal family himself, it was accepted etiquette, a part of life. He had greater problems with the weighty traditions of the British court and its resistance to change – the 'men with moustaches' who resented him as a foreigner. Elizabeth realised this and to bolster up his position and compensate as far as she could for the hurt caused by the controversy over the Mountbatten/Windsor name she had made several public gestures. In September of the year of her accession she had granted him precedence next to herself and in December she had informed the Cabinet that she wished her husband to be appointed to the highest rank in each of the three services. He should be Admiral of the Fleet, Field Marshal and Marshal of the Royal Air Force.[11] Philip appeared at the Coronation in the heavily gold-braided dress of Admiral of the Fleet, but, in a gesture of independence, when he attended the Queen at the State Opening of Parliament he wore a plain naval officer's uniform. In the early summer of 1953, shortly before the Coronation, she had informed the Cabinet that she wished the Duke of Edinburgh to be appointed Regent in the event of her death or incapacity before Prince Charles (then referred to as the Duke of Cornwall) became eighteen. The Duke of Edinburgh as Regent would delegate the royal functions to Counsellors of State, among whom the Queen specifically wished the Queen Mother to be nominated.[12] The Government decided that the Regency Bill should be introduced into the Houses of Parliament in November and passed before Elizabeth's departure on her Commonwealth tour. The timing was unfortunate: the press chose to interpret this as a snub to Margaret because of the Townsend affair.

Philip's most recent promotion, agreed in Cabinet on 22 February

1957, was the title of Prince of the United Kingdom. This had not been Elizabeth's idea but the suggestion of Churchill, who told the Cabinet on 2 March 1955 that he had put it forward 'in informal conversation with the Queen' and that she had been favourably disposed towards it.[13] Elizabeth, perhaps significantly however, did nothing to follow it up for nearly two years, not until February 1957. In Cabinet Prime Minister Harold Macmillan characteristically claimed the credit for it. He had, he said, proposed the idea to the Queen 'in recognition of the great services which HRH has provided to the country and of his unique contribution to the life of the Commonwealth, culminating in the tour which he has just concluded'.[14] What Macmillan did not say, but which was almost certainly his intention, was that this should knock on the head all the rumours about rifts in the royal marriage by making Elizabeth be seen publicly to reward her husband for his services.

If there had been a rift, there was certainly a reconciliation on Philip's return later in 1957. Philip's behaviour, not least in taking the prolonged tour, suggested that he had been feeling the constrictions of marital Palace life. After ten years of marriage, Elizabeth wanted more children and she now felt she could cope with the demands of her job. She and her husband were very much together in the international public eye that spring and summer – the Portuguese state visit in February was followed by a visit to Paris in April, where the couple were mobbed by the Parisians. Outside the Opéra the welcoming crowds pressed so close that they had to be driven back by mounted guards with drawn swords, and at a reception for 2,000 at the Louvre distinguished guests clambered on the pedestals of statues for a better view of them. In October they were in the United States for the 350th anniversary of the founding of the State of Virginia. Macmillan, anxiously concerned to repair the breach in Anglo-American relations caused by Suez, arrived in Washington to find 'the whole country still enthralled by the visit of the Queen'; the British Ambassador, Harold Caccia, told him that Elizabeth had 'buried George III for good and all'.[15]

One result of the 'rift' episode was that Philip was increasingly seen to exercise a dominant rule in the field in which it was open for him to do so – his own family. Elizabeth felt that because, as she explained to friends, 'he has never had any family life of his own', this was particularly important to him. Beyond that, her anxiety to adjust the balance between their relative positions in their public and their private lives was to make him the ultimate arbiter where their children were concerned. Her own upbringing had taught her that traditional roles in the family should not be reversed. The Queen Mother had been the stronger personality of the two, but she had never tried to usurp her husband's position as head of the family, although in those areas about which she felt strongly, like the Windsors and the German relations, her feelings had dominated. In Elizabeth's view the family should be run on traditional lines; her role as mother was to be kept distinct from her position as Queen and because of this she fought far harder than her mother and her father had to preserve her children's privacy. Commander Colville was her employee and his views, however unpopular they may have been with the public and the press, were her views.

Elizabeth's instinct to let her husband 'run the show' as far as the family was concerned was to have serious consequences for her eldest son in particular. 'Motherhood is not the Queen's long suit,' a friend said. 'She likes getting on with her job and she is extremely busy.' She kept an hour for the children in the morning and another for bathtime, but otherwise saw no harm in their spending most of their time in the company of nannies and governesses just as she and Margaret had. Allegations that Philip was a distant arm's-length father when the children were small are untrue according to his children and their former nanny (backed up by the evidence of Mike Parker and other people working at Buckingham Palace at the time). Princess Anne told her father's biographer how Philip always tried to spend time with them before bedtime, a pattern which she has set for herself. Charles's adored nanny, Mabel Anderson, described him as 'a marvellous father. When the children were younger, he always used to set aside time to read to them, or help them put together those little model toys.'[16] The staff remember him as 'more unbending than the Queen' at the time, playing hide and seek with them before bedtime to the accompaniment of delighted shrieks. Elizabeth could appear distant and sometimes even formidable. Once at Balmoral when Charles was a very small boy, he asked his great-aunt, the Princess Royal, to get down a jar of sweets for him, but then they heard Elizabeth coming. Charles froze with fright and Princess Mary hastily put the jar back on its shelf.

Charles was depicted as a lonely little boy dressed by his nanny in faintly old-fashioned children's clothes of a style and cut which had not changed since the 1930s and which were made for him by two exclusive Bond Street shops – Rowes and The White House. The inevitable consequence of his mother's prolonged absences was that he, like many upper-class children, was closer and more accustomed to his nannies, first Helen Lightbody and then Mabel Anderson, than to his mother. His fourth birthday, in 1952, was the first his father had attended; on his fifth his parents were at Sandringham finalising plans for the great Commonwealth tour while Charles spent the day with his grandmother and his Aunt Margaret at Windsor. His mother gave him a helmet and a sword; his grandmother presented him with a set of garden tools, gifts which were somehow symbolic of their differing views of Charles and his future. Preparatory to saying goodbye, Elizabeth went to Harrods and bought his Christmas presents, a red, white and blue glider and some mud-pie moulds, to be given to him on Christmas Day, when she and his father would be in New Zealand. On 22 November she tucked her children up in bed – Charles, responsible as ever, promising 'to look after Anne'; outside the nursery door she burst into tears. Her son had already been taught why his mother had to leave him so often. 'Mummy has an important job to do,' he told a friend, pointing at the globe newly installed in the nursery so that he could follow his parents' progress. 'She's down there.' It was 2 May before he saw her again, piped aboard *Britannia* at Tobruk, and then he had to wait while she shook hands with a line of dignitaries whom he tried to join. 'No, not you, dear,' were Her Majesty's first words to her son after their six-month parting before the later, private reunion. It was his first lesson in the royal rule that private emotion is not shown in public. Elizabeth was behaving according to tradition. When her own father and mother had returned from a five-month tour of Australasia in 1927, her grandfather's instructions had been, 'We will not embrace at the station before so many people. When you kiss Mama take yr. hat off . . .'

In the frequent absence of his parents Charles's world was essentially ruled and inhabited by women, principally his two nannies, while in the background there was always his beloved grandmother and lifelong supporter, the Queen Mother. He was a timid, sensitive child and, in his parents' eyes, often suffered in comparison with his more forceful younger sister. 'If you raised your voice to him,' his governess, Miss Catherine Peebles, known as 'Mispy', recalled, 'he would draw back into his shell and for a time you would be able to do nothing with him.' 'He was never as boisterous and noisy as Princess Anne,' Mabel Anderson said. 'She had a much stronger, more extrovert personality. She didn't exactly push him aside, but she was certainly a more forceful child.'[17] 'Princess Anne was a very naughty little girl, a regular monkey,' a member of Philip's staff recalled. 'She used to come into our room, very assertive and ask, "Are you writing letters for Papa?" Prince Charles always tried to be correct and take her away but she would shake him off.' On one occasion when she was only about four years old, she let Charles's pet rabbit, Harvey, out of its hutch and stood with her hands on her hips laughing as the gardeners chased around trying to catch it.

Elizabeth and Philip had decided that their children should be brought up to have as 'normal' a life as possible, but Elizabeth realised that, even though they planned later to send him to school, Prince Charles was not yet ready for the rough and tumble of competition in the outside world. She employed the nursery governess Miss Peebles to teach him at home in the Palace. At five, Prince Charles was used to a world of grown-ups, less so to interaction with children of his own age. Like Elizabeth he was shy and reserved, but he was also sensitive, lacking his parents' inner toughness. Charles and his sister were never close as his mother and her sister had been even though the age gap was far smaller – less than two years. Charles was very much alone on his pinnacle as heir to the throne and had to work out the implications of his position for himself. The dawning realisation that his mother was the Queen and that there was a 'royal' way to behave had an obviously inhibiting effect. He knew that he was 'different' – the most difficult thing for any child to sense in its relations with the outside world. Even on a visit to a friend's farm it was noticed that his reactions were contained, not spontaneous, his interest polite almost as if he were on a royal visit.

Charles's early childhood was very like his mother's but unlike those of most of his contemporaries – for a boy to be taught by a governess instead of going to nursery school was very unusual by the mid-1950s. Like his mother's, his curriculum included history, which he loved, and geography made relevant to him by his parents' travels; he was poor at mathematics, but as his future job would be unrelated to commercial considerations that hardly seemed to matter. Like her, he began French at an early age and like hers, his education was supplemented by expeditions to museums and historical monuments. And, also like hers, his expeditions were curtailed because of public interest. Elizabeth was taken aback by the publicity given to his visits and instructed Colville to write a personal letter to all newspaper editors: 'The Queen trusts that His Royal Highness will be able to enjoy this in the same way as other children without the embarrassment of constant publicity . . .' That was in April 1955; Elizabeth's appeal produced temporary relief for her son, but it was not to last long. She was preparing to launch Charles on the beginning of his career as a schoolboy. In preparation for this change, at Christmas 1956 a male tutor-companion, Michael Farebrother, replaced Miss Peebles at Sandringham. Mrs Lightbody retired – according to Charles's authorised biographer, Jonathan Dimbleby, Philip sacked her because she mollycoddled him and showed too much favouritism towards him over Anne. Both Mispy and Mabel Anderson were transferred to Anne. Charles's real childhood was over.

'Mummy, what *are* schoolboys?' the Prince had reportedly asked his mother. On 28 January 1957 he became the first heir to the throne to begin primary school education. Dressed in his school uniform of ochre sweater and ginger corduroy shorts, the Prince (with Mispy in attendance) was driven in one of the less ostentatious of the Palace cars to a crowded red-brick building in Hans Place, an expensive square just behind Harrods. This was Hill House, his first school, recently founded and run on highly individual lines by Colonel Townend, a former artillery officer with a sporting background as an Oxford football blue and an athlete for England. Entry to Hill House was governed by the Colonel's personal approval. If he liked the mother, the boy was in. It was unsnobbish and academically not too competitive. The teachers were almost all women, most of them young and pretty, and there was no corporal punishment. The school motto was 'A boy's mind is not a vessel to be filled but a fire to be kindled.' There were sports at the Duke of York's Barracks playing fields on the nearby King's Road and swimming with his classmates in the Buckingham Palace pool.

Charles's first day passed off without incident as neither the press nor the public had as yet caught up with this latest development, but next morning large crowds crammed the narrow thoroughfares round the school and Elizabeth almost lost her nerve about sending him. He went, but had to run the gauntlet of the crowd both going in and going out – not an agreeable experience for an eight-year-old. On the third day Elizabeth kept him at home while Colville personally telephoned the newspaper editors with her plea that they withdraw their men and let her son go to school in peace. Once again it worked and at the end of term Elizabeth and Philip attended the school's Field Day. Charles took a competent part in dismantling and setting up a field gun, earning a 'Well done, Charles,' from his father. It seemed as if this first experiment had been a success and his parents prepared to extend it. Philip had made it plain in an interview he gave in the States that year (1956) what their educational objectives were for Charles. 'The Queen and I', he said, 'want Charles to go to school with other boys of his generation and learn to live with other children, and to absorb from childhood the discipline imposed by education with others . . .'[18]

But for a boy like Charles whose upbringing and background had been so different from his contemporaries, this was never going to be easy. From Hill House, Charles had always been able to retreat within the familiar walls of Buckingham Palace and to the security of Mabel Anderson. But on 23 September 1957, two months before his ninth birthday, his parents deposited him at Cheam, the preparatory school in Hampshire which had been attended by all the Mountbatten males including his father. He was about to set his foot on the first rung of the ladder which represented the beginning of the brutal rite of passage from childhood to adolescence of every British boy whose parents could afford it – the British boarding-school. His mother went through the same miserable time that every other mother does on sending her child off on that formidable experience – a mixture of guilt at inflicting it, misery at the parting, apprehension about how he would react and hope that everything would turn out all right. In Elizabeth's case the feelings were acute; it was only too evident that Charles was dreading the prospect. She saw him shuddering with horror on the long train journey down from Balmoral; Charles later remembered the first days at Cheam as the loneliest of his life. Just a few hours after his arrival, the young maths master who had been detailed to keep an eye on him looked out of a window and saw one small boy standing conspicuously apart, 'a solitary and utterly wretched figure'. At Cheam the boys were just that much older and therefore less innocent and more formidable than they had been at Hill House. They had all been told that the Queen's son was one of the twelve new boys that term and that the Queen wanted him to be treated just like anyone else, but it was just not possible for them to do so. 'Charles himself', his biographer Anthony Holden wrote, 'had no experience at all of forcing his way into a group of strangers, winning the acceptance of his peers . . .' Elizabeth knew that her son was miserable during his first years at Cheam, but felt that it was something he would have to bear in order to prepare himself for his future position.

The boys were not hostile, but the herd instinct made them wary of someone so obviously 'different'; the unwritten code of honour made them unwilling to be seen to 'suck up' to the Queen's son. Charles learned then that it was often the nicest boys whom he would have most liked to make friends with who hung back and the ones who approached him were often those he liked least. It didn't help that he was rather plump and not particularly good at sport, the quickest road to popularity. Nor did it help his self-esteem to have his father's example before him – Prince Philip of Greece had been first team goalkeeper and captain of the cricket XI. The behaviour of the newspapers made life difficult for him and for everyone at the school. Journalists hung round reportedly offering bribes for stories about Charles. 'Even the school barber was in the pay of the newspapers,' Philip raged, and Elizabeth sent Colville into action again. During the school holidays a meeting was held at Buckingham Palace for national newspaper editors at which Colville warned them that either they stopped their harassment at Cheam and printed only stories of genuine interest or the Queen would withdraw her son and educate him at the Palace and the press would get the blame. It worked, although the foreign paparazzi kept on trying and had to be chased off by the Prince's detective who had accompanied him to school. Charles got on all right, although his best friend at school was the headmaster's daughter, Mary Beck, the only girl there.

Much of the attempt to pretend that he was just like the others was spoiled by the announcement while he was still at Cheam at the end of the summer term of 1958 that Elizabeth had decided to create her son Prince of Wales. Elizabeth was ill after an operation for sinusitis, but she had tape-recorded a message to be broadcast at the opening by Philip of the Commonwealth Games in Cardiff:

I want to take this opportunity [she said] of speaking to all Welsh people, not only in this arena, but wherever they may be. The British Empire and Commonwealth Games in the capital, together with all the activities of the Festival of Wales, have made this a memorable year for the principality. I have therefore decided to mark it further by an act which will, I hope, give as much pleasure to all Welshmen as it does to me. I intend to create my son Charles Prince of Wales today. When he is grown up I will present him to you at Caernarvon . . .

The nine-year-old boy sitting in front of the television with a group of classmates in the headmaster's study at Cheam had become Prince

of Wales, Earl of Chester and Knight Companion of the Most Noble
Order of the Garter. Nobody had even thought of warning him about
it beforehand, which seems an extraordinary lack of sensitivity on
Elizabeth's part. Perhaps she thought it would come as a welcome
surprise, but if she really wanted her son to be treated like any other
schoolboy this television announcement was hardly the way to do it.
Elizabeth had had no school experience herself and had very little
idea of what schoolboys were like. Charles later recalled the feelings
of acute embarrassment he had felt at the time. There was no particular reason why Elizabeth should have chosen this moment to
create her son Prince of Wales; the decision had been taken only a
month before and its timing was due to the public relations instincts
of Harold Macmillan. At his audience on 25 June 1957 Elizabeth had
asked Macmillan's advice about the creation of Charles as Prince of
Wales. Macmillan told her that 'for the Queen to declare at some early
date that it is Her intention to create Prince Charles Prince of Wales
would give very great pleasure, not only to the people of Wales, but of
course especially to them. It must be remembered that no one under
the age of 25 has ever known a Prince of Wales in existence, and the
creation would not therefore be merely an expected formality, but a
truly significant event.' He advised her that her planned visit to Cardiff
to speak at the closing ceremony of the Empire and Commonwealth
Games would present an ideal opportunity for the announcement. He
also thought that there should be no question of the investiture
ceremony for several years, at least until Prince Charles was eighteen.[19]
Elizabeth agreed on both counts, but the decision was kept a secret
even from the Cabinet until just two days before the Cardiff announcement.[20] No doubt it pleased the Welsh – some 36,000 Welshmen in the
stadium cheered, threw their hats in the air, danced on the terraces
and sang 'God Bless the Prince of Wales' – but its immediate result
was to focus the spotlight even more fiercely on Charles by underlining
his position as future King, a heavy burden for a nine-year-old child
to bear.

His mother was looking even further ahead; early in 1959 she
suggested to Macmillan that she should hand over Marlborough House
as a Commonwealth Centre. Marlborough House was a royal palace
maintained by the Ministry of Works at public expense for occupation
by a member of the royal family. Its last occupant had been Queen
Mary, who had died there in March 1953. The house had huge rooms,
no central heating and few bathrooms. Modernisation would cost a

great deal of money and Elizabeth felt that she could not ask for public money for such a purpose. As a royal residence it was at that time surplus to requirements, but she did, however, think of providing a house for Prince Charles when he got married and cannily asked Macmillan if he could give her an assurance that when this happened the government of the day would ask Parliament to provide a 'suitable residence' in return for the surrender of Marlborough House.[21]

Early in June 1959 Martin Charteris was despatched to Accra on a special mission. The Queen had just told him that she was expecting a baby and would have to cancel her planned visit to Ghana later that year. She was afraid that if Dr Kwame Nkrumah, President and virtual dictator of Ghana, a notoriously tricky personage, was just told the bald facts in a cable he might be offended and fall into a rage with dire results. Charteris was to tell Nkrumah the intimate truth, which was that she and the Duke had been trying for another baby for a long time. Charteris flew to Accra on the pretext that he was to discuss the question of decorations with the Presidential administrator, an Englishman named 'Jacko' Jackson. When Jackson heard that he was to tell Nkrumah that the tour was off, he told Charteris, 'I wouldn't be in your shoes for anything – you could well end up in prison!' Apprehensive, Charteris went to meet Nkrumah in the Christiansborg Castle looking down over the old slave quarters and out to the Atlantic. When he told Nkrumah the news, there was a heavy silence as the President stared steadily with flat brown eyes at the Private Secretary; then Charteris gave him a friendly pat on the knee to ease the tension. Finally Nkrumah said, 'If you had told me my mother was dead, you couldn't have given me a greater shock. I have put all my personal happiness into it [the royal tour] . . .' Then he said, 'I must go and see the Queen at Balmoral', and to Balmoral he went. When she did get to Ghana, Charteris said, Elizabeth 'twisted him round her little finger'.[22]

Elizabeth's pregnancy was still a secret when she arrived in Canada towards the end of June for a mammoth six-week 15,000-mile tour in the course of which as Queen of Canada she officiated at the opening of the St Lawrence Seaway in the presence of the Canadian Premier, John Diefenbaker, and his wife and President Eisenhower accompanied by his wife, Mamie. She also visited Chicago on *Britannia* for what *Time* described as 'the most lavish 14 hours in Chicago's history', and the warmest reception she and Philip had so far enjoyed on their North American tour. She had had to take two days off resting at Whitehorse in the Yukon, ostensibly with stomach trouble, but otherwise, as *Time*

put it, her long, sometimes too arduous tour had been more of a
personal success than a triumph of monarchy in highly independent,
increasingly nationalistic Canada. As the Whitehorse *Star* informed
her, 'QUEEN, YOU ARE OK BY US.' Elizabeth flew back by Comet
to reveal what only the courtiers and heads of the relevant states
already knew – her pregnancy. The family were reunited at Balmoral
for the annual holiday, joined briefly by the Eisenhowers – the
President, his wife, their son John and grandchildren – who spent the
night and enjoyed the inevitable picnic tea at Loch Muick.

Elizabeth and Philip were delighted with her pregnancy. At Balmoral observers recalled 'how happy the prospective mother and father
were – teasing each other. The Queen was saying how extraordinary it
was after so long. They were frightfully pleased and happy with each
other – after all they had had their ups and downs.' They had been
trying for a baby for two or three years since Philip returned from the
four-month *Britannia* cruise to the Lisbon reconciliation. Earlier that
year he had once again been on a long sea voyage on *Britannia* circling
the globe, visiting India and Pakistan, then crossing the Pacific from
20 January to 30 April. The new baby was the product of their reunion.
(Years later 'insiders', ignoring the dates, spread rumours that Prince
Andrew was Porchester's child, conceived while Prince Philip was
away.) The birth of Andrew at Buckingham Palace on 19 February
1960 was widely seen as setting the seal on a successful marriage,
reinforced by the revelations in a Sunday tabloid of a former superin-
tendent at Windsor, now publican of a Hertfordshire pub, the Plough
and Dial, about the royal couple's sleeping arrangements (together in a
huge 7ft 6in Victorian bed with a tightly packed horsehair mattress),
which earned the man an injunction. Asked the reason for the almost
ten-year gap between the birth of Princess Anne and her younger
brother, friends gave various explanations – from 'she was too busy
when she first became Queen – then she got broody over having more
babies', to 'Prince Philip thought two was enough'. The baby was
named Andrew after his paternal grandfather in a further gesture
towards Philip.

Eleven days before the baby was born Elizabeth had made another
public gesture intended to repair some of the hurt caused by the 1952
decision not to allow Philip's family name to be passed on to their
children. Queen Mary was dead, Churchill in retirement; the Queen
Mother's reservations about the name change probably remained the

same, but Elizabeth now offered a compromise. On 8 February 1960 she issued a statement in Council:

> Now therefore I declare my Will and Pleasure . . . while I and my children will continue to be styled and known as the House and Family of Windsor my descendants, other than descendants enjoying the style, title or attributes of Royal Highness and the titular dignity of Prince or Princess, and female descendants who marry and their descendants, shall bear the name Mountbatten-Windsor . . .

It concluded:

> The Queen has always wanted, without changing the name of the Royal House established by her grandfather, to associate the name of her husband with her own and his descendants. The Queen has had this in mind for a long time and it is close to her heart . . .

The Mountbatten-Windsor name change episode is clouded in confusion. On 27 January 1960 Rab Butler, acting as Deputy Prime Minister as Macmillan was absent on his 'winds of change' tour of southern Africa, telegraphed the Prime Minister reporting a conversation he had had with Elizabeth:

> I have this weekend apprehended what was on foot at the Palace. The Lord Chancellor rang me in Gloucestershire on Saturday afternoon and from the parables I was able to understand that a change of name was envisaged for the children . . . today the situation was made clear by a talk with the Queen . . . She clearly indicated that the 1952 decisions [re keeping the family name of Windsor] had been reached, and that she accepted them, but she did not indicate that she accepted them in spirit. She stressed that Prince Philip did not know of the present decision, on which she absolutely set her heart.[23]

Macmillan had been at Sandringham to see the Queen after Christmas and discussed the subject with her then (although he had not seen fit to tell Butler anything about it). According to his biographer, Alastair Horne, Macmillan 'liked to make a good story' out of meeting the Duke of Gloucester there: 'greatly disturbed. "Thank Heavens you've come, Prime Minister. The Queen's in a terrible state; there's a fellow called Jones in the billiard room who wants to marry her sister, and Prince Philip's in the library wanting to change the

family name to Mountbatten . . ."' And, according to a source close to
Butler, at the time he said privately that when he discussed the
question with Elizabeth, 'it was the first time he had seen the Queen
in tears'.

It seems likely that, whatever Elizabeth may have diplomatically told
Butler, there had been some heavy lobbying from Mountbatten and
Philip, just as there had been in 1952. Elizabeth still stood by the
original decision not to substitute 'Mountbatten' for 'Windsor'. What
she was prepared to do was not to change the name of the royal family
as such, which was to remain the House of Windsor, but only to give
a surname to more distant descendants who, not being Royal Highnesses, would need one. It was not conceding what Mountbatten and
Philip had wanted in 1952, but it was a symbolic gesture in that
direction and would mean that Philip's name would appear as the
name of some at least of his descendants. Macmillan claimed the credit
for the compromise 'Mountbatten-Windsor', predicting (wrongly as it
turned out) that, as in the case of Spencer-Churchill, the first part of
the double barrel would quickly be dropped. One of the royal aides at
the time, however, remembers that the name was a solution put
forward by Martin Charteris. Whether Elizabeth was pressured into
it, or whether the idea was, as she said, 'close to her heart', she sent a
private message of gratitude to Macmillan via Butler saying that the
decision had taken 'a great load off her mind'.

When consulted on 2 February, some members of the Cabinet
'expressed serious regret that this step had to be taken but, while
recognising the dangers of criticism and unpopularity, particularly
attached to the husband, none felt that the Queen's wishes should be
refused'.[24] None the less, they did insist that the royal declaration
should 'make it quite clear that the Queen and her children would
continue to be styled and known as the House of Windsor'.[25] Suspicions of Mountbatten's ambition were strong, rightly as it turned
out. In 1973 when Princess Anne married Captain Mark Phillips, her
name appeared on the marriage register as 'Mountbatten-Windsor' in
direct contravention of Elizabeth's declaration of February 1960.

The year 1960 had begun well for Elizabeth, not only because of the
birth of Prince Andrew and the delight of having a baby in the nursery
again, but also because the perennial problem of her sister's love life
seemed to have come to a happy conclusion. After the Townsend affair
had ended, one by one all Margaret's male friends had married and by
1956 it seemed that only the archetypal chinless wonder, Billy Wallace,

the millionaire son of one of George VI's wartime ministers, was left. After he repeatedly asked the Princess to marry him, she finally consented as much out of the fear of finding herself left 'on the shelf' at twenty-six as from any real desire to become Wallace's wife. Then, to her outrage, the foolish fellow had a fling on holiday in the Bahamas, neglected to tell his royal fiancée that he was home until she tracked him down, and then blurted out the truth to her. To his great and continuing surprise she threw him out. Margaret was on her own again.

Elizabeth felt as responsible for her sister as she had when they were both in the nursery at No. 145 Piccadilly. Now that 'us four' had become 'us three' and the headship of the family had descended upon her, she felt even more responsible. Indulging Margaret had become a family tradition, even when she was behaving badly, as she often did. 'Ever since the breach with Townsend,' Lascelles told a friend, '[the Princess] has become selfish and hard and wild.' 'She [Elizabeth] gets angry with her but Family is all important to her and from that point of view Princess Margaret is one of the First Eleven,' a friend said. Subconsciously jealous of her sister, Margaret was not above cocking the occasional snook at her even now that she was Queen. Their relationship was much the same as it had been when they were children. At a picnic at Balmoral, Margaret might throw a dishcloth into her sister's face. One woman minister found Margaret's manner to Elizabeth 'informal to the point of coarseness'. After one state banquet at the Palace the women retired together as was the custom. The minister thought that the Queen looked particularly pretty in a gossamery evening dress with the Garter Ribbon as a sash across the bodice and complimented her upon it. Whereupon Margaret said to her sister, 'Darling, that does show your bosom up too much...' On 20 November 1957 Elizabeth celebrated her tenth wedding anniversary with a ball at Buckingham Palace, but on that evening her sister chose to take a party to the Coliseum to see *The Bells Are Ringing*. Afterwards she had supper at the Savoy and then arrived at the Palace only around midnight, an hour and a half after the dance had begun, and stayed for less than an hour. The press saw it as a deliberate slight to Elizabeth; Margaret still felt bitter about Townsend and resentful that she had been forced to give him up because of her sister's royal position. Elizabeth could celebrate ten years of marriage with a handsome husband and two children, but Margaret was still unmarried and alone.

She had not forgotten Townsend, who had gone on a prolonged round-the-world trip (seventeen months, 60,000 miles) to recover from the trauma of 1955. In March 1958 he was back and telephoned her to arrange a meeting; on the 26th the pair met at Clarence House with the Queen Mother's blessing. The Queen Mother behaved again much as she had during the famous affair, indulging her daughter and her own desire to see Townsend again, regardless of the consequences. Next day the meeting was headline news. Elizabeth, 'tight-lipped' on a state visit to the Netherlands, was reportedly furious as her visit was relegated to the back pages by her sister's indiscretion. None the less, Margaret went on seeing him and taking the initiative in doing so. Returning from a successful tour of the Caribbean in May, she traced Townsend to his sister's home in Somerset and invited him to a lunch the Queen Mother was giving at Clarence House; they met there again twice the following week. Marriage rumours began again; this time the Palace stepped in, an exercise in damage limitation. A firm denial was issued; the couple took the hint and after one more meeting Townsend left. Just over one year later, Margaret was to receive a letter from Townsend informing her that he had fallen in love with, and was to marry, a nineteen-year-old Belgian girl, Marie-Luce Jamagne. The fact that many people remarked how Townsend's new love resembled his old was no consolation. According to her biographer, Christopher Warwick, Margaret felt it was 'a betrayal of an understanding they had reached concerning remarriage after divorce'.

Curiously, Townsend's letter arrived when Margaret herself had fallen in love and was considering getting married. The man was Antony (always known as 'Tony') Armstrong-Jones. Armstrong-Jones, only five months older and just a few inches taller than the Princess, was completely unlike her first love, Peter Townsend, apart from the fact that, like Townsend, he did not come from the high aristocratic circles in which her friends like Johnny Dalkeith, 'Sunny' Blandford and Colin Tennant moved. His father, Ronald Armstrong-Jones, was a successful barrister whose family home, Plâs Dinas, was in Caernarvonshire (now Gwynedd). His mother, Anne Messel, was the beautiful daughter of a wealthy stockbroking family, owners of a famous garden at Nymans in Sussex, and sister of the designer and decorator Oliver Messel. His parents had divorced when Armstrong-Jones was five and both had remarried, Anne to the Earl of Rosse, an Irish landowner with estates in both England and Ireland, with his principal residence at Birr Castle, County Offaly. Armstrong-Jones's father had married an Australian from whom he was then separated.

Tony Armstrong-Jones had been to Eton and Cambridge, but he was completely different from the products of those two temples of education who adorned the Queen's household. At Cambridge he had taken no interest whatsoever in his academic work; his one achievement had been to cox the winning boat in the annual Oxford and Cambridge boat race, unnerving his more gentlemanly opponent by shouting at him, 'Why don't you f—ing move over?', when the two boats touched. He had a slight limp, the result of a severe case of polio when he was a child. He was artistic, a streak inherited from the Messels, bohemian and unconventional with a wide range of friends and lovers. He was intelligent and amusing, tough, determined and ambitious; his friends at Cambridge included the equally tough and determined heir to part of the Hulton publishing fortune, Jocelyn Stevens. Armstrong-Jones had enjoyed himself at Cambridge, left without a degree and turned his hobby, photography, into a career, learning his trade in Baron's studio and then setting up on his own. When Jocelyn Stevens bought *Queen* magazine as a twenty-fifth birthday present to himself in 1957, he invited Armstrong-Jones to help him liven up the magazine's stuffy image. 'Tony's' breakthrough into royal circles had come with a commission to photograph the young Duke of Kent for his twenty-first birthday – a job which he had gained by the simple means of writing a letter to the Duke's mother. From there he had graduated to photographing Prince Charles and Princess Anne before earning the final accolade of photographing Elizabeth herself.

Margaret met Armstrong-Jones at a dinner-party given by her friend and lady-in-waiting Lady Elizabeth Cavendish, the youngest sister of the 11th Duke of Devonshire, in the autumn of 1958. The party was intended to cheer her out of a fit of *weltschmerz* which had overtaken her after the unhappy final ending of the Townsend saga in May. Lady Elizabeth was a highly intelligent woman, the friend of John Betjeman, and her circle was artistic and intellectual as well as aristocratic. On that particular evening she had invited Armstrong-Jones, probably with the hunch that he was just the type of young man who might interest and amuse the Princess. Armstrong-Jones was uninhibited, relaxed and in no way intimidated by royalty; he had the easy, friendly but authoritative manner which all top photographers have with their subjects. Jocelyn Stevens said of Margaret, 'I have always regarded her as a bird in a gilded cage. She would have loved to break free but was never able to.' The young photographer appealed to that side of her and it soon became obvious to all their friends that there was a strong mental and physical attraction between them. Margaret was lovely and sexy, enchanting when she wanted to turn on the charm. Tony was interested in sex and very attractive to women; one of his first girl assistants had left when she accidentally developed a roll of film showing his Eurasian girlfriend in pornographic poses.

Margaret introduced Tony to her mother, who was charmed by him. In order to keep their affair secret he rented a room looking over the Thames at Rotherhithe. The house was dilapidated eighteenth-century, its bow window straight on the river; Tony's room, which he painted and furnished in white, became known to her as the 'little white room'. It was romantic and magical: 'One walked into the room and there was the river straight in front,' she recalled. 'At high tide swans looked in. And because it was on a bend of the river, you looked towards the Tower and Tower Bridge with the dome of St Paul's behind them . . .'[26] Here and at Tony's studio in the Pimlico Road, Margaret enjoyed an informal style of living and entertaining which she had never experienced before, with the emphasis on wit and amusement rather than flowers, food and fine wine, and she could enjoy herself on equal terms with Tony's artistic friends. In the early summer of 1959 Tony took a series of official photographs to mark her twenty-ninth birthday, which were published in August. Elizabeth invited him to stay at Balmoral, but still the press suspected nothing; his profession providing the perfect cover. It was while he was staying there in October that Margaret received the letter from Townsend telling her of his engagement to Marie-Luce Jamagne. Two months later in December 1959 the couple became privately engaged. The Queen Mother was told to her great delight, but it was not until January at Sandringham that Tony formally asked the Queen if he might marry her sister.

Elizabeth was almost maternally delighted by her sister's happiness, a joy undoubtedly tinged with relief that *that* difficult problem seemed to have been finally solved. The inescapable feeling of guilt which she had felt towards her sister since the Townsend affair was assuaged. News of the engagement was held back until after the birth of Prince Andrew, but when Clarence House issued the announcement on the evening of Friday, 26 February, precisely one week after Prince Andrew was born, the surprise was almost total. Among the public at large there was a general feeling of delight that the Princess had found happiness at last and among the young that she had married someone outside the 'tweedy' circle, whose talent and not his birth had made his career. Not everyone was pleased. Noël Coward noted a '*froideur*' when the subject of the engagement was raised while he was lunching with the Duchess of Kent and Princess Alexandra. If the Queen Mother and the Duchess of Gloucester, one the daughter of an earl and the other the daughter of a duke, had not been considered blue-blooded enough by Princess Marina to marry into the royal family, still less did she welcome a man called Jones who earned his living as a photographer. (When Patrick Lichfield told his mother, a Bowes-Lyon married to Prince George of Denmark, that he wanted to be a photographer, she sniffed that he might as well be a ballet dancer or a hairdresser.) Many of the European royals refused invitations to the wedding on the same grounds. There was a good deal of snobbishness about it in older aristocratic and courtly circles, whose members enjoyed retailing the story of how Lady Pembroke had made Armstrong-Jones eat with the servants when he came to take photographs at Wilton. One old courtier told Harold Nicolson that he lamented the whole thing and especially the announced plan for a honeymoon on the royal yacht. 'The boy Jones has led a very diversified and sometimes a wild life and the danger of a scandal and slander is never far off.'[27] The royal family, however, a friend said, 'liked him a lot' and were 'relieved'.

While the Princess's friends were happy to see the couple undoubtedly in love – 'We are *so* happy and blissful with each other,' Margaret wrote to a friend – and the Princess's mother and sister seemed prepared to suspend judgement in aid of seeing her safely married, some of Tony's friends had serious reservations. Jocelyn Stevens went so far as to cable instead of congratulations a sombre prophecy: 'Never has there been a more ill-fated assignment.' The bridegroom's father told him roundly that he was too free a spirit to put up with the restrictions of royal life. Tony could never properly belong to the royal family, his bohemian temperament would never allow it, and Margaret, try as she might to adapt to Tony's way of life, could never be anything but a part of the royal family. It was the only world she knew.

The wedding of Princess Margaret and Antony Armstrong-Jones was held at Westminster Abbey on 6 May 1960 – staged might have been a better word. It was the first great royal spectacular since the Coronation, designed at least in part by the bridegroom himself.

Norman Hartnell, whose speciality was the heavily embroidered grand occasion gown such as he had produced for the Coronation and the Queen's own wedding, was under strict instructions from Armstrong-Jones to keep it simple. The dress was spectacularly plain, depending for effect on simplicity of line and the subtle deployment of thirty yards of white silk organza. A silk tulle veil ordered from Paris by Hartnell fell in clouds from the magnificent Poltimore tiara, bought for the Princess at auction for £5,000, skilfully placed on her dark hair swept up into a chignon. Margaret looked the part of a fairy-tale princess as she was driven to the Abbey in a glass coach, the focus of television cameras sending her image around the world. The sniping of the press at the bridegroom's unconventional circle of friends, at his ex-girlfriend Jacqui Chan's choice of that moment to cut a pop record and at the last-minute embarrassment of the withdrawal of his best man, Jeremy Fry, ostensibly because of jaundice but actually due to rumours circulating about an alleged homosexual incident in his past, was eclipsed by the glamour of the occasion. The wedding cost £26,000 and questions had been raised in Parliament over the use of *Britannia* with its crew of twenty officers and 237 ratings for the six-week honeymoon, when the weekly cost of running the yacht was underwritten by the taxpayer to the extent of some £10,000 a week. The Queen Mother defused this by announcing that she would pay for it out of her own purse. However, the Macmillan Government, eager to cash in on the 'feel-good factor', contributed without a qualm. Suez, the criticisms of Altrincham, Osborne and Muggeridge, faded into the past as the public indulged in one of its periodic orgies of mass participation in and identification with royal family occasions. The occasion was splendidly stage-managed by the Lord Chamberlain, and interpreted by the Great Royal Communicator, Richard Dimbleby, without whose voice no royal occasion would have seemed complete. Dimbleby had recently been diagnosed as having cancer (he died five years later), but his choice of phrase to project the image which the public saw on camera and the reverential tone of voice confirming the ritual nature of the occasion were, as always, perfect:

For one moment we see the bride now as she looks about her at the Abbey in this lovely gown of white silk organza, with the glittering diadem on her head, the orchids in her hand, and the comforting, tall, friendly, alert figure of the Duke of Edinburgh on whose right arm she can rely . . .

The sun shone, the bride was beautiful; only the gender roles of the old fairy-tale had been reversed. The bridegroom played the Cinderella part, symbolically connecting the traditional royal family with the new talented generation which was to dominate the next decade. The 1960s was the era of the image, with the photographers acting as high priests to its gods the models and the rock stars. In the West Indies, destination of the honeymoon cruise, a Trinidadian calypso singer had already composed a song of welcome. It ran: 'Our lovely Princess thought it was stupidness ... why shouldn't a Princess marry a Camera-man? ...'

12

Advise, Consult and Warn

'She [the Queen] took her Commonwealth responsibilities very
seriously and rightly so, for the responsibilities of the UK
monarchy had so shrunk that if you left it at that you might as
well have a film star.'

Harold Macmillan to Harold Evans, 18 November 1961

The era of the jet plane plus her role as head of the Commonwealth
had already made Elizabeth the most travelled monarch of the House
of Windsor. Her widespread tours during the 1960s should be seen
against the background of the Cold War as Britain and the United
States battled with the Soviet Union for the hearts and minds of newly
independent developing nations in Asia and Africa. As a personal
symbol whom people regarded with affection and respect disassociated
from the taint of a former colonial power, she was a potent card for
her Prime Ministers to play. Macmillan was a statesman of the old
school, who thought in global terms and who found the transition from
Empire to Commonwealth an easy one. He saw Britain's role as the
leader of the Commonwealth as giving her a degree of power and
status to which her economic resources no longer entitled her, but he
was also pragmatically (some would say cynically) preparing to change
allegiances. It was during this period that Britain began her awkward
minuet with the developing European Common Market under the
aegis of the formidable General de Gaulle.

Macmillan had been looking towards Europe as a possible solution
for Britain since the end of 1959, when he wrote Elizabeth a long letter
telling her that, 'in the present state of Europe, if we are to reach
agreements helpful to this country, so long as de Gaulle remains in
power the French are the key'. A magnificently staged state visit by de
Gaulle to London took place in April 1960. It was an outstanding

success; de Gaulle knew very well how firmly Elizabeth's father had supported him in the war years, even against Churchill. He spoke with emotion at the banquet in Buckingham Palace of 'the most precious encouragements' he had received from the royal family. 'Where else, Madame, better than in your presence could I bear witness to my gratitude?' he said, as great Crosses of Lorraine in fireworks blazed outside Buckingham Palace. At the end of the summer parliamentary session in 1961 Macmillan wrote to Elizabeth reporting the debates on Europe:

The great majority feel that our position in the Commonwealth should we weaken industrially and economically would ultimately fade away. Could we in the second half of this century seize our opportunities and become, in association with Europe, a strong, active, and well-balanced country economically? We should become for that very reason a better member of the Commonwealth and more fit to lead it . . .[1]

There was not a great deal Elizabeth could do about Europe beyond charming de Gaulle with her fluency in French. In May, as if to underscore Britain's interest in good relations with the Continent, she made a highly successful state visit to Italy, meeting the Pope and being cheered by 100,000 people in Naples. The Commonwealth visits were more strenuous; in 1961 she undertook two major tours – to India and to Africa. En route to India at the end of January she and Philip stopped off in Cyprus to drink orange juice with President Makarios whom her Government had once deported to the Seychelles. In New Delhi more than a million Indians turned out to welcome her, the first British monarch to visit the country since her grandfather, George V, fifty years before. President Rajendra Prasad recalled: 'Our relationship with the United Kingdom is part of our history of the past 200 years . . .' Elizabeth attended a Republic Day parade and laid a wreath of 500 white roses on the tomb of Mahatma Gandhi. In Jaipur she rode on a ceremonial elephant and Philip took part in a tiger hunt. There was outrage in London when he killed a magnificent 9ft 8in tiger with a single shot. The *Daily Mirror* parodied Blake:

> Tiger, Tiger, burning bright
> In the forests of the night,
> Tell me, was it just a fluke
> You got potted by the Duke?

There was more bad press when, after a visit to Pakistan, the royal party moved on to Nepal, where King Mahendra had laid on an even more elaborate *shikar*: 305 hunting elephants had been corralled by local tribesmen and a camp prepared for the Queen's reception. Two square miles of soil had been removed to a depth of six inches to rid the area of snakes and insects and had been replaced by turf watered by a sprinkling system. 'Buckets of bugs' were taken away and the entire area sprayed with DDT. Elizabeth's two-bedroom tent was equipped with a white enamel bathtub with running hot water, and a flush lavatory topped with a royal red velvet seat cover. While drinks were dispensed from the backs of elephants, an agitated tigress was marshalled into a 'hunting zone' by eight elephants. Elizabeth refused to handle anything more deadly than an 8mm cine camera, while Philip, perhaps fortunately, had a boil on his shooting finger. The honour of despatching the tigress fell to the unwilling British Foreign Secretary, the Earl of Home, who missed three times before asking Sir Michael Adeane and the Duke's Treasurer, Rear Admiral Christopher Bonham Carter, to help. Bonham Carter and Adeane fired simultaneously, dropping the tigress in her tracks. Home missed again, explaining apologetically, 'I've never ridden an elephant before, never seen a tiger outside the zoo . . .' He did, however, manage to shoot a female rhino, depriving its calf of its mother and earning extremely bad press back home when he said he might make the feet into wastepaper baskets.

The problems of southern Africa rather than Asia were to occupy most of Elizabeth's attention as head of the Commonwealth over the next three decades. In October 1959 Macmillan had told a colleague that Africa was the biggest problem looming on their horizon and in January 1960 he had flown out to investigate the situation for himself, to Accra, Salisbury and finally to Cape Town, where he made his famous 'Wind of Change' speech warning the white South Africans of the strength of African national consciousness which they must now accept as 'a political fact'. On 21 March, less than two months after he left, sixty-nine black demonstrators were killed and another 180 wounded at Sharpeville. Macmillan told Elizabeth:

> The rigidity, and even fanaticism, with which the Nationalist
> Government in South Africa have pursued the apartheid policy have
> brought about – as I feared when I was there – a dangerous, even
> ominous situation in that country . . . I must warn Your Majesty that I

see a very difficult period facing the Commonwealth . . . my supreme
task is to try to avoid anything in the nature of disintegration.[2]

In October 1960 white South Africa voted to become a republic; Prime
Minister Verwoerd's application for renewed membership of the
Commonwealth in March 1961 foundered on his refusal to abandon
apartheid and the stage was set for the controversies of the next thirty
years.

The royal visit to Ghana which had been postponed due to
Elizabeth's pregnancy with Prince Andrew finally took place in
November 1961, by which time Ghana had become a republic and
there were fears that Nkrumah might also leave the Commonwealth.
Dr Nkrumah had become increasingly dictatorial and, it appeared,
anti-Western. He had returned from a visit to Moscow in October in a
hostile mood, sacked most of his Western advisers and thrown a
number of his opponents into jail. The internal situation in Ghana was
volatile and there were fears for Elizabeth's life in case she might be
the victim of an assassination attempt on Nkrumah while she was in
his company. Beyond that, liberal British public opinion was against
the tour as seeming to endorse an undemocratic regime. 'It is really
dreadful that the Queen should be going there, after the way that
Nkrumah has behaved and is behaving,' Lord Salisbury wrote to Lord
Swinton on 28 March 1961.[3] No previous royal tour had been
accompanied by what government advisers described as such a 'hulla-
baloo' in the press and argument in Parliament. The situation became
even more critical when, five days before Elizabeth was due to leave,
there were two bomb explosions in the capital, Accra, one of which
blew the legs off Nkrumah's statue in front of the Parliament building;
as a result, the British Government considered cancelling the visit.
The head of Special Branch had already been sent out there and the
Commonwealth Secretary, Duncan Sandys, made a second visit to test
the atmosphere for himself. Their conclusion was that, on balance, the
Queen should go ahead. Macmillan was willing to take the risk. Both
he and the new US President, John F. Kennedy, were playing for high
stakes in Africa, and keeping Ghana out of the Soviet sphere of
influence was their objective. To this end Kennedy was considering
providing the finance for the Upper Volta dam; Elizabeth's visit was
Macmillan's trump card.

Elizabeth insisted on going. She had given Nkrumah her word that
she would and she saw it as her duty to do everything possible to keep

Ghana in the Commonwealth. 'How silly I should look', she said, 'if I was scared to visit Ghana and then Khruschev went and had a good reception.' As Macmillan wrote in his diary:

> The Queen has been absolutely determined all through. She is grateful
> for MPs' and Press concern about her safety, but she is impatient of
> the attitude towards her to treat her as a *woman*, and a film star or
> mascot . . . She has great faith in the work she can do in the
> Commonwealth especially . . . she loves her duty and means to be a
> Queen and not a puppet.[4]

This was the first-ever visit to Ghana by a British sovereign. The British Government had taken care to smooth her way by returning the ceremonial stools and chairs captured by British soldiers in the Ashanti wars during her great-great-grandmother's reign. There was huge public excitement over the visit. The Principal Secretary of the State Functions Secretariat, Dr David Awotwi, in charge of the social side, was forced to go to ground in a secret office to escape pressure from the politicians who wanted themselves, their families and friends included in everything. On the eve of the visit a junior minister stole several hundred tickets to the most coveted event, the 'High Life' ball, and gave them to his friends so all the tickets had to be reissued in another form. At Kumasi in the central part of the country there was a magnificent Durbar of chiefs hosted by the Asantehene, Otumfuo Sir Osei Agyeman Prempeh II, King of Ashanti, who brought with him in a huge black Rolls-Royce the Golden Stool of the Ashanti rarely seen in public. At Accra Hospital Elizabeth and Philip managed to visit the seven-year-old Kwame Appiah, son of the imprisoned Opposition leader and his English wife, Peggy, daughter of the former Labour Chancellor, Sir Stafford Cripps. 'Last time I was here,' Philip told the boy, 'I had luncheon with your mother. Give her my regards.' Nkrumah was less than pleased.

The Government-directed local press called the tour 'Our Greatest Hour' and hailed it as heralding a 'fascinating change' in the current of relations between Great Britain, the Commonwealth and Ghana, 'a bridge over which the traffic of the future will pass toward the building of a new and more prosperous world'. All Ghana, the neo-Marxist *Evening News* declared, had been moved by this 'most modest, lovable of Sovereigns'. It bestowed on her the ultimate accolade – 'the world's greatest Socialist Monarch in history'. The British press, however, according to the report of the Acting High Commissioner, did their best to stir up trouble 'in their customary surly manner', abusing Nkrumah and reporting scare stories of alleged bomb plots including one to attach a limpet mine to *Britannia*, which so enraged the Ghanaian Government that the correspondents of the *Daily Mail* and the *Daily Express* were prevented from leaving the country and had to be bailed out by the High Commissioner.

The Acting High Commissioner's report reflected the exasperation of officialdom with what it regarded as the irresponsible attitudes of the British press and its increasingly anti-establishment stance. This attitude on the part of the press was a new factor which Elizabeth would have to face. Her immediate predecessors had been used to deferential coverage (with the exception of Beaverbrook's newspapers). Even the pre-Murdoch *Times* was guilty: 'it was particularly pleasing to see *The Times* making some amends for their irresponsible articles earlier this year,' the High Commissioner commented. 'On the other hand,' he continued, 'the *Daily Telegraph* and the *Daily Express*, no doubt out to prove their habitual thesis that when black men govern themselves they make a mess of things, remained incorrigible to the end . . . We pay a heavy price for a free Press and it is an appalling thought that, because a small group of British journalists are determined to abuse the host Government, the good effects of a Royal tour which has turned out to be an undisputed popular success, may be completely undermined . . .'[5] The royal family had been trained to ignore the press – 'those filthy rags of newspapers,' as George V used to call them. Unfortunately for Elizabeth, the press and the developing communications media would become the screen though which she was interpreted to her people. Personal contact was to be important to her as she tried to reach through the screen to the people in an increasingly arduous series of royal tours.

Macmillan, who would have been held responsible had anything happened to Elizabeth, had been reassured as to the tour's success by twice-daily telegrams from Michael Adeane detailing the warmth of her reception at the events of the day. From his point of view the Ghana visit had been a success (it was followed by visits to other West African countries including Sierra Leone, where Elizabeth, in response to criticism of her unbejewelled daytime appearance, wore tiaras and diamonds at every opportunity). Elizabeth had proved her value (and therefore Britain's) on the international scene and as a weapon in the Cold War. Her success in Africa, the cockpit of the Cold War during the 1960s, gave a fillip to her Prime Minister's hand in his wooing of President Kennedy. He had been in touch with Kennedy over the Ghana visit underlining the risk Elizabeth was running and implicitly connecting it with the financial one the President would have to take with the Upper Volta dam scheme. When she returned, he telephoned the President: 'I have risked my Queen,' he told Kennedy, deliberately hinting at an international chess game, 'you must risk your money!' It was gambling language which Kennedy understood. While responding to the British Prime Minister that he would match the Queen's courage with his own, he used the same terms to the international economist Barbara Ward when, on 12 December 1961, the United States formally announced participation in the Volta project: 'We have put quite a few chips on a very dark horse but I believe the game is worthwhile.'[6]

Elizabeth never wavered from her dedication to the Commonwealth, a view which Macmillan did not share. With his mind focused on relations with the United States and Europe and the invisible battle-fields of the Cold War from Cuba to Berlin, the Commonwealth to him was more an ideal to which he paid lip-service than a reality. The crunch came with the Commonwealth Conference in London in September 1962, when Macmillan attempted to justify to the assem-bled Prime Ministers the rationale behind his approaches to the EEC. Although backed up by a very able exposition of Britain's negotiating position by Edward Heath, Macmillan was not surprisingly unable to satisfy the Conference that 'Britain's entry into the EEC would not be incompatible with the Commonwealth, the two associations being complementary'. Even Sir Robert Menzies, the Australian Prime Minister, an old and trusted friend, made what Macmillan described as 'a very damaging speech'. Elizabeth, having received all the Prime Ministers individually that week, was probably better informed as to their real views than Macmillan was. At his weekly audience with her, Macmillan found her 'sympathetic' but 'worried about Commonwealth feeling'. The final communiqué made it clear that the Commonwealth leaders had the gravest reservations about Britain's negotiations to join the EEC and thought that the price she was being made to pay was too high, both from her own as well as the Commonwealth's point of view.

In the end, early in 1963, de Gaulle, to Macmillan's total dismay, issued a thunderous veto against Britain's entry into Europe. The Government's response to this rebuff was to give the General a slap on the wrist by cancelling a proposed visit to Paris in March by Princess Margaret and her husband, now the Earl of Snowdon, to attend a charity gala premiere of *Lawrence of Arabia* and lunch with de Gaulle. Sir Pierson Dixon, British Ambassador in Paris, had strongly advised cancellation on the grounds that the French Government would use it as an opportunity to play politics. He proposed using as an excuse the fact that as the Queen was absent on a tour of Australia and New Zealand, Princess Margaret's constitutional responsibilities as a Counsellor of State prevented her also from being out of the country. 'The excuse might be transparent,' the Ambassador advised, 'but that did not really matter . . .'

Across the world in Australia and New Zealand, Elizabeth's tour was affected by the sense of hurt and betrayal felt as a result of Britain's approach to the Common Market. The 'Faerie Queene' aura which had surrounded her almost ten years earlier on her post-Coronation tour of 1954 was no longer there. She was older and a more familiar phenomenon. Television had lessened the impact of seeing her and the crowds were far smaller than they had been in 1954. Elizabeth was to find diminishing returns on all her overseas tours of the 'Old Commonwealth' as her reign continued.

Back home in England Elizabeth and Philip endured for the first time the experience of being booed in public during the controversial state visit in July of King Paul I of the Hellenes and Queen Frederika. The visit had been intended as a symbol of reconciliation between Greece and the United Kingdom after their protracted breach over the independence of Cyprus. The omens for success had not been good. In April that year Queen Frederika, in England to attend the marriage of Princess Alexandra to the Hon. Angus Ogilvy, had been accosted outside Claridge's by Mrs Ambatielos, British-born wife of an imprisoned Greek politician. The Government knew that demonstrations were planned by anti-nuclear and other left-wing groups; the Greek Prime Minister, Constantine Karamanlis, had advised King Paul against the visit and resigned when the King rejected his advice. A good deal of bad feeling centred on Queen Frederika, daughter of the Duke and Duchess of Brunswick-Lüneburg, who was resented by conservative opinion in Britain for her ardent espousal of the union of Cyprus with Greece and by the left wing for her supposed 'Nazi' sympathies. As a girl she had been a member of the Nazi league of German Girls although she had had an English governess and had attended a well-known English girls' boarding-school, North Foreland Lodge. Recently, a newspaper editor who had printed gossip about her difficult relations with her eccentric mother, the old Duchess of

Brunswick, had been jailed. Queen Frederika was outspoken, tactless and interfering and, therefore, unpopular in political circles in Athens. As a descendant on her father's side of Queen Victoria's uncle, the King of Hanover, and on her mother's as a great-granddaughter of Queen Victoria, she was doubly related to Elizabeth while King Paul was Philip's first cousin.

The demonstrators, described by the fiercely anti-Communist *Time* as a 'motley collection of Communists, Socialists, anti-monarchists, ban the bombers [headed by Bertrand Russell] and beatniks', were initially given some countenance by the Labour Party's leader and deputy leader, Harold Wilson and George Brown, who boycotted a state banquet for the Greek royal couple. On the first night a chanting crowd of 1,500 people wearing black sashes demonstrated in Whitehall, but were prevented by police from reaching Buckingham Palace where Elizabeth was giving a banquet. The Foreign Office had taken the precaution of buying up every ticket for a special performance of *A Midsummer Night's Dream* on the following evening, but when the royal party arrived and left they were greeted by a chorus of boos and shouts of '*Sieg heil!*' Elizabeth herself was described as looking 'startled and dismayed' despite a volume of counter-cheering. It was the first time a British monarch had been subjected to such treatment since Edward VII had been hissed at Ascot by racegoers shocked by his part in a recent divorce scandal. In general the press condemned the demonstrators; the *Daily Mirror* took the leaders of the Committee of 100 to task for 'providing a shield for mischievous Communist agitation' and pointed out that Greece was practically the only country in eastern Europe not ruled by a totalitarian dictatorship.

Reminders of the royal family's foreign blood were not popular in Britain. In 1958 when President Heuss of West Germany came to London on an official visit, the reception was noticeably cool with most commentators harking back to the war. The President's gift of £5,000 towards the rebuilding of Coventry Cathedral was greeted with a snarl from the *Daily Mirror*'s star columnist, Cassandra: 'We want no apologetic tips on our national tombs . . . All I want of them is to wait for a generation to pass before they come sidling up to us saying it was all just a big mistake.' Elizabeth's speech at the state banquet at Buckingham Palace in the President's honour recalling her own and her husband's German ancestry went down badly with the public. 'Our German Blood' was the headline in the *Daily Express* next morning; it was not meant politely. The visit of King Paul and Queen Frederika was yet another reminder. The new satirical magazine, *Private Eye*, liked to refer to Philip as 'Phil the Greek'. Another visit by a head of state which roused a certain amount of hostility was that of the Emperor of Japan, Hirohito, in October 1971. Elizabeth, seated beside the Emperor as they drove up the Mall in an open carriage smiling and waving in customary fashion, could hear the comments of the crowd all too clearly. 'I'm glad the Emperor couldn't understand English . . . ,' she confided later.

Elizabeth's own first experience of the land of her ancestors was a ten-day tour of the then Federal Republic of Germany, planned in 1963 as part of Macmillan's European policy but undertaken only in 1965. It would be the first state visit by the royal family to Germany since before the First World War, a fact which was becoming embarrassingly obvious. By 1963 the Queen was the only head of a major state not to have visited the Federal Republic, nor had she returned the visit to Britain of President Heuss. Kennedy had made his famous speech at the Berlin Wall in the summer of 1963, while de Gaulle had made frequent visits, on one of which he had made much of his partial German ancestry – a field in which, as the British Ambassador pointed out, 'the Queen could outplay him with ease'. In comparison with Franco–German relations, particularly the two countries' collaboration in the EEC, Anglo–German relations were very much in eclipse.

The state visit took two years to organise, one not negligible difficulty being the royal couple's numerous German relations. Philip warned the British Ambassador, Sir Frank Roberts,[7] of the protocol problems which had arisen during a recent visit to Germany by the King of Greece and Queen Frederika. Princely Germans who had no status under republican protocol had none the less taken severe umbrage at finding themselves seated below relatively junior government officials at dinners for their 'Greek' cousins. To avoid trouble, Philip had suggested that Roberts should explain the position to the German President, Herr Lübke, and say that the Queen would understand if her relatives were not invited on formal occasions. Lübke absolutely refused to countenance this, explaining in his down-to-earth way to the Ambassador that in his native Sauerland, when a girl of the country returned after no matter how many years, her relatives must be invited to meet her and, therefore, he certainly intended to invite them. Prince Ludwig of Hesse and the Rhine, married since 1937 to a

British woman, Margaret Geddes, one of the few German relations frequently invited to stay at Windsor and Buckingham Palace and therefore accepted as an authority on the British royal family by the others, produced the solution. German 'royals' should be invited only when the Queen visited their particular area of Germany; this would reduce the previous protocol difficulty of having hordes of them attending functions at the same time. That, however, was not the end of delicate situations. Philip's relations, whose estates were principally in West Germany, still had their castles and large houses in which to entertain the royal couple, whereas the estates of some of Elizabeth's relations had been in the Communist East.

The Queen's first visit to the land of her forefathers would be an emotional experience for her which she was not at all sure she was going to enjoy. She did not speak the language, and through her most impressionable years when she was growing up during the war, anti-German feeling had been strong, even within her own family where her fiercely patriotic mother had experienced not only the Blitz but the First World War and the agony of having one brother killed and another wounded and captured. Elizabeth, like most people of her age, had been taught to hate the Germans and had, in the ATS, been trained to fight them. Her father had not been keen on his German relations and used to complain loudly about their always wanting to be invited to stay. Some, like the Coburgs, were considered completely beyond the pale since the old Duke had been a Nazi *gauleiter*. The Duke of Brunswick, the head of the House of Hanover, was not popular with his royal British relations, while his wife had been a Hitler *mädchen* and had recently all too obviously transferred her loyalties to General de Gaulle. The Duke of Brunswick made a point of having his servants dressed in Windsor livery when he held a grand-banquet – something which, despite the fact that he was entitled to do so, did not go down well with the British House of Windsor. He and his mother were not on speaking terms and at a reception in Hanover for the Queen, at which both had to be present, the Ambassador and his wife had to look after them separately after they had met the Queen.

Prince Ludwig of Hesse and his wife, known in the family as 'Princess Peg', were old friends of the royal couple. Prince Ludwig was an extremely talented man, very musical and a friend of Benjamin Britten, whose operas he translated into German. Before the Second World War he had been anti-Nazi and had planned to live in England after marrying his English wife; he had only reluctantly gone back to Germany to fulfil family responsibility when his elder brother, Philip's brother-in-law, Prince George Donatus, had been killed in an air crash en route to his wedding in 1937. Elizabeth was very fond of Philip's youngest sister, Sophie, known as 'Aunt Tiny', and her second husband, Prince George of Hanover, younger brother of the Duke of Brunswick and of Queen Frederika of Greece, and while in Germany she took time off to visit Philip's family and see the two places, Wolfsgarten and Salem, where he had spent so much of his youth before the war.

In the end Elizabeth genuinely enjoyed the German visit and the warmth of her reception. At Schloss Bruhl near Bonn she triumphed, looking, as one observer remarked, 'devastatingly beautiful' coming down the double staircase to a fanfare of trumpets, the embroidery on her pale blue dress echoing the rococo swirls of the plasterwork ceiling. 'Oh,' said Cecil Beaton, standing beside Hardy Amies, designer of the dress, 'she looks like *real* royalty.' At one Embassy reception the Ambassador, taking Elizabeth round, and thinking to give her a break, introduced her to Baroness Oppenheimer who shared her interest in breeding horses. It was, he said, a slight mistake: 'I couldn't get her to move on.' At Munich the Minister–President of Bavaria, with the Duke of Bavaria present, entertained the Queen to an opera gala. 'She doesn't like operas very much,' an official said, 'so we insisted it was a light opera – *Rosenkavalier*.' Curiously, the Duke of Bavaria, as the head of the Wittelsbach family, was the Stuart claimant to the throne. The Duke had been slightly nervous previously, having been asked to address the Stuart Society as guest speaker at their annual dinner the following January. Wanting to accept but equally not wishing to seem discourteous to the present incumbent of the British throne whom he was to meet, he – through an intermediary – consulted the Duke of Edinburgh, whom all the German princes seem to have used as a channel to Buckingham Palace. Philip replied to the intermediary in his famously blunt style: 'Well, you can tell him that we don't mind but it's a damn dull occasion, I'm told.'

Elizabeth had one free evening after a reception in Duisburg. To the Ambassador's surprise and delight when he said to her how much she would be looking forward to a quiet private evening, she said, 'Yes, but don't you think it would be nice to invite our German suite who have been so good to us?' 'I'm sure they'd love it,' the Ambassador replied, 'but I don't see that there's any obligation on your part to do so.' 'No, no,' she said. 'I'd like to do that . . .' At Cologne Cathedral the elderly Cardinal spoke not a word of English, but when he received the Queen he managed to deliver a speech of about five minutes 'in beautiful English' which he had learned by heart. When the Ambassador told the Queen this, she said, 'it was one of the nicest speeches that had ever been done in her honour'. Finally, in Hamburg, the great port which had once been part of the democratic Hanseatic League, there was a delicate question of her reception at the town hall, which had an enormous staircase. There was a tradition that even in the days of the Empire, the Mayor of Hamburg would stand at the top of the stairs and would never descend to greet the Emperor. There was considerable discussion about this and finally the Mayor said, 'I cannot go down to greet even the Queen of England but I will go down to greet a lady.'

Meanwhile, a series of events had led to the resignation of Macmillan. 'Supermac', as cartoonists had come to depict him in the earlier years of his premiership, had been losing his grip on the public and the party, a loss of touch emphasised by his panicky and ruthless sacking on 12/13 July 1962 of his Chancellor of the Exchequer, Selwyn Lloyd, and other Cabinet colleagues, including the Lord Chancellor, Lord Kilmuir, and David Eccles, the Minister of Education, an episode that has gone down to history as 'The Night of the Long Knives'. 'Greater love hath no man', commented the Liberal politician, Jeremy Thorpe, 'than to lay down his friends for his life.' The sacked Ministers had made no secret of their dismay in their valedictory audiences with Elizabeth, whose confidence in Macmillan and his reputation for 'unflappability' was shaken. To soften the blow, in a break with precedent Elizabeth invited their wives to accompany them to the Palace. Macmillan had acted quickly and brutally in order to avoid protracted press speculation over the approaching weekend (a tactic he was to repeat in October 1963 to secure the succession of the Earl of Home to the premiership). Some of the unfortunate men, a royal aide remembers, 'were on the verge of tears'. Lord Kilmuir had had so little notice of his dismissal that he arrived in white tie and tails complete with the Grand Cross of the Royal Victorian Order given him by the Queen because he had been booked to address a meeting of the Dairy Society as Lord Chancellor that night.

Later the same year, in October 1962, the Vassall case involving a homosexual civil servant entrapped by the Russians into passing on

defence secrets began the sex and spy mania which was to characterise
the next few years. Two journalists were subsequently jailed in March
1963 for refusing to disclose their sources and the press declared war
on Macmillan. Then in June 1963 the Profumo scandal broke. John
Profumo, the Secretary of State for War, had been sleeping with a call
girl, Christine Keeler, among whose other lovers was a Russian naval
attaché named Ivanov, who was also a Russian intelligence officer. The
whole affair had taken place against a backdrop of society scandal;
Profumo and Keeler had met at Cliveden, where Viscount Astor
hosted nude parties by his swimming-pool and Stephen Ward, a
society osteopath, had a weekend cottage to which he invited Keeler
and her fellow call girl, Mandy Rice-Davies. Following a court case
involving Keeler and one of her lovers who was accused of assaulting
her, rumours reached such a pitch that Profumo had been forced to
make a statement formally denying in Parliament that there had been
any 'impropriety' in his relationship with Keeler. In June, several
months later, Profumo confessed the truth to his wife and decided
to come clean about his lie to Parliament; he resigned his office
and retired from public life to devote himself to charity work in the
East End. Understandably he begged to be excused the customary
valedictory audience with Elizabeth. Stephen Ward was charged with
offences under the Sexual Offences Act of 1956 including brothel-
keeping and procuring a living on the earnings of prostitutes. Abandoned by his society friends, he took an overdose of Nembutal. He had
been a participant in the Thursday Club lunches and had drawn
portraits of the Duke of Edinburgh and other members of the royal
family. When Ward's drawings were put up for sale by his supporters
to pay his legal costs, Sir Anthony Blunt, Surveyor of the Queen's
Pictures since April 1945, quietly bought them to save the royal family
embarrassment.

At the same time another of Macmillan's ministers, Duncan Sandys,
was about to become involved in the fall-out of a salacious divorce case
between the Duke and Duchess of Argyll. The whole scenario shocked
Macmillan; sex was a subject from which he recoiled, involving as it
did the central tragedy of his life, his wife's affair with Boothby, a man
known for the eccentricities of his sexual attachments. Macmillan was
appalled by the seamy underside revealed in these scandals and hesitant
in his public approach to them. The American Ambassador in London,
David Bruce, described Macmillan's statement in Parliament as 'piti-
able and extremely damaging' when he claimed ignorance of the whole

affair, ending lamely, 'I do not live among young people much myself.'
On 23 June he wrote to Elizabeth what his biographer describes as 'an
almost painfully apologetic letter suggestive of a truly stricken man',
expressing his deep regret at 'the development of recent affairs' and
his feeling that he should apologise 'for the undoubted injury done by
the terrible behaviour of one of Your Majesty's Secretaries of State
upon not only the Government but, perhaps more serious, one of the
great Armed Forces . . .' He repeated the pathetic exculpatory tone of
his House of Commons statement: 'I had, of course, no idea of the
strange underworld in which other people, alas, besides Mr Profumo,
have allowed themselves to be entrapped . . .' He ended, with a touch
of paranoia, that he had begun 'to suspect in all these wild accusations
against many people, Ministers and others, something in the nature of
a plot to destroy the established system . . .'[8]

Elizabeth was reassuring, sympathising with him over the 'horrible
time' he must be experiencing and comforting him with her assurance
that she was well aware how difficult it was for people with high
standards to suspect colleagues of unworthy behaviour. She knew
Cliveden, the setting for the Profumo scandal, well, having often been
over to tea there with her mother and sister during the reign of Bill
Astor's mother, the formidable Nancy. Although she was nearer Bill's
age than she was Macmillan's, she was probably as shocked as her
Prime Minister by the goings-on revealed daily in the press. Unlike
Macmillan, however, she appeared relatively relaxed to find herself
one of the targets of the new-wave satirists. The year before she had
been reported as 'chuckling her way through' the review *Beyond the
Fringe*, accompanied by two other targets, the Foreign Secretary, the
Earl of Home, and the Lord Chamberlain, the Earl of Scarbrough.
The cast felt that they had failed; one was reported as saying that if
they had wounded the establishment as much as they had intended to,
the Queen's advisers would not have let her come.

In the midst of the welter of society and spy scandals, the counter-
intelligence service, MI5, learned through the FBI that there was
definite evidence that the distinguished art historian Sir Anthony
Blunt was a Soviet spy. It had been Blunt who had tipped off the
spies Guy Burgess and Donald Maclean, enabling them to escape to
Moscow in 1952 (after a telephone call from Kim Philby, who had
himself fled to Russia in February 1963). After the defection of
Burgess, one of Blunt's closest friends, MI5 had questioned Blunt on
fourteen occasions, but it was not until 1964 that suspicions they

harboured about him were confirmed. On the surface it appeared extraordinarily unlikely that a man like Blunt, a member of the Queen's household, a favourite of the late Queen Mary, and a popular and respected director of the Courtauld Institute since 1947, should have been a spy for the Soviets since 1936–7. He had worked for MI5 from 1940 to 1945 and in 1956, for his services as Surveyor, had been made a Knight Commander of the Royal Victorian Order, which is in Elizabeth's personal gift.

Blunt was a very English spy. Tall, thin, blond and charming, immensely intelligent and cultivated, he had been born in the respectably dull seaside town of Bournemouth in 1907, the son of a clergyman and of the daughter of a member of the Indian Civil Service. 'His father was a kinsman of the poet, anti-imperialist, and libertine Wilfrid Scawen Blunt, his mother a friend of the future Queen Mary,' wrote his biographer; 'both these connections were to have a curious significance for Blunt's future career.'⁹ While at Trinity College, Cambridge, he had been a member of the exclusive society, the Apostles, dedicated to the cult of the intellect, freedom of thought and the denial of all moral restraints beyond loyalty to friends. An influential minority of the Apostles was, like Blunt and his friend Burgess, homosexual, a secret network at a time when homosexual acts were illegal. Like Burgess and other Cambridge friends he was recruited by the Russians at Cambridge during the 1930s. Blunt appears to have been inspired by hatred of fascism, devotion to Burgess and the thrill of secret betrayal of a philistine establishment. All this made his long service at the Palace, the very heart of the establishment, all the more paradoxical.

To Elizabeth, he was a familiar if distant figure. He had been recruited by the Royal Librarian, Sir Owen Morshead, to assist with the cataloguing of the Old Master drawings in the Library at Windsor and had published a catalogue of the French drawings in the royal collection in 1945. By the spring of 1945 he was sufficiently trusted by the royal circle to be sent by King George VI with Morshead on a mission to Germany. A good deal of unfounded mystery has been woven around this mission. The reason why the King sent Morshead and Blunt to Germany was the recent capture by Patton's Third Army of the area surrounding the Friedrichshof, the castle built by Queen Victoria's eldest daughter, German Empress and Queen of Prussia, the seat of the Landgrave of Hesse and his family. Philipp of Hesse, head of the family, had been arrested by the Americans for his Nazi connections and his family evicted to a villa in the nearby village while the castle was requisitioned as a club for officers. The King was obviously concerned about the safety of family documents (rightly so, for one of the American officers and his lover looted cases of jewellery and other objects from the castle, which were later recovered in Chicago). With the permission of the Landg-ravine, Morshead and Blunt removed from the castle a trunk of correspondence between Queen Victoria and her daughter, the Empress Frederick, part of which had already been removed years earlier by another Windsor courtier, Sir Frederick 'Fritz' Ponsonby, who had annoyed both George V and the Kaiser by publishing the Empress's letters to her mother, the Queen, in an unauthorised version in 1927. The papers removed by Blunt and Morshead, known as the Kronberg Papers, were deposited in the Royal Archives at Windsor in August 1945 and were subsequently returned to the Landgrave of Hesse in 1951.

The mystery which later surrounded the Morshead/Blunt expedition arose from a confusion over the discovery at about that time of a huge cache of German Foreign Office documents buried in the Harz Mountains, among which was a file, later known as the Marburg file, concerning the Duke of Windsor's relations with the Germans including the episodes in Lisbon in July 1940. Despite Churchill's attempts to suppress them, these were later published in the volumes of Captured German Documents in 1957. Rumour had it that Blunt had abstracted the most damaging of these letters and used them to blackmail the royal family. Additional embroideries were that Blunt had been parachuted behind enemy lines to lay hands on these incriminating documents. According to Edward VIII's official biogra-pher, however, not one single paper brought back from Germany by Blunt and Morshead related to the Duke of Windsor.

In December 1945 the King entrusted Blunt with another delicate rescue mission to Germany. This time it concerned family treasures belonging to the Hanovers which the King feared might be looted by the Russians. After discussions with Prince Ernst August, a number of valuable objects including the diamond crown of Queen Charlotte, wife of George III, and the Gospel of Henry the Lion were spirited out of Germany in a secret operation which horrified the Foreign Office and deposited for safe-keeping at Windsor. (They were sub-sequently returned in equally secretive fashion to the Hanover family during Elizabeth's reign.)[10] Two years later, in August 1947, the King sent Blunt and Morshead to the Kaiser's former home in Holland, Haus Doorn, where he had died in exile. This time there was a connection; John Wheeler-Bennett, appointed to do the first sifting of the Marburg file, reported that he had found a reference in the file to the role played in the Duke of Windsor saga by the Kaiser, whose son Frederick William and his wife Cecilie were both used by Hitler as royal intermediaries. There can have been no other serious explanation for the King's anxiety to search Haus Doorn, which was no longer in any danger from enemy looting. In fact no serious documentary material at all was discovered, only the Kaiser's Garter Star and Field Marshal's baton, a Cosway miniature of the Duke of Clarence and some copies of nineteenth-century letters. Further suspicions about the significance of the Blunt/Morshead mission were raised by Spycatcher Peter Wright's statement that when he interrogated Blunt twenty years later in 1967, the Palace put an embargo on any questions about his missions to Germany. That in itself could seem suspicious to anyone unfamiliar with Palace methods and sensitivities. Palace officials simply wanted to keep the royal family out of a case in which they were not in fact embroiled, but which could raise, as it has, all sorts of unpleasant questions. It could be assumed that they were concerned not, as has been implied, with the Windsor connection, but with questions about the import and export of the collections.

The intelligence authorities decided on an immunity deal for Blunt. There were several reasons for this decision, not least that the unmasking of the 'fourth man' in the wake of the Philby defection and the Profumo scandal would be profoundly damaging and embarrassing. The revelation that the royal art historian and Knight of the Royal Victorian Order had been yet another highly placed Soviet spy was simply not to be contemplated. Further, counter-intelligence officers advised that it would be best to leave him alone and extract from him the confession that MI5's officer, Nicholas Elliot, had failed to get from Philby: a full list of those recruited and how they operated. The deal was approved by the Home Secretary, Henry Brooke, with the co-operation of Michael Adeane. The Palace, it must be assumed, took all these reasons into account in agreeing to play along – 'Blunt sang like a canary,' a courtier said. From then on until 1979, when he was finally publicly unmasked by Mrs Thatcher's statement in the House of Commons, stripped of his knighthood and disgraced, Blunt never came into the Private Secretaries' Office. He knew, and they knew, but it was a well-kept secret. At one point it was only by the use of some

delicate footwork that Martin Charteris managed to avoid the automatic granting of a further promotion for Blunt within the Royal
Victorian Order to GCVO (this did not mean any special favour:
'Promotion within the Royal Victorian Order', one courtier said, 'is as
inevitable as death').

Elizabeth knew about Blunt and the immunity from the beginning,
as Roy Jenkins discovered when a civil servant remembered that,
as Home Secretary, he should be told about it in 1966 – six months
after he had actually taken office. In October 1967 when Richard
Crossman, visiting Balmoral, attempted to discuss the Philby story, he
found himself cut short. He asked whether the Queen had read the
revelations in the Sunday newspapers that Philby, who had fled to
Moscow four years previously, had been a Soviet agent since before
the war. The answer was, 'No, she didn't read that kind of thing.' 'I
was suddenly aware', Crossman wrote, 'that this was not a subject
which we ought to discuss.'[11] At the Palace, apart from Elizabeth
and her Private Secretaries, nobody knew about it, not even Blunt's
deputy, Oliver Millar, who succeeded him as Surveyor in 1972. Millar
recalled:

> From quite early in my time as his deputy the day-to-day running of
> the office was left to me. He came, in fact, very seldom to the office in
> St James's Palace and I used to go up to the Courtauld for a talk or we
> would ring each other up. He was absolutely charming to work with,
> always encouraging and receptive. He had the gift of handing over 'sole
> charge' to those whom he trusted and to whom he had given
> responsibility. In his early days as Surveyor he had been especially
> concerned to initiate a programme of conservation – cleaning and
> restoration – and to put in hand the compilation of detailed catalogues
> of the different sections of the collection. By the time he resigned he
> had become a rather distant figure, but he had always, so far as I can
> remember, avoided big formal occasions . . . he always got out of it by
> claiming to be too tired or busy.[12]

Elizabeth, therefore, hardly saw the traitor whom she was harbour-
ing within her gates. The last public occasion with which he was
involved was the opening of the Queen's Gallery in 1962. It was none
the less for her, and indeed for Blunt, a piquant situation which was
perfectly portrayed in Alan Bennett's 1988 play, *A Question of
Attribution*. Her acceptance of the Blunt deal certainly saved the
establishment a good deal of embarrassment, as the row which followed

the unmasking of Blunt in 1979 showed. The admission of Blunt's guilt even then was forced out of the then Prime Minister, Margaret Thatcher, by the revelations of the investigative author Andrew Boyle, and it was only then that Elizabeth stripped him of his knighthood.

The Profumo affair, coming as it did on the heels of the spy scandals of 1962 and 1963, foreshadowed the end of the Macmillan era. Elizabeth had perhaps learned more from Macmillan than she had from her previous Prime Ministers. Although he had found their early contacts at the Tuesday audiences 'somewhat difficult' and forced, he came to lay great store by them and to take care that the discussions should be as full as possible, sending Elizabeth an agenda of the points he wished to discuss beforehand. 'This gave Her Majesty an opportunity to consider the issues involved, and frame her own views,' his biographer wrote. Macmillan approached Elizabeth in much the same spirit of formal gallantry which Disraeli had used towards Queen Victoria, with a touch of Disraelian flourish and occasional floridity in his style. He was genuinely impressed by the depth of her knowledge, the assiduity with which she absorbed the vast mass of documentation sent to her and, even after relatively few years on the throne, her remarkable accumulation of political experience. Apart from the weekly audience they carried on a frequent correspondence. Macmillan wrote long reports giving her inside knowledge of events as they happened, particularly when he was abroad at meetings and conferences. Elizabeth responded in what Macmillan described as 'a very informed and informal style', writing in her own hand and addressing the envelopes herself even though she had plenty of people to do it for her. Macmillan no doubt exaggerated the closeness of his relationship with her; he could never resist making a good story out of his latest sojourn at Windsor or Sandringham to regale and impress friends at the smarter London clubs or grand country-house parties. At times, he once told Mountbatten, he 'almost felt as if he were eavesdropping'; on one occasion he was summoned to Windsor to see the Queen and was talking to her in her sitting-room when the door opened and Princess Margaret, wearing a dressing-gown, came in, saw him, said crossly to her sister, 'No one would talk to you if you weren't the Queen', and went out again slamming the door, leaving the Prime Minister greatly embarrassed.

He was always sensitive to her feelings and careful not to infringe on her prerogative as when the idea of giving Rab Butler the title of Deputy Prime Minister was raised in September 1961. Elizabeth's father, George VI, had been quick to pounce on this when it had been raised by Churchill in the context of giving it to Anthony Eden in 1951. The King had pointed out that the title implied succession and, as such, was an infringement of the royal prerogative of choosing the Prime Minister. Elizabeth, very much her father's daughter, had, according to Macmillan, objected once before. 'The Queen has in the past rightly pointed out that there is *no* such official post, for which queen's approval is required . . .'[13] None the less, in the wake of the Night of the Long Knives, according to Butler's biographer, Macmillan gave Butler an 'unofficial intimation', conveyed to the parliamentary correspondents and published in their respective newspapers on 14 July 1962, 'that he would from now on in effect be Deputy Prime Minister'.[14] According to a recent constitutional authority, Vernon Bogdanor, Elizabeth again refused to grant the title to Butler and Macmillan therefore told the Commons that it was 'not an appointment submitted to the sovereign but is a statement of the organisation of Government'.[15] The Palace position remains that the office of Deputy Prime Minister 'has no constitutional significance'.

Curiously, for all Macmillan's reverence for Elizabeth and her office, the final act of his premiership was to link her even more closely and damagingly with the 'establishment' and to lead to a curtailment of her prerogative in choosing her Prime Minister. At his weekly audience on 20 September 1963, he told her of his decision not to lead the party into the next general election and that this would involve a change in the leadership in January or February. He noted in his diary that:

> The Queen expressed her full understanding. But I thought she was
> very distressed, partly (perhaps) at the thought of losing a PM to
> whom she has become accustomed, but chiefly (no doubt) because of all
> the difficulties about a successor in which the Crown will be much
> involved. We discussed at some length the various possibilities. She
> feels the great importance of maintaining the prerogative intact. After
> all, if she asked someone to form a government and he failed, what
> harm was done? It often, indeed at one time almost invariably,
> happened in the first half of the 19th century. Of course, it would be
> much better for everything to go smoothly, as in my case . . .[16]

According to his biographer, 'Macmillan declared himself determined at all costs to preserve this prerogative, the Queen's right to select her Prime Minister', but as it turned out, his handling of the question of his successor was to have the opposite effect.

Later, he vacillated, discussing the leadership possibilities with colleagues, ultimately concluding that he would fight the general election after all. On 7 October he was struck by acute prostate trouble; in great pain and always tending towards the hypochondriacal, he convinced himself that he could not continue to lead the party. On the eve of his prostatectomy, writing from his hospital bed in the King Edward VII Hospital, he told Elizabeth he must of necessity resign. She telephoned constantly to ask after his health in the days after his operation – three times on one day – but in a state of post-operative wooziness he could not understand what she was saying. Meanwhile the Conservative Party Conference at Blackpool opened in confusion with four leading contenders to the succession, Hailsham, Butler, Maudling and Home. Hailsham and Butler appeared to rule themselves out, the first from over-confidence the second from apparent diffidence (he had apparently been told three months previously by the chairman of the 1922 Committee representing all Conservative back-bench MPs that 'the chaps won't have you'). Macmillan had already sounded out Home as a possible leader; from his hospital bed the ailing Prime Minister determined to be in charge of the process of choosing his successor. Conscious of the accusations at the time of his own succession that the choice had been virtually in the hands of two peers and limited to the views of the Cabinet, he ordered the Lord Chancellor to consult the Cabinet, the Chief Whip to talk to other ministers and Conservative MPs, while the Chairman of the Conservative Party was to sound out the constituencies and Lord St Aldwyn the politically active Conservative peers. After these consultations and communications with the four leadership candidates, Macmillan spent the day, 17 October, writing a long letter to Elizabeth meticulously setting out the course of events of the past days. 'I am anxious', he told her, 'that everything done so far should be amply recorded in writing and not give rise to the kind of confusion by which previous crises have afterwards been poisoned with very ill effects to all concerned . . .' He had also dictated a 'top secret' memorandum, which he intended to give her if she asked for his advice, putting the case for Home:

The important fact in my view is that Lord Home's candidature has not been set forward on his own merits but has been thought of as a last-minute method of keeping out Mr Butler now that Lord Hailsham

has (according to the pundits) put himself out of court by his stupid
behaviour (at Blackpool) . . .

Apart from Home's actual lead, I am impressed by the general
goodwill shown towards him, even by those who give reasons in favour
of other candidates, and I cannot fail to come to the opinion that he
would be the best able to secure united support . . .[17]

That afternoon news of the advice to be given the Queen that Home
was to be Macmillan's successor leaked out. A revolt threatened
overnight and the Palace was lobbied against Home, but the lobbyist
was firmly told that the Queen must not be put in the position of
having to choose the leader of the Tory Party. According to one
source, Macmillan asked the Palace to advance his audience with the
Queen, which had been scheduled for 11.45 a.m., in order to forestall
any move by the rebels, and on the morning of the 18th at 11.00, in an
unprecedented move for a British sovereign, the Queen arrived at the
hospital for the farewell audience accompanied by Adeane. She went
alone into the hospital boardroom, where a tense and unhappy Prime
Minister waited for her, dressed in a white silk shirt for the occasion
but with a bottle in his bed and a pail underneath into which bile
dripped through a tube. His doctor, Sir John Richardson, waited
outside, his ear to the door in case of an emergency, but Elizabeth
spoke in such a low voice as to be almost inaudible. The doctor noted
that 'there were in fact tears in her eyes, and perhaps why I could not
hear was because her voice was not very steady'. 'What are you going
to do?' she asked Macmillan, who noted that she was very upset. 'Well,
I'm afraid I can't go on,' he replied. Then she said, 'Have you any
advice to give me?' Macmillan then read to her the prepared memorandum and handed it over to her for preservation in the Royal
Archives.

There was some concern at the Palace over the constitutional
correctness of Macmillan's behaviour. 'Macmillan was exercising a
right he thought he had to advise the Queen on her successor,' one of
the royal secretaries said, 'but technically he hadn't because he had
already resigned.' Given the unrest in the Conservative Party over the
decision, of which the Palace was well aware, it was also by no means
certain that Home would be able to form a government. Precedents
were consulted, notably George V's invitation to Baldwin after the
retirement of Bonar Law in 1923; Elizabeth then invited Home to the
Palace and offered him the premiership. The fourteenth Earl of Home

became Prime Minister of Great Britain, renouncing his earldom to become plain Sir Alec Douglas-Home under recently passed legislation. The resulting row even exceeded the controversy when Macmillan had been appointed. In a three-page article in the *Spectator* Iain Macleod claimed that the leadership had been settled by eight or nine Tory grandees – the 'magic circle' – all but one of whom had gone to Eton, in favour of one of their own and that Macmillan's memorandum had left the Queen with no option of choice. Enoch Powell made the same charge, that Macmillan had deliberately deprived the Queen of the exercise of her principal prerogative. There was some truth in this: Macmillan seems on the evidence of his published diaries to have taken the initiative in getting Home to present himself as a candidate with a view to having him as his successor. The Palace had made no attempt to take their own independent soundings but asked Macmillan to do so, the main objective being to keep the Queen from having to choose the leader of the Tory Party, which was certainly not her constitutional duty. The British passion for official secrecy meant that the results of the canvassing of the Conservative Party were not generally known. Macmillan argued that he acted as he did to protect the Queen, shouldering the responsibility for himself, but the end result left an unfortunate impression in the public eye. Either it appeared that the Queen was bamboozled out of pity for the old wizard into accepting his recommendation of an undoubted member of the grouse-moor set or that she acquiesced because of her own personal 'tweedy' leanings and the fact that Home was an old family friend of her mother's, who, as Chamberlain's Parliamentary Private Secretary, had seen eye to eye with the Queen Mother over Munich. Neither explanation did the image of the monarchy good in the new contemporary anti-establishment Britain.

It could certainly be argued that Home, an honourable man for whom no one who knew him had anything but respect and liking, was perhaps the best compromise candidate from the party unity point of view, but he carried with him too much old-fashioned baggage for the current climate. Elizabeth had appeared to have allowed herself to be led into accepting an outgoing Prime Minister's advice on his successor, which was against constitutional practice, however much Macmillan had dressed it up with documentation of soundings taken by Tory grandees. Michael Adeane, as the Queen's Private Secretary, it is argued, should have advised the Queen to exercise her independent right of consultation but he was anxious above all to keep her from any

involvement in choosing the leader of the Conservative Party. Moreover, despite the popular impression that Butler was the obvious
candidate, in fact Home was the choice of a majority within the party
and succeeded in forming a government including his rivals for the
leadership. In public relations terms, however, the outcome was
unfortunate for Elizabeth. The choice of the fourteenth Earl of Home
as Prime Minister against the background of the changes in social
attitudes which were taking place in the early 1960s showed the Palace
and the 'magic circle' as belonging to another era. Moreover, the
change which then took place in the method of choosing the leader of
the Conservative Party from private consultation to direct election was
further to limit the Queen's choice and, therefore, her prerogative.

A year later the fourteenth Earl lost his job to 'the fourteenth Mr
Wilson' (as he once retorted to the Labour leader) in the general
election of October 1964. Elizabeth's four previous Prime Ministers –
Churchill, Eden, Macmillan and Douglas-Home – all had a more or
less similar background with shared interests which she understood.
Wilson provided a new experience, coming as he did from an entirely
different social planet, a northern, provincial lower middle-class
background. Despite a brilliant academic record at Oxford, he had
remained endearingly, some thought deliberately, close to his roots.
He still spoke with a Yorkshire accent and followed the fortunes of his
local football club, Huddersfield Town. He was rarely seen without a
pipe in his mouth, which, as their relationship became cosier, he would
smoke during their weekly meetings. He was, however, the first of her
Prime Ministers to be almost of her own generation; born in 1916 he
was only ten years older, and he was a man who liked the company of
women and respected their intelligence.

In a breaking with tradition, Wilson arrived for his first formal
meeting with Elizabeth – to 'kiss hands' and receive his seals of office
as her First Minister – with two carloads of family and supporters, his
father, wife and two sons, and his confidential secretary, Marcia
Williams. Normally, a Prime Minister arrives alone. The Wilson party
sat on a sofa in the Equerries' Room and were given sherry by Patrick
Plunket. Marcia Williams's recollection of the occasion was not very
flattering:

> A number of anonymous Palace individuals were there. To me they all
> looked exactly alike. As I recall it, the conversation centred on horses.
> Perhaps it was assumed that everybody was interested in horses,

though my knowledge of them was minimal and the Wilson family's less. It struck me at the time as an ironic beginning to the white-hot technological revolution and the Government that was to mastermind it . . .[18]

At his very first Tuesday audience with Elizabeth, Wilson had got off to a spectacularly bad start when she asked him about something in the Cabinet Minutes and caught him completely on the wrong foot, unprepared and unbriefed on the subject. After that experience, Wilson would let the Private Secretary know beforehand the subjects he proposed to discuss with Elizabeth and he spent some time going over them with him before he went in to see her. He also used to bring his Private Secretary with him so that the two could liaise while the audience was going on and then, after it was over, Wilson would come down to the Private Secretary's room for a quick drink and another discussion. Elizabeth soon took to Wilson, enjoying his cosy manner, his wit and the expertise with which, as a born teacher, he could present the issues. 'Harold did get on very well with the Queen and she was very fond of him,' an aide recalled. 'His Audiences got longer and longer. Once he stayed for two hours, and was asked to stay for drinks. Usually prime ministers only see her for twenty or thirty minutes, and it is not normal for them to be offered drinks by the Monarch.'[19] 'I think the Queen talked very freely to Wilson,' one of her former Private Secretaries said. It was a rapport on a personal level which had nothing to do with shared interests, for they had none in common. Wilson never went racing, he neither rode nor shot; yet he offered Elizabeth a window on a world of which she had no experience, of provincial life, Labour beliefs and trades union politics. He made her feel in touch with her people in a way which his aristocratic predecessors could not. In return Wilson found in her a confidante whom he could trust. 'Harold was very fond of her and she reciprocated it,' his colleague Barbara Castle said. 'He made her feel at ease, kept her well-informed, probably quite racy in his reports. He really enjoyed his visits to her and reporting to her.'

In Barbara Castle's view his fondness for Elizabeth could obscure his political judgement and the detachment a Labour Prime Minister should maintain vis-à-vis the throne. When it came to discussions on an increase in the Civil List in 1975, Wilson agreed to the Palace proposals without even putting it to the Cabinet, she recalled. 'There was rumbling on the Labour side.'[20] When he finally left office in 1976, his Tuesday meetings with Elizabeth were the thing that he was to miss most about politics at the top. Richard Crossman, one of Wilson's ministers, also felt that sometimes relations between Queen and Prime Minister were too close, to the latter's disadvantage. When Emrys Hughes, Labour MP for South Ayrshire, wanted to put forward a bill for the abolition of hereditary titles, Crossman considered that it would be better to let him go ahead as no one took him seriously and any attempt to gag him might be misunderstood. Elizabeth, however, took a different view. Adeane went to see Wilson, who then made it clear he wanted the bill stopped. 'This is a good example of the Queen and the PM hobnobbing together,' Crossman wrote on 15 February 1967. (Later, however, Roy Jenkins and Crossman managed to persuade Wilson of the dangers of this course and Hughes was allowed to go ahead.) Elizabeth, ever alert to any potential threat to the monarchy, saw the abolition of titles as the first step towards an egalitarianism which could eventually threaten the throne, telling Crossman when he went to see her on Privy Council business at Windsor at Easter that she had 'looked through all the Sunday papers rather anxiously' for a report of the session in which the Bill had been introduced. Crossman could not resist saying that there had been two reports in *The Times* and the *Guardian*, both of which had said what a flop it had been, adding that he was glad he and Jenkins had been right in their advice to the Prime Minister. 'It was a mistake to say this as she didn't reply.'

It is a truism that Labour Prime Ministers get on better with their sovereigns than most of their Conservative counterparts. Elizabeth, like her father (but not her mother), is truly apolitical; ideology is not and cannot be a part of her mental make-up. Richard Crossman asked the Clerk of the Privy Council, Sir Godfrey Agnew, 'whether she preferred Tories to us because they were our social superiors'. 'I don't think so,' Agnew replied. 'The Queen doesn't make fine distinctions between politicians of different parties. They all roughly belong to the same social category in her view.' 'I think that's true,' Crossman added. Queen Victoria notoriously got on better with the working classes and servants like John Brown and the Munshi than she did with the aristocracy and High Society. The High Aristocracy with Whig traditionalists like the Dukes of Devonshire has tended to look down on the royal family as middle-class philistines. Hence the Queen got on far better with Harold Wilson than she did with Anthony Eden.

Their shared view of Britain was patriotic and conservative with a small 'c'. She could hardly be expected to feel cosy with a radical socialist like Tony Benn, who had discarded his inherited viscountcy and whose intellectual background and policies aimed at the destruction of the House of Lords and ultimately the monarchy. She saw and sees it as her job to get on with politicians of whatever party as the elected representatives of her people. 'I respected her as a true professional,' Barbara Castle said. 'She was most conscientious, did her homework. I particularly admired the skill with which she adapted to each situation, changing ministers and governments.' 'It can't be easy for the Queen when a Cabinet leaves office,' she said. 'She can't commiserate because that would reflect a judgement on an incoming government but equally she mustn't be cold. The way she got over it was by remembering everything connected with a minister – in my case, when I was dismissed by the new Labour Prime Minister, Jim Callaghan, it was "How is X hospital [which the Queen had opened] going?" – which kept the conversation going in a perfectly safe, politically neutral way.' Alone with her women guests after dinner at the Palace Elizabeth would inject just the right note of informality. 'On one occasion she said to me, "Poor Prince Charles has got his 'O' level tomorrow and I must just go and say goodnight."' Asked if she ever got an inkling of what Elizabeth was really thinking, Barbara Castle replied that she never gave anything away: 'She was professionally discreet above everything.' She felt too that there was a price being paid: 'You felt as though she never relaxed for a moment – there was a lot of repression there', that Elizabeth worked too hard to be correct and that 'a bit of human frailty would have been welcome'.

Her consort, on the other hand, was less successful at concealing his opinion of politicians. Baroness Castle described him as 'cocky' and was taken aback by his behaviour at the official opening of the Severn Bridge. While the band played the national anthem, Barbara Castle attempted to stand to attention as Philip muttered at her out of the corner of his mouth, 'When are you going to finish the M4? You've been a long time at it . . .' The radical Tony Benn, on the other hand, liked his iconoclastic ideas about various aspects of the royal role. Philip argued, in terms that were unlikely to have pleased his wife, about the necessity for changing the Queen's Commonwealth role, by which he meant the Queen being Queen of Canada as well as of Britain: 'They don't want us and they will have to be a republic or something,' he told Benn in February 1968.[21] He also said that he thought the Privy Council meetings were 'an absolute waste of time' and that the Prime Minister's audience should be broadened to include other ministers who could explain departmental issues to the Queen. Curiously, he thought government should be decentralised and showed himself to be a warm supporter of Scottish and Welsh nationalism. All this was music to Benn's ears: 'He is a thoughtful and intelligent person,' he noted of Philip. He was more suspicious of Elizabeth, whom he regarded as a siren figure luring members of the Labour Party away from their attachment to pure democracy and the working class. 'She is not very clever but is reasonably intelligent and she is experienced,' he wrote. 'She has been involved in Government now for eighteen years . . .' He was surprised at the vehemence with which she was prepared to express her views – 'You *can't* cancel Concorde,' she told him – and her honesty: when he asked her what she thought of Pierre Trudeau as Canadian Prime Minister, she replied that she had found him 'rather disappointing'.[22]

Richard Crossman, too, deplored Elizabeth's seductive influence over his colleagues and members of his party. After a meeting held to discuss a statement on the Queen's finances on 11 November 1969, he wrote:

> Barbara [Castle], Roy [Jenkins] and I are republicans. We don't like the royal position, we don't like going to Court or feel comfortable there, and we know the Queen isn't comfortable with us. Fred Peart, on the other hand, gets on with the Queen just like George Brown and Callaghan do . . . Harold is a steady loyalist and, roughly speaking, it is true that it is the professional classes who in this sense are radical and the working-class socialists who are by and large staunchly monarchist. The nearer the Queen they get the more the working-class members of Cabinet love her and she loves them . . .[23]

Some of the more intellectual left-wing ministers found the historic pantomime of royalty hard to take. Crossman, like Wilson a former Oxford don but unlike him a journalist, became Lord President of the Council in Wilson's first Government in 1964, a post which put him in frequent contact with Elizabeth. He was outraged by the custom which required busy ministers to attend meetings of the Privy Council in remote Balmoral or Sandringham if that was where she happened to be. 'The Privy Council is the best example of pure mumbo-jumbo you can find,' he wrote in his diary on 20 September 1966. 'It's interesting to reflect that four Ministers, busy men, all had to take a night and a day off and go up there [Balmoral] with Godfrey Agnew [the Clerk of the Council] to stand for two and a half minutes while the list of Titles [of Orders in Council] was read out. It would be far simpler for the Queen to come down to Buckingham Palace but it's *lèse-majesté* to suggest it.' One of his duties as Lord President involved attending Elizabeth for the 'pricking of the Sheriffs', when she actually pricked with a bodkin the names of these honorary local officials written on a document – 'a bodkin', Crossman recorded with quasi-disbelief on 23 March 1967, 'because Queen Elizabeth I did it with a bodkin and the tradition has been carried on'.

Crossman made a great show of disliking the 'mumbo-jumbo' which the involvement of the monarchy in the workings of government entailed. When Lord President he upset the traditionalist Duke of Norfolk by refusing to attend the State Opening of Parliament and backed down only when Michael Adeane pointed out that he could ask the Queen to excuse him, but added, 'Of course, the Queen has as strong a dislike of public ceremonies as you do. I don't disguise from you the fact that it will certainly occur to her to ask herself why you should be excused when she has to go, since you're both officials...' Crossman was fascinated by Elizabeth, who figures largely in his highly indiscreet diaries. At Sandringham he noted her skill at doing an enormous and very difficult jigsaw puzzle which was always laid out on a round table: 'while she was standing there talking to the company at large, her fingers were straying and she was quietly fitting in the pieces while apparently not looking round'. He was surprised by her sensitivity to other people's feelings. 'She asked me how morning sittings were going and I looked at her in surprise. "Oh, I'm sorry," she said, "I wasn't really criticizing." And I realised how sensitive she is and that my face must have revealed my irritation.' In June 1967 seeing the Queen on the eve of her departure for Canada for Expo 67, he said he hoped she would enjoy it although the exhibitions were terrible. She said, 'I'm too small to see them', and he had a sudden picture of the tiny little woman looking upwards and only seeing the soles of the feet of the statues above her as she was traipsed miles and miles around the red carpet. Some courtiers thought him hypocritical when he asked if he could bring his family to see round Buckingham Palace and then made rude comments about the monarchy in the press.

Nineteen sixty-four was in many ways a watershed year. Prince Edward, Elizabeth's last child, was born on 10 March. Early in the new year, 1965, Winston Churchill, now aged ninety and for long an extinct volcano, suffered a massive stroke and he died a fortnight later on 24 January. At Elizabeth's instigation he was given a state funeral, the coffin lying in state in Westminster Hall, as more than 300,000 people filed past. At St Paul's Cathedral for the funeral service, Elizabeth, as Mary Soames, Churchill's daughter, wrote, 'waiving all precedence, awaited the arrival of her greatest subject'. At the end of the service again the family preceded her out of the church, following the coffin, before it was taken to the simple country churchyard at Bladon, Oxfordshire, less than a mile from his birthplace at Blenheim. At the graveside was a wreath of white flowers on which Elizabeth had written in her own hand, 'From the Nation and the Commonwealth. In grateful remembrance. Elizabeth R.' In the same year Richard Dimbleby, the great interpreter of the royal show, died of cancer. Neither the Queen nor her entourage seem to have acknowledged the part Dimbleby had played in putting across the image of the monarchy. He was not given a knighthood; however, the Queen did send him six half-bottles of non-vintage champagne on his deathbed. In a sense Dimbleby's death was as symbolic as Churchill's, marking the end of an era of public deference, and even reverence, towards the monarchy. When Elizabeth celebrated the tenth anniversary of the Coronation in 1963 it had barely been noticed. 'The English', Malcolm Muggeridge told America via the Jack Parr show in 1964, 'are getting bored with their monarchy.'

13

Head of the Family

'The Queen has shown firmness in every area of her life except with her children . . .'

Anonymous

With the birth of Prince Edward, Elizabeth's family was complete. 'Goodness what fun it is to have a baby in the house again!' she told a friend. 'He is a great joy to us all, especially Andrew who is completely fascinated by him. In fact he considers him his own property, even telling Charles and Anne to "come and see *my* baby"!' In the 1960s, when Anne and Charles were teenagers and Andrew and Edward still young children, she seemed to have found a satisfactory balance between the demands of her work and her children. Prince Charles went on record as saying that he thought of his family as 'very special people'. 'I've never wanted to get away from home,' he said. 'We happen to be a very close-knit family. I'm happier at home with my family than anywhere else.'

Later, as his private life turned spectacularly and publicly sour, he blamed his mother's remoteness and his father's impatient strictness for the disaster. The Prince protested too much, but there was more than a little truth in what he was to say to his biographer, Jonathan Dimbleby. Elizabeth was noticeably more relaxed with her two younger children, Andrew and Edward, than she was with him. This was especially true with Andrew, an uncomplicated, rumbustious child, who was her favourite. 'She began to feel that she ought to do more about the children when Andrew was born,' a relation said. Elizabeth loved Charles and he her, but he was in awe of her and she was undemonstrative in her affection. One courtier remembered being in the room when Charles came to say goodnight to his mother as she was working on her papers. After he had kissed her goodnight, he was on his way out when Elizabeth said, absentmindedly, 'Goodnight, darling.' Charles stopped in his tracks and turned round saying in a surprised voice, 'You called me darling!' This did not mean that the children were not an important part of her plans, just that she had less time to give them than most mothers. When Charles caught chickenpox just before Easter 1959, she was forbidden to see him as she had never had the disease, but as soon as he was no longer infectious, she refused invitations in order to be with him. 'As it means I won't have seen him very much,' she wrote, 'I feel that to go away just as Charles is getting visible again would be unfair . . .'

Although Elizabeth seemed superficially impervious to the changes taking place outside the Palace walls as the Swinging Sixties gathered pace, she knew that in one important area of her life – her children – the outside world was going to have its effect. Hard as she struggled to protect their privacy, she knew that eventually they could not be screened from the world of their contemporaries and that as media interest in them grew ever more insatiable so the pressure on them would grow. She longed for them to be able to lead 'normal' lives while realising that ultimately this would not be possible. Knowing that their 'royalness' would inevitably make them suffer, she over-compensated for this by letting them do what they liked as much as she could. This was particularly true of the two younger children, born at the beginning of the age of permissiveness. It was true too of Anne, her father's girl, in whose presence Philip's face lit up, a confident, independent and strong-willed individual who would never have to shoulder the burden of kingship. It could never be as true of the Prince of Wales, born to be King and therefore subject to the rules imposed by his destiny.

Elizabeth and Philip saw it as their duty to bring Charles up to be equal to his future role. The fact that he was a sensitive and diffident child was, therefore, not a plus in their eyes, nor was what they perceived as weakness outweighed by his qualities of affection and goodness of heart. The lack of steel and tendency to self-pity in his nature dismayed them. Initially he had been a clumsy and unathletic child who brought out all his father's impatience, never far from the surface. An aura of 'wimpishness' hung over him which his parents were determined to eradicate. When go-karts were introduced, Anne and Charles had been given one. Anne leapt eagerly into hers; Charles initially refused even to get in his. 'Windy' was the word his parents used to describe his behaviour; 'lacking courage' would be a polite translation of its meaning. As it happened, Charles was later to prove them wrong on that count. Already he found warmth and appreciation in women other than his mother: his nanny, Mabel Anderson, his mother's lady-in-waiting, Lady Susan Hussey, and his beloved 'Granny', Queen Elizabeth, who recognised in him the vulnerability of her much-loved husband and encouraged him to appreciate music, art and books. Philip (although perversely capable of great kindness) was by nature a bully and he bullied Charles, sometimes bringing tears to his eyes. Elizabeth, like Queen Mary in a similar situation, never moved to protect her son, principally because she believed her husband to be right and secondly because she believed that his masculinity gave him the right to have the principal say in his eldest son's upbringing.

Elizabeth herself, brought up by governesses, had had no personal experience of public education. The Mountbattens were the deciding factor in the choice of a school for Charles – that meant Gordonstoun, the spartan school on the north-eastern Scottish coast which Philip had attended. The Queen Mother was firmly of the opinion that he should go to Eton as the school most suited to his temperament and where the boys, more used to the proximity of royalty, would be more at ease with him and he with them.

As Elizabeth's future Foreign Secretary, Lord Carrington, wrote, 'As schools go Eton was, I think, a tolerant place. There were none of the daunting rituals for new boys, the institutionalized bullying, about which one has heard or read of other places. One had one's own room – a small bedroom/study – from the first day one arrived ...'[1]

Elizabeth worried whether the proximity of the school to Windsor Castle and London might make him more homesick, although most people would have thought that a home-loving boy like Charles would have found its nearness reassuring. Perhaps she hoped against hope that far away from home it would be easier for him to adapt to his new environment. Whatever she might have thought, she had very little say in the matter. 'The Queen was not allowed to have a view at that stage,' a confidant said. 'She was constantly saying – "my view has to be checked over". It was quite awkward. Prince Philip was very obstinate and wouldn't come round to Eton ... The Queen was easily overborne, she had no knowledge of schools and gave in to Prince Philip because he was so anxious for his son to follow [in] his footsteps.' Philip also argued, not unreasonably, that Eton was too close to Fleet Street for comfort. The Dean of Windsor, Robin Woods, and Mountbatten, of course, were also consulted. No one took Lord Altrincham's suggestions of sending the heir to a state school seriously.

Neither Philip nor Mountbatten seem to have recognised that Charles had a very different and much more sensitive nature than theirs. No doubt the view they took was that 'it would make a man of him' and, as so often, they prevailed. When it came to the family, Elizabeth tended to revert to the traditional, wifely, submissive role. Whereas in her executive capacity she had a sureness of touch which surprised even the most experienced politicians, in personal matters she was reserved, even diffident, and would do anything to avoid confrontation. And Philip was determined to have his way on this. As early as 1959, in the opinion of his son's biographer,[2] he was 'clearly forcing the pace in the family argument', contributing £1,000 towards a rebuilding scheme at Gordonstoun and writing to his brother-in-law, Prince George of Hanover, 'Wouldn't it be nice if my son could take advantage of all these improvements?' Prince George himself had been a headmaster at Salem, Gordonstoun's 'twin' school in Germany. In the same year Dr Kurt Hahn, founder-headmaster of Gordonstoun, came to London to address a meeting chaired by Mountbatten's eldest daughter, Patricia Brabourne, where the vote of thanks was proposed by Lady Rupert Nevill, wife of one of the Queen's closest friends, and the audience included James Orr, Philip's Private Secretary, also an old Gordonstoun boy.

And so on 1 May 1962 Charles travelled north in an aircraft of the Queen's Flight with his father at the controls. He was extremely apprehensive; everything he had heard about the place made it sound 'pretty gruesome', and it was not made more attractive by the fact that the Duke of Bedford's son, Lord Rudolph Russell, had recently run away from it. On a visit earlier with his parents he had found it spartan even compared with Cheam. As it turned out, it was worse than he had expected. While Elizabeth might have taken comfort from the fact that three of his cousins, Prince Welf of Hanover, Prince Alexander of Yugoslavia and Mountbatten's grandson, Norton Knatchbull, were there, that did not protect him from the bullies. Officially bullying was strictly forbidden, but good intentions cannot control the aggressive instincts of adolescent boys and Charles with his sensitive temperament was a natural victim. The jug-ears, which have been mercilessly portrayed by cartoonists, did not help. Charles's parents showed considerable insensitivity in not taking Mountbatten's advice to have them operated on before subjecting him to public school life. Charles was, according to contemporaries, picked on 'maliciously cruelly, and without respite'; he was intensely and conspicuously lonely because any boy who made any attempt to walk with him or befriend him would find himself followed by a crowd making slurping noises indicating that he was 'sucking up' to the Prince. On the football field boys made it their business to cannon into the heir to the throne as hard as they could. The writer William Boyd, a fellow-pupil, overheard a gang of rugby thugs boasting, 'We did him over. We just punched the future King of England.'[3]

Such experiences mark a person for ever; it made Charles feel that no one would ever like him for himself and even more painfully conscious of the gulf which separated him from his peers. The ugliness and discomfort which characterise British public schools make them more like prisons or corrective institutions. For someone brought up in a Palace with every detail of life subtly attended to, Gordonstoun represented an extreme culture shock. Windmill Lodge, the house to which Charles was assigned, was a low stone and timber building with the most basic accommodation. Boys slept fourteen to a dormitory in unpainted rooms with hard wooden beds, bare floorboards and naked lightbulbs. The windows were left open at night, even when gales would blow in wind and rain horizontally from across the North Sea.

Charles did not mind the discomfort or the emphasis on physical fitness and outdoor activities nearly as much as he did the hostile atmosphere. Although he dutifully later said in public that Gordonstoun had been good for him, he confessed that he had loathed his time there and his letters to his friends at home make sad reading. The school was good for him, perhaps, in the sense of making him self-sufficient and toughening him up, which was what his father wanted. He took refuge in the countryside and the sea, in music and in visits to his grandmother at Birkhall on the Balmoral estate. The Queen Mother's heart bled for her favourite grandchild. 'He is a very gentle boy, with a very kind heart,' she said of him, 'which I think is the essence of everything.' When he pleaded with her to get his parents to take him away from Gordonstoun, however, she refused. In Charles's case the embarrassing consequences and bad publicity for everyone which would have followed such a move made it unthinkable. The press did not make his life easy even at that distance from Fleet Street. A book of his essays was stolen, sold and eventually published in a German magazine. Worse still, on one occasion when he took refuge in a bar to escape from the curious crowds pressing round him, he panicked when asked what he wanted to drink and said 'Cherry brandy' because he had drunk it before while out shooting. He was overheard by a journalist and the story of the underage Prince (he was fourteen) illegally buying alcohol made the headlines, causing a major uproar which deeply embarrassed Charles and gave him his first bad experience of press coverage. Not only was Charles humiliated by the episode but he was upset when the Metropolitan Police removed his friend and protector, his detective, Donald Green, from royal duty. 'He defended me in the most marvellous way and he was the most wonderful, loyal man,' he later told his biographer. The whole incident made him think 'it was the end of the world'.

Charles shrank every time he had to leave home for Gordonstoun. 'There were tears, and you could never find him when the car was waiting – he might be upstairs bathing Prince Edward or something,' a courtier remembered. Philip tried to get the whole miserable process over as quickly as possible. 'Papa rushed me so much on Monday when I had to go, that I hardly had time to say goodbye to Mabel and June [the nursery assistant] properly,' Charles complained. 'He kept hurrying me up all the time.' The experience took its toll on Philip too; a friend remembers him coming back from taking Charles to school, white-faced and, unusually for him, walking wordlessly to the drinks tray to pour himself a stiff drink. By now Elizabeth and Philip had come to admit that the Gordonstoun experiment had not been a success. Dermot Morrah, in his 'privileged account' of the young Charles, was authorised by Elizabeth to write:

> The contrast between their son's naturally introspective temperament
> and the determinedly outward-looking ideals promulgated by Kurt
> Hahn for his foundation was driving him still further in upon himself
> ... The Prince spent three years trying with his innate
> conscientiousness ... to follow in his father's footsteps in all school
> activities ... but he was doing it against the grain.[4]

In 1965, when he was seventeen, he was given a respite from Gordonstoun by being sent to school in Australia. In keeping with the ideas behind his education, he was not going there for his own pleasure but because Elizabeth felt that the heir to the throne should begin to have some first-hand experience of the Commonwealth, and in fulfilment of a promise she had made on her Coronation tour of Australia in 1954. Charles was to spend six months at Timbertop, the country branch of Geelong, often known as the 'Eton of Australia' (although it was in fact modelled on Gordonstoun lines). The decision was taken by Philip, in consultation with Sir Robert Menzies, the Anglophile, monarchist Prime Minister of Australia, and Dr Robin Woods, who, as Dean of Windsor, was the clergyman closest to the royal family (and whose brother happened to be Archbishop of Melbourne and Chairman of the Board of Governors at Geelong).

Charles was apprehensive about Australia and a new school environment as, from past experience, he had every right to be. At seventeen he was still pathetically attached to the nursery. 'It is an awful long way away and I shall hate leaving everyone for so long, especially Edward and Mabel [Anderson],' he wrote. He told his grandmother that he was taking two wristwatches with him, one of which would always be geared to English hours so that he would know what the time was at home and what everyone there would be doing. Elizabeth understandingly ruled that the decision whether he should spend one or two terms at Timbertop should be left to him. Just as his shy grandfather, George VI, had had when he entered unfamiliar territory at Cranwell and Cambridge, Charles was provided with a 'minder' (a protector from the outside world), in the form of one of his father's equerries, thirty-five-year-old Squadron Leader David Checketts, a man who was to be the mainstay of the Prince's life for the next thirteen years. Checketts established himself with his wife and children on a farm not far – in Australian terms – from Timbertop. As a trained public relations man, he was ideally suited to handle press enquiries as well as to provide a home environment for the Prince at weekends. Checketts not only protected the Prince but also prodded him into confronting his public duties. On one occasion when in transit on a refuelling stop, a large crowd gathered to see Charles. Charles's instinct was to remain out of sight on the plane, praying for it to leave, but Checketts forced him to get out and talk to the people. It was a formative experience; having once faced a crowd like that, he never feared it again. On the school's annual visit to the missionary stations of Papua and New Guinea, he was impressed by the magnificent feather head-dresses of the ritual dancers, the customs and skills of the tribesmen; it was the dawning of his interest in anthropology. He was also deeply moved by the Christian spirit of the missionary churches. Charles genuinely enjoyed his time in Australia; the family love of the countryside was strong in him. He had met friendliness and none of the hostility which he had encountered in his British public schools. Away from home, he grew up, although when he left he was still unsure enough of himself to insist on Checketts reading out the farewell statement which he had written himself.

He returned more confident to the dreaded Gordonstoun, this time driving himself with his father sitting in the back, underlining a distinct progress from boyhood to being an adult. He was made 'Guardian' of the school, a rather watered-down Gordonstoun version of head boy. Three terms later he left, having passed his A-level exams with grades good enough to win him a university place. He had also proved that he could act – putting on a masterly performance as Macbeth – and developed a passion for the cello. He made no lasting friends at Gordonstoun. It had been a brutal rite of passage which had left scars on his psyche.

Elizabeth realised to her dismay that the experiment in sending Charles out into the world to get along with his contemporaries had failed. She and Philip had hoped that the experience would have developed his character and drawn him out of his shy, unconfident self. But instead of drawing him out, it had made him more introspective and more of a loner than ever. With her usual honesty, she passed what Morrah had to say about Charles, now at the age of eighteen. Morrah wrote:

> His naturally introspective character seems to engender barriers which he himself recognizes and would like to remove, but which still baffle him as they have done since his early days at Cheam. He continues to feel that others who should be his intimates are constrained by the fear that any spontaneous advances they might make would be set down as toadying. It is still with those who are too old or too young to be suspected of such motives that he feels most comfortable. All who see him in their company agree that he has a wonderful way with children. He gets on excellently with older people, paying graceful deference to seniority but speaking his own mind frankly. But with his own contemporaries, outside his near kindred, he has yet to achieve any deep relationship. He suffers perhaps more than he knows from one of the inevitable inhibitions of royalty.[5]

Dermot Morrah, a Fellow of All Souls, a leader writer on *The Times* and, as Arundel Herald Extraordinary, a member of the Royal College of Arms, enjoyed an unusually privileged position as a member of the establishment who was also a journalist writing about the royal family.

His book, *To Be a King*, was subtitled, 'A privileged account of the early life and education of HRH the Prince of Wales, written with the approval of HM the Queen'. What he wrote, therefore, can be taken as reflecting what Elizabeth thought about her son. It is clear from hints by Morrah that as early as August 1966 Elizabeth had doubts whether he would even make captain of his house, let alone head of the school. 'They didn't appreciate what a gem they'd got,' a friend said. Elizabeth's response to a friend who told her how delighted she was that Charles was going to Trinity College, Cambridge, was the dampening, 'If he gets in.' Philip's behaviour at his son's confirmation in the royal chapel at Windsor in 1964 was odd by any standards and hardly calculated to make the sixteen-year-old boy feel that he occupied a central position in his father's thoughts. Throughout the Archbishop's address at the service he was seen reading a book. Whether this was a gesture of protest at Charles's confirmation in the Church of England (Philip's own religious history has been chequered – from a Greek Orthodox childhood through German Protestantism to his in-laws' Anglicanism), or aimed at discomfiting Archbishop Ramsey whose relations with the royal family were uneasy, it was, as the Archbishop later said to the Dean of Windsor, 'bloody rude'. Rude not only to the Archbishop of Canterbury, the spiritual head of the Anglican Church, but to his son whose day it was and who had approached the occasion with real religious feeling.

His parents' obvious lack of confidence in his abilities did not help the naturally diffident Charles, who hero-worshipped his father and copied him even to the extent of his habit of walking with his hands behind his back. By sending him to Cheam and Gordonstoun they had ensured that he would be measured against his father's achievements there and found wanting. At Gordonstoun Philip had been captain of cricket and, according to the experts, was good enough to play at club level. He was a natural athlete, good at every sport he took up, even when he came to it relatively late as he did to shooting and polo. Charles as a boy was not a 'natural', although through courage and perseverance he achieved a good deal, and as he grew up he followed his father in his passion for shooting and polo, although he never liked sailing. He showed no interest in science or technology, to his father's disappointment, which hurt him. Essentially a loner, he loved his grandmother's favourite sport, fishing, and, according to Morrah, any older friend of the family who came to visit (often Bishop Woods who would be sent up to Gordonstoun to take Charles out when his parents were too busy – it would often be six weeks before they could manage a visit) would find himself 'taken for long walks with the Prince among the lonely mountain rocks and burns of Morayshire, while his young host pointed out to him, with deep concentration and apparent expert knowledge, every pool, backwater and eddy where a fish might be expected to rise to the fly'.

On his eighteenth birthday in November 1966 after his return to Gordonstoun, Charles became officially of age to succeed his mother and rule of his own authority should she die, displace his father as Regent if she became incapacitated, and act as one of the Counsellors of State entitled to carry out her functions when she was abroad. It was something of a re-run of his experiences of 1957, when, as an embarrassed Cheam schoolboy, he had unexpectedly seen the news of his promotion to Prince of Wales announced on television. Again, no one had thought to tell him. He heard the announcement of his new powers on the 6 p.m. news.

On 22 December 1965, a year before Charles was to leave Gordonstoun, Elizabeth and Philip had held a dinner-party at Buckingham Palace. The participants were the Prime Minister, Harold Wilson, the Archbishop of Canterbury, Michael Ramsey, the Dean of Windsor, Robin Woods, the Chairman of the Committee of University Vice-Chancellors, Sir Charles Wilson, Mountbatten, representing the services in his capacity as Admiral of the Fleet, and Michael Adeane. Its purpose was to chart the next stage of the Prince's education. He had shown that he had reached university level and here at least there were no father's footsteps for him to follow. At this conference Mountbatten seems to have taken the lead. 'Trinity College [Cambridge] like his grandfather,' he said. 'Dartmouth like his father and grandfather; and then to sea in the Royal Navy ending up with a command of his own.' Mountbatten was an inveterate planner or plotter when it came to the royal family; he was not one to pass up the opportunity offered by his relationship to them. He was always popping in to the Palace proffering advice; sometimes Elizabeth accepted it, sometimes she did not. Now he was being offered a say in the career of the heir to the throne. The naval emphasis was his and Philip's; the choice of college and university, however, was due more to the wishes of the Queen Mother. Not only had Trinity College, Cambridge, been the college which her late husband had attended during his brief and undistinguished university career, but the Master of Trinity was an old and trusted friend of hers, Rab Butler. At Cambridge George VI and his brother, the Duke of Gloucester, had not been allowed to live in college but in a rented house on the outskirts run by his minder, Louis Greig, and his wife. As a result, they had had a very dull time, courted by dons but meeting very few undergraduates. The Queen Mother was determined that, after her grandson's experiences at Cheam and Gordonstoun, he should have the opportunity of meeting intelligent and civilised people of his own age and have the chance to lead a normal, enjoyable university life. Rab Butler was represented as being the ideal man to take charge of the Prince and the decision was taken that Charles should live in college at Trinity. Again, Elizabeth had played a passive role in charting her son's future, but this time Philip, also never having been to university, had had little input. He did, however, make an inspection visit, incognito, piloted by Bishop Woods, whose son was at Trinity. But while Philip later adapted to university life and very much enjoyed staying with the Butlers on informal visits to Trinity, Elizabeth was never at home there and seemed ill at ease on her first visit, quiet and sitting on the edge of her chair at lunch. She did, however, despatch the Palace 'tapissier' (the official in charge of furnishings) down to Cambridge to do up Charles's rooms.

Charles went up to Trinity in the autumn of 1967 to study archaeology and anthropology, subjects well suited to the descendant of the God Wotan, to whom almost all the rest of the world seemed like an unfamiliar and different breed. He had his own set of rooms, including his own kitchen, and more privacy than he had had anywhere away from home hitherto. Kindly, relaxed and highly intelligent, the Master and his wife, Mollie, provided a refuge for the Prince in the Master's Lodging to which he had his own key. First-year students were not supposed to have cars, but Butler turned a blind eye to the Prince's MGB, realising that he would need to get away. The Butlers introduced him to Lucia Santa Cruz, Butler's research assistant and the daughter of the Chilean Ambassador. She seems to have been Charles's first real girlfriend; the Prince, Mollie Butler remarked, 'cut his teeth on' her. Elizabeth was always 'very nice to her'; she was a suitable girl and it was time that Charles lost his diffidence with girls of his age. Charles worked hard and enjoyed university life – acting, music and dining clubs. To Butler's disappointment he did not make friends outside the upper-class circle to which he was accustomed; he was too diffident to make the effort to cross such bridges although he was temporarily almost converted by a socialist undergraduate on his staircase and asked Butler whether he thought it would be a good idea if he joined the Labour Club. Butler was anxious that the Prince should be given the time and space to achieve a good, civilising university education, something unknown in his family. While George VI had picked up a useful grounding in Dicey's *The English Constitution* and the ultimate treatise (with the same title) on the British monarchy by Walter Bagehot, the Duke of Gloucester had been reduced to killing mice to relieve the tedium and the future Edward VIII at Oxford had concentrated on sport and left with his Warden's opinion, 'Bookish he will never be . . .'

For all three a university education had been merely a gesture; Charles took it seriously and was determined to succeed on his own terms. But in this as in every other attempt to lead a normal life, his destiny got in the way. Elizabeth's promise to the Welsh made at Cardiff in 1957 to present Charles to the people as their Prince of Wales had to be fulfilled and a date had been set in June 1969 for his formal investiture. As the date approached she realised that the future Prince of Wales had hardly set foot in his principality. *Britannia* had called briefly at Holyhead in 1958, when Mountbatten and his daughter Pamela had taken the nine-year-old Prince ashore and, as Mountbatten characteristically put it, 'We thus had the unique privilege of bringing the newly created Prince of Wales to Wales for the first time.' To Welsh nationalists the idea of an English Prince of Wales was abhorrent; the original presentation of the Black Prince as Prince of Wales in Caernarvon, the castle of the defeated Welsh prince, Owen Glendower, had been a blatant act of triumphalism. Now they were going to be presented with a Prince who had a mere smattering of Welsh blood (through the Queen Mother), who neither spoke Welsh nor had ever lived in Wales. Elizabeth's solution was to transfer Charles (to Butler's fury and the Prince's dismay) to the University of Aberystwyth to study Welsh. It was all part of a plan to relaunch the monarchy in the year 1969. From now on the emphasis was to be on the younger generation.

When Charles left Gordonstoun, his sister Anne was sixteen and in her last year at Benenden, one of the top girls' boarding-schools in the country. With her forceful extrovert personality, she had found few problems in mixing with her contemporaries in a new environment despite having been brought up and educated at Buckingham Palace by Mispy, and having her only contact with girls her own age through the Buckingham Palace Brownie Pack. As a child she had been a tomboy uninterested in dolls – once when a visitor had happened to see a doll in her pram and asked its name, the Princess had glared and said abruptly, 'No name.' 'Having an elder brother,' she later said, 'I was rather more interested in playing the sort of games that he was playing . . .' She was competent, confident, athletic. Her father had taught her to swim, her mother to ride; she had the natural affinity with animals, particularly dogs and horses, which her mother had. A revealing set of photographs shows the young Princess handling an unruly young calf with ease, while her worried-looking older brother tussles ineptly with his animal at the end of a rope. As the second child and a girl, she never felt the same pressures upon her which her brother experienced as heir to the throne, but equally, she told an interviewer, she 'always accepted the role of being second in everything from quite an early age'. While she may have accepted that role in the family hierarchy, that did not mean that she did so in her daily life. She was fiercely competitive and, as far as her family was concerned, a rebel like her father had been, 'naughty but not nasty', as his Gordonstoun headmaster had put it. 'As a child and up to my teens', she said, 'I don't think I went along with the family bit, not until later than anyone else. I know its value now but I don't think I did up to my middle teens . . .' Later she was grateful: 'The greatest advantage of my entire life is the family I grew up in. I'm eternally grateful for being able to grow up in the sort of atmosphere that was given to me – and to have it continue now that I'm grown up.'[6]

Elizabeth's relationship with Anne was an exceptionally easy one, as her own relationship with her mother had been. Since she had been able to accommodate her husband's forceful personality, she had few problems with her daughter, who was in many ways almost his clone; there was none of the conflict that characterises many mother–daughter relationships. There was mutual admiration and respect for each other's abilities and shared interests. Like her mother and – to a lesser extent – her father, Anne had a passion for horses. Charles later claimed that he often felt left out at home when his mother, father and sister discussed the finer points of equitation or breeding and that they laughed at him when he made some elementary mistake in the subject. 'Oh, Anne's so practical,' Elizabeth would say delightedly, 'she always knows what to do', when one of the dogs was hurt. They even owned the same dogs; Anne had a black labrador and a corgi – a male refugee from the royal pack which was exclusively female. The relationship with her father was equally easy; Anne fulfilled in many ways the son's role to him but without the underlying element of male competitiveness. It was she, rather than Charles, who enjoyed sailing with him at Cowes on *Bluebottle* and *Bloodhound*.

Like her father, Anne had leadership qualities; in her last year she was made captain of her House, and her headmistress's description of her attitude might as easily have been applied to him. Anne, she said, was capable and able to 'exert her authority in a natural manner without being aggressive. If there was any failing at all it was possibly her impatience. She was extremely quick to grasp things herself and couldn't understand anyone else not being able to do so.' Like her father, Anne was not academically minded; she worked just hard enough at her lessons to get by and concentrated on sport and, above all, riding. She left school with two low-grade A-level passes in History and Geography and no ambitions whatsoever to go to university, which she pronounced 'a highly overrated pastime'. At school she had succeeded in crossing the invisible royal barrier between herself and her contemporaries far better than Charles had, but she was none the less deluding herself when she claimed (as did the girls and teachers who were at school with her) that she was treated just like any other girl. 'Fortunately children aren't so stupid,' Anne said of her first days at Benenden. 'They accept people for what they are rather quicker than adults do. They have no preconceived ideas, because how could they have? They accepted people for what they were and they had other things to do, so they weren't bothered.'[7] While the girls might have come to accept Anne, the idea that at the age of twelve her fellow pupils had no idea that she was the daughter of a woman called the Queen, whose pictures appeared constantly on television, in the newspapers, on stamps, coins and banknotes, is simply disingenuous. An ordinary girl does not attend boarding-school accompanied by her own detective nor is she addressed as 'Princess' by teachers.

Anne would have made a success of anything she took on even if she had not been a royal and she has, first as a top rider of Olympic standards, then as President of the Save the Children Fund. She owed her introduction to the world of the horse to her parents and specifically to her mother's Crown Equerry, Colonel Sir John Miller, who had his own gelding, Purple Star, sent to the top-class eventer and trainer, Alison Oliver, to be trained for her to ride. Sir John, who rode for England in the 1952 Olympics, as Crown Equerry was officially in charge of the Royal Mews, which meant all the Queen's horses and carriages and all her motor transport as well as the royal stud at Hampton Court and Prince Philip's polo ponies. Educated at Eton and Sandhurst, he was the owner of a large house and estate near Oxford, and had commanded the 1st Battalion of the Welsh Guards until appointed the Queen's Crown Equerry in 1961, a post which he held until 1987. A man of few but pithy words, he masterminded the royal horses (but not the racehorses), both for the family's sporting activities and for official occasions, with military precision and the perfectionism and attention to detail which is a feature of royal service. Sir John was a law unto himself; if he thought something needed doing, he would telephone the Queen directly and he was in the habit of dropping in on her to discuss things without warning. In the case of Anne, it was he as much as anybody who set her course for three-day eventing. After leaving Benenden Anne began training at Alison Oliver's stables at Brookfield Farm, Warfield, with the fierce dedication and self-discipline which she showed in anything she wanted to do. She made her eventing debut with Purple Star in 1968, coming a creditable fifth at the Eridge Horse Trials, and from then on she was launched on the eventing circuit, travelling the country with Alison Oliver, staying in the large country houses in whose parks the events were held and getting to know the horsy world in which she felt most at home. It was in this hard-riding, raunchy circle that she was to meet her future husband, Captain Mark Phillips, one of the principal eventing stars.

Since her eighteenth birthday in August 1968, Anne had been promoted, on Elizabeth's orders, to being referred to as Princess Anne and addressed by the household as 'Ma'am' and by the staff as 'Your Royal Highness'. She had her own suite of rooms at Buckingham Palace, sharing a sitting-room with her brother, and was entitled to £15,000 from the Civil List. She had her own car, a Rover 2000, and was already an expert driver, having learned early, like her brother, driving round the family estates. She had carried out her first solo official engagement in March, when she presented the 1st Battalion, the Welsh Guards, with the Welsh emblem, the leek, on St David's Day; for that and for subsequent solo engagements, the Queen 'lent' her one of her younger ladies-in-waiting, Lady Susan Hussey.

From being a dumpy schoolgirl, criticised by *Women's Wear Daily* for her puppy fat, her 'frumpy fur stoles and middle-aged evening gowns', she began to slim down, wearing contemporary clothes – even trouser suits – and was seen dancing on stage at the controversial musical *Hair* to the consternation of a senior duke, who described himself as 'very surprised with her. She's not particularly pretty, yet she was wearing a trouser suit, of all things. I've seen the show myself. Dreadful . . . People doing all sorts of things under that blanket, and standing naked . . .'[8] She was developing her own life, apart from her brothers. She hardly saw Charles, although their rooms were at opposite ends of the same corridor; Andrew and Edward were nine and fourteen years younger than she was and she did not entirely relish their company. Seeing them during their school holidays was 'enough, quite frankly', she admitted during a television interview on the children's programme *Blue Peter*, when she implied that she thought they were rather spoiled: 'you always consider that they're not always getting the sort of discipline you got when you were small'.

Meanwhile, she had gone from strength to strength in her favourite sport – three-day eventing – so that by 1971 she had qualified for the Badminton horse trials, a royal family occasion hosted by the Duke of Beaufort at his magnificent house in Gloucestershire. Riding one of Philip's former polo ponies, Doublet, and competing with top British and European riders, she managed to come in fifth while her future husband, Mark Phillips, won the championship. Later that year she won the European individual championship at Burghley in front of her parents and 50,000 people; Elizabeth proudly presented her with the trophy. She was only twenty-one and had been eventing for just three years before she reached the top. BBC TV viewers voted her Sports Personality of the Year and she polled the highest votes from the British Sportswriters' Association as 'the person who has done the most to enhance British sporting prestige internationally'. She was completely fearless, a natural athlete and as expert at handling a London bus on the Metropolitan Police skid-pan as she was at driving or even firing a gun from a Chieftain tank when visiting the regiment of which she was Colonel-in-Chief, the 14/20 Hussars.

Despite her sporting successes, Anne was not popular with the public. Like her father, she was outspoken, often rude, and had no patience with the media circus for which she refused to perform. She was determined to be herself and made no attempt to conceal her feelings or to play to the gallery as her grandmother did. She was uninterested in clothes and had no fashion sense. Like her mother, she could seem forbidding when she was not amused. On a joint visit with Charles to President Nixon at the White House in 1970, she singularly failed to charm the American media; the *Washington Post* dubbed her the 'Royal Sourpuss' and accused her of being 'sullen, ungracious and plain bored'. The British public regarded her as arrogant; she and Princess Margaret regularly came at the bottom of the royal popularity table for much the same reasons. The nadir of her relations with the British press was still to come: when at the Badminton horse trials in 1982 she famously told a photographer to 'Naff off!' According to the dictionary, although Anne was probably unaware of it, the term is mid-nineteenth-century slang for 'fuck'. Later that year at another horse trials she told two *Daily Mirror* reporters to 'piss off'. Elizabeth, who, despite all rumours to the contrary, is a permissive mother, was reluctant to attempt to control her daughter's behaviour. Although, like any other mother, she worried about her taking risks driving (Anne was fined at least twice for speeding) and would plead with her to be careful, reproving her was quite another matter. When, after the 'Naff off' furore, a courtier suggested that she really ought to speak to her daughter about her language, Elizabeth replied gloomily, 'I suppose it'll *have* to be me that does it.'

Despite her rather horse-faced looks (the member of the family whom she most resembled was her great-aunt, the Princess Royal), Anne, with her powerful, direct personality and healthy interest in sex, was attractive to men. She had many boyfriends, among them the well-connected Andrew Parker Bowles, future husband of Camilla Shand. But Anne was no snob; neither of her husbands was to be either aristocratic or rich. She tended to prefer the men she found on the eventing circuit, like Richard Meade, an immaculately handsome man with curly blond hair and an impeccable profile who was also a brilliant horseman, a double Olympic Gold Medallist who had won every major title in the eventing calendar. Meade described her as 'humorous, amusing and very exciting to be with', but denied they had ever discussed marriage. Mark Phillips came from the same eventing circle; he was a strong, expert horseman who had been chosen by the Badminton Committee to ride the Queen's big grey eventer, Columbus, otherwise known as 'the Monster' or 'the Brute'. Anne herself had suggested him to her mother as 'the most sympathetic of the good men I had seen riding'.

With Charles and Anne drawing most of the media attention, Elizabeth was more successful in guarding her two younger children from publicity. Virtually no notice was taken of them until they grew up and even then they were never to be the media stars that their elder brother and sister were. Elizabeth was delighted in the new dimension which having two new babies had given the family. 'Andrew has been a source of great fun this Christmas with everything being new and wonderful for him,' she had written to a friend in 1961. 'The tree and presents and the masses of people ready and only too willing to play with him – absolutely perfect.' She treasured her children's childhood and was devastated when it was discovered that Charles's nanny had accidentally thrown away all the letters she had written to him when he was small. Charles too loved babies – 'I wish I had one of these,' he said wistfully one day on a visit to his brothers' nursery.

Elizabeth has a great sense of family duty. She has been very generous to Philip's relations, his sisters and their families and to his mother, Princess Alice, who spent the last three years of her life at Buckingham Palace until her death in 1969. After the war, Princess Alice had started a nursing order of nuns in Athens. The order was perennially short of money and dependent on rich contributors, Elizabeth among them. When Princess Alice was ill in Athens, her daughters tried to persuade her to leave and go to London, but she adamantly refused until told that 'Lilibet said she should go'. 'Oh well, in that case let's go tomorrow,' she replied. Elizabeth was, Princess Alice's daughter, Princess George of Hanover, said, 'absolutely divine' to her.[9] She enjoyed talking to her mother-in-law, who had a sharp intelligence and a great knowledge of family history and relationships. Princess Alice had been born at Windsor and remembered Queen Victoria well – she was eighteen when the old Queen died. Princess Alice had a temperament somewhat like Philip's. 'They were both undemonstrative, and would talk quite roughly to each other,' a courtier said, 'but there was a deep bond.' She used to treat her brother, Mountbatten, like 'that naughty little boy'. She was great friends with Prince Edward, who could shout at the right tone so that she could hear him. 'He used to sit on the edge of her bed and she would read books to him and play Halma.' Unworldly to the end, she was determined to be buried in Jerusalem, 'because it's the centre of the Christian world'. When her children protested that it was too far away and that it would be difficult for them to visit her grave, she replied briskly, 'Not at all, there's a very good bus service from London.' Elizabeth has a reputation for meanness, but it is thrift rather than miserliness. She hates waste and the stories about her going round Buckingham Palace turning out the lights and sending Prince Charles out to hunt for a dropped dog lead are illustrations of that. She also hates to give things away or to pay too much for anything (a royal trait), but when it comes to supporting her extended family she is generous. 'She pays for everyone,' a courtier said. 'The Kents and people like that.' 'Really,' Elizabeth used to complain wryly, 'what with my mother and her castles and my mother-in-law and her nunneries . . .'

Cautiously through the 1960s Elizabeth was making moves towards healing the breach with the Duke and Duchess of Windsor. The situation was a tricky one for her: as the sovereign she could not approve of the Abdication; as the loyal daughter of King George VI and Queen Elizabeth, brought up to disapprove of Uncle David and particularly of Wallis Simpson, she could not welcome them with open arms without upsetting her mother, nor did she particularly want to do so. But Uncle David was still 'Family' with a capital 'F' and the continuance of the Windsor feud was doing the royal family no good in the eyes of the public, a majority of whom were now too young to remember the events of 1936. A poll organised by the *Express* in 1962 at the time of the Windsors' twenty-fifth wedding anniversary showed an overwhelming percentage in favour of the Duke and Duchess being allowed to return to live in England.

Relations had remained cool through the first ten years of her reign. The Duke had been furious when she had declined to continue the £10,000 a year allowed him by George VI. The royal family had not liked the stream of publications emanating from the Windsors, inspired by their desire to set the record straight, their constant delusions of impending poverty and the need for large sums to underwrite their extravagant lifestyle. The Duke's memoirs, *A King's Story*, had appeared in 1951 while George VI was still alive and the family had not enjoyed the raking-up of the Abdication story with all its painful memories and dangerous implications. The royal view was that it was highly undignified for an ex-sovereign and member of the family to 'do a Crawfie'. The Duchess's autobiography, *The Heart Has Its Reasons*, came out in 1956 and like the Duke's was a best-seller. 'Considering the malice in her mind, her book was surprisingly mild in effect,' wrote Charles Murphy, who had ghosted this book as he had the Duke's and persuaded her to suppress her ill will. More and unpleasant revelations from the Duke's past came with the publication in 1957 of Volume X of the captured German documents relating to the Duke's relations with the Nazis during his sojourn in Lisbon in July 1940. Although there was no actual proof in the documents that the Duke had contemplated treason, the papers did make plain at the very least that

the Germans believed that the embittered Duke could be persuaded to
betray his brother by acting as a substitute king in the event of a
negotiated peace or a successful German invasion of Britain. Churchill
had attempted to have the papers destroyed in 1945 and in 1953, under
pressure from the Queen Mother, and then to delay their publication.[10]
When the time came, the Duke, advised by lawyer Walter Monckton,
and the Foreign Office, managed to play down the papers as coming
from 'a much-tainted source' and being 'in part complete fabrications
and in part gross distortions of the truth'. In Elizabeth's eyes, the
Windsors were at best a nuisance and at worst an embarrassment.

There had been more trouble over the official biography of the late
King by Sir John Wheeler-Bennett, published in 1958. The Duke had
given Wheeler-Bennett several interviews and access to his archive; he
was understandably furious when the Palace refused his request to see
in typescript the passages which referred to him. After all, he argued,
'in the references to me . . . you are actually writing part of the history
of a living former Sovereign'. Wheeler-Bennett replied cautiously that
he would first have to consult Elizabeth, who after all had commissioned the book. She told him that she would read the book before
deciding which other members of the family should see it before
publication. An authorised biography of a sovereign is like an official
monument; Elizabeth felt that only she should exercise the right of
final decision as to how her father's life should be presented. The
Duke took her decision as yet another slight, writing furiously to his
lawyer in July 1956, 'I am incensed over this latest display of rudeness
towards me from the Palace, and am determined that, unless my niece
has the common courtesy to give me an opportunity of reading all
references to myself in Wheeler-Bennett's official biography of my late
brother, then no mention of me whatsoever shall appear therein.'[11]
According to the Duke's biographer, Michael Bloch, it was only after
a threat of legal action that Elizabeth allowed him to see relevant
portions of the text and then only at proof stage. Otherwise, he can
have had little to complain of in Wheeler-Bennett's book. Elizabeth
had seen to it that the wounds caused in the family by the Abdication
had not been reopened. References to Wallis Simpson were sketchy in
the extreme. (The Windsors' marriage at Candé rated a footnote of
one-and-a-half lines in which the name of the Bedaux château was
misprinted as Landé.) All family anguish and controversy were
suppressed. Elizabeth obviously preferred not to have the family's
dirty linen washed in public. The papers of Baldwin and Chamberlain

relating to the financial settlement were placed under embargo. (When H. Montgomery Hyde wrote his life of Baldwin, he saw everything which was closed to subsequent historians; Elizabeth blue-pencilled a passage in his book referring to a letter written by the King which made unfavourable references to the Duchess of Windsor.) Wheeler-Bennett made no more than a passing reference to the bitter quarrel between the royal family and the Duke of Windsor which had followed the King's decision in 1937 to withhold the title of Royal Highness from the Duchess, the one single factor which divided the family irrevocably. It was not until the 1980s when the researches of various historians produced documentary evidence of these quarrels that Elizabeth finally allowed Philip Ziegler, official biographer of Edward VIII, to print letters which showed all too clearly the gulf between the two sides.

Two years later Elizabeth had made amends for the difficulties over the Wheeler-Bennett book by giving the Duke and his co-author, Lord Kinross, access to the Windsor archives to research a slim volume of memoirs to be published as *A Family Album*. At the time of *A King's Story*, George VI, deeply unhappy about his brother's project, had refused him and his assistants any such facilities. *A Family Album* promised to be a far less controversial book and Elizabeth was anxious not to exacerbate relations with her uncle unnecessarily. Even then, as *Time* magazine noted, she did not avail herself of the opportunity to see him. Just before Christmas 1959 the Duke and Lord Kinross had turned up at Windsor Castle to visit the archives. Elizabeth, who must have known that they were coming and the time of their visit, had left one hour earlier to join Philip at a shooting lunch, preferring not to have a faintly embarrassing meeting with her uncle whom she had not seen since 1953. Some hours later the Duke and Kinross emerged from the rear entrance as Elizabeth and Philip were arriving at the Sovereign's Entrance. Elizabeth's unwillingness to meet her uncle may not have been unconnected with the knowledge of the Duke's illegal, possibly even criminal, currency dealings on the black market of which she had been informed that summer and which had at one moment threatened a scandal which would have affected 'the position and reputation of the Crown'.[12]

When the Duke was at Windsor in the late summer of 1959 (the family was once again not there to meet him, being away on holiday at Balmoral), he had walked into a dust-sheeted room. It was almost as if he had opened the door of the chamber in which the Monster of

Glamis had been shut up, a shameful secret hidden from the public eye. It was the room from which he had made his famous Abdication broadcast in 1936. Nothing had changed. 'There in the window was the chair in which I sat on that occasion, and the desk on which I had placed my script,' he wrote. He had been moved by an excursion to Frogmore, an elegant Regency house a few minutes down the hill from the castle. Frogmore in its peaceful setting beside a lake had been his childhood home when George V and Queen Mary were still Prince and Princess of Wales. It was there that the children had enjoyed peaceful holidays with their mother while their father was off sailing or shooting. In his absence the children and their mother had amused themselves playing silly jokes on the tutors, like giving the French teacher, M. Hua, a tadpole sandwich or dressing up some of the more lugubrious family busts in shooting clothes. Frogmore had a special significance in the iconography of the royal family; it was mausoleum territory established by Queen Victoria, whose obsession with death and funerary mementoes was excessive even by the high standards of her age. The small hill above the lake was crowned by the memorial built by the Queen in memory of her mother, while the garden was dominated by the mausoleum she had erected after the death of Albert in which the marble images of the couple lay side by side under a canopy of stars. Walking in the romantic garden beside the lake with its water lilies shaded by huge cedar trees and weeping willows, the Duke conceived the idea of himself and, above all, Wallis joining the family in death as they had never been in life. With this in mind he put in a request to Elizabeth that he and Wallis should be buried in a private mausoleum at Frogmore, following funeral services in St George's Chapel, Windsor. His request, involving as it did the ultimate recognition of Wallis as a member of the royal family, was treated with some caution but finally agreed to in December 1960.

Elizabeth took a major step towards reconciliation in March 1965 when the Duke was in London for an eye operation at the London Clinic, where he spent three weeks. One evening she visited him there and met the Duchess, their first sight of each other since at least 1936. After twenty-five minutes she left, seeming in the best of spirits, no doubt relieved that the ordeal of meeting the family bugbear was over. A spokesman described the meeting as 'very private but very pleasant indeed'. In family terms this was a huge step forward; in the following days, as the Duke convalesced, he and Elizabeth began to get to know each other, walking together in the gardens of Buckingham

Palace. On 7 June 1967, four days after their thirtieth wedding anniversary, the Duke and Duchess attended a royal family ceremony together for the first time when they stood in the front row with Elizabeth, Philip, the Queen Mother, the Kents and Gloucesters, at the unveiling of the memorial plaque to Queen Mary on the wall of Marlborough House opposite St James's Palace. All eyes were surreptitiously watching to see if the Duchess would curtsey to her old enemy, Queen Elizabeth. She did not. An observer described the Duchess as 'incredibly nervous', the Queen Mother as 'civil'. As Philip Ziegler remarked, it was a curious touch of irony that so intimate a family occasion, honouring the woman who had done most to ensure that the Duchess of Windsor should never be accepted as a member of the royal family, should be the first time the Duchess took her place in their midst. This public reconciliation was still only partial; the Windsors were not invited to luncheon with the royal party but lunched instead with Princess Marina at Kensington Palace before returning to Paris on an aircraft of the Queen's Flight. 'The young couldn't understand what all the fuss was about,' a courtier commented.

The Duke attended the next royal occasion, the funeral of Princess Marina in 1968, alone. The occasion seems to have acted as a *memento mori* for him; he finalised his ideas for a last resting-place for himself and Wallis, asking Elizabeth for permission for them to be buried in the family plot at Frogmore. He knew that on his death the £10,000 which had been negotiated by Walter Monckton before the war in lieu of rent for his life interest in Sandringham and Balmoral would cease and he had already written to Elizabeth on 17 August asking her to continue to pay it to Wallis during her lifetime. He raised the matter again with her at Windsor following Princess Marina's funeral on 30 August. It took Elizabeth nearly six months to give her decision, an indication of the extreme reluctance with which she approached such personal questions, but when she did reply on 26 February 1969, her tone was charming and friendly. 'Dear Uncle David,' she wrote:

> I am very sorry that it has taken me so long to answer your letter of August 17th, about which we spoke at Windsor in September, but it has taken time to find out the details.
>
> I appreciate the points you make and what I am prepared to do is this: Should Wallis survive you, I will make her a voluntary allowance

of £5,000 per annum, and if I die in her lifetime I feel sure my
successor would continue it. This is on the basis that the two blocks of
War Loan to which you refer are not reduced by Estate Duty when you
die . . .

 In any case, I hope that the question of any provision for your widow
is many years away yet!

 I do hope this will help ease your mind.

She was halving what the Duke had asked for, but, in view of the
hardline attitude of her parents towards his wife, the fact that she was
prepared to extend a continuing responsibility for her represented a
sea change. Elizabeth was behaving as decently and responsibly as she
could. She was not mean enough to hint that the gross extravagance of
the Windsors' life could perhaps be moderated if he was as worried as
he appeared to be about his financial position. Nor did she point out
that the Duchess would be a very rich woman when her husband died
or that she would still own a fortune in jewels paid for out of his
revenue as Prince of Wales, which derived from his former Duchy
lands and rents in England.

With this promise of help, Elizabeth cautiously extended an invitation to the next great royal occasion, the investiture of Charles as
Prince of Wales at Caernarvon Castle on 1 July 1969. 'As you know,'
she wrote, 'Charles's Investiture at Caernarvon takes place on July 1st,
but I have hesitated to enquire whether you would like an invitation
considering all the circumstances. But if you would reply to this
indirect form of invitation in whatever way you feel, I shall quite
understand.' As an invitation it could hardly be described as a pressing
one. The phrase 'considering all the circumstances' appeared as a
positive deterrent – what did she mean by it? The fact that the
Duchess had not been included? The inevitable press speculation
which even the Duke's presence would arouse, damaging Charles's big
day? There is no doubt that the Abdication was a subject which the
royal family would prefer to have forgotten and, indeed, the ranks of
those who did remember it were already getting thinner. The younger
generation neither knew nor cared about it, but every time the Duke
appeared at a royal occasion he represented living proof of the skeleton
in the family cupboard, the Duchess even more so. The Queen
Mother, everyone knew, had by no means forgiven the woman whom
she had once called 'the lowest of the low'. All this was presumably at
the back of Elizabeth's mind when she extended the 'indirect form of

invitation' implicitly excluding the Duchess, an exclusion which she must have known would make it impossible for the Duke to accept. Caernarvon could have presented the opportunity for a public reconciliation of the Windsor family, but the past still stood in the way. As if to make amends, the Queen ended her letter with a reference to Wallis: 'I hope you are both keeping well and with love and affectionate thoughts from Lilibet.'[13]

The Duke replied generously. 'As I do not believe that the presence of his aged great-uncle would add much to the colourful proceedings centred upon Charles,' he wrote, 'I do not feel that I should accept,' adding, 'At the same time I do appreciate your nice thoughts.' When, however, a few weeks later, he received an invitation to the dedication of the King George VI Memorial Chapel in St George's, he refused on the grounds that he would be on his way to the United States at the time, adding what his biographer described as 'a mild rebuke'. 'Although you did not include Wallis by name in the invitation,' he wrote, 'I presume that you expected her to accompany me. You see, after more than thirty years of happy married life, I do not like to attend such occasions alone.'[14] Privately, at least, a semblance of proper relations within the family had been restored.

Charles's investiture as Prince of Wales at Caernarvon Castle duly went ahead despite the fact that, unfortunately for the royal family, the atmosphere in Wales had changed dramatically since the day in 1957 when the announcement of Elizabeth's intention to make her son Prince of Wales had raised cheers from thousands of loyal Welsh subjects at Cardiff. The Welsh Nationalist movement, Plaid Cymru, had become much more vociferous and indeed violent; there were bomb attacks on public buildings in Wales and Elizabeth told Harold Wilson that she feared for her son's safety. None the less, two years previously she had decided that Charles should go to the ultra-Welsh college of Aberystwyth for the summer term preceding his investiture and she could not now change her plans without causing deep offence. The Welsh Nationalists were prepared for Charles's sojourn in their country and so was the Home Office, which mounted a highly visible security operation at Aberystwyth, billeting seventy-odd police officers in the town and infiltrating undercover men into the university disguised as cleaners and students. In the circumstances Charles showed real courage in going ahead; four Aberystwyth students went on hunger strike in protest against his arrival, a bomb destroyed an RAF radio station nearby and an attempt was made to saw off the head of a statue of the previous Prince of Wales, Charles's great-uncle David, on the town's promenade.

Unlike his great-uncle, for whom this mock medieval ceremony of investiture had been reinvented to boost the popularity of the Welsh Chancellor of the Exchequer, David Lloyd George, Charles took the whole idea seriously. Prince Edward had rightly protested about the whole thing and particularly the 'preposterous rig' which had been designed for him; Charles took an enthusiastic part in the preparations, which were masterminded by the Duke of Norfolk and Lord Snowdon. While Norfolk planned the details of the ceremonial, Snowdon, created Constable of Caernarvon by the Queen in 1963, superintended the design aspects, which included a dark green uniform with drainpipe trousers and zip-fastened roll-collared jacket for himself, a modernistic Perspex canopy and thrones of Welsh slate for Elizabeth, Philip and Charles. He did not, however, design the Prince's uniform or his coronet. Charles, apprehensive of being forced into some modern version of the 'preposterous rig', wore his Commander-in-Chief's uniform with a purple surcoat trimmed with ermine as a concession to theatre. Unfortunately Snowdon was defeated over the princely coronet, which he had wanted to be a simple classical band of gold. The eventual crown was an elaborate modernistic version of the Prince of Wales's traditional crown studded with jewels and replete with crosses and fleur-de-lys.

As the day approached, Elizabeth must have regretted her decision to follow the precedent set in 1911. Although Charles had won over a good deal of public sympathy by learning enough of the language to make a speech in Welsh at the League of Youth Eisteddfod in Aberystwyth, there had been complaints voiced about the amount of money to be spent on this 'mini-coronation' and it was quite clear that numbers of Welsh people were opposed to the idea of it. Worse still, from Elizabeth's point of view, was the possibility of a bomb attempt on the Prince. But, having gone thus far, it had to go ahead. As the Secretary of State for Wales, George Thomas, put it, 'There should be no part of the United Kingdom where the Royal Family cannot go', but, he stressed, 'It will require great moral courage from that young man.' Both on the eve of the investiture and the day itself there were bombs. The royal train was held up en route by a hoax bomb, but the next morning a real one exploded in a town thirty miles from Caernarvon, killing the men who were planting it. In London the BBC organised prerecorded obituary tributes to the Prince to be broadcast in the event of his assassination. As Charles travelled in the ceremonial carriage towards the Castle with the Welsh Secretary and his equerry, David Checketts, a loud bang was heard – another bomb.

At the Castle, the elaborate ceremony began with the arrival of Elizabeth dressed in a primrose yellow Norman Hartnell coat and hat. Patrick Plunket, Master of the Household, knocked on the Water Gate, which was opened by Snowdon bearing a fifteen-inch key. 'Madam, I surrender the key of this Castle into Your Majesty's hand.' Elizabeth touched it, saying, 'Sir Constable, I return the key of the Castle into your keeping.' She then proceeded to the dais with the slate thrones under the canopy before the Prince made his appearance with his own procession, which included six Welsh peers carrying his insignia – the sword used by his great-uncle, a golden rod or sceptre, a gold ring engraved with Welsh dragons, the velvet mantle and the coronet. As the Home Secretary, James Callaghan, intoned the Letters Patent – 'Elizabeth the Second by the Grace of God of the United Kingdom of Great Britain and Northern Ireland . . . by these Our Letters Do make and create our most dear Son Charles Philip Arthur George Prince of the United Kingdom of Great Britain and Northern Ireland Duke of Cornwall and Rothesay Earl of Carrick Baron of Renfrew Lord of the Isles and Great Steward of Scotland Prince of Wales and Earl of Chester . . .' – Elizabeth invested her son with the insignia and he then knelt in an act of homage. Placing his hands between hers, he swore: 'I, Charles, Prince of Wales, do become your liege man of life and limb and of earthly worship, and faith and truth I will bear unto you to live and die against all manner of folks.'

Charles later said he found this moment extremely moving, while Elizabeth told George Thomas that it had been a 'wonderful day'. Thomas's response was significant: '. . . it was a far greater triumph than we had a right to expect. He really was the Prince Charming. Wales has been in a state of euphoria, and at least half a million dollars came to Caernarvon itself.' The previous Prince of Wales had taken a more realistic view: 'I got the impression that if I did what was asked of me, it would help Papa in his dealings with the difficult Mr Lloyd George.' The ceremony of 1911 had been designed to boost the ruling party, that of 1969 was to boost the monarchy. It succeeded because it was evident that the Queen and the Prince believed in what they were doing. It might have been planned as a public relations exercise by their advisers, but to them it was part of their job as icons of the continuing myth of monarchy. Royalty have to believe in that myth or they will not be convincing; it is their way of communicating with the people. Via the television cameras their sincerity came across and the ceremony evoked the uplifting wave of emotion which is the *raison d'être* of such occasions. The investiture at Caernarvon was part of an unprecedented public relations campaign to relaunch the monarchy.

14

Daylight upon Magic

'You're killing the monarchy you know, with this film you're making. The whole institution depends on mystique and the tribal chief in his hut. If any member of the tribe ever sees inside the hut, then the whole system of the tribal chiefdom is damaged and the tribe eventually disintegrates.'

David Attenborough, anthropologist and maker of wildlife films, to Richard Cawston, producer-director of *Royal Family*

Elizabeth's deepest instinct was for privacy and for the preservation of her family life as far as possible from the public gaze. She had, like her father, been trained in the principles of Walter Bagehot, who had warned of the fragility of the monarchy's mystique: 'We must not let in the daylight upon magic.' Her advisers, however, were concerned that in the context of the 1960s, the monarchy was seen as boring and outdated. The answer, it seemed to them, was to bring the monarchy closer to the public by allowing them to peer through the keyhole by means of television cameras. First they were invited into the palaces to view the royal collections in a joint BBC/ITV collaboration, *Royal Palaces*. With *Royal Family*, in 1969, the public were permitted not only to look into the palaces, but also over Elizabeth's shoulder on private as well as public occasions.

The Mountbatten family persuaded Elizabeth to overcome her reservations about the idea. Mountbatten himself was always an eager publicist (two years earlier Independent Television had made a film about him, *The Life and Times of Lord Mountbatten*), while his son-in-law, Lord Brabourne, was a successful film producer (although not he but Lord Windlesham was to be the producer on this film). Philip was, as always, in favour of new ideas and change as far as the monarchy was concerned. A new element had been introduced at the Palace with the arrival in 1965 of a young Australian, William Heseltine, as

Assistant Press Secretary and the retirement in 1968 of the stonewall-
ing Commander Colville, whom he then replaced. Heseltine, unlike
the Commander, saw his job as giving the press easier access to the
royal family and the film was timed to coincide with Charles's highly
stage-managed investiture at Caernarvon. The film commentary promoted it as a revolutionary step in allowing the royal family to be seen
as human beings, speaking and acting normally where before they had
always appeared as icons behaving, and above all speaking, in a formal
'royal' way. The idea of presenting the royals as 'normal' and
'ordinary', ignoring the extraordinary circumstances under which they
have to operate, was to prove a dangerous step, although it did not
appear so at the time.

From its first showing in July 1969 and over no fewer than five
repeats over the next eighteen months the film attracted forty million
viewers in the United Kingdom alone. Elizabeth, always so stiff in
the Christmas broadcasts, appeared absolutely natural, just as she was
seen in her own circle, relaxed, radiating happiness and enjoyment,
making jokes, always smiling. She was, however, not the only principal
player; the object of the film was to promote Charles as the hope of
the future. The opening shots showed the twenty-year-old Prince
waterskiing and then on a bicycle in a London street. The images were
clearly intended to emphasise his contemporariness, but Charles, with
his serious, rather sad expression, conventional clothes and haircut,
came across as the reverse of 'with it', light years away from most
young people his age. There was a distinct air of Elgar rather than the
Rolling Stones. The old-fashioned aura which he presented through
youth into middle-age was to lead later commentators to dub him 'a
social dinosaur'.

The camera switched to his heritage, focusing on his mother in
uniform, solemn and erect, taking the salute on her charger, Burmese,
at her official birthday parade, Trooping the Colour. The atmosphere
of grand informality throughout the film was epitomised by the next
clip which showed a footman holding out a salver of carefully prepared
carrots which Elizabeth, dismounting with a skilful flick of her
cumbersome riding habit, fed to the horses. Tradition and continuity
were represented by the kilted piper marching at 9 a.m. under the
Queen's windows on the west side of Buckingham Palace, a custom
begun by Queen Victoria to remind her of her beloved Highlands. The
same ceremony takes place at Balmoral and at Windsor but not at
Sandringham. (On the Queen's official visit to Tokyo in 1975 the

Japanese with characteristic thoroughness arranged for a kilted Japanese piper to entertain her outside her windows at the Akasaka Palace
and make her feel at home.)

Elizabeth was seen at work with her Private Secretary, Sir Michael
Adeane, her manner very crisp and executive as she opened personal
mail and ran over the speech which had been prepared for her to
deliver in Brazil. 'Too much history which I would think they know
already,' she said, 'and not enough thanks. It seems a bit churlish not
to thank them for it . . .' The forward planning which went into her
official year was impressive. She was shown seated with Bobo standing
at her elbow, both with similar hairstyles and the regulation three
strands of pearls, putting together outfits for future tours using
coloured sketches for the dresses – 'I think I'd like to keep that one for
Australia.' Elizabeth fished in a leather box and came up with a
startling necklace of gold set with magnificent pigeon's egg-size
cabochon rubies, formerly belonging to the 'Persians', as she called
them – presumably the Mogul emperors of India – sent as a present to
Queen Victoria. 'Rather fascinating,' she says, using the qualified,
understated 'Windsorspeak' characteristic of the royal family. Apparently she had never worn this splendid object. 'One ought to get a
dress designed to wear it with . . .' The use of 'one' as a more indirect
form of 'I' is another feature of royal conversation.

Morning audiences were filmed. The presentation of a gold medal
to the poet Robert Graves was a somewhat awkward occasion.
Although Graves was accompanied by the Poet Laureate, C. Day
Lewis, neither of them seemed to have any idea how to conduct
themselves in a royal *tête-à-tête* and compensated with a rather
uncomfortable jokey familiarity – Elizabeth, smiling and informal and,
after all, used to such occasions, certainly comes out of it best. A quick
press of the buzzer and the elderly poets are ushered out. A more
formal ceremony was the reception of a recently appointed ambassador.
This involved the despatch of carriages from the Royal Mews to fetch
the ambassadorial party and an impressive display of uniforms by
various officials including the Marshal of the Diplomatic Corps, whose
dress would not have been out of place at the Congress of Vienna in
1815. The Marshal was the handsome Sir Lees Mayall; the Ambassador was the new US representative, the millionaire anglophile Walter
Annenberg. The Ambassador was noticeably nervous as the Marshal,
who had done the job a hundred times before, explained exactly what
to do. 'When the doors of the Queen's audience room open,' he said,

'you take one pace forward with your left foot, then stop and bow.
Then you walk up to the Queen who is standing about 6 or 7 paces
away. As she holds out her hand, you bow again, another little bow as
you shake hands. Then you transfer your credentials to your right
hand and give them to her . . .' The etiquette was as formal and precise
as if it had been the court of the Chinese emperor. There were streams
of other ambassadors either presenting credentials or taking their leave,
introduced by the Master of the Household, Patrick Plunket, in his
smart, high-collared uniform: 'The Venezuelan Ambassador, Your
Majesty . . . The Italian Ambassador, Your Majesty . . .'

Shots show the royal lunch on its long journey from the basement
kitchen. The dishes stand on an old-fashioned, high and heavy two-
tiered wooden trolley, which looks as if it had been in service since at
least before the First World War. Things are made to last at
Buckingham Palace; in 1969 there were sheets still being used which
dated from Queen Victoria's reign and even blankets from the reign of
her uncle and predecessor, William IV. The trolley lumbers along 200
yards of corridors and up two floors in the lift before reaching the
private dining-room where Elizabeth is lunching with Philip before
one of the annual summer garden-parties. There will be 9,000 guests
at this one, staring at the royal family – Charles and Anne are also
there – and at the pink flamingoes in the lake. At this and various other
receptions, Elizabeth actually manages to look as if she were enjoying
herself, smiling and quite unlike her public image.

She was forty-three when this film was made and still extremely
pretty, seemingly utterly at her ease when tracked by the cameras
behind her shoulder in the Land-Rover driving a five-year-old Prince
Edward at Sandringham in the snow or picnicking among the pine
trees and barking corgis beside Loch Muick at Balmoral. Philip and
Anne are in charge of the barbecue, a cast-iron contraption which
looks as if it has been made by the local blacksmith; their methods of
lighting it seem positively boy scout – newspapers are rolled up by
Elizabeth and Anne and placed in the bottom with tidy little heaps of
kindling over them, then lit carefully with a match. 'Doomed to
failure,' Anne jokes, but apparently not, as later shots show her and
her father grilling large fillet steaks. Charles seems particularly fond of
Edward, showing him how he makes his special salad dressing (with
cream, curiously) and putting up with endless 'whys'; another shot
shows him explaining to his brother how a cello works. A string snaps
painfully against Edward's cheek; he doesn't cry but gets extremely

cross: 'What did you do that for?' Elizabeth is photographed on *Britannia*, maternally holding Margaret's daughter, Lady Sarah Armstrong-Jones, in her arms. It is August and the family are on their way to Balmoral; the Snowdons are presumably somewhere in the Mediterranean. 'I think sometimes the Snowdon children used to think of the Queen as Mum,' a friend said. Charles, Anne and their father are portrayed very much in sporting 'Action Man' mode, Charles and Anne being winched over a rough sea between *Britannia* and the accompanying destroyer. We are told that Charles's favourite sports are 'shooting, skiing, waterskiing and his father's favourite sport – polo'. Philip is pictured helicoptering on to the lawn at Buckingham Palace, at the controls of an aircraft of the Queen's Flight – 'he has flown 55 different types of aircraft'. His private office is staffed by upper-class girls in what appears to be a uniform of grey lambswool sweaters and twin rows of pearls.

Elizabeth works on the move. The royal train has ten coaches including three working offices, three dining-rooms, five bathrooms and three kitchens. En route to Scotland she is seen going through papers with Martin Charteris, her Assistant Private Secretary, while Bobo irons her clothes in preparation for the public engagements she will face during her annual stay at the Palace of Holyrood in Edinburgh early in July. Sir Hugh Casson, commissioned to redesign the interior of the train, had been given minute instructions by Bobo – 'Bobo was the client really,' he said. Even at Balmoral Elizabeth's official 'boxes' follow her; at least a dozen a day are loaded on to a trolley at the back door and trundled through the hall with its life-size statue of Prince Albert and up the stairs past antlers and trellised thistle-flocked wallpaper to Elizabeth's office on the first floor. When on holiday, she works on them in the evening before dinner and even at Balmoral she cannot escape the traditional annual visit of the current Prime Minister and spouse.

Britannia is different; for a family on whom cameras are trained as soon as they emerge into the daylight, the royal yacht is a refuge with the particularly holiday atmosphere of being at sea. Elizabeth wears trousers and a twinset. The crew take orders in hand signals so as not to disturb the royal family on the decks below. As *Britannia* steams into some foreign port at the beginning of a state visit (in this case Brazil), there is a resounding oompahing of Sousa marches from a Marine band in white uniforms and pith helmets, an ear-splitting whistling as Elizabeth is piped either on board or into the royal barge, and a huge spray of white water from accompanying speedboats official and unofficial. On shore, Elizabeth is on duty every hour of every day; she can never see what she wants to see, only what her hosts are determined she should. There is a good deal of official eating both on shore and on board. Sometimes, as on the state visit to America, she would give a state banquet in a big hotel, when all arrangements, down to the last coffee spoon, would be brought out from Buckingham Palace. The Palace Steward, who rarely travelled except for the big occasions, would be there to supervise and bring the necessary staff with him. Often the royal chef went too. Everything had to be planned for months in advance, not only the menu but also the plate, the dinner services, the cutlery, candelabra, table decorations, flower holders and cruets, all of which had to be carefully packed as the items were so valuable – a dessert plate could be worth £500. This would be done for banquets in places as diverse as Lusaka and Nepal, a huge feat of organisation and logistics. Elizabeth herself would take care that everything was suitable for the place where the banquet was to be held. On one occasion when the Steward and his staff disagreed with their boss, the Master of the Household, over whether some particularly grand candelabra and gilt service should go, Elizabeth backed their opinion, saying it was too ostentatious for its destination: – 'it would be all right for Spain where they expect a banquet to be a big, lavish event, but not there'.

The most important thing on these occasions is Elizabeth's health. Although she is very strong physically and normally suffers only from colds, a carefully planned visit could be ruined if she went down with food-poisoning. Staff ensure that the ice for her drink is made with Malvern water and that if there is a tray of glasses she takes the one with the Malvern cubes. She will give the Steward a quick glance and know that her drink is safe. For the same reason, she never eats shellfish on tour. Although she occasionally eats lobster at Balmoral, she doesn't like oysters or mussels or even avocado pears – 'they taste like soap'. She likes chicken, lamb and, in the family tradition, game, particularly partridge. At Balmoral the late King insisted on grouse almost every night and in post-war austerity years when meat was rationed, the staff at Balmoral ate so much venison that, as one remarked, 'it's a wonder we didn't grow antlers'. All over the world people have marvelled at Elizabeth's stamina and how she can actually endure the punishing schedules of these state visits without apparently tiring. 'She has two great assets,' said one of her Private Secretaries, 'first of all she sleeps very well and secondly she's got very good legs and she can stand for a long time . . . The Queen is as tough as a yak.'

The final scenes of the film are overtly 'family' ones with Elizabeth, Philip and their two elder children sitting round a family lunch table telling not very funny stories. Elizabeth was talking about Queen Victoria's 'incredible control'; when at a Durbar an Oriental potentate fell over and shot towards her throne feet first, the Queen restrained her giggles and was seen to give a 'slight shiver but that was all'. Her own worst moment, she said, had come at an audience, when the Home Secretary had come in with his hand over his mouth and said, 'The next one's a gorilla. And he was . . . you know, long arms hanging down . . .' Philip countered with a story about his father-in-law, the late King: 'He had very odd habits, sometimes I thought he was mad.' Once Philip had gone down to Royal Lodge to see the King and, on asking for him, was told that he was in the garden. He went out and saw no one, then heard the most incredible explosion of bad language coming from a rhododendron bush; peering into the centre of the bush, he saw the King hacking away with a pruning knife and wearing on his head the full bearskin in which he would have to be on parade for Trooping the Colour.

The overwhelming impression given by the film was of a woman happy and busy in her public and private life, enjoying her job as much as she did the company of her four children. The image was one of a contented, united family, rather charmingly old-fashioned in their kilts, pullovers and shortish haircuts, surrounded by horses and dogs in their traditional British upper-class way of life. The project, which seemed to have fulfilled all the highest hopes of the royal advisers in its presentation – or re-presentation – of the royal image, with hindsight seems fraught with dangers. The emphasis on the ideal family was to return to haunt Elizabeth twenty years later when her children's marital disasters revealed the cracks in the fabric. The film innocently whetted the public's appetite for the royal soap opera, which was to reach epidemic proportions with catastrophic consequences when this began to go wrong.

The *Evening Standard*'s television critic, Milton Shulman, warned:

Richard Cawston's film, *Royal Family*, could not have had a better critical reception if it had been the combined work of Eisenstein, Hitchcock and Fellini. But the making and showing of such a film with the Monarch's co-operation may have constitutional and historical

consequences which go well beyond its current interest as a piece of
TV entertainment.

What has actually happened is that an old image has been replaced
by a fresh one. The emphasis on authority and remoteness which was
the essence of the previous image has, ever since George VI, been
giving way to a friendlier image of homeliness, industry and relaxation.

But just as it was untrue that the royal family sat down to breakfast
wearing coronets as they munched their cornflakes, so it is untrue that
they now behave in their private moments like a middle-class family in
Surbiton or Croydon.

Judging from Cawston's film, it is fortunate at this moment in time
we have a royal family that fits in so splendidly with a public relation's
man's dream.

Yet, is it, in the long run, wise for the Queen's advisers to set as a
precedent this right of the television camera to act as an image-making
apparatus for the monarchy? Every institution that has so far attempted
to use TV to popularise or aggrandise itself has been trivialised by it.

Nineteen sixty-nine was a key year for the monarchy, which started
two potentially dangerous trends. First, by bringing the television
cameras into the Queen's private family life, they not only let in
daylight on the magic but whetted the public appetite for more
intimate detail. From being allowed in to the drawing-room, they
would soon be expecting to be let in to the bedroom as well. Secondly,
Philip brought the question of the cost of the monarchy into the public
arena by announcing on NBC's *Meet the Press*:

> We go into the red next year, now, inevitably if nothing happens we
> shall either have to – I don't know, we may have to move into smaller
> premises, who knows? We've closed down – well, for instance we had a
> small yacht which we had to sell, and I shall probably have to give up
> polo fairly soon, things like that . . .

It was an extraordinary piece of what Philip himself called 'donto-
pedalogy' (putting his foot in his mouth). By going public on the
always sensitive question of financing the monarchy which was already
being secretly discussed at the time, Philip was inviting publicity on a
subject which both the Government and the Palace would have
preferred to see handled as quietly as possible. What he was saying
was in essence true; the effect of inflation on the Civil List had meant
that the sum settled on Elizabeth's accession in 1952 (£475,000 a year

including an inflation allowance of £70,000) would no longer cover costs and the balance would indeed, as he said, go into the red in 1970. The flippant manner in which he put it, and particularly the phrases about being forced to give up polo, embarrassed both the Government and Buckingham Palace. It made the worst possible public impression. A group of dockers in a Bermondsey pub wrote sarcastically to the Prince offering to take up a collection to buy him a polo pony. Even Elizabeth's devoted Harold Wilson criticised the speech in Cabinet, while Barbara Castle recorded a general lack of sympathy for cries of poverty coming from the husband of 'one of the richest women in the world'.

Previous monarchs' complaints about the size of the Civil List had been kept strictly private. Now Philip had started a public argument on the most sensitive subject of all, the cost of the monarchy, and begun a debate which would rumble on increasingly dangerously until it burst out with republican violence in the recession-hit early 1990s. On 11 November 1969 Harold Wilson informed the House of Commons that detailed discussions with the royal household had taken place on the subject, as a result of which a new select committee would be appointed at the beginning of the next Parliament. The discussions were still going on when Wilson's Government was defeated at the general election in June 1970 (the Prime Minister's resignation had to be delayed because the Queen was at Royal Ascot). On 20 May 1971, in response to a message from the Queen (described by republican Willie Hamilton, the Labour MP for Fife, as 'the most brazenly insensitive pay claim made in the last 200 years'), the House of Commons, now headed by the new Conservative Prime Minister, Edward Heath, resolved to appoint a select committee to enquire into and report on the subject.

The situation had become critical for the Palace the previous year. The annual sums agreed for the maintenance of the Queen in her public role had been fixed nearly twenty years ago on her accession in 1952. But over the two decades since 1952 wages had risen by 126 per cent and consumer prices by 74 per cent; just under ten years earlier, in 1962, the total Civil List expenditure had for the first time exceeded the statutory figure of £475,000 provided under the 1952 Act, and from that point on the contingency funds provided had been drawn upon to make up the increasing deficits each year. By 1970 the Civil List expenditure had reached £745,000 and only £30,000 remained in reserve. The resulting deficit was met by the Privy Purse, which by the end of 1971 was expected to provide £600,000. The Committee was composed of a mixed bag of MPs from all parties and sides of the political spectrum ranging from such stalwarts as William Whitelaw to the anti-monarchist Willie Hamilton and provided the most wide-ranging public discussion of the cost of the monarchy ever held. On Elizabeth's side evidence was given by her Private Secretary, Sir Michael Adeane, as to the extent of her official duties and on finance by the overall head of her household, the Lord Chamberlain, Lord Cobbold. Information on Elizabeth's private income was withheld, provoking reasonable complaints that, without such information, the amount really required by the Palace would be based on guesswork. The question of her tax immunity was also publicly raised for the first time. It was categorically stated by the Palace that the royal palaces, royal jewels, and royal collections, whose value 'could be regarded as astronomical', are vested in the sovereign and are, therefore, inalienable. (These also specifically included the immensely valuable stamp collections accumulated by George V and George VI.) Suggestions that the Queen owned private funds worth £50 million were, the Committee was assured, 'wildly exaggerated'.

Mountbatten, always more sensitive to public relations than either Elizabeth or Philip and their advisers, had been particularly anxious that this point should be cleared up. He was concerned by the bad impression given by the ever-increasing public cost of the monarchy, particularly when contrasted with what was widely believed to be Elizabeth's huge private fortune. The fact that she regularly appeared on the American magazine *Fortune*'s list of the world's richest women caused, in his view, immense damage in the public eye. Mountbatten thought the Palace's traditional secrecy on such matters a great mistake. 'Unless you can get an informed reply published making just one point, the image of the monarchy will be gravely damaged,' he told Prince Philip on 5 June 1971. 'It is true that there is a fortune, which is very big, but the overwhelming proportion (85%?) is in pictures, objets d'art, furniture, etc. in the three State-owned Palaces. The Queen can't sell any of them, they bring in no income.' He recommended an authoritative article in *The Times* which would be picked up by the world's press, otherwise people would resent being asked to pay more and more while Elizabeth economised on her '£100m fortune'. 'So will you both please believe a loving old uncle and NOT your constitutional advisers, and do it,' he pleaded.[1] Four days later

Jock Colville, now a banker, made a statement in *The Times* in which he said that the Queen was worth about £12 million.

Mountbatten, it seemed, had been over-optimistic; *Fortune* continued to count Elizabeth's palaces, jewels and collections as her assets, while facts and figures given to the Select Committee revealed the true cost of the monarchy to the taxpayer as being considerably more than the published amounts for the Civil List and the Privy Purse. These showed that, quite apart from the Civil List allowance, many of the costs of the royal activities were also borne by government departments:

Marshal of the Diplomatic Corps	£ 6,000
Overseas visits at request of government departments	214,000
Gentlemen-at-Arms and Yeomen of the Guard	13,000
Palaces occupied by the Queen and members of the royal family	974,000
Rail travel including royal train	36,000
Stationery and office equipment	46,000
Orders of Knighthood	25,000
Refund of purchase tax	5,000
Equerries	22,000
Royal yacht	839,000
Queen's Flight	700,000
Postal and telecommunications (paid by Post Office Corporation)	52,000
Total	£ 2,932,000

(The Crown Estate payments to the Consolidated Fund were £3,800,000.)[2]

The royal finances are divided into three parts: 1. The Civil List paid for by the Government, which meets the cost of staff and expenses incurred wherever the court is in residence, in provision for the Queen as head of state, charity donations and contributions to certain other members of the royal family. 2. The Privy Purse, which meets the cost of private expenditure arising from the Queen's responsibilities as head of state, pensions for employees, maintenance of Sandringham and Balmoral, charity and welfare and amenity of members of the royal household. (The Queen had made considerable donations from her private resources to expenses of other members of the royal family, and on this occasion offered to refund £60,000 to the Privy Purse.) The Duchy of Lancaster, then a tax-free estate belonging to the Queen as sovereign, contributed a proportion of its income to the Privy Purse, payments which had risen from £110,000 in 1952 to

£300,000 in 1970. 3. Elizabeth's private income, exempt both from estate duty and income tax.

At Committee sessions a good deal of criticism was aroused at the proposals for increased annuities chargeable to the Civil List for members of the royal family apart from the Queen: Queen Elizabeth, the Queen Mother, £95,000 from £70,000; Duke of Edinburgh, £65,000 from £40,000; Princess Anne, £15,000 from £6,000; Princess Margaret, £35,000 from £15,000; Duke of Gloucester, £45,000 from £35,000. In addition it was proposed that younger sons from the age of eighteen and before marriage should receive £20,000, rising after marriage to £50,000; daughters from the age of eighteen £15,000 and after marriage £35,000; a widow of the Prince of Wales, £60,000; and provision for the Duchess of Gloucester or younger sons' widows of £20,000. A global sum of £60,000 was to be allowed for remaining members of the family. The case for the annuities being paid for out of the Civil List was that those members of the royal family shared the royal duties and because of their close relationship to the sovereign were precluded from any gainful employment. It was pointed out that Elizabeth had had to make contributions to the expenses of other royals on public duties out of the Privy Purse and her private income.

'No explanation had been given as to how the Queen Mother's £70,000 allowance had been arrived at,' the Committee objected. The Lord Chamberlain, Lord Cobbold, expressed it as 'his personal view' that it should be regarded 'as something of the nature of payment for services rendered over years of peace and war'. The Committee unsentimentally took the view that as the Queen Mother's duties would inevitably contract with age, so would the necessity for 'such an extensive household' and suggested that her annuity should not be in excess of the pension awarded to a retired prime minister. If the most popular member of the royal family could receive such treatment, it was hardly surprising that the Duke of Edinburgh should fare even worse, despite recognition that he worked extremely hard. The report complained that insufficient information had been provided:

> Your Committee received evidence of the scope of the Queen's
> activities, but as in other cases found it impossible to distinguish
> between the public and private spending. Nor was it possible to
> determine to what extent any current financial difficulties were due to
> inflation or to additional commitments voluntarily undertaken. No
> accounts were requested or offered.

The Committee queried whether Philip needed a separate household and recommended that he share one with Elizabeth and receive £20,000 a year for his expenses. As for Anne, the Committee thought her present annuity of £6,000 should be retained, but the rise to £15,000 on marriage should not be given automatically but be reviewed if necessary (presumably depending on the wealth of her husband). 'She is remote from the Throne and has shown a marked desire for greater individual freedom than is normally granted to the daughter of the Monarch,' the Committee noted. While they went on record as welcoming this trend, the implication clearly was that the Princess could not expect to have her cake and eat it.

Margaret received rougher treatment. She had had an annuity of £15,000 since her marriage and in addition about £80,000 spent on her apartment at Kensington Palace. In 1970, the Committee noted, she had spent 'only 31 days' outside London on official engagements. In their opinion, 'Since the Princess has a working husband and since her public engagements appear to be extremely limited in number, scope and importance, Your Committee do not feel it right to ask the taxpayer to continue the annuity; free housing should be adequate recompense for services rendered.' The Queen's uncle, the Duke of Gloucester, was similarly dismissed. The Duke, apparently, had been receiving an annuity of £35,000 since the accession of George VI in 1937, a sum unaltered in 1952. However, the Committee commented, 'The Duke and his family are very remote from the Throne. No evidence was produced as to the amount of public work engaged in over the last 19 years'; they therefore saw no good reason for continuing this annuity and recommended its abolition. They also recommended the abolition of the £10,000 annual payments to Andrew and Edward, calling them 'indefensible'.

The Committee's recorded proceedings continued on similarly radical lines. The Prince of Wales should be given a salary and deprived of the revenues of the Duchy of Cornwall. It was a misconception, the Committee declared, that the Duchy was a private estate. The Revolution of 1688 had transformed the contract between the monarchy and Parliament and therefore the monarch's former private estates thereafter ceased to be their private estates. 'No royal personage should be entitled to the total proceeds of what has become a public estate,' they declared. Furthermore, when it came to the Crown Estate, handed over to the Government by George III in 1760 and used as justification for the public funding of the Civil List, the

Committee described its links to the monarchy as 'tenuous, dating back to the plunder which followed the Norman Conquest'. In view of this, they continued, 'the charade enacted at the beginning of each new reign, when the Monarch is presumed to hand over all claims to the revenues from the Crown Lands in exchange for a Civil List, should be ended'. Their recommendation was that the Crown Estate, with the Duchies of Lancaster and Cornwall, should be jointly administered as 'the Public Estates' to save costs of duplication and their income accrue direct to the Consolidated Fund.

They tackled the question of the Queen's immunity from taxation, regretting that more precise information on the value of the tax-free private income had not been provided. Such information would be 'clearly relevant to any reconsideration of the size and value of the Civil List, since the private fortune must have been accumulated in very large measure by virtue of the uniquely favourable treatment in respect of all forms of taxation'. Their conclusion, prompted by Mr Hamilton, was defiant to the point of rudeness:

Your Committee may have received much information previously unknown. A great deal still remains shrouded in mystery. What is abundantly clear, however, is that considering the enormous scale of the tax [remission] granted to the Royal Family, the Gracious Message of May 19 1971, represented the most insensitive and brazen pay claim made in the last two hundred years.

Their final recommendations, had they been carried out, would have represented the greatest revolution in the relationship between sovereign and Parliament since 1688. They included: abandonment of the term 'Civil List' in favour of 'Expenditure on the Royal Family' under which all payments to individual members of the royal family would be shown; Elizabeth to be paid an annual salary of £100,000 a year, salaries of Her Majesty's household to be put on the Treasury vote, and household expenses on a new vote with an additional £80,000 for postal and telecommunications services; the Queen Mother's annuity to be reduced to the equivalent of a retired prime minister's pension; Philip's annuity to be reduced to £20,000 a year and his separate household to be abolished; Anne's present annuity to be retained, but its automatic increase to £15,000 on marriage to be abolished and the situation reviewed when necessary; Margaret's and the Duke of Gloucester's annuities were to be abolished and payments to other members of the royal family were to be made out of the £100,000 provided for the Queen; the Prince of Wales was to be paid a salary not greater than the Prime Minister and his Duchy of Cornwall and the Queen's Duchy of Lancaster merged with the Crown Estates into one entity, the Public Estates; that all royal income should be liable to all tax law, and that royal expenditure under the renamed Civil List should be subject to five-yearly reviews by the House of Commons. Finally, a Labour member of the Committee, Douglas Houghton, proposed that the royal household should be reconstituted as a government department. His intention was to avoid the necessity for the Queen repeatedly to ask the Government for expenditure on her household incurring the stigma of being seen to get large pay rises. Houghton argued:

> The central issue appears to be one of control. Who is to be in ultimate control of the Royal Household? Is it to be the Queen or Parliament? . . . If the Monarchy could manage without coming to Parliament, there could be only one answer . . . she would run her own Household and pay for it . . . [but] the expenses of a constitutional monarchy are the responsibility of the state.

Elizabeth, through Lord Cobbold, made it absolutely clear that Houghton's plan was unacceptable:

> although the [royal] Household is in one sense a Department of State, it is also a family administration and the two things are slightly intermingled and it is not a straightforward department . . . It is almost an item of principle that the Queen regards these people as her own servants and they regard themselves as her servants. I think they have the idea of the dignity of the Monarchy, which is supported by the idea that the Queen is controlling her own Household.

When it came to the debates in the House of Commons, the Conservative majority saw to it that not one of the Select Committee's recommendations was adopted. Elizabeth got her Civil List increased in 1972 from £475,000 to £980,000, with corresponding increases for other members of her family, and retained control of her household, but the revelations that the Civil List was merely the tip of the iceberg as far as the cost of the monarchy was concerned since so much of the expenditure was absorbed by various government departments laid the foundations for future trouble. (According to a recent expert, Philip

Hall, the Civil List accounted for only about 30 per cent of government expenditure on the monarchy, with the other 70 per cent coming from departments such as Defence and Environment.) While the general public remained unaware of this and the subject of the Queen's immunity from taxation was not yet an issue, the need for the rise in the Civil List was not generally understood. According to an opinion poll taken at the time of the December debates, 31 per cent of Conservative and 74 per cent of Labour supporters thought the proposed increase too high.

Inflation rocketing after the rise in oil prices ensured that by 1975 the situation had again become precarious. Once again Elizabeth had to apply to the Government for help, her Prime Minister this time being Harold Wilson, now in his second and last term. Obligingly, the Labour Government arranged for yearly upratings of the Civil List to maintain its value in real terms. Once again this resulted in disagreeable debate in the House of Commons, with rebellious members on the Labour side demanding full disclosure of the facts about the Queen's personal fortune and tax immunity and suggesting a royal commission into the financial position of the monarchy. This, however, was a can of worms which no Government felt prepared to open.

All this inquisition was hardly a pleasant experience for Elizabeth. Facts emerged from the Select Committee evidence which were seized upon by the press. The cost of the royal yacht had provided abundant ammunition for any editor who felt it his duty to cut the monarchy down to size. During the 1950s and 1960s the Beaverbrook press had been particularly hot on the subject; the Canadian press lord's newspapers were then as frequently accused of being anti-monarchist as the Australo-American Rupert Murdoch's titles have been in the 1990s. Evidence to the Committee revealed that *Britannia* had cost £2.15 million to build and that its running costs had risen from £29,188 in 1953–4 to £757,300 in 1970–71, and that it required 189 crew on an everyday in-harbour basis and 279 when the royal family was on board. Unfortunately, despite the attention lavished upon it by Mountbatten and Philip, who had been closely involved in the non-technical side of its design, the yacht's construction had not proved long-lasting and it was subject to relatively frequent refits at very considerable cost to the Ministry of Defence. In 1960, only seven years after she was commissioned, *Britannia* already needed a refit costing £9 million. (Elizabeth summoned the Minister for Defence when this was mooted. 'I see,' she said wryly. 'You pay and I get the blame.') She was always very conscious of the effect of the royal yacht as a floating symbol of privilege and used it as rarely as possible for any trip which could be construed as for private pleasure only. The Snowdons' honeymoon cruise on *Britannia* had met with very little criticism, but when Anne and Mark Phillips were to do the same there was an outcry. Questioned about it on television, the royal bride rudely dismissed it as 'none of their business', and justified its use on the grounds that the Queen intended to travel on it from the West Indies to New Zealand where she was to open the 1974 Commonwealth Games. None the less, Elizabeth, a creature of habit, continued to use *Britannia* once a year on holiday in Scotland; sailing on board the yacht to visit the Queen Mother at her Castle of Mey on the remote coast of Caithness became an annual ritual. The Queen Mother was also given use of *Britannia* for three weeks every summer, often for holiday trips to the Mediterranean.

Whatever criticism there might be of the monarchy in the press, Elizabeth knew that she could count on the support of her Prime Ministers, be they Conservative or Labour. Not one leading politician who has worked with her has anything but admiration and fondness for her; admiration for her total professionalism, her dedication to her job, the friendliness and support she offered them and her total absence of partisanship. Her relationship with Wilson's successor, Edward Heath, lacked the warmth of her relationship with the Labour leader. Heath's biographer, John Campbell, has described it as 'correct but cool'.[3] Partly this was a result of the Conservative Prime Minister's personality. 'Ted' Heath, as he is always known, has no small talk and little time for women; wives of his colleagues seated next to him at dinner have found conversation with him uphill work. Politics apart, Elizabeth and Heath had nothing whatsoever in common. He came, like Wilson, from a background with which she was utterly unfamiliar, born in a small seaside resort town on the south-eastern coast of England into a family described by his biographer as 'the upwardly mobile, socially aspiring skilled working class just where it merges into the lower middle class'. But unlike Wilson he was an introvert, inhibited and formal, temperamentally incapable of entertaining Elizabeth with jokes and dazzling expositions. According to Heath's own account given to Elizabeth Longford, their meetings were extremely businesslike:

> I believed in telling the Queen everything. There was always an agenda
> drawn up in agreement with the private secretary. She had it on a card
> on the table beside her to make sure that the items were covered, but I

believed in telling her a good deal else of what was going on, which I
hadn't mentioned to the private secretary, because I knew she would be
interested . . . She talks about her own visits and what she has observed
herself there. Reactions of different people. She gives you a lead . . .[4]

Anything further removed from a conversation, say, between the
Queen and Winston Churchill could hardly have been imagined. Heath
was no countryman; he was a good amateur musician and successful
international yachtsman; Elizabeth is interested in neither. 'The
Queen', a member of the household said, 'found Heath hard going.'
Their only common ground was politics. And on one important issue
there was a major divergence of interests. In Elizabeth's eyes she has
two main roles, complementary and to her of equal importance: she is
Queen of Great Britain and head of the Commonwealth, both sacred
trusts inherited from her father. While Macmillan had been the first
British Prime Minister to attempt to join Europe and the most
committed – since Churchill – to the maintenance of the 'special
relationship' with the United States which had so aroused de Gaulle's
suspicion, Heath was the first of Elizabeth's Prime Ministers to be a
passionate European to the exclusion of all other connections. He had
no time for the Commonwealth and showed it. Elizabeth, according to
Campbell, was 'deeply unhappy with Heath's undisguised disrespect
for the institution in general and most African leaders in particular,
and greatly upset by the rows which disfigured the 1971 Commonwealth conference in Singapore'. The *casus belli* was the Government's
decision to resume arms sales to South Africa, provoking a string of
African leaders to visit Britain to denounce the Government's support
of apartheid. Elizabeth's old friends Julius Nyerere and Kenneth
Kaunda came, threatening to withdraw from the Commonwealth;
Kaunda declared on arrival at Heathrow that he had come to appeal to
the British people over the heads of their Government (and, no doubt,
privately to Elizabeth). At a stormy dinner given by Heath for Kaunda
at Downing Street, Heath denounced the Zambian leader for hypocrisy
in condemning Britain while Zambia itself continued to trade with
South Africa. While Heath treated African threats to 'expel' Britain
from the Commonwealth with disdain, Elizabeth, although outwardly
imperturbable, did not enjoy the situation. She would, apparently,
have liked to have attended the Commonwealth Heads of Government
Conference in Singapore in January 1971, but Heath would not allow
her to go. On 21 January 1972 Heath signed the Accession treaty

marking Britain's entry into the EEC to take effect from 1 January 1973. In her Christmas 1972 broadcast just a few days before the critical date, Elizabeth reached out to reassure the Commonwealth. Unlike the Queen's Speech at the State Opening of Parliament, when she is merely the mouthpiece of the Government of the day, the Christmas broadcast is her own which she writes with Philip's help. 'The new links with Europe will not replace those with the Commonwealth,' she said. 'They cannot alter our historical ties and personal attachments with kinsmen and friends overseas. Old friends will not be lost. Britain will take her Commonwealth links into Europe with her.' In terms of *realpolitik* and, indeed, the views of her Government it made no sense, but Elizabeth meant what she said; it was her coded message of personal support to the Commonwealth. Later that year, according to Campbell, 'she positively insisted, against Heath's wishes, on attending the next [Commonwealth] meeting in Ottawa'.

Much of Elizabeth's time over this and the following years was to be devoted to overseas tours intended to reassure the 'white' countries of the 'Old Commonwealth' – Canada, Australia and New Zealand – that Britain's new European commitment would not diminish the links between them. The fact was that they already had been weakened by the strains and shock of Britain's earlier abortive attempt to enter the EEC; as far as the 'Old Commonwealth' was concerned, things could never be the same again. Britain had signalled that her interests lay with Europe and that the 'historical ties and personal attachments' of which Elizabeth had spoken would inevitably weaken. In Canada the *Toronto Star*, hitherto a supporter of the Crown connection, for the first time editorialised as to whether the time had not come for Canada to have its own head of state instead of one who belonged to a foreign country. On a six-day visit to Australia that year, 1973, Elizabeth signed what was designed as a first formal step towards cutting the umbilical cord with Britain, the Royal Styles and Titles Bill, introduced by the Labour Prime Minister, Gough Whitlam. This stated categorically that when the Queen was in Australia, she would be referred to only as 'Queen of Australia' and not, as hitherto, as 'Queen of the United Kingdom and of Her Other Realms and Territories'. In 1975 the dismissal of Gough Whitlam by the Governor-General, Sir John Kerr, the Queen's representative in Australia, gave further impetus to anti-British sentiment and a questioning of the validity and desirability of the connection with the British Crown.[5]

In Britain the industrial unrest which was to dog the remaining years of the decade had caused Heath to call a crisis election to be fought on the issue 'Who Governs Britain?' (the Government or the unions). Elizabeth flew back from Canberra on 28 February 1974 in time to hear the result. To general astonishment the Government lost, involving her in a constitutional question. The Labour Party, headed by Wilson, won 301 seats, the Conservatives 297 with 14 Liberals and 9 Scottish and Welsh nationalists holding the balance. But, although the Labour Party had won four more seats than the Conservatives, it had received fewer votes and achieved a smaller share of the popular vote than at any general election since 1931. The result had produced the first hung Parliament since 1929. Heath, therefore, decided to try to form a government with the support of the Liberals, asking Elizabeth's permission to do so. Elizabeth could have refused, but she did not. As incumbent Prime Minister Heath was perfectly within his rights to act as he did. Denis Healey, who was to be Chancellor of the Exchequer in Wilson's next Government, says that the Palace was infuriated by Heath's suggestion, giving as it did the impression that the monarchy was the property of the Conservative Party,[6] but Martin Charteris, who had succeeded Adeane in 1972 on the latter's retirement, denied there was any such feeling. It was characteristically kind of Elizabeth to give Heath the chance to form a government if he could. There is absolutely no reason for thinking, as some senior Conservatives gave the impression, that she would have preferred a Conservative Government to a Labour one; on personal terms she probably liked Wilson the best of all of her Prime Ministers. When the Liberals refused to join a coalition with Heath, Heath resigned and Elizabeth invited Wilson to become her Prime Minister once again.

The Harold Wilson of 1974 was a very different man from the feisty figure who had bounced in to No. 10 Downing Street in 1964. Eleven years of a tightrope party leadership had worn him out although he was only fifty-eight:

> He had lost none of his acuteness [his biographer wrote], but he no
> longer had the same energy, the same aggression, or the same ambition.
> He took less exercise, drank more brandy, spoke at greater length.
> Rumours about his health reflected changes in his appearance. He
> looked older than his years and he was slower in gait. In his first
> administration it had been hard for officials to keep up with him. In his
> second, he gave those closest to him an impression of being worn out,

sometimes even of listlessness . . . He began to tell people that he had
seen it all before . . .[7]

Elizabeth was soon made aware of the change in Wilson; she knew
too that he was already planning his retirement and that he intended
to bow out of political life on or around his sixtieth birthday on 11
March 1976. Wilson confirmed it to her in the winter of 1975; it was a
secret he kept from everyone except his closest advisers. On 5 April
1976 she and Philip attended Wilson's retirement dinner at No. 10
Downing Street – a signal honour since the last occasion she had set
foot in Downing Street had been for Winston Churchill's retirement
dinner twenty-one years before. On 23 April it was announced that
Elizabeth had bestowed upon him the highest honour in her personal
gift, making him Knight Companion of the Garter. The fact that she
had granted it to all her retiring Prime Ministers (Harold Macmillan
had refused it) made no difference; Wilson saw it as setting the seal on
an entirely happy professional relationship.

James 'Jim' Callaghan, Wilson's successor as Prime Minister and
leader of the Labour Party, had been one of Elizabeth's strongest
supporters in the Labour Cabinets of the 1960s and 1970s. A tough
pragmatist with strong trade union links, Callaghan gave one of the
most perceptive summings-up of Elizabeth, fond, admiring and
extremely level-headed. Unlike Wilson, he was never under the illusion
that he was singled out in any way for special favour. His audiences
with the Queen lasted from an hour to an hour and a half – 'no drink
– that was the rule apparently – all treated the same. But each thinks
he is treated in a much more friendly way than the one before! Though
I'm sure that's not true. The Queen is more even-handed. What one
gets is friendliness but not friendship.' Callaghan told Elizabeth
Longford:

One gets a great deal of friendliness. And Prime Ministers also get a
great deal of understanding of their problems – without the Queen
sharing them, since she is outside politics. I think she weighs them up,
but doesn't offer advice. She listens. Of course she may have hinted at
things, but only on the rarest occasions do I remember her ever saying,
'Why don't you do this, that or the other?' She is pretty detached on all
that. But she's very interested in the political side – who's going up
and who's going down. But not so passionate about MLR [Minimum
Lending Rate].

Elizabeth, Callaghan said, showed a real awareness of her position and its implications and, like any wise dynast, of what it takes to ensure the survival of the monarchy:

> The Queen has a deep sense of duty and responsibility in this [the political] area, and also sees it as a means of preserving the Royal Family as an institution. If her Prime Minister liked to give the Queen information and gossip about certain political characters, she would listen very attentively, for she has a real understanding of the value of a constitutional monarchy. I think she is absolutely right to be on the alert. I think the prestige of the monarchy could deteriorate if she didn't work so hard at it . . . She really knows about preserving the monarchy and how to conduct herself on public occasions. When to step into the limelight and when to step out. She really is professional in her approach, and I admire her, and am very fond of her.[8]

David Owen, Foreign Secretary in the Callaghan Government, also spoke of Elizabeth's friendliness; her ability to behave naturally in a formal setting, the skilful way in which she can have a knowledgeable and intelligent conversation about a subject without giving a hint of her real views:

> On *Britannia*, when the last guest goes, the Queen kicks off her shoes and tucks her feet under her skirt on the sofa and talks about the people who've been there that evening in a vivacious way – her face lights up and she becomes really attractive – so you realise how much is kept under control. She gets confidentiality from people because they are treated in such a welcoming and considerate way.

He was impressed by the naturalness with which Elizabeth behaved under the scrutiny of hordes of cameramen – she simply was not bothered with her image and had no 'side' to her.[9] This too was how she struck the wife of Owen's predecessor as Foreign Secretary, Anthony Crosland, on the state visit to the United States in 1976 to commemorate the bicentenary of the signing of the Declaration of Independence. At a banquet held on 6 July in Philadelphia's Museum of Art, Elizabeth was seated beside Mayor Frank Rizzo, who frequently got up and went round the tables gladhanding the guests. Elizabeth's two ladies-in-waiting, the Duchess of Grafton and the Hon. Mary Morrison, were outraged and complained to her afterwards about the Mayor's behaviour. Elizabeth herself remained completely unruffled.

'What a fascinating man he is,' was all she would say. After spending three days on *Britannia* sailing from Bermuda to Philadelphia, lunching and dining every day with Elizabeth and Philip, Susan Crosland, like Owen, described it as 'positively cosy'. She noted the great affection between Elizabeth and her two ladies-in-waiting – 'intimacy and little jokes'; she also noted the complete naturalness of Elizabeth's behaviour in front of her Foreign Secretary and his wife. On one occasion when Philip was sounding off about something, Elizabeth said to him 'quite sharply', 'Oh Philip, do shut up. You don't know what you're talking about.'[10]

On the second day out of Bermuda a Force 9 gale came up. *Britannia* rocked and rolled in a welter of huge waves. Assembled for pre-dinner drinks the passengers speculated as to who would turn up. Elizabeth, it was believed, did not enjoy rough seas. She appeared, however,

> looking philosophical, almost merry, twenty yards of chiffon scarf flung over one shoulder. Half a pace behind her was her Consort, his face less fresh than usual, ashen and drawn, in fact. We didn't spend long at table that evening, and soon after returning to the drawing-room for coffee, the Queen rose to say goodnight, resting one hand against the handle of the open sliding door which at that moment began sliding shut, *Britannia* having failed to take a breathing spell before heaving over again. The Queen gripped the handle firmly, pressed her back to the door and moved with it as it slid slowly shut, the chiffon scarf flying in the opposite direction. 'Wheeeeee,' said the Queen. *Britannia* shuddered, reeled again. The chiffon scarf flew the other way. 'Wheeeeee,' said the Queen. *Britannia* hesitated before the next heave. 'Goodnight,' said the Queen, slipping through the door, Prince Philip half a pace behind her . . . When we foregathered in the drawing-room before lunch, complexions were better than the evening before. 'I have *never* seen so many grey and grim faces round a dinner table,' said the Queen. She paused. 'Philip was not at all well.' She paused. 'I'm glad to say.' She giggled. I'd forgotten that her Consort is an Admiral of the Fleet.[11]

The heat in Philadelphia and Washington that July was appalling, the temperature hovering around 100° Fahrenheit at night and in the shade, the humidity suffocating. The schedule worked out between the royal household and the US authorities was punishing. In Washington it involved in one day an arrival ceremony on the White House lawn, a reception at the British Embassy for foreign heads of mission, a reception and a luncheon at the Capitol, followed by an inspection of the Magna Carta in the Rotunda, a visit to the Smithsonian Institution and an exhibition of London Treasures, and to the National Gallery for the 'Eye of Jefferson' exhibition, a presentation at the District Building, and a dinner and reception at the British Embassy for President and Mrs Ford. 'The Queen never faltered in the day's walkabout under a remorseless sun, crowds stretching their arms out to her,' Susan Crosland wrote. On the Monday evening before the first day of the visit, the Queen had shown her how to stand for hours without tiring. '"One plants one's feet like this," said Her Majesty, hoisting skirt above ankles to demonstrate. "Always keep them parallel. Make sure your weight is evenly distributed. That's all there is to it."'

State visits by the Queen have a glamour which no politician can rival, an intangible value which is symbolic rather than real, but valuable none the less. Elizabeth is very conscious of being the representative of the British people and 'the condition of Britain' is something which concerns her deeply. Just occasionally, in the late 1970s when Britain seemed to be slipping into irreversible decline with the economy diving and unemployment rising, she let her preoccupations show in odd asides, usually when some visit with an historical context brought it home to her. On the German state visit of 1978, when the representatives of the German Navy dined on board *Britannia* with the British Navy, there was a sense of how things might have been before 1914. Elizabeth flew to Berlin; still the city of the Wall, of East and West and Checkpoint Charlie. There were echoes of 1945; she could not help but be conscious of the decline in her country's standing since her father's reign. Huge changes had taken place in Anglo-German relations since her last state visit in 1965, and in 1975 Britain had voted in a referendum to stay in the EEC. Elizabeth had accepted this as the official policy of Her Majesty's Government. Asked what her feelings on Europe were, a former minister said: 'I would be surprised if she didn't have mainstream views. Instinct tells me she isn't hostile.' Another thought that she was 'rather pro-Europe'. When the recently appointed President of the Commission of the European Community, Roy Jenkins, had a half-hour audience with her in July 1977, he found her 'friendly and forthcoming':

> Her Europeanism did not extend to an uncritical acceptance of the major European leaders. She got Giscard right, but underestimated Schmidt, perhaps too influenced by his having stubbed out his

cigarettes all over the Buckingham Palace plates. None the less, her European commitment seemed very strong and when I broached the question of her paying a visit to the Community, she was positively enthusiastic, and said that something in the new year ought to be possible.[12]

'My quite strong impression was that she leant in a pro–Europe direction but Prince Philip didn't,' a source said. The tradition at the Brussels Commission Headquarters was for a visiting head of state to ask questions of the Commission. Elizabeth's Private Secretary intimated that he didn't think she would want to ask any questions. To the suggestion that Philip might like to, he replied, 'That's what we're afraid of.' When the visit did take place in November 1980, Elizabeth apparently enjoyed herself and was described as being 'in a very good temper throughout'.

The year of the Silver Jubilee, 1977, marking Elizabeth's twenty-five years on the throne was an unexpected high point, both for her and for the country. Twenty-five years after her accession the omens for any kind of celebration had not been auspicious. Britain was wallowing in the worst economic trough since 1945 with inflation at 16 per cent and 1.5 million unemployed. The Chancellor had been forced to go to the International Monetary Fund for a huge loan which imposed severe cuts in public expenditure. Under the circumstances nobody felt much like celebrating; the Government had no money to spend and Elizabeth was anxious that no grandiose schemes should be embarked on in her honour. 'The Government's line was "We don't want to overdo this",' Martin Charteris said. 'I told them – look, you've never done what I've done – followed the Queen round in Birmingham and Sheffield and places like that and seen the glow she spreads around and how people empty out into the streets to see her.' The Government was also worried about the potential danger to Elizabeth of the proposed Jubilee tour of Britain, which had been planned since 1975 to include Northern Ireland. In April they asked Charteris what Elizabeth wanted to do about it – did she still intend to go to Ulster? Charteris went to her and said, 'They're worried about Ulster – indeed as we all are.' 'She looked at me very straight', he recalled, 'and said, "Martin, we said we're going to Ulster and it would be a great pity not to."' Despite all the foreboding the celebrations in June were a spontaneous explosion of popular feeling. Flags and slogans were everywhere – there were bonfires and street-parties, a

huge national coming-together which no one had expected, least of all
Elizabeth, who was bombarded with bouquets and cheers wherever
she went. 'She was floored,' said her domestic chaplain. 'She could not
believe that people had that much affection for her as a person, and
she was embarrassed and at the same time terribly touched by it all.'
Her reaction was just like that of her grandfather, George V, at the
time of his Jubilee, when he couldn't believe that the people really
liked him for himself. People recognised that Elizabeth, like her
grandfather, was decent, honourable and totally dedicated to her job,
and they loved her for it, feeling a common sense of gratitude at having
someone like her to represent Britain. Martin Charteris said, 'The
Queen had a love affair with the country.'

Charteris attended Elizabeth on all her domestic tours in Jubilee
Year and for most of the 56,000 miles that she travelled visiting the
countries of the Commonwealth. Among them, curiously, was Papua
New Guinea, which had never been a part of the British Empire but
from having been a mandate of Australia had elected to invite Elizabeth
to be its head of state. The inhabitants had been invited to write their
own endogenous constitution by former Australian Prime Minister
Gough Whitlam while he was in power and had opted for a republic
with independence on 1 August. In February Charteris had a visit
from the Australian High Commissioner, Sir John Bunting. 'You're
not going to believe this,' Bunting said, 'but they want the Queen to
be their Queen and sit on [their] throne.' 'Why?' Charteris asked.
'First of all because they like her and know her because she's been
there. Second, they want someone who will be above local squabbles.
Third, they want to go on getting British decorations. But they only
want her for ten years.' 'The Queen was tickled with the idea and
accepted,' Charteris recalled. 'Now it's twenty-five years on and they're
still devoted to her . . .'

Otherwise there were increasing signs that enthusiasm for the
British monarchy was on the wane, in the 'Old Commonwealth' at
least, as was demonstrated in Canada in 1978, when she spent two
weeks there, the principal reason for her visit being the opening of the
Commonwealth Games. Familiarity had lessened the impact of her
visits; she could no longer expect the ecstatic receptions which had
greeted her in the 1950s. The French-Canadians disliked the British
connection and in 1978, in order to distance himself from it, Trudeau
was not there to greet Elizabeth when she arrived. He went on holiday
to Morocco, a deliberate breach of the Commonwealth and United

Kingdom custom that when the monarch enters or leaves the country, the Prime Minister is in attendance.

At home 1979 saw the beginning of an entirely new direction in British politics as Callaghan's Government went down in a turmoil of industrial unrest and economic instability and Margaret Hilda Thatcher stepped on to the political stage. For Elizabeth, dealing with another woman at the highest level in British politics was a new experience. Not only was Margaret Thatcher the first woman Prime Minister and the first woman to lead the Conservative Party, but she was the first Prime Minister of Elizabeth's own generation, being only six months older. Although she was rumoured to have aristocratic blood in her veins through Harry Cust, a strikingly handsome Lincolnshire aristocrat who was reputedly the father of Lady Diana Cooper, Thatcher's background was small town, like Wilson's and Heath's, and, like theirs, dominated by religion (her parents were Methodists) and the work ethic. Like Elizabeth, she had worshipped her father, her role model in life. Alderman Roberts had been a successful grocer in Grantham, described by his daughter's biographer as 'the epitome of middle England'; Margaret and her sister were both born above the family corner shop. He was not only hard-working and hard-headed in his conduct of his business, but he was also a considerable figure in local municipal politics, eventually becoming Mayor of Grantham. He had brought up his daughter with a strong sense of public duty and a clear-cut view of right and wrong. 'They were all very serious-minded and they worked too hard,' a friend said of the Roberts family. 'Life was a serious matter to be lived conscientiously.'[13] That, indeed, is how Margaret saw it; she was bright, shone in the school debating society for the relentlessness with which she put across her views, read chemistry at Oxford, an unusual achievement for a woman at the time, plunged early into politics as a member of the Oxford University Conservative Association, married a man of means and gave birth to twins, became a lawyer and then a Member of Parliament in 1959 at the age of thirty-two. She became Secretary of State for Education and Science in the Heath Government in 1970, when she was famously and unfairly pilloried as 'Thatcher the Milk-Snatcher' for ending free school milk for older primary schoolchildren (a policy which had not even originated with her) and labelled as 'The Most Unpopular Woman in Britain'. In February 1975 she had ousted Edward Heath, regarded as a loser by his party after two successive electoral defeats, as leader of the Conservative Party.

The relationship between Elizabeth and Mrs Thatcher has fascinated the British public. In Thatcher's more arrogant later years the
press took to calling Thatcher the Deputy Queen, implying that she
was usurping Elizabeth's position, as on some occasions, quite unconsciously and tactlessly, she appeared to be. From the beginning
Elizabeth was curious about this woman who was so different from any
other in her experience. Superficially they had things in common –
they were both highly professional and dedicated to their jobs; as
executive women with huge responsibilities they had both had to put
their jobs before their families. They both had husbands who understood their position and supported them and managed to walk a pace
behind without losing their own personalities. Mrs Thatcher's determination to arrest the decline of Britain, to pull the country up by its
boot-straps and make it respected in its own eyes and those of the
world, appealed to Elizabeth.

The similarities ended there. Thatcher was revolutionary and
missionary where Elizabeth was conservative and distrustful of change.
Elizabeth was a countrywoman, while Thatcher was irretrievably urban
(the unkind might say suburban). When she became Prime
Minister, her sister wrote an article saying that Margaret had never
worn anything but patent leather court shoes and she packed them
even for stays at Balmoral. On her first visit there as Minister for
Education, Patrick Plunket and a lady-in-waiting had taken the
Thatchers out for a walk. Mrs Thatcher had no country shoes and had
to be forced to put on a pair of the towering lady-in-waiting's hush
puppies with multiple pairs of socks. It was a battle of wills. 'I didn't
know how determined she was,' the courtier recalled. On another
occasion she actually managed to get her into a pair of green wellington
boots. Mrs Thatcher did not relish the resolutely outdoor life which
the family led at Balmoral. 'The royal family', a courtier said, 'will go
out in weather you wouldn't put a dog out in.' It was noted that when
the time came to leave Balmoral, Mrs Thatcher would be poised,
suitcases packed well ahead of time, longing for the off. Denis Thatcher
and the Duke of Edinburgh had a good deal in common beyond their
roles as consorts, enjoying golf-club jokes over a drink and seeking
solace in each other's company at such occasions as Commonwealth
conferences. Elizabeth and Mrs Thatcher were not entirely comfortable with each other on a social basis, perhaps because Mrs Thatcher
regarded royalty not just with loyalty but with reverence. 'She had a
rather exaggerated respect for the institution of monarchy,' a friend

said. 'Nobody would curtsey lower – no one would be more supportive of the monarchy even when it was engaged in attacking her. She had great sympathy for any of the royal family who got into trouble. Even if it was their fault, it never was as far as she was concerned.' Elizabeth enjoys people with a sense of humour, which Mrs Thatcher manifestly does not possess. Elizabeth remained puzzled by her and was once heard to enquire, half-humorously, 'Do you think Mrs Thatcher will ever change?'

Both the Palace and loyal Thatcherites protest that the two women got on very well, but the indications are that while Elizabeth was always perfectly professional and correct in her relations with her Prime Minister, in her heart of hearts she did not like her or approve of all the changes she was making in the fabric of Britain. In the company of Commonwealth leaders who were also old friends, she would refer to her (as did leading anti-Thatcherites) as 'that woman'. The widest area of divergence between them, as with Edward Heath, was over the Commonwealth, and in the late 1970s and 1980s that meant principally the questions arising from inter-racial conflict in southern Africa. 'The Queen was sympathetic to the Black cause in Rhodesia and southern Africa,' the Hon. Lee Kuan Yew, Senior Minister of Singapore, wrote.[14]

For the past fifteen years successive Foreign and Colonial Secretaries and heads of government had been preoccupied with the settlement of the situation in Rhodesia since in 1965 the white minority Government under Ian Smith had unilaterally declared independence from Britain. Britain, still theoretically responsible for the territory, had imposed sanctions on Rhodesia, but had hitherto failed to reach a settlement. In an effort to placate international hostility and produce a semblance of legality, Smith had held elections in the spring of 1979 which had returned a black Prime Minister, Bishop Abel Muzorewa, but Muzorewa was widely regarded as merely a Smith stooge, the black nationalist leaders having been excluded from the electoral process and the civil war continued. Lord Carrington, Thatcher's appointee as Foreign Secretary, was determined that a proper settlement should be achieved in Rhodesia once and for all. Since Margaret Thatcher at that time was almost entirely ignorant of foreign affairs, she listened to Peter Carrington – up to a point. She was not entirely convinced that Muzorewa should not be given a chance and she had no sympathies either with black nationalism or the sanctions policy against Rhodesia. The biennial Commonwealth Heads of Government

Conference was fixed for August in Lusaka at which the question of a
new settlement would be discussed. Unfortunately, in the meantime
on a visit to Canberra, she made a point of emphasising publicly that
she would not be able to push economic sanctions against Rhodesia for
that year through the House of Commons. 'She made some very silly
remarks in Canberra which very nearly torpedoed the whole way we
were building up to this Conference,' said a British official. All this,
together with what was known of her character and opinions, resulted
in her demonisation in the press of the African Commonwealth
countries who would be involved in the Conference, notably Zambia,
under the control of Dr Kenneth Kaunda. At this moment the
Rhodesian Government chose to bomb Lusaka, and the New Zealand
Prime Minister, Robert Muldoon, on a visit to London came forward
with the unhelpful statement (designed for his domestic right-wing
electorate) that he might advise Elizabeth, as Queen of New Zealand,
not to go to Lusaka as it was in a war zone. The Commonwealth
Secretary-General, Sir Shridath 'Sonny' Ramphal, stepped in and with
Kaunda's help persuaded the nationalist leader, Joshua Nkomo, unilaterally to declare a ceasefire during the period when Elizabeth would be
in Zambia. Ramphal was therefore able to defuse the issue of her
personal safety as a right-wing ploy to disrupt the Conference. 'In my
conversations with the Queen,' Sir Sonny said, 'it was perfectly clear
to me that whether that issue had been removed or not, there was no
way she was about to allow Muldoon or anybody else to stop her.'[15]

Elizabeth was determined to use her unique position and contacts to
save the Lusaka Conference. In London she was in close touch with
Sir Sonny Ramphal, who had the right of access to her as head of the
Commonwealth. When Commonwealth heads of state came to London,
even on private visits, she made time to see them. She had grown up
with the concept of the Commonwealth and, said Ramphal, was aware
that acceptance of her role as head of the Commonwealth in a post-
imperial situation depended on those countries' perception of her as
genuinely caring about them:

> She did care and she did convey that caring. And I believe that this is
> the key to her unquestioned success in the Commonwealth . . . there
> was a genuine measure of caring about the Commonwealth, about its
> people, about its Governments, about its leaders, about its general
> situation, about its influence in the world. It mattered to her, these
> were not formalities, this was an important side of her life . . . All that

was understood in the Commonwealth and in return there was this easy acceptance of the Queen as Head of the Commonwealth.

Elizabeth never took sides publicly, unlike the Queen Mother, who, during the Rhodesia years, would urge Foreign Ministers 'not to be nasty to Smithy [Ian Smith]'. She is emphatically not a racist. 'I found her enormously principled on all these issues,' Sir Sonny said.

Whether we were talking about poverty or about racism, apartheid, UDI, she was always on the high moral ground and she was very wise to the degree to which politicians would try to manipulate her into situations in which she might be compromised. There was never any doubt in my mind where she stood on issues like Rhodesia or apartheid but nobody wanted to get her into the controversy with Mrs Thatcher. Sometimes she came so close that it was only her moral strength that saw it through . . . at Lusaka, it was very important that the Queen should be there and be able to use her influence with Kenneth Kaunda if things got tricky . . .

Elizabeth flew off to Africa several days in advance of the Lusaka meeting, visiting Kenya, Malawi and Tanzania before arriving in Lusaka to be greeted by thousands of Zambians and the plaudits of the government-owned *Zambia Daily Mail*, which contrasted her 'extra-ordinary loving heart' with what they saw as the Iron Lady's unsympathetic feelings. Thatcher arrived late that night accompanied by Lord Carrington, who graphically described her apprehension and also her courage as their plane descended towards Lusaka airport. She was well aware of the feeling that had been stirred up about her and, as the plane taxied to a halt, she took a pair of sunglasses out of her handbag and put them on. 'She was afraid of having acid thrown in her face,' said Carrington. 'Don't worry,' he told her, 'they're going to love you.' She put them away and they did love her – temporarily at least. Softened up by Elizabeth, Kenneth Kaunda swept Margaret Thatcher on to the dance floor after the opening banquet. At Lusaka Malcolm Fraser, the Australian Prime Minister, who had been instrumental in persuading Mrs Thatcher to sign the communiqué confirming that the heads of government 'were wholly committed to genuine black majority rule for the people of Zimbabwe', earned her deep resentment by leaking its substance to the media before the formal signing. Elizabeth had remained, as she always did on these occasions, in the background.

She takes no part in the actual conference sessions. As had now become traditional, at various intervals during the day individual Commonwealth leaders slipped away to have a private talk with her. Sir Sonny Ramphal said of those meetings:

> Nobody was ever indifferent to that because of what she brought to it. First of all because for a long time she had been friends of these people, many of them had grown up with her in office. Julius Nyerere and Kenneth Kaunda and people like that from Africa were young men when she became Queen, making their way in political life. She knew them as young Prime Ministers, and young Presidents and so over many years they were friends. Secondly, she did her homework prodigiously – the one comment I got from all of them was, 'My goodness, how aware the Queen is of our situation.' She would know who was in the clutches of the IMF, who had got what political scandal raging, she'd know the family side of things, if there were children or deaths in the family. She'd know about the economy, she'd know about elections coming up. They felt they were talking to a friend who cared about the country, the people concerned . . . It was that sort of informality and, to me, it made a lot of difference to the meeting because it was another bit of glue that made them a collective, and the Queen was very conscious of this kind of valuable role she was playing . . .

The success of the Lusaka Conference, at which both Mrs Thatcher and the Africans made concessions, led to the constitutional conference at Lancaster House and the eventual peaceful transference of power to an independent Zimbabwe on 17 April 1980, a turning-point in the post-colonial history of southern Africa.

The Rhodesian question was merely the introduction to Mrs Thatcher's prickly relationship with the Commonwealth, which was to erupt into extreme turbulence six years later at the Nassau Conference in 1985, dominated by the controversy over sanctions against South Africa as a means of ending apartheid and minority rule. Even before Nassau, a cost-cutting exercise by the Thatcher administration had upset both Queen and Commonwealth. Previously students from Commonwealth countries had come to Britain for university education on the same basis as British undergraduates. In 1979, within six months of the Thatcher Government taking office, it was announced that differential overseas student fees would be introduced, higher than those for British undergraduates; from 1983 they were to pay the

Happy and glorious:
Elizabeth on a walkabout
during the Jubilee summer
of 1977 – 'The Queen had a
love affair with the people . . .'

Queen of all her peoples:
Elizabeth being carried by
the islanders of Tuvalu
during her tour of the
South Pacific in 1982

Elizabeth with her racing
manager and old friend,
Henry George Reginald
Molyneux Herbert, then
Lord Porchester, now
7th Earl of Carnarvon,
but always known as 'Porchy',
at the Derby, June 1985

The glitter and the gold:
state banquet during the 1989
Commonwealth Conference
in Kuala Lumpur,
Malaysia

'Those bows':
Elizabeth with President
Ronald Reagan at the
De Young Museum,
San Francisco, on her
state visit in March 1983

Elizabeth and Philip with
President Nelson Mandela
in Capetown, 20 March 1995;
her first visit to a free
South Africa, once again a
member of the Commonwealth,
after almost fifty years

Balmoral Castle,
set in the green valley
of the River Dee,
Aberdeenshire, Scotland

Sandringham House,
Norfolk, England.
'Reminiscent of a Scottish
golf hotel', but beloved
of Elizabeth as 'an escape
place' where she can carry
out her childhood dream
of farming with 'lots of
horses and cows and dogs'

The image that shocked
the world: Windsor Castle
ablaze on the night of
Elizabeth's forty-fifth
wedding anniversary,
Friday, 20 November 1992

The morning after:
Elizabeth views the
wreckage of her childhood
home

Elizabeth and Philip with their senior grandchildren,
Princes William (on Elizabeth's right) and Harry
(sitting on her left) and Peter Phillips and his
sister Zara (children of Princess Anne and
Captain Mark Phillips), December 1987

Elizabeth and her Prime Ministers: at a dinner held at Spencer House
(ancestral London home of the Princess of Wales) held to celebrate
Elizabeth's forty years on the throne. From left to right: Margaret Thatcher,
Harold Wilson, John Major, Elizabeth, Edward Heath, James Callaghan

Brothers and sisters-in-law:
Charles, Diana, Sarah and
Andrew on a skiing holiday
in 1987

The Wales War:
Diana at the
Serpentine Gallery on
the evening of her husband's
television interview,
29 June 1994

'That's what it's all about': Elizabeth, with the Queen Mother and Margaret,
on the balcony of Buckingham Palace watching the fly-past
during the VE Day Commemoration, 8 May 1995

An 'Awayday': Elizabeth on her way to Edinburgh by Intercity, June 1991

The Queen: smiling, relaxed and regal,
Elizabeth aged sixty-nine in 1995

full rate. To the fury of both the Foreign and Commonwealth Office and the Commonwealth itself, the Ministry of Education announced the decision with no previous consultation. It worried and upset Elizabeth deeply, as she confessed with unprecedented frankness to Commonwealth representatives. Mrs Thatcher's economising had hacked at the roots of the British connection and the cultural basis of the English–speaking Commonwealth. As a member of the Commonwealth Secretariat said:

> It was totally destructive because one of the things about the Commonwealth is that all the ruling groups have been educated here. In the early '70s you'd have, say, ten Prime Ministers around the table who knew each other as students in Britain, because they all went to the LSE [London School of Economics] or Cambridge, Oxford and so on. And she [Thatcher] wiped that out . . . Now you have the situation where European students are treated as if they were natives of this country. They all come from rich countries whereas students from the developing nations do not, so people have stopped coming to Great Britain. Many of them go to the United States . . . even Germany is giving out a lot of scholarships . . . We encourage people to go to India.[16]

From the Nassau Conference onwards, Mrs Thatcher handbagged the Commonwealth heads of government at their biennial meetings. Thatcher's position was that imposing sanctions on South Africa would harm British exports and throw black South Africans out of work. The leaders of the Commonwealth, both black and white, took the view that the sanctions were an important weapon in the battle to end apartheid. Discussions became acrimonious and personal, particularly when it came to issuing press communiqués. Mrs Thatcher either, as at Kuala Lumpur, issued a separate text contradicting what the other members of the conference believed had been agreed, or, as at Nassau, publicly belittled the concessions she had made, when in a television interview she told the press that she had only made a teeny-weeny concession, accompanying this statement by a graphic gesture. She quarrelled both with Malcolm Fraser at Lusaka and with his successor, Bob Hawke, the Labour Party leader, at Kuala Lumpur in 1989, when she summoned a press conference and publicly disassociated herself from the previously agreed communiqué on South African sanctions.

Elizabeth was aware of Commonwealth unhappiness with Mrs Thatcher's stand and would have been sympathetic. Commonwealth sources believe that whenever possible she acted as a restraining influence on the Prime Minister, perhaps counteracting the anti-Commonwealth attitudes in the Thatcher entourage. 'The Queen could have been concerned about the Commonwealth,' a Thatcher aide said, 'but it didn't make sense to say that the Commonwealth would fall apart. The practice of the Commonwealth is to insult Britain at every turn, take its money and ask for more. Therefore there was no chance of its falling apart.' On one Commonwealth crisis, Elizabeth and her Prime Minister certainly did see eye to eye: when in 1983 President Reagan ordered the US invasion of Grenada (of which Elizabeth was Queen) with no prior consultation, Mrs Thatcher was 'incandescent' over the telephone to Reagan; staff called the Grenada episode 'very turbulent – an Atlantic storm'.

Mrs Thatcher's view of the Commonwealth matured over time. An aide commented:

> Both of us set out with the view that the Commonwealth was something we had been brought up with, maps on the wall at school with red patches on them, something to be proud of, the remnant of Empire that had been painlessly dissolved and that it had something to commend it to the family of nations. But on closer inspection we saw the extent to which it depended on British forbearance and commitment to uplifting the world's condition – what kind of legacy we had to endure as being an ex-Colonial power. It required considerable forbearance and Mrs T was not very good at forbearing . . . She came to realise that it was a valuable institution embracing one of the world's smallest democracies, Tuvalu, to the world's largest, India. She recognised that they got a great deal out of it. Mrs T began to realise some of the problems of the New World and of course one hit her between the eyes in 1982 with the Falklands – how do you ensure the security of the small states? She could also see it [the Commonwealth] had a role to play in defending the world from militant Islam.[17]

That there were tensions between the Palace and Downing Street was highlighted by what became known as the *Sunday Times* affair. On 20 July 1986, just before the Commonwealth Games were to be held in Edinburgh, having been boycotted by a number of nations in protest against Britain's stubbornness over sanctions against South Africa, the *Sunday Times* ran a front-page story that Elizabeth was deeply unhappy with Mrs Thatcher's policies over a wide number of issues: 'Sources close to the Queen let it be known to the *Sunday Times* yesterday that she is dismayed by many of Mrs Thatcher's policies. This dismay goes well beyond the current crisis in the Commonwealth over South Africa. In an unprecedented disclosure of the monarch's views, it was said that the Queen considers the Prime Minister's approach to be uncaring, confrontational and divisive.' Elizabeth was horrified and Mrs Thatcher, always sensitive to the multiplying stories in the press that she and Elizabeth did not get on, was deeply hurt – so much so that she did not even mention the episode in her memoirs. The Queen's Private Secretary, Sir William Heseltine, in time-honoured fashion, wrote a letter to *The Times* in which he asserted the Queen's constitutional right to counsel, encourage and warn her ministers: 'She is entitled to have opinions on Government policy and express them to her chief ministers.' Whatever personal opinions the sovereign may hold or may have expressed to the Government, he said, 'she is bound to accept and act on the advice of her Government'. Lastly, the Queen was 'obliged to treat her communications with the Prime Minister as entirely confidential between the two of them'. It was 'preposterous' to think that the Queen after thirty-four years' experience would have departed from those basic principles, he wrote. He admitted that the Queen's Press Secretary, Michael Shea, had talked to Simon Freeman, the journalist concerned, but claimed that he had 'said nothing which could reasonably bear the interpretation put upon it by the front-page article of July 20'. The claim that the contents of the article were based on information coming from Palace sources close to the Queen 'constitutes a totally unjustified slur on the impartiality and discretion of senior members of the Royal Household'.

The idea that Shea could have been authorised by Elizabeth to 'leak' the views attributed to her in the *Sunday Times* piece was, as Heseltine said, 'preposterous'. Michael Shea, ex-Gordonstoun, ex-Edinburgh University, a former diplomat and Director-General of British Information Services in New York, had been recruited by the Palace after Elizabeth's successful bicentenary visit to the United States and had joined as her Press Secretary in 1978. A writer in his spare time, he was a different breed from the Eton–Sandhurst brigade of Guards–City traditional Palace elite. An intelligent and approachable man of liberal views, he had shared rooms at university and later in London with David Steel, leader of the Liberal Party, and had been best man at Steel's wedding. Shea was well aware of Commonwealth concerns and in close touch with Commonwealth sources, who later described him as having been 'betrayed' by Freeman. He did not know Freeman, had never met him and the interview had not been face to face but over the telephone in response to Freeman's request for an interview on the general theme of 'The Monarchy in 2011'. According to Shea, the journalist extrapolated what he said into sensational claims about Elizabeth's unhappiness with Mrs Thatcher's policies. The interview had run on the lines of 'Is the Queen concerned about the Commonwealth?' 'The Queen is always concerned about the Commonwealth.' 'Is the Queen unhappy about the coal strike?' 'The Queen is always unhappy when the country is in turmoil.' People close to Mrs Thatcher at the time, however, believe that, although Shea certainly never consulted Elizabeth about any inspired 'leak' of her views and that she would never have authorised any such thing, 'there is no smoke without a fire'. They are convinced (although Thatcher herself refused to believe it) that there was hostility to Mrs Thatcher at the Palace.

No one at No. 10 Downing Street at the time suspected Elizabeth of being involved in any way, but they did think it unlikely that Shea would have taken it upon himself to brief this journalist without any consultation with his colleagues, i.e. that there was some conversation with some member of the Private Secretaries Office and an agreement that a carefully placed hint might 'do some good'. 'We thought we were being rubbished by the Palace,' one insider said, 'but Mrs T. was determined not to believe it.' Among those suspected of being anti-Thatcher were the Private Secretaries and professional staff (but not Sir William Heseltine, the Principal Private Secretary), 'real courtiers', i.e. those holding posts in the household and 'friends of the Queen'. Others included members of the royal family who were 'fed up with opening hospital wards only to have them closed and then receive hundreds of letters as a result'. Shea, they thought, must have believed himself to be expressing a widespread opinion within the Palace; much of Freeman's article appeared to be conjecture, but 'the nub of the story – about the Commonwealth – was true'. The Queen loyally stood by her Press Secretary. At Holyrood House just after the story broke, Shea sat between Elizabeth and Mrs Thatcher, both of whom told him to pay no attention to the media rumpus, but none the less his position in relation to Downing Street had become difficult. Accompanying Elizabeth on the state visit to China, during which Philip made a widely publicised remark about 'slitty eyes', Shea became involved in a televised scuffle with Chinese security guards. He decided that he had had enough and six months later left to join Hanson plc.

Eighteen months previously in 1984–5, Thatcher had taken on the British coalminers in a prolonged battle which ended in defeat for the National Union of Mineworkers. It had been a period of anguish for Britain, with horrendous violence between the pickets and the police, tales of families' divided loyalties, of thuggery and poverty. At the very end of the strike Elizabeth and Philip visited *The Times* on the occasion of the newspaper's bicentenary. While Prince Philip, in his customary forthright way, is alleged to have denounced the miners' leader, Arthur Scargill, as 'a shit', Elizabeth was introduced to the paper's labour editor, Paul Routledge, as the man covering the miners' strike. She volunteered that she had been down a coal mine in Scotland that had closed soon afterwards and, after a pause, added, 'It's all about one man, isn't it?' Routledge replied that perhaps it wasn't about one man and that, knowing the miners and having been brought up among them, he didn't think one man could bring out 100,000 men on strike for a whole year. 'There was a pregnant pause,' Routledge recalled, and the party moved on. Eight years later, having written an unauthorised biography of Scargill, he had become more familiar with the megalomaniac tendencies of the man. 'With the hindsight that has come from writing this book,' he admitted, 'I now feel that I owe the Queen an apology. By that stage, at any rate, the strike *was* about one man. Scargill may not have started the strike, but one word, one signal from him could have called it off before the struggle plumbed the depths of misery, violence and failure to which it sank . . . The Queen was right.'[18]

Elizabeth, therefore, did not blame Thatcher for the miners' strike. No one has ever discovered what her feelings were when Mrs Thatcher took the salute of the returned Falklands veterans in the parade through the City of London in October 1982. She may have reflected that the Falklands victory was very much Mrs Thatcher's, but other people thought it odd to see the Prime Minister standing on the dais instead of the Queen who is head of the armed forces. Not one member of the royal family was invited to be present at this ceremonial occasion, in contrast to the 1945 parade celebrating the end of the Second World War, when the King took the salute with Churchill and Attlee at a discreet distance. Mrs Thatcher did not, however, attend the fortieth anniversary celebrations of D-Day in 1984 because she considered it very much the Queen's occasion and perhaps to avoid the repeated conjecture that she was upstaging the monarch. The newspapers accused Mrs Thatcher of ambulance-chasing and elbowing the royal family out of the limelight by dashing to be the first on the scene of disasters like the sinking of the ferry *Herald of Free Enterprise* at Zeebrugge or the destruction of the Pan-Am airliner over Lockerbie. IRA outrages found the Prime Minister swiftly comforting victims (she had, after all, nearly become a terrorist statistic herself in the Brighton hotel bombing). 'She wanted to demonstrate solidarity with the people who suffered and to show that terrorists would never break British determination,' an aide said. None the less, Downing Street was conscious of the impression that was being given and sensitive about it; there seems to have been a breakdown in communication between Prime Minister and Palace as to who should go where and when. 'The royal family couldn't be relied on to go,' a Thatcher aide said defensively and indeed there was widespread resentment when Elizabeth did not go to the Lockerbie disaster area but sent Prince Andrew instead.

Mrs Thatcher is sparing in her references to the Queen in her memoirs of her Downing Street years. The most she would say about her audiences with the Queen was:

Anyone who imagines that they are a mere formality or confined to social niceties is quite wrong; they are quietly businesslike and Her Majesty brings to bear a formidable grasp of current issues and breadth of experience. And although the press could not resist the temptation to suggest disputes between the Palace and Downing Street, especially on Commonwealth affairs, I always found the Queen's attitude towards the work of the government absolutely correct.[19]

Suggestions that Mrs Thatcher might be interviewed on the subject were met by the Palace response, 'I doubt if she'd say anything, she's too loyal.'

The impression persists among politicians and Commonwealth members that Elizabeth did act as a restraining influence on Mrs Thatcher in some of her more intransigently tactless moods. There is speculation that it was advice from the Palace which widened the celebration of the Downing Street anniversary from a dinner to which Mrs Thatcher and her Cabinet invited Elizabeth, an occasion with strictly party overtones, to one to which all party leaders and descendants of former Prime Ministers were invited. Another occasion was the

Cenotaph ceremony held on Armistice Sunday in Whitehall, at which the Queen and the leaders of the political parties lay wreaths. Mrs Thatcher originally refused to allow the newly formed SDP to take part. A leading member let the feelings of his party at being thus excluded be known – indirectly – to the Palace. Mrs Thatcher gave way. Mrs Thatcher, however, could be obdurate on certain issues. Elizabeth would have liked to have visited the European Parliament in Strasbourg; her Prime Minister resolutely opposed the idea of giving royal countenance to that despised institution. Elizabeth did not go.

Mrs Thatcher's major innovation in British politics has been the fearless determination with which she set about attacking the sacred cows and ancient institutions of Britain. Doctors, lawyers, the universities, the trades unions, the nationalised industries, the BBC and the National Health Service – none of them escaped her reforming zeal and her determination to cut costs, reduce public spending and get value for money for the taxpayer. It was only a matter of time before the same spotlight would be turned on the monarchy again. The free market economy which Mrs Thatcher so cherished ushered in a free-for-all in communications in which she permitted a dominant share to be taken by her favourite press tycoon, the republican Rupert Murdoch. It is ironical that this most 'loyal' of the Queen's Prime Ministers, whose attitude towards the monarchy was the most reverential, should have set in train a revolution in British life which would touch the Queen herself in the next decade.

15

Extended Family

'A *family* on the throne is an interesting idea . . . It brings down
the pride of sovereignty to the level of petty life . . .'

Walter Bagehot, *The English Constitution*

Elizabeth celebrated her son's twenty-first birthday in November 1969
with a ball for 400 people. Pyramids of out-of-season syringa trees in
huge malachite pots perfumed the air as she kicked off her shoes and
danced with abandon until the early hours, her joy perhaps tinged with
relief that her son had at last reached manhood, releasing her from
responsibility for him. Over the next ten years family ties would begin
to loosen and then unravel with frightening speed.

By the mid-1970s the close-knit image fostered by the *Royal Family*
film would be increasingly an illusion. Anne's marriage took her out of
the family circle, Charles was away for long periods in the Navy,
Andrew went to boarding-school first at Heatherdown in 1969 and
then to Gordonstoun in 1973, and Edward followed in his footsteps to
Heatherdown in 1972 and then on to Gordonstoun in 1977. The family
were together for the traditional holidays – Christmas at Windsor
followed by a spell at Sandringham, Easter at Windsor, August and
September at Balmoral – but even when they were in London they
were rarely together except on formal occasions, such as the Diplomatic
Corps reception in November. The size and nature of Buckingham
Palace influenced the way they lived. Each of them had their own
suites and their own servants divided from one another by long
corridors or on different floors. It was more like a hotel than a private
house and the family tended to live in it that way.

Anne was the first of Elizabeth's children to be married. Her mother
had played no part whatsoever in her choice of husband, a pattern that
was to be repeated, as was her unquestioning acceptance of her child's

decision whatever her private feelings might have been. Queen Victoria, the sovereign whom she most admired, had interfered ceaselessly, even plotting the marriage of her favourite son, Prince Arthur, while he was still in the cradle and despatching him as soon as he was old enough on a European tour of inspection with a list of recommended potential brides. This, however, was not Elizabeth's style – she rarely interfered; many of her courtiers would say she did not interfere enough. Moreover, the 1960s were a different world from the 1860s. None of Elizabeth's children would have accepted an arranged marriage; the class revolution begun in the 1960s and epitomised to a relative degree by Margaret's marriage to a man who earned his living taking photographs (even if his mother had married an earl) was in full flood. Captain Mark Phillips, a professional soldier with decent, reasonably well-off parents and a respectable middle-class background, was an acceptable husband; whether he was a long-term prospect or merely a passing phase in the Princess's life was another matter. A remark Elizabeth is said to have made at the time indicates that she had diagnosed the true cause of his attraction: 'I shouldn't wonder if their children are four-legged.' The Queen Mother, displaying a similar flippancy, delivered the verdict that 'They could almost have been computer-dated.'[1] Privately it seems that Anne's parents were not overly impressed by her choice ('they were frightfully against it', a relation said), but relieved to see her safely married. Charles received the news of his sister's engagement in a letter from his father while serving in the Navy in the Caribbean. He experienced, he told a friend, 'a spasm of shock and amazement' at the prospect of 'such a ghastly mismatch'; later, according to reports, he dubbed his brother-in-law 'Fog', because he was 'thick and wet'. The general opinion at court was that once the physical attraction had passed, Anne might find her husband dull, but, since childhood, what Anne wanted she got. They hoped that the shared interest in horses would carry the couple through. In an informal engagement photograph of the two families together with the engaged couple, Elizabeth, characteristically, seemed more interested in their 'his and hers' black labradors, Flora and Moriarty.

Mark Phillips had appealed to Anne as the man who could beat her at eventing and whose superior horsemanship she could admire. Outsiders might find his conversation limited – 'if you ever sat next to Mark Phillips you had to know about army manoeuvres or dressage,' a royal relation said, 'and if you didn't know about either of those subjects you'd had it . . .' For Anne, however, such things were a mutual interest. Mark Phillips was handsome enough to be attractive and, being quiet, calm and rather shy and inarticulate, he could never compete with her on a personal level. Their engagement was announced on 30 May 1973, and they were married with due royal splendour in Westminster Abbey on 14 November, Charles's twenty-fourth birthday. Beforehand the royal image-makers had been at work; Norman Parkinson photographed Anne, a contemporary fairy princess in a filmy Zandra Rhodes long dress, a diamond tiara set on her fashionably coiffed long blonde hair, standing in the Long Gallery at Windsor Castle, loving and submissive in front of her handsome soldier husband, gallant in regimental mess kit and spurs. There was a television interview with the couple, when a clearly camera-shy Phillips stumbled through (perhaps unnerved by his army instructor's advice to 'keep quiet and keep smiling'), but Anne, utterly relaxed and direct, demonstrated to a wider public for the first time that she was a television natural.

Suddenly she was popular again, a popularity briefly renewed by her cool bravery in the face of a determined kidnap attempt by an armed man in the Mall the following year. It was a serious incident; the attacker, with a history of mental illness, seized Anne by the arm and tried to drag her out of the car. Her detective, the chauffeur, a policeman and a journalist were shot, the detective three times.

'Her story was just like a nightmare,' a shocked Charles wrote in his journal on 20 March 1974 after Anne had telephoned him in California, where he was on a visit with his ship, the *Jupiter*,

and she told me about it as if it were a perfectly normal occurrence. Her bravery and superb obstinacy were unbelievable – imagine refusing continually a kidnapper's demands for her to get out of the car and climb into his with all the time a pair of pistols being waved at her? Imagine seeing four people shot in cold blood in front of you and still refusing to get out; to struggle to prevent the man pulling you out of the car while Mark held on to your other arm until, after what must have seemed an eternity, the police arrived in sufficient numbers to overpower the man? My admiration for such an incredible sister knows no bounds!

All seemed well, however, with the Phillipses' marriage. After a stint as an instructor at Sandhurst, Mark moved to the Ministry of

Defence and Elizabeth bought them a country estate, Gatcombe Park in Gloucestershire, in 1976. The vendor, Rab Butler, complained humorously that 'the Queen drove a hard bargain'; the price for the eighteenth-century house and 733 acres, rumoured in the press to be £750,000, was nearer £500,000. The couple naturally built stables and Elizabeth loaned them the money to buy a neighbouring farm. There was a good deal of public muttering and the usual confusion between Elizabeth's private fortune and the monies paid her under the Civil List arrangements (Anne's Civil List allowance had been increased on her marriage from £15,000 to £35,000); rumours went around that they had built a swimming-pool for the horses and Captain Phillips's comment that they were 'just like any other couple with a mortgage' was greeted with understandable derision. On 15 November 1977, the morning after their fourth wedding anniversary, Anne gave birth to Elizabeth's first grandchild, Peter Phillips. Elizabeth was thrilled; confined, as usual, by her public duties, she could not be at the hospital for the birth. She was due to hold an investiture in the Throne Room at Buckingham Palace that morning and could not disappoint the several hundred people waiting for her. At 10.46 a.m. (the investiture was due to start at 11) Mark Phillips telephoned her to give her the news; as a result, she did allow herself to be ten minutes late and apologised: 'I have just had a message from the hospital. My daughter has given birth to a son, and I am now a grandmother.' (She did not, as Mrs Thatcher notoriously did in the same circumstances, use the royal 'we'.)

Elizabeth's relationship with her eldest son was growing more and more distant, partly of necessity, since he spent most of his time away from home in the Navy after leaving Cambridge, but more importantly from a lack of communication on a deep personal level. 'He worshipped the Queen but was in awe of her,' Mountbatten's private secretary, John Barratt, wrote.[2] Their relations were superficially smooth and easy, based on private jokes and shared experiences, but avoiding anything more serious or personal as was the established custom in the royal family. Elizabeth, her days and often also her evenings occupied with unavoidable routine, never took the initiative in inviting her children's confidences. Although she was their mother, she was still the Queen and that invisible aura of distance surrounded her. She could laugh, joke, mimic when she felt relaxed and in the mood, but she was still self-contained and reserved, finding it impossible to discuss emotional issues. In the stiff-upper-lip tradition of her family, she regarded displays of emotion or complaints as weakness. 'Never explain, never complain' could have been the family motto. When a dog belonging to one of her Private Secretaries died, she wrote a four-page letter of condolence, but when one of her former Private Secretaries died, she could not bring herself to write to his widow although the man had served her loyally for many years. It was not callousness but an inability to express, and an unwillingness to face up to, deep emotion. By contrast, Margaret, to whom the death of their father had come as the greatest blow of her life, was always ready with sympathy in such circumstances; when the father of one of her ladies-in-waiting died, Margaret's was one of the two most touching letters of sympathy which his daughter received. Elizabeth's children (and other people) did not confide in her, partly because she was the Queen and partly because of a reluctance to break through her reserve. She herself would sometimes complain that her children 'never talked to her', seemingly not realising that perhaps the initiative could lie with her. The situation was not made any easier for her by the fact that her husband and her son did not get on and that she tended to agree with Philip in his criticism of Charles.

In the circumstances Charles turned to people other than his parents. He was fond of but not close to his sister, who was too like his father for comfort. He had a surrogate mother in his former nanny, Mabel Anderson, an elder sister (or, as one relation described her, 'a female Mountbatten') in Lady Susan Hussey, who was only eleven years older than he was, and, the most important of all his relationships, a surrogate father in Mountbatten. Mountbatten by this time was coming to occupy in the Prince's life the place of both his father and his mother. His had been the influential voice in the plotting of the Prince's education, something in which Elizabeth, unsure of herself because of her own lack of life experience in the field, had acted passively, leaving the initiative to her husband and his uncle. After Cambridge, it had been Mountbatten who pressed upon the Prince the importance of joining the Navy rather than any other service. Philip, naturally, who had regarded his period in the Navy as the happiest time of his life, was keen to have his son follow in his footsteps. He took the greatest trouble to consult senior naval officers on the subject and to report the results of these meetings in handwritten notes to Charles, but it was Mountbatten, rather than his father, who had urgently lobbied the Prince to choose the Navy above the other services, even while Charles was still at Gordonstoun. He could spend some time in the other services if necessary, Mountbatten argued, but 'you must have a "mother service" that you really belong to and where you can have a reasonable career. Your father, Grandfather, and both your Great Grandfathers had a distinguished career in the Royal Navy. If you follow in their footsteps this would be very popular . . .'[3]

Mountbatten enjoyed illuminating for the Prince the history of his family and the ways of Whitehall. With his career record, notably as the last Viceroy of India and Chief of the Defence Staff, he was, as Charles's biographer wrote, uniquely placed to instruct the Prince with authority and intimacy about the governance of Britain and to help him interpret the duties and opportunities which faced him. 'He communicated his *aperçus* in anecdotes which were invariably self-serving but so turned to hold the wayward listener. For hour after hour Prince Charles was entranced by these insights and the morals that Mountbatten drew from them.' 'You really are becoming exactly like Queen Victoria in her old age and nobody will know what to do when you aren't there to help and advise,' Charles told him on 11 August 1970. He learned far more about the taboo subject of Uncle David from Mountbatten than he did from anyone else in his family. While Mountbatten angled for conciliation between the Windsors and the Prince, hoping that affection for the heir to the throne might persuade them to bequeath him their property, and was successful in presenting Uncle David to his great-nephew in a more sympathetic light, he never ceased to hold him up to Charles as a dreadful example of selfishness and dereliction of duty. 'The Prince rarely forgot anything that his great-uncle told him, and he was invariably disposed to believe him,' the Prince's biographer wrote. Nevertheless Charles, as he grew towards middle age, began to display certain characteristics in common with the Duke of Windsor, as Mountbatten did not fail to point out.

Philip, who had been familiar with his uncle's *modus operandi* since adolescence, warned Charles against letting Mountbatten interfere too much with his naval career, but no warnings could dent the developing hero-worship and almost filial love which the young Prince had for his great-uncle. 'You are the most astonishing "Great-Uncle" ever,' he wrote to Mountbatten. By the time Charles was twenty-three, Mountbatten had become his closest confidant and the greatest single influence on his life. The Prince called him 'grandpapa' to his face and 'honorary grandfather' in his letters; in return Mountbatten referred to him as 'honorary grandson'. To Charles, Broadlands was 'the best and most welcoming of homes' and it was there, rather than to his parents' houses, that he took girlfriends for relaxing, unsupervised weekends. Later, after Mountbatten's death, he was to write of him:

> I have lost someone infinitely special in my life; someone who showed enormous affection, who told me unpleasant things I didn't particularly want to hear, who gave praise where it was due as well as criticism; someone to whom I knew I could confide anything and from whom I would receive the wisest of counsel and advice. In some extraordinary way he combined grand-father, great uncle, father, brother and friend . . .

Mountbatten's relationship with Philip was difficult and often stormy. As Charles grew closer to Mountbatten, the gap between Philip and his uncle widened and their relationship was strained until the last few years of Mountbatten's life, when Mountbatten commented that Philip had become 'more like his old self again' and something like their old easy friendship was restored. Elizabeth, on the other hand, did not mind Mountbatten's interference in her son's life. Absorbed as she was in her own duties, she welcomed the fact that he had a mentor and one whom she personally liked and trusted. Unlike her mother, who always kept him at arm's length and who, like Philip, was suspicious of his influence over Charles, she regarded Mountbatten as an integral part of the family. With her father dead at an early age, he was the only senior member of the royal family to whom she could feel close. She called him Dickie and he called her Lilibet; she was always very relaxed in his company and used to go down to Broadlands as often as once a week to ride with him. 'She was always mildly amused by his inclination to exploit his entrée [to the Palace] . . . and his obsession with protocol, titles and honours also amused her, but usually she was happy to indulge him,' his secretary wrote. This indulgence even extended to allowing him successfully to pursue the adoption of Mountbatten-Windsor as the family name to an extent which had not been envisaged under the declaration of 1960.

Mountbatten was thrilled to find himself responsible for moulding the character and guiding the career of the heir to the throne; through Charles his hold on the royal family became firmer and closer than hitherto. He had never lost sight of his ambition to see his family name at least be linked with and if possible supersede the name of Windsor and he was determined to build upon the success he had achieved in

1960. Anne's wedding had provided him with the occasion. He wrote to Charles pointing out that Anne's marriage certificate would be 'the first opportunity to settle the Mountbatten-Windsor name for good' and asking him to intervene to ensure that 'her surname is entered as Mountbatten-Windsor . . . I hope you can fix this.' Dutifully, Charles wrote to the Lord Chamberlain, Lord Maclean, asking him to remind Elizabeth that 'the names on the marriage certificate . . . should be "Mountbatten-Windsor"', adding, 'The Queen already knows about this and has asked to be reminded about it in good time.' Three years later, having heard that Andrew, then only sixteen, was confused about the matter, Mountbatten wrote once more to Charles asking him to make it quite clear to his younger brother that 'when the time came he should sign the marriage register as "Mountbatten-Windsor" and not "Windsor" alone'.[4]

Elizabeth's central relationship is with her husband. Despite the fact that, as friends admit, 'he is a difficult man and the Queen finds him difficult', she adores him and defers to him, which seems all the more strange to observers in that everyone else defers to her. 'He shouts at the Queen sometimes like he shouts at other people and she doesn't seem to mind. It's as if she thinks that that's how husbands behave,' a friend said. On one occasion after Elizabeth had ordered something to be done in the park at Windsor, Philip exploded at luncheon: 'What bloody fool arranged for that?' Elizabeth said, 'I did.' 'Well,' her husband shouted, 'it was a bloody stupid thing to do.' A brave courtier intervened. 'Excuse me, Sir, but Her Majesty was quite right.' 'Well,' said Elizabeth, 'I'm glad somebody's standing up for me around here.' When he pays her a rare compliment, such as telling her she looks lovely in a particular dress, 'she looks like a child, looks like you'd given her the world'. This does not prevent her telling him sharply to 'Shut up!' if he is sounding off about something he knows very little about or in a way she thinks is tactless, usually in a Commonwealth context. In return he is protective of her; nothing makes him angrier than a gesture which he might detect as the faintest disrespect towards her. 'Keep that bloody camera away from the Queen!' he exploded during the filming of *Royal Family*, when he thought the cameraman was getting intrusively close to her. They understand each other on a deep level and the marriage works, despite the fact that Philip has not remained faithful through all their nearly fifty years of marriage.

The question of Philip's fidelity is, like the real extent of Elizabeth's

personal fortune, the last bastion which courtiers will defend –
metaphorically – to the death. Money and sex, the two questions which
most excite the public interest, are naturally the ones which the
courtiers least want to see exposed. In defence of their Queen, even
the most open, frank and truthful of courtiers is prepared to lie or
feign ignorance. The advent of the author Kitty Kelley with millions
to spend in pursuit of Philip's adventures has caused a great fluttering
of the dovecotes, not only at the Palace but in certain quarters of his
circle. Since the alleged 'party girl' affair in the mid-1950s, Philip has
learned to carry on his flirtations and relationships in circles rich and
grand enough to provide protection from the paparazzi and the
tabloids. So discreet has he been that scurrilous accounts of his
adventures have had to be published abroad for fear of legal action.
His defence has always been that the presence of his detectives would
prohibit any extra-marital activity, but the exploits of the Prince of
Wales with Mrs Parker Bowles while similarly guarded has blown
holes through that particular line. The women are always younger than
he, usually beautiful and highly aristocratic. They include a princess, a
duchess, two countesses, and other titled and untitled ladies, some of
them in the society horsy set.

Elizabeth notices; she is an exceptionally observant person. At a
party given in Scotland, Elizabeth was seated at a table beside the
dance floor, ostensibly talking about racing, but her eyes were
elsewhere, and, as the dancers parted, she could see her husband
dancing very close to the hostess's daughter. She sees but she does not
want to know, taking it all in her stride. Nor, like anyone else in similar
circumstances, does she want to be told.

Theirs is a very royal marriage; Elizabeth's generation was not
brought up to expect fidelity but loyalty. Affairs are one thing, passion
another. Philip is not the man to fall hopelessly in love; his affairs
make no difference to a marriage as firm and indeed fond as theirs.
Elizabeth understands his desire for independence and to be his own
man and makes allowances for it. Philip goes his own way, driven,
restless, always on the move. He makes his own plans, often without
consulting his wife. Mountbatten's secretary recalled how on several
occasions Elizabeth had accepted invitations for the couple to spend
the weekend at Broadlands and would later have to telephone to say
they couldn't come because Philip had made other arrangements.
'After one of these calls, Lord Mountbatten said, "God, the poor

Queen really does have a tough time, because Philip never tells her what he's doing."' This, he said, was because Philip never wanted to be dictated to and throughout their married life had striven to keep some independence. But despite all the rumours, Philip's often obvious flirtations and his affairs, they still share a bed and always have done. 'The marriage works physically,' a relation said. 'I think they've built up the most extraordinary relationship, they've made it work.'

Towards the end of his life, Mountbatten told his secretary and confidant, John Barratt, that he believed Elizabeth's greatest achievement was holding the family together and coping with the family's problems. 'Most people can hide their family difficulties but hers are always the focus of public attention,' he said prophetically. Elizabeth took her inherited role as head of the family seriously. It was, therefore, destined to reflect on her when, under the microscope trained by the media, its members behaved no better, and in some cases rather worse, than most families do.

From the late 1960s the private life of her sister once again presented a major headache for Elizabeth. The grim predictions of the bridegroom's family and friends before the Snowdons' marriage were turning out to be disastrously true. The couple had two children, David, Viscount Linley, born 3 November 1961, and Lady Sarah Armstrong-Jones, born in May of the same year as Prince Edward, 1964. (Tony Armstrong-Jones, who had refused a title on his marriage, accepted the Earldom of Snowdon so that Margaret's children should not remain commoners.) Although the couple were physically passionate, there had been strains in their marriage almost from the beginning. Snowdon made a determined effort to fit in to the royal family, even to the extent of learning to shoot under the tutelage of Philip, and walking with his hands behind his back as Philip did. He made himself agreeable to the family, successfully with the Queen Mother who liked amusing young men, less so with Philip with whom he had nothing in common. Snowdon, like Philip, had some difficulty adjusting to his new role of walking two paces behind his wife. In the household at first, Margaret, royal provider of both the house and the money, dominated a situation which, as a free spirit, he found hard to take. His determination to take control was signalled by the abrupt departure of the butler and, more significantly, Ruby MacDonald, Bobo's sister, Margaret's dresser almost since childhood. Ruby called the Princess 'Margaret' and was possessive and jealous of anyone who came too

close to her. She would abuse the ladies-in-waiting who carried out
Margaret's orders which she thought should have been given to her;
'She was the bane of my life,' said one. 'She was in a very powerful
position and was awful to the rest of the staff, and on tour to ADCs
and practically to Governors . . . a tray of drinks always had to be sent
up to her.' 'Ruby was a fiend – royaller than the royals. Tony got rid
of her and quite right too,' said another. The butler sold his story to a
Sunday newspaper; his chief complaints seem to have been about the
tightness of his employer's trousers and his refusal to employ three
charwomen instead of one, shortcomings which he claimed it was his
duty to reveal in order to preserve 'the dignity of the royal family'.
Margaret, used since childhood to have people dancing attendance on
her, expected her husband to do the same. As she had almost nothing
with which to occupy herself, she wanted him always with her. Their
six-week honeymoon was something which she had regarded as normal;
for Tony Snowdon, active and used to working for a living, such royal
lounging was hard to take. 'She was terribly possessive of him,' a
friend said. 'We warned her. "Be careful, he's a bohemian . . ." She
didn't understand. She wanted him all for herself and couldn't accept
that he was bohemian and wouldn't necessarily turn up at eight on the
dot.' Snowdon's increasing success as a photographer and his job on
the *Sunday Times Magazine* gave him the necessary independence, but
a battle of wills began which eventually turned into a war and destroyed
the marriage.

In the early to mid-1960s the Snowdons were a popular, glamorous
couple, undertaking numerous public engagements which reduced the
pressure on Elizabeth. Both of them were indefatigable; so much so
that *Private Eye* unkindly dubbed them 'The two highest-paid performing dwarfs in Europe'. In recognition of their growing family and
their active royal role, Elizabeth gave them a larger twenty-room
apartment at Kensington Palace, No. 1A. It had been unoccupied for
some time and the bill for redecoration was estimated at £65,000, of
which Elizabeth offered to pay £20,000 personally. Even when the
final bill totalled £85,000 there were no complaints in the press; the
Snowdons, she the most glamorous member of the royal family, he the
symbol of 1960s success as a photographer, were still enjoying a
honeymoon with the newspapers. They were very much a part of the
jet set, holidaying free with the Aga Khan to promote his new resort,
the Costa Smeralda in Sardinia; with Margaret's old friend and former
escort, Colin Tennant, at *his* resort on the West Indian island of

Mustique; with Harold Acton at Villa La Pietra near Florence; and with Jocelyn Stevens at the magnificent rented Palladian villa, La Malcontenta, on the outskirts of Venice. As an alternative, second-league court, the Snowdon circle was a microcosm of fast-track 1960s life. Unlike Elizabeth's, their friends were people in the arts, the media and showbusiness, like Peter Sellers and Britt Ekland. Sellers was dazzled by the Snowdons; his wife later complained that he sold them his pale blue Aston Martin for a throwaway price and even gave them his daughter's favourite Palomino pony. He became court jester to the royal family at Windsor and Kensington Palace and made a spoof home-made movie for Elizabeth's thirty-ninth birthday in 1965.[5] Sellers was frequently at the Royal Lodge with the Queen Mother for weekends, where parties were less circumscribed than Elizabeth's and Margaret had the security of the royal setting and the freedom to see the people who amused her. It was the perfect compromise for a woman who would have liked to find her identity outside the royal fence but never quite had the courage to do so.

Elizabeth had always felt enormous sympathy for her sister, who could apparently never find her role in life. She understood the wilfulness which was really the futile beating of wings against a wall and she could not help feeling the contrast between her own position both as Queen and as a successful wife and mother and her younger sister's distinctly rocky path. As the Snowdon marriage began to unravel more and more publicly, she hoped against hope that her sister would not be left alone again. 'It oughtn't to have gone wrong – there's still deep affection there now,' a friend said. The trouble was, as their friends had diagnosed from the start, that the two of them were 'too alike, almost the same person. Sometimes it works in a relationship, but in their case it didn't.'[6] 'They had a showbusiness quality and when it worked it was sensational,' Snowdon's friend Jocelyn Stevens said. 'But when it didn't, there was an atmosphere you couldn't kick your way through.' Margaret's cousin, the Earl of Lichfield, following in Snowdon's footsteps as a photographer, described them as 'trading insults like gunfire'. Infidelities were matched by infidelities, cannon shots in the mutual battle for supremacy. They were both self-centred, devious, manipulative and capable of being sadistic. Neither was prepared to yield, but where Margaret's 'royalness' had initially given her the edge, in open warfare it was a seriously inhibiting factor. She had nowhere to go beyond the palace walls whereas Snowdon had an infinity of possibilities. He could go to greater lengths in the war than

she could. Once in Sardinia when the Aga Khan was about to drive
them out to dinner from the Hotel Pitrizza, where they always stayed
at his expense, Snowdon lay down underneath the car as a gesture of
defiance, certainly not one that his wife would have been able to
employ. In the end he was to be tougher than she was and to suffer
less. He had his own life independent of the family while she had
banked hers on the success of her marriage. Anything less than success
would mean defeat.

For Elizabeth, the explosive state of her sister's marriage was a
source of private worry and public concern. Margaret's infidelities
were more public than her husband's. She had an affair with Robin
Douglas-Home, the piano-playing nephew of the ex-Prime Minister,
Sir Alec, and married to the model Sandra Paul; he later committed
suicide. Unambiguously passionate letters written to him by the
Princess surfaced in New York and were published by a foreign
magazine. There were other affairs, fortunately less publicly known;
while only one of Snowdon's, with the beautiful young daughter of a
peer, became common knowledge. The word divorce was already in
the air as far as the Snowdons themselves were concerned but as yet it
seemed unthinkable. In 1967, Elizabeth's first cousin, the Earl of
Harewood, eighteenth in succession to the throne, became the first of
George V's direct descendants to divorce after being sued for adultery
by his first wife. Not only was he divorced, but he intended to marry
the mother of his son, Patricia Tuckwell, an Australian violinist, herself
a divorcée. Under the terms of the Royal Marriages Act he needed to
obtain Elizabeth's consent for his remarriage; advised by the Privy
Council she granted it, but as a compromise and to avoid embarrassing
his family further, Harewood married Patricia Tuckwell in a civil
ceremony in the United States. But although George Harewood might
seem to have paved the way forward, a Snowdon divorce, touching as
it did Elizabeth's own immediate family, would be a more serious
affair.

In private the Snowdons' marriage had deteriorated so much by the
early 1970s that they led virtually separate lives. Snowdon would
refuse to speak to his wife even in front of the children, would spy on
her through a hole in the wall and leave insulting notes in drawers
where she would find them: 'You look like a Jewish manicurist and I
hate you.' He reverted to his bohemian life, often spending nights
away from Kensington Palace. Margaret, constrained by her birth from
retaliating in kind, took refuge in her favourite whisky, Famous

Grouse, and conspicuously put on weight. Wretchedly unhappy and increasingly frustrated, she seemed no longer to care about the effects of her behaviour on the public. Opponents of the monarchy and its cost, notably Labour MP Willie Hamilton, made her the target of their criticism over the sensitive years during which the Palace was negotiating a rise in the Civil List with the Government.

Elizabeth's patience with her sister finally snapped over the Roddy Llewellyn affair, which began in 1973, when Margaret was forty-three and Roddy Llewellyn only twenty-five. Roddy was introduced by Margaret's most faithful friends, Colin and Anne Tennant, who were hard put to it to divert her in her misery. The Tennants did not know him personally but took him on the recommendation of a friend, the London hostess Mrs Violet Wyndham. As the son of the famous eventer Colonel Harry Llewellyn, a Welsh landowner, Roddy seemed eminently suitable. He was blond, good-looking and sweet natured and the Tennants could afford to overlook the fact that he had led a chequered life, at one time sharing the house of a well-known decorator. Five months after their first meeting, Margaret invited him to Les Jolies Eaux, her villa designed by Snowdon's uncle, Oliver Messel, on Colin Tennant's resort island of Mustique. The couple enjoyed what the Princess's biographer described as a 'loving friendship' and the relationship was to continue with ups and downs over the next four years.

A year after their relationship began, Llewellyn found the situation too much to cope with and began to behave irrationally, taking off for Turkey on the spur of the moment without telling Margaret, then having a nervous breakdown in Barbados. Margaret also suffered a brief breakdown in the autumn of 1974, 'brought about by Tony's silences and insensitivity'; Lord Rupert Nevill and a friend became so concerned about Margaret's mental state during the marriage break-up that they arranged to bug the room where she and Snowdon had a confrontation and sent the tape anonymously to a Harley Street psychiatrist who was not given the identity of the couple. His verdict was, 'This lady needs help and needs help soon.' One weekend when a friend was having a house-party, Margaret telephoned threatening suicide: 'If you don't come over, I'll throw myself out of the window . . .' The friend rang Elizabeth, who coolly told him, 'Carry on with your house-party. Her bedroom is on the ground floor . . .' Margaret's marriage was in its final throes. On returning from Mustique after her holiday there with Roddy, she had asked her husband to move out of their Kensington Palace apartment, but he remained there although during that time he was to begin an affair with the woman he was later to marry, Lucy Lindsay-Hogg. 'There he was, living in my house, thinking he could have a lovely affair,' Margaret said. 'I asked him for a separation but he laughed in my face. He was becoming a virtual stranger and we would meet on the stairs and growl at each other. And I had to go on behaving as if nothing was happening.'[7]

Unfortunately for Margaret and the royal family, events conspired to make her appear publicly as the guilty party. So far her relationship with Roddy had remained unknown to the general public although it was well known in royal and society circles; she had been lucky to 'get away with it' for so long. Early in 1976 the *News of the World* published what appeared to be an intimate photograph of the Princess and Roddy, in swimming costumes, sitting side by side at a beach bar in Mustique. The implications were obvious – the profligate Princess on holiday with her toyboy. The newspaper had cut out the Princess's friends, Viscount Coke and his wife Valeria, sitting opposite, but that fact was considered irrelevant. The spotlight was now turned on Roddy and his unroyal way of life on a rural commune at Surrendell, a forty-seven acre farm in Wiltshire, where, it emerged, Margaret had not only lunched but also spent the night. Margaret had thoroughly enjoyed these excursions into a different world, but the image of a middle-aged hippy princess mixing with upper-class drop-outs was not one which commended itself to the public. The photograph precipitated the public crisis in the Snowdon marriage which had been threatening for so long. On its publication, Snowdon moved out, taking advantage of a situation which had been handed to him by his wife on a plate. Two days later a statement was issued from Kensington Palace:

> Her Royal Highness The Princess Margaret, Countess of Snowdon, and the Earl of Snowdon have mutually agreed to live apart. The Princess will carry out her public duties and functions unaccompanied by Lord Snowdon. There are no plans for divorce proceedings.

Elizabeth's Press Secretary, Ronald Allison, told the press, 'The Queen is naturally very sad at what happened', adding that there had been 'no pressure' from her on 'either Princess Margaret or Lord Snowdon to take any particular course'.

This was literally the truth. Elizabeth was indeed desperately sad at the failure of the marriage. She doted on the Snowdon children, who had spent so many of their holidays with her at Balmoral, Windsor and Sandringham while their parents were in some exotic location. She loved her sister, who seemed doomed never to find happiness. Even while she disapproved of the Roddy Llewellyn connection, describing it privately as 'my sister's guttersnipe life', she had not attempted to forbid it. Like the rest of Margaret's inner circle, she felt somehow that the unhappy Princess's personal well-being was a responsibility on all of them. The Queen Mother, just as she had over Townsend, had not interfered, despite the fact that she had become extremely fond of Snowdon, consenting to a joke 'royal opening' of his country retreat, 'The Old House', of which Margaret had disapproved. Margaret had taken Roddy down to the Royal Lodge to introduce him to her mother, but in general the royal family had not welcomed him; he had been tolerated at a distance as yet another of 'Margot's' whimsical fancies and as long as the friendship remained private they were prepared to go along with it. He was never invited to Windsor and while Elizabeth was on one of her Caribbean tours Mustique had been out of bounds to him. Private confrontation and interference in her sister's life was not Elizabeth's style, but once the *News of the World* had brought the Llewellyn affair into the public domain, impinging on the image of the monarchy, she felt compelled to act. Even then, she tried to avoid personal confrontation, deploying a sophisticated man about town to 'deal with' the Roddy problem. She remained, as ever, totally protective of her sister.

From her point of view, however, the fall-out from the Roddy affair became worse and worse. He was pictured travelling to Heathrow in Margaret's Rolls-Royce; while in the Caribbean he fell ill and was hospitalised in Barbados, where a concerned Margaret was photographed visiting him. He became involved in trying to start a career as a pop-singer and then was persuaded to act as front man for a night-club in Battersea, which was much resented by the local people and resulted in extremely bad publicity. Outraged Labour politicians seized on the subsequent headlines to attack Margaret and her Civil List allowance. Willie Hamilton pointed out that the Elizabeth Garrett Anderson Hospital for Women was threatened with closure for lack of funds while Margaret's Civil List allowance had risen to £55,000 a year. Why not deduct at least £30,000 from her pay to help the hospital, he asked. 'If she thumbs her nose at taxpayers by flying off to Mustique to see this pop-singer chap, she shouldn't expect the workers of this country to pay for it.' He pointed out that she had been on just eight public engagements in the first three months of the year, during which time she had drawn £14,000, 'not bad for eight performances'. After a near-riot outside the night-club Bennett's, on 13 April 1978, Elizabeth and her advisers came to the conclusion that Roddy must temporarily disappear from the scene. The final act of Princess Margaret's doomed marriage was about to be played. On 10 May it was announced from Kensington Palace that the Princess was seeking a divorce; the statement stressed that she had no plans to remarry and intended to live her life as the Queen's sister to the full. It was not, however, the end of her friendship with Roddy upon whom she was now even more dependent for amusement and companionship.

Elizabeth's arm's-length attitude to Roddy and his relationship with her sister was made perfectly plain in the difficulties over the organisation of Margaret's fiftieth birthday party in 1980. Elizabeth made it clear that she could not attend any party for her sister at which Roddy was present as it would therefore appear that she was countenancing the relationship. Margaret wanted him at the dinner; Elizabeth did not want him there at all. There were rows and eventually a compromise was reached: the Tennants, who, as Margaret's oldest and most loyal friends, would otherwise have been seated at one of the top tables, were detailed off to give Roddy dinner elsewhere and he would be allowed to come in after 10.30 with the after-dinner guests. It was a clear signal that there could be no future in the friendship which had already lasted seven years. To everyone's surprise it was ended not by the Princess but by Roddy a year later when he fell in love with and married Tania Soskin. The story ended happily for Roddy, who by this time had made a name for himself as a garden designer; he and Tania had two children and lived happily in an idyllic cottage in Oxfordshire. Margaret was alone again. 'I'm back to where I started with Peter,' she admitted, 'but this time I'm divorced . . .'

Elizabeth remained on good terms with Snowdon after the divorce. However badly he might have behaved towards her sister when their marriage was on the road to ruin, his comportment afterwards was impeccable and he proved to be an excellent father, although sometimes showing his cruel streak. Elizabeth was very fond of the Snowdon children, particularly Lady Sarah Armstrong-Jones; 'she virtually brought them up,' a friend said. 'They love the Queen and she loves them.' For all their failings together, the Snowdons have produced admirable children. Margaret used to complain that 'Tony was so oily to my mother and sister', and was not amused when the Queen Mother suggested that Tony be asked to Sandringham for Christmas after they were divorced. '*Really*, my mother!' Margaret exploded.

As another sign of changing times in the royal family, in 1976 Elizabeth was persuaded to give permission for her first cousin, Prince Michael of Kent, to marry Marie-Christine Troubridge (born Baroness Marie-Christine von Reibnitz), who was not only divorced but also a Catholic. Elizabeth felt sorry for Michael as a boy whose father had been killed soon after his birth and whose mother had died relatively young. But she was far from overjoyed by the prospect of the marriage and would have preferred a less exotic bride. She was persuaded into it by Mountbatten, the royal matchmaker, who felt paternal towards Michael and was charmed by Marie-Christine – 'the worst piece of advice Mountbatten ever gave the Queen,' according to several senior courtiers. Realistically, Elizabeth had little room to act; rejection of a bride for a minor member of the family on the grounds that she was divorced and of the wrong religion would understandably have led to a good deal of criticism, and so, after approval by the Privy Council, she gave her formal agreement. The wedding took place abroad (as the Royal Marriages Act of 1772 specifically prevents members of the royal family being married in civil ceremonies in England) in June 1978 in Vienna, the birthplace of the bride's mother, a Hungarian countess. At the last moment the Pope, who had granted an annulment of Marie-Christine's first marriage, refused a dispensation for a church wedding, almost certainly because the children of the marriage were to be brought up as Protestants in order to preserve their position in the line of succession to the throne (which Michael, then sixteenth, would have to renounce because of his marriage to a Catholic).

'Even if her behaviour had been exemplary, I do not believe that Princess Michael would ever have established a cosy relationship with the Queen,' Mountbatten's secretary, who also later worked for Prince and Princess Michael, wrote. 'The royal family is very inward-looking and finds it hard to welcome strangers; and the Queen, particularly, finds it very difficult to relax unless she is surrounded by those with whom she feels at home.' Elizabeth did not feel at home with Marie-Christine. Despite her looks, chic and the powerful charm she could

exert, the glamour which she brought to the royal family was not
appreciated nor regarded as a plus in public relations terms. The inner
circle royal family saw her as an adventuress and her behaviour seemed
to confirm their suspicions. Not content with life on the outer fringes
of the family, the new Princess Michael was determined to push
herself in. She made it known that she expected to be invited to join
the family for Christmas. Elizabeth gave in, but was surprised to find
her unwanted guest complaining about the rooms allotted to her
children and their nanny. She did not care for the public complaints
about not being allotted money on the Civil List or of poverty when
she gave Prince and Princess Michael the house in Kensington Palace
formerly occupied by the Snowdons (as a result of which there were
constant complaints about and quarrels with the PSA, the Public
Services Agency, which was then responsible for the royal palaces,
over decoration) and Marie-Christine then spent almost half a million
pounds on doing up the Gloucestershire manor house, Nether Lypiatt,
which they subsequently acquired. Charles, who particularly disliked
her, tried to prevent their moving into the same county as his new
country home, Highgrove, but failed and at Kensington Palace both he
and Margaret made it clear that they did not like their neighbour,
whom the family referred to as 'Princess Pushy', 'the Valkyrie' and
'You Know Who'. After a spate of bad publicity involving wigs and
Texan millionaires, Princess Michael kept a lower profile, but was left
in no doubt that the family had frozen her out. Queen Elizabeth, an
expert at the unspoken put-down – 'she could chill you with her eyes'
– was once observed at a reception at St James's Palace, on being
approached by Princess Michael, skilfully revolving so that she always
kept her back turned to her while appearing supremely unconscious of
her presence. The final embarrassment came with the revelation in
1985 that Marie-Christine's father, Baron von Reibnitz, had been a
member of the SS, a fact of which the unfortunate Princess Michael
(born in 1945) was herself unaware. Elizabeth, who, not unnaturally,
hates to be surprised by unpleasant news about her family by reading
it in the newspapers, was not amused.

Elizabeth, like her mother, has never been close to the Kents, with
the exception of the much-loved Princess Alexandra. She is loyal to the
people she likes and, according to a courtier, one of the few times she
was seen to explode with rage was at the scathing revelations by
Alexandra's daughter, Marina, about her parents in the tabloids. As a
boy, the young Duke of Kent used to stay with her and Philip at Birkhall

when they were first married and she attended his marriage in 1961 to Katherine Worsley, daughter of a great Yorkshire landowner. She subsidises the Kents' public activities – among other things they save her the necessity of presiding at sporting events not involving horses such as the Wimbledon Lawn Tennis Championships (a job inherited from Princess Marina) and the Football Association Cup Final.

In the mid-1970s Elizabeth was not only the head of the family but almost its most senior surviving member, apart from her mother and Princess Alice, Duchess of Gloucester. Her maternal uncle, David Bowes-Lyon, had died at Birkhall in 1961. Her father's younger brother, the Duke of Gloucester, Uncle Harry, a simple, uncomplicated soldier and farmer to whom public life had been anathema, suffered a series of strokes which left him paralysed and unable to talk from 1968 until his death in 1974. Uncle Harry was extremely forthright and often unconsciously funny. Although he had served conscientiously as Governor-General of Australia, he did not enjoy the duties that came as his birthright. 'Public speaking did not come naturally to him,' George V's biographer, Kenneth Rose, wrote of him, 'nor had he a fund of amiable small-talk with which to engage strangers. At the opening of a fruit and flower show he spoke only once. "What a bloody big marrow," he said, "glad I don't have to eat it", and at a performance of *Tosca* during a state visit he watched as Maria Callas plunged over the battlements, then his distinctive high-pitched voice rang round the opera house: "Well if she's really dead, we can all go home."'[8] His eldest son, the dashing, handsome and reckless Prince William of Gloucester, was killed piloting his own plane in 1972.

The Duke of Windsor also died that year, 1972. In November 1971 a biopsy revealed that the Duke was suffering from inoperable cancer of the throat; painful cobalt treatment produced no result and through that winter his condition deteriorated so that he could have died at any time. According to his doctor, Jean Thin, he was aware of this but 'it did not affect his general composure' and 'his courage and resignation compelled general admiration'. He seemed concerned only that the Duchess should not be made too anxious. He was largely confined to bed, with his favourite pug dog close by him for company. Elizabeth saw him not long before he died. She was due to make an important state visit to Paris in May 1972 designed to 'improve the atmosphere' for Britain's membership of the EEC. Shortly before the visit an anxious Sir Christopher Soames, the British Ambassador in Paris, called in Dr Thin to discuss the state of the Duke's health. Nothing, the Ambassador said, should be allowed to interfere with the Queen's carefully arranged schedule. 'If the Duke's death occurred during the visit, it would upset this schedule and possibly affect the outcome of the Queen's mission,' the surprised and somewhat disgusted doctor heard the Ambassador say. 'The Ambassador came to the point,' Thin recalled, 'and told me bluntly that it was all right for the Duke to die before or after the visit, but that it would be politically disastrous if he were to expire in the course of it. Was there anything I could do to reassure him about the timing of the Duke's end?' The doctor told Soames plainly that he could give him no such reassurance and it was perfectly possible that the Duke would indeed die during his niece's stay in Paris. They then arranged that after Elizabeth's arrival, the Ambassador would call Thin every evening at six o'clock for a bulletin.[9]

In the event the Duke did not die during the visit and on the fourth day Elizabeth, accompanied by Philip, Martin Charteris and the Duchess of Grafton, paid the expected call on her uncle. The Duke, although still lucid, was by now extremely weak, bedridden and on an intravenous drip, but he insisted on getting up to receive her. It was out of the question, he told Dr Thin, that the Queen should see him in his bedroom or wearing his bedclothes. She was his sovereign, and the least he could do was to receive her, properly dressed, in the adjoining sitting-room which separated his room from the Duchess's. When Thin objected because of the drip, he simply replied, 'That's your problem.' Gallantly, the Duke sat waiting for his niece, a drip tube hidden under his shirt and attached from the back of his collar to fluid flasks concealed behind a curtain. When Elizabeth arrived, she was greeted with extreme formality by the Duchess, who said, 'His Royal Highness is waiting to see Your Majesty.' To the doctor's horror, when Elizabeth entered the room the old man made a supreme effort and stood up, bending his neck in the traditional bow, oblivious to the risk of detaching the drip tube. She asked him to sit down and 'they chatted affectionately for about a quarter of an hour'. The doctor noticed that as Elizabeth left the Duke's room there were tears in her eyes; she was deeply moved by the dying man's gallantry and the sight of him brought back thoughts of her own father. 'The Queen was very shaken at how like Uncle David was to her father,' an observer said. 'She was very overcome – and would have liked to have got out of going to see him.' Then she went downstairs for what one of the party described as 'the most extraordinary tea-party I've ever attended'.

Wallis presided over a round table placed in front of the fireplace. Above her hung her portrait painted in the 1930s; 'she looked like a mummified version of it,' a member of the party recalled. On a visit some six months previously Charles had described her as 'flitting to and fro like a strange bat', unable to speak due to facelifts 'except by clenching her teeth all the time and not moving any facial muscles'. It was an awkward occasion; the Duchess's hand shook terribly when handling the tea-cups, and one was dropped. The pugs snuffled round the company; Elizabeth, normally a dog-lover, does not like the breed. The house reeked of joss sticks and from out of the walls came the muffled sound of scratchy piped-in music. The male servants wore the scarlet and black livery of Elizabeth's own footmen at home and on the hall table lay a red box marked 'The King'.

The Duke died nine days later in the early hours of 28 May 1972. Three days later his body was flown by the RAF to Britain and on 1 June he lay in state in St George's Chapel. Sixty thousand mourners filed past over the following two days, not a bad total for an ex-King whose reign had ended nearly forty years before. The Duchess arrived on the second day to stay at Buckingham Palace. Mountbatten was deputed to meet her at the airport and found her extremely nervous at having to confront the entire royal family without her husband's support. She was 'particularly worried about Elizabeth, the Queen Mother, who, she said, never approved of her'. Mountbatten assured her that she had nothing to worry about. 'Your sister-in-law will receive you with open arms,' he declared with his customary hyperbole. 'She is so deeply sorry for you in your present grief and remembers what she felt like when her own husband died.' He took her to her husband's lying-in-state at Windsor. 'At the end she stood again looking at the coffin', he recalled, 'and said in the saddest imaginable voice: "He was my entire life. I can't begin to think what I am going to do without him, he gave up so much for me, and now he has gone. I always hoped I would die before him."'[10] Charles, who was also there, does not seem to have heard this moving speech. At dinner at Buckingham Palace, he had found the Duchess's behaviour decidedly odd and wondered 'what sort of strain she was suffering under – whether all the social chatter was part of a brilliant façade or whether she was really like that all the time and didn't really notice Uncle David's departure'. At Windsor, beside the coffin, 'she kept saying "He gave up so much for so little" – pointing at herself with a strange grin'.[11]

The funeral service took place on Monday, 5 June, at St George's Chapel, Windsor; 3 June had been the Queen's official birthday which is traditionally celebrated by the ceremony of Trooping the Colour with all its accompanying panoply of guardsmen in uniforms and huge black bearskins, and the sovereign riding her charger side-saddle to the accompaniment of regimental brass bands. There had been an awkward moment when the question had arisen as to whether it should be cancelled as a mark of respect, as it certainly would have been had the Duke still been a reigning sovereign. Elizabeth and her advisers were reluctant to do so and a compromise was reached by which the ceremony went ahead but a lament was played by pipe bands, an effective tribute to the Duke who had been an enthusiastic piper himself. At Windsor the funeral was performed with the state befitting an ex-King. The officiating priests were the Archbishops of Canterbury and York, the Moderator of the Church of Scotland and the Dean of Windsor. The entire royal family was there except for the Duke of Gloucester, who was too ill to attend. Few foreign royalties apart from King Olav V of Norway, a close relation, had, however, made the effort to be at the funeral ceremony of one who, in royal terms, had betrayed his class. There was a handful of his English friends. Garter King of Arms proclaimed the dead man's high-sounding titles: Knight of the Garter, of the Thistle, of St Patrick, Knight Grand Cross of many chivalric orders, once King Edward VIII of Great Britain, Ireland and the British Dominions beyond the Seas, Emperor of India. 'To everyone in the congregation', his biographer wrote, 'this roll-call of heraldic honours must have provided a vivid reminder of how much he had given up; the slim, wasted figure of the widow in black recalled with equal vividness why he had made the sacrifice . . .' Had he not abdicated, he would have rested with the other sovereigns in the family vault under St George's. As it was, by his own wish his coffin was later taken to Frogmore to be interred under a simple stone in the grass to await the day when his wife would be buried by his side.

A photograph of the time shows the Duchess in black, anguished, confused, staring out from behind a lace curtain at the window of Buckingham Palace, an unfamiliar and hitherto hostile environment. She was, perhaps, beginning to suffer the effects of the mental and physical paralysis which was to overtake her, the result, some people unkindly said, of too much anaesthetic for too many facelifts over the years. She appeared confused during the funeral at which she sat beside Elizabeth. The Countess of Avon, wife of the former Sir Anthony Eden, noted that 'she seemed very strange . . . did nervous things with her hands and kept talking, "Where do I sit? Is this my seat? Is this my prayer book. What do I do now? . . ."' Elizabeth was concerned, showing what Clarissa Avon described as 'a motherly and nanny-like tenderness and kept putting her hand on the Duchess's arm or glove.' Afterwards there was a luncheon for forty people at the Castle where the Queen Mother drew the Duchess aside to sit chatting with her on a sofa while drinks were served. At the luncheon the Duchess sat on Philip's right, with Mountbatten on her right. The final ceremony of interment took place that afternoon at Frogmore, where the Duchess, under the influence of sedatives given by her doctor, seemed even more disorientated, wandering from person to person asking 'Where's the Duke?', or 'Are you having a good time?' and 'Why isn't the Duke here?' The Queen Mother took her arm. 'I know how you feel,' she said. 'I've been through it myself.'

The whole family later saw her off from the Castle. 'She kept on telling me what a charming young man Charles was and what a comfort to her,' Mountbatten recalled. 'Charles certainly was splendid in supporting her . . . I must say I am desperately sorry for her – she is so lonely and sad, and yet kept saying how wonderful the family were being to her, and how much better the whole thing had gone than she had expected.'

Just over a year later on 11 July she was back at Windsor to visit her husband's grave, arriving on an aeroplane of the Queen's Flight to be met at the airport by Mountbatten and the Duke of Kent. She had tea at the Castle although Elizabeth was absent on duty in Edinburgh and never saw her aunt-by-marriage again. The Duchess returned to Paris and the house she had shared with the Duke surrounded by mementoes of him; his bedroom an untouched shrine into which every night she would go and say 'Goodnight, David'. Although convinced of her poverty, she remained an extremely rich woman with liquid assets of some £3 million and millions more in jewellery, paintings, furniture and objects. (Her jewellery and various objects belonging to the Duke when sold by Sotheby's in Geneva in April 1987 made over $50 million, with the engagement ring made from the emerald of the Great Mogul selling for $2.1 million.)

After the Duke's death, Mountbatten became involved in a protracted and ultimately losing battle with the Duchess's French lawyer,

Maître Suzanne Blum, for control of the final disposition of the Windsor assets. He did succeed in having some of the Duke's uniforms and military insignia returned to Windsor and in 1972 made an arrangement with the late Duke's private secretary (who received a CVO from Windsor and the sack from his employers) for all the Duke's papers to be removed from the Paris house and taken to the Windsor archives. Maître Blum later in 1979 alleged that 'two individuals' authorised by Mountbatten and acting on royal authority 'burgled' the Duke's filing cabinets, removing his private correspondence and other papers. This was absolutely denied by the Palace, but some of his papers were then returned. Mountbatten, however, failed in his attempt to set up a Foundation headed by Charles to administer the Duke's income to various charities or to induce the Duchess to make Charles and other members of the royal family the beneficiaries of her will. At one time it seemed as if the Duchess intended to do so. She was charmed by Charles and once told a friend that 'all this' (indicating her possessions) would go to Charles because he had written her such a 'beautiful letter' after the Duke's funeral. Mountbatten had to admit defeat after receiving a final communication from her in 1974:

> As to the depositions in my will, I confirm to you once more that everything has been taken care of according to David's and my wishes, and I believe that everyone will be satisfied. There is therefore no need of your contacting my advisor in Switzerland. It is always a pleasure to see you, but I must tell you that when you leave me I am always terribly depressed by your reminding me of David's death and my own, and I would be grateful if you would not mention this any more.[12]

The Duchess was not invited to Princess Anne's wedding in 1973, but the Queen Mother did make an effort to pay a personal visit to her when on an official visit to Paris in October 1976. At the last moment the Duchess was too ill to receive her; she was suffering from senile hallucinations (which would almost certainly have produced hostile comments and behaviour towards the Queen Mother, whom she had always relentlessly denigrated in private conversations). Queen Elizabeth, with a graceful but possibly not heartfelt gesture, sent a bouquet of two dozen red and white roses with the message, 'In friendship. Elizabeth'. This was the last contact between the senior royal family and the Duke's widow. The Duchess lingered on in the shuttered house in the Bois de Boulogne, increasingly incapacitated mentally and physically, until she died there in a vegetative state on 24 April 1986, aged 89.

Her body was flown to London escorted by the Lord Chamberlain and met by the young Duke of Gloucester (Prince William's younger brother, Prince Richard, had inherited the title on their father's death), who accompanied it to Windsor. The short private service in St George's Chapel was attended by sixteen members of the royal family, the American Ambassador and the few surviving friends of the Duchess. Her coffin lay in the place previously occupied by her husband, Queen Mary and the preceding Kings of England, and on it rested a wreath of yellow and white lilies from Elizabeth. It was noticeable, however, that the title 'Her Royal Highness' was not on the plaque; even more curiously her name was not mentioned even once during the ceremony. Afterwards her coffin was followed out of the Chapel by the principal members of the royal family to be taken to its final resting-place in the lawn at Frogmore beside the Duke. In death there was final reconciliation between the family and the woman who had shaken the British throne to its foundations. Elizabeth was seen to weep.

Elizabeth was fifty in April 1976, settled in her job and way of life and looking distinctly middle-aged. On the social side the atmosphere at court became perceptibly duller after the death in 1975 from cancer of Patrick Plunket aged only fifty-one. Plunket was a life-enhancer who loved parties, which he endeavoured successfully to make both lively and splendid. Elizabeth was an excellent hostess who took care that every detail of any guest's stay was looked after. Intensely practical and with an eye for detail, she enjoyed overseeing the running of her houses and feeling that she kept in touch. Friends found it endearing to see how much she delighted in laying the table for informal meals in the log cabin at Balmoral and doing the washing-up afterwards, almost as if it were a therapeutic change from the remote grandeur of her everyday life. She was not, however, a natural party-giver and had relied on Patrick Plunket to organise the social side of the family's life. It was he, with the help of Elizabeth's cousin, Lady Elizabeth Anson, who had organised the teenage parties for Anne and Charles, drawn up the guest lists, found suitable and amusing people, overseen the food, flowers and lighting and set up a discotheque for the night in the heart of Windsor Castle.

It is a fact of royal life that the family do not have a wide circle of friends as most families do and the Master of the Queen's Household

is responsible for drawing up lists of the people they invite. 'When
they have their shooting-parties and other parties at Balmoral, Sandringham, Windsor or wherever,' a friend said, 'the Queen doesn't
think of the people – the Master of the Household comes with a list
and says, "Would you like these people asked?"' The circumstances of
being royal made it difficult for the children to make friends in the
normal way; while Anne got on all right at Benenden, Charles had no
Gordonstoun friends and not many from Cambridge. The people they
knew well tended to be the children of courtiers or royal relations; it
was difficult for them to have friends round on an informal basis to
Buckingham Palace or Windsor. The importance of Patrick Plunket in
the social life at court was in his wide circle of friends and his ability
to put people together so that they would enjoy themselves. He could
make a party go and he made sure that Elizabeth enjoyed herself.
While Philip was off dancing with one of his woman friends, Plunket
would whirl Elizabeth on to the floor. 'He'd notice at parties if she was
looking lonely, scoop her up and dance with her until she saw
somebody she wanted to be dropped off with and drop her off. Always
keep an eye, always be there if she looked a bit lonely.' He was almost
like a brother to her and, for the children, he, like Susan Hussey,
formed a bridge between the generations. 'It was a tragedy when
Patrick Plunket died,' a family friend said, 'because he made sure
amusing and interesting people were invited and the Queen listened to
him. It was disastrous for the whole of the household. It was disastrous
for her as a friend.' Many people later thought that had he lived he
might have helped avert some of the worst of the disasters which were
to overtake the family in the 1980s.

It was he who had organised the memorable party in Ascot week
1970 to celebrate the seventieth birthdays of the Queen Mother,
Mountbatten and the Dukes of Gloucester and Beaufort. The initiative
had come from him, not from the family, and it was he who had put
on the party for Prince Charles's twenty-first birthday in 1969. With
his premature death the court began to lapse into the traditional ways
which belonged to previous reigns. Even at Balmoral, where the royal
family went into kilts and holiday mode, women guests would find
themselves having to change their clothes four times a day from
something to wear down for breakfast into sporting clothes for lunch
and out with the guns, back to change for tea and then into a long
dress for dinner. (At Birkhall, where the Queen Mother keeps up the
state of former royal days, the women wear full-blown evening dress

and jewels for dinner even when it is only a small house-party.) Even picnics and barbecues had a strict routine; Philip has a specially designed trailer to hold the food – 'woe betide anyone who did not put things back in the right place,' a guest said – and transgressions were received with much impatient shouting from Philip and sometimes also from Elizabeth. Tradition was so strongly imprinted on Elizabeth's mind that at Balmoral she would cancel a house-party if there were no grouse on the moors, regardless of the inconvenience to the guests who had planned their holidays round it (and in some cases bought clothes for it). It never occurred to her that guests could be invited if there were no shooting or that there might be other ways of spending the day on Deeside. 'She could have had such fun with other people who liked walking, who liked fishing, who liked gardening, anything like that – but instead it would be, "What are we going to do with them? There's no shooting . . ."'

The loss of the charming, worldly-wise Patrick Plunket was a serious blow to Elizabeth, depriving her of an important connection to the world outside her rather blinkered, ultra-traditionalist horsy set and of a friend who might have guided her in her dealings with the younger generation over the next decade. His death was followed by the retirement in 1977 of an even wiser counsellor and old friend, Martin Charteris, her Private Secretary since 1950, a man whom she knew to be utterly devoted to her and who could be relied on to tell her what he thought necessary, even when it might not be palatable to her. Charteris had known Elizabeth's children all their lives and had a rapport with them that his successors could not have.

Even before Charteris's retirement, the traditional friction between the monarch and the heir to the throne had begun to develop. Charles had completed the last part of his parents' preordained training plans by spending almost five years in the Navy. Before that he had spent four months with the RAF at Cranwell qualifying as a jet pilot, which he had thoroughly enjoyed. He had also made his first parachute jump, an unpleasant and dangerous experience when the rope tangled round his feet immediately he leapt from the plane. None the less, when he became Colonel-in-Chief of the Parachute Regiment in 1977, he insisted on going on the regimental parachute training course. Despite his personal diffidence and timidity, he was physically brave and seemed to enjoy testing his courage to its limits, and although not naturally athletically gifted he showed real grit in his determination to succeed in physical tests and in sports such as skiing and polo. He did not, however, much enjoy his naval career and hated his preparation for it at Dartmouth Royal Naval College, an experience which he found like going back to school, describing it as 'irritating . . . incomprehensible . . . demeaning'. Once on board ship he felt himself inadequate and was haunted by the naval achievements of his father and his great-uncle, both of whom had shown outstanding ability in the service. He felt as though he were constantly being measured against them and when his father visited him on his ship after he obtained his own command, he was so nervous he forgot his own officers' names when introducing them. Mountbatten did his best to help to bolster his great-nephew's confidence. When Charles was sent on a training course at Portsmouth, he coached him in navigation, a subject for which, being utterly unmathematical, the Prince showed little aptitude. Charles lacked the gregariousness necessary for naval life; while at Portsmouth he refused to be billeted in the mess with the other trainees and commuted daily to Broadlands. He felt extremely uncomfortable aboard HMS *Jupiter*, his second ship, where, according to a fellow officer, the wardroom conversation was 'pretty revolting'; his shipmates found him 'diffident, unsure, wary, vulnerable'. As commanding officer of his own ship, HMS *Bronington*, however, he was popular with his crew; he never shouted at them. His kindness and soft-heartedness made him unsuited for service life; when one of the seamen on *Jupiter* was killed in a road accident, the Prince was distraught and telephoned home in tears. 'Charles really must learn to be tougher,' Elizabeth commented.

The objectives of Charles's education as drawn up by his parents and Mountbatten had been ultimately to fit him for his job as future King. Cheam and Gordonstoun had been the first steps in the toughening-up process, taking him away from the warm embrace of home, pitching him into daily contact with his contemporaries and teaching him self-reliance. Elizabeth and Philip had already had to face up to the fact that that part of his education had not been a startling success. Charles had emerged from his ordeal with what self-confidence he had thoroughly dented; Geelong under the tutelage of Checketts and his formative contact with the primitive peoples of New Guinea had given him, as Elizabeth had hoped, a lasting fondness for Australia. The Navy had been supposed to teach him discipline and leadership and give him work experience of the armed forces of which he would one day be titular head. Outwardly, the image of Charles flying jets, making parachute jumps and commanding his own ship had portrayed him as the dashing Action Man Prince of Wales. Inwardly, to judge from the letters and journals reproduced in his authorised biography, the experience appeared not to have changed him much and, worse, to have left a festering resentment at having his life mapped out for him.

Charles emerged from the Navy in 1976 to find himself with no role in life beyond his ceremonial functions as the heir to the throne. He was twenty-eight and had somewhat unwisely publicly set a limit for getting married 'by the time I'm thirty'. The precedents for the role of Prince of Wales were not encouraging: the Duke of Windsor, after a brave stint in France during the First World War and then a series of punishing Empire tours, had become increasingly spoiled, selfish and dissolute; Charles's great-grandfather, George V, an altogether more placid and pliable young man, had spent his seventeen years as Prince of Wales doing nothing but 'killing animals and sticking in stamps', to quote his official biographer; Edward VII's conduct as Prince of Wales had been a byword for self-indulgence.

Elizabeth, busy and successful in her public role as monarch, had given her son little help in his search. There was, after all, no role marked out for the heir to the throne until he succeeded and with the Queen a healthy fifty-year-old that eventuality was going to be a long way away. She gave him his own office in St James's Palace and his own advisers, among whom David Checketts still featured, and expected him to get on with his life. There were desultory discussions between Buckingham Palace, Downing Street and the Prince's staff about finding him a 'proper job'. Checketts suggested the possibility of the Governor-Generalship of Australia, but the bitter row which took place in 1975 over the sacking of the Australian Prime Minister, Gough Whitlam, by the Queen's official representative, the Governor-General, Sir John Kerr, put paid to that plan. Lord Carrington and Sir Christopher Soames suggested he might be appointed Ambassador to Paris, an idea which was quickly shot down. Later, when James Callaghan succeeded Harold Wilson as Labour Prime Minister in 1976, he suggested a programme of instruction in government, but was disappointed by the Prince's lack of enthusiasm. 'Jim Callaghan was obsessed with the idea of getting Prince Charles a job,' a fellow minister said. 'We put him on the board of the CDC [Colonial Development Corporation] and the idea was that he would be chairman, but he didn't bother to turn up and wouldn't take it seriously. He wasn't interested – he wanted to be a dabbler ...' Checketts endeavoured to interest the Prince in the running of his Duchy of Cornwall without success. There was concern at the Palace about the apparent lack of focus to the Prince's life and public comment about the fact that he seemed to spend much of his time in high-profile elitist sports such as polo, shooting and skiing. The hero prince seemed to be turning into a playboy.

The Prince resented Buckingham Palace's efforts to control him; difficulties between them over the Trust to be established to celebrate the Queen's Silver Jubilee in 1977 marked the beginnings of a rift between the two households which was to become more marked over the years. In the summer of 1974 Martin Charteris warned the Prince's Private Secretary, Checketts, that the Trust, which the Prince was in the process of establishing to help inner-city projects, might conflict with the already established George V Jubilee Trust (set up under the chairmanship of Charles's predecessor as Prince of Wales) and the proposed Trust for the Queen's Silver Jubilee, particularly as the Queen was intending to ask her son to be chairman of both Jubilee Trusts. 'I think', Charteris wrote on 26 June 1974, 'the message is go steady on the Trust Prince Charles has in mind until the dust settles . . .'[13] Martin Charteris was almost certainly acting after consultation with Elizabeth and pointing out in a perfectly reasonable manner the dangers of a major muddle, or, as he tactfully put it, a potential 'conflict of interest' over the various Trusts. Lord Charteris, as he later became, remembers no conflict with Charles, of whom he was and is very fond. Only on one, delphic occasion was the message transmitted from Elizabeth to her son: 'Tell him to leave the throne alone.'

Charles, however, according to his biographer, Jonathan Dimbleby, was apparently infuriated at the implication that he was to be reined in by the Palace and was not prepared to take direction even from someone as wise as Martin Charteris. 'Though the Prince disguised his growing resentment – except from his intimates', Dimbleby wrote, ' – he was quick to detect any apparent slight from the Queen's officials and began resolutely to distance himself from them.' The truth was that the Prince, reacting to years of Palace control, was becoming something of a wild card in the royal pack. In his determination to assert himself he was entering the kind of period of rebellion against his parents which most people go through at the teenage stage. With his own huge income from the Duchy of Cornwall (on his twenty-first birthday the entire income of the Duchy – £248,000 – was made over to him, although by arrangement with the Treasury he handed over 50 per cent in lieu of income tax) and his own staff, he was flexing his muscles, uncertain as to which direction he wanted to go but obstinate to any outside pressure.

Released from the hierarchical discipline of the Navy to which even a Prince had to conform, he was becoming a spoiled, rich young man whose innate good qualities and real seriousness were frustrated by a consciousness of the aimlessness of his life. His personal servants and his valets – first James MacDonald and then Stephen Barry – had indulged him and he took any kind of criticism badly. Checketts was later to be the first victim. The self-pity, pessimism and complaining note which ran through both his private correspondence and his journals, the 'weakness' which his parents had tried to eradicate, now turned into petulance when he was crossed. He allowed the temper fits, or 'gnashes', which he had inherited from his grandfather, George VI, to burst out in what his biographer described as 'alarming displays of uncontrolled temper, his face [being] suffused with intense emotion'.

> Unable to find a suitable challenge for his ill-focused energy, the Prince had more time on his hands than he either wished or cared to admit. To his friends he seemed troubled by anxiety and discontent, which he sometimes allowed to affect his behaviour towards his staff. Easily provoked by minor irritations, he became uncharacteristically impatient and peremptory. Whereas a decade earlier his comments about the official programmes put before him had been innocent and dutiful, in the late seventies his response to yet another 'Away Day' [i.e. official engagement] could seem reluctant and jaundiced . . .[14]

Even Mountbatten, now in his late seventies, was not listened to with quite such reverence by the headstrong Prince, bent on self-enlightenment and on finding a spiritual direction to his life, something on which his worldly great-uncle was hardly equipped to advise him. In the mid-1970s Charles found a guru in one of Mountbatten's friends, the elderly South African writer Laurens van der Post, author of *The Lost World of the Kalahari*, which celebrated the myths of the bushmen. In the words of his biographer, Charles now began to undertake a voyage of spiritual enquiry away from the cultural certainties into which he had been born. Van der Post apparently detected a 'missing dimension' in the course of education and training plotted for the Prince by his parents and his father in particular. 'I think one should be outward bound the inner way,' he told Charles, who now began to record his dreams for his guru to interpret. Van der Post also proposed a seven-week 'retreat' into the Kalahari desert for 1977, a dotty scheme which was quickly sat upon by the Foreign Secretary, Tony Crosland, much to the relief of the Palace. Charles found his personal guru in the Old Man of Lochnagar, the character who, in the stories he had invented for his younger brothers, lived in a cave on the brooding mountain above Balmoral, and he developed a belief in reincarnation. This sort of thing did not appeal to his parents; Elizabeth with her traditional Anglican Christian faith regarded it as yet another example of her son's waywardness. It was another form of rebellion against the narrow certainties which had hitherto shaped his life. In 1979 he became bewitched by a young Indian woman, former wife of the film director John Huston, who introduced him to Buddhism and to a book called *The Path of the Masters*, a guide to the spiritual wisdom of the Eastern gurus. At the age of thirty, the future pillar of the Established Church of England was wallowing in the kind of mystical experience which most people had been through in the 1960s. His parents and their friends were unaware of the extent to which he was infatuated with his new spiritual guide and her guidance which led him towards vegetarianism and against the killing of animals. 'We were surprised when he suddenly gave up shooting,' a member of Philip's Norfolk sporting circle said. The Prince's household, however, became thoroughly alarmed. The Hon. Edward Adeane, son of the Queen's former Private Secretary, and now the Prince's Private Secretary, told friends, 'it's got to be stopped'; fortunately for their peace of mind it did.

Charles's emotional life was equally wayward and a source of concern to his parents. Since 1970 there had been only one woman in his heart, Camilla Shand. Camilla was a sparky, confident blonde, eighteen months older than he was and already sexually experienced. Although not titled, she was well-connected; the Shands were what was called in those days 'a good county family'. Her father, Major Bruce Shand, was a well-to-do ex-cavalry officer and wine merchant who listed hunting and gardening as his 'recreations' and acted as Vice Lieutenant of Sussex. Her mother was a daughter of Lord Ashcombe, descendant of the great builder Thomas Cubitt, who built most of Belgravia. The most significant fact about Camilla's ancestry was that her great-grandmother on her mother's side, the Hon. Mrs George Keppel, had been Edward VII's longest-serving mistress.

Camilla had always been fascinated by Alice Keppel, who was to be her role model in her relationship with the Prince of Wales. Alice was witty, down-to-earth and knew how to keep men happy just as her great-granddaughter did. Camilla and Charles shared a sense of humour and a passion for the *Goon Show* – their nicknames for each other, 'Gladys' and 'Fred', are *Goon Show* names – and a love of country life, riding and hunting.

Charles had met Camilla through his first girlfriend, Lucia Santa Cruz, and fallen for her almost immediately. Their affair was encouraged – up to a point – by Mountbatten, who saw Camilla as ideal mistress material, a girl who could bring his shy nephew out and make him happy. Charles used Broadlands for romantic weekends away from what Mountbatten's secretary described as 'the prying eyes of the Buckingham Palace staff'. He and Camilla often went there with no questions asked. Camilla was nice, unpretentious and had no ambitions towards becoming the future Queen Consort, while at the back of her mind she was still besotted with her future husband, Anne's former boyfriend, Andrew Parker Bowles. Charles had not been able to bring himself to tell her how he felt about her, he was only twenty-four and too uncertain of himself to make the commitment to marriage. There were doubts as to whether Camilla would have been considered by the then demanding court standards as entirely worthy of the heir to the throne. Mountbatten gently warned him off getting too serious about her. She would not have fitted the part of virgin bride whom he recommended for Charles and anyway he had his own granddaughter, Amanda Knatchbull, daughter of Patricia and John Brabourne, in mind for the role. 'I believe, in a case like yours,' Mountbatten was to write to Charles some eighteen months later, advice which was to have momentous consequences, 'that a man should sow his wild oats before settling down. But for a wife he should choose a suitable and sweet-charactered girl before she meets anyone else she might fall for.' The Prince hesitated and lost Camilla, who became engaged to Parker Bowles after Charles left to join his ship, HMS *Minerva*, in the West Indies and married him in July 1973. His indecision was to cost himself and the monarchy dearly. Andrew Parker Bowles's status as the son of old friends of the royal family – and of Charles's grandmother in particular – meant that Camilla would remain very much within the Prince's orbit.

Mountbatten was, as Elizabeth teasingly described him, an old-fashioned matchmaker; he could not resist the temptation of guiding the Prince into matrimony. Having succeeded so spectacularly with Philip, the prospect of pulling off the double by making his granddaughter the wife of the heir to the throne was certainly alluring. After the loss of Camilla to Parker Bowles in 1973, Mountbatten pointed him in Amanda's direction. In 1974 after a visit to the Brabournes' house on Eleuthera in the Bahamas, where he had found Amanda 'disturbingly attractive', Charles had begun to consider her as a possible marriage prospect and had even raised the subject with her mother, but Amanda was then not yet seventeen. Mountbatten – without consulting Amanda's parents – did what he could to further the match just as he had with Philip, writing 'how to woo' letters to Charles and even going to the lengths of enlisting his favourite goddaughter, the chic Sacha Abercorn, to take Amanda to Paris on a clothes-hunting trip to smarten her up. Elizabeth and Philip approved; when told of his uncle's matchmaking plans for Charles, Philip apparently said, 'Good, it beats having strangers coming into the family.' Charles continued to see Amanda and suggested marriage to her five years later, but she, although fond of him and sorry for his loneliness, was only too well aware of what marriage into the royal family involved and turned him down.

Through all this time Charles dated a string of beautiful upper-class and not so upper-class girls – including Lady Jane Wellesley, daughter of the Duke of Wellington, Georgiana Russell, Sabrina Guinness, Davina Sheffield and Anna Wallace – and proposed to at least one of them. Elizabeth and Philip favoured the lovely and sweet-natured Lady Leonora Grosvenor, but she married Elizabeth's cousin, the Earl of Lichfield, instead. Mountbatten persisted with his dream of seeing his granddaughter destined for the throne of Great Britain and concocted a scheme whereby he and Amanda should accompany the Prince on an official tour of India envisaged for 1980. When he put the idea to Elizabeth and Philip, however, Philip was adamantly against it, pointing out that the presence of the former Viceroy would overshadow the purpose of the visit which was to introduce the heir to the British throne to the Indian public. Elizabeth thought of the effect upon Amanda, whose presence on the tour would make her an object of speculation to the press, who had, until now, taken no notice of her, regarding her simply as Charles's cousin, and remained unaware of the frequency of his visits to Broadlands to see her. Amanda's parents were of the same opinion and that if she were to go an engagement would have to be announced or denied in circumstances which would ruin any chance of the couple getting together. In the event, as we have seen, Amanda Knatchbull chose freedom, confirming the lonely Prince in his belief that marriage into the House of Windsor was a sacrifice which no one should be expected to make.

In the interim he carried on a series of short-lived affairs and one-night stands, so much so that by 1978 Mountbatten began to admonish him against 'beginning on the downward slope that wrecked your Uncle David's life and led to his disgraceful abdication and futile life ever after'. On an official visit to Australia Checketts had to warn him against spending the weekend with two former girlfriends because inevitable press speculation about it would spoil his visit; Charles, again like his Uncle David, insisted obstinately that his private life was his own affair, and gave in only when Checketts threatened to consult the Queen. Where once he had been the epitome of kindness and consideration, he now began to display an inconsiderate selfishness, changing his plans when he felt like it with no thought for his hosts. When he did this to the Brabournes, Mountbatten told him angrily that he was 'showing no signs of pulling yourself together' and that his behaviour was 'typical of how your Uncle David started'.

On the morning of 27 August 1979 the IRA detonated a bomb planted in Mountbatten's fishing boat as he left harbour at Mullaghmore on the west coast of Ireland on a fishing trip with his family. They were about to collect lobster pots when the bomb exploded almost under Mountbatten's feet, killing him instantly with his grandson, Nicholas Knatchbull, aged fourteen, and a local boy, Paul Maxwell, aged fifteen. His daughter, Patricia, and her husband, Lord Brabourne, were severely injured, and Brabourne's eighty-three-year-old mother died the next day. Elizabeth was at Balmoral when she heard the news. She was terribly shocked; a piece of her past had been violently torn away from her. (It had been unwise, to say the least, for a member of the royal family who had so notably served in the armed forces regularly to spend holidays in the South of Ireland. On the same day, 130 miles to the east, the IRA blew up twenty British soldiers at Warrenpoint in County Down.) Mountbatten's death touched Elizabeth deeply and personally. She went down to Broadlands for the funeral, but once again, in a matter which meant so much to her emotionally, could not bring herself to express her feelings in letters of condolence to his daughters. For the family, their one consolation was that Mountbatten had died instantly and dramatically before old age could take its inevitable toll. Mountbatten had interfered ceaselessly but always with the good of the family in view. There was now no one who could replace him as an adviser outside the Palace who would tell the family what they might not want to hear. A vital channel of communication between Elizabeth and her eldest son had disappeared.

16

Grim Fairy-Tales

'If the Queen had spent as much time over the mating of her children as she does on her horses all this might not have happened . . .'

A courtier

By 1980, with the deaths of Mountbatten and Plunket and the retirement of Martin Charteris, Elizabeth had lost trusted counsellors who were not only vital links with the outside world beyond Whitehall but also with her children. The most important question facing the monarchy for its dynastic future and its survival into the next reign was the marriage of the heir to the throne, now becoming increasingly urgent. The Prince was thirty-two and still besotted with a married woman, Camilla Parker Bowles, to whom he had once again turned for consolation after the death of Mountbatten. Perhaps because of this the women to whom he had proposed marriage had turned him down. Elizabeth was aware of the relationship and that the officers of Andrew Parker Bowles's regiment were unhappy about it, breaking as it did the convention that no officer should have an affair with a brother officer's wife. 'Ma'am,' an old friend had told her, 'the Prince of Wales is having an affair with the wife of a brother officer and the Regiment don't like it.' She looked down and did not answer; it is doubtful whether she took any action over it, adopting the family ostrich stance in the face of unpleasant personal situations. Philip, however, always the most pro-active of the two, put pressure on his son to marry and produce an heir.

Charles agonised, torn between what he saw to be his duty and his love for Camilla. The bride, according to Mountbatten's precepts, would have to be a virgin with no sexual past – something which automatically excluded his girlfriends hitherto. In the summer of 1980 the ideal solution seemed to have presented itself in the form of Lady Diana Spencer, sister of a former girlfriend of the Prince, Lady Sarah Spencer. The Spencers were not only impeccably aristocratic and connected to the great families of England, but even had royal blood, tracing back to the first Duke of Richmond, the illegitimate son of King Charles II by his mistress, Louise de Kéroualle. They were rich, owning acres of Northamptonshire surrounding their stately home, Althorp, and a palatial London house, Spencer House, filled with superb collections of paintings, furniture and works of art. The Spencers had had a special relationship with the royal family and a tradition of being courtiers. Diana's great-grandfather, the 6th Earl, had been Lord Chamberlain to both Edward VII and George V; her grandmother, Lady Cynthia, wife of the 7th Earl, had been Lady of the Bedchamber to the Queen Mother, as had her great-aunt, Lady Delia Peel, who had been much beloved by both Elizabeth and Margaret; while another great-aunt, Lady Lavinia, was a great friend of and exactly the same age as the Queen Mother, having shared a governess with her as a child. The Spencers, said a descendant, had a special voice when talking about royalty – '*They're* coming.' Diana's family on her mother's side, the Fermoys, were also closely linked to the royal family, having been their next-door neighbours at Sandringham since George V had rented out Park House on the estate to Diana's grandfather, the 4th Baron Fermoy. Diana's grandmother, Ruth, Lady Fermoy, had been a lady-in-waiting to the Queen Mother since 1956 (one of Queen Mary's first thoughts on leaving the deathbed of George V had been to inquire about 'Lady Fermoy's new baby' – Frances, Diana's mother). Diana's father, the 8th Earl, always known as 'Johnnie' Spencer, had been equerry to the Queen's father and to the Queen herself.

'On paper', as one of Elizabeth's friends later said bitterly, 'it seemed the ideal match.' There were, however, family characteristics on both sides of Diana's parentage that had she been a brood mare might have given Elizabeth reason to question the desirability of such a mating. 'The Spencers are difficult,' a relation said. 'It's the Sarah Jennings[1] genes. As a family they like to live among dramas. There's never a moment when they're all speaking to each other. Spencers are not as others – they're not straightforward.' Had Elizabeth studied Diana's immediate family on her mother's side and the recent formbook of both her parents, she might not have been so pleased. It was not a happy story. Her father, Johnnie Spencer (then known as

Viscount Althorp), had been on the worst possible terms with his father, the 7th Earl, 'Jack' Spencer, who had lived at Althorp, resolutely guarding the house and its past and rarely seeing his grandchildren. Diana's family on her mother's side, the Anglo-Irish Fermoys, had shown signs of instability; her uncle, who was to surprise the world at the time of her engagement by issuing press statements stressing his niece's virginity, later shot himself. In Norfolk society, perhaps the most traditional, unchanging and 'backwoods' in the whole of England, Diana's mother was condemned as a 'bolter' – a phrase taken from Nancy Mitford's novel *The Pursuit of Love*.

Diana's mother, the former Hon. Frances Roche, is the parent she most resembles, in looks and character. She was and is, as one of the Spencer relations testified, 'one of the strongest personalities I've ever met. She is attractive and full of vitality, she is funny and very outspoken. Men are bowled over by her physical presence.' As a debutante Frances was a year younger than the rest, but 'took the place by storm'. 'She could have done anything she wanted but became engaged at 17.' The man she wanted was Johnnie Althorp, despite the fact that he was twelve years older than she was and already engaged to the beautiful Lady Anne Coke, daughter of the 5th Earl of Leicester, a great friend, shooting companion and Norfolk neighbour of King George VI. (Lady Anne, a maid of honour at Elizabeth's Coronation, later married Margaret's friend Colin Tennant.)

Althorp was tall, good-looking and, although no intellectual, amusing company. He was older than Frances, but she was brighter than he was and, when they were first married, richer – her grandmother had been a New York heiress – and instead of living on the Althorp estate they lived at Park House, which was Frances's. Friends described him as becoming boring after his marriage, utterly devoted to his wife and obsessed with his children to an unusual degree. They were married in 1954; over fifteen years later the marriage deteriorated to a bitter divorce. The strain of producing a Spencer heir had not helped. Frances, after the birth of two daughters and the death of a weakly son, had been subjected to humiliating fertility tests; Diana was the third daughter, followed three years later by the longed-for son. Diana was only six when her parents' marriage fell apart in painful circumstances in 1967 after a series of bitter rows, some of which she witnessed. Frances Althorp had become infatuated with a married man eleven years her senior, Peter Shand Kydd, whom she later married. In the subsequent divorce case in 1969 Frances was denied custody of her children; her own mother, Lady Fermoy (some people said out of snobbery), testified against her and did not subsequently speak to her for thirteen years. The children were left deprived of their mother and in the company of their father, who, relations say, was 'utterly destroyed by Frances's bolting'. His bitterness against his former wife never left him and he spent his time in virtual silence, speaking only to his chauffeur and his gamekeeper. The youngest of his children, Charles, sobbed his heart out every night crying for his mother; Diana, the next oldest, tried to mother him. All the children felt responsible for their father, left alone and lonely. Diana was his particular favourite. They were also very possessive of him, regarding any pretty woman who came near him as an interloper who might usurp their mother's place. Girls employed as nannies for the children might find pins stuck in their chairs or their clothes thrown out of the window. This possessiveness was to be carried to extreme lengths when, in 1976, their father married Raine Dartmouth. Diana's initial response, in a fit of rage, was to hit her father across the face. Later, on a family occasion at Althorp, she seemingly caught her stepmother from behind and sent her crashing down some stairs in full view of astounded Spencer staff.

The divorce affected all of them, except apparently the second eldest, Jane, the 'sensible' member of the family, who has been described as 'saintly, good with everyone, kind and thoughtful'. Diana, according to sources both hostile and sympathetic, was a compulsive liar or, to put it more kindly, a fantasist. Her brother, Charles Spencer, told Diana's biographer, Andrew Morton:

> I don't know whether a psychologist would say it was the trauma of the divorce but she had real difficulty telling the truth purely because she liked to embellish things. On the school run one day the vicar's wife stopped the car and said: 'Diana Spencer, if you tell one more lie like that I am going to make you walk home.'[2]

'Leopards don't change their spots,' a Norfolk neighbour commented cryptically of the adult Diana, while her grandmother told a friend of a school report on Diana aged six: 'Diana Spencer is the most scheming little girl I have ever met.' Holidays when the children were young were split between Park House and their mother's new home in Sussex, a fair-sounding arrangement which none the less put an intolerable emotional strain on the children, exchangeable pawns between two bitter parents. At her first school, Silfield, Diana dedicated all the pictures she did in art class to 'Mummy and Daddy'. At that school, Diana and Charles were the only children in their class whose parents were divorced; divorce was a disgraceful thing which did not happen in good county families. When her father sent her to her first boarding-school, Diana interpreted it as a rejection, pleading and threatening him, 'If you love me, you won't leave me here.' Photographs taken of her in adolescence show her with a sad, wary look, as if suspicious of the outside world – even in puberty the famous Spencer legs are already in evidence. According to Morton, Diana's overwhelming memory of her childhood is one of rejection and abandonment, of her mother driving away from Park House and out of her life when she was six years old.

Diana's reaction was to fantasise. 'I'm going to *Be* somebody,' she would say. Her stepfather nicknamed her 'Duchess' and she was known in the family as 'Duch'. 'She always knew what she wanted and how she wanted it done,' a nanny said of her. From the age of fifteen she wanted the Prince of Wales, who came into her life in 1977 through her sister, Sarah. Sarah was a pretty redhead; as the goddaughter of one of the Queen's ladies-in-waiting, she seemed an eminently suitable choice to join the traditional royal party at Windsor for Ascot week. Unfortunately she suffered from the binging and vomiting disorder, bulimia, which was also to affect Diana. Charles was aware of this; Sarah was painfully thin, but he was apparently sympathetic and gentle with her and she was soon being tipped as a possible bride. Two years later Charles met Diana for the first time at Althorp, to which the Spencer family had moved after the death of the 7th Earl in 1975. He was invited by Sarah; he noticed Diana, a slightly plump, pretty teenager, as the 'jolly' and 'bouncy' younger sister. Although they had been next-door neighbours when the family lived at Park House, Charles had been so much older that Diana had not known him at all. Occasionally she used to go over to tea with Prince Andrew, who was in her own age group. Her nanny, Janet Thompson, remembered walking into the drawing-room at Sandringham to find Elizabeth playing hide-and-seek with the six-year-old Andrew and five-year-old Diana. At tea, Charles walked in, very much the elder brother. 'Everything all right? Looks like a good party to me.' It was to be his future wife's first memory of him. Even at that age she was made aware that he was more than just Andrew's elder brother.

Apart from those early contacts, however, Elizabeth hardly knew

Diana. Diana's much-loved paternal grandmother had died in 1972, and in that year Johnnie and his children had moved to Althorp so that they were no longer Sandringham neighbours. Diana was not close to her maternal grandmother, Ruth Fermoy, who was not on speaking terms with her mother and, if court sources are to be believed, was not in favour of the Prince of Wales marrying either of her younger Spencer granddaughters. 'It's got to be stopped,' she had said when the possibility of the Prince's marrying Sarah had been discussed. In 1978 Jane, the second eldest, married Robert Fellowes, then the Queen's Assistant Private Secretary and son of the Queen's popular Sandringham land-agent, Sir William 'Billy' Fellowes. The wedding took place in the smart Guards' Chapel at Wellington Barracks, the Guards' headquarters a stone's throw from Buckingham Palace. Later Diana was overheard to say, 'It'll be Westminster Abbey for me.' It was perfectly understandable that she should already have had the Prince of Wales in mind as a potential husband. She was of an age when women dream of marrying men who are not just powerful or attractive but inhabit a plane above everyday life. Charles, as the future King, was the world's most eligible bachelor, and, since Diana's elder sisters had entered the royal orbit, he was not just a distant impossible star but an accessible one. Her sights were set. She began to court the limelight. At her sister's wedding she bounced up to James Whitaker, doyen of the royal reporters known as the 'ratpack': 'I know you – you're the wicked Mr Whitaker, aren't you?' she said. 'I'm Diana.'[3] Her love affair with the press had begun.

Two years later in July 1980, moved by Diana's sympathy and compassion when they had a long conversation sitting on a hay bale at a Sussex barbecue, Charles began to consider her as a possible bride. Her feelings were not feigned; Diana had always had an instinctive capacity to sense suffering and pain and a vocation to reach out towards the victim. According to Charles's account of the conversation to his authorised biographer, 'she said how sad he had seemed at the Mountbatten funeral and how she had sensed his loneliness and need for someone to care for him'. That she had an ulterior motive for this approach does not make it any the less heartfelt. She thought she could help him, that she could provide the solace he was seeking and that they could be happy ever after. The sympathetic approach worked; less than a month later, during Cowes week in early August, Charles confided to a friend that he had met the girl he intended to marry and described Diana's warmth, ease of manner and, less perceptively, 'her enthusiasm for rural life'.

From then on things began to snowball and acquire a momentum that none of the participants would be able to stop. That same summer Charles had had a spectacular scene with Anna Wallace, one of the women to whom he had proposed, another beautiful, strong-willed blonde with a rich landowning father, at the Queen Mother's eightieth birthday ball, and another at a ball at Stowell Park when he had danced the night away with Camilla Parker Bowles. The sweet, sympathetic and apparently pliable Diana Spencer seemed the perfect antidote; he invited her to join the house-party at Balmoral that September. Among the Prince's house-party were his great friend Nicholas Soames, and Andrew and Camilla Parker Bowles. Diana, Soames and Parker Bowles flew back to London later on, leaving Camilla behind with the Prince. A few days later, on 17 September 1980, photographers gathered at the nursery school where Lady Diana Spencer worked, caught the famous shot of her in a filmy skirt against the sunlight – a virgin madonna with child in her arms and sexy legs below. It was an unforgettable image and the beginning of a media superstar.

A month later Diana was photographed again, watching the Prince ride his horse, Allibar, at a meeting in Ludlow, Shropshire. With them was Camilla Parker Bowles; they spent the next two days as her guests at Bolehyde Manor, where she was then living. Diana was aware of the Prince's closeness to Camilla; their affair had already reached the pages of *Private Eye*, where it was hinted how much the Prince had been seeing of his friend's wife while Parker Bowles was on an assignment to protect Lord Soames as Governor of Rhodesia. In November the 'royal train' scandal hit the newspapers – it was reported that the Prince of Wales had spent the night with a blonde woman on the royal train in a Wiltshire siding after a West Country engagement in his Duchy of Cornwall. At first the press assumed it was Diana; Elizabeth ordered her Press Secretary, Michael Shea, to issue a denial, which she no doubt believed. The editor concerned, Bob Edwards, was generally condemned. Later he was told that there had indeed been a blonde woman on the train that night but that it had been Camilla not Diana. Diana must have had her suspicions, but she was in no position to confront the Prince. For the moment she was prepared to put up with Camilla's patronage in return for her good opinion; naïvely she apparently thought that once the Prince was officially hers, her older rival would fade away. James Whitaker, with whom Diana began a series of conversations during this period, wrote that she was 'doggedly determined' to marry the Prince. Her mother appealed to the press to leave her daughter alone; but privately Diana told Whitaker she did not agree – 'I like to think I get on well with most of you,' she told him. 'Already,' Whitaker wrote, 'she had learned to deploy one of the most powerful assets in her armoury – how to handle the press.'

While the British press had made up its mind that Diana was 'the one', the Prince apparently had not. He flew to India on an official visit and on his return did not see Diana for a week. Elizabeth and Philip began to worry about the possible fall-out as a result of their son's dithering and its effects on Diana, whom they now regarded as compromised both by his attentions and that of the press. Elizabeth wrote to a friend saying how worried they were that he had not yet proposed. She did not, however, personally interfere. Nor did her mother; it was not the family way. The Queen Mother, according to one theory, was directly responsible for the Charles–Diana engagement in a Machiavellian plot cooked up with her lady-in-waiting, Ruth Fermoy, to frustrate Mountbatten's attempt to strengthen the Mountbatten connection with the next generation of the royal family by foisting his granddaughter, Amanda Knatchbull, on Charles. It sounds plausible, but there is no evidence of any deep-laid plot involving Ruth Fermoy, who, according to a courtier, was 'always horrified at the prospect of the engagement, asking "Is it true?", and complaining, "Nobody tells me anything."' The Queen Mother, like the rest of Prince Charles's family, was anxious for him to marry a suitable girl and was prepared to take Diana at face value. As his closest family confidante she felt that she should, for once, give him a push in the way of a decision. One day at Royal Lodge she told him, 'There's Diana Spencer – that's the girl you should marry. But don't marry her if you don't love her. If you do, grab her because if you don't there are plenty of others who will . . .' Ruth Fermoy, like most courtiers, does not seem to have been prepared to share her doubts with her employer. The same applied to Diana's father, who later, when the marriage began to go sour, admitted to one of Charles's confidantes, 'We were all terrified of her [Diana].' Just before her death, Ruth Fermoy told Jonathan Dimbleby that she had been against the marriage but had thought it pointless to intervene. 'If I'd said to him, "You're making a very great mistake," he probably wouldn't have paid the slightest attention because he was being driven,' she said.

Driven, it seems, not only by some of his friends and confidantes (with the exception of Mountbatten's grandson, Lord Romsey, and his wife Penny, who diagnosed that Diana was in love with the role rather than the man, while Nicholas Soames publicly declared that it was 'a terrible mismatch'), but principally by his father. Philip, aware of his son's tendency to indecision, pointed out to him that he must act and as soon as possible, either by proposing to Diana and 'pleasing his family and the country', or by ending the relationship immediately. Given Charles's past record, anyone might think that this was wise advice, but Charles, according to his biographer, felt 'ill-used and impotent' as a result. The royal family spent New Year's Eve as usual at Sandringham, attended by a complete roll-call of the ratpack, who observed that the royal nerves seemed to be on edge. Even Elizabeth was moved to shout, 'Go away. Can't you leave us alone?', while Charles offered 'another unseasonal greeting'. The ratpack was there for a sighting of Diana; when she did arrive, she stayed only twenty-four hours because the enormous press interest was making life impossible for the family. A courtier did, however, observe that when they rolled back the carpet in the saloon and Charles and Diana danced together, you could see 'an electricity between them'. Still the Prince did not propose or take 'la grande plonge', as he quaintly referred to it in letters to his friends. He was, he wrote on 29 January 1981, in

> a confused and anxious state of mind. It is just a matter of taking an
> unusual plunge into some rather unknown circumstances that
> inevitably disturbs me but I expect it will be the right thing in the end.
> It all seems so ridiculous because I do very much want to do the right
> thing for this Country and for my family – but I'm terrified sometimes
> of making a promise and then perhaps living to regret it.

To be fair to the Prince, he was prepared to do something which Uncle David so conspicuously had not done, to sacrifice his love for his country; he also wanted a home with children and someone always there with whom he could share the burdens of his life. He was attracted by Diana's sweetness, her concern for him and what he saw as her enthusiasm for life. He convinced himself they were compatible. Still he did not propose but went on a skiing holiday to Klosters to stay, as usual, with his friends, the Palmer-Tomkinsons; boosted by their support he finally made up his mind. He returned from Klosters on 2 February 1981 and two days later he proposed and was instantly accepted.

Elizabeth and Philip were delighted. A friend who went to see the Duke before the official announcement three weeks later on 24 February found him 'so pleased' and saying, 'Isn't it wonderful that they're going to get married? . . . We're delighted.' And they were, the friend added, 'It all seemed so perfect . . . They were so anxious for him to get married that they didn't look beneath the surface. They knew she came from a broken home but they thought a family atmosphere would be the answer . . .' For Diana, it was a case of answered prayers, but even she was beginning perhaps to be touched by doubt. Replying in her large, rounded, rather childish writing to one of the many people who had sent letters of congratulation to the couple on their engagement, she said, 'it's amazing how many people have said that married life is the best', adding, 'I wonder if I'll be saying that in twenty years time!' Both of them could be seen as victims of public expectation, but of the two, Diana was undoubtedly the most willing. The truth was not exactly the romantic fairy-tale the public wanted to believe in. 'The "fairy-tale love affair" was a calculated act by two people who both thought they knew what they wanted and went after it without considering the long-term consequences,' one of Diana's biographers wrote. 'By the time the couple announced their engagement in February 1981 Charles had, for the best part of a decade, known that he had found his soulmate in Camilla Parker Bowles. Diana knew it too and went along with it . . . he needed someone suitable to produce a future King, she desperately wanted to be Princess of Wales.'[4] Both were readers of the novels of Barbara Cartland, Diana's step-grandmother, on the themes of virginity and romantic love and both of them were determined to be in love, Diana wholeheartedly, Charles more reluctantly. A television interview with the couple after the engagement was announced revealed the unreality of the couple's views of each other:

Charles: Diana is a great outdoor-loving person.
Diana: We both love music and dancing and we both have the same sense of humour.
Charles: You'll definitely need that.

The Prince's response to a query about being in love was the disquieting 'whatever that may mean'.

At first the signs seemed good as Diana showed herself not to be the 'shy mouse' people had once thought her but determined to assert her power over her Prince, firmly and in public. On a visit to some royal relations, Diana, who had been showing off her engagement ring, found as she was leaving that she had left it behind in the drawing-room. Peremptorily she ordered Charles to go back and fetch it. Her hosts were surprised but pleased, thinking that that was the way to treat the spoiled royal bachelor. Later, they saw the incident in a different light. Diana had moved into Clarence House for a few days over the time of her engagement to escape the press siege at her flat in Coleherne Court. She then was given a suite of rooms at Buckingham Palace. On the night she had left Coleherne Court for Clarence House the Scotland Yard inspector assigned to her, a favourite of Prince Charles's who shared his 'alternative' view, told her, 'I just want you to know this is the last night of your freedom, so make the most of it.' Those words, Diana later said in somewhat melodramatic terms, 'felt like a sword through my heart'. Arriving at 4 p.m. she was left on her own. A few days later she moved into the intimidating anonymity of Buckingham Palace.

Elizabeth did little to make her daughter-in-law feel at home. Diana, she quickly realised, was not her type of girl. She was turning out to be emphatically not the country lover Charles had thought she was. She was interested in clothes, pop music, dancing and shopping while horses and dogs, hunting, shooting and fishing, the royal pastimes, bored her. 'The Queen didn't really like Diana very much,' an aide said. Later, when her behaviour became eccentric to the point of rudeness, Elizabeth simply did not understand her. Although a kind person, she is not an imaginative one. Since Buckingham Palace had never seemed intimidating to her, she assumed that Diana would adapt to its atmosphere. She was unused to close contact with girls of Diana's age and had little idea of how they might react to these unusual surroundings; she could not comprehend the feelings of smallness and insignificance which invades outsiders within those walls. For 'Duch' Spencer, who felt destined to command and be in control, the experience was devastating. Diana felt that no one had bothered about her, no one was assigned to really show her the ropes.* A month later Charles left for a five-week official visit to Australia and New Zealand, then to Venezuela and the United States, leaving his fiancée officially in the care of four men who were supposed to help and guide her in

---

* Senior Palace staff regarded these allegations on the part of Diana as 'monstrous'. 'We were all so delighted with her and longing to help her – she was so pretty and charming. The Queen allocated Sue Hussey . . .'

her role as prospective Princess of Wales. They were his Private Secretary, Edward Adeane, son of the Queen's former Private Secretary, Michael Adeane, two ex-Foreign Office men, Francis Cornish, the Prince's Assistant Private Secretary, and Oliver Everett, who had been specifically recalled to the Prince's staff to act as Diana's unofficial Private Secretary; then there was Michael Colborne, a former Petty Officer in the Navy who had left the service in 1975 to join the Prince. Their field of advice could, however, be limited only to public life. Diana had a desk in Colborne's office and, having virtually nothing else to do, was frequently there. She seemed, to their embarrassment, haunted by Camilla Parker Bowles. She would openly seek their help: 'I asked Charles if he was still in love with Camilla Parker Bowles and he didn't give me a clear answer. What am I to do?' Elizabeth, busy and remote in her area of Buckingham Palace, was unaware of this aspect of her son's fiancée's problems. The Prince's staff were too loyal to tell her and, if they had, it is doubtful whether she would have been sympathetic. Her attitude would have been, 'Charles has asked her to marry him. He has told her about Mrs Parker Bowles and has given her up. Diana must get on with it.' She also thought that Frances Shand Kydd, who was helping her daughter over her wardrobe, was the person to be responsible for her daughter's morale.

Increasingly, however, Diana's problems obtruded themselves on Elizabeth's notice, although she attributed them to the normal bride's pre-wedding nerves and the huge pressure of publicity upon a nineteen-year-old girl who was being treated like a film star. Diana lost weight and was frequently in tears. During Ascot week at Windsor, just two weeks before the wedding, the problems were obvious to everyone. 'Diana was going through a terribly difficult time of adjustment and was feeling very claustrophobic,' an observer said. During tea at the back of the royal box at the races she was practically in tears and had to be escorted home early. The Prince was clearly worried and did not hide his concern. 'She's so much younger than me, do you think that matters?' he asked. A friend commented:

> It was not like talking to somebody who was just about to get married
> and was thrilled to bits and longing for his life with her. And I – if
> it had been anybody else – I think I would have said, 'Look, for
> heaven's sake' . . . I mean if it had been one of my children and they
> weren't quite sure – I would have said to them, well, if you're not
> sure, don't do it. But you couldn't say it to him really because

everything was planned. Mugs being made with their faces on and all these kinds of things. You can't suddenly abandon something like that with ease. And I don't think he actually wanted to – I think he felt that he wanted it to be right but I could tell there were doubts and it was very sad . . .

Ten years later when their 'fairy-tale' marriage collapsed, both Charles and Diana were to stress their doubts beforehand; Charles insisting that his father had pressured him into the match, Diana saying that the day before the wedding the Prince had told her that he did not love her and that in consequence when she was halfway down the aisle she had felt like turning back. Charles also told a friend that he wanted to call the whole thing off but that his father had told him he could not. Almost at the last minute Diana's obsessive jealousy was aroused when she found in Colborne's office the now notorious bracelet with initials GF specially ordered as a farewell present for Camilla by Charles. When she confronted Charles with it, he explained that he did not intend to see Camilla privately in future but insisted on giving it to her personally at a last meeting. Diana was understandably distraught; and, as it turned out, she had every reason to be. Camilla's shadow darkened her marriage. On the Monday of the wedding week Charles, unaccompanied even by his detective, went to give the bracelet to Camilla; in her suite at Buckingham Palace Diana, lunching with her sisters Sarah and Jane, told them that she was afraid Charles did not love her but was still in love with Camilla Parker Bowles. Her sisters tried to cheer her up. 'Bad luck, Duch,' one said, 'your face is on the tea towels now so it's too late for you to chicken out.' At the pre-wedding ball held at Buckingham Palace, while most of the guests and royal family greatly enjoyed themselves, some people noticed that the Prince danced only one dance with Diana. Diana was seen to be in tears. Charles danced all night with Camilla and, after Diana left for her pre-wedding night at Clarence House, disappeared with her. The Prince's valet, Stephen Barry, told Andrew Morton that Charles spent the night before his wedding with Camilla while Diana slept at Clarence House. The story was vehemently denied by the Prince's biographer and by his royal relations.

Events had begun to roll forward with an unstoppable momentum; the plans for a huge television spectacular had long been laid. The wedding on 29 July 1981 was in terms of world television the biggest royal event ever staged; three-quarters of a billion people would

participate via satellite. Everything seemed to be all right on the day;
the sun shone. Diana had been reassured the previous evening by a
present from Charles of a signet ring engraved with his crest of the
Prince of Wales feathers and a loving message: 'I'm so proud of you
and when you come up I'll be there at the altar for you tomorrow. Just
look 'em in the eye and knock 'em dead.' Any misgivings Elizabeth
and her courtiers might have had faded in the radiance of the occasion
as the bride, dazzling in yards of ivory silk, tulle and diamonds, walked
up the aisle of St Paul's Cathedral on the arm of her father, gallantly
performing this very public duty after recovering from a near-fatal
stroke two years before. There had been behind-the-scenes difficulties:
to avoid trouble threatened by the Spencers, Barbara Cartland, the
bride's step-grandmother, had stayed away; and Diana had banned her
husband's two married confidantes – Lady Tryon and Camilla – from
attending the wedding breakfast which was to be given for 120 people
at the Palace although she had not been able to prevent Camilla from
being among the 2,700 congregation in the Cathedral. But now there
was an atmosphere of glamour, happiness and love echoing the words
of the Archbishop of Canterbury, Robert Runcie, 'This is the stuff of
which fairy-tales are made . . .' He also went on to say, ironically as it
turned out, 'Those who are married live happily ever after the wedding
day if they persevere in the real adventure which is the royal task of
creating each other and creating a more loving world . . .' The question
at the back of Elizabeth's mind as she sat listening to her Archbishop
must have been, 'But will they?'

At the time, the royal wedding seemed to set the seal on the future
of the monarchy as the focus of the nation; an occasion of superb
ceremonial centring round the figures of a handsome Prince and a
beautiful Princess. Polls showed that its popularity stood as high as it
had at the time of the Queen's Coronation and Jubilee. When, after an
elaborate-sounding wedding breakfast of quenelles of brill with lobster
sauce, chicken breasts stuffed with minced lamb, strawberries and
cream, the couple appeared on the Palace balcony and the Prince,
prompted by the crowd, kissed his bride full on the lips, it seemed as
if love had triumphed and the future could be nothing but bright. Just
as Elizabeth and Philip had after their wedding, the couple drove to
Waterloo Station to spend the first two days of their honeymoon at
Broadlands and their first night in the same four-poster bed in which
the Prince's parents had slept in 1947. Borne along on the wave of
popular enthusiasm, the Prince and Princess had returned to the

euphoria of the time of their engagement when Charles had written to friends, 'I do believe I am very lucky that someone as special as Diana seems to love me so much . . .'

Charles's letters home from *Britannia*, on which the couple spent a fifteen-day honeymoon, conveyed the picture of married life which his parents and friends wanted to hear: '. . . marriage is very jolly'. It also presented an unconscious portrait of a middle-aged fogey and his child bride: 'Diana dashes about chatting up all the sailors and the cooks in the galley etc. while I remain hermit-like on the verandah deck, sunk with pure joy into one of Laurens van der Post's books.' He might just as well have been describing a puppy as a wife. Reviewing the official biographer's account of the honeymoon, Robert Harris described the Prince's behaviour as 'selfish and peculiar': 'Bookish older husband, high-spirited young wife: it is like a scene out of Boccaccio.' In the *Decameron*, however, it is the young wife who cuckolds the elderly husband and not the reverse. The couple joined Elizabeth at Balmoral for the usual family holiday, where Elizabeth expected Diana, whom she had been led to believe was a country-lover, to fit in with the family ways and was surprised and secretly irritated when she did not. She was puzzled by her and innately suspicious of her over-emotional behaviour. Diana, whose intellectual diet had been the novels of her step-grandmother, expected and believed in 'love and romance'. What she got was an introduction to a family in which duty took first place and in which emotion had perforce to be suppressed. It was the price they paid for their privileged position.

The royal family is not an easy one for an outsider to enter. A relation described them as

a very odd family. They're not welcoming and cosy. They'll never ask you how you are or what sort of day you've had . . . They're probably the least close-knit family that I have ever come across. The Queen Mother is the knitter of the whole thing but I often wonder whether one half is pleased to see the other half. I think it's personalities really . . .

Suddenly, which is terrifying, there's the Queen Victoria look – all of them, even the minor ones . . . You'd be larking about and suddenly you'd gone too far and you hadn't realised it and you'd get this chilling po-face. Princess Margaret's very good at it. You'd expect it of her, but you wouldn't expect it of the younger ones and they've all got it . . . It's such a fine line. They like to be treated as human beings until it just doesn't suit them . . .

Diana had imagined that she could 'reform' the royal family from within, 'building bridges' between Charles and his parents. When this proved to be an illusion and she found that her husband and his family regarded her as an immature and potentially unstable girl, the strain began to tell and her efforts to assert herself appeared hysterical and often rude. She would try and ingratiate herself with her mother-in-law by giving her little presents of china birds, but their effect was negated by her sometimes defiant and discourteous behaviour when she would refuse to come down to dinner or otherwise would appear at public functions five minutes after Elizabeth, something which no one is allowed to do. She was suffering from bulimia, an eating disorder with which Elizabeth, who, in any case, had very little sympathy with illness or physical weakness, was quite unfamiliar. All she felt she could do to help was to reduce the strain of media attention on her daughter-in-law by appealing to the media editors to leave her alone after the announcement of her pregnancy on 5 November 1981. Her Press Secretary, Michael Shea, set up the meeting in the second week of December between Elizabeth, Fleet Street editors, TV and radio representatives. After Shea had complained that photographers had even pursued Diana into the village shop at Tetbury near Highgrove, Barry Askew, editor of the tabloid *News of the World*, a man nicknamed 'the Beast of Bouverie Street', impertinently asked Elizabeth, 'Wouldn't it be better to send a servant to the shop for Princess Diana's wine-gums?' 'Mr Askew,' Elizabeth replied icily, 'that was a most pompous remark.'

Elizabeth's appeal fell on deaf ears. Diana had become a media phenomenon; she was now the member of the royal family the public most wanted to see. Her popularity had at first pleased Elizabeth and the rest of the family, then all of them, and the Prince of Wales in particular, found themselves upstaged and not a little jealous. In February 1982 the *Sun* published a photograph of the pregnant Princess in a bikini on holiday with the Prince at the Brabournes' house on Eleuthera in the Bahamas. Elizabeth called it 'a black day for British journalism', but she had reckoned without her daughter-in-law's fondness for seeing her own image in the papers; Diana let it be known to the offending newspaperman that she had not minded at all. Just before the Eleuthera holiday, Elizabeth was shocked to hear that the Princess had either slipped or thrown herself down a staircase at Sandringham; one distressing incident in the black moods of despair that seemed to grip her, although there were periods of happiness such as Christmas at

Windsor, when the Prince had written to a friend, 'We've had such a lovely Christmas – the two of us. It has been extraordinarily happy and cosy being able to share it together.' Elizabeth hoped that the birth of their son might change things and calm her daughter-in-law's erratic behaviour. Prince William was born on 21 June 1982. Elizabeth is said to have remarked in one of her not-so-happy one-liners, 'Well, at least he hasn't got his father's ears.' For the moment at least, there was joy and contentment in the Wales family.

From the beginning of 1982, Elizabeth had had more important affairs to worry about than her daughter-in-law's mood swings. On 5 April the British naval task force had put to sea destined for the Falkland Islands, invaded by the Argentines three days before. On board HMS *Invincible*, which had sailed with the task force, was the twenty-two-year-old Prince Andrew, serving as a helicopter pilot. Andrew was Elizabeth's favourite child, the baby she had been determined to have despite her husband's qualms about adding to the already sufficient number of 'royals'. He had been born eight years after her accession to the throne, when she had been less overwhelmed by her royal duties and a more practised hand at pacing her private and public lives than she had been during the childhood of her first-born. She adored him, so much so that courtiers referred jokingly to him as 'the love-child'. When Prince Edward was born four years later, he was generally thought to have been intended as a companion for Andrew.

Andrew had grown up to be an uncomplicated soul, rumbustious, a little spoiled and more than a little arrogant. He had inherited the family penchant for practical jokes – in Los Angeles in the 1980s he had shocked the American press by squirting them with red paint, much as his father had 'accidentally' sprayed newspapermen with a hosepipe at the Chelsea Flower Show. There has always been far less pressure upon him to achieve than on his elder brother as heir to the throne and he had sailed through life hitherto with none of the tortures suffered by Charles at the hands of an apparently hostile world. From the nursery presided over by Charles's favourite nanny, Mabel Anderson, he had progressed to lessons with Mispy, Charles's governess, and a few other children of his age, including Margaret's son, Viscount Linley, then to a smart preparatory school, Heatherdown. The staff at Heatherdown were apparently rather relieved when he left; at his best he could be diligent and polite, at his worst aggressive, rude and obstinate. At home he would place whoopee cushions on chairs and set off stink bombs; he once poured large bottles of bubble bath into the

Windsor Castle swimming-pool. Unlike Charles, he had an easy relationship with his father, even though he was more than a little in awe of him. In 1973 he had followed Charles to Gordonstoun, which by then was co-educational and generally more relaxed than it had been when his brother had left it six years earlier. Unlike Charles, he arrived at Gordonstoun 'full of bounce' and the boys retaliated. After one dormitory fight he got a crack on the head which put him in the school sanatorium for two days; 'he's a very tough and independent fellow,' a master commented. His father appreciated his toughness, saying, 'he's a natural boss', and seems not to have realised that some of the aggressive self-confidence was assumed as a natural defence and that beneath the surface Andrew was more sensitive and less confident than he appeared. Like Charles, Andrew had been sent for a spell of 'getting to know the Commonwealth' – in his case, Canada – attending Lakefield College School in Ontario in the intervals of his time at Gordonstoun. Like Charles, he had taken a parachute training course and learned to fly, but instead of sending him to university his father decided that he should become a full-time naval officer and enrolled him at Dartmouth Royal Naval College in 1979. He was to sign up for a naval commission for twelve years with special training as a helicopter pilot. At twenty-one he qualified as a helicopter pilot and joined 829 Naval Air Squadron, flying Sea Kings from the carrier HMS *Invincible*.

Elizabeth herself became the focus of the growing media interest in the Palace which had been fed by the Wales's marriage. At 7.15 a.m. on the morning of 9 July 1982, she awoke to hear the door being opened and footsteps approaching her bed. Instantly she was aware that it was not her footman, Paul Whybrew, who was out exercising the corgis. So she said in a loud headmistressy voice, 'It's too early yet for tea', hoping that it was some innocent person who had opened the door by mistake and who would be frightened off when they heard her voice. Instead, someone crossed the room, opened the curtains and then sat on her bed. It was a thirty-one-year-old schizophrenic, Michael Fagan, wanting to talk to her about his family problems. She pressed the night alarm button which rings in the corridor outside. No one heard it; the policeman had gone off duty as usual at 6 a.m. when the domestic staff arrived. The footman was out with the dogs and the housemaid hoovering in another room with the door closed in order not to disturb Her Majesty. She made two telephone calls asking for police to be sent, but there was no immediate response. According to Fagan, she did not appear either nervous or worried and when he asked her for a cigarette she used that as a pretext to manoeuvre him out into the corridor where they met a maid with a hoover. 'Bloody 'ell, Ma'am, what's he doing here?' the maid exclaimed – Fagan, apart from anything else, was barefoot – and took him into a nearby pantry to look for cigarettes. The footman returned with the corgis to see Elizabeth standing outside the pantry with her finger to her lips, 'Ssh', then she pointed for him to go in, where he talked to Fagan and offered him a drink. Finally a policeman came along and started to rough Fagan up, then a plain-clothes man sauntered along the corridor to be startled by Elizabeth shouting, 'Get in there!' Elizabeth, according to staff, remained cool as a cucumber while they were shaking like leaves and returned calmly to bed to have her tea. On the bed was a large fragment of a broken glass ashtray and blood – Fagan later said that he had intended to slash his wrists in front of the Queen.

Elizabeth gave strict instructions that the incident was not to be mentioned, but the police report was leaked to the newspapers the next day, Saturday, and after waiting for confirmation the press broke the story on Monday. The report to the Home Secretary revealed that Palace security, as Fagan claimed to have told Elizabeth, was indeed 'diabolical'. This was not the first time he had been in the Palace; on the previous occasion he had taken a bottle of wine. This time he had been spotted on the railings near the Ambassador's Entrance on the south front of the Palace, and again climbing through the Master of the Household's office window which had been opened by a housemaid. He was seen in the corridor outside by a housemaid, who assumed he must be a workman, and from then on he had been able to traverse the corridors halfway round the Palace to the Queen's bedroom on the north front. Within two weeks another security scandal broke when it was announced that Commander Michael Trestrail, the Queen's police officer, who had served her for years and of whom she was very fond, had confessed to having a homosexual relationship over a number of years with a male prostitute and had resigned from the Metropolitan Police. Elizabeth, who was in hospital after having had a wisdom tooth out, was very upset, not so much at the security angle but at the loss of Trestrail. Within that week the IRA blew up a squadron of the Household Cavalry in Hyde Park on its way to the changing of the guard at Buckingham Palace and a military band in Regent's Park. Elizabeth's coolness when faced with Fagan recalled her courage just over a year earlier, on 13 June 1981, when a young man had stepped out into the road as she rode down the Mall for the Trooping the

Colour ceremony and fired six shots at her, which luckily turned out to be blanks (although she was not to know that at the time). Elizabeth merely ducked, patted her horse, Burmese, and rode on. The royal family has a fatalistic attitude towards the possibility of assassination and reacts accordingly, as did Anne during the Mall kidnap attempt (the most serious of the three incidents) and Charles in Australia in 1995.

While the Trestrail affair inspired the press to one of its periodic field days about the number of homosexuals in royal service, the Fagan episode also gave rise to speculation about the state of Elizabeth's marriage and the royal couple's sleeping arrangements. Elizabeth is held to have said soon afterwards that her one concern while talking to Fagan was that Philip might burst into the room and all hell break loose.[5] This cannot be true as she knew that by the time Fagan was sitting on her bed, Philip had left the Palace at 6 a.m. for a distant official engagement, and, in order not to wake her up, had spent the night in the dressing-room of his apartment. Had he not had that engagement, he would have been in Elizabeth's bed – they always sleep together when under the same roof – and Fagan might have had rather a different reception.

The Falklands war, the first major military conflict of Elizabeth's reign, had ended with the surrender of the Argentine forces on 14 June 1982. When Andrew returned from the Falklands that summer, he was already, unknown to his mother, in love with the actress Koo Stark. Andrew, ruggedly handsome, had taken over his brother's title of royal heart-throb; he had been competed for by girls at Gordonstoun and in Canada; soon the British press would dub him 'Randy Andy'. Andrew took Koo to stay at Balmoral and introduced her to Elizabeth, who liked her and seemed utterly relaxed about Koo's past love affairs and her part in a soft-porn movie directed by the Earl of Pembroke. The British press, however, greatly relished publishing stills of Koo in what the papers described as 'steamy' scenes from the film. Despite Andrew's love for Koo, who subsequently behaved with great dignity over the ending of the relationship, the 'soft-porn actress' label effectively finished any chance of her becoming a princess. Andrew's frolics in Barbados with an older woman (already well known to the tabloid press) and photographs of him necking in the sea with another girl caused a major royal dust-up. Elizabeth was upset by his evident naïveté and penchant for 'vulgar' women; Philip was furious that he had brought scandal on the family. It was obviously time to marry Andrew off.

Sarah Ferguson came into Andrew's life in the summer of 1985. Once again, Elizabeth was delighted with her son's choice of bride; once again, had she considered it, the formbook as far as Sarah's background and immediate past were concerned held out some warning signs. Again, at first glance, the match looked promising. Sarah was well bred. The Fergusons were a landowning family with a record of distinguished service in one of the Household Cavalry Regiments, the Life Guards, and Sarah's maternal grandmother, a first cousin of Princess Alice, Duchess of Gloucester, widow of Elizabeth's Uncle Harry, could trace her bloodline back to Charles II. Sarah herself had close court connections, being second cousin to Robert Fellowes, through his mother, the former Jane Ferguson, aunt of Sarah's father, Ronald. Ronald Ferguson, or 'Major Ron' as he was to become known to the tabloids, had come into contact with the royal family through polo, the game to which Philip and Charles were addicted. Ferguson played on Philip's polo team through the 1960s and consequently he and his wife Susie were occasionally invited to shoot at Sandringham and once to stay at Windsor for Ascot week. According to the Major, his first wife, Susie, Sarah's mother, and Philip were particularly friendly and remained so beyond the Fergusons' divorce. His own relations with Philip did not go outside polo. He became Deputy Chairman of the Guards Polo Club in 1971 and, after Charles took up polo seriously in 1970, became his honorary Polo Manager.

'I was responsible for his ponies, his sticks – even his moods,' Ferguson was to write in his autobiography, *The Galloping Major*:

There were occasions when he arrived at the ground and you could almost see smoke coming out of the top of his head, he was so uptight. If he was low and tired, I had to boost him up, either by making a comment or getting him angry. On other occasions he was buoyant and I'd need to subdue him slightly to make him concentrate. I don't think the Prince of Wales realized when I was trying to manipulate his moods. I would do it by giving him the wrong stick, for example. 'Why on earth can't you give me the right stick,' he'd yell. That was exactly the sort of angry reaction I wanted, to get the adrenalin flowing. I was a useful whipping boy. The Prince couldn't shout and scream at just anyone, but he could and did take it out on me . . .

Sarah was the Fergusons' second daughter, born on 15 October 1959. She was just fourteen in 1972 when her mother left home, leaving her and her elder sister, Jane, in the custody of his father. Susan Ferguson later married an Argentine polo-player, Hector Barrantes, and went to live with him on his ranch in the Argentine. The Fergusons' marriage was a victim of the randy, glamorous world of polo, later depicted in Jilly Cooper's best-seller *Riders*. Ronald Ferguson could have walked straight out of Cooper's pages. Just like the Spencer children, the Ferguson girls were possessive of their father and at first bitterly opposed to his second marriage in 1976, although they later came round to it. Sarah, who so closely resembled him – not only in looks – was particularly close to him. In 1985 she was a typical Sloane Ranger – as upper-middle-class girls like herself had been dubbed – with a none-too-demanding job, no intellectual interests and a range of friends like herself who said 'Yah' instead of 'Yes', gave parties and often acted as chalet girls in winter ski resorts such as Klosters and Verbier. Sarah was unusual only in that she had a lover twenty-two years older than herself, racing driver Paddy McNally, who showed no signs whatsoever of intending to marry her. Among Sarah's circle had been Lady Diana Spencer, whose wedding she had attended. There were differences between the two girls: Diana was an earl's daughter living in an expensive flat in a millionaire's area, The Boltons, while Sarah had no stately home in the background and an overdraft at the bank. There were considerable character differences too. Sarah Ferguson was flamboyant, outgoing, greedy for life and its experiences, careless of appearances. She was a woman who would hurtle headlong where angels fear to tread. Diana was her opposite in almost every way; nevertheless as her marriage continued on its miserable downward path, she found in Sarah an ally. It was Diana who had engineered an invitation to stay at Windsor for Ascot week in 1985 and she who had seen to it that Sarah sat next to Andrew at lunch in the state dining-room. He fed her chocolate profiteroles and the romance was on.

By the new year 1986, when the Queen invited her to Sandringham, Sarah had finally given up on Paddy McNally. It was only too obvious that Prince Andrew was in love with her and they seemed well suited, both of them given to the kind of boisterous bread-throwing antics which distinguished dinner-parties given by Sloane Rangers and their male equivalents, the 'Hooray Henrys'. There were differences in their habits: Andrew neither smoked nor drank, Fergie did both; she was gregarious and a real party-girl, while he preferred golf or a quiet evening in when he was at home. Her sexual past and general behaviour certainly did not qualify her for membership of the royal family under previous rules. (What, one wonders, would George V or Queen Mary have thought of her?) 'Sarah Ferguson', Martin Charteris, who liked her despite describing her as a 'vulgarian', pronounced on television, 'was not cut out to be a royal princess in this or any other age.' As in the case of Diana, those courtiers who did know her and her father well did not come forward to express their doubts. Elizabeth and the other members of the royal family welcomed her as they had never welcomed Diana. Elizabeth liked her high spirits and the fact that she was a country girl who would go riding with her and who took to the outdoor life at Sandringham and Balmoral like a duck to water. It was enough for her that Andrew loved Sarah and, knowing her son as she did, she was anxious to see him safely married. Philip appreciated Sarah's feisty exuberance and her refusal to be intimidated by him. Charles contrasted her uncomplicated enjoyment of life with his wife's tantrums and black depressions. 'Why can't you be like Fergie?' he would ask Diana. Those courtiers who knew Major Ferguson and his daughter rather better had their reservations. 'You know you won't be able to go on as you always have,' one warned. 'You'll have to put an act on, conform.' 'Oh, I'll just be myself,' Sarah replied airily.

And so there was another fairy-tale wedding, this time at Westminster Abbey, in July 1986, and another apparently passionate kiss on the Palace balcony in front of cheering crowds to set the seal on a royal romance. Elizabeth created Andrew Duke of York on the morning of his wedding day and as a present paid for a new house to be built on the Sunninghill estate, where she and Prince Philip had once planned to live. In 1989 the Yorks began to build their dream home at a cost of £3.5 million. The Queen Mother, apparently, cautioned against such excess, but Elizabeth, indulgent as always, made no attempt to inhibit them. The conspicuous consumption represented by Sunninghill, dubbed South York by the press after the Ewing ranch in *Dallas*, made a particularly bad impression on the public and the timing of its completion in 1990 could hardly have been worse, coming as it did at the beginning of a severe and prolonged recession, during which thousands of people lost their homes and livelihoods. Publicity about 'Fergie's' free-loading habits made frequent headlines; she was rumoured to have haggled with tradesmen and suppliers during the building of Sunninghill for special prices and then left them hanging on for months without being paid. The press zeroed in on the number of days she spent on holiday and the mountains of luggage with which she would return from American trips. In an effort to outshine her sister-in-law, who wisely bought British, Fergie patronised Yves Saint Laurent. There were rows over the royalties for her books, on Queen Victoria's Osborne and *Budgie the Helicopter*; she was rumoured to have tried to claim all credit for the first, although it was in fact written by Benita Stoney, the niece of the Royal Librarian, and it was alleged that 'Budgie' was a plagiarisation of a book published in the 1960s. Later she was to bring out an illustrated book on Queen Victoria's travels, of which the notable feature was photographs of herself posed against various backgrounds. The implication was that she was using her position for all that she could get. The press, having built her up at the time of her wedding, now turned on her. Headstrong as ever, she gave them plenty of material – charging *Hello* magazine £200,000 for the privilege of taking photographs of herself and Andrew with their children. In the disastrous charity TV show *It's a Royal Knockout* (1987), she stood out for her un-royal behaviour. Once again, when it came to her children, Elizabeth's indulgence (in this case of Edward, whose brainchild it was) blinded her to the dangers. Anne was bullied by the others into doing it. Charles, to his credit, would not allow his wife to take part.

Edward is the most retiring and least known of Elizabeth's children. Four years younger than Andrew and fifteen years younger than Charles, he had grown up very much on his own. His education had been much the same as his brothers' – his personal Commonwealth stint had been two terms as junior master at the Collegiate School, Wanganui, in New Zealand. He had been to university at Cambridge where he read history and his tutor, Robert Rhodes James, considered him to have a first-class ability although he emerged with a second-class degree. Like Charles, he showed a talent for acting; indeed he longed to take up acting as a profession, but it was closed to him because of his royal birth. Instead he joined the Royal Marines, the toughest of all the branches of the Services and one utterly unsuited to a sensitive young man who dreamed of being an actor. To most people this seemed an incomprehensible choice. He could, after all, have simply joined the Army in a less demanding area or one of the regiments linked with the royal household. Instead, in June 1986 he was thrown in at the deep end into a routine of gruelling physical activity with an unsympathetic commanding officer. In January 1987

Edward had the courage to resign from the Marines before his time was up, enraging his father and earning himself a public and undeserved reputation as a wimp, which fuelled rumours that he was gay. Concerned friends of his mother's questioned a former master at Wanganui, who assured them that the Prince had always been surrounded by girls. Contemporaries of Edward at Cambridge testify to at least one affair with a woman undergraduate. None the less, rumours persisted even down to the naming of names, an allegation which the man in question resolutely denied. The story was started by an expatriate Briton in New York, who telephoned a London tabloid with the story that Prince Edward had had an affair with one of his valets, offering it for £25,000. Buckingham Palace staff absolutely deny that there is anything in the story and say that Edward, who is extremely discreet, has had several relationships with women and that his parents try to be as helpful over this as they can, inviting his friends to meals and making sure that there is a week free at Balmoral for Edward to ask his own friends. He is popular with the staff towards whom his manners are a good deal better than his siblings'. While Elizabeth, the Queen Mother and Margaret are polite to their staff, Elizabeth's children are not. 'Why are you all so bloody rude to the servants?' Charles's friend, the late Major Hugh Lindsay, was heard to explode at Balmoral. Charles himself, once such a polite little boy, is now known for losing his temper and tearing a strip off footmen in public, a humiliating experience for the person concerned.

Even when Edward was seen to be close to a public relations girl, Sophie Rhys-Jones, insinuations went on that she had only been used as a front to protect Edward's reputation. Edward's relations with the press were unfortunate; he behaved in a notably petulant way in public, stamping out of the press conference when reporters failed to enthuse over the embarrassing *It's a Royal Knockout*. When newspapers published photographs of Edward kissing Sophie Rhys-Jones, the Prince, backed by Elizabeth, complained to the Press Complaints Commission on the grounds of invasion of privacy, but then later, on the advice of a public relations firm much patronised by the younger royals, called a few editors together and said he would withdraw the complaint if they didn't publish the photographs, a manoeuvre hardly calculated either to deter the newsmen or earn their respect and cutting the ground from under the PCC. Edward has been, however, the only royal who has been allowed to take up a normal civilian job, first with Sir Andrew Lloyd Webber's theatre production company

and then on his own as an independent TV producer. It is the nearest
he can get to his dream of acting, but in an overcrowded and
competitive field he runs the risk of jealousies and accusations of
trading on his privileged position. He lives at Buckingham Palace, a
life fairly distant from his parents; even when at one of their holiday
homes he prefers to go out riding by himself rather than accompany
his mother. Elizabeth has comparatively little contact with her youngest
son (who, surprisingly, is his father's favourite), but the romance with
Sophie Rhys-Jones, an ordinary British working girl with a background
utterly remote from the royals, has her approval. She feels that some
level-headed commonsense would not come amiss in the younger
generation of the family. Sophie at least shows so far no signs of the
navel-gazing media mania which has affected the more glamorous
women members of the family.

In the 1980s Elizabeth began to fight back against media intrusion
into the family's affairs. In 1987, when the *Sun* published a private
letter written by Philip to the Commandant General of the Royal
Marines about Edward's decision to give up his career in the service,
Elizabeth initiated proceedings against the newspaper for breach of
copyright; she did the same thing when the *Sun* published a photograph of her with her new-born York granddaughter. The problem for
her was that the stories leaking through into the British press from
1985 onwards, particularly those relating to the Waleses' marriage,
were based on fact, although the general public was not yet prepared
to take them seriously. In an article entitled 'The Mouse that Roared',
Tina Brown, the New York-based but well-informed British editor of
Vanity Fair, wrote that 'the heir to the throne is pussy-whipped from
here to eternity' and that both the Waleses had lost touch with reality.
By 15 September 1984, when Prince Harry was born, the marriage was
a shell and the Prince had once more taken up with Camilla Parker
Bowles, whose new home was conveniently near to Highgrove. Diana's
jealousy of Camilla and the Prince's resentment of the public adulation
of his wife (which had first become acute during their joint tour of
Australia and New Zealand) had poisoned the atmosphere between
them. With their total lack of compatibility there was no common
ground on which they could meet. There was an exodus of staff who
could no longer cope with the 'two camps' atmosphere within the
Wales household. Oliver Everett, the Princess's Private Secretary, was
the first to go, cold-shouldered by the Princess but rewarded by
Elizabeth with the coveted post of Royal Librarian as some compensa-

tion for the diplomatic career which he had given up to join the Wales household. Even the faithful Michael Colborne, wearied of being the victim of the Prince's moods, handed in his resignation. The chef left because the couple's social life was too boring; both ate sparingly and gave no joint dinner-parties (how could they when they had no joint friends?). Diana got rid of Stephen Barry, whom she regarded as having far too strong a hold over the Prince, then Charles's favourite labrador, and tried to distance him from his friends. 'He's got to give up everything for me' was her attitude.

The Wales situation was developing towards danger-point, but neither Elizabeth nor her household seems to have realised it. One problem was the lack of communication on a deeper level between Elizabeth and her eldest son, a point emphasised by the Prince's biographer, perhaps even over-emphasised in an attempt to excuse the Prince's return to his mistress.

> . . . he was unable to turn to his parents to discuss the misery of his private life or of his public persona [Dimbleby wrote]. Their response to his charitable endeavours was incurious, while he was rarely left in doubt that they did not entirely welcome his contributions to controversial debate. The emotional gulf between the Prince and his parents was hard to bridge, while communication between them was normally limited to the exchange of social pleasantries and the formal business of family enterprise. In the family, only his grandmother seemed able to give him the understanding and support for which he had always turned to her.[6]

Other factors were the unwillingness of people to tell her. One courtier said:

> The Queen is an extremely well-informed person. My mother always drummed into me that they [the royals] knew far more about you than you thought they did . . . There were an awful lot of people who would tell the Queen things about people who were further removed than her own children, which she might be interested in hearing. But I'm not certain that when it comes to somebody who's very near they actually would.

And there was always the family habit of 'ostriching'.

Elizabeth could not fail to notice, however, that Diana was 'difficult'. Diana's calculated power games, using her beauty and attraction for the media – demonstrated by such occasions as when she chose the televised state occasion of the opening of Parliament by the Queen in November 1984 to air her new, short hairstyle and thus became the focus of all the camera shots – did not endear her to her mother-in-law. A year earlier, on the occasion of the British Legion concert in memory of the dead of two world wars at the Albert Hall, the Princess had first sent a message that she would not be going and had then appeared twenty minutes after the Queen, a public discourtesy on a solemn occasion. Privately, Elizabeth now regarded Diana as 'that tiresome girl' and her behaviour as childish. For someone as totally dedicated to public service and royal duty as she was, such antics were inexplicable.

To the Princess of Wales, however, what she saw as the royal family's apparent approbation of her husband's mistress and *her* husband seemed equally strange. The Parker Bowleses were frequent guests of the Queen Mother at Birkhall when Charles was on holiday nearby in Balmoral. Derek Parker Bowles, Andrew's late father, had been an old friend of the Queen Mother's. Andrew, his eldest son, remained on easy terms with the royal family; there was at that time never any outward sign that he resented his wife's relationship with the Prince of Wales except when taunted with it in public, as happened to him once at Ascot when a fellow member of the Turf Club repeatedly shouted 'Ernest Simpson' at him. The Parker Bowleses' was an open marriage in which each apparently accepted the other's affairs. All the same, many people unfamiliar with the ways of the court thought it strange when in 1987 Parker Bowles was appointed Silver Stick in Waiting, not realising that this is an honorary post held automatically by the lieutenant-colonel commanding the Household Cavalry which involves attendance at state functions, Trooping the Colour and the arrival of a head of state on a state visit. It was a royal family tradition that the Prince of Wales should have mistresses – the only recent exception being George V, who was utterly monogamous as far as Queen Mary was concerned (but then he had not been brought up to consider himself as the heir to the throne). Charles's affair with Camilla was almost a re-run of Edward VII's long romance with Camilla's great-great-grandmother, Alice Keppel, but with one important difference. Queen Alexandra had been annoyed and puzzled by her husband's fondness for Mrs Keppel (whose handsome husband, Colonel Keppel, was also a cavalry officer), but she had put up with it and never, ever made a scene. In the pre-divorce era of private infidelity and public composure, Edward VII's behaviour was nothing out of the ordinary. Diana, however, was the product not only of a different era but a different generation even than her husband and the Parker Bowleses. She wanted sole and acknowledged possession of her husband (at least until she finally gave up on him) and came to passionately and dangerously resent her situation. 'She worshipped him with a calf-like adoration and he kicked her in the gutter,' one Palace aide said. It was outstandingly a case of 'Hell hath no fury like a woman scorned'. Elizabeth and her family closed their eyes to it at their peril.

Increasingly too there was a lack of communication between Elizabeth's advisers at Buckingham Palace and the Prince's staff at St James's. The resignation early in 1985 of the Prince's Private Secretary, Edward Adeane, whose relations with the Queen's household were excellent, did not help matters. This is Dimbleby's account of the split. Adeane, he said,

> belonged to the old school of courtiers, honourable and cautious . . .
> Adeane had always found it hard to reconcile himself to the Prince's
> unconventional enthusiasms and outspoken contributions to public
> debate and he did not hesitate to say so . . . he grew more and more
> unhappy at his failure to corral the heir apparent . . . Early in 1985
> after a long succession of disagreements that grew ever sharper with
> the Prince, Adeane finally tendered his resignation . . .[7]

A Palace aide put it rather differently:

> Adeane had very good relations with the Palace. He and Colborne
> didn't get on because Colborne was the provider of secret cuff-links
> and flowers for ladies and Adeane didn't approve. Adeane tried to get
> the Prince to work and stick to his plans but it was like nailing jellies to
> a wall to get him to stick to a programme and a lot of deceit used to go
> on to make out he was doing a lot of work when he wasn't – he was off
> playing polo or something.

'The Prince of Wales sacks anyone who tells him what to do,' a friend of the family said.

The Prince, despite his kind heart, essentially gentle nature and good intentions, was not an easy man to work for and was, his biographer admitted, demanding of his staff. He frequently changed his mind and then was furious when his staff could not keep up with new arrangements. 'The Prince's enthusiasm', Dimbleby wrote, 'too often bore the imprint of the last person he had spoken to [his father apparently called him an 'intellectual pillow'] and he had a tendency to reach instant conclusions on the basis of insufficient thought', relying too much on intuition rather than logic. The increasing tension in his private life did not help his temper and there would be scenes in the office when papers would be thrown round the room. The result of this was chaos:

> In these circumstances, the impression of order and precision conveyed by the Prince's entourage on public occasions concealed a disarray in his private office that he found hard to comprehend and impossible to rectify. Under pressure to meet the Prince's ever-shifting needs, a team of four officials supported by a dozen secretaries and typists found themselves reacting haphazardly to the flow of princely enthusiasms. No one thought to complain but disorder was rife. Letters, which arrived each week in their hundreds, piled up, unsorted and unanswered . . . Classified documents sent over from the Foreign Office were frequently left in the office unread for days . . .

It was all a little too reminiscent of the Duke of Windsor in his early days as Edward VIII. Unsurprisingly, the search for a successor to Adeane took six months; the Prince's Assistant Private Secretary, David Roycroft, seconded from the Foreign Office to induce order to the chaos, 'lacked rapport with the Prince' and left. The Prince was unwilling to have an 'insider' foisted upon him by his mother's entourage, but eventually lighted upon Sir John Riddell, who, as a baronet and a merchant banker, fitted in perfectly well with Buckingham Palace where the senior staff, who had been fearing that the candidate would have been bearded and possibly even wearing sandals, were relieved to recognise the familiar dark pin-striped suit.

The lack of communication between Prince and Palace was embarrassingly revealed on a visit to Italy by the Prince and Princess of Wales in the spring of 1985. The Prince of Wales had always been an advocate of ecumenism and had eagerly accepted an invitation from the Archbishop of Canterbury to an ecumenical service in Canterbury Cathedral on the occasion of the Pope's visit in 1982, an occasion which had aroused the suspicion and opposition of the extreme wings of the Protestant Church. In Italy in 1985 he planned to further the movement towards reconciliation between the two Christian churches not only by visiting the Pope, a standard courtesy to a head of state, but also by attending a religious service. Adeane had consulted both the Archbishop of Canterbury and the Home Office (the government department responsible for advising Buckingham Palace on the constitutional implications of inter-faith relations). It was agreed that the best way of accomplishing this would be if the Prince and Princess attended a mass in the Pope's private chapel but did not take Communion. There would therefore be no breach of the heir to the throne's position as supreme governor-designate of the Established Church, avoiding criticism by all but the 'lunatic fringe'. The suggestion was conveyed to the Pope and a date agreed for the morning of 30 April, the day after the Waleses' audience with the Pope.

Suddenly and without warning two weeks before the planned mass, the Palace launched a pre-emptive strike by leaking an item to *The Times* diary which appeared on 16 April: 'A request by Prince Charles to attend a papal mass in the Vatican has been refused after a top level decision taken in the past 24 hours, involving Buckingham Palace, Church leaders and the diplomatic corps.' The trouble was that after all the careful negotiations and arrangements between the Prince, Archbishop and Pope, the involvement of the Home Office and Her Majesty's representative at the Holy See, the one person who had not been consulted was Elizabeth, an omission which even the Prince's biographer called a serious breach of protocol: 'with only a fortnight to go, the Supreme Governor of the Church of England had been given no opportunity fully to consider the constitutional implications of her son's attendance at the Pope's mass'. As soon as Elizabeth was informed of the plan and prior to the *Times* leak, she had a long meeting with Prince Charles, at which it can be assumed that she expressed herself forcefully at this extraordinary oversight. The outcome of the meeting was that on 15 April a message was sent by the Prince's office to the Vatican that the Prince would not, after all, be attending the mass on which, according to Dimbleby, 'he had set his heart so many months before'. The result was an embarrassing confusion; while Adeane and the Deputy Private Secretary, Sir William Heseltine, back-pedalled and obfuscated, their hopes of concealment were wrecked by Vatican sources who let it be known that, but for the last-minute cancellation, the Prince would have taken part in an historic act of reconciliation with the Church of Rome. The news of the cancellation provoked the predictable reaction from Dr Paisley, leader of the Free Presbyterian Church of Ulster, and the Moderator of the Free Church of Scotland, who warned in a letter to the Prince that 'reconciliation to the see of Rome could jeopardise Your Royal Highness' right to succession'. The Prince dashed off a furious response to this which his staff marked 'on no account is this letter to be sent'.

The row over the papal mass indicated not only a lack of communication between Elizabeth and her son on an official as well as a personal level but the Prince's increasing tendency to pursue his own initiatives without pausing to think of the possible consequences, constitutional or otherwise, of his actions and to do so without consultation with the Palace. From 1985 after the departure of Adeane the Prince's activities expanded, many of them admirable, not all of them wise, and he acquired a number of unconventional and environmentally minded advisers. On the inner-city front he set up not only the Prince's Trust but the Prince's Youth Business Trust and Business in the Community, using his influence to lobby politicians and leading business-men on their behalf. The Prince's view that his position as a Privy Counsellor, Member of the House of Lords and heir to the throne gave him a right to 'warn, protest and advise' was not necessarily constitutionally correct; some of the people and vested interests he attacked saw it as an abuse of his influential position. The Prime Minister, Mrs Thatcher, was incandescent when informed of a scheme of the Prince's to establish closer links between himself personally and the rulers of the Gulf and Middle East generally, which, it seemed, would involve setting up some kind of secretariat. The Prince's attacks on ministers, while well-meaning, were not welcomed, particularly if they were made in public as when, in 1987, he condemned Nicholas Ridley's policies on the environment at the opening of the North Sea Conference. While many people agreed with his green views on the environment, to the politicians it seemed that he was appealing to a constituency over their heads. The Ministers for Energy were particular targets; while the Prince spoke from the heart and was generally in line with public feeling on such subjects as stubble-burning by farmers, he did not always make the equation between pollution-removal and human employment as in the case of CO_2 emissions and the effect of regulation on coalminers' jobs. There were battles with the Royal Institute of British Architects when the Prince publicly attacked schemes for a new wing of the National Gallery – 'a carbuncle on a beloved face' – and Paternoster Square in front of St Paul's: 'architects have done more damage to London than the Luftwaffe'. He took on the advanced wing of the Church of England with attacks on the New English Bible and the Alternative Service Book, applauded by many but perhaps not necessarily in line with his mother's official position as Supreme Governor of the Church whose policy she must officially support (although those who know Elizabeth suspect that her views on both are in line with her son's). In 1991 he delivered the Shakespeare Birthday Lecture with a passionate plea for the teaching of the Bard, combined with an attack on the Government's policy on primary education, which infuriated the then Education Secretary, Kenneth Clarke.

While the Prince was earning himself an international reputation as an environmentalist, holding an unofficial environment conference in the run-up to the Rio Summit in 1991, inviting the Brazilian President Collor and Senator Albert Gore to talks aboard *Britannia*, and lashing architects, politicians and misguided 'modernisers' in the Church and the teaching profession, the behind-the-scenes struggle between the Queen's courtiers and the Prince's to retain the Prince within the ambit of palace control ended with a definite defeat for the Palace. In this the key figure was Commander Richard Aylard, RN, the Prince's Assistant Private Secretary, a grammar school boy with a degree in Applied Zoology and Mathematics who had served as a naval officer on board HMS *Invincible* during the Falklands war.

> From the late '80s Aylard had been responsible for co-ordinating the preparation of some of the Prince's most outspoken and influential speeches [Dimbleby wrote]. When some raised their eyebrows on the discovery that the likes of Jonathon Porritt [a leading environmentalist, then director of the Friends of the Earth] had the Prince's ear, Aylard affected innocent concern about their anxieties but ignored them. Porritt, supported by Aylard, became an increasingly influential figure at the Prince's environmental court; but it was Aylard who held the threads together and, with a finely tuned ear for the Prince's verbal mannerisms, wrote increasingly effective drafts for the Prince to work on.[8]

Aylard's background was quite unlike that of the Queen's courtiers; he had no 'social' connections. He is good-looking rather in the Peter Townsend mode, lean, of medium height, with dark, slightly curly hair and finely cut features. Aylard, as Dimbleby admits, 'was indeed more ambitious than his modest demeanour would suggest'.

In 1990 Sir John Riddell departed the Prince's office six months before his contract ran out and returned to the more familiar and agreeable pastures of the City. His successor, Major-General Sir Christopher Airy, who had recently completed a stint as General Officer Commanding London District and Major-General Commanding the Household Division, might have been hand-picked by the Palace, where he was well known and regarded as a 'safe pair of hands'. The Prince consulted Aylard and, curiously, Sir James 'Jimmy' Savile, an eccentric TV personality and charity fund-raiser who acted as unofficial adviser to some of the younger royals, asking them to 'sound out' Airy. Undeterred by this unusual pair, the Major-General accepted the job, but within a few months he had been sidelined by Aylard who was destined to succeed him. Before the Prince's departure from London for the official visit to Brazil culminating in the *Britannia* environmental seminar, Aylard suggested that it would be better for the Private Secretary, Airy, to remain in London holding the fort as there would be little for him to do on the tour. Airy, not unnaturally, since Private Secretaries always accompanied their employers on official visits, resented this advice and did not take it. According to the official biographer:

> During the seminar, it was painfully obvious that he [Airy] had
> nonetheless been reduced to the role of a bystander, able only to engage
> in a kind of courteous small talk that did not quite measure up to the
> needs of the moment. It was this episode which finally convinced the
> Prince that, whatever his other qualities, Airy should be replaced by
> Aylard.

The Prince, apparently, shrank from sacking him, but his hand was forced in the spring of 1991 when Aylard warned that the *Sunday Times* was about to run a story 'Prince sacks Airy' and told him that 'either we will have to deny it or make it fact very quickly'. The deed was done, however, not by the Prince, who hated sacking people, but by Allen Sheppard, chief executive of Grand Metropolitan and a member of the Prince of Wales Co-ordinating Committee, which oversees the Prince's 'overlapping and often rivalrous charities'. 'The Prince went for a walk in the garden while Sheppard took Airy to one side to inform him that the time had come to write a letter of resignation . . .'

His successor was, of course, Aylard, in whom 'the Prince detected, if not a kindred spirit, at least someone who appreciated his purpose and, as an environmental specialist, understood his vision. To an unusual degree, Aylard combined reticence and intensity, his deference concealing a resolute and calculating intellect.' His qualities, however, do not seem to have been equally appreciated by his colleagues, who, according to Dimbleby, motivated by jealousy of Aylard's 'closeness' to the Prince, alleged that he had engineered his own preferment at their expense and consequently 'for many weeks the atmosphere at St James's was to be soured by this jealousy'. By the time Aylard had been in charge for three years, the social mix among the Prince's senior staff included two public school boys, three with a grammar school background and two from comprehensive schools, which, says Dimbleby, 'sharply delineated St James's from Buckingham Palace'. He credits Aylard with a 'sharp eye for public relations' and as sharing 'the Prince's frustration with the failure of Buckingham Palace to "get the message across"'. Inevitably, as he pursued this course, Charles was bound to come up against his mother, who, according to a former Press Secretary, 'has a lot of input on PR at the Palace and is extremely alert . . .' A major part of the St James's Palace public relations offensive spearheaded by Aylard two years later would be the promotion of a two-and-half-hour telebiography of the Prince and related book by Jonathan Dimbleby. Elizabeth was to be consulted about neither project. As the new decade opened she was about to experience the most difficult years of her entire life on both the public and the personal fronts.

17

Family at War

'We have come to regard the Crown as the head of our *morality*
... We have come to believe that it is natural to have a virtuous
sovereign ... But a little experience and less thought show that
royalty cannot take credit for domestic excellence.'

Walter Bagehot, *The English Constitution*

In November 1990 Margaret Thatcher made a forced exit from
Downing Street in an atmosphere of betrayal, bitterness and back-
stabbing, which might have formed the plot of a Shakespearean
tragedy. In July that year she had performed her last act of loyalty to
the monarchy by piloting through Parliament a Civil List increase
from £5.09 million to about £7.9 million a year, which was intended
to last for the decade. This ended the system of yearly increases which
had been established in 1975 with its recurrent accompaniment of
hostile articles about 'pay rises for royals' in the press. By obtaining
the agreement of the Labour Opposition leader, Neil Kinnock (who in
1975 had voted against the Labour Government's Civil List Bill), and
announcing the Bill at the end of the summer sessions, Mrs Thatcher
pushed it through with the minimum of discussion. MPs learned of it
only two hours in advance and were allowed twenty minutes to ask
questions. Increased allowances for other members of the royal family,
such as Prince Edward (from £20,000 to £100,000), were not read out
but merely printed in the parliamentary record, *Hansard*. None the
less, the question of the Queen's exemption from income tax was
raised by a Tory MP and was, for the first time, to become a subject
for widespread public discussion and to damage Elizabeth's standing
with her people almost as much as the scandals within her family
which were about to erupt. The family, which should have been a
source of strength, was becoming Elizabeth's Achilles heel, just as the

whole fabric of the monarchy, its cost, even the necessity or desirability of its existence, was increasingly coming into question.

By 1990 Elizabeth could no longer remain oblivious to the stress within her family. The Waleses, on the rare occasions when she saw them together on family holidays or special celebrations, were openly at war. Sarcastic remarks would fly, unpleasant exchanges in which Diana usually got the upper hand because she was prepared to be more unrestrained. At Balmoral in August 1990, when the family gathered to celebrate Princess Margaret's sixtieth birthday, the atmosphere was notably edgy. Nerve-endings were close to the surface, there were nasty asides and raised voices. When Fergie and Diana clowned around on a picnic, the Prince of Wales was heard to mutter 'little things please little minds'. Even Elizabeth seemed affected, shouting not only at the corgis but even at Prince William. Both grandparents were more impatient with him than they were with the Yorks' little girl, Beatrice. It was the heir to the throne syndrome repeating itself. Prince William would eventually be King; therefore his upbringing and behaviour mattered more than the other children's. When Prince William out riding one day gave his groom the slip and came home early, his grandmother, who was only too aware of what the implications might be, tore a strip off him. In her view, which contrasted with her daughter-in-law's, the eventual heir could not be brought up exactly as other boys. However, as far as the grandchildren were concerned, the regime at Balmoral was much less spartan and more relaxed than it used to be. Instead of bathing in the freezing burns, they were allowed to go to a local swimming-pool and to the cinema if there was a film specially suited to them.

There were frictions with Charles too. Although on the whole Elizabeth could laugh and joke with her son as before, on more important levels she doubted his judgement, while he, for his part, felt excluded from major decisions by her household. Elizabeth felt distanced from him by his obvious reliance for advice upon his inner circle of friends, even over such questions as the treatment of the arm which he broke playing polo in June 1988. Philip always had little patience with his son; now both he and Elizabeth felt both anguished and irritated over the obvious failure of the marriage. Charles seemed oblivious to Palace advice. Sir Robert Fellowes and his predecessor as Private Secretary, Sir William Heseltine, had attempted in vain to get the Prince either to give up or cut down on his polo commitments. They felt, correctly, that polo was bad for his image and that this reflected generally on the monarchy. Polo is essentially a sport of the rich played for an elite audience of people who attend either because they are genuinely interested in it or because they like the snobbery associated with it and the feeling of rubbing shoulders with the rich and the royal. The vast majority of the population find it incomprehensible and boring. Where George V and George VI had always made a point of attending the Cup Final, the annual high point of the national game, association football, Elizabeth nowadays never went. The job was left to the Kents, hardly first-circle royalty, and the implication was that the real royals couldn't care less about popular sport. In recession–hit Britain, the Prince of Wales's association with the sport of rich playboys was hardly helpful to his family's public image. Yet he insisted on continuing for therapeutic reasons. 'Without polo', he said, 'I'd go stark, staring mad.' He has now given up top-level competitive polo and plays only charity matches. (Philip has swapped the more dangerous excitements of the game for carriage–driving.) When Charles did finally attend the 1995 Cup Final, as part of the campaign to refurbish his image, he attempted to present the Cup to the losers, a *faux pas* which suggested that his attention had hardly been riveted to the game.

Elizabeth's affection for Fergie was waning in the face of the Duchess's self–indulgent behaviour. In March 1990 the Yorks' second daughter, Eugenie, had been born, but the birth was not enough to compensate for the fissures in their marriage. Sarah was evidently bored with her husband, whose frequent and prolonged absences on naval duty left her at a loose end. Sarah told a friend that in 1988 Andrew had spent only forty-two nights at home out of a year. Once Sunninghill was finished she was not prepared to live as an ordinary naval wife in married quarters or even in a rented house near Andrew's base to be near her husband, and when he was home she found his preferred way of relaxation dull. Andrew liked to watch videos and play golf and, when the couple entertained, Sarah found his behaviour embarrassingly boorish. At dinner-parties Andrew was served first and gobbled down his food regardless of the other guests, and he had a fondness for telling loud and unfunny naval jokes. Sarah was definitely the dominant partner in the relationship; to Elizabeth's household it seemed that he had no control over his wife's behaviour, while to Sarah equally it appeared that Andrew was not prepared to stand up for her to his mother's courtiers. Andrew, sadly, was still in love with his wife, but, as Sarah's father had told his mistress, she had been in love with the royal family rather than her husband. Now both 'love affairs' were cooling from Sarah's point of view.

The Ferguson family connection was proving an embarrassment for the family. In May 1988 newspapers broke the story of Major Ron's visits to the Wigmore Club, a gentlemen's 'massage' parlour which the papers hinted was little more than a brothel. Ferguson left the Guards' Polo Club when his position as deputy chairman was not renewed. Philip, President of the Club, always protective of Elizabeth, was not amused by the scandal and refused the Major's repeated attempts to see him, despite the intercessions of the Duchess of York and the Prince of Wales. In November the following year the Duchess had met the first of two Texans who were to bring about her downfall. Steven Wyatt was the son of Lynn Sakowitz Wyatt, heiress to the Saks stores fortune, by a disastrous first marriage to a man who killed his girlfriend while on an acid trip and served time for manslaughter. His stepfather, Oscar Wyatt, was one of the richest and toughest men in Texas, while his mother, a Lauren Bacall look-alike, fashionably thin and eternally young, was a star on the international jet-set circuit and a frequent favoured guest at the Reagan White House. Princess Margaret was an occasional guest at the Wyatts' house, Allingham, and continued to be so even after the scandal which involved Steven Wyatt and her niece-in-law. In Europe at Somerset Maugham's former Cap Ferrat villa, La Mauresque, the Wyatts used to entertain Prince Rainier and Princess Grace of Monaco to barbecues with steaks flown in by private jet from Texas. There had even been rumours that Lynn would have liked to succeed Grace as Princess of Monaco after Grace died. Lynn had been hostess at her house in Houston when the Duchess of York was invited to a British festival at the Houston Grand Opera and Steven Wyatt had been there to help entertain the royal guest. Sarah afterwards flew to New York in the Wyatts' private plane, stayed at their expense at the Plaza Athenée and dined with Steven at the fashionable restaurant Mortimer's, in a group which included the Queen Mother's cousin, John Bowes-Lyon.

The friendship did not end there. Back in England Wyatt, now working for a petroleum company associated with his stepfather's oil interests, was with Sarah again at a shooting-party in Yorkshire; later she introduced him to the unsuspecting Andrew. After the birth of Princess Eugenie in March, the affair continued even more openly. Sarah and her daughters spent a holiday with the Wyatts at Cap Ferrat, during which the photographs that helped finally to sink her marriage with Andrew were taken. Later that summer the extent to which Sarah had become involved with Wyatt was blatantly revealed one summer evening. Sarah, having refused an invitation to dinner with Lord McAlpine, the construction millionaire, friend of Lady Thatcher and former Treasurer of the Conservative Party, and his wife, Romilly, at London's top French restaurant, Le Gavroche, was persuaded by Wyatt to give dinner in her second-floor Buckingham Palace apartment to Dr Ramzi Sultan, an Iraqi oil-marketing dealer, whose country had invaded Kuwait on 2 August and who as such was certainly *persona non grata* to the British Government. Afterwards, she joined the McAlpines, bringing with her, uninvited, both Wyatt and Ramzi Sultan, and indulged in an obvious and intimate display of affection with Wyatt. Sarah later saw to it that Wyatt was invited to the Christmas ball held at Buckingham Palace to celebrate the ninetieth, sixtieth and thirtieth birthdays that year of the Queen Mother, Princess Margaret and Prince Andrew. It was the high point of his social mountaineering. Sarah had ignored the scolding of her cousin, Robert Fellowes, to whom she contemptuously referred as 'Bellows', and the warnings about Wyatt from her father (who at one point was sharing his mistress, Lesley Player, with Wyatt). But Wyatt, shying away from potential scandal, removed himself to Washington. As he moved offstage another Texan, the smooth, English-educated John Bryan, took his place in the Duchess of York's life.

For some time the royal household had been dismayed at Elizabeth's indulgence of her daughters-in-law and her refusal to interfere. The Private Secretary was at a disadvantage not only because of his relationship to both of them but because they could circumvent him by their direct access to their mother-in-law. When they wanted anything, Sarah and Diana would simply go to her over the heads of the household and wheedle, 'Oh, Ma'am, please, just this once ... The household hate me ...' etc. If approached from the other side, Elizabeth would say, 'I can't interfere in my children's lives.'

Although by now aware of the rumours about her daughter-in-law's behaviour with Wyatt (which Andrew steadfastly refused to believe), Elizabeth did not know of the pact which both her daughters-in-law had made to separate from their husbands, according to Major Ferguson, who told Lesley Player about it in the spring of 1991. There had already been one marital split in the family when in 1989 Anne had separated from Mark Phillips; there had been a certain amount of scandal, first concerning one of Anne's detectives, then when letters written to her by one of the Palace equerries, her future husband, Commander Tim Laurence, were stolen and taken to a tabloid newspaper. Meanwhile Mark Phillips had his own problems with allegations of affairs and a love-child. But Anne's popularity as one of the hardest-working members of the royal family (and particularly for the Save the Children Fund) had seen her through. Mark Phillips behaved with dignity, the split had been amicable and the marriage was to be legally dissolved in April. But as she delivered her 1991 Christmas broadcast Elizabeth was unaware of the extent to which her family life was crumbling round her. One phrase of that broadcast, intended as an affirmation of her continuing determination to go on serving the nation after forty years on the throne, was to come back to haunt her: 'With your prayers and your help, and the love and support of my family, I shall try and help you in the years to come.' (This was interpreted by various sections of the press as a slap in the face for Charles, sending a public signal that she did not intend to abdicate in his favour. It was no such thing: Elizabeth never has had any intention of abdicating and never will.)

In January 1992 the photographs of Wyatt and Sarah in the South of France were found on top of a wardrobe by a window-cleaner and 'odd-job' man cleaning up Wyatt's Cadogan Square flat. This time the naïve, long-suffering Prince Andrew, in his father-in-law's words, 'hit the roof'. 'The pictures are only holiday snaps,' Major Ferguson told Lesley Player, invited by Sarah to act as her 'lady-in-waiting' on a charity visit to Palm Beach with the instruction: 'You must understand you've really got to *be* with Dads [Major Ferguson] this time ...' 'But', the Major went on, 'they show that Texan fellow in a basket chair with his arm around her – and the one that really annoyed Andrew was little Beatrice with no clothes on being cuddled by him.'[1] When the pictures were published in the tabloid *Sun*, every British 'bloke in the street' understood why Andrew had 'hit the roof'.

Six days after the publication of the photographs, Andrew and Sarah agreed to separate. On the following morning, 22 January, they travelled up to Sandringham to tell Elizabeth of their decision. She looked, Sarah later wrote, 'sadder than I had ever seen her,' expressing her disappointment and asking them to reconsider before taking an irrevocable decision. Privately, however, she was stunned. 'I can't understand my children,' she told a friend. 'She [Sarah] didn't even try to be a naval wife ...' For Elizabeth, the period she had spent in

Malta as a young naval wife had been one of the happiest experiences
of her life. Although there were other aspects of the marriage which,
sadly, she did comprehend, her daughter-in-law's selfish have-it-all,
grab-it-all attitude was simply alien to her. Her eyes were beginning to
be opened as far as the Duchess of York was concerned. 'Fergie isn't
as nice as you think she is,' a royal relation said. Sarah wanted sex,
money, fun and excitement and she was prepared to sacrifice everything in order to get it. Incredibly, this woman was capable of self-
delusion to the extent that she told her father later, 'I'm thirty-four,
nearly thirty-five, and I haven't lived my life at all . . .'[2]

Elizabeth was now aware of the prospect of a second marriage
failure; she was as yet unprepared for the third. As the new year of
1992 opened, the year which was intended to celebrate the fortieth
anniversary of her accession, she was about to experience the worst
period of her entire life. The image of decency, honour and duty which
she had created around the monarchy over the past forty years was
about to be shattered by the scandalous antics of the younger
generation.

At this point the warring younger royals began seriously to deploy
the newspapers as weapons in their individual struggles to get the
upper hand, thus putting the situation beyond the control of Elizabeth
and her advisers. 'Always make friends with the press,' Sarah had told
Lesley Player. 'As you get to know them you'll find your favourites
who will really look after you . . .' James Whitaker, royal correspondent
of the *Daily Mirror*, claims that in the spring of 1992 he had been
visited at his London home by John Bryan,

> masquerading as merely a consultant to the Duchess of York. Cocky
> and determined, he maintained he was acting as a broker in the
> negotiations between the Queen's solicitors, Farrer's, and the Duchess
> of York's over the financial terms of her separation from the Duke. He
> described Farrer's and their senior partner, Sir Matthew Farrer, as 'a
> bunch of assholes' and he claimed to be playing a central role in the
> negotiations. 'They can't do a damned thing without me,' he bragged,
> 'and the Queen has said I have got to be involved at every single level
> of negotiation. My word is final.'[3]

On 15 March there was a lawyers' meeting at Sunninghill between
Sir Matthew Farrer, representing the Queen, and Charles Doughty of
Withers & Co. representing the Duchess of York, at which Bryan was

present. According to Ronald Ferguson, Bryan was holding out for a house for Sarah in England, plus £5,000 a week income for herself for life. However, to their disappointment, although under English law Sarah was entitled to half the marital home, Sunninghill belonged to Elizabeth, while Andrew himself was not a rich man. He had his naval pay and his Civil List income, which, being provided by the taxpayer for the performance of his royal duties, could hardly be used to support his ex-wife, and in any case was soon to be abolished. Sarah, however, had her daughters, Beatrice and Eugenie, to whom Elizabeth was devoted and whom Sarah had been heard to describe as 'my security' – and her silence. For Elizabeth it was an exercise in damage limitation. ('Those girls [by which he meant Sarah and Diana]', a courtier was to opine two years later, 'are going to cost the Queen a fortune.')

The first public breach between the Duchess and the Palace came as a result of further manipulation of the media, when the *Daily Mail* leaked the fact that the Duchess of York had consulted lawyers about a separation from her husband. The Palace – the Queen's Private Secretary, Sir Robert Fellowes, and her Press Secretary, Charles Anson – believed that Sarah had done this deliberately on the advice of Tim Bell Associates, the PR firm favoured by the Yorks and Prince Edward, although why they should have thought she had anything to gain by such a move is questionable. On 19 March Charles Anson summoned six court correspondents, including the BBC's Paul Reynolds, and issued a statement announcing the Yorks' separation and told them to come to his office if they wanted further guidance. Reynolds accepted the invitation and, after five minutes' conversation with Anson, broadcast on the BBC's *World at One* to the effect that, 'The knives are out for Fergie at the Palace.' According to Reynolds, Anson told him that the rift between the Yorks had begun the previous year and that the Duchess was being advised by Sir Tim Bell's firm. The *Daily Mail* leak was followed up by a story in the *Sunday Telegraph*, one of the few newspapers actively supporting the royal family, that Sir Robert Fellowes was thought to have confided that the Duchess was not in control of herself, that both the Queen and the Queen Mother had tried to 'calm her', but that the entire family now thought it was 'time to wash their hands of her'. Both Fergusons were paranoid about their cousin Robert at the Palace, but while they demanded and got a public apology from Anson, the York camp felt that whatever the Palace might have said in its subsequent statement, the leak to the *Mail* had come from Diana, who was close to its editor-in-chief, Sir David English, and subsequently became even closer to its royal correspondent, Richard Kay. Anson did not, as was widely reported, offer his resignation to Elizabeth, but he did apologise to the Queen and the Duchess of York for the embarrassment caused. The episode was a disagreeable foretaste of what was to come as the monarchy was to become embroiled in the maelstrom of the Waleses' marital troubles.

Diana, idolised by the public, had been increasingly calling the shots in the media war between herself and her husband. Charles found himself cast not only as an uncaring husband (which was the truth), but as a bad father (which was not). Incidents such as Prince William's accident in June the previous year – when he was hit on the head with a club while playing golf with a schoolfriend – were highlighted in the press as evidence of Charles's selfishness. While Diana kept vigil at the Great Ormond Street Hospital for Sick Children as their son underwent a minor operation and spent the night there, Charles attended the opera, where he was host to a party including two European Commissioners, and then travelled overnight to Yorkshire for an official visit with his European guests. 'What kind of dad are you?' asked the *Sun*. While Diana made a point of emphasising her love for her children in public as well as in private, Charles refused to perform for the cameras, with predictable results. There had been more bad publicity earlier in the year when Diana's father, Earl Spencer, died suddenly on 29 March while the couple were for once on holiday together at Lech in Austria with their sons. Diana at first refused to travel with her husband, then relented as far as the flight to London was concerned, but was adamant that she would not travel to the funeral in Northamptonshire with him. She went by car; he travelled by helicopter after his anxious staff had hurriedly reinstated a cancelled meeting for him to provide a plausible excuse for their separate journeys. The occasion was another publicity coup for Diana, pictured grieving and apart from her husband. Reporters focused on her wreath: 'I miss you dreadfully, darling Daddy, but will love you forever.' At the service she made a public gesture of reconciliation, reaching out for her stepmother's arm. According to Countess Spencer's assistant, the whole thing was a sham. 'She hardly ever saw him. She hadn't been to Althorp since her brother's wedding in 1989 and she made very little effort to see him in London.' As for touching Raine Spencer's arm, it was no secret that the Spencer children hated 'Acid' Raine, as they called her, blaming her for the sale of treasures from

Althorp and for vulgarising the Spencer name and royal connections for commercial ends (even to the extent of selling replicas of Diana's wedding dress to the Japanese). When Countess Spencer returned to Althorp to retrieve her belongings after her husband's death, she was told that she would have to provide proof of purchase before anything could be removed, and when her maid had attempted to remove four suitcases with the Countess's clothes, Diana and her brother Charles stood by the door, searched the cases and forced her to transfer the contents into black plastic binbags.[4]

In February 1992 the cruellest images of all hinted at what the world was soon to be told in detail, that the 'fairy-tale marriage' was definitely over. The pictures of a pensive Diana seated alone in front of the Taj Mahal, the monument erected by the grieving Shah Jehan to his beloved wife, sent the message loud and clear. It was followed up by the famous 'kiss that wasn't', when Charles after a polo match went to kiss his wife's cheek and Diana, with flawless timing, turned her head away at the last moment so that he was left looking a fool leaning in the direction of her earring. Four months later, with the serialisation of Andrew Morton's book *Diana: Her True Story*, on 7 June in the *Sunday Times*, the world learned the truth, albeit a somewhat slanted version of it. The book presented Diana as a cross between Mother Teresa and New Age Woman, caring but assertive, a victim struggling to free herself from the crushing weight of an ultra-traditional family and an uncaring, adulterous husband. It paraded the difficulties she had suffered: the bulimia, the depression, the suicide attempts.

The trouble about the book from the Palace point of view was that the essential presentation of Diana as a virgin sacrifice offered up on the altar of the dynasty, used and abused by her husband, was near enough to the truth to be believable. The real problem which it presented was that it could not be dismissed as a journalistic fabrication. Diana had authorised her closest friends to speak to Andrew Morton and when, on the eve of publication of the serialisation, Elizabeth's Assistant Private Secretary, Robin Janvrin, and Richard Aylard prepared a disclaimer for Diana, she refused to sign it. Andrew Knight, a director of News International, owners of the *Sunday Times*, was told by one of Morton's sources that she had indeed talked to Andrew Morton 'and had done so at the instigation of the Princess, who had told her to hide nothing because she wanted "to end the fairy-tale"'. Diana herself tipped off a photographer about her visit to Carolyn Bartholomew, her old flatmate at Coleherne Court and one of

Morton's principal sources, a visit which was intended to underline her seal of approval of what Carolyn Bartholomew had done. All this gave the lie to the assurances given by Robert Fellowes (who as Diana's brother-in-law was in a particularly awkward position) to the head of the Press Complaints Commission, Lord McGregor, and to the Cabinet Secretary, Sir Robin Butler, that the Princess of Wales had not authorised the book and had given him her word that she had not. Sir Robert, accompanying Elizabeth on a state visit to Paris at the time, was forced into humiliating apologies as a result. As in the case of Charles Anson, he offered his resignation, which was refused.

The publication of the Morton book ended any sympathy Elizabeth might have had for Diana. She had been aware of her daughter-in-law's difficulties and had had several private talks with her over the past years. She herself had often found her son's behaviour unsatisfactory. Philip had also been sympathetic to Diana as he had to Sarah in his own way. Because of his own position he had an insight into their problems on marrying into the royal family and he was always responsive to pretty women. As Ronald Ferguson had written insinuatingly, even when the Wyatt photographs had surfaced the Duke's response had not been hostile but rather, 'There, but for the grace of God, go I.' At times when Diana, in the throes of her psychological difficulties, had fits of panic about going into a room to meet a crowd of strangers, Philip had jollied her along, seizing her round the waist and whirling her in. Now Diana had 'gone public' in a way which the royal family found impossible to forgive. The whole royal myth which Elizabeth had worked so hard to build up had started to unravel because of the 'me' impulses of two young women who had voluntarily entered the circle and enjoyed all its privileges and then turned on the system when they found that it did not suit them. Sarah's indecent, uncontrolled blunderings seemed more forgivable than Diana's shrewd manipulation of the media and her appeal to the wider public who adored her. Neither of them seemed to have given a moment's thought to the institution which had made them rich and celebrated, nor to the feelings of the millions of people who had revered it and found these revelations painful and indeed shocking.

Elizabeth went on as usual, publicly serene but privately both furious and deeply troubled. The traditional ceremony for the celebration of her official birthday, the Trooping the Colour, went ahead with the Princess of Wales part of the family party on the Palace balcony for the RAF fly-past as if nothing had happened. Privately, however, both Elizabeth and Philip, who had been at pains not to take sides, rallied to Charles, and Philip wrote him a 'long and sympathetic letter' praising his 'saint-like fortitude'. At Royal Ascot the following week, Philip for the first time showed hostility towards Diana, refusing either to look at her or speak to her. In private, Elizabeth and her son discussed for the first time whether he should take the initiative and separate from his wife. He consulted Lord Goodman, a celebrated lawyer and 'fixer', about the implications of such a move, but for the moment did nothing. At Ascot the disgraced Sarah took her daughters to wave to their grandmother as the royal procession moved down the course before the races. Elizabeth waved but inwardly she must have felt despairing at yet another public manifestation of what the press now liked to call her 'dysfunctional' family. (On the following race day, Andrew loyally joined his wife and daughters on the rails.) The royal show went on as if nothing had happened, but behind the scenes the atmosphere could have been cut with a knife. Guests at lunch at the Castle noted that Elizabeth, unsurprisingly, seemed to be 'in a pretty bad temper'. There was an awkward atmosphere and before lunch the Queen stood alone with a semicircle of guests around her, none of whom were brought up to talk to her. With the exception of Blair Stewart Wilson, the Master of the Household, royal staff made no attempt to put the guests at their ease. When she did talk to her guests, Elizabeth was less than her usual gracious self and in the royal box at the races after lunch again no one spoke to her. At the end of the month the Waleses attended a dinner to celebrate the Queen's fortieth anniversary at which five British Prime Ministers were present and in August after a brief, disastrous attempt at a family holiday on the Greek millionaire John Latsis's yacht, they joined the family at Balmoral.

While the Waleses' marriage staggered on, superficially at least, fate was preparing another distasteful surprise for Elizabeth. On 20 August the *Daily Mirror* published compromising photographs of Sarah and John Bryan taken earlier that month while they were on holiday with Beatrice and Eugenie at a rented villa in the South of France, after which the term 'financial adviser' was to become the standard euphemism for something completely different. Amazingly, at Balmoral nothing was said at breakfast when Andrew, forewarned by his wife, went down to face his family, the newspapers with their blaring headlines and explicit photographs scattered over the table. Elizabeth and Philip digested them alone upstairs, before Sarah went in for a meeting with Elizabeth at 9.30. Elizabeth, feeling utterly let down, was, Sarah recalled, 'furious'. While the general public was shocked that she could have carried on in that way with her lover in the presence of her children, at the Balmoral family gatherings it was as if nothing had happened. Sarah remained for a further three days, sitting in her usual place beside Andrew at meals; but for her it would be her last holiday in the bosom of the royal family. Andrew, in the face of incontrovertible evidence that Bryan and his wife had deceived him, behaved as the gentleman that his wife's two ex-lovers emphatically were not. As John Bryan admitted, 'Andrew really showed his colours. He was just as supportive as could be . . .'

Four days later the *Sun* delivered another body-blow with the publication of the 'Squidgygate' tapes. These recordings of a telephone conversation on New Year's Eve 1989 between Diana at Sandringham and James Gilbey (a well-connected sports-car dealer) in his car in an Oxfordshire lay-by made clear Diana's feelings about her husband and her resentment about her treatment as an outsider after all she had done 'for that fucking family'. The *Sun* censored parts of the tape including references to a media personality and some of the more explicitly sexual innuendo, but what remained (added to what was subsequently published elsewhere) implied what amounted to an affair or 'heavy petting'. Gilbey's relationship with Diana ended with the publication of the tape; he proved to be one of a number of men with whom Diana consoled herself as a result of her husband's neglect and then strategically discarded. The Squidgygate tapes (named after Gilbey's pet name for Diana, 'Squidgy') made no difference to the state of her marriage, although they did apparently shock Charles.

Elizabeth, faced with the worst revelations about the family's private life since the scandal of George IV and Queen Caroline over one hundred and seventy years previously, had decided on a policy of containment. She hoped against hope that the marriage could be patched up enough to hobble along in public at least and to save the monarchy from the pain and disgrace of the heir to the throne separating from his wife and the mother of his children. While at Balmoral, she persuaded the couple to continue, at least in public, to keep up appearances and go ahead with plans for a joint visit to South Korea scheduled for October. At first Diana refused point-blank to consider it. Charles then bluntly told her that she would have to come up with her own explanation why she was not going; at this she backed down, saying that as the Queen had asked her to go, she would. In the event, the tour was an absolute disaster; the entire attention of the world's press was focused on the state of the Waleses' marriage and it was only too evident from the couple's body-language that they could not bear each other's company. The policy of 'keeping up appearances' had gone on too long and had served only to prolong their agony and the media interest in it.

Morton's book had blown a hole in this policy so devastating that it made the end inevitable. It foundered also because of the absolute refusal of both sides to consider any form of reconciliation. A churchman called in to attempt to bring the couple together said that he had never met a case in which an estranged husband and wife had been so adamantly against it. Elizabeth was always cautious and conservative in her reactions to situations; her advisers, who should have been more aware of the real state of affairs between the couple, followed her lead. With hindsight, the policy had proved a disaster; it would have been better if Elizabeth had sat down with the couple years earlier and told them 'either get on together or lead officially separate lives'. At least it would have stopped the steady trickle and then the flood of media stories about the marriage. As it was, the couple went on torturing each other. Diana would taunt Charles with her popularity, 'It's me they want to see, not you', and tell him, 'You're never going to be King.' He would riposte that he didn't want to live with her and refuse to accept the blame for her jealousy: 'I'm not the first Prince of Wales who's had a mistress.' Elizabeth and Philip, none the less, went on hoping that something could be salvaged; the Duke indulged in his habit of writing personal things he could not bring himself to say face to face on his laptop computer. His letters to Diana since the Balmoral discussions were, apparently, helpful and constructive.

Nothing helped; Diana wanted 'out' and the space to live her own life. The Prince simply could not bear being with her. It was, as so often, to be a quarrel over the children that brought things to a head in November 1992. Charles had arranged a shooting-party at Sandringham to coincide with the Princes' exeat from their school, Ludgrove. A week beforehand, he discovered that the Princess refused to go to Sandringham and intended to take the boys to Windsor to stay with their grandmother instead. In the circumstances, however, it does seem odd that he should think such a weekend a good plan; it might be his idea of a perfect way to spend his boys' days out, but, knowing Diana's dislike of Sandringham and shooting, he could hardly have expected her to share it. 'Dismayed by this news,' the Prince's biographer writes, 'the Prince had a long conversation with his mother, after which the Princess came under strong pressure to reconsider her refusal.' Her answer was that under no circumstances would she go and that if she could not stay with the boys at Windsor, she would go to Highgrove and take the children with her. The Prince, for his part, was equally adamant in refusing to cancel his shooting-party. It was the moment of truth: 'Eventually, when it became clear that she was not going to relent, he snapped. Unable to see any future in a relationship conducted on those terms, he decided he had no choice but to ask his wife for a legal separation,' Dimbleby wrote.

Friday, 20 November 1992, the date of the Prince's cherished shooting weekend at Sandringham, was to be a fateful day in more ways than one. On the morning of that Friday, clouds of smoke could be seen rising from the area of Windsor Castle near the Queen's private chapel; within hours the blaze, started by a restorer's lamp which had set a curtain alight, was roaring almost out of control, running through wall-spaces, licking and devouring the beams in St George's Hall, setting the sky alight with a huge red glow which silhouetted the ancient towers against the night sky. To those watching the scene on television, it seemed almost unbelievable: Windsor Castle, the symbol of the monarchy, on fire. Fortunately Prince Andrew was there and with his naval training organised a successful rescue operation. As a result, very few works of art were lost, but the damage to the Castle and particularly to the great St George's Hall was serious. Elizabeth was at Buckingham Palace celebrating her forty-fifth wedding anniversary (without her husband, who was in the Argentine). Alerted by Andrew she rushed down to Windsor, where, a small, bowed figure in headscarf and mackintosh, she inspected the dreadful scars in the heart of her childhood home. She was, in her son's words, 'absolutely devastated'. She loved Windsor more than anywhere else; for her it was particularly associated with that happy childhood which now seemed like a lost paradise. It was not just memories that had been destroyed but a part of the royal heritage which had been entrusted to her; the fire hurt her not only as a person but as monarch, enhancing the sense of bewilderment and even of failure which she felt in the face of the ruin of her children's marriages. Charles drove over from Sandringham on Friday night to inspect the damage, but returned to join his house-party in the early hours of Saturday. With her husband in the Argentine and her family – apart from Andrew –

elsewhere, Elizabeth was left alone to contemplate a disaster which was not only real but symbolic.

The reaction of the public to the television statement by the Secretary of State for the Department of National Heritage, Peter Brooke, pledging public money to pay for the damage, then estimated at £60 million, was a further slap in the face. The *Daily Mail*, a widely read, middle-of-the-road newspaper, which usually opposed the anti-monarchist line taken by the Murdoch press, voiced the general feeling in a front-page editorial headed, 'Why the Queen must listen', asking: 'Why should the populace, many of whom have had to make huge sacrifices during the bitter recession, have to pay the total bill for Windsor Castle, when the Queen, who pays no taxes, contributes next to nothing?' On 26 November, six days after the Windsor fire, Thatcher's successor as Prime Minister, John Major, made a surprise announcement in the House of Commons that the Queen and the Prince of Wales had volunteered to pay tax on their private incomes and that the Queen would reimburse the Civil List annuities to five of the royal family – Princess Anne (who had since 1987 enjoyed the title of the Princess Royal, customarily bestowed on the eldest daughter of the sovereign), the Duke of York, Prince Edward, Princess Margaret and Princess Alice, Duchess of Gloucester – who would be paid from the revenues of the Duchy of Lancaster. As a public relations exercise the affair could hardly have been worse handled, the timing of the announcement making it seem as if Elizabeth had been panicked by the public reaction into agreeing to pay tax.

The reality was rather different, although the essential point was true: that Elizabeth was agreeing to pay in order to deflect criticism of the monarchy and was indeed responding to public opinion. The issue of the tax exemption on Elizabeth's private income had been gathering strength, fuelled by Britain's bitterest recession since the 1930s, since the last settlement of the Civil List in 1990. A hostile editorial in the Murdoch-owned *Sunday Times* written on 10 February 1991 by the republican editor, Andrew Neil, at the time of the Gulf War, attacked the behaviour of the younger royals for carrying on a privileged lifestyle financed by the public while the British people were losing their jobs and homes and, some of them, even their lives at war for their country. A *World in Action* TV programme in June 1991, based substantially on the work of Philip Hall, whose book on the subject, *Royal Fortune*, was published in January 1992, had revealed the circumstances of the royal tax exemption. Hall's important argument based on ten years' research was that there was no justifiable historical basis for the exemption and that income tax had been paid by all Elizabeth's predecessors except her father, who had been the first monarch to enjoy such exemption. It had not been until late 1991 that Elizabeth, in response to the rising strength of public opinion and, apparently, urged on by Charles, had authorised her advisers to begin discussions with the Treasury on the subject. According to a senior courtier, the decision that she should pay tax on her private income and remove all members of the royal family except for the Queen Mother and the Duke of Edinburgh from the Civil List – the Prince of Wales had his own income from the Duchy of Cornwall – had been taken in April 1992, but the Palace and the Treasury had moved extremely slowly, intending to announce the final arrangements early the following year. The result was that they were caught out not once but twice. Palace dilatoriness made it look as though Elizabeth was moving only in response to pressure from the Prime Minister when he visited Balmoral in September – that indeed was the impression gained from various leaks and floaters in the press. Then came the Windsor fire and the hostile public reaction to the Heritage Secretary's pledge that the loyal public would pay up.

Four days after the fire Elizabeth made a speech at London's Guildhall at a luncheon given to mark her fortieth (and most inauspicious) year on the throne. She was suffering from a heavy cold and the after-effects of the smoke and fumes at Windsor. She looked – and sounded – sad as she made a plea for understanding, although the formal language in which her speech was couched lessened its impact, as did the fact that, instead of making a direct appeal, she read it from a paper. (Unlike her daughter, the Princess Royal, or her husband, Elizabeth has never been able to, or felt confident enough to, memorise a speech.) 'I am quite sure that most people try to do their jobs as best they can, even if the result is not always entirely successful,' she said. '. . . There can be no doubt . . . that criticism is good for people and institutions that are part of public life . . . But we are all part of the same fabric of our national society and that scrutiny, by one part or another, can be just as effective if it is made with a touch of gentleness, good humour and understanding . . . This sort of questioning can also act, and so it should do, as an effective agent of change.' The speech also contained veiled but bitter allusions to the press, which confirmed suspicions that the 'Queen's advisers' were still not taking the media seriously as the voice of the public; it might also have been better received had the announcement of the Queen's decision to pay tax been made earlier instead of only hinted at as it was in the speech. The *Daily Mail* editorialised:

> We sympathise with the Queen. Of course we do. But these are hard times for most people. Many of them have had a truly horrid year. They have lost their livelihoods. Even been driven from their homes. The Queen should pay some tax on her income. And fewer members of her family should be a charge on the Civil List. She should offer to contribute to restoring the fabric of Windsor Castle . . . If we read it right, this intense and complex speech is not only a cri de coeur, but a prologue for change.

It was dubbed the 'annus horribilis' speech: '1992 is not a year I shall look back on with undiluted pleasure,' Elizabeth said. 'In the words of one of my more sympathetic correspondents [her former Assistant Private Secretary, Sir Edward Ford], it has turned out to be an annus horribilis . . .' Sir Edward, a classical scholar, had invented the phrase to distinguish 1992 from 'annus mirabilis', which is used to describe a particularly outstanding year as the Queen's fortieth anniversary might have been expected to be. The *Sun* translated it into the vernacular: 'One's Bum Year'. It was a low point in her life, not just because of what had happened with one disaster after another, but because of the lack of gratitude, even derision, with which her forty years of dedication seemed to have been crowned.

Elizabeth had moved in response to public feeling but she had moved too late. The public impression was given that the decision had been hastily forced upon her as a result of public outcry and the Windsor fire. At the same time John Major told Parliament that the National Audit Office would be looking into expenditure on the royal palaces, something which the Palace had hitherto striven to avoid. For once, Elizabeth's cautious instincts had let her down; by moving too slowly in response to public feeling, she had allowed a head of steam to build up and a hue and cry about the expense of the monarchy to develop which might have been avoided by swifter action. Part of her unwillingness to move on the income tax issue had been reverence for her father. George VI, who had inherited the throne in unusual circumstances after the Abdication, which had entailed his brother's removal of large sums and pay-offs, had been left 'virtually without two beans to rub together', according to one of the royal courtiers. He it was who, in order to ensure the future of the monarchy, had negotiated the exemption with the Treasury under the sympathetic eye of Neville Chamberlain in 1937. And it was he, in effect, who had impressed on his daughter that she should retain that exemption if she wanted to maintain the independent position of the monarchy.

On 11 February 1993 the Lord Chamberlain, Lord Airlie, took the unprecedented step of holding a press briefing on the new fiscal arrangements for the royal family, while Michael Peat, for whom the new title of Finance Director had been created, announced them on television. The main thrust of the statement was that the Queen and the Prince of Wales had agreed to pay income tax and capital gains tax *on a voluntary basis* (author's italics) on their private income, including the Queen's Privy Purse income and the Prince of Wales's Duchy of Cornwall revenues after the deduction of expenses. In one important area, however – that of inheritance tax – the Queen was exempted. Although Airlie stated that her estate would be subject to this tax 'as a matter of general principle' (whatever that might mean in the circumstances), 'bequests left Sovereign to Sovereign will be exempt'. When John Major announced this in the Commons, he said that this was to prevent the royal assets being 'salami-sliced' away. Although it was glossed over, the exemption was in fact crucial; without it the royal family and their way of life would not survive the end of Elizabeth's reign. The Lord Chamberlain also promised increased public access to the royal collections and the setting up of a fund (self-generating through tourist income and not therefore publicly financed) for their maintenance. In April, in a further statement, he announced that restoration of Windsor Castle, estimated to cost between £30 and £40 million spread over five years, would be met without recourse to public funds, with 70 per cent envisaged as coming from the proceeds of opening Buckingham Palace and imposing charges for entrance to the Windsor precincts and the remainder from savings made on the annual grant-in-aid provided by the Department of National Heritage for the royal palaces.

The announcement was welcomed 'with relief by monarchists and grudgingly by commentators' – the timing of the whole initiative had given the unfortunate impression that it had been forced on the Palace by public opinion (which was substantially true). Critics continued to denounce the cost of the royal train, the Queen's Flight and the royal yacht and commented unfavourably on the royal family's 'lifestyle', which included 'expensive peregrinations between Buckingham Palace, Windsor Castle, Sandringham and Balmoral'. The next target for critics would be the cost of the grace-and-favour residences inhabited by royal pensioners and servants, a vulnerable area for Elizabeth since it was an important way in which she could keep her servants and retain their loyalty, now increasingly under threat from the siege of the tabloids.

It was an undoubted fact that, while criticism of the cost of the monarchy was a perennial problem for the Palace, the behaviour of the younger royals had brought it to the forefront. A Gallup poll published early in 1993 found that four out of five respondents thought 'too many members of the family lead an idle, jet-set kind of existence'. The monarchy, Rebecca West had once claimed, is 'a presentation of ourselves behaving well', which in the early 1990s the younger generation of the family manifestly was not. The real catalyst for the storm of criticism of the monarchy as an institution was the failure of the 'princely marriages'. 'None of this would have happened', bewailed an elderly former courtier, 'if the Wales marriage hadn't gone wrong.'

And on that particular front things were going from bad to worse. The day after Elizabeth's Guildhall speech the Prince and Princess of Wales agreed that separation was the only option. Elizabeth and the Prime Minister were consulted and it was agreed that the announcement should be made by the Prime Minister on 9 December. Although the grim facts of the marriage were already widely known or guessed at, the announcement, made in Parliament and carried on all the television networks, was still profoundly shocking:

It is announced from Buckingham Palace that, with regret, the Prince and Princess of Wales have decided to separate. Their Royal Highnesses have no plans to divorce and their constitutional positions are unaffected. This decision has been reached amicably and they will both continue to participate fully in the upbringing of their children.

Their Royal Highnesses will continue to carry out full and separate programmes of public engagements and will, from time to time, attend family occasions and national events together.

The Queen and the Duke of Edinburgh, though saddened, understand and sympathise with the difficulties that have led to this decision. Her Majesty and His Royal Highness particularly hope that the intrusions into the privacy of the Prince and Princess may now cease. They believe that a degree of privacy and understanding is essential if their Royal Highnesses are to provide a happy and secure upbringing for their children, while continuing to give a whole-hearted commitment to their public duties.

That said, the Prime Minister went ahead to underline that

> the decision to separate has no constitutional implications. The
> Succession to the Throne is unaffected by it; the children of the Prince
> and Princess retain their position in the line of succession; and there is
> no reason why the Princess of Wales should not be crowned Queen in
> due course. The Prince of Wales's succession as head of the Church of
> England is also unaffected.

The implications of this last statement brought a collective gasp
from the MPs who heard it, and no wonder. It was not merely papering
over the cracks but wallpapering them with fluffy flock. The idea that
the Princess of Wales, living apart from her husband and at daggers
drawn with him, might be crowned Queen Consort struck most people
as absurd. The bald statement that the Prince of Wales's succession as
head of the Church of England was also unaffected, although strictly
constitutionally correct, also required some swallowing and it was not
long before leading clerics came out publicly to say so. The Archbishop
of Canterbury, when officially consulted before the announcement,
had taken the following view:

> . . . a formal separation within marriage would be likely to win
> widespread understanding, as it would signal the importance of the
> institution of marriage and the seriousness of the marriage vows made
> before God. By putting that consideration above their emotions as
> individuals, the royal couple would be widely admired for their
> dedication to serving the public interest. According to the Archbishop,
> there were two important provisos: both parents would have to be seen
> to maintain close bonds with their children; and extra-marital love
> affairs that might be brought to public attention would need to be
> avoided. Assuming the conditions were met, then respect and
> gratitude, touched by sadness, would be widely shared sentiments in
> the Anglican communion.[5]

The sensational announcement overshadowed the wedding at Balmoral that month of the Princess Royal to Commander Tim Laurence.
Anne, apparently, had wanted to slip off quietly and get married at
Crathie, where, under the dispensation of the Church of Scotland, she
could, although a divorced person, marry in church. Her family,
including her mother, had been taken by surprise, Elizabeth, to her
daughter's embarrassment, learning of it only a week before from the

BBC ('Bloody press,' Anne is held to have exploded, 'you know what Mummy's like about surprises'). The Queen Mother had a house-party fixed for that date and had to leave her guests to fly up to Scotland and back at short notice. The Castle itself was closed. Anne then moved with her husband to a flat in the uncosy anonymity of the huge blocks of flats called Dolphin Square on Chelsea Embankment. Since Laurence had held the relatively humble position of equerry at Buckingham Palace and incurred a certain amount of jealousy and hostility over his romance with the Princess, it would have been awkward for the couple to start their married life 'at the office'. Discreet, quiet, yet with a will of his own, Laurence is liked by the family. He is 'terribly nice and frightfully kind', a royal relation said.

Unfortunately for the Prince and his family, within weeks of the announcement, the leaking of yet another taped conversation, this time between the Prince and Mrs Parker Bowles, made it all too clear that the Archbishop's second proviso as to the avoidance of extra-marital love affairs was certainly not being met. The conversation, curiously, dated from December 1989, just a few weeks before the Squidgygate tape. This one was labelled, inevitably, 'Camillagate', and its effects on the public who read it was immeasurably greater. While Squidgygate may have slightly dented Diana's madonna image, the Camillagate tape made it quite clear that Diana's fears about Camilla being her husband's mistress were completely justified. While to the sophisti-cated Charles's dirty talk about living inside his lover's trousers or being a Tampax appeared pathetic and puerile, the backbone of middle Britain was shaken to the core. The mums and dads in the provinces, the traditional support on which the monarchy had relied, hated it. The man at the *Mirror* whose job it was to transcribe the tape told his colleagues, 'This tape is going to stop Charles ever becoming King.' It was going to take a lot of living down. Much hypocritical nonsense was talked about Charles's adultery making him unfit to be King, but to many people it did seem that Charles, like his great-uncle, Edward VIII, had put his private life before his public duty in continuing his relationship with Mrs Parker Bowles.

For Elizabeth, it was a nightmare. The war between the Waleses recreated the fears of her father when he found himself at war with the Windsors – 'two camps', as Wallis had described it. The fall-out represented a continuing danger to the image of the monarchy as the two sides sought to win points against each other through the media. Elizabeth's concern was to minimise the damage. 'Considered inaction'

has always been her watchword. Diana represented a huge problem.
Since Camillagate she enjoyed the backing of the majority of the
British public, who saw her as the wronged wife. With her beauty, her
modern attitudes, her caring rapport with the sick, her glamour and
her refusal to kow-tow to the Palace, she represented a walking
reproach to the family. Like the Queen Mother, she has that invaluable
commodity lacking in 'real' royalty, the common touch. Attempts by
royal officials to downgrade her or limit her exposure merely made
them look ridiculous; through the newspapers, Diana could appeal to
the public over their heads. Elizabeth's is too cool a head to support
any kind of dirty tricks campaign. 'The Queen sees that she mustn't
be undermined,' a courtier said. Diana, for her part, is too clever to
defy Elizabeth, who holds the purse strings and has the ultimate
sanction over the whereabouts of the Waleses' children. She knows
that she can telephone her mother-in-law without interference from
the Private Secretaries, and the two women do talk. None the less,
Diana remains a loose cannon, unpredictable and with the capacity to
cause immense damage should she so wish. 'They're all terrified of her
at the Palace,' a courtier said, and, apparently, unable to control her.
When she made her famous statement 'withdrawing' from public life
in December 1993, she insisted on making it as dramatic and public as
possible despite all the efforts by Elizabeth and even the Prime
Minister to persuade her to make it low-key. The best-selling novelist
Jeffrey Archer was drafted in to make sure that it kept within limits.
In the end, Diana paid tribute to the 'support and understanding of
the Queen and the Duke of Edinburgh', conspicuously refraining from
mentioning her husband. The inference was therefore drawn that this
too was somehow his fault, that he and his officials had forced her out
of public life.

    Bereft of advice, except from her friends in the media and a circle
of rich London businessmen, Diana began to score own goals.
Some newspapers, jealous of her close connections with the *Daily
Mail*'s Richard Kay, began to target her. The *Sun* published photographs of her at a rendezvous with Kay captioned 'Two-faced Diana',
and the *News of the World* revealed the story of her 'nuisance calls' to
Oliver Hoare. Her relationship with James Hewitt was revealed in
Princess in Love. Photographs of her exercising in a West London gym
were published in the *Mirror* and resulted in a lawsuit by the Princess
which mysteriously never came to court. More photographs, of the
Princess sunbathing topless in the south of Spain, were bought up by

the loyal proprietor of *Hello* (allegedly at the instigation of the Palace), but while Diana told Richard Kay of her 'utter humiliation' over the pictures and that it had felt 'like a rape', the rumours in the *Hello* circle were that Diana did not appreciate their act of generosity. 'The Princess of Wales was furious,' a leading editor said. 'She didn't want us to buy the photographs because she wanted to be seen – she's obsessed with her body.' Pressure from the media on both the Waleses was, a courtier said, driving them mad. The Waleses' children, particularly Prince William, apparently blame the media for their parents' separation.

It was having its effect on the senior members of the family. Even Elizabeth, who invited Diana to Sandringham for Christmas 1993, was seen to be 'fuming' when the photographers massed to take pictures of Diana and packed up as soon as they had done so, ignoring the rest of the family. Although normally uninterested in publicity, she now took their attitude as a slight. Inside the house the atmosphere was tense and quarrelsome. At tea over Victorian tables loaded with delicious cakes and scones, there were family spats. Charles, the proud father, boasted how William had shot twenty pheasants. 'That's rubbish,' shouted Andrew. 'I know it was only fifteen.' Philip, who in the wake of the Waleses' separation had written his son some tough and unpalatable letters, for once leapt to Charles's defence: 'Andrew, why do you always have to be so tiresome?' Easter that year had been a low point for Elizabeth. For a person who so rarely revealed her feelings, she made it clear at small private dinner-parties how depressed she was by the family situation and its repercussions. By the following Easter, 1994, when things seemed to be quietening down or at least the missiles were not coming over the battlements at such regular intervals, her courtiers noticed a distinct lightening of her spirits. She was not to be given much respite.

Elizabeth was concerned about the effect which the failure of his marriage and the tabloid persecution of him as a result of it was having upon Charles. It seemed to people, both friends and acquaintances, who met him over the following months that he was self-obsessed, thrashing about within himself to find an explanation for what had gone so horribly wrong. Elizabeth and Philip were themselves searching for an answer, wondering whether they were to blame for the failure of not just one, but all of their children's marriages. 'What did we do wrong?' they asked friends, and again, 'What have we done to become such bogeymen to our daughters-in-law?' The answer that

Charles eventually came up with, or rather his authorised biographer Jonathan Dimbleby did with his approval, was the one which was to hurt Elizabeth most as a parent.

The Prince was desperate to explain himself, to win back the approval of the public which he had so spectacularly lost; the method he deployed first was to use television to appeal to the people over the heads of the tabloids. The image-maker he chose was Jonathan Dimbleby, son of the great presenter of the royal occasion, Richard Dimbleby. As an experienced television interviewer with impeccable 'green' credentials and a man who had once worked on the Windsor estate, Dimbleby seemed the perfect choice. He got on well with Richard Aylard and 'empathised' at once with the Prince himself. Over the next eighteen months he prepared a television documentary aimed to celebrate the Prince's twenty-fifth anniversary of his investiture as Prince of Wales.

The result, *Charles: The Private Man, the Public Role*, appeared on British television on 29 June 1994. Elizabeth had not been consulted over the project; her gut reaction and that of her friends and courtiers was that it was a mistake and that no good could be done by taking a high profile. Their opinion was that the sensible thing was to take the long view, to maintain a dignified silence and let time heal the wounds that had been caused. The Prince of Wales could do himself no good, they thought, by exposing himself on television. While he argued that he was taking a 'pro-active' stance, they thought he was letting the media dictate his agenda. Several of his advisers thought the same, including Camilla Parker Bowles, who begged him not to do it; one of them resigned over it. 'He's on a hiding to nothing' was the general opinion. The Prince is not a good television performer; his self-deprecating air and 'Windsorspeak' do not come across well in the age of the sound-bite. None the less, Dimbleby had done a sympathetic and expert job and his portrait of the Prince rang true. The programme was aimed at the young, the future King's constituency. The Prince was shown at his best as an environmental crusader, speaking articulately, passionately and without notes. With pop star Phil Collins at a holiday camp organised by his inner-city help organisation, the Prince's Trust, he appeared as a good communicator in contrast with his diffident television interview manner. The 'hook' of the programme was the Prince's response to Dimbleby's question about his marriage: 'Did you try to be faithful . . . ?' The Prince answered, 'until the marriage had irretrievably broken down'. The episode, with its painful confessional aspect, was aimed at stopping the continual speculation about his marriage and his affair with Camilla, whom he described as a 'dear friend' he would continue to see. Viewers responded favourably to the programme; press commentators who had indicated the opposite were forced to backtrack when street polls produced a 'thumbs-up' reaction to the Prince for his honesty and for his 'caring' image.

Elizabeth, however, who, her entourage claimed, 'had not watched the programme', and other commentators thought that the prince, in baring his soul as he had, had given hostages to fortune and not only with his confession of adultery, which was so vague in its timing as to be misleading. It was all very well for the Prince to complain about his concern for his sons' reading newspapers with 'Charles and Di' stories, but the programme revealed the Prince, immediately after being shown in father and son shots at Balmoral, as confessing to a television interviewer that he had been unfaithful to their mother. There had been other aspects which, as the future constitutional monarch, he should have avoided. An early sequence of the programme showed the Prince at one of his 'dreaded' programme meetings objecting to being asked to be present at the Royal Command Film Performance. Pulling a face, he said, 'I thought the Queen always did it.' The occasion is a traditional charity fund-raising event always patronised by royalty; the Prince's implication that it was too boring for him to attend was offensive to the organisers and raised a fundamental question as to what he thought he was there for anyway. It was a symptom of the Prince's increasing impatience with public duties which did not suit him and his failure to comprehend, as his mother did, that fulfilling these duties was one of the principal purposes of a monarchy. Perhaps the saddest, most revealing moment in the whole programme came when the Prince, asked by a little Malaysian boy, 'Who are you?', responded 'I wish I knew.'

From Elizabeth's point of view, the television programme had been bad enough but at least it seemed to have succeeded in its object of winning back some sympathy for the heir to the throne. Counteracting the tabloid image of him as a 'social dinosaur', Charles had presented himself as a man with a vision of the future and what he saw as a monarchy consonant with a changed Britain, as when he said he wanted to be known as 'Defender of Faith' (i.e. of all religious denominations in the United Kingdom) rather than 'Defender of the Faith' (limited to the Protestant faith in its Anglican, Church of England, form). Dimbleby followed up the television programme with a major biography of the Prince, which went far beyond being 'the book of the film'. He had already, on the Prince's recommendation, interviewed all his friends and confidants, taking statements on the subject of the Prince's marriage to be deposited in the royal archives. Camilla Parker Bowles did not co-operate on the book, nor, to her credit, did the Waleses' ex-nanny, Barbara Barnes, who refused to take sides despite an appeal by the Prince for her co-operation. Elizabeth was aware of the interviews, but when she discovered, as the book was nearing completion in September 1994, that the Prince had given Dimbleby access not only to all his correspondence and diaries but also to state papers without checking what they were, there was an explosion. She insisted that he take the papers back and ensure that Dimbleby did not have access to official material which he had no right to see. At Balmoral on his annual visit the Prince stayed with his grandmother at Birkhall. 'He'll only be coming here for one day,' Elizabeth remarked dryly; the day which Charles chose was the Ghillies' Ball, when there would be no occasion for a conversation with his mother.

The Prince of Wales: A Biography, finally published in November to a fanfare in the press and three weeks' serialisation in the *Sunday Times*, was an important book based on original material which under normal Palace conventions would not have been released until after Charles's death. But both its tenor and its timing could hardly have been worse from Elizabeth's point of view, hurting her in both her private and her public role. The serialisation, coming as it did on the eve of her visit to Russia, the first ever by a reigning British sovereign, diverted media attention from this historic royal event to sensational revelations with all the most controversial material lumped together. It was, of course, the Case for Charles and was intended as a heavyweight riposte to Andrew Morton's Case for Diana.

According to Dimbleby, blame for the unhappy state of the monarchy as a result of the failure of the Waleses' marriage could not be laid at Charles's door. In common with almost everyone since Philip Larkin wrote his memorable line, 'They fuck you up, your mum and dad', the Prince and Dimbleby blamed what Charles saw as inadequate parenting. His mother had been remote, his father a bully. Both of them had been 'unable or unwilling to proffer . . . the affection and appreciation' which Charles craved. His wife had been neurotic; one passage described an occasion when she had sat all day in Colborne's office 'her head bowed in silent despair'. Only Camilla Parker Bowles emerged with credit as, in the words of one reviewer, a kind of virginal Mills & Boon heroine: 'Her warmth, her lack of ambition or guile, her good humour and her gentleness endeared her to the household.' (But not, it should be said, to the British public; housewives spat at her when she stopped in her local supermarket.) Within months of the book's publication the Parker Bowles's twenty-year-old marriage ended. The Prince's initiative in making his TV confession had made it untenable.

It is terrible for any parent to be accused publicly of being a bad mother or father. Elizabeth had done her best in a difficult situation – to be a mother and a head of state, head of the Commonwealth and head of a household is a unique experience. She has had to put her job first and the reason why she has been so successful at it is because she not only enjoys it but also because she is a dedicated, self-contained personality. Charles may have felt excluded from areas of his mother's life and subject to the rigorous standards expected of the heir to the throne, but, except at boarding-school, he had been surrounded by love, from his nannies and his grandmother, let alone his mother's courtiers like Lady Susan Hussey and Martin Charteris, who were extremely fond of him. The fact that there was a certain amount of truth in Charles's self-pitying account did not excuse it. Elizabeth is good with small children but not with adults. She is not a hugger or a communicator on a personal level. Out of consideration for her adored husband in his difficult position as consort, she over-compensated by allowing him absolutely free rein in the upbringing of his son. But the inescapable fact that she is the Queen sets her apart from everyone, even her own children. Charles was a victim of his royal birthright; he seems unwilling to accept, as his mother has, that there is a price to pay for privilege and the greater the privilege the higher the price. Charles's siblings, Anne, Andrew and Edward, were outraged by this public portrayal of their parents and told him so. Outwardly, Elizabeth put a brave face upon it. No one seeing her in Moscow could have thought her less than delighted to be there. In London on her return one foreign ambassador on taking his formal leave of her found her laughing, joking and seemingly without a care in the world.[6] Only those who knew her well could diagnose how wounded she felt.

Predictably, almost exactly a year later, the Princess of Wales determined to have her say on television and to put her case to the nation over the heads not only of her own advisers but also of Buckingham Palace. Elizabeth learned of the planned broadcast only shortly before the BBC announced it for the following week. (The date of the announcement, 14 November, was an unwelcome forty-seventh birthday surprise for Charles, on an official visit to Tokyo. Photographs showed him cutting a celebratory cake, his face expressing total dismay.) The broadcast went out on the BBC's flagship current affairs programme, *Panorama*, on Monday, 20 November 1995, yet another unhappy wedding anniversary for Elizabeth. The interview by the BBC's Martin Bashir (the BBC had naturally been chosen as the vehicle since Charles's programme had featured on the opposition ITV) revealed the Princess, unlike her husband, to be a consummate television performer, but, like him, she was in confessional mode. She confirmed all the facts in Morton's book – the bulimia, the depression, her anguish over Camilla Parker Bowles. She had been the victim of attempts by her 'enemies' to isolate her, to represent her as 'a basket case'. Like Charles, she confessed publicly to adultery – with James Hewitt (although she denied other affairs). Defiantly she announced (referring to herself in the third person) that she 'would not go quietly', that she did not want a divorce and that she intended to reign not officially but, to use a phrase borrowed from the works of her step-grandmother, Barbara Cartland, as 'Queen of Hearts'. The interview was a public relations triumph for Diana, but yet another family embarrassment for Elizabeth. Diana had publicly cast doubts on whether Charles was fit to be King in an obvious bid to promote Prince William as next in line to the throne, a proposal which, if taken seriously, would strike at the heart of the hereditary monarchy. Elizabeth, with the welfare of the future of the monarchy and her Wales grandchildren at heart, decided on a policy of containment and conciliation as far as Diana was concerned; in line with that, Buck-ingham Palace announced its willingness to offer support to the Princess and have talks with her on her proposed role as roving ambassador. In return, Diana made it clear that for her children's sake she would join the family party at Sandringham for Christmas. Later she changed her mind and rejected Elizabeth's invitation.

Thus far Elizabeth had been determined not to become personally involved in the Waleses' war nor to be seen to take sides. She still saw both her estranged daughters-in-law and spoke to them on the telephone. But ultimately for her the monarchy must come first. Much as it went against the grain for her, she reluctantly came to the decision that a divorce would be the most sensible way to end the painful public battle between Charles and Diana that had done so much damage to the image of the institution to which she had devoted her life. After three years' separation, the Waleses showed no signs of either reconciliation or of either of them taking steps to initiate a divorce. With the situation in danger of spinning out of control, Elizabeth finally took the initiative. Just before Christmas 1995 she wrote separately to both Charles and Diana advising them that they must begin divorce proceedings. In order to avoid any misunderstandings, the Palace let it be known that she had done so. In not only countenancing but actually initiating the divorce of the heir to the throne, she was taking the monarchy a long way down the road towards adaptation to the modern world.

Elizabeth R

'With the monarchy here, it is a little like Solomon's temple. There is much to be penetrated before you get to the centre – long passageways, both literal and figurative, and it is an elaborate circumstance for an outsider ... It's unusual, and there's the protocol, there are courtiers, long passageways, carpets and chandeliers, enormous rooms and guards. That is part of the requirement and mystique of royalty. And by the time you actually hack your way through all of this and get to the centre of it, it can be a pretty intimidating thing. And what is so wonderful about the Queen is that when you do get through all of this and get to the centre she's a perfectly delightful person – natural, funny, interested, professional ...'

Raymond G. H. Seitz, former Ambassador
to the Court of St James's[1]

Buckingham Palace stands, dauntingly huge and elephant grey, at an aloof distance from the high iron railings against which the tourists press. The rows of windows give nothing away; only the presence or not of the royal standard on its roof-top flagpole indicates whether Elizabeth is in residence. At the gate one of two policemen checks your identity and your appointment by telephone with someone within. Set in the ground behind them, an iron flange is raised unobtrusively, concealed with red gravel, a protection against terrorist attack. (In Elizabeth's private apartments the windows are covered by hideous ruched net curtains, designed to catch the glass splinters if a bomb exploded. These are the everyday realities of her life.) Once you are passed, the flange sinks back into the ground and you are waved through to the Privy Purse Entrance, where the red carpet starts and footmen stand ready to usher you into the waiting-room furnished with beige silk wall-hangings, gilt chairs covered in a lime-green material recognisable as the work of a distinctly establishment decorator. On the walls are two handsome Victorian paintings by William Frith – *Life at the Seaside* and *Departure, Paddington Station*. Unsurprisingly, since this is Elizabeth's territory, however remote from her it may be, there is a horse picture, *Arab Stallion*, by Sperling, 1843. There is a selection of broadsheet newspapers, but no tabloids.

Outside on the hall table neatly furled umbrellas are laid out in a row. Even when the temperature outside is rising towards the eighties by 11 a.m. the umbrellas will still be there; on rainy days they will be spread open round the floor like black mushrooms. Symbolically, their permanent presence could signify that the Palace is always ready for a rainy day. They also convey the message that it is the last bastion of the English gentleman. Waved by Neville Chamberlain at Munich, carried by Lord Halifax on a visit to Hitler at Berchtesgaden, the umbrella which once ruled the world even now still symbolises Whitehall, the machine of government with which the Palace is closely linked. Elizabeth is the constitutional cog in the workings of government; together, her Private Secretary, the Prime Minister's Private Secretary and the Secretary to the Cabinet are known as 'the Golden Triangle'. They are the three men who really know what is going on in the political world.

Elizabeth, although she has no real political power, is the Queen Bee at the centre of this Alice in Wonderland world of passages and mirrors. No ordinary member of the public will reach her inner sanctum except through the carefully controlled access of the television cameras, most recently in the television film *EIIR*, made for the BBC by Ed Mirzoeff and scripted by Antony Jay (who also wrote *Royal Family*). The official 'hook' for the programme was Elizabeth's ill-fated fortieth anniversary and, although Sir William Heseltine, as Private Secretary, was involved in the original discussions with the BBC (as he had been over *Royal Family* when Press Secretary), the thrust of the film was entirely different and reflected the changes which had overtaken the monarchy's relationship with the people in the intervening twenty or so years. Switching understandably from the focus on the family, the Palace wanted this film to put across the range of the sovereign's activities. Put crudely, against the background of the Civil List furore and the rising tide of republican grumbling the film was intended to show the people what the monarchy was for and how they were getting value for their money.

The problem about featuring Elizabeth in her role as constitutional monarch is that the British Constitution, being unwritten and based

largely on precedents, is almost inexplicable and certainly not visually
in a popular film. *EIIR*, therefore, concentrated on Elizabeth herself
in her role as head of state, receiving ambassadors, pinning on medals,
discussing the Gulf War with John Major. (Talking of her audiences
with her Prime Ministers, she says: 'they unburden themselves – tell
one what's going on – sometimes one can help – one's a sort of sponge
– Occasionally you can put your point of view which they hadn't seen
from that angle...') She is seen posing for one of the hundred
portraits painted of her since her accession, putting on the style with a
state visit to Windsor for President Walesa of Poland, peering from an
army helicopter over rainswept Belfast, invisible under the famous
'Hat of State' on the White House lawn, where the speaker's lectern
had been set for the much taller President Bush. (Elizabeth's speech
to the Houses of Congress two days later was made by her opening
crack, 'I hope you can all see me today...') Later on the same 1991
state visit, she is shown at a banquet on *Britannia* with the Reagans.
Nancy looks anguished, perhaps fearful that poor failing old Ron will
make a gaffe, but in the end it is Elizabeth who, somewhat unguard-
edly, makes a remark about the impossible burdens the welfare state
puts on democracies, a view which has distinct political overtones. As
a constitutional monarch, Elizabeth is supposedly impartial and apolitical. This is why her Privy Counsellors (who include all her leading
ministers, past and present) are sworn to secrecy and are supposed not
to reveal the content of their conversations with her. 'It is a fundamental condition of royal influence that it remains private,' a recent
constitutional authority stated.[2] It is for this reason that the Palace
presents such a consistently negative attitude towards 'outsiders'. One
former Press Secretary remarked of the Press Office that it was the 'no
comment' office.

An unusual feature of this film and one which presents Elizabeth
as a person rather than a puppet is that she does the voice-overs in
a conversational tone unlike the stilted sounds we are accustomed
to hear on Christmas broadcast or occasions like the State Opening
of Parliament. She is pictured opening letters – she gets 200–300 a
day:

> Being rather remote it gives one an idea of what's worrying people and
> how they think I can help [she says], and sometimes I can help . . . pass
> things on to the right authorities or organisations. I've always had the
> feeling that people are writing to me and I like to see what they're

writing to me about. There is a feeling that the buck stops here . . . A man wrote that I was the only person who could stop the circle he was in – I rather liked that . . .

Elizabeth is fascinated by ordinary family situations. On shoots at Balmoral she will often sit beside a soldier from one of the Scottish regiments assigned to protection duty there, who also act as beaters, and question him about his life. The soldiers, down-to-earth Scots often from the slum estates of Glasgow, have no hesitation about telling her. Later on, at dinner, she will startle an officer from the same regiment by expressing her concern about Private X's wife or girlfriend.

She is thirsty for information; she likes to *know*. She can ask virtually anyone she likes in for a private conversation. 'Audiences are my way of meeting people without anyone else listening,' she says, 'and that gives one a broad picture of what's going on either in Government or the Civil Service. They feel they can say what they like and that's the basis of my information.' She is seen at work signing remissions of prison sentences. It is not merely a formality for her – she is interested in the circumstances and asks about them: 'Oh,' she will say, 'these are about Strangeways [a much-publicised prison riot] . . .' Investitures are another way for her to meet people. While the protocol for knighthood is often complicated – rehearsed beforehand with the stool on which the recipient is to kneel before Her Majesty, he is told, 'Grasp the handle with your right hand, stand on your left leg and bend your right knee on to the stool. Afterwards, the Queen's handshake is the signal your time's up' – for Elizabeth, it is not just an antiquated formality but another chance for her to glimpse a different world. 'I'm always fascinated by people who come and the things they've done,' she says.

Sometimes, however, her queenly slip shows. At Windsor Castle, President Walesa, the former electrician from Gdansk, arrives among the panoply of a carriage procession up the Long Walk to the Castle, preceded by the Household Cavalry, in immaculate uniform, booted, spurred and wearing gleaming helmets with nodding plumes. Elizabeth seems surprised that Walesa, once accustomed to life in a tiny, crowded flat in a tower block, should find Windsor Castle so big ('so sweet', she tells Princess Anne), and equally that a man brought up behind the Iron Curtain in Communist Poland should speak 'only two words of English'. When President Walesa and his wife come in to the room where the entire royal family is assembled, however, she treats him as head of state to head of state and there is no formality over the introductions: 'My mother . . .' When Prince Michael of Kent attempted – rather tactlessly – to tell Walesa in Russian, 'I don't speak Polish, I only speak Russian but they're pretty close,' Elizabeth tells him crisply, 'Stop showing off.'

A 'dine and sleep' at Windsor in the spring of 1991, the royal equivalent of a house-party, is shown. The guests include the former Labour leader, Neil Kinnock, and his wife Glenys. Elizabeth is filmed showing the party the treasures of the Royal Library after dinner. She pulls out an edition of J. M. Barrie – 'We used to have tea there when we were small children. He was the most wonderful story-teller . . .' They look at a volume of Queen Victoria's diaries, rewritten and bowdlerised by her prudish youngest daughter, Princess Beatrice. Elizabeth confesses that she too keeps a diary ('but not as detailed'). An unfortunate bishop gushes, 'You write it in your own hand?' She looks surprised, an eyebrow is raised, 'Yes. I can't write it in any other way . . .'

Bishops are very much a part of Elizabeth's official life as constitutional monarch. As sovereign she is supreme Governor of the Church of England, the established church. She appoints, on the advice of the Prime Minister, the archbishops and diocesan bishops who take an oath of allegiance to her on their appointment and pay homage to her after their consecration. In actual fact nominations for bishoprics are made by a Church body, the Crown Appointments Committee, which submits two names to the Prime Minister, who makes his choice (or can ask for other names to be submitted). He then submits it to the sovereign. Elizabeth takes a good deal of interest in church affairs and, according to a recent authority, was dismayed by Mrs Thatcher's promotion in 1981 of Graham Leonard over John Habgood as Bishop of London. She apparently went to the length of contacting the Archbishop of Canterbury, Dr Runcie, to see if it could be reconsidered and was 'told politely, "No."'[3] Constitutionally there is nothing she can do if a Prime Minister submits a name she is not happy with, but, as she told a dean of St Paul's, 'I can always say that I should like more information. That is an indication that the Prime Minister will not miss.' According to Kenneth Rose, writing in 1985, there have been at least two occasions in recent years when Elizabeth has used this technique over controversial appointees.[4] And when it came, moreover, to an appointment closer to home, that of a successor to the retiring Dean of Windsor, the clergyman closest to the royal family, she successfully circumvented the choice of the then Prime Minister, Ted Heath, by consulting the outgoing Dean and putting forward his suggestion, The Rt Rev. Michael Mann.

The Home Secretary is obliged to attend the swearing-in of bishops when the bishop kneels and puts his hands out to be clasped by the Queen while the Home Secretary recites the oath of allegiance. 'It's very complicated,' a former Home Secretary said, 'and if you want to trip the bishop up you whiz through it. It's very Erastian in sentiment and can't have changed much since Henry VIII's day – it knocks out both the Pope and God in two phrases: "I . . . renouncing all foreign princes and prelates [i.e. the Pope] acknowledge that I hold the said bishopric in spirituality [i.e. not from God] and temporality only from Your Majesty . . ."' Elizabeth is very conventional in her religion; when the new prayer book was substituted for the old Book of Common Prayer, she accepted it, but in her heart of hearts she prefers the old version; it is used in Sandringham Church on the Sundays when she is there and Scripture readings are taken from the old Bible and not the modern version. Four different bishops are invited to preach at Sandringham in January when Elizabeth is there and it is noticeable that the less orthodox tendency appear only when she is not. Although not a great communicant (usually only on the big festival days of Easter, Christmas and Whitsun), she is attentive and sincere when in church. When at Windsor she goes to eleven o'clock service in the Private Chapel in the Great Park near the Royal Lodge every Sunday and then back to drinks and usually lunch with the Queen Mother. Philip has become more serious and interested in religion over the last thirty years. He is 'much less sarcastic, more tolerant and prepared to listen', a clergyman said. With Elizabeth, Philip was deeply involved in the setting-up of St George's House as a Centre for Christian Consultation, a religious 'think-tank' for laymen, clergy and clergy in training.

As a traditional Anglican Christian with an exceptionally stable family background over two generations – her parents and her grandparents – Elizabeth is particularly hurt by and in some ways uncomprehending of the failure of her children's marriages. Just as she views her anointing and the vows which she made at her Coronation as sacred, so too her marriage – and particularly where children are concerned – involves a commitment. Divorce is the last resort. Members of her family who come to her to tell her of their marital failures are always advised to wait, to give the situation time to heal before making the irrevocable decision. Before Elizabeth's accession, divorcees were not admitted to court functions and (with the notable exception of Peter Townsend) were excluded from the upper echelons of the royal household. Since 1955 divorcees are no longer prohibited from entering the (enlarged) Royal Ascot Enclosure – undischarged bankruptcy or a criminal record being the only grounds for exclusion. Forty years ago even old friends of Elizabeth's who might have breached the no-divorce rule, even innocently, would not have expected to be invited to the Palace; it has been many years since that particular taboo operated. Elizabeth understands but she has an inherited gut feeling that divorce is both sad and wrong, which makes the failure of her children's marriages all the more tragically ironic.

In artistic and intellectual circles Elizabeth is generally regarded as a philistine. She practically never reads a book unless it is horse-related. She does not enjoy the opera, theatre or concerts – not even ballet for which her mother and sister are enthusiasts. Science and technology bore her; Philip is credited with having told somone who suggested the Queen might like to visit some high-tech plant: 'Unless it eats grass and farts, she isn't interested.' This is, however, an exaggeration. Elizabeth is knowledgeable and appreciative about the great royal collections, which she regards herself as holding in trust for future generations and has become increasingly so. Nor is it true that she only likes animal pictures, although some of her favourite paintings which hang in the private dining-room and the corridor at Windsor do include, among views of Rome and Venice by Canaletto, a set of Stubbs painted for George IV, and over her bed at Sandringham hangs the only known antique painting of a corgi. According to a former Surveyor of the Queen's Pictures:

> She's enormously proud of her pictures and takes very seriously her role as custodian of the royal collection. She has an exceedingly penetrating eye – an inherited asset – and her assessment of a picture is invariably honest and often shrewd. She has a good visual memory. She will never pretend to appreciate something she doesn't like or understand – and here she's often over-modest. I think she is very moved by a good painter of certain kinds of pictures. When we were hanging pictures for her in the private dining-room at Buckingham Palace, she picked out from the Picture Gallery some of the finest, most appealing Dutch, Flemish and English paintings.

Elizabeth likes to look at pictures by herself, but is rarely given the chance to do so at public exhibitions where her private enjoyment is often spoiled by the intrusive remarks of a well-meaning curator or trustee. 'I remember one exhibition in particular – of Stubbs at the Tate – she knew a great deal about the artist and I could see this person interposing himself ruining it for her. All she wanted was to look at the pictures and occasionally remark what she liked, and I could see the experience was actually unenjoyable for her,' a friend said.

The size and quality of the Queen's collection is of vast importance. It contains more than 7,000 paintings as compared with the 2,000 or so owned by the National Gallery, 3,000 miniatures (the largest collection in existence), 30,000 Old Master drawings and watercolours (including a bird's-eye view of Tuscany by Leonardo da Vinci), 500,000 engravings and etchings, thousands of works of art and the world's greatest collection of Sèvres porcelain. Like most of the Queen's possessions, the royal collections are controversial. Although collected by her ancestors, they are not her personal property; and although often included among her assets, they are hardly that in real terms since she cannot sell them. Yet although they do belong in theory to the nation and Elizabeth is a generous lender to exhibitions, the vast proportion of the collection is not visible to the general public except briefly, such as during the recent opening of Buckingham Palace and at the adjacent Queen's Gallery (which has been criticised as a 'hideous, windowless bunker which is only a half-hearted, temporary space . . . a public art gallery as appealing as the foyer of a seedy provincial cinema'). Robin Simon, the editor of the influential art magazine *Apollo*, recently criticised the lack of imagination in the presentation of the royal collection in a stinging attack not on the Queen but on her court:

> The problem is the Palace itself. The Court is still a court – with all the sluggish, timid, bureaucratic, purblind, amateurish incompetence that has been present since the days of Ethelred the Unready.
>
> As anyone knows who has ever had to deal with the Palace, the experience is like swimming in treacle. To get anything done takes years of absurd negotiations. The moment one meeting comes to a decision, another is called to reconsider.
>
> All around courtiers watch each other, afraid to take any initiative that might incur the smallest imagined frown of displeasure from the

monarch or her minions. As Dr Johnson wrote of the 18th-century
Court of St James's: 'They mark the keen glance, and watch the sign to
hate . . .'[5]

Estimates of Elizabeth's wealth vary wildly from the billions reached
by lumping together all the palaces and their contents, the private
estates, the Crown Jewels and those in the royal collection which the
Queen wears. Again the jewellery is a grey area when it comes to
assets; although the Crown Jewels are obviously inalienable, a good
deal of the other jewels are almost certainly family property, acquired
with private funds and handed down from generation to generation
(the resplendent objects given to Elizabeth by the Sheikhs of the Gulf
are presumed to be 'Crown' property, however). Sandringham and
Balmoral are family estates handed down from Edward VII and Queen
Victoria respectively. Elizabeth is not, as often claimed, one of the
richest women in the world, but, according to an informed private
source, she is worth about £50 million in two funds managed by two
different people who are not allowed to communicate with each other.
The chances of anyone outside the Inland Revenue reaching an
accurate estimate of her assets and income are, therefore, remote.

Elizabeth is not an extravagant person; she does not enjoy spending
money on herself or anybody else, nor does she have expensive tastes.
The Palace cars might be Rolls-Royces, but they are certainly veterans.
'Two of the big ones are thirty-two years old,' a court official said.
'One she still uses is forty years old; it was a wedding present from the
Royal Air Force . . . She hadn't had a new car for twenty years or so
when the Association of Motor Manufacturers and Traders made one
for her as a Jubilee present . . . That was the last car she had and that
was delivered in '78, so they're not run in any extravagant manner . . .'
At Buckingham Palace, however, the ancient wooden food trolley has
at last been replaced by a lighter modern metal one. Although she has
very fine wine cellars at Buckingham Palace and Windsor, she and her
children are very abstemious. No wine is served in the private dining-
room unless the family are entertaining guests, and then Elizabeth will
have a gin and Dubonnet before lunch and two Martinis in the evening
(mixed by Philip), one of which she will take in with her. Normally
when they are together at lunch she will have water and Philip a glass
of beer. Neither of them eats cooked breakfast and when they are alone
they have just one course and cheese, with which Elizabeth always
likes to have a piece of celery. Her weakness, like her mother's, is for

chocolate, and tea is her favourite meal. She likes to make the tea herself using the swivel-mounted kettle which Philip designed for her.

Elizabeth's one extravagance is her racing and even that is kept as far as possible on a business-like basis. She is no longer one of the leading owners either in terms of number of horses in training or of prize money. Racing today is a big-money business and has changed out of all recognition since the advent of the really big players like the al-Maktoum brothers a decade ago. The Arabs have 500 mares, Elizabeth only twenty. Three-quarters of the Arabs' horses are bought at public auction with money no object in order to improve their stock and their chances of winning the big races. Elizabeth rarely buys – partly because she can't compete in financial terms and partly because there would be political repercussions were she to be seen spending vast sums on horses. She races the horses she breeds. As far as breeding goes, she has one of the small to middling stud farms in the country, about 5 per cent of the size of those owned by the al-Maktoums. She has the studs which she inherited, two in Norfolk on the Sandringham estate, and one at Polhampton, which she bought from the Wills family in 1972, where she keeps her yearlings. In 1982 she bought West Ilsley training stables from Sir Michael Sobell and Lord Weinstock for about £750,000, recouping the money from the sale of her good filly, Height of Fashion, to Sheikh Hamdan al-Maktoum for between £1.5 and £1.8 million. Some of her horses were already being trained there by Major Dick Hern (who was given a seven-year lease terminating in 1989), but Elizabeth decided she would like to own a racing stables and feel involved in that aspect as well. In 1989 Elizabeth – and her racing manager, Lord Carnarvon – earned a good deal of bad publicity over the Dick Hern affair, when Elizabeth refused to grant an extension of his lease on West Ilsley. Hern was in a wheelchair after a hunting accident in 1984 and then had open heart surgery in 1988. His retained jockey, Willie Carson, and some of the racing press thought that Hern had been badly treated. Others, less sentimental, thought that Carnarvon and Elizabeth had taken a level-headed decision, that the stables had been in chaos, there was uncertainty and the prognosis for Hern was not good. He still lives in the same house belonging to Elizabeth and trains at Lambourn at a yard offered to him by Sheikh Hamdan.

Since 1970 Elizabeth has had a racing manager, her old friend Lord Carnarvon, and a stud manager, Michael Oswald, married to one of the Queen Mother's ladies-in-waiting and based at Sandringham.

Carnarvon's duties are to represent Elizabeth at race meetings, to liaise with her three trainers, the Earl of Huntingdon, Roger Charlton and Ian Balding, and to advise on the buying and selling of thoroughbreds and mating of royal mares. Oswald's brief is to supervise the royal bloodstock at Sandringham, Wolferton and Polhampton, supervise the management of the syndicated stallions and advise on the mating, buying and culling of mares (he is also racing manager to the Queen Mother). Since the early 1970s Elizabeth has been sending mares over to America (she had to give up sending them to Ireland because of the Troubles) to stallions which could give the royal stud speed and class. She keeps the mares at stud in the Bluegrass country of Kentucky with Will Farish at Lane's End, and with Mrs Chandler at Mill Ridge. She has made private visits to Kentucky to check out her horses and the available stallions, usually staying with the Farishes at Lane's End. 'She's been, I think, three times and seen the different stallions,' her racing manager said, 'leaving it for a year or two with gaps because obviously with the gaps you see new horses, otherwise you'd see the same each time.' She has visited stud farms in Normandy twice, once to stay with the Duc de Daudufret-Pasquet at Sassy and secondly with the famous racing trainer and breeder Alec Head at Le Haras de Quesnay, where she enjoyed the unusual pleasure of eating out in local restaurants. These, unlike Sandringham and Balmoral, are her real holidays and she seems conscious of that, saying guilelessly, 'People don't seem to mind my horse trips...' From 1974 to 1984 Paul Mellon left the great stallion Mill Reef in the UK and made sure that Elizabeth's mares had nominations to him every year. The Maktoum family of Dubai is also generous to her in that respect. Nowadays, with the improving situation in Ireland, her mares are sent there again to the class stallions at Irish studs.

As the Queen's income is now taxed, the studs are a business and have to be profitable. 'This is difficult to achieve and if the exercise comes out all square, that's what we're aiming for,' Lord Carnarvon says. The stud operations rather than the prize money produce the main income for the royal racing venture. Elizabeth has a quarter share in Shirley Heights which stands at Sandringham stud – in 1990 Shirley Heights earned £40,000 for every successful covering, of which there are about forty per year, and some free nominations for her own mares. She also has a share in Bustino at Wolferton while Sheikh Mohammed's Belmez, also at Wolferton, no doubt pays his way. Philip Hall, the leading outside expert on the royal finances, wrote in his book published in 1992 that an overall look at the Queen's racing activities in the 1980s and 1990s with the relatively low prize money from her horses would see her making a loss. As late as 1977 she was second leading owner in terms of prize money and second in the league table of breeders that year, but it is unlikely that she will be able to occupy those positions again. All she can really hope for is to break even. 'If you've lost the speed, you've got to put it back again. You can't put it back again overnight. It takes two generations...', Carnarvon said. It is a highly competitive, international business: Elizabeth's horses have won in America, Germany and France. She cannot compete on equal terms with the really big players, but she won £306,000 in 1993.

Elizabeth is very 'hands-on' when it comes to racing. If she can, she attends the sales at Newmarket to study the finer points of the horse-flesh on offer; usually, however, either Carnarvon or Oswald is there on her behalf, watching even if they don't buy – they bought two fillies for her recently, one at Newmarket and one at Keeneland, Kentucky. Carnavon's son-in-law, John Warren, helps her with the buying and selling of yearlings and she has some unconventional connections in the horse world who help her with difficult animals. (One of them was surprised when she recommended him an obscure book about horse-trading in East Anglia. The secret is that she loves horses of any kind and pursues her knowledge with her usual professionalism.) She slips down to Polhampton, an easy drive from London, to check out on her yearlings. 'The idea is to keep somewhere between eighteen or twenty mares and that would produce normally about fifteen foals and fifteen yearlings – so that's the sort of number the Queen feels she can cope with,' Carnarvon said.[6]

She likes going racing, as any teleshot of her at Ascot will show, when she comes alive as she never does on ceremonial occasions. A shot from *EIIR* shows her watching a race with her stud manager, Michael Oswald, on the monitor. 'Look,' she says professionally, 'it's on the wrong leg – no wonder it can't corner.' Then, as the horses thunder down the final straight, Elizabeth, despite her sixty-five years, runs like a girl out to the front of the box to catch the finish. She would probably prefer to see one of her own two year olds or fillies running on a less prestigious occasion, but work prevents her doing so. Carnarvon, her eyes and ears in the racing world, telephones her to give reports. She is the ultimate boss: 'The recommendations would come either through me or Michael Oswald,' Carnarvon says, 'or through the trainers themselves, and then the Queen having made up her mind gives me instructions.' If she is out of the country, she is still consulted unless out of reach, as apparently on *Britannia*, where communications are far from perfect. If she has a runner at one of the courses, she'll tape it or even telephone dial race call anonymously. Before and after each race in which one of her horses is running, she will get a call from either Carnarvon or her trainer. She does not bet (nor, contrary to rumour, does the Queen Mother).

For Elizabeth, the science of breeding is more than the mere thrill of the sport. Her understanding with Carnarvon is on code wavelength: 'She's very knowledgeable and when you get to her age and have started very young, like she and I did . . . You send a mating up to the Queen and suggest something and straight away she'll see what a fascinating ingredient it might be – "I love that idea."' 'Where the mating of broodmares is concerned,' wrote a recent historian of the royal studs, 'in the majority of cases it is the Queen herself who plays the principal role, putting her own ideas to Lord Porchester [Carnarvon] and Michael Oswald who both proffer their advice, but the final decision is always Her Majesty's.'[7] Elizabeth is such an expert on thoroughbred bloodlines that she instinctively knows a pedigree, usually without checking it in a book. The kind of expertise which her grandmother, Queen Mary, would apply to the spider-like web of German princely genealogy, Elizabeth concentrates on the permutation of breeding thoroughbred racehorses. It needs knowledge and flair. 'You've got to have a book with all the stallions in stud in the top half and then a second half for your own mares,' says Carnarvon, 'and you can switch, keep the mare in front of you and keep switching until you get the right mix.'

Elizabeth, as a quasi-professional owner and breeder, does not really enjoy the purely social side of racing or the new glitz with which it has become associated. When she wants to talk about the finer points of a race and of a horse's performance with people who really know what they are talking about, she is not particularly amused to find herself caught up with the Ascot Hat Brigade and the trophy wives. She likes her own expert team and the old-school owners, people with whom she stays for race meetings, although many of them nowadays are the children or grandchildren of the parents she used to know, like Lord Halifax, her host for the race meeting at York.

There is no glitz either about her racing establishments. The main buildings at Sandringham stud (Michael Oswald's headquarters) remain as they were in Edward VII's day, a neat one-storey complex built of the local brown carstone pointed with brick, topped with a traditional stable clock. In front, and almost dwarfing the building, is a life-size bronze of Edward's Derby winner, Persimmon, now green with verdigris. There is no atmosphere of luxury about the offices or the stables. Oswald, perhaps because of the fierce financial scrutiny now focused on the Queen's affairs, emphasises Elizabeth's thrift, how she communicates with him on scraps of paper. The envelope which this author received from him was not franked as Palace stationery is (and, therefore, free as On Her Majesty's Service), but normally stamped. The heart of the operation is the gynaecological 'suite', no place for the imaginatively squeamish, the central object of which is a padded green rectangular structure into which the mares are put for the various gynaecological observations, including scanning done by a portable scanner the size of a small TV set. The stud groom, dressed like all the royal stud employees in a blue anorak with Elizabeth's cypher in red, told me how a 6ft 4in policeman had fainted when told the details. On the walls a scanning chart showed embryos at various stages – and other key plans, ovulation, cysts, etc. Scanning is used to spot optimum chances of pregnancy – this, after all, is what the big money operation is all about. Twins are no good; one is either born dead or is too weak to survive, therefore one is aborted early – 'like squeezing a pea'. Next door to this gynaecological chamber is a large shed with wood-chip floor covering and a large rectangular unglassed window with a very battered piece of plastic padding beneath it. This area is used to 'tease' the stallion; mares are let in here and the stallion outside the window tries to get at them. The kicks in the plastic panelling testify to the mares' reaction, often furiously unenthusiastic. The stallion when suitably aroused then performs next door (at around £40,000 a shot if successful) attended by four men, who hold the mare's bridle and generally facilitate the stallion's access to her. 'It only takes a few minutes.' The mare is subsequently regularly and minutely surveyed with the scanner and if the impregnation has not been successful, the process will be gone through again until it is. A mare spends a season – 15 February to 15 July – at the stud. 'If it doesn't work, it's usually the fault of the mare not the stallion,' the men in charge say. 'It's in everyone's interest that she should be pregnant.' Fertility rates for the Queen's stallions are advertised in the stud brochure as 91 per cent over sixteen seasons for Bustino and 92 per cent over fifteen seasons for Shirley Heights.

Apart from her brief 'horse visits' to America every three years or so, Elizabeth never has a holiday as such, despite hostile press reports about her 'six weeks' at Balmoral and Sandringham. Wherever she goes, her boxes and her secretarial staff follow her. 'Sandringham is an escape place but it's also a working place,' she says in *EIIR*. 'It's a commercially viable bit of England. I like farming, I like animals. I wouldn't be happy if we just had arable farming, I think that's very boring . . . Because it's an inherited place, one's known it since one was a child. I know how much my father loved it . . . we are very involved with the people on the estate – you have a responsibility towards them.'

Sandringham is very much a family place for Elizabeth. It was built by her great-grandfather; both her grandfather and her father died here, and her father was born in York Cottage, now the estate office, an ugly villa in the grounds. While the family and their staff love it, to outsiders the Big House is quite frankly hideous. It looks, as Queen Mary's biographer, James Pope-Hennessy, wrote, like a Scottish golf hotel, built in Edwardian–Jacobean style in aggressive red brick trimmed with stone, with a touch of fantasy in the elaborate stone *porte-cochère* modelled on a Loire château and tall trellis-patterned mock Elizabethan chimneys and towers with a weather-vane. The house looks huge and once had 365 rooms, but forty or so were demolished when a wing was pulled down in 1974–5. That was a servants' wing with a huge dormitory where the more junior male staff slept in cubicles, a warren of small bedrooms and the usual hierarchical set of dining-rooms for the various ranks of staff. It was pulled down as an economy as it was leaking and falling down; during Queen Alexandra's long occupation and during the war years practically no maintenance had been carried out. Plan after plan was put up to Elizabeth, who was, a former employee said, 'very concerned that the staff should not be affected by the changes'. Philip came up with the idea to amalgamate the three staff dining-rooms to save space (just as, at Buckingham Palace, he ended the system of different kitchens for the preparation of royal and staff meals), but there were difficulties in that the same type of service was required but the pantry space was no longer there. Sir Peter Ashmore, the then Master of the Household, attempted to decree that there would be no more tray service to bedrooms. Staff held their breath for the arrival of 'Miss MacDonald', Princess Margaret and her guests. Tray service was resumed. The result was below-stairs confusion; the wretched pantry boys would be dealing with the breakfast trays piled up higgledy-piggledy all over the place because there was no space to put them so that often good china got broken, while they also had to wash up the main dining-room breakfast as the chefs shouted at them to prepare the shooting lunches. As an economy, the wall where the old wing had been was not properly faced with stone but just red bricks; it is visible only to the staff and tradesmen, who refer to it as 'the out-patients' department'. There are still strong traces of the old regime. When Philip asked if they could change the way the flowers were arranged in the bedrooms, the old gardener told him that they were done that way because that was how Queen Mary liked them, detailing exactly where she had wanted them put, and of her fondness for carnations, the fashionable flower of before the First World War. When Pope-Hennessy visited the house in 1956, something else more macabre had not changed:

> Across the head of the main stairs is situated a truly sinister warren of small rooms, looking on to the main front of the house . . . the first door on the left is where the Duke of Clarence died. This dim and cheerless hole is surprisingly small . . . so that you could touch the mantelpiece with your hand if lying on the bed. How fourteen people, including the [enormous] Duchess of Teck, crammed into his room on the morning of 14 January 1892 foxes me completely [he wrote]. Queen Alexandra kept this room as a shrine, visiting it almost daily, strewing fresh flowers on the bed, looking at his uniforms and clothes ranged in a glass cabinet along the wall opposite the fireplace. Even the soap and hair brushes were left as on the day he died . . .
>
> To sum up [Pope-Hennessy went on], this is a hideous house with a horrible atmosphere in parts and in others no atmosphere at all. It was like a visit to the morgue; and everywhere were their faces, painted, drawn or photographed: few pictures not directly relating to themselves: most curiously *borné* [limited] their horizon seems to have been, ringed in by their own family and their own likenesses, with an outer constellation of 'servants' of *every* class.[8]

'Creepy' and 'somehow frightening' were other words he used to describe the house. The main staircase is, as he wrote, 'almost incredibly gloomy, a great windowless well of tangerine-coloured wood'. The passages are painted in nile green while the carpet is ugly, blotched with red. Elizabeth's office is very 1950s with pale washed walls and brocade curtains to match.

Each generation of the family has left its mark on the house, although the spirit of the place is Queen Alexandra's, particularly in the drawing-room, '1860 masquerading as 1760', as Pope-Hennessy puts it, rather like the Ritz Hotel in London with rococo plasterwork and pretty painted ceiling panels of sky, balustrades, peacocks and vases of flowers. One can imagine the Edwardian ladies there after dinner, Mrs Keppel among them, with their streamlined, heavily embroidered evening dresses, their pearl chokers and diamond ornaments on their piled-up hair, fluttering like doves in a dovecote for the arrival of the bearded, paunchy King with a pungent aura of Havana cigars. A celebrity screen is a microcosm of the Edwardian era from Gladstone to Nellie Melba and the first 'Gibson Girl', and there are vitrines of Alexandra's collection of Fabergé animals, many of them given to her by her nephew, the last Tsar. There are, of course, serried ranks of royal photographs, many of them of Christmas past, notably 1951 (George VI's last) and 1901 (the last of the Victorian era). The dining-room next door, again reminiscent of the Ritz, has been, as Pope-Hennessy says, 'effectually disinfected' by the Queen Mother, painted pea-green and hung with Goya tapestries. She also lightened the panelling of estate oak lining the 'saloon' – the social centre of the house where everyone meets for tea, and which is disconcertingly off the hall so that nervous non-royal guests come right into the midst of the family. The almost obligatory Edwardian stuffed bear (usually Russian, upright and proffering a tray for visiting cards) has been swept away, but in the hall two weather machines, the focus of George V's daily interest, still remain.

Within walking distance from the Big House down an avenue of Scots pines is the little Sandringham church built out of the rich reddish-brown carstone quarried on the estate and cut into small tiles inserted horizontally, with stone trimming. Inside it is the normal English parish church of its time with an oak vaulted roof supported by angels and a mosaic-tiled floor of the Edwardian period. It is full of family plaques: to Edward VII's sisters, Alice of Hesse and the Empress Frederick of Prussia, to his haemophiliac brother, Leopold, and to his eldest son, Prince Eddy. Outside the church are two pathetic graves: those of Prince Alexander John Charles Albert, '3rd son of Edward and Alexandra b. 6 April 1871 d. 7 April 1871', and next to his under a red granite stone, Elizabeth's sad, afflicted uncle, Prince John, 'b. 12 July 1905 d. 18 January 1919'. In the graveyard too are the tombstones of the local families who have worked on the estate and occupy the purpose-built villages like Dersingham – 'Benefer, Parker, Marrington, Stratton, Amos'. Nowadays the Big House is open from

Christmas until February; Elizabeth goes there in the springtime when the thoroughbred breeding season is at its height, and the Queen Mother always goes there with her own house guests at the end of July. Generally, during the rest of the year, Elizabeth uses Wood Farm at Wolferton (where Prince John died), a charming two-storey brick and stone farmhouse which has been renovated. Philip and other members of the family use it for weekends and shooting-parties and there is a special place built there for shooting lunches.

At 20,000 acres, the Sandringham estate is one of the biggest in Norfolk. There is a land agent (who rejoices in the name John Major), but Philip is in overall control of the estate and particularly the shooting, although the studs are Elizabeth's province. Apart from horses, gun-dogs, cattle and pigs, Elizabeth breeds and races racing-pigeons (one of her father's birds won the Dickens Medal, the animal's Victoria Cross, for its exploits in the Second World War). There are woods of tall, elegant Corsican and Scots pines and towards the sea flat lands retreat towards the sea wall built in 1860; beyond it is rough grass covered by the sea at high tide and laced with creeks at low tide. The sky is huge over the great stretch of water called the Wash and to the north the coast of Lincolnshire shimmers like a mirage. Samphire, a sort of salty sea-asparagus, grows in the mud under water and can be harvested at low tide as it has been since medieval times. Boiled and eaten with mayonnaise or hollandaise, it is served as a course on its own. The royal family love it and samphire from Sandringham was served at the wedding breakfast of the Prince and Princess of Wales. The retired head-keeper, Montague Christopher, and his wife gather two harvests of samphire each year to send up to Balmoral and to the Prince of Wales in London. Once they harvested 30lb for a state banquet given to the President of Mexico. Philip is particularly fond of hazelnuts from a nutgrove at Appleton, the old house (now pulled down) where Queen Maud of Norway lived. As the Duke is never there at nutting time, the keeper gathers them in and buries them, like squirrels do in the wood, but in hessian bags so that they can breathe, and about a foot down to escape the frosts. They keep so well that eaten in January they are as good as they were in October. Venison from the estate – the original fallow deer and now munjak escaped from Woburn and roe deer – is sent up to London for the Palace kitchens. Elizabeth likes the country things – quince jelly from the quince tree at Wood Farm, little baskets of game fowl eggs presented to her by the keepers. Although Philip is in overall charge of the estate,

Elizabeth notices everything and has the final say in such things as tiles for the re-roofing of the barns. 'She has a mastery of detail,' one of her employees said, 'is very observant and has an incredibly retentive memory (which the Queen Mother has too) a trained memory for facts.'

Balmoral is the other place where Elizabeth can fulfil her childhood dream of being 'married to a farmer and having lots of horses and cows and dogs'. She calls her annual visit there 'hibernating'. 'It's nice to be able to sleep in the same bed for six weeks,' she says. 'And there is a certain fascination in keeping the place as Queen Victoria had it . . .' As one looks up the valley of the Dee from the castle, the view is not so very different from Victoria's day as the long-horned and long-haired Highland cattle browse in the distance. Elizabeth is patron of the Highland Cattle Society and started the Balmoral herd soon after her accession in 1953. She has had three male champions in a row recently and has a 'fold' of thirty breeding cows. She also breeds Highland ponies (and has had the champion stallion at the Royal Highland Show for several years), fell ponies and Austrian Halflingers, which have chestnut coats and blond manes and tails like palominos. While Philip is responsible to Elizabeth for the private estate here (as he is at Sandringham), and the day-to-day management is overseen by the Factor, she takes a great interest in it and rides out every day to see what is going on. The red deer which Victoria found so picturesque are today a problem at Balmoral as they are on every Highland estate. The Balmoral estate is a founder member of the Grampian Deer Management Group; there are some 4,500 deer roaming the estate, kept out of newly planted areas by 6ft fences. There are 72,000 acres of forestry managed according to conservation principles – trees lie where they have fallen as shelters for beetles and other forms of wildlife. Philip is interested in regenerating the native forest: the deer are kept out by fencing and native pines replanted. Elizabeth finds small saplings and puts protective covers round them, the Prince of Wales puts up tree shelters. The huge ant-heaps are carefully preserved because the ants clean the trees and eat aphids off them.

Shooting is an important part of the Balmoral day as it is at Sandringham, and Elizabeth brings her gun-dogs with her. At Balmoral, however, when the Queen's Piper plays round the castle for twenty minutes each morning, the labradors and spaniels in the royal kennels put their noses in the air and howl in protest. The cherished corgis of course accompany their mistress and are allowed to hunt rabbits out of the small space of cultivated garden close to the castle. There are

problems when Elizabeth goes to see her mother at Birkhall (or anywhere else). Her mother's corgis love her, but the two packs don't get
on and on one occasion there was a fatality when the two packs fought.
Both Elizabeth and her mother adore their dogs and will not have a
word said against them. It is the custom for the corgis to have dog
biscuits thrown to them after lunch. On one occasion, apparently, a
nervous bishop took a biscuit from the footman's tray and ate it; on
another, a guest, taken by surprise when a footman's white-gloved hand
appeared next to Her Majesty and biscuits were cast round him on the
floor like manna and feeling a sharp furry swirling round his feet and –
dangerously – his lap, attempted a joke: 'My dogs beg too, Ma'am.'
Elizabeth's retort was icy, 'My dogs don't beg.' Intimations that they
might yap or snap are also unwelcome. Corgi duty, the preserve of the
Queen's footman, is not generally popular. The pack can vary from
seven to eleven. They are taken out for a walk every morning. Elizabeth
feeds them herself at 5 p.m., their main meal – the food is prepared
and she mixes and gives it to them. Then they are taken for another
walk – this can be difficult as they never like leaving Elizabeth and tend
to resent the efforts of a subordinate trying to tell them what to do.
Moreover, they will be scattered all round a room, under a curtain,
behind a sofa, and all have to be retrieved. Mealtimes can be embarrassing for guests as there may be noisy canine altercations under the
table and the guests don't know how to react. Corgis are such an
inseparable part of Elizabeth's image that they rate a longer entry in
the *Royal Encyclopedia* than do the court correspondents – the respectable end of the royal media ratpack. Here we learn that Elizabeth's
current pack of seven represents the tenth generation descended from
Susan, a particularly long-lived animal given to her on her eighteenth
birthday in 1944, which died at Sandringham aged fifteen and is buried
there. There are also two 'dorgis', the result of mating one of Elizabeth's
corgis with a dachshund belonging to Margaret. Wherever she goes on
tour, Elizabeth is accustomed to being confronted by the yapping
representatives of the local corgi club, and at the exhibition designed
to celebrate her forty years on the throne, a somewhat dull affair of
uniforms in showcases and Elizabeth's dresses looking lifeless on dum-
mies, a stuffed corgi lying on the floor of a mock-up of one of her
sitting-rooms was among the liveliest of the exhibits.

Whenever Elizabeth goes on her 'expensive peregrinations' to
Balmoral and Sandringham, about thirty of her domestic staff go with
her; otherwise the houses have a skeleton staff of housekeeper, cleaners,

maintenance men and gardeners. The staff – Elizabeth hates the word servant and will not allow it to be used – enjoy the change as much as the family does. The atmosphere is more relaxed and so are their employers. 'The Queen expects us to relax a bit and enjoy ourselves at Balmoral,' a member of the staff says. 'She'd say, I don't bring my staff up here to be unhappy.' She built a new recreation hall at Balmoral for the staff and always likes to be asked to the annual end-of-holiday fancy-dress dance there. She is considerate when there are staff parties, either taking her guests out to a barbecue or making sure that dinner is early so that the staff can get away. When there are staff barbecues, she is careful to have the royal barbecue somewhere else so as not to embarrass them. Elizabeth is a thoughtful employer and staff conditions have become easier since her accession. Ascot week in particular had always been an exhausting occasion for the staff, who, at the end of a demanding week, would have to stay up until about six o'clock in the morning for the Friday night ball, with the guests not leaving until Saturday. Elizabeth saw to it that the Friday dance was phased out and the guests left on Friday. Again for grand occasions like Ascot week, the male staff used to have to powder their hair, which they hated, and wear knee breeches and huge aiguillettes on their uniforms, which made it very difficult for them to wait at table. At night the custom always used to be that two staff, a page and a footman, had to be in attendance after dinner – 'the Queen would go to bed at about half past eleven, twelve o'clock, but Princess Margaret would stay up until half past two . . . When the Queen realised what was happening she said that once she went to bed the staff should say goodnight to the remaining guests and leave them with what they needed.' Yet if staff misbehave, Elizabeth can be intimidating. 'At Sandringham once,' one said, 'the Queen came into the dining-room and found some young footmen larking around. She really tore a strip off them.'

Elizabeth likes to keep her finger on the pulse of her household and her various houses. She enjoys overseeing the decoration and likes to be involved. She really enjoys doing up bedrooms without professional advice – 'Not always a great success,' said a courtier. One friend recalls:

I remember one occasion when she'd just done up three of the bedrooms for state visits and she was rather like a child because, you know, she's never had an opportunity of really doing up any of those rooms and she was so excited. She'd found big chintzes to go into these rooms. She'd done a bedroom in Laura Ashley and she was so thrilled by that. And equally at Balmoral she's like a housewife *manquée*. She loves laying the table in the log cabin and putting out the sandwiches which come out of these old-fashioned biscuit-tin boxes . . . you don't dare help . . .

The writer Daphne du Maurier, after staying at Balmoral, said of Elizabeth, 'She's so practical. She'd have made a marvellous head of the WI [Women's Institute].'

She is not interested in gardens as her mother and her eldest son are ('I'm only a weeder really,' she told a guest at a Holyrood party for gardeners), but she keeps an eye on things none the less. When a friend asked her if he might photograph herbaceous borders at Holyrood for a book, she said, 'Yes, but you mustn't do it before the 15th July, or it won't be ready . . .' A former courtier has remarked:

Many, many times, I have heard the Queen say, 'Well, nobody ever tells me anything', but in fact she is much better informed than almost anybody I've ever known anywhere. Everybody who thinks they know something nobody else knows loves being the one to tell the Queen first. I mean not least of all her famous page for many years, Mr Bennett, who knew or gleaned everything from upstairs and downstairs. He was a great supplier of information, but that is something which I think there is a danger within the Queen's household now of being rather eroded. They've been going through a period in recent years of financial reorganisation headed by Michael Peat who was appointed Financial Adviser to the Queen . . .

Mention the name Michael Peat to any member of Elizabeth's staff or non-clerical employees and the most mild-mannered will become quite vitriolic. 'Ruthless' is the word most often used to describe him. Under the regime of the Lord Chamberlain, the Earl of Airlie, and Mr Michael Peat, the royal household, most traditional of British institutions – hierarchical, patriarchal, and yet extremely personal and based on loyalty to Elizabeth herself – is being subjected to the kind of bruising, cost-cutting, management-orientated, performance-related, pay-minded, memorandum-based exercise which has cut the heart and soul out of many companies. A former courtier recalled:

All the Members of the Queen's Household when I first went there put the Queen first. I remember once at the Lord Chamberlain's lunch we

were arguing about something and the very dry voice of Sir Michael
Adeane said, 'Does anybody know what the Queen wants?', and there
was dead silence and he said, 'Well, I think somebody should ask her
and we won't waste any more time discussing it.' Lord Plunket said he
was seeing her tomorrow. 'Well, you ask her tomorrow and I shall be in
on Tuesday . . . let me know what the answer is and don't let's waste
any more time on it.' And that's how it should be. There's a lot going
on now of . . . well, they've instituted a lot of civil service sort of things
whereby we're called upon to make an annual report and to carry out
an annual interview with all staff and there has been a feeling
permeating the lower regions of the Queen's Household, amongst
officials and staff, that the atmosphere and the feeling's different and
that they don't get the feeling the only person they're working for is
the Queen. They feel they're being given orders by other people which
may or may not have been approved by the Queen . . . It was said to
me by staff at the Royal Palace. It's a rather sad situation.

Michael Charles Gerrard Peat, aged forty-six, educated at Eton and
Trinity College, Oxford, with an MBA from the top European business
school, INSEAD and an FCA, has a background in accountancy as a
partner from 1972 to 1993 in KPMG Peat Marwick, the firm founded
by his father. Since 1990 he has been Director of Finance and Property
Services, an entirely new Household title created specifically for him,
and since 1996 he has also taken over the office of Keeper of the Privy
Purse. He had already begun his scrutiny of the royal household in
1986 after being called in by the new Lord Chamberlain, the 13th Earl
of Airlie, who was appointed to the top Palace job in 1984 after a City
career principally in merchant banking, having worked thirty-four
years for K. Schroder Wagg. Airlie, tall, slim and immaculate, is the
grandson of the famous Mabell Airlie, Queen Mary's lady-in-waiting
and friend who acted as Cupid to King George VI and Queen
Elizabeth, and whose memoirs, *Thatched with Gold*, pre-dated Crawfie
and were not entirely approved of in court circles. His wife, Virginia,
daughter of the celebrated socialite 'Nin' Ryan and John Barry Ryan
of Newport, is lady-in-waiting to the Queen. Airlie, through his
'hands-on' approach to his job and his patronage of Peat, is far and
away the most influential member of the household. 'Lord Maclean
[the previous Lord Chamberlain]', one member of the staff said
plaintively, 'used to leave us alone.'
   Lord Airlie's connection with Mr Peat began while he was chairman
of Schroder's working on an overall review of the organisation

worldwide. Peat's firm was also acting as auditors at Buckingham Palace and was therefore familiar with the financial set-up there. Having spent six months 'looking and listening' after taking up his appointment as Lord Chamberlain, Airlie decided on a similar review of the household operations to bring the Palace into line with 'the best business practices' as operated in the outside world. Elizabeth, apparently, agreed that 'perhaps it would be a useful exercise'. As a result of Lord Airlie's administration, the royal household (which in practical terms means Airlie and Peat) has more control over its affairs than it did before. The Civil List agreement, substituting a ten-year timescale for an annual review, has made longer-term planning possible. The unoccupied palaces, such as Hampton Court and the public part of Kensington Palace, are now no longer under the direct control of the Department of National Heritage but the Historic Royal Palaces Agency, while the occupied palaces – Buckingham Palace, Windsor Castle and the properties in the Home and Great Parks, St James's Palace, Clarence House and Stable House Yard, Clarence House and Marlborough House Mews – are no longer maintained by the Property Services Agency but are directly under the control of Michael Peat and financed by an annual grant-in-aid of around £20 million a year from the Department of National Heritage.

The latter arrangement has been a mixed blessing as far as the royal household is concerned. MPs campaigning to have royal finances opened up further to public scrutiny have targeted the numerous grace-and-favour residences which are in the Queen's gift and are occupied by present and former employees, or their widows. This has been the subject of an investigation by the parliamentary Public Accounts Committee, which is in essence another episode in the long-running battle by Parliament to gain more control over the Palace. The grace-and-favour residences are a means by which senior and junior members of the royal household are compensated for their far from lavish salaries, enabling them to live, often in very desirable properties in Central London, at below-market rents. And if your employer is also your landlord, it is an additional guarantee of your loyalty. The death in 1985 of the elderly Lady Gale in a fire which started in her grace-and-favour apartment at Hampton Court and later badly damaged the palace first brought the system to public attention (although no grace-and-favour accommodation has been granted since 1991 and the system is being phased out). This was followed in 1994–5 by reports of the large sums spent on refurbishing for the use of Mr Peat a six-bedroom apartment at Kensington Palace formerly occupied by Princess Alice, which had been vacant for twenty years. The total for the redecorating of this apartment and one for Mr Peat's deputy next door was reputed to be £1 million, although according to the Palace the final figure for decoration for Mr Peat's apartment amounted to £142,000. Mr Peat pays £450 towards the rent of this apartment as compared with £2,000 plus paid for similar sized housing in the area. It was announced in May 1995 that he had been paid a £13,000 bonus on top of his £116,000 salary (already high by household standards). Royal officials have stated that Mr Peat's economies will make savings of more than £50 million by the end of the century in the running of the household and in maintaining the palaces.

Mr Peat's earnings and perquisites did not go down well with chambermaids in the royal household whose wages had actually been reduced in his reforms. The domestic staff has resented the clerical employees' getting higher wages than they do and feel that performance-related pay is unfair and impossible in the circumstances of their own employment. The official response is that change was long overdue and in any case is always unpopular. That is true, but one could question the wisdom of damaging an ethos built up over the years: the sense of being a community and of belonging to a family which royal service had engendered. Elizabeth is a traditionalist; although she has agreed to the reforms, people question how much she is now aware of what is going on. Memoranda are not a substitute for personal contact and there is little consultation between the Personnel Service and senior staff when it comes to new recruitment. Bobo Macdonald and 'Bennie' Bennett, who would have told Elizabeth what the feeling was, are both dead. No one else would dare to interfere. And outside the Palace the newspapers are ever present, ever hungry for news and ready to pay for it.

Elizabeth and Philip are totally discreet. They never discuss family matters in front of the staff, nor does Elizabeth ever leave anything that should be private lying around where it might provide a temptation. In fact their own staff have been notably loyal – leaks in recent years have come primarily from officials. The younger royals have been less careful. The Princess of Wales had to be told off in her early days for going in to the royal kitchens and chatting to the staff, and she shocked courtiers with the frankness with which she spoke and behaved in front of the servants. Some of the worst offenders, as far as leaks go, in recent years have been Charles's two valets, Stephen Barry and Ken

Stronach. Charles gave Barry far too much leeway and it went to his head. He would invite his gay friends into the palaces and show them round – even the Queen Mother's home, Clarence House – while at Buckingham Palace he would give parties in his rooms with footmen serving drinks and canapés. He was to provide much of the material for recent royal books – apart from writing his own after he was sacked by the Princess of Wales. The Princess of Wales is tricky with her staff, the Prince of Wales spoiled and demanding, given to writing tetchy little notes of instructions about minor things ('This sponge is dry. Please see that it is watered immediately'), or sending staff back from Highgrove to London to fetch a single pair of cuff-links. He has a tendency to the right royal rages so graphically described by Stronach. His grandfather, George VI, before his behaviour was modified by the calming influence of his wife, used to kick the furniture (in one Northamptonshire house where he used to stay for hunting, they had to remove the decent antique furniture from his room and replace it with something more expendable before his arrival). Charles, under the stress of his failing marriage, apparently went so far as to pull a handbasin from the wall. Stronach, who had been 'bequeathed' to Charles by Mountbatten, had been outstandingly loyal and surprised everyone by going public in the way he did. He gave as his reason for doing so that he felt 'let down' by Charles's admission of adultery with Camilla Parker Bowles after the Prince's staff had been under such a strain to keep it private both from the Princess and the press.

It is unimaginable that anyone close to Elizabeth or Philip would behave in this way. They have earned the loyalty of their staff. Even Philip with his explosive temper is liked by those who work for him. Elizabeth's ladies-in-waiting and friends are less enamoured of him, regarding him as difficult and a bully. Like many men, while he can be warm and charming to a pretty woman even when he knows her to be a tabloid journalist (a breed which tops his hate list), he can be noticeably ungracious to middle-aged women or those he does not find attractive. Both he and Elizabeth are good judges of people who work for them; Elizabeth's ladies-in-waiting are, almost without exception, particularly charming, quick-witted and kind. They are unsnobbish, unpompous and – some of them – independent-minded, and often subversively amused by the stuffier attitudes of Elizabeth's male officers of the household.

The top men at Elizabeth's court – the Lord Chamberlain, the Private Secretary, the Keeper of the Privy Purse, Master of the

Household, Deputy Private Secretary and Press Secretary – are, most of them, in the traditional mould: upper-class family, good public school (usually Eton), a Guards regiment, and the City or the Foreign Office. The ethos of the Palace is very much that of the Guards: suits as immaculate as their manners, unemotional, relaxed approach to life, membership of an exclusive London club (usually White's), and traditional hobbies like shooting and watching cricket. Somewhat surprisingly, since Philip is usually not so conventional in his choice, his chief aide, Sir Brian McGrath, is also Eton, Irish Guards and a member of White's Club, with shooting among his hobbies.

The Queen's Principal Private Secretary is the most important figure in the Palace hierarchy despite his lowly sounding title. He is her channel of communication with the outside world, her eyes and ears in Downing Street and Whitehall. Everything important which reaches Elizabeth goes through him; he is the filter sifting the relevant from the irrelevant. His is the face which important visitors see when they go to the Palace although the vast majority of Elizabeth's subjects don't know his name and wouldn't recognise him if shown his photograph. The calibre of the Queen's Private Secretary is of immense importance in the relations of the Palace with the outside world, both in the image which the Palace presents and the type of advice and information he gives the sovereign. The Private Secretary's job, as defined by Harold Laski, requires exceptional qualities:

> He must know all that is going on; he must be ready to advise upon all
> . . . He is the confidant of all Ministers, but he must never leave the
> impression that he is anybody's man. He must intrude without ever
> seeming to intrude . . . Receiving a thousand secrets, he must
> discriminate between what may emerge and what shall remain obscure
> . . . It is a life passed amid circumstances in which the most trifling
> incident may lead to major disaster . . . The royal secretary walks on a
> tightrope below which he is never unaware that an abyss is yawning . . .
> Half of him must be in a real sense a statesman, and the other half
> must be prepared, if the occasion arises, to be something it is not very
> easy to distinguish from a lacquey.[9]

The present incumbent of this extremely tricky job, since 1990, is Sir Robert Fellowes (Eton, the Scots Guards, the City). He is assisted by Robin Janvrin (Marlborough, Oxford, the Royal Navy, the Foreign Office), Deputy Private Secretary since 1995, and Mary Francis, the first woman ever to be appointed (in 1995) as Assistant Private Secretary. Mary Francis, aged forty-eight, comes from outside the 'magic circle' of courtiers. She read history at Newnham College, Cambridge, and has spent her career in public service, as private secretary to various ministers, a two-year spell at a merchant bank and another two as Financial Counsellor at the British Embassy in Washington, then a three-year stint as Private Secretary to the Prime Minister with special responsibility for economic affairs. The Press Office (subordinate to the Private Secretary) includes the Press Secretary, since 1990 Charles Anson (Lancing, Cambridge and Johns Hopkins University, the Foreign Office, two years in Margaret Thatcher's Press Office at Downing Street, and City PR), a Deputy Press Secretary and two Assistant Press Secretaries, one of whom, Geoffrey Crawford, is Australian, plus a band of women somewhat unkindly dubbed by the tabloid royal ratpack 'the Camillas'.

Most of the top officials, the Private Secretaries in particular, are highly intelligent, shrewd and well equipped with the necessary diplomatic skills. The core composition of the court has not changed since Altrincham attacked it as 'a tight little enclave of ladies and gentlemen' in the 1950s. They are all decent, honourable, loyal people, who see themselves as defenders of the monarchy, a position which of itself implies negativity. The prevailing atmosphere, even more marked in the junior secretarial ranks, is defensive and the most innocuous questions take on a preternatural importance. This is partly the fault of an increasingly intrusive press and public interest, when even a modest snippet of scandal about the sexual behaviour of a royal detective can be worth upwards of £500, but the traditional court attitude of not letting the light in upon the magic still rules at Buckingham Palace. And it comes from the top. No one, except Philip, is in a position to tell Elizabeth what she will not like to hear. After more than forty years on the throne, her experience of public affairs and guarding the position of the monarchy is so superior to any of her employees' and her aura so formidable that no one would dare. Quite apart from anything else all her advisers are considerably younger than she is. Her principal adviser, Sir Robert Fellowes, born in 1941, is only seven years older than her eldest son. Her present Prime Minister, Tony Blair, is even younger.

The court is the way it is because Elizabeth likes it that way, and, as courts go, it is a happier organisation than many of its equivalents. It would not necessarily be improved by the introduction of thrusting go-getters (and, in any case, the taxpayer would be unwilling to stump up the salaries they would demand as parity with the private sector or even Whitehall at the higher levels). The Prince of Wales's office, run on less traditional and ostensibly more open lines, has been more discordant. Not all the 'best business practices' brought in by Mr Peat have yet proved their validity. The presentation of the unoccupied palaces and such tourist attractions as the Crown Jewels has improved out of all recognition, but the grumbling and disruption in the Queen's own household has yet to subside and may have changed its fragile ethos irreparably.

Although there are no black faces in evidence within the Palace walls, no one could accuse Elizabeth of being racist. The Commonwealth Secretariat is set up just down the Mall from Buckingham Palace in Marlborough House and its head, the Secretary-General, today the Nigerian Chief Emeka Anyaoku, has the right of direct access to the Queen as head of the Commonwealth. To anyone who attends Commonwealth occasions, such as the annual Commonwealth Day reception, it is obvious how happy Elizabeth is in that ambience, and how much she is genuinely loved and appreciated there. Many Commonwealth people have been surprised and offended by the recent sustained British attacks on the monarchy. The warmth of Elizabeth's reception by President Mandela on the 1995 state visit to South Africa after its readmission to the Commonwealth was an eloquent testimony to how he viewed her contribution to the ending of apartheid.

One thing about the court, however, is offensive to many people and that is its bias against women in any top executive capacity. Until the arrival of Mary Francis as Assistant Private Secretary, no woman had ever been appointed to the Private Secretaries' Office. (This epoch-making event in Palace history passed almost unnoticed in the media.) Women in their traditional role, gracious, well-dressed, charming, are acceptable as ladies-in-waiting or, on a lower level, as secretaries – 'lady clerks' – dressers, housekeepers and chambermaids (chefs are always male). The senior women in the royal family – Elizabeth, the Queen Mother and Margaret – are as much responsible for this attitude as are the senior male members of the household. While the senior royal ladies show good judgement in the women they choose to be ladies-in-waiting and have an excellent rapport with them (Margaret, the most demanding, difficult and capricious of the royal women, has the most intelligent ladies-in-waiting), they all of them prefer men as companions and conversationalists and in a professional capacity.

The Queen Mother, who was young in the 1920s and 1930s, probably the most bitchy and competitive era as far as society women were concerned, tends to the traditional view that all beautiful women are stupid and intelligent women ugly, although she will admit the biographer Elizabeth Longford as the one exception.

As far as her private, as opposed to her public, social life is concerned, Elizabeth's evenings are – surprisingly – often unoccupied. Paradoxically, since she is just about the most famous woman in the world, she will be free to come to dinner more often than you would realise – provided, that is, that you are one of the people she feels at home with and can count upon to invite a small number of guests she would like to see. Philip has far more official evening engagements than she has and she is, therefore, often alone. That does not mean that she is necessarily lonely. She will have seen numbers of people in her official capacity during the day. A quiet evening with the television news, her racing/breeding books and piles of photographs to be stuck into her photograph albums and captioned provide the necessary relaxation. She often talks on the telephone to her mother and sister – 'us three' remain close, closer indeed than she is to her children, who lead their own lives.

Elizabeth has been through family troubles in the past few years which would have shattered someone more emotionally fragile than she is. Worst of all for her as a private person, and also as one with the reputation and preservation of the monarchy so close at heart, has been the public exposure, the almost daily trawling through the dirty linen (literally as well as figuratively). For her personally there has been just one consolation. The events of the *annus horribilis* and its aftermath have drawn her and her husband even closer together. Philip has gone out of his way to show his affection and support for her. 'They have come together very much lately,' a courtier said. On occasions when Elizabeth carried out some evening function without him, she would return to find him waiting up for her even if it was after midnight. 'I think he's been apparently absolutely wonderful to her and incredibly supportive and sort of around,' a relation said. 'And during all those horrors except during the fire when he wasn't there, he has tried not to leave her on her own too much.' 'He is unsung for the total support he gives to the Queen,' a member of staff said. 'They're like Darby and Joan now – it's very sweet really.' Elizabeth has a dream, a fantasy that she knows she can never realise. There is a valley in Lancashire, near Clitheroe and the beautiful Forest of Bowland, where, she once told a friend, 'Philip and I would like to retire to . . .'

Epilogue

'Everyone thinks what fun to be the Queen if you can be Queen for a day: but for a lifetime . . .', Elizabeth's cousin, Lady Pamela Hicks's face expressed her horror at the prospect of such a fate. There can be no retirement for Elizabeth. She will remain in office until she dies or is mentally incapacitated. Even in the latter case, she will still be Queen until the day of her death.

Already her reign has been one of the longest in British history – and one of the most difficult of recent times. Despite her hard work and total dedication, she has seen the standing of the monarchy as an institution diminish from the high peak of glamour and adulation which it reached in her Coronation year so that as the millennium approaches, serious questions have been asked as to whether it will survive her. The 1990s have witnessed an unprecedented wave of criticism and, perhaps worse, derision directed at Buckingham Palace. Republicanism has become fashionable again although it is still confined largely to intellectuals, eccentrics and, more dangerously, a few powerful and influential people in the media.

The trigger for this disaffection has undoubtedly been the behaviour of the younger royals and the break-up of the marriage of the Prince and Princess of Wales in particular. As the novelist Julian Barnes wrote in his *Letters from London* in 1992:

When I was growing up, the Royal Family still operated as a normal and domestic exemplar for most of Her Britannic Majesty's subjects. This function is currently in abeyance. You could try to argue that Elizabeth's children are showing how democratically close to ordinary people they are by their ability to screw up their own lives; but that would be sophistry. Part of the unspoken deal between the Royals and the populace is that the Royals, in return for privilege, wealth and adoration, must occasionally be seen to suffer, or give the appearance of suffering; they must also indicate from time to time that they are subject to burdensome duty, to long-term conditions and restrictions that the rest of us do not envy. They can't be seen to wallow in the benefits and then walk away when things get sticky. Otherwise the Royal Family will quickly decline into mere illustrators of what is known in advertising as an aspirational life-style: this is how we plebs could and would live, had we the luck, the history, the tax breaks. Whether this would be a strong enough philosophical justification for the House of Windsor's continuance is doubtful.[1]

'The sexual and marital tomfoolery' of what Barnes calls the Queen's 'whelps' has indeed been terrible PR for Windsor Inc., but it has not been the only cause of the trouble. The social revolution which began in the late 1950s has ended the age of deference. As a result, almost every major Western country including the United States has suffered from what the former US Ambassador in London, Raymond Seitz, called 'institutional melancholy'. The general public is increasingly cynical about the integrity and wisdom of such established institutions as Parliament, the Church and the Law, and the monarchy was bound to be affected. Margaret Thatcher's reforming zeal undermined the traditional aspects of just about every British establishment and her advocacy of the free market ushered in the greed and excess of the 1980s, in which money, profit and cost were the criteria by which everything was to be judged.

The cost of the monarchy has always been a sensitive point and the Thatcherite requirements of cost-effectiveness and value for money are particularly difficult to apply to the 'magical' and ceremonial organisation which it represents. Could such an expensive establishment – the total cost of the monarchy to the public is estimated at £79.1 million a year – be justified in a Britain which was no longer a world power? Financial arguments about the monarchy are complicated and tedious, but abolishing it and replacing the Queen with a republican president as head of state would not necessarily save a great deal. The head of state could no doubt make do with a far smaller entourage than the monarch does at present and might, therefore, cost half the present sum to maintain, but it has been estimated that presidential elections would cost some £45 million a time every five years. A constitutional monarch is apolitical in a way which no president can be. Every non-royal person has some political views or connection, a situation which would inevitably create difficulties. He or she would be very unlikely to possess the glamour or aura which the sovereign does as the symbol of the nation. In any case the cost to the taxpayer of the Queen in terms of value for money compares favourably with the money which the British taxpayer contributes to the European Union's common agricultural policy merely for the destruction of the farmers' surplus produce. In 1993 the EU paid farmers £439 million for their surplus produce and then buried it. Britain contributed £57 million of this although British farmers were responsible for only 34,000 tonnes of the surplus. Among the fruit and vegetables destroyed were nearly a million tonnes of apples, more than 700,000 tonnes of peaches, some 165,000 tonnes of nectarines and nearly 127,000 tonnes of cauliflowers.[2]

Republican arguments against the monarchy are that it props up the class system and stands in the way of true democracy and the modernisation of Britain. Republicans object to the way that the prerogative powers of the Queen are deployed by the executive to implement objectives without consulting Parliament. The answer to most of these points, as an eminent constitutional expert put it in a television programme on the monarchy, is 'Rubbish'. The real divide in British society is not between the titled and the untitled but between the rich and the poor and the monarchy can hardly be held responsible for that. Abolishing it would not make the executive less powerful or undemocratic and might pave the way to political dictatorship. It is perfectly possible to reform the constitution, exclude the hereditary element from the House of Lords, and the other things that reformers would like to see without abolishing the monarchy. It really is up to Parliament to decide these things and deprive the executive of the prerogative power if it wants to, but under present conditions when the Whips are all-powerful and the Prime Minister has so many jobs in his gift, it seems extremely unlikely that the House of Commons would do any such thing. Equally, it is hard to see why 'modernisation' cannot be achieved without getting rid of the Queen. As an American observer put it, 'You tamper with institutions at your peril.' The British monarchy has lasted 1,200 years. Dismantling it would not be easy, nor would the finding of a satisfactory and safe alternative. It would be extremely difficult to disentangle the monarchy from the constitution and such a leap in the dark could be dangerous. Indeed recent polls suggest that around 80 per cent of the British people still want the monarchy, or at least they want Elizabeth as Queen.

Feelings about the Prince of Wales as a future King are more equivocal as a result of his marital troubles, but he will have to atone for his 'sins' as far as the public is concerned by sticking rather more closely to the Julian Barnes prescription than he has in the immediate past. The passage of time will help and people will forget. The Prince's willingness to accept change and his charitable work for the inner cities and the environment will help to restore his image. If the Queen survives as long as her mother has, the poor man will be a septuagenarian by the time he succeeds. The probability is that he will be King of Great Britain at least and head of the Commonwealth, but unlikely that he will be King of Australia, Canada or New Zealand.

The British monarchy has survived where others have not because of its adaptability. As a recent constitutional authority put it,[3] George Washington would recognise the position of Bill Clinton as similar to his own as President of the United States, whereas George III would certainly not be able to equate the powers of the monarchy in his day with those of his great-great-great-great-granddaughter, Elizabeth II. The constitution can be adapted to changing circumstances. The monarchy need no longer be identified with the Anglican Protestant Church of England, as indeed Charles recognised when he spoke of preferring 'Defender of Faith' rather than 'Defender of the Faith' to be included in his title on his accession. Some people have suggested eliminating the religious element altogether as outdated and substituting 'Defender of the Constitution'. The Act of Settlement with its emphasis on Protestantism and exclusion of Catholics would and should be changed. The Royal Marriages Act, which only came into being at the whim of George III who thought it unfair that his brothers should marry whom they liked where he could not, should be abolished.

Quite apart from Elizabeth's constitutional role as a safeguard against dictatorship – the armed forces, for instance, swear allegiance to her and not to the Government or the state – there is her real, although intangible importance as a focus of national identity and continuity in a rapidly changing, increasingly internationalised world. On Monday, 8 May 1995, Elizabeth with her mother and sister stood on the balcony of Buckingham Palace watching the VE Day commemoration celebrations. Below and in front of them, the Mall was packed with 300,000 people, gathered, just as they had been fifty years ago, in a spontaneous celebration of national unity. The Queen Mother was seen to wipe away a tear, no doubt remembering that day when she had stood there with her husband and Winston Churchill to acknowledge the cheering crowds, shouting 'We want the King!' Then, Elizabeth and Margaret had been just two young girls among the sea of faces. Now the Queen Mother was within three months of her ninety-fifth birthday, Elizabeth had celebrated her sixty-ninth birthday a few weeks earlier, Margaret was nearing her sixty-fifth. In the words of one young media commentator, 'The sight of those three old women on the balcony brought home to me what it was all about . . .' It was not clear whether he was referring to VE Day or to the monarchy. It could have been either or both. VE Day, in the eyes of those celebrating it, represented a victory, however brief, of good over evil. It was a commemoration of men and women who had sacrificed their lives for that victory. Elizabeth represents values which most people still recognise even if they don't either practise them or aspire to them themselves – courage, decency and a sense of duty.

POSTSCRIPT

After the turbulent years from 1992 to 1996 life for Elizabeth and the royal family has settled down to a more even tenor, although it could not yet be called 'happy ever after'. The divorces of first the Yorks and then the Waleses were made absolute on the 30 May and 28 August 1996, the first amicably, the latter, predictably, less so. Of the two, Diana emerged with the best settlement and the most dignity, with a £17 million lump sum, a generous allowance for her private office, retention of her Kensington Palace apartments, and a firm declaration by the Palace that she would continue to be regarded as a member of the family as far as state occasions were concerned. But she too, like Sarah, Duchess of York, was stripped of the title of Her Royal Highness, which had come with her marriage and implied membership of the royal family. To Elizabeth, the divorces meant that the two women were no longer married to their husbands and therefore no longer entitled to be Royal Highnesses, but while the public approved the removal of HRH from the Duchess of York, who was pilloried in the Press for her debts, her extravagance and the continuing revelations about her private life, many people thought that the Princess of Wales, as mother of the future king, should have been allowed to retain it instead of being known merely as Diana, Princess of Wales. Her name was also dropped from the official prayers of the Established Church. The public made it clear in an overwhelming response to newspaper polls that it was still unprepared to see Camilla Parker Bowles appear at the Prince of Wales's side, a verdict apparently accepted by the Prince and the Palace.

Diana, Princess of Wales, made outstandingly successful fund-raising charity trips to the United States and Australia while her ex-sister-in-law, Sarah, Duchess of York, wallowed in a trough of bad debt and worse publicity. The publication in 1996 of her self-exculpatory autobiography, *My Story*, was preceded by scandalous revelations by her fortune-teller, Vasso Kortesis, and John Bryan's former business partner Allan Starkie and followed by what many people saw as undignified promotion tours and television interviews with chat-show hosts and comediennes in a desperate attempt to improve her image and retrieve her finances. Elizabeth and Andrew were almost the only people to emerge unscathed. All three authors described Andrew as 'a gentleman' although it was not altogether certain that they knew what that meant. Sarah went out of her way to emphasise how generously her mother-in-law had treated her and her own affection and respect for her. While the rest of the royal family refused to have Sarah stay with them at Sandringham at Christmas, Elizabeth would make sure that she visited her at nearby Wood Farm and continued to have her to tea at Windsor on Sundays with her two York granddaughters. For Elizabeth the welfare of her grandchildren is of paramount importance. Prince William, despite the public and private traumas of his parents' divorce, appeared to settle down well at public school, Eton College, within sight of his grandmother's Windsor Castle, showing his closeness to his grandparents by preferring to remain at Sandringham for the Christmas following the divorce than to go skiing with his father.

There was a changing of the guard at Buckingham and St James's Palaces as some of the principal protagonists of the years of turbulence retired from the scene. Commander Aylard, the Prince's devoted Private Secretary, was sacked, being made the scapegoat for the controversial Dimbleby TV programme and biography and the rift between Buckingham Palace and St James's. At Buckingham Palace Charles Anson, the Queen's Press Secretary, after six years in what had been the hottest seat in royal public relations took a job in private industry, to be replaced by the likeable Australian Geoffrey Crawford, who had been his deputy and, until he resigned over the *Panorama* interview, press secretary to the Princess of Wales. Sir Robert Fellowes, who, with Anson, had been denounced as the villain of the piece by the Duchess of York, also announced his decision to retire after six years in the post, to be succeeded by Robin Janvrin.

The lessons of 1992–6 were not lost on Elizabeth. Chief among them was the evident need not to be once again taken by surprise and at the mercy of events. A body of the inner circle of the family and their principal advisers was set up on an informal basis to chart the future of the monarchy. Known as the Way Ahead Group, its brief was to plan the future on the organisational and public relations level and to maintain awareness of wider issues of concern to the monarchy and its future profile. One of their most important immediate concerns was the projection of the image of the Prince of Wales as the natural successor to Elizabeth, repairing the damage done by the failure of his marriage. He is to take over more of her public engagements and to be seen to be doing so. Changes under national discussion include not only the abolition of the Royal Marriages Act and modification of the Act of Settlement but also altering the English rule of male primogeniture to allow the Crown to devolve on the first-born child of either sex. In view of the fact that the Prince of Wales is Elizabeth's first born and that both his two children are boys, this particular change would not take effect in the foreseeable future, but such a move would be in line with modern thinking. Some of the most popular and successful sovereigns in the post-medieval age have been women – Elizabeth I, Queen Anne, Victoria and Elizabeth herself.

Among the more radical suggestions is that the sovereign should take back the Crown Estates, which, since the accession of George III, have been formally surrendered to Parliament at the beginning of each reign in return for the taxpayers subsidy, the Civil List. At present the annual revenues of the Crown Estates outstrip the value of the Civil List and other subsidies to the monarchy by some £30 million. The initial advantages to both monarchy and tax-payer seem obvious but the dangers are hidden. Just over three hundred years have passed since a king's head was cut off and his successor but one exiled in order to found a constitutional monarchy in which the sovereign was dependent upon the people for funds and therefore, by implication, on their consent. The ending of that contract between Crown and people is simply not on the cards. In the air-raid shelter at Windsor Castle where Elizabeth, Margaret and Crawfie used to spend dark hours of the night were some of the key relics of the monarchy, including one of the two shirts which her distant ancestor Charles I wore at his execution. As a keen student of the history of her country and her family, the lesson would not be lost on her. Elizabeth's security is in the sureness of her response to what her people want.

Elizabeth has always been cost-conscious, increasingly so since recent discontent over the expense of the monarchy. The royal travel arrangements are to be run on a budget from a block grant and organised by the Palace, instead of being offloaded onto various Ministries, principally Defence. Lastly, her beloved yacht *Britannia*, an instantly recognisable symbol of her reign for over forty years, is to be de-commissioned because of the huge costs of an overhaul. It will probably be replaced by a similar ship which will not be exclusively for the use of the Royal Family. It is part of a general slimming-down process which is what most of the public want. The questions recently asked about the monarchy have had beneficial effects, jolting Elizabeth and her advisers, however uncomfortably, towards the twenty-first century.

Acknowledgements

By kind permission of Her Majesty The Queen I was given access to papers in the Royal Archives at Windsor dealing with her life prior to her accession. I am indebted to Oliver Everett, the Librarian and Assistant Keeper of the Queen's Archives, to the Registrar, Lady de Bellaigue, and to Bridget Wright of the Royal Library for their guidance, help and kindness. I am grateful to the following librarians and archivists for facilitating access to their collections: Melanie Barber, Deputy Librarian and Archivist, Lambeth Palace Library; Alan Bell, Librarian, and the staff of the London Library; Dr B. S. Benediksz, former Sub-Librarian Special Collections, University of Birmingham; K. V. Bligh, Archivist (Modern Collection), and the staff of the House of Lords Record Office; Michael Bott, Archivist, and the staff of the Archives, Reading University Library; Peter B. Boyden, Head of Archives, Photographs, Film and Sound, National Army Museum; Michael Brunton, Librarian, *Time* Magazine; Dr Penelope Bullock, Librarian, Balliol College, Oxford; Mary Clapinson, Keeper of Western Manuscripts, Bodleian Library, University of Oxford; Raymond H. Geselbracht, Supervisory Archivist, Harry S. Truman Library; Alan Kucia, Archivist, Churchill Archives Centre, Churchill College, Cambridge.

I am more grateful than I can adequately express to all those who have helped me towards an understanding of my subject. For obvious reasons I have preserved the confidentiality of everyone connected with the royal family and household. I am also deeply grateful to the following: Larry Adler, the late Sir Godfrey Agnew, Mrs Fiona Asquith, Sir Reginald Bennett, Michael Bloch, Anthony Blond, Peter Blond, the late Lord Bonham-Carter, Lady Butler, Dame Barbara Cartland, Sir Hugh Casson, Nicholas Courtney, Rohan Daft, Lord Deedes, Professor David Dilks, Lady Margaret Douglas-Home, Margaret Forster, Lady Fraser, Geoffrey Gibbs, Martin Gilbert, Robert Golden, John Grigg, Mrs Eileen Hall (Eileen Heron), Philip Hall, the late Dowager Viscountess Hambleden, The Hon. R. J. L. Hawke AC, Tim Heald, Lord Healey of Riddlesden, Lord Jenkins of Hillhead, Jereen Jones, Robert Lacey, Mrs Derek Lawson, Dr Hugh L'Etang, the Countess of Longford, the late Lady Alexandra Metcalfe, Edward Mirzoeff,

Andrew Morton, Peter Nahum, Tim O'Donovan, Lord Owen, John Pearson, Roland Pym, The Honourable Sir Shridath Ramphal, Sir Robert Rhodes James, Andrew Roberts, Sir Frank Roberts, Mrs Patsy Robertson, Kenneth Rose, The Hon. Sir Steven Runciman, Giles St Aubyn, R. G. H. Seitz, Lord Sherfield, William Sitwell, Noreen Taylor, D. R. Thorpe, Peter Townend, the late Group Captain Peter Townsend, Hugo Vickers, Lord Wakeham of Maldon, Christopher Warwick, Viscount Whitelaw, Alan Williams MP, the Rt Rev. Robin and Mrs Woods, James Whitaker and Philip Ziegler.

I am especially indebted to Vernon Bogdanor for allowing me to see the typescript of his important book, *The Monarchy and the Constitution* (1995); to Pat Gannon-Leary for lending me her as yet unpublished thesis, *Royalty Represented: A Contemporary History of Imagery of Royalty and National Identity in Media Discourse*; and to Frances Montgomery for her MA Report for the Courtauld Institute of Art, *The Crowning of David: A Study of the Images of David as King in the Tiberius and Cambridge Psalters.*

This book would have been impossible without the help and support of everyone involved in its production: my agent, Gillon Aitken, who provided the original inspiration, and Sally Riley of Aitken, Stone & Wylie Limited; my editors, Helen Fraser and Roger Cazalet, at Heinemann, and Jonathan Galassi at Farrar Straus & Giroux, Inc. Linda Osband has provided invaluable support and expertise in editing yet another of my books. Douglas Matthews kindly agreed to do the index and David Williamson produced not only the family trees on the endpapers of the book but also the right answers to many complex questions. The archival expertise of my researcher, Dr Saul Kelly, has been a mainstay of this biography as it was for my previous book on George VI. I am grateful to my picture researcher, Lynda Marshall, for her skill in hunting out the right pictures to accompany the text, and to Bernadette Dunning for her patience in transcribing interviews and dealing with correspondence. But most of all I owe a debt to my husband, William Bangor, who not only bore with me over the long months of working on the book, but provided essential help and support in transcribing difficult interviews and reading proofs.

PERMISSIONS

Her Majesty The Queen for gracious permission to quote from the Royal Archives; Her Majesty Queen Elizabeth The Queen Mother for gracious permission to quote from her correspondence; and HRH the Princess Margaret, Countess of Snowdon, for gracious permission to quote from her correspondence. HRH Princess George of Hanover, for permission to quote. HarperCollins

Publishers for the Nicolson Papers; Lambeth Palace Library for the Fisher Papers; the Clerk of the Records on behalf of the Beaverbrook Foundation for the Beaverbrook Papers in the House of Lords Record Office; extract from Julian Barnes, *Letters from London*, reprinted by permission of the Peters Fraser & Dunlop Group Ltd.

Sources

All royal letters and diaries cited in the text are located in the Royal Archives at Windsor unless otherwise noted. Many are quoted in the authorised biographies, notably Sir John W. Wheeler-Bennett, *King George VI*, James Pope-Hennessy, *Queen Mary*, and Philip Ziegler, *King Edward VIII* and *Mountbatten*. Michael Bloch has had access to the Duke of Windsor's private papers and his *Wallis & Edward, Letters 1931–1937*, and *The Secret File of the Duke of Windsor*, contain original material not printed elsewhere. Jonathan Dimbleby's authorised biography, *The Prince of Wales*, is the source for the Prince's correspondence and diaries.

By gracious permission of Her Majesty The Queen I have consulted the Royal Archives concerning the period up to her accession in February 1952. Subsequent papers are reserved for the eventual authorised biography.

Apart from private sources, I have researched the following archives: House of Lords Library, Beaverbrook Papers; Columbia University Libraries, Bakhmeteff Archive; Archives du Ministère des Affaires Etrangères, Quai d'Orsay, Paris; Bodleian Library, Monckton Papers (Dep. Monckton Trustees); Public Record Office of Northern Ireland (PRONI), Londonderry Papers; University of Birmingham, Chamberlain Papers; Public Record Office (PRO) is the official source for state papers cited in this book: CAB, PREM, WORK and DO being the sections consulted; Royal Army Museum, Diary of Eileen Heron; Lambeth Palace Library, Don Papers, Fisher Papers; Balliol College, Oxford, Nicolson Papers; University of Reading, Astor Papers; Churchill College, Cambridge, Cadogan Papers, Swinton Papers.

Much of the book where sources are not quoted is based on oral testimony.

1: *Destiny*

1. cited in Noble Frankland, *Witness of a Century: The Life and Times of Prince Arthur, Duke of Connaught 1850–1942* (1993), p. 24
2. cited in Sarah Bradford, *King George VI* (1989), p. 19

3. *Ibid.*, p. 4
4. *A King's Story: The Memoirs of HRH the Duke of Windsor, KG* (1951), pp. 187–8
5. Mabell, Countess of Airlie, *Thatched with Gold* (1962), p. 21
6. Private unpublished memoir
7. Interview with the Hon. Lady Lindsay of Dowhill, 28 July 1986
8. Stanley Olson (ed.), *Harold Nicolson, Diaries and Letters, 1930–1964, Part Three* (1980), p. 338
9. Lord Harewood, *The Tongs and the Bones* (1981), p. 270
10. Robert Rhodes James, *Victor Cazalet* (1976), p. 255
11. Private collection, HM Queen Elizabeth the Queen Mother to Osbert Sitwell, 18 December 1944
12. Dorothy Laird, *Queen Elizabeth the Queen Mother* (1966), p. 34
13. Lord Gorell in Elizabeth Longford, *The Queen Mother* (1981), p. 18
14. Robert Rhodes James (ed.), *Chips: The Diaries of Sir Henry Channon* (1967), p. 397

2: *Princess in an Ivory Tower*

The main source for Elizabeth's childhood and adolescence is Marion Crawford's *The Little Princesses*, first published in 1951 and republished in a new edition in 1993.

1. cited in Robert Lacey, *Majesty* (1983), pp. 70–1
2. cited in Martin Gilbert, *Winston S. Churchill: The Exchequer Years* (1979), p. 1349
3. cited in Kenneth Rose, *King George V* (1984), p. 389
4. cited in Osbert Sitwell, *Rat Week* (1984), p. 44
5. Unpublished private memoir
6. Interview with Dame Barbara Cartland, 17 March 1994
7. Beaverbrook Papers, BBK H/165 (1954), John Gordon to Beaverbrook, 23 March 1954
8. cited in Osbert Sitwell, *Queen Mary and Others* (1974), p. 23
9. Columbia University Libraries, Bakhmeteff Archive, HRH Duke of Kent to Prince Paul Karageorgevic, 26 September [1934]
10. Dugdale Typescript Diary, 'Constitutional Crisis November to December 1936 by Nancy Dugdale', written from material supplied by Thomas Dugdale, Private Secretary to the Prime Minister, Stanley Baldwin
11. Rose, *op. cit.*, p. 92
12. Archives du Ministère des Affaires Etrangères, Quai d'Orsay, Direction d'Europe 1930–1940, Grande Bretagne, Z 274.3, File no. 176, f. 34

13. Lambeth Palace Library, Diaries of Dr Alan Campbell Don, Lambeth MS 2864, 22 January 1936
14. Airlie, *op. cit.*, p. 198
15. Interview with the Earl of Harewood, 23 April 1988

3: *Heiress*

1. Norman Hartnell, *Silver and Gold* (1955), p. 94
2. Hugo Vickers, *Cecil Beaton* (1985), pp. 226–7
3. Information on the Guides in this paragraph is based on interviews with members of the group.
4. RL/HRH Princess Elizabeth, 'The Coronation, 12 May 1937'
5. cited in Sir John W. Wheeler-Bennett, *King George VI* (1958), pp. 312–13
6. Unpublished private memoir
7. Bodleian Library, Dep. Monckton Trustees, MS9 f. 52, George VI to Monckton, 1 March 1942, cited in Bradford, *op. cit.*, p. 408
8. Michael Bloch (ed.), *Wallis & Edward, Letters 1931–1937* (1986), p. 238
9. Nigel Nicolson (ed.), *Sir Harold Nicolson: Diaries and Letters 1930–1939* (1966), pp. 297–8
10. PRONI, Londonderry Papers, D.3099/13/26, Queen Elizabeth the Queen Mother to Edith, Marchioness of Londonderry, 31 May 1937
11. Beaverbrook Papers, BBK G/23, Folder XIII
12. cited in John Vincent (ed.), *The Crawford Papers* (1984), pp. 617–18
13. cited in 2nd Earl of Birkenhead, *Walter Monckton* (1969), p. 169
14. University of Birmingham, Chamberlain Papers, NC 7/4/8, HM Queen Elizabeth the Queen Mother to Chamberlain, 2 July 1938
15. cited in Philip Ziegler, *Mountbatten* (1985), p. 102

4: *Windsor War*

1. cited in Trefor Evans (ed.), *The Killearn Diaries* (1972), p. 107
2. cited in Wheeler-Bennett, *op. cit.*, p. 304
3. Chamberlain Papers, NC 7/4/10, HM Queen Elizabeth the Queen Mother to Chamberlain, 17 May 1940
4. PRO PREM 4/10/4, Hailsham to Churchill, 19 June 1940
5. PRO WORK 29/1052, 27 September 1941
6. Mark Girouard, *Windsor: The Most Romantic Castle* (1993), p. 8
7. Eleanor Roosevelt, *This I Remember* (New York, 1949), p. 209
8. RA GVI PS 5850

9. RA GVI PS 222/23, Sir Gerald Wollaston to Lascelles, 6 January 1944; 222/52 memo. by Lascelles
10. Beaverbrook Papers, BBK H/165, John Gordon to Beaverbrook, 23 March 1954
11. cited in Ziegler, *op. cit.*, p. 308
12. Private collection, HM Queen Elizabeth the Queen Mother to Osbert Sitwell, 21 June 1944
13. National Army Museum WRAC Archive, diary of Eileen Heron, 1945
14. Interview with the Earl of Carnarvon, 25 January 1989

5: *A Princely Marriage*

1. In conversation with Basil Boothroyd, 1970
2. John Dean, *HRH Prince Philip, Duke of Edinburgh: A Portrait by his Valet* (n.d.), p. 35
3. Interview with the Countess Mountbatten, 5 May 1993
4. Sir John W. Wheeler-Bennett, *Friends, Enemies and Sovereigns* (1976), p. 137
5. cited in Ziegler, *op. cit.*, p. 457
6. cited in Bradford, *op. cit.*, p. 391
7. Peter Townsend, *Time and Chance* (1978), pp. 177–8
8. Private diary
9. The Act of Settlement of 1701 provided that in the event of Queen Anne dying without issue, the Crown was to be settled on the nearest Protestant heir, the Electress Sophia of Hanover (mother of George I). As the youngest daughter of Elizabeth of Bohemia, the Winter Queen, eldest daughter of James I, the Electress Sophia was a direct descendant of the Stuart kings. By Act of Parliament she and all her descendants were given British nationality. This appears not to have been generally known; in 1955 Prince Ernst August of Hanover went to court and eventually to the House of Lords to prove his British nationality. The Government was dismayed to find that some 400 persons, mainly German, were therefore British. PRO PREM 11/4438, minute by J. G. Phelps for the Prime Minister, Harold Macmillan, 24 July 1959
10. Private collection, HM Queen Elizabeth the Queen Mother to Osbert Sitwell, 10 July 1947. The Queen Mother is referring to the repeated UN vetoes of Allied proposals by Molotov, then Foreign Minister of the USSR.
11. cited in Bradford, *op. cit.*, p. 386
12. cited in Ziegler, *op. cit.*, p. 458
13. Beaverbrook Papers, BBK H/121, John Gordon to Beaverbrook, December 1947

14. Private information
15. RA GVI PS 8644(5), 18 November 1947, Lascelles to Press Secretary;
    13 February 1948, Lascelles to Secretary to Governor-General of Canada
16. Lambeth Palace Library, Fisher Papers, vol. 276, ff. 1–11

6: *The Edinburghs*

1. Balliol College, Oxford, Nicolson Papers, Harold Nicolson to Vita Sackville-
   West, 8 June 1948, unpublished postscript
2. PRO WORK 19/1175, 13 November 1947
3. PRO WORK 19/1175, minute dated 1 October 1947
4. *Loc. cit.*, correspondence and documents concerning the Clarence House
   cinema
5. John Parker in *The Queen* (1992), p. 21, states that the cost of refurbishing
   Clarence House reached four times the original estimate of £50,000. This is
   refuted by the evidence of documents in PRO WORK 19/1175, notably a
   minute of March 1951 giving details of the actual expenditure involved.
6. cited in Ziegler, *op. cit.*, p. 458
7. Elizabeth Longford, *Elizabeth R* (1983), p. 123
8. John Colville, *The Fringes of Power: Downing Street Diaries 1939–1955*
   (1985), pp. 625–6
9. RA GVI PS 9091, Lascelles to James Chuter Ede, 21 August 1948; Lascelles
   to Chuter Ede, 4 November 1948; Lascelles to George VI, '5.xii[xi] 1948'
10. RA GVI PS 9091(2), H. A. Strutt to Colville, 23 August 1948; Lascelles to
    George VI, '9.x.1948'; Letters Patent of 9 November 1948; Edward Ford
    to Sir Terence Nugent, 31 December 1948; George V's Letters Patent of
    30 November 1917
11. Christopher Hussey, *Clarence House* (1949), p. 102
12. University of Reading, Astor Papers, MS 1416/1/4, Queen Elizabeth the
    Queen Mother to Lady Astor, 19 October 1949
13. *Ibid.*, MS 1416/1/3/16, Major Thomas Harvey to Lady Astor,
    n.d. [October 1949]
14. *Ibid.*, Lady Astor to Mr and Mrs Bruce Gould, 8 November 1949
15. RA PP GVI 7606
16. Beaverbrook Papers, BBK H/152, John Gordon to Beaverbrook,
    4 March 1952
17. *Loc. cit.*, BBK H/136, Gordon to Beaverbrook, 6 January 1950
18. Interview with Noreen Taylor in the *Spectator*, 7 January 1995
19. Ziegler, *op. cit.*, pp. 491–2
20. *Ibid.*

21. RA GVI PS 1231, Norman Brook to Attlee, 14 June 1950; Lascelles to Brook, 21 June 1950

7: *Sovereign Lady*

The hitherto unpublished facts and opinions in this and the following chapters have been given to the author in confidence and are, therefore, not attributed.

1. Private collection, Queen Elizabeth the Queen Mother to Osbert Sitwell, 3 May 1952
2. cited in Victoria Glendinning, *Edith Sitwell: A Unicorn among Lions* (1988), p. 229
3. Astor Papers, MS 1416/1/4/10, HRH Princess Margaret to Lady Astor, n.d. [early 1952]
4. James Cameron, *News Chronicle*, 7 February 1952
5. Ziegler, *op. cit.*, p. 509
6. cited in Michael Bloch, *The Secret File of the Duke of Windsor* (1988), p. 261
7. *Ibid.*, pp. 261–2
8. cited in Philip Ziegler, *King Edward VIII: The Official Biography* (1990), p. 537
9. Bloch, *op. cit.*, pp. 264–5
10. *Ibid.*, p. 265
11. PRO CAB 128/24 CC(52), 18th Conclusions, Item 1, 18 February 1952
12. *Loc. cit.*, 20th Conclusions, Item 2, 20 February 1952
13. *Loc. cit.*, 36th Conclusions, Item 4, 3 April 1952
14. PRO CAB 129/51 C (52) 114, 7 April 1952
15. Beaverbrook Papers, BBK H/155, Arthur Christiansen to Beaverbrook, 13 March 1952
17. Longford, *op. cit.*, p. 157
18. Nicolson Papers, Harold Nicolson Diary, 19 February 1952 (unpublished passage)
19. PRO PREM 11/319 CC(52)39, minute 6, 8 April 1952, Lascelles to Colville, 10 April 1952, Colville to Duke of Norfolk, 10 April 1952
20. Kenneth Rose, *Kings, Queens & Courtiers* (1985), pp. 227–8
21. PRO PREM 11/34 CC(52)87
22. Churchill College, Cambridge, Cadogan Papers, ACAD 1/23, Diary 1952, 21 and 22 October
23. Beaverbrook Papers, BBK H/156, E. Pickering to Beaverbrook, 30 October 1952
24. Lambeth Palace Library, Fisher Papers, vol. 123, ff. 12–13, Diary of Coronation Preparations, 6 November 1952

25. PRO CAB 129/40 CC(52), 98th and 99th Conclusions, 18 and 20 November 1952
26. Bloch, *Secret File*; for this and the immediately following quotes, see pp. 277–9. 'The Unknown Soldier' was the Windsors' nickname for the Duke of Gloucester.
27. Colville, *op. cit.*, p. 713
28. Fisher Papers, *loc. cit.*, 2 June 1953

8: *Dark Princess*

1. Townsend, *op. cit.*, p. 189
2. The attribution of this painting has been questioned but most experts believe it to be at least in part by Leonardo.
3. Townsend, *op. cit.*, pp. 116–17
4. Interview with Group Captain Peter Townsend, 21 May 1993

9: *'The World's Sweetheart'*

1. PRO CAB 128/26 PART 1 CC(54), 8th Conclusions, Item 11, 10 February 1954; CAB 129/65 C(54)48, 8 February 1954, and C(54)49, 9 February 1954
2. PRO DO 35/5141, UK High Commissioner in New Zealand to Secretary of State for Commonwealth Relations, 25 February 1954, and DO 35/5139, UK High Commissioner in Australia to same, 9 April 1954
3. cited in Longford, *op. cit.*, p. 169
4. RA GVI 332/16
5. RA GVI 332/17, Lascelles to Duff Cooper, 4 July 1938
6. RA GVI 332/62, 29/5/51
7. RA GVI 332/68, Mountbatten to First Sea Lord, 1 June 1951
8. cited in Andrew Morton, *The Royal Yacht Britannia* (1984), pp. 32–3
9. cited in Martin Gilbert, *Winston S. Churchill*, vol. VIII: 1945–65, *Never Despair* (1988), p. 976
10. Colville, *op. cit.*, p. 654
11. Gilbert, *op. cit.*, p. 823
12. *Ibid.*, p. 849
13. *Ibid.*, p. 852
14. *Ibid.*, p. 897
15. *Ibid.*, p. 1117
16. *Ibid.*, p. 1124
17. *Ibid.*, pp. 1126–7

18. Interview with Professor David Dilks, 15 November 1994
19. cited in Robert Rhodes James, *Anthony Eden* (1986), pp. 600–1
20. Harold Macmillan, *Riding the Storm 1956–1959* (1971), p. 182
21. John Grigg, *The Monarchy Revisited*, W. H. Smith's Contemporary Papers No. 9 (1992), p. 4

10: *Tweed and Diamonds*

1. Nicolson Papers
2. Rose, *op. cit.*, p. 52
3. Interview with the Earl of Carnarvon, 4 October 1994
4. *Ibid.*
5. Interview with the Earl of Carnarvon, January 1989
6. Nicolson Papers, unpublished diary entry, 7 December 1955
7. Lacey, *op. cit.*, p. 230
8. Nicolson Papers, unpublished diary entry, 16 October 1957

11: *Mountbatten-Windsor*

1. cited in Alistair Horne, *Macmillan 1957–1986* (1989), p. 170
2. Interview with Larry Adler, 6 October 1994
3. 'Baron, Pat and the Duke – her story', *Independent on Sunday*, 4 April 1993
4. 'How Baron took Royal Photographs', *Illustrated*, 2 May 1953
5. Foreword to *Baron by Baron* (1957), p. xi
6. cited in Ronald Allison and Sarah Riddell (eds), *The Royal Encyclopedia* (1991), p. 451
7. Tim Heald, *The Duke: A Portrait of Prince Philip* (1992), p. 306
8. Beaverbrook Papers, BBK C/82, Arthur Christiansen to Beaverbrook, 29 July 1963
9. Nicolson Papers, diary, 12 July 1955
10. Beaverbrook Papers, BBK H/217, Gordon to Beaverbrook, n.d. [1961]
11. PRO CAB 128/25 CC(52), 106th Conclusions, Item 3, 18 December 1952
12. *Loc. cit.*, CAB 129/64 C(53) 301, 28 October 1953. According to the *Royal Encyclopedia*, whenever the sovereign is unable to attend a meeting of the Privy Council either through absence abroad or through temporary illness, two or more other members of the royal family stand in as Counsellors of State to exercise the functions of the sovereign. Under the Regency Acts, 1937–53, the Queen is empowered to appoint six Counsellors of State: the Duke of Edinburgh, the Queen Mother, and the four persons next in line of succession provided they have reached the age of twenty-one. At present

these four are the Prince of Wales, the Duke of York, Prince Edward and the Princess Royal.

13. PRO CAB 128/40 CC(55), 19th Conclusions, 2 March 1955
14. *Loc. cit.*, CAB 128/31 PART 1 CC(57), 13th Conclusions, Item 1, 22 February 1957
15. Macmillan, *op. cit.*, p. 318
16. cited in Anthony Holden, *Charles, Prince of Wales* (1979), p. 75
17. *Ibid.*, p. 72
18. *Ibid.*, p. 96
19. PRO PREM 11/441, Macmillan to Adeane, 27 June 1958
20. *Loc. cit.*, CAB 128/32 CC(58), 64th Conclusions, Item 7, 24 July 1958
21. *Ibid.*, PREM 11/4102
22. Interview with Lord Charteris of Amisfield, 16 June 1993
23. cited in Anthony Howard, *Rab: The Life of R. A. Butler* (1987), pp. 275–6
24. *Ibid.*
25. PRO CAB 128/40 CC(60), 4th Conclusions, 2 February 1960
26. Christopher Warwick, *Princess Margaret* (1983), p. 93
27. Nicolson Papers, diary, 28 April 1960

12: *Advise, Consult and Warn*

1. Harold Macmillan, *At the End of the Day 1961–1963* (1973), p. 27
2. cited in Horne, *op. cit.*, p. 203
3. Churchill College, Cambridge, Swinton Papers, SWIN 174/7/6
4. Harold Macmillan, *Pointing the Way 1959–1961* (1972), 13 November 1961, p. 472
5. PRO PREM 11/3509, Acting British High Commissioner in Ghana to Secretary of State for Commonwealth Relations, 11 December 1961
6. cited in Horne, *op. cit.*, p. 399
7. Interview with Sir Frank Roberts, 16 November 1993
8. cited in Horne, *op. cit.*, pp. 485–6
9. Michael Kitson in *The Dictionary of National Biography 1981–1985*, ed. by Lord Blake and C. S. Nicholls (1990), pp. 41–3
10. Report by Martin Bailey in *The Art Newspaper*, vol. v, no. 42, November 1994
11. Anthony Howard (ed.), *The Crossman Diaries: Selections from the Diaries of a Cabinet Minister 1964–70* (1979), p. 341
12. Interview with Sir Oliver Millar, 12 October 1994
13. Macmillan, *At the End of the Day*, p. 41
14. Howard, *Rab*, p. 292

15. Vernon Bogdanor, *The Monarchy and the Constitution* (1995), p. 87
16. cited in Horne, *op. cit.*, p. 533
17. *Ibid.*, pp. 556–7
18. Marcia Falkender, *Inside Number 10* (1972), p. 17
19. cited in Ben Pimlott, *Harold Wilson* (1993), p. 524
20. Interview with Baroness Castle of Blackburn, 26 January 1994
21. Tony Benn, *Office without Power: Diaries 1968–72* (1988), p. 38
22. *Ibid.*, pp. 190–1
23. When asked about Crossman's claim that he was a republican, Lord Jenkins replied that he 'wouldn't have gone as far as that' and that as Home Secretary, when he often saw the Queen in the course of his duties, he certainly did not 'feel uncomfortable' with her. Interview with Lord Jenkins of Hillhead, 2 November 1994

13: *Head of the Family*

Quotations from the Prince of Wales's letters and diaries in this and following chapters are from the authorised biography by Jonathan Dimbleby (1994) unless otherwise stated.

1. *Reflect on Things Past: The Memoirs of Lord Carrington* (1988), p. 16
2. Holden, *op. cit.*, p. 110
3. cited in Jonathan Dimbleby, *The Prince of Wales* (1994), p. 63
4. Dermot Morrah, *To Be a King* (1968), pp. 114 and 116
5. *Ibid.*, pp. 134–5
6. Nicholas Courtney, *Princess Anne* (1986), p. 22
7. *Ibid.*, p. 30
8. *Ibid.*, p. 38
9. Interview with HRH Princess George of Hanover, 12 May 1994
10. Private information
11. Bloch, *Secret File*, p. 399
12. Andrew Roberts, *Eminent Chuchillians* (1994), p. 282
13. Partly published in Ziegler, *King Edward VIII*, p. 555
14. *Ibid.*

14: *Daylight upon Magic*

1. Ziegler, *Mountbatten*, pp. 683–4
2. The information on this and the following pages comes from the *Report from the Select Committee on the Civil List, 1971–2*
3. John Campbell, *Edward Heath* (1994), p. 493

4. Longford, *op. cit.*, p. 276
5. In November 1975 the Governor-General of Australia, Sir John Kerr, dismissed the Prime Minister, Gough Whitlam, in consequence of the latter's inability to obtain supply. Kerr, quite rightly, did not consult the Palace since the Australian Constitution vested the power of dismissal in the Governor-General and not the sovereign, and he loyally did not wish to involve the Queen in an Australian political and constitutional crisis in which she had no legal powers. Constitutionally, therefore, the Queen was not involved, but because the Governor-General was her representative and she was, as Queen of Australia, head of state, the controversy raised Australian hackles and generated nationalist feeling about the anomaly of having an absentee head of state.
6. Denis Healey, *Time of My Life* (1989), p. 373
7. Pimlott, *op. cit.*, p. 648
8. Longford, *op. cit.*, pp. 278–9
9. Interview with Lord Owen, 22 November 1994
10. Interview with Susan Crosland, 1994
11. Susan Crosland, *Tony Crosland* (1982), p. 345
12. Roy Jenkins, *European Diary, 1977–81* (1989), p. 130
13. Hugo Young, *One of Us* (1990), p. 12
14. Letter to the author, 4 March 1995
15. Interview with Sir Shridath Ramphal, 20 December 1993
16. Interview with the author, 18 November 1993
17. Interview with the author, 18 July 1994
18. Paul Routledge in the *Observer*, 5 September 1993
19. Margaret Thatcher, *The Downing Street Years* (1993), p. 18

15: *Extended Family*

1. Courtney, *op. cit.*, pp. 61 and 57
2. John Barratt, *With the Greatest Respect*. The book, written with Jean Ritchie, was to have been published in 1991 but was withdrawn. John Barratt recently died of Aids.
3. cited in Dimbleby, *op. cit.*, p. 155
4. *Ibid.*, p. 193
5. see Roger Lewis, *The Life and Death of Peter Sellers* (1995), pp. 933–6
6. cited in Nigel Dempster, *HRH The Princess Margaret: A Life Unfulfilled* (1981), p. 127
7. *Ibid.*, pp. 119–20
8. Rose, *Kings, Queens and Courtiers*, p. 132

9. Bloch, *Secret File*, pp. 301–2
10. Ziegler, *Mountbatten*, p. 680
11. Dimbleby, *op. cit.*, p. 180
12. Ziegler, *Mountbatten*, p. 681
13. Dimbleby, *op. cit.*, p. 236
14. *Ibid.*, p. 244

16: *Grim Fairy-Tales*

1. Sarah Jennings (1660–1744), wife of John Churchill, 1st Duke of Marlborough, is described by the *DNB* as 'not an amiable woman, spiteful and untrustworthy but none the less shrewd and of remarkable ability'. She feuded with everybody from her former friend, Queen Anne, to both her daughters. The Spencers are descended from her daughter, Lady Anne Churchill, grandmother of the 1st Earl Spencer.
2. Andrew Morton, *Diana: Her True Story* (1992), p. 21
3. James Whitaker in conversation with the author
4. James Whitaker, *Diana v. Charles* (1993), p. 93
5. Douglas Keay, *Elizabeth II: Portrait of a Monarch* (1992), p. 238
6. Dimbleby, *op. cit.*, p. 392
7. *Ibid.*, p. 358
8. *Ibid.*, p. 497

17: *Family at War*

1. Lesley Player, *My Story: The Duchess of York, Her Father and Me* (1993), p. 251
2. Ronald Ferguson, *The Galloping Major: My Life in Singular Times* (1994), p. 207
3. Whitaker, *op. cit.*, p. 76
4. After her separation from Charles, Diana was reconciled with Raine, now Comtesse de Chambrun, and could be seen lunching with her at Claridge's.
5. cited in Dimbleby, *op. cit.*, p. 491
6. Private information

18: *Elizabeth R*

1. Interview with HE Ambassador Raymond G. H. Seitz, 3 February 1994
2. Bogdanor, *op. cit.*, p. 71
3. Bernard Palmer, *High and Mitred* (1992), p. 291

4. Rose, *Kings, Queens and Courtiers*, p. 92
5. Robin Simon in *Daily Mail*, 29 May 1995
6. Carnarvon interview, 4 October 1994
7. Arthur Fitzgerald, *Royal Thoroughbreds: A History of the Royal Studs* (1990), p. 249
8. James Pope-Hennessy, *A Lonely Business* (1981), p. 231
9. see Wheeler-Bennett, 'The Sovereign's Private Secretary', in *King George VI*, pp. 820–1

Epilogue

1. Julian Barnes, *Letters from London, 1990–1995* (1995), p. 159
2. *The Times*, 8 August 1995
3. Bogdanor, *op. cit.*, p. 302

Select Bibliography

Of the biographies of Elizabeth II now available, the most useful are: Kenneth Harris, *The Queen* (1994), Antony Jay, *Elizabeth R* (1992), Douglas Keay, *Elizabeth II* (1992), Elizabeth Longford, *Elizabeth R* (1983), and Robert Lacey, *Majesty* (1977). Authorised biographies of previous sovereigns and members of the royal family which contain original source material are cited at the head of the Sources section.

Airlie, Mabell, Countess of, *Thatched with Gold* (1962)

Allison, Ronald, and Riddell, Sarah (eds), *The Royal Encyclopedia* (1991)

Bagehot, Walter, *The English Constitution*, new edn with introduction by Richard Crossman (1993)

Baron by Baron [Baron Henry Stirling Nahum] (1957)

Barry, Stephen, *Royal Service, my twelve years as valet to Prince Charles* (1983)

Benn, Tony, *Office without Power: Diaries 1968–72* (1988)

Birkenhead, 2nd Earl of, *Walter Monckton* (1969)

Bloch, Michael (ed.), *Wallis & Edward, Letters 1931–1937* (1986)

Bloch, Michael, *The Secret File of the Duke of Windsor* (1988)

Bogdanor, Vernon, *The Monarchy and the Constitution* (1995)

Boothroyd, Basil, *Philip: An Informal Biography* (1971)

Bradford, Sarah, *King George VI* (1989)

Brendon, Piers, and Whitehead, Philip, *The Windsors, a Dynasty Revealed* (1994)

Campbell, Lady Colin, *Diana in Private: The Princess Nobody Knows* (1992)

Campbell, John, *Edward Heath* (1994)

Carrington, Peter A.R.C., Baron, *Reflect on Things Past: The Memoirs of Lord Carrington* (1988)

Colville, John, *The Fringes of Power: Downing Street Diaries 1939–1955* (1985)

Costello, John, *Mask of Treachery* (1988)

Courtney, Nicholas, *Princess Anne* (1986)

Crawford, Marion, *The Little Princesses* (new edn, 1993)

Crosland, Susan, *Tony Crosland* (1982)

Dean, John, *HRH Prince Philip, Duke of Edinburgh: A Portrait by His Valet* (n.d.)

Dempster, Nigel, *HRH The Princess Margaret: A Life Unfulfilled* (1981)

Dempster, Nigel, and Evans, Peter, *Behind Palace Doors* (1993)

Dimbleby, Jonathan, *The Prince of Wales* (1994)

Donaldson, Frances, *Edward VIII* (1974)

Duncan, Andrew, *The Reality of Monarchy* (1970)

Evans, Trefor (ed.), *The Killearn Diaries* (1972)

Falkender, Marcia, *Inside Number 10* (1972)

Ferguson, Ronald, *The Galloping Major: My Life in Singular Times* (1994)

Fitzgerald, Arthur, *Royal Thoroughbreds: A History of the Royal Studs* (1990)

Frankland, Noble, *Witness of a Century: The Life and Times of Prince Arthur, Duke of Connaught 1850–1942* (1993)

Gilbert, Martin, *Winston S. Churchill*, vol. V: 1922–39 (1976)

Gilbert, Martin, *Winston S. Churchill*, vol. VIII: 1945–65, *Never Despair* (1988)

Girouard, Mark, *Windsor: The Most Romantic Castle* (1993)

Glendinning, Victoria, *Edith Sitwell: A Unicorn among Lions* (1988)

Hall, Philip, *Royal Fortune: Tax, Money & the Monarchy* (1992)

Harewood, the Earl of, *The Tongs and the Bones* (1981)

Harris, Kenneth, *The Queen* (1994)

Hartnell, Norman, *Silver and Gold* (1955)

Haseler, Stephen, *The End of the House of Windsor, Birth of a British Republic* (1993)

Hawke, Bob, *The Hawke Memoirs* (1994)

Heald, Tim, *The Duke: A Portrait of Prince Philip* (1992)

Healey, Denis, *Time of My Life* (1989)

Hoey, Brian, *All the Queen's Men: Inside the Royal Household* (1992)

Holden, Anthony, *Charles, Prince of Wales* (1979)

Horne, Alistair, *Macmillan 1957–1986* (1989)

Howard, Anthony (ed.), *The Crossman Diaries: Selections from the Diaries of a Cabinet Minister 1964–70* (1979)

Howard, Anthony, *Rab: The Life of R. A. Butler* (1987)

Hussey, Christopher, *Clarence House* (1949)

Ingham, Bernard, *Kill the Messenger* (1991)

Jay, Antony, *Elizabeth R: The Role of the Monarchy Today* (1992)

Jenkins, Roy, *European Diary, 1977–81* (1989)

Jenkins, Roy, *A Life at the Centre* (1991)

Keay, Douglas, *Elizabeth II: Portrait of a Monarch* (1992)

Lacey, Robert, *Majesty* (1983)

Laird, Dorothy, *Queen Elizabeth the Queen Mother* (1966)

Lewis, Roger, *The Life and Death of Peter Sellers* (1995)

Longford, Elizabeth, *The Queen Mother* (1981)

Longford, Elizabeth, *Elizabeth R* (1983)

Macmillan, Harold, *Riding the Storm 1956–1959* (1971)

Macmillan, Harold, *Pointing the Way 1959–1961* (1972)

Macmillan, Harold, *At the End of the Day 1961–1963* (1973)

Morrah, Dermot, *To Be a King* (1968)

Mortimer, Penelope, *Queen Elizabeth, a Life of the Queen Mother* (1986)

Morton, Andrew, *The Royal Yacht Britannia* (1984)

Morton, Andrew, *Diana: Her True Story* (1992)

Nairn, Tom, *The Enchanted Glass, Britain and its Monarchy* (1988)

Nicolson, Nigel (ed.), *Sir Harold Nicolson: Diaries and Letters 1930–1939* (1966)

Olson, Stanley (ed.), *Harold Nicolson, Diaries and Letters, 1930–1964, Part Three* (1980)

Parker, John, *The Queen* (1992)

Pearson, John, *The Ultimate Family* (1986)

Pimlott, Ben, *Harold Wilson* (1993)

Player, Lesley, with Hall, William, *My Story: The Duchess of York, Her Father and Me* (1993)

Pope-Hennessy, James, *Queen Mary 1867–1953* (1959)

Pope-Hennessy, James, *A Lonely Business* (1981)

Prochaska, Frank, *Royal Bounty: The Making of a Welfare Monarchy* (1995)

Rhodes James, Robert (ed.), *Chips: The Diaries of Sir Henry Channon* (1967)

Rhodes James, Robert, *Victor Cazalet* (1976)

Rhodes James, Robert, *Anthony Eden* (1986)

Roberts, Andrew, *Eminent Churchillians* (1994)

Roberts, Sir Frank, *Dealing with Dictators: The Destruction and Revival of Europe 1930–70* (1990)

Roosevelt, Eleanor, *This I Remember* (New York, 1949)

Rose, Kenneth, *King George V* (1984)

Rose, Kenneth, *Kings, Queens & Courtiers* (1985)

Seward, Ingrid, *Prince Edward* (1995)

Shaughnessy, Alfred, *Both Ends of the Candle* (1978)

Sitwell, Osbert, *Queen Mary and Others* (1974)

Sitwell, Osbert, *Rat Week* (1984)

Thatcher, Margaret, *The Downing Street Years* (1993)

Townsend, Peter, *Time and Chance* (1978)

Vickers, Hugo, *Cecil Beaton* (1985)

Vincent, John (ed.), *The Crawford Papers* (1984)

Warwick, Christopher, *Princess Margaret* (1983)

Warwick, Christopher, *George and Marina, Duke and Duchess of Kent* (1988)

Watson, Sophia, *Marina: The Story of a Princess* (1994)

Wheeler-Bennett, Sir John W., *King George VI* (1958)

Wheeler-Bennett, Sir John W., *Friends, Enemies and Sovereigns* (1976)

Whitaker, James, *Diana v. Charles* (1993)

Whitelaw, William, *The Whitelaw Memoirs* (1989)

Wilson, A. N., *The Rise and Fall of the House of Windsor* (1993)

Windsor, HRH Duke of, *A King's Story: The Memoirs of HRH the Duke of Windsor, KG* (1951)

Woods, Robin, *An Autobiography* (1986)

York, Sarah, Duchess of, with Jeff Coplon, *My Story* (1996)

Young, Hugo, *One of Us* (1990)

Ziegler, Philip, *Crown and People* (1978)

Ziegler, Philip, *Mountbatten* (1985)

Ziegler, Philip, *King Edward VIII: The Official Biography* (1990)

Ziegler, Philip, *Harold Wilson* (1993)

Index

NOTES. The following abbreviations are used: ER = Queen Elizabeth II; EQM = Queen Elizabeth the Queen Mother. Ranks and titles are generally the highest mentioned in the text

Abdication (1936), 2, 56–7, 69
Abdul Karim ('the Munshi'), 5, 320
Abercorn, Alexandra (Sacha), Duchess of, 426
Aberystwyth, 336, 349–52
Acton, Sir Harold, 403
Adeane, Edward, 424, 440, 457, 459–60
Adeane, Sir Michael: as Private Secretary, 179, 244; and Churchill's resignation, 226–7; favours Suez War, 233, 245; and Macmillan's accession as PM, 236; Altrincham criticises, 240; background and character, 244–5; on ER's TV manner, 262; denies ER–Philip marriage difficulties, 268; on tiger shoot, 296; on ER's Ghana visit, 299; and Blunt case, 311; and Macmillan's resignation and succession, 316, 318; and ER's relations with Wilson, 320; and formal ceremonies, 323; and Charles's education, 334; in TV film *Royal Family*, 355; gives evidence to HC Select Committee on Civil List, 362; retires, 372; and ER's wishes, 516
Adelaide Cottage, Windsor, 197–8, 201
Adler, Larry, 265–6
Aga Khan, 402, 404
Agnew, Sir Godfrey, 320, 323
Ainslie (Palace butler), 30, 137, 143, 149
Airlie, David Ogilvy, 13th Earl of, 482, 515–17
Airlie, Mabell, Countess of: relations with Queen Mary, 14–15, 22–4, 41–2, 52;

Christmas present for ER, 30; on George V's relations with ER, 31; on Buckingham Palace, 60; compares ER with Victoria, 98; and ER–Philip courtship, 105; on Philip, 121; and George VI's funeral, 183; *Thatched with Gold*, 516
Airlie, Virginia, Countess of (*née* Ryan), 516
Airy, Major-General Sir Christopher, 462
Alanbrooke, Viscount *see* Brooke, Field Marshal Sir Alan
Albert, Duke of Bavaria, 305
Albert, Prince Consort, 4–5, 7, 40, 73–4, 143, 271
Alexander, Duke of Württemberg, 11
Alexander, King of Serbia, 7
Alexander, Prince of Yugoslavia, 328
Alexander, Ulick, 258
Alexandra, Princess, 209, 291, 301, 410–11
Alexandra, Queen of Edward VII, 9, 13, 28, 51, 456, 507–9
Alfred the Great, King of West Saxons, 3
Alfred, Prince, Duke of Edinburgh, 8
Alice, Princess of Greece (Philip's mother), 81–3, 128, 342
'Allah' *see* Knight, Clara
Allanbay Park (house), Berkshire, 209–10
Allison, Ronald, 406
al-Maktoum brothers, 503
Althorp (estate), 432–4, 472–3
Altrincham, John Grigg, 2nd Baron, 239–43, 245–6, 253–4, 260–3, 328, 521
Ambatielos, Betty, 301

Amies, Sir Hardy, 251–2, 305
Ancaster, Gilbert Heathcote-Drummond-
Willoughby, 2nd Earl of, 67
Anderson, John, 251
Anderson, Mabel, 146–7, 276–7, 279–80,
327, 330–1, 396, 445
Andrew, Prince *see* York, Duke of
Andrew, Prince of Greece, 81–2, 113
Anne, Princess Royal: birth and
christening, 159; childhood, 163; meets
ER in Tobruk, 217; meets Churchill,
226; character and behaviour, 277–8,
336–8, 340; surname, 286, 399; relations
with parents, 326, 337–8; upbringing,
326; education, 336–8; achievements,
duties and appointments, 338–9; riding,
338–40; appearance and dress, 339–41;
early unpopularity, 340–1; in TV film,
356–7; Civil List allowance, 364–6, 395;
Britannia honeymoon criticised, 369;
marriage, 392–5, 399; kidnap attempt on,
394, 448; regains popularity, 394; child,
395; at Gatcombe Park, 395; social life,
418; separation and divorce, 468–9;
letters stolen, 469; ER pays allowance to,
479; marriage to Tim Laurence, 484–5;
protests at Charles's portrayal of parents,
491
Annenberg, Walter, 355
Anson, Charles, 471–2, 520, 530
Anson, Lady Elizabeth, 417
Anyaoku, Chief Emeka, 522
Appiah, Kwame, 298
Appiah, Peggy (*née* Cripps), 298
Archer, Jeffrey, Baron, 486
Argyll, Margaret, Duchess of, 307
Armstrong-Jones, Antony *see* Snowdon, 1st
Earl of
Armstrong-Jones, Ronald, 246
Armstrong-Jones, Lady Sarah, 357, 401,
408
Arthur, Prince (Victoria's son) *see*
Connaught, Duke of
Ashmore, Vice-Admiral Sir Peter, 508
Askew, Barry, 444
Asquith, Margot, Countess of Oxford and
Asquith, 8, 15
Astor, Nancy, Viscountess, 151–2, 171, 308
Astor, William Waldorf, 3rd Viscount,
307–8

Athlone, Alexander Cambridge, Earl of,
136, 149
Athlone, Princess Alice, Countess of, 136,
149, 198
Attenborough, (Sir) David, 353
Attlee, Clement, 1st Earl, 118, 122, 141,
161
Australia (and New Zealand): royal visits
to, 164–6, 331–2, 371; Charles at school
in, 330–1
Austria: Hitler annexes, 76
Avon, Anthony Eden, 1st Earl of: and
Margaret–Townsend romance, 208, 210,
213; undergoes surgery, 222–3; and
Churchill's stroke, 223–4; and
Churchill's delayed resignation, 225–6;
succeeds to premiership, 227–8; relations
with ER, 228–9, 232–3, 320; and Suez
crisis, 230–5, 239; resigns, 232, 234–6;
divorce, 265; proposed as Deputy Prime
Minister, 314
Avon, Clarissa, Countess of (*née* Churchill),
208, 226, 415
Awotwi, David, 298
Aylard, Commander Richard, 461–3, 473,
488, 530

Baden, Margravine of *see* Theodora,
Princess
Badminton (estate), Gloucestershire, 91,
148
Bagehot, Walter: *The English Constitution*,
96, 336, 353
Balding, Ian, 504
Baldwin, Lucy, Countess, 35
Baldwin, Stanley, 1st Earl, 49, 54, 56,
344–5
Balmoral: Victoria at, 5; ER's childhood
visits to, 36, 73; Mrs Simpson at, 53;
George VI–Duke of Windsor dispute
over, 71; life and style at, 73–5, 418–19;
Churchill visits, 221; Eisenhowers visit,
284; Privy Council at, 322–3; in TV film,
356–7; Thatcher at, 380; Diana at, 443;
Charles–Diana children at, 465; Duchess
of York at, 476; ER at, 508, 512–14;
described, 512–13; shooting, 512
Baring, Helen ('Poppy'), 46
Barnes, Mrs (cook), 144, 149
Barnes, Barbara, 490

Barnes, Julian: *Letters from London*, 524–5, 527

Baron (photographer; i.e. Baron Henry Stirling Nahum), 138, 265–8, 270

Barrantes, Hector, 450

Barrantes, Susan (*formerly* Ferguson; Duchess of York's mother), 449–50

Barratt, John, 401

Barry, Stephen, 423, 441, 455, 518–19

Bartholomew, Carolyn, 473–4

Bashir, Martin, 492

Battenberg, Admiral Prince Louis of *see* Milford Haven, 1st Marquis of

Battle of Britain (1940), 92

Beaton, Cecil, 46, 61, 101, 305

Beatrice, Princess (Yorks' daughter), 469, 475

Beaufort, Henry Somerset, 10th Duke of, 240, 258, 418

Beaufort, Mary, Duchess of, 57, 91

Beaumont family, 43

Beaverbrook, William Maxwell Aitken, 1st Baron, 124, 153–4, 177, 224, 265, 368

Beck, Mary, 281

Bell, Sir Tim, 471

Benenden school, Kent, 336–8

Benn, Tony (Anthony Wedgwood Benn), 317, 321–2

Bennett, Alan: *A Question of Attribution*, 312

Bennett, Ernest ('Bennie'), 149, 249, 515, 518

Benning, Osla, 112

Berlin: ER visits, 376

Bermuda, 375

Bernhard, Prince of the Netherlands, 267

Berthold, Margrave of Baden, 83

Betjeman, (Sir) John, 289

Betty (kitchenmaid), 148–9

Bevin, Ernest, 122

Bill, Charlotte ('Lalla'), 14

Birkhall, Balmoral, 36, 53, 87–8, 130–1, 418, 456, 513

bishops (Church of England): appointment of, 498–9

Blanc, Louis, 82

Blandford, John Spencer-Churchill, Marquis of (*later* 11th Duke of Marlborough; 'Sunny'), 195, 288

Blitz, The, 92

Bloch, Michael, 72, 344

Bluebottle (yacht), 269

Blum, Maître Suzanne, 416

Blunt, Alfred Walter Frank, Bishop of Bradford, 55

Blunt, Anthony, 307–13

Blunt, Wilfrid Scawen, 309

Bolshevism, 18

Bonham Carter, Admiral Christopher, 296

Bonham Carter, Mark (Baron), 100

Boothby, Robert, Baron, 237, 307

Bowes-Lyon, Sir David, 21, 114, 143, 257, 411

Bowes-Lyon, Fergus, 22

Bowes-Lyon, John, 467

Bowes-Lyon, Michael, 22

Boyd, William, 329

Boyd-Rochfort, Cecil, 255

Boyle, Andrew, 313

Brabourne, John Knatchbull, 7th Baron, 117, 128, 148, 353, 425–7

Brabourne, Patricia, Lady *see* Mountbatten, Patricia, Countess

Bracken, Brendan, Viscount, 224

Brazil, 461–2

Britannia (royal yacht): replaces *Victoria & Albert*, 217–19; on Philip's tours, 264, 268–70, 284; on, 1959 Canada–US tour, 283; Margaret honeymoons on, 292; on Ghana visit, 299; in TV film, 357; cost, 363, 368–9; used for state visits, 375–6; Charles–Diana honeymoon on, 443; environmental seminar on, 462; entertaining on, 496; decommissioning, 531–2

British Expeditionary Force, 90

Broadlands (house), Hampshire, 130–1, 397–8, 400, 420, 425, 442

Bronington, HMS, 420

Brooke, Field Marshal Sir Alan (Viscount Alanbrooke), 92

Brooke, Henry, 311

Brooke, Peter, 479

Brown, George (*later* Baron George-Brown), 302, 322

Brown, John, 5, 74, 320

Brown, Tina, 454

Browning, General Sir Frederick ('Boy'): as Comptroller, 138–9; on Charles's name, 143; and Charteris, 155; on Mountbatten,

157; at ER's Coronation, 189; and
Townsend, 201; and Bobo MacDonald,
250; collapse and resignation, 270
Bruce, David, 307
Bruce Lockhart, Robert, 70
Bruton Street, Mayfair, 26, 30
Bryan, John, 468, 470–1, 475–6, 530
Bryant, Mrs Warwick, 146
Buckingham Palace: ER moves to as child,
58–60; organization, life and style at,
58–60, 62–3; air raid shelter, 91;
bombed, 92–3; household, hierarchy and
protocol, 136–7, 243–50, 253; ER and
Philip move to, 176; Diana moves into,
439; Michael Fagan breaches, 446–7;
opened to public, 482; described, 494–5
Bunting, Sir John, 378
Burgess, Guy, 308–9
Bush, George, 496
Business in the Community, 460
Buthlay, Major George, 125–6, 152–3, 155
Buthlay, Marion ('Crawfie') *see* Crawford,
Marion
Butler, Mollie, Lady, 335
Butler, Richard Austen, Baron ('Rab'), 223,
236–8, 261–2, 285–6, 313–15, 317,
335–6, 395
Butler, Sir Robin, 474
Bwthyn Bach, Y ('The Little House'), 36

Caccia, Harold (Baron), 275
Cadogan, Sir Alexander, 182
Caernarvon, 349–52
Callaghan, James (Baron), 259–60, 321–2,
351, 373–4, 379, 421
Callas, Maria, 411
Cambridge: Trinity College, 333–6
Cambridge, Adolphus, Marquess of, 47
Cambridge, Lady Mary, 43, 47
Camden, John Charles Henry Pratt, 5th
Marquis of, 201
Camden, Marchioness of *see* Townsend,
Rosemary
Cameron, James, 172
'Camillagate', 485
Campbell, Sir Harold, 100
Campbell, John, 369, 371
Campbell, Patrick, 265
Camrose, John Seymour Berry, 2nd
Viscount, 224

Canada: proposed separation from Crown,
37, 378; royal visits to, 78, 162–3, 283
Carey, George, Archbishop of Canterbury,
484
Carl Eduard, Duke of Saxe-Coburg and
Gotha, 125
Carnarvon, Henry Herbert, 6th Earl of, 257
Carnarvon, Henry Molyneux Herbert, 7th
Earl of (*formerly* Baron Porchester;
'Porchy'): on VE Day, 109; friendship
with ER, 256–9; rumoured to be father
of Andrew, 284; and ER's racehorses,
503–6
Caroline, Queen of George IV, 4, 8, 476
Carrington, Peter Carington, 6th Baron,
327, 381–2
Carson, Willie, 503
Carter, Howard, 257
Cartland, Dame Barbara, 39, 438, 442, 492
Cassandra (i.e. William Connor), 302
Casson, Sir Hugh, 218, 357
Castle, Barbara (Baroness), 319, 321–2, 361
Catherine II (the Great), Empress of
Russia, 42
Cavendish, Lady Elizabeth, 64, 289
Cavendish-Bentinck, Revd Charles
William, 21
Cawston, Richard, 353, 359
Cecile, Princess of Greece (*later* of Hesse
and the Rhine), 83
Cecilie, Princess of Germany, 311
Chamberlain, Ida, 70
Chamberlain, Neville: and Duke of
Windsor's allowance, 70, 344; agrees to
George VI's tax-free income, 71, 482;
visits Balmoral, 75; and Axis dictators,
76; and death of Lady Strathmore, 77;
and war threat, 78, 86; resigns, 89–90
Chan, Jacqui, 292
Chandler, Alice, 504
Chandos, Oliver Lyttelton, 1st Viscount,
236, 238
Channon, Sir Henry ('Chips'): on Glamis,
23; on Princesses' dress, 35;
homosexuality, 46; on Edward-Simpson
affair, 51, 54; on EQM's style, 61; on ER
and Philip, 102, 104–5, 139, 145; on
death of Queen Mary, 183; on Margaret,
199
Charles I, King, 2, 96, 143, 531

Charles: The Private Man, the Public Role
(TV interview), 488–9

Charles, Prince of Wales: temper, 11, 423,
453, 458, 519; birth and christening,
141–3; genealogy, 142; cello playing, 143,
332; nursery and nannies, 146–7;
devotion to EQM, 158; and birth of
Anne, 159–60; belief in homeopathy,
161; third birthday, 163; home, 176;
meets parents in Tobruk, 217; Churchill
praises, 221; meets Churchill, 226;
relations with parents as child, 276–7,
279–80; upbringing, 276–8, 326–7, 490;
character and behaviour, 277–8;
education, 278–80, 327–32, 420; made
Prince of Wales, 281–2; home life,
325–6; introspection and diffidence,
326–7, 332–3; acting, 332; at Cambridge,
333–5; confirmed, 333; sports and service
activities, 333–4, 419–21; comes of age,
334; romances, 335, 425–7; invested as
Prince of Wales, 336, 348–51; studies at
Aberystwyth, 336, 349–52; in TV film
Royal Family, 354, 356–7; finances
revised (1970), 365–7; 21st birthday, 392,
418; naval career, 392, 394–7, 419–21;
relations with ER, 395–6, 419, 455, 491;
relations with Mountbatten, 396–8, 420;
relations with Philip, 396, 491; relations
with Camilla Parker Bowles, 400, 424–5,
429, 435, 438, 440–1, 454–7, 485, 489,
519; dislikes Princess Michael, 410; and
Duchess of Windsor, 413, 415–16; few
friends, 418; role and duties, 421–3;
Duchy of Cornwall income, 422–3, 480,
482; spiritual questing, 423–4; meets and
courts Diana, 433–6; engagement,
436–8; and Diana's problems, 440–1;
wedding and honeymoon, 441–3;
children, 445, 454; plays polo, 449,
465–6; deteriorating marriage relations,
454–5, 457, 464, 469, 472–7, 524–5; and
staff, 454–5, 457, 519; visit to Italy and
Pope (1985), 458–60; expanding
activities and views, 460–1; advisers,
461–3; environmental concerns, 461–3;
TV biography of, 463; and ER's refusal
to abdicate, 469; receives bad press, 472;
relations with children, 472, 477–8;
father supports over Diana, 475; visit to
South Korea, 476–7; separation, 478,
483–4; pays income tax, 479–80, 482;
and Church, 484, 527; taped conversation
with Camilla leaked, 485; TV interview
with Dimbleby, 488–90; Dimbleby
biography of, 490–1; and Diana's
Panorama interview, 491; divorce, 492–3,
527, 529; and succession, 492, 526–7, 531

Charlotte, Queen of George III, 4

Charlton, Roger, 504

Charteris of Amisfield, Martin, Baron:
appointed ER's Private Secretary, 155,
372; on state visit to Canada and USA,
162–3; on George VI's health, 164; and
George VI's death, 166–7; relations with
Adeane, 179; on Margaret–Townsend
romance, 214; and Suez crisis, 233;
background and character, 245–6; 1959
mission to Accra, 283; suggests Windsor-
Mountbatten surname, 286; and Blunt,
312; in TV film, 357; on Heath and 1974
election result, 372; on ER's Silver
Jubilee, 377–8; retires, 419, 429; and
Prince of Wales Trust, 422; and Duchess
of York, 451; affection for Charles, 491

Cheam school, Hampshire, 83, 280–1

Checketts, Squadron Leader Sir David,
331–2, 351, 420–3, 427

Chequers, HMS, 156, 203

Chicago, 283

Childs, Wyndham, 27

China: state visit to, 388–9

Cholmondeley, George Cholmondeley, 5th
Marquis of, 179

Christiansen, Arthur, 177, 265, 273

Christopher, Montague, 510

Christopher, Prince of Hesse, 113

Church of England, 484, 489, 498–9, 527

Churchill, Clarissa *see* Avon, Countess of

Churchill, Clementine, Lady, 31, 204, 225

Churchill, Sir Winston S.: and ER's
accession on return from Kenya, 1, 167,
174; and ER as child, 31; on Edward and
Mrs Simpson, 56, 67, 89; and Duke of
Windsor's allowance, 70–1; and George
VI's visit to Paris, 77; succeeds
Chamberlain as PM, 89; and fall of
France, 90; at Windsor, 100; and ER's
title, 102; on ER's wedding, 121; 1945
election defeat, 122; condemns Paul of

Yugoslavia, 124; on George VI's decline and death, 160–1, 165, 220; re-elected, 163; in USA, 164; and ER's Coronation, 175, 180, 182; and George VI's funeral, 175; on ER's occupying Buckingham Palace, 176; on Mountbatten family ambitions, 177; opposes Duke of Windsor's presence at Coronation, 184; and Margaret–Townsend romance, 203–4; welcomes ER from 1953/54 tour, 219–20; relations with ER, 220–2, 224–5, 227–8; accepts Garter, 221–2; portrait bust, 221; suffers stroke, 222–5; resignation, 225–7; declines dukedom, 227; and Macmillan's appointment as PM, 236; and Philip's title, 275; and Duke of Windsor's Nazi association, 310, 344; death and funeral, 324; and VE Day, 528

Civil List: introduced, 3; George VI's voluntary cuts, 35; and Duke of Windsor's savings and allowance, 70, 73; Wilson approves 1975 revisions, 319; effect of inflation on, 360–1; 1970 Commons Select Committee on, 361–8; 1975 increases, 368; and Anne's marriage increase, 395; 1990 increases, 464; 1992 curtailments and revisions, 479–81; and Crown Estates, 531

Clarence, Edward, Duke of ('Eddy'), 10–12, 15

Clarence House, London, 134–6, 145–6, 149–51, 157, 175–6

Clark, Jane, Lady, 222

Clark, Kenneth, Baron, 258

Cleveland Street scandal, 10

Clinton, Bill, 527

Coates, Major Jimmy: 'mission', 91–2

Cobbold, Cameron Fromanteel Cobbold, 1st Baron, 261, 362, 364, 367

Coke, Edward Douglas, Viscount, and Valeria, Viscountess, 406

Colborne, Michael, 440–1, 454, 457

Collins, Phil, 488

Collor de Mello, Fernando, 461

Colville, Lady Cynthia, 90, 138, 183

Colville, Sir John ('Jock'): on ER's first broadcast, 93; on incident at Patricia Mountbatten's wedding, 128; and ER's wedding, 129; as ER's Private Secretary,

137–8; and ER's Paris visit, 139–41; writes ER's speeches, 139; returns to diplomatic service, 155; resumes as Churchill's Private Secretary, 174; and Mountbatten's family claim, 176–7; and ER's coronation, 180, 182, 185; and court life, 197; on Margaret–Townsend romance, 204; on Churchill's reaction to George VI's death, 220; on Churchill's relations with ER, 220–1, 227; and Churchill's stroke, 223–4; and Churchill's proposed dukedom, 227; on ER's working methods, 229; on ER's private wealth, 363

Colville, Margaret, Lady (*formerly* Egerton; 'Meg'), 138, 155

Colville, Commander Richard: and Margaret–Townsend romance, 204, 209; character, 246–7; and Parker's resignation, 265; and ER's family role, 275; and Charles's upbringing, 278–9, 281; retires, 354

Commonwealth: and national independence, 122; ER's devotion to, 186, 294, 300, 321, 381–3, 388, 522; ER's 1953/54 tour of, 215–19; sovereign as Head of, 215; Philip tours (1956), 264; ER's 1961 tour of, 295; Heath's antipathy to, 370; and Britain's EC entry, 371; Thatcher and, 384–6, 388

Commonwealth Conference, London (1962), 300

Commonwealth Games: 1958, 281–2; 1974, 369; 1978, 378; 1986, 386

Concorde (aircraft), 322

Connaught, Prince Arthur, Duke of, 6, 28, 44, 99, 134

Conservative Party: 1963 leadership succession, 315–18

Cooper, Alfred Duff (1st Viscount Norwich), 25, 74, 217, 258

Cooper, Lady Diana, 25, 77, 379

Cooper, Jilly: *Riders*, 450

Coppins (house), Iver, Buckinghamshire, 104–5

Corbett, Jim, 166

Corbin, René, 49

Cordet, Hélène, 267

corgis, 38–9, 148, 512–13

Cornish, Francis, 440

Cornwall, Duchy of: revenues, 365–7, 422, 480, 482; Charles and, 422

Coronations: George VI (1937), 58, 64–8; ER (1953), 180–92

Coty, René, 62

Coventry: bombed, 93–4

Coward, Noël, 46, 69, 98, 257, 291

Crawford, Geoffrey, 520, 530

Crawford, Marion (*later* Buthlay; 'Crawfie'): on George VI and ER, 34; on Margaret, 34; appointed governess, 37, 39; on ER's orderliness, 39; and Princesses' education, 40–1; and Princesses' upbringing, 42–3; and death of George V, 50; at Buckingham Palace, 59–60; on ER and Margaret at garden parties, 62; and Buckingham Palace Girl Guides, 63–4; on ER at 1937 Coronation, 66; and ER's emotional reaction to death of grandparents, 77; and return of ER's parents from USA, 79–80; on Philip, 84; and outbreak of war, 87, 89; at Windsor in wartime, 90, 95, 100, 531; teaches ER, 97; on death of Duke of Kent, 99; on ER's adolescence, 101; remains on staff, 111; and ER's engagement, 116; marries and leaves service, 125–6, 152–3; on ER's growing self-reliance, 150; retires and writes on Princesses, 150–5; death, 155; and Margaret's education, 199; *The Little Princesses*, 38, 152–3

Crosland, Charles Anthony Raven, 374, 424

Crosland, Susan, 374–6

Crossman, Richard H. S., 312, 320, 322–3

Crowley, Aleister, 100

Crown Estates, 363, 366–7

Cunard, Maud Alice, Lady ('Emerald'), 69

Cunningham, Admiral Andrew, Viscount, 103

Curzon House, London, 93

Cust, Harry, 379

Cyprus, 295, 301

Czechoslovakia: Germany occupies, 78, 86

D-Day celebrations (1994), 389

Daily Express, 265, 273

Daily Mail, 241, 471, 479, 481, 486

Daily Mirror, 470, 475, 485, 486

Daily Sketch, 206

Dalkeith, John Montagu Douglas Scott, Earl of, 195, 288

Dalton, Hugh, 90, 122

Dalton, Revd John Neale, Canon of Windsor, 15

Danzig, 86

Darling, Fred, 255, 257

Dartmouth: Royal Naval College, 19–20, 84, 334, 420, 446

Daudufret-Pasquet, Duc de, 504

Dawnay, Oliver, 209

Dawson of Penn, Bertrand Edward, Viscount, 49

Day Lewis, Cecil, 355

Dean, John, 114, 129–30, 136–7, 144–50, 163, 165, 167, 175

de Bellaigue, Antoinette ('Toni'), 96–7, 111, 139

de Bellaigue, Sir Geoffrey, 97

debutantes, 261

Derby, Frederick Arthur Stanley, 16th Earl of, 15

Devonshire, Deborah, Duchess of, 249

Devonshire, Edward Cavendish, 10th Duke of, 128

Diana, Princess of Wales *see* Wales, Diana, Princess of

Dickman, Cyril, 95, 111, 130–1, 249

Diefenbaker, John, 283

Dilks, Professor David Nevill, 229

Dimbleby, Jonathan, 279, 422, 436, 455, 457–9, 463, 478, 488–90; *The Prince of Wales: A Biography*, 490

Dimbleby, Richard, 292, 324

Disraeli, Benjamin, 6, 176

Dixon, Sir Pierson, 301

Don, Rt Revd Alan Campbell, Dean of Westminster, 24, 50, 68

Donoghue, James, 184

Doughty, Charles, 470

Douglas-Home, Sir Alec *see* Home, Baron

Douglas-Home, Robin, 404

Driberg, Tom, 123, 192

Dudley Ward, Freda, 24

Dudley, William Ward, 3rd Earl of, 184

Duke of Edinburgh's Award Scheme, 272

Duke of York's camps, 18–19, 78, 86

du Maurier, Daphne (Lady Browning), 138, 258, 262, 270, 515

Dunkirk evacuation (1940), 90

Durham, John George Lambton, 3rd Earl of, 27

EIIR (TV film), 495–6, 505, 508
Eccles, David, 1st Viscount, 187, 306
Ede, James Chuter, 121, 141
Eden, Sir Anthony *see* Avon, 1st Earl of
Edgar, Donald, 270
Edinburgh, Dukes of *see* Alfred, Prince; Philip, Prince
Edward III, King, 94
Edward VII, King, 5–9, 44, 59, 61, 144, 421, 456–7
Edward VIII, King *see* Windsor, Edward, Duke of
Edward, Prince (ER's son): born, 323, 325; home life, 341; and Princess Alice, 342; in TV film, 356; allowances, 365, 464, 479; education, 392, 452; career, 452–4; character and behaviour, 452–3; sex life, 453–4; protests at Charles's portrayal of parents, 491
Edwards, Bob, 435
Egbert, King of Wessex, 3
Egypt: and Suez War, 231–3
Eisenhower, Dwight D., 164
Eisenhower, John, 284
Eisenhower, Mamie, 283–4
Ekland, Britt, 403
Eldon, John Scott, 4th Earl of, 114, 257
Elizabeth II, Queen: and father's accession, 2, 57; genealogy, 2–4; appearance, 10, 141; birth and christening, 25–8; childhood, 30–2, 37–8; character, 31–4; relations with George V, 31–2; first pony, 32; relations with Margaret, 33–5, 100–1; corgis, 38–9, 148–9, 512–13; interest in riding and horses, 38, 97, 158, 254–8; orderliness, 39; education, 40–1, 63, 96–7; childhood daily routine, 43; childhood friends, 43; and Edward–Mrs Simpson relationship, 47–8; dress as child, 49, 66; and death of George V, 50; at Glamis, 53–4; and Abdication crisis, 56; on parents' Coronation, 65–8; consents to pay tax, 71, 479–82; and position of Duke of Windsor, 72–3; at Balmoral, 73, 75; and deaths of Strathmore grandparents, 76–7; first meets Philip, 80, 84–5; cries at

Chamberlain's resignation, 90; first broadcast, 93; in wartime Windsor, 93–6, 99–100, 531; as Girl Guide, 97; confirmed, 98; Grenadiers Colonelcy, 99; shyness and innocence of world, 101–2, 109–10, 156; devotion to Philip, 102–3, 110, 116; made Counsellor of State, 102; style and title as Princess, 102; serves in ATS, 106–8; driving, 109; given own suite at Buckingham Palace, 111; engagement, 116–17, 121; reserve, 117; on 1947 South Africa tour, 118–20; wedding, 121, 123–4, 126–7, 129–30; official allowance, 124; awarded Garter, 128; honeymoon, 130–1; marriage relations, 133, 145, 156, 178–9, 264, 278, 399–401, 448, 523; pregnancy and birth of Charles, 133, 140–2, 144; early homes and household, 134–8, 144–6; 1948 Paris visit, 139–40; popular appeal, 140–1; and adoption of Mountbatten-Windsor surname, 142, 285–6; food and drink, 148–9, 359, 501; relations with staff, 149–50, 513–15, 517–19; dependence on Philip, 150; in Malta, 158–9; pregnancy and birth of Anne, 158–9; 1951 Rome visit, 160; increasing official duties, 160–2; belief in homeopathy, 161; 1950 visit to Canada and USA, 162–4; 1952 aborted trip to Australia and New Zealand, 164–6; accession on father's death, 165–71; at father's funeral, 172; entertains Duke of Windsor, 173; proclaims confirmation of Windsor surname, 177; and planning of Coronation, 180–4; titles, 181; self-dedication, 185–6, 192; and Commonwealth, 186, 294, 300, 321, 370–1, 381–3, 386, 388, 522; and Coronation ceremony, 187–92; and Margaret–Townsend romance, 194, 202–11, 214, 239, 263; 1953/54 Commonwealth tour, 215–19; and royal yacht, 218–19; relations with Churchill, 220–2, 224–5, 227–8; interest in horse-racing, 222, 224, 503–7; and Churchill's stroke and resignation, 223–4, 226–7; working methods, 229–30; and speechmaking, 230; and Suez War, 233–4; and Macmillan's premiership,

237–8, 239; criticised, 240–2; courtiers and household, 243–51, 253, 483; social and domestic duties, 250; dress and style, 251–3; interest in dogs, 254; lacks intellectual interests, 258–9; friends, 259; self-containment, 259–60; humour, 260; Christmas speeches, 262; public persona, 263; relations with children, 275–9; and Charles's education, 279–80, 327–8, 330–3; creates Charles Prince of Wales, 281–2; 1956 Canada–US tour, 283–4; and birth of Andrew, 283–4; meets Armstrong-Jones, 290; as Head of Commonwealth, 294, 300; 1960 visit to Italy, 295; 1961 Commonwealth tours, 295–6, 301; visits Ghana, 297–300; and EC entry, 300–1, 371; booed by demonstrators, 301–2; 1965 visit to Germany, 303–4; and Blunt, 311–13; approves post of Deputy Prime Minister, 313–14; and succession to Macmillan, 315–18; relations with Harold Wilson, 319–21, 372–4; opposes abolition of hereditary titles, 320; and Labour Party, 322–3; and birth of Edward, 323, 325; and Privy Council, 323; home and family life, 325–7, 337, 341–2; thrift, 342–3; softens attitudes to Windsors, 343–9; and Charles's investiture as Prince of Wales, 350–1; in TV film, 353–60; health, 358–9; finances reviewed, 361–8; private wealth, 362–3, 368, 501; taxation immunity, 366, 368, 464, 479–80; uses *Britannia*, 369, 531; friendliness, 373–5; 1976 US state visit, 374–6; visits Berlin, 376; Silver Jubilee, 377–8, 422; relations with Thatcher, 379–81, 386–91; attends Lusaka Conference, 382–4; and Charles's 21st birthday party, 392; and children's marriages, 392–3; emotional reserve, 395–6; first grandchild, 395; relations with Charles, 395, 419, 422, 455, 463, 465, 491; and family, 401, 429; and Margaret's marriage difficulties, 403–9; keeps relations with Snowdon, 408–9; and death of Duke of Windsor, 412, 414–15; 50th birthday, 417; and death of Duchess of Windsor, 417; Jubilee Trust, 422; and Charles's marriage prospects, 426; and

assassination of Mountbatten, 427; and Charles's courtship of Diana, 436–8; relations with Diana, 439–40, 443–4, 455–6, 474, 485–7; disturbed by intruder, 446–7; and Andrew's romances, 448; apparent assassination attempt on, 448; relations with Duchess of York, 451, 466, 469, 474; resents press intrusion, 454, 480–1, 487; and Charles's deteriorating marriage, 455, 457, 464, 469; and Charles's proposed visit to Pope, 459–60; and Church of England reforms, 461; family problems, 464–5, 469–77, 485–8, 499, 524–5; eschews abdication, 469; and Windsor Castle fire, 478–81, 481; pays allowances to family, 479–82; concedes tax payments, 479–92; criticised for cost of monarchy, 482–3; and Charles's Dimbleby interview and biography, 488–92; visit to Russia, 490–1; and Diana's *Panorama* interview, 491; and Wales's divorce, 492–3, 529–30; TV film (*EIIR*), 495–7; contact with others, 496–8; and prime ministers, 496; and Church appointments, 498–9; and divorcees, 499–500; religious observance, 499; cultural and artistic tastes and collections, 500–1; memory, 512; household and court, 519–22; attitude to women, 522; prerogative powers, 526–7; symbolic powers, 528

Elizabeth the Queen Mother: background and upbringing, 19–21; courtship, 20, 22–3; and birth of ER, 25–7; marriage, 25; 1927 Australasian tour, 29; on childhood adulation of ER, 31; and birth of Margaret, 32; family life, 35–6; at Royal Lodge, Windsor, 36; and daughters' education, 39–40; hostility to Duchess of Windsor, 47, 53, 348–9; pneumonia and influenza, 50, 56–7; on George V's death, 51; life at Buckingham Palace, 60–1; appearance and dress, 61, 68; Coronation, 64–7; adopts Queenly role, 68–9; attitude to Duke of Windsor, 72–3, 125; supports husband, 72; fishing, 74–5; and mother's death, 77; 1939 visit to USA and Canada, 78–80; reserve over Mountbatten, 81; and outbreak of war, 87–8; and Chamberlain's resignation, 90;

and bombing of Buckingham Palace,
92–3; entertains at Windsor, 100; and VI
attacks on London, 105–6; visits ER in
ATS, 108; on 1947 South Africa tour,
119–20; and ER's engagement, 121; and
Crawfie's marriage, 126; and Crawfie's
book, 151–2; devotion to Charles, 158,
277, 327, 329; and George VI's health
decline and death, 161, 164, 169–72;
relations with ER as Queen, 170–1;
entertains Duke of Windsor at George
VI's funeral, 173; and
Margaret–Townsend romance, 194, 202,
205–11, 213–14; tour of S. Rhodesia,
205; Altrincham criticises, 240–1; gives
jewellery to ER, 252; intellectual
interests, 258–9; and Charles's university
education, 334–5; Civil List allowance,
364, 366; and Rhodesia crisis, 383;
friendship with Snowdon, 401, 409; and
Margaret's marriage difficulties, 407;
attemps to visit Duchess of Windsor,
416; 70th birthday, 418; social style, 418;
and Charles–Diana engagement, 436;
supports Charles, 455; and Duchess of
York's behaviour, 471–2; remains on
Civil List, 480; and Anne's marriage to
Laurence, 485; non-betting, 506;
memory, 512; corgis, 513; attitude to
women, 522–3; at VE Day 50th
anniversary, 528
Elizabeth, Princess of Greece *see* Toerring-
Jettenbach, Countess of
Elizabeth, Queen of Bohemia ('The Winter
Queen'), 3
Elliot, Dominic, 207
Elliot, Nicholas, 311
Elliot, Walter, 51
Elphinstone family, 43
Elphinstone, Jean *see* Wills, Jean
Elphinstone, Margaret, 38
Elphinstone, Mary Frances, Lady (*née*
Bowes-Lyon), 28
Empire, British *see* Commonwealth
Empress of Britain (ship), 79, 161
English, Sir David, 472
Entente Cordiale (France–England), 10
Ernst August, Duke of Brunswick, 304
Ernst August, Prince of Hanover, 176, 310

Esher, Reginald Baliol Brett, 2nd Viscount,
18
Eton College, 327
Eugenie, Princess (Yorks' daughter),
466–7, 471, 475
European Community (Union), 294–5, 300,
370–1, 376–7, 526
Euston, Hugh Fitzroy, Earl of (*later* 11th
Duke of Grafton), 100, 102, 259
Evans, Mrs (housekeeper), 30
Everest, Mount, 186
Everett, Oliver, 440, 454

Fagan, Michael, 446–8
Falklands War (1982), 386, 389, 445, 448
Farebrother, Michael, 279
Farish, William F., 504
Farrer, Sir Matthew, 470
Fellowes, Jane, Lady (*née* Spencer), 432,
434, 441
Fellowes, Sir Robert: marriage, 434;
relationship to Duchess of York, 449;
advises Charles against polo, 465;
counsels Duchess of York, 468; and
Duchess of York's marriage breakdown,
471–2; on Morton's *Diana*, 474;
background, 520–1; retires, 530
Fellowes, Sir William, 434
Ferguson, Mrs (Palace housekeeper), 143
Ferguson, Major Ronald, 449, 467, 468–9,
474
Ferguson, Sarah *see* York, Sarah, Duchess
of
Ferguson, Susan (Duchess of York's
mother) *see* Barrantes, Susan
Fermoy family, 430–2
Fermoy, Ruth, Lady, 430, 432, 434, 436
Festival of Britain (1951), 160
Fisher, Geoffrey, Archbishop of
Canterbury, 183, 191–2, 212
Fitzalan-Howard, Alathea, 43, 97
Fitzherbert, Maria Anne, 4
Fleming, Ian and Ann, 232
Ford, Sir Edward, 142, 166, 178–9, 197,
233, 245–6, 481
Ford, Gerald and Betty, 376
Forster, Margaret, 270
Fort Belvedere, 37
Fortune (US magazine), 362–3
Fox, Frederick, 251

Fox, Uffa, 269
France: George VI visits (1938), 76–8; 1940 defeat, 90; and Suez War, 231–4
Francis, Mary, 520–2
Franz, Prince, Duke of Teck, 11, 45
Fraser, Malcolm, 383, 385
Frederick William, Prince of Germany, 311
Frederika, Queen of the Hellenes, 160, 301–3
Freeman, Simon, 387–8
Friedrichshof, Germany, 309
Frogmore (house), Windsor, 346–7
Fry, Jeremy, 292
Furness, Thelma, Viscountess (*née* Morgan), 35, 37, 44–5

Gaitskell, Hugh, 122
Gale, Daphne, Lady, 517
Game Research Association, 257–8
Gandhi, Mohandas Karamchand, 127
Gasperi, Alcide de, 222
Gatcombe Park, Gloucestershire, 395
Gaulle, Charles de, 294–5, 300–1
Geddes, Margaret *see* Margaret, Princess of Hesse and the Rhine
Geelong High School, Australia, 331, 420
General Strike (1926), 27–8
George I, King, 3
George II, King, 3
George III, King, 3–4, 58, 143, 527, 531
George IV, King, 4, 8, 58, 65, 476
George V, King: removes John Brown's statue, 5, 74; relations with son Edward, 7, 44; appearance and character, 12–13; marriage, 12; relations with children, 13–16, 19; success as king, 16; in World War I, 16–17; disapproves of newspapers, 25; and names for ER, 28; and ER's childhood, 29, 31–2; convalesces at Bognor, 31; economises on Civil List, 35; on Princesses' education, 40; and Mrs Simpson, 47; popularity, 48–9; Silver Jubilee (1935), 48–9; health decline and death, 49–51; settles money on sons, 71; stamp collection, 71; rescues Philip's family, 81; learns Bagehot's *English Constitution*, 96; Letters Patent on style and names of royal children, 142; smoking, 144; on family surname, 176, 178; and Stamfordham, 244; horses, 254;

as Prince of Wales, 421; Jubilee Trust, 422; marital fidelity, 456
George VI, King: death and funeral, 1, 165–75; accession, 2; dress and appearance, 7, 10; temper ('gnashes'), 11, 15, 196, 423; birth and upbringing, 14–16; stammer, 15–16, 19, 65, 87; in World War I, 16, 18; post-World War I work, 18; education, 19; courtship, 20, 22–3; marriage, 24–5; 1927 tour of Australasia, 29; occupies Royal Lodge, Windsor, 34–5; relations with children, 34–5; Civil List allowance, 35; economises on hunting, 35; family life, 36; at father's death, 50; unease at Edward's behaviour over Mrs Simpson, 53–4; and Abdication crisis, 56; proclaimed king, 56–7; Coronation, 58, 64–8; at Buckingham Palace, 59; and wife's dress, 61; grooms ER for public life, 63; decline in relations with Edward, 69–70; money allowance to Edward, 70–1; tax-free income, 71, 481–2; shooting, 74, 257–8; 1938 visit to Paris, 76; 1939 visit to USA and Canada, 78–80; and Chamberlain's peace hopes, 78; and war threat, 86–7; wartime broadcasts, 88–9; refuses evacuation to Canada, 91; and bombing of Palace, 92–3; popularity, 93; learns Bagehot's *English Constitution*, 96; relations with Margaret, 101; declines ER's early engagement, 104; protectiveness towards ER, 106; visits ER in ATS, 108; and end of World War II, 109–10; and ER's engagement, 116, 120; on 1947 South Africa tour, 118–20, 143; on loss of Empire, 122; fears of republicanism, 123; and official allowance for ER, 124; grants Garter and titles to ER and Philip, 128; at ER's wedding, 130–2; and birth of Charles, 141; as Charles's godfather, 143; health decline, 144–5, 155, 160–1, 164; devotion to Charles, 158, 163; and Margaret–Townsend romance, 194–6, 198; controls Garter, 221–2; diligence, 229; and racehorses, 255; friendship with 'Porchy', 257–8; opposes Deputy Prime Ministership, 313–14; at Cambridge, 334–6; and Duke of Windsor's

autobiography, 345; Memorial Chapel, 349; eccentricities, 359; finances, 481–2
George I, King of the Hellenes, 81, 103–4
George II, King of the Hellenes, 113
George, Prince of Greece, 81, 143
George, Prince of Hanover, 113, 305, 328, 342
George Donatus, Prince of Hesse and the Rhine, 83, 305
Germany, 86–7, 90, 303–6
Ghana, 283, 297–300
Gibbs, Hon. Mrs Vicary, 111
Gibson, John, 137
Gilbey, James, 476
Girl Guides, 63–4
Giscard d'Estaing, Valéry, 376
Glamis Castle, 20–2
Gloucester, Princess Alice, Duchess of, 24, 49, 114, 411, 479
Gloucester, Prince Henry, Duke of: born, 14; marriage, 24, 49; character and interests, 45, 411; invested Grand Master of Bath, 160; appearance, 164; meets ER from Kenya, 167; at George VI's death, 173; invites Duke of Windsor to stay, 185; and change of royal surname, 285; at Cambridge, 335–6; Civil List allowance, 364–6; death, 411; at EQM's 70th birthday, 418
Gloucester, Prince Richard, Duke of, 411, 417
Gloucester, Prince William of: killed, 411
Godfrey, Prince of Hohenlohe-Langenburg, 83
Goering, Hermann, 76
Goodman, Arnold, Baron, 475
Goon Show (radio programme), 425
Gordon, John, 124, 153–4, 171, 177, 182, 218, 273
Gordonstoun school, 83, 327–30, 332, 334, 392, 446
Gore, Senator Albert, 461
Gothic, SS, 166, 215–16
Gould, Bruce and Beatrice, 151–2
Grace, Princess of Monaco (*née* Kelly), 467
Grafton, Fortune, Duchess of, 374, 412
Graham, Joan, 267
Graham-Hodgson, Sonia, 43
Grampian Deer Management Group, 512
Graves, Robert, 355

Great Depression (1930s), 35
Greece, 301
Green, Donald, 330
Greig, Sir Louis Leisler, 335
Grenada, 386
Grenadier Guards, 99, 100
Greville, Mrs Ronald, 37, 145
Grigg, John *see* Altrincham, 2nd Baron
Grosvenor, Lady Leonora, 426
Guards Chapel, London: bombed, 105
Guinness, Sabrina, 426

Haakon VII, King of Norway, 89–90, 92, 143
Habgood, John, Archbishop of York, 497
Hahn, Kurt, 83, 272, 328, 330
Hailsham, Douglas McGarel Hogg, 1st Viscount, 90–1
Hailsham, Quintin McGarel Hogg, Baron, 315–16
Halifax, Charles Edward Peter Neil Wood, 3rd Earl of, 506
Halifax, Edward Frederick Lindley Wood, 1st Earl of, 15, 76, 89, 211
Hall, Philip, 367–8; *Royal Fortune*, 479, 504–5
Hamilton, Lord Claud, 32
Hamilton, Willie, 361–2, 366, 405, 407
Hampton Court Palace, 517
Handley, Tommy, 99
Hardinge family, 43
Hardinge, Sir Alexander (*later* 2nd Baron; 'Alec'), 51, 53–4, 93, 100, 144
Hardinge, Elizabeth, 97
Hardinge, Helen Mary, Lady, 51
Hardinge, Winifred, 75, 97
Hare, Augustus, 41
Harewood, 6th Earl of *see* Lascelles, Henry George Charles, Viscount
Harewood, George Lascelles, 7th Earl of, 16, 27, 32, 42, 52, 56–7, 109, 404
Harewood, Patricia, Countess of (*formerly* Tuckwell), 404
Harris, Robert, 443
Harry, Prince *see* Henry, Prince
Hartnell, Norman: designs for EQM, 7, 49, 61, 68, 77; designs ER's wedding dress, 126–7, 129; designs for ER, 140; and ER's Coronation robes, 186; and Bobo MacDonald, 251; designs Margaret's

wedding dress, 292; designs outfit for Charles's Prince of Wales investiture, 351

Harvey, Major Thomas, 151

Haus Doorn, Holland, 311

Hawke, Robert James Lee, 385

Head, Alec, 504

Heald, Sir Lionel, 204

Heald, Tim, 267, 272

Healey, Denis (Baron), 372

Hearst, William Randolph, 247

Heath, (Sir) Edward, 236, 238, 300, 361, 369–72, 379, 499

Heatherdown (school), 392, 445

Hélène, Princess of France, 10

Hello (magazine), 487

Henry III, King, 94

Henry, Prince (Wales's son; 'Harry'), 454, 477–8

Hern, Major Dick, 502

Heron, Eileen, 107–8

Heseltine, Sir William, 354, 387–8, 459, 465, 495

Heuss, Theodor, 302–3

Hewitt, James, 486, 492

Hicks, Lady Pamela (*née* Mountbatten), 98, 216, 524

Highgrove (house), Gloucestershire, 410

Highland Cattle Association, 512

Hill House school, London, 279–80

Hillary, (Sir) Edmund, 186

Hirohito, Emperor of Japan, 303

Historic Royal Palaces Agency, 517

Hitler, Adolf, 76, 78, 86–7, 90

Hoare, Oliver, 486

Holden, Anthony, 280

Home, Sir Alec Douglas-Home, Baron (*formerly* 14th Earl of), 96, 196, 306, 308, 315–17

homeopathy, 161

Horne, Alastair, 285

Horsley, Squadron Leader Beresford ('Peter'), 167, 189

Houghton, Douglas, 367

Howes, Peter, 158

Huggett (Windlesham gardener), 147

Hughes, Emrys, 320

Hungary, 238–9

Huntingdon, William Hastings Bass, 16th Earl of, 504

Hussey, Lady Susan, 327, 396, 418, 439n, 491

Huston, Mrs John, 424

Hyde, Harford Montgomery, 345

Imperial Poona Yacht Club, 269

In Which We Serve (film), 98

India: independence, 122; 1961 visit to, 295

Industrial Welfare Association, 18

Invincible, HMS, 445–6

Iraq, 233

Irish Republican Army (IRA), 43, 427, 447

Israel: and Suez War, 231–4

Italy, 295, 458–9

ITMA (radio programme), 99

It's a Royal Knockout (TV programme), 452–3

Ivanov, Colonel Eugene, 307

Iveagh, Rupert Guinness, 2nd Earl of, and Gwendolyn, Countess of, 105

'Jack the Ripper', 10

James II, King, 2

Janvrin, Robin, 473, 520, 530

Jay, Antony, 495

Jenkins, Roy (Baron), 312, 320, 322, 376

Jennings, Sarah, 430

Jerram, Thomas, 136, 143

John Paul II, Pope, 459

John, Prince: birth and death, 14

Joyce, William ('Lord Haw-Haw'), 88

Joynson-Hicks, Sir William, 27

Juliana, Queen of the Netherlands (*formerly* Princess), 128, 198

Jupiter, HMS, 394, 420

Justice, James Robertson, 265

Karamanlis, Constantine, 301

Kaunda, Kenneth, 370, 382–4

Kay, Richard, 472, 486–7

Kaye, Danny, 147

Keeler, Christine, 307

Kelley, Kitty, 400

Kelly, HMS, 98, 103

Kelly, Sir Gerald, 100

Kennedy, John F., 297, 300, 303

Kensington Palace, 136, 402, 517–18

Kent, Edward, Duke of (Victoria's father), 4

Kent, Prince Edward George Nicholas
Patrick, Duke of, 410–11
Kent, Prince George, Duke of: birth and
upbringing, 14, 16; handwriting, 40;
relations with mother, 41; art collecting,
45; career, 45–6; drug-taking, 46;
marriage, 46, 259; sexual proclivities,
46–7; banned from seeing Lady Cunard,
69; killed, 99, 157
Kent, Katherine, Duchess of (*née* Worsley),
411
Kent, Princess Marina, Duchess of:
marriage, 46–7; appearance, 62;
genealogy, 81; widowed in war, 99;
encourages Philip's courtship, 104;
family pride, 114; visits Windlesham
Moor, 147; disapproves of
Margaret–Snowdon engagement, 291;
death and funeral, 347; entertains
Windsors, 347
Kent, Prince Michael of, 99, 409, 498
Kent, Princess Michael of (*née* Marie-
Christine von Reibnitz), 409–10
Kenya, 165–6
Keppel, Alice, 9–10, 424–5, 456, 510
Kerr, Sir John, 371, 421
Keyser, Sister Agnes, 22–3
Kilmuir, David Maxwell Fyfe, 1st
Viscount, 236, 306
Kinematograph Renters Society, 135
King (royal steward), 143
Kinnock, Glenys, 498
Kinnock, Neil, 464, 498
Kinross, Patrick Balfour, 3rd Baron, 345
Kirkwood, Pat, 267
Knatchbull, Amanda, 425–7, 436
Knatchbull, Nicholas, 427
Knatchbull, Norton, 328
Knight, Andrew, 473
Knight, Clara ('Allah'), 29–30, 33, 43, 66,
78, 88, 95, 110, 145
Korean War, 161
Kortesis, Vasso, 530
Krock, Arthur, 79
Kronberg Papers, 310

Labour Party, 122–4, 320–2, 374
Lacey, Robert, 154, 229, 233, 253, 262
Ladies Home Journal, 151, 153
Lakefield College School, Ontario, 446

Lambart, Lady Elizabeth (*later* Longman),
43
Lampson, Sir Miles, 63, 87
Lancaster, Duchy of, 363, 366–7
Landseer, Sir Edwin, 74
Lang, Cosmo, Archbishop of Canterbury,
22, 48–9, 53, 65, 67, 98
Langtry, Lillie, 9
Larkin, Philip, 490
Lascelles, Sir Alan ('Tommy'): and Duke
of Windsor's behaviour, 44, 72; at
Windsor in war, 100; opposes Philip as
ER's suitor, 114–15; liking for Philip,
133; and Colville, 137, 155; and birth of
Charles, 142; and George VI's health,
165; meets ER as new Queen, 168; on ER
occupying Buckingham Palace, 176;
Philip's attitude to, 179; and Coronation
economies, 180; and televising of ER's
Coronation, 182–3; on
Margaret–Townsend romance, 194,
202–5, 213, 287; death, 214; and
Churchill's retirement, 220; and
Churchill's stroke, 223–4; diary, 243–4;
and ER's visit to Scotland, 243;
retirement, 243–4
Lascelles, George *see* Harewood, 7th Earl of
Lascelles, Gerald, 27
Lascelles, Henry George Charles, Viscount
(*later* 6th Earl of Harewood), 23
Laski, Harold, 520
Latsis, John, 475
Laurence, Commander Timothy, 469,
484–5
Law, Andrew Bonar, 316
Learmonth, Sir James, 144
Lee of Fareham, Arthur Hamilton,
Viscount, 26
Lee Kuan Yew, 381
Legh family, 43
Legh, Diana, 64, 75
Legh, Sir Piers ('Joey'), 64, 100, 114, 125,
179, 197
Lennox-Boyd, Alan (*later* 1st Viscount
Boyd), 229
Leo IV, Pope, 3
Leonard, Graham, Bishop of London, 498
Leveson-Gower, Lady Rosemary, 43
Lewis, 'Diamond Joe', 247

Lichfield, Patrick Anson, 5th Earl of, 291, 403

Lightbody, Helen, 145–6, 163, 277, 279

Lillie, Beatrice (Lady Peel), 98

Lindsay, Major Hugh, 453

Lindsay, Sir Robert, 72

Linley, David Armstrong-Jones, Viscount, 401, 445

Llewellyn, Roderick, 405–8

Llewellyn, Tania (*formerly* Soskin), 408

Lloyd, John Selwyn (*later* Baron Selwyn-Lloyd), 234, 306

Lloyd George, David (1st Earl), 17, 48, 316, 350

Lloyd Webber, Sir Andrew, 453

Logue, Lionel, 65, 87

Londonderry, Edith, Marchioness of, 69

Longford, Elizabeth, Countess of, 97, 140, 369, 373, 523

Lorne, John Campbell, Marquis of (*later* 9th Duke of Argyll), 8

Louise, Princess, Duchess of Fife, 13

Louise, Princess, Marchioness of Lorne, 8

Lübke, Heinrich, 303

Ludgrove school, 477

Ludwig, Prince of Hesse and Rhine, 83, 303–5

Lusaka Conference (1979), 382–4

Lynn, Dame Vera, 99

McAlpine, Alistair, Baron, 468

McCorquodale, Raine *see* Spencer, Raine, Countess

Macdonald, Mrs (cook), 30

MacDonald, James, 136, 139, 423

MacDonald, Margaret ('Bobo'): as ER's nurserymaid, 30, 65–6; relations with ER, 33, 249; at Windsor in war, 95; remains as ER's dresser, 111; and ER's wedding, 129–31; relations with John Dean, 136; at Charles's christening, 144; tipping, 148; at Clarence House, 149; in Canada, 163; on dying George VI, 165; on royal yacht, 219; power and status, 249–51; in TV film, 355, 357; death, 518

MacDonald, Ramsay, 48

MacDonald, Ruby, 33, 144, 401–2

McGrath, Sir Brian, 520

McGregor, Oliver Ross McGregor, Baron, 474

Maclean, Charles Hector Fitzroy, 399, 516

Maclean, Donald, 308

Macleod, Iain, 265, 315

Macmillan, Lady Dorothy, 237, 307

Macmillan, Harold (*later* 1st Earl of Stockton): and Churchill's stroke, 223; and Churchill's delayed resignation, 225–6; on ER's grasp of business, 229; as PM, 235–8; relations with ER, 237, 313–16; and Philip's title, 275; and Charles as Prince of Wales, 282; and provision of house for Charles, 283; and adoption of Mountbatten surname, 285–6; EC negotiations, 294–5, 300, 370; view of Commonwealth, 294, 300; in southern Africa, 296; and ER's Ghana visit, 297, 299; resignation and succession, 306, 314–18; and scandals, 307–8; declines Garter, 373

McNally, Paddy, 450

McNeil, Jane (*later* Countess of Dalkeith and Duchess of Buccleuch), 195

Magpie, HMS, 159–60

Mahendra, King of Nepal, 296

Major, John, 479–82, 483–4, 496, 521

Makarios III, Archbishop, 295

Malan, Daniel François, 165

Malta, 156–9, 161

Mandela, Nelson, 522

Mann, Rt Revd Michael, Dean of Windsor, 499

Margaret, Princess: born, 32–3; character and behaviour, 33–5, 41, 101, 200, 287; relations with ER, 33–5, 101, 287; childhood, 38; education, 40–1, 97, 199; dress as child, 49, 66; at Glamis, 53–4; and Buckingham Palace, 60; at father's Coronation, 66; appearance, 80, 199–200; and war, 87–8, 531; visits Elstree, 98; precocity, 101; comforts mother in war, 105–6; envies ER's ATS service, 106; visits ER in ATS, 108; on senior courtiers, 115; and ER's engagement, 116; on 1947 South Africa tour, 118, 120; and ER's wedding gifts, 127; social aplomb, 156, 171; at father's death, 165, 169, 171; role, 171, 199, 213; romance with Townsend, 193–214, 239, 263, 287–8; 1954 visit to S. Rhodesia, 205; 1955 West Indies tour, 206; and ER's jewellery, 252; and Regency Bill, 274; courtship, engagement and marriage, 285–6, 289–92, 393, 402; wedding, 291–3; Paris visit cancelled, 300–1; and Macmillan's visit to ER, 313; unpopularity, 341; Civil List allowance, 364–6, 407, 479; marriage relations, 393, 401–6; emotional warmth, 396; children, 401; life-style, 402–3; affairs, 404–6; drinking, 404–5; separation and divorce, 406, 408; forbidding manner, 443; 60th birthday, 465; and Wyatts, 467; ladies-in-waiting, 522

Margaret, Princess of Hesse and the Rhine (*née* Geddes; 'Princess Peg'), 83, 304–5

Margarita, Princess of Greece (*later* of Hohenlohe-Langenburg), 83

Marie, Duchess of Edinburgh (*formerly* Grand Duchess of Russia), 8

Marie, Queen of Romania ('Missy'), 8, 17

Marie Adelaide, Princess of Teck (Queen Mary's mother), 11

Marie Louise, Princess, 96

Marlborough House, London, 9, 60, 282–3

Marlborough, Susan, Duchess of (*née* Hornby), 195

Marten, Sir Henry, 96–7, 199

Martyn, Charles, 252

Mary, Princess Royal, 14, 16, 27–8, 108, 125, 184–5, 276

Mary, Queen: background, 10–11; marriage, 10; dress and style, 13, 61, 252; relations with children, 13–15; and EQR's engagement to George VI, 24–5; on birth of ER, 27; gifts to ER, 32; character, 34, 41–2; on Princesses' education, 40–1; Silver Jubilee, 48; and George V's death, 50; and Edward's relations with Mrs Simpson, 52; on Abdication and proclamation of George VI as King, 57, 69; moves to Marlborough House, 60, 282; at George VI's Coronation, 66–8; at Balmoral, 73; and Chamberlain's resignation, 89–90; wartime evacuation, 91; attends ER's confirmation, 98; on ER–Philip courtship, 105; on post-war economies, 122; and Crawfie's marriage and departure, 125–6; Edward visits, 125; and ER's wedding, 127; at Brabourne

wedding, 128; and birth of Charles, 142–3; smoking, 144; on George VI's illness and death, 145, 167, 172; health decline, 164; and ER's accession, 167–8; and Duke of Windsor at George VI's funeral, 173; and Mountbatten family ambitions, 176; death, will and funeral, 183–5; offends Margaret, 199; at launch of *Queen Mary*, 230; memorial plaque, 347

Maud, Queen of Norway (*formerly* Princess), 13, 511

Maudling, Reginald, 315

Maxwell, Paul, 427

Mayall, Sir Lees, 355

Meade, Richard, 341

Meet the Press (NBC programme), 360

Melbourne, William Lamb, 2nd Viscount, 6

Mellon, Paul, 504

Menzies, Sir Robert, 180, 300, 331

Mersham-le-Hatch, Ashford, Kent, 148

Messel, Oliver, 405

Mey, Castle of, Caithness, 170

Michael, King of Romania, 123

Middleton, Guy, 266

Milford Haven, David Mountbatten, 3rd Marquis of, 84, 103, 128–9, 266–7

Milford Haven, George Mountbatten, 2nd Marquis of, 83

Milford Haven, Admiral of the Fleet Prince Louis Alexander Mountbatten, 1st Marquis of, 81, 129, 145–6

Milford Haven, Nadejda, Marchioness of, 83, 143

Milford Haven, Victoria, Marchioness of, 83, 128

Millar, Sir Oliver, 312

Miller, Colonel Sir John, 338–9

Mills, Florence, 46

Minerva, HMS, 425

Mirman, Simone, 251

Mirzoeff, Edward, 495

Mispy *see* Peebles, Catherine

monarchy: constitutional powers and limitations, 3, 525–6; Protestantism, 3; post-World War I status, 18; in Empire and Commonwealth, 54–5; as theatre, 61; cost, 360–8, 482–3, 525; declining esteem for, 483, 524–5

Monckton, Walter (*later* 1st Viscount), 68, 73, 344, 347

Montague-Browne, Anthony, 236

Montaudon-Smith, Mrs ('Monty'), 41, 97, 100

Moore, Charles, 255

Moran, Charles McMoran Wilson, 1st Baron, 161–2, 220, 223–5

Morgan, John Pierpont, 75

Morrah, Dermot, 188, 240, 330, 332; *To Be a King*, 333

Morrison, Mary, 217, 374

Morshead, Sir Owen, 16, 309–11

Mortimer, Raymond, 98

Morton, Andrew, 432–3, 441; *Diana: Her True Story*, 473–4, 477

Mosbacher, Buz, 269

Mosley, Sir Oswald, 56

Mountbatten family, 17, 43

Mountbatten, Edwina, Countess, 81, 162

Mountbatten, Admiral of the Fleet Louis, 1st Earl: shuns Edward's wedding, 69; character, 80–1; introduces ER and Philip, 80; interest in Philip, 84; and film *In Which We Serve*, 98; promotes ER–Philip marriage, 103–4, 112, 117; and sinking of HMS *Kelly*, 103; court suspicions of, 114–15; and Indian independence, 122; and post-war Labour government, 123; at ER–Philip wedding, 129, 131; Beaverbrook's hostility to, 131; recommends Browning, 138; sharp practices, 152, 157–8; in Malta, 156; relations with ER, 157–9; relations with Philip, 156, 398, 400; meets ER on return from Kenya, 167; at George VI's funeral, 172; relations with Duke of Windsor, 173–4; ambitions for family, 176–8; and replacement royal yacht, 218; and Suez crisis, 233–4; and royal adoption of surname, 286, 398–9; and Charles's education, 327–8, 334, 396; and Princess Alice, 342; in TV film, 353; on ER's private wealth, 362–3; influence on Charles, 396–8, 420, 423; and Prince Michael of Kent's marriage, 409; and Duchess of Windsor at husband's funeral, 413, 415; and Duke of Windsor's effects, 415–16; 70th birthday, 418; and

Charles's romances, 425–7, 436; killed, 427, 429

Mountbatten, Lady Pamela *see* Hicks, Lady Pamela

Mountbatten, Patricia, Countess (*formerly* Lady Patricia Brabourne), 64, 98, 117, 128, 143, 148, 157–8, 258, 328, 425–7

Mountbatten-Windsor: adopted as surname, 142, 285–6, 398–9

Mowatt, Marina, 219, 410

Mowbray, Segrave and Stourton, Captain William Marmaduke Stourton, 25th/26th Baron, 192

Muggeridge, Malcolm, 239, 241, 324

Muldoon, Robert, 382

Munich crisis (1938), 76, 78

'Munshi, The' *see* Abdul Karim

Murdoch, Rupert, 368, 391

Murphy, Charles, 343

Mussolini, Benito, 76

Mustique, West Indies, 403, 405–8

Muzorewa, Bishop Abel, 381

Nahlin (yacht), 52

Nahum, Jack, 266

Nash, John, 58

Nassau Conference (1985), 384–5

Nasser, Gamal Abdel, 231, 233, 238–9

National and English Review, 239

National Gallery, London, 460

Nazi–Soviet Pact (1939), 86–7

Neil, Andrew, 479

Nelson, Admiral Horatio, 1st Viscount, 96

Nemon, Oscar, 221, 245

Nepal, 296

Nether Lypiatt (house), Gloucestershire, 410

Nevill, Lady Rupert, 212, 248, 259, 328

Nevill, Lord Rupert, 212, 248, 259, 405

Newnes (publishers), 153–4

News of the World (newspaper), 406–7, 444, 487

New Zealand *see* Australia (and New Zealand)

Nicholas II, Tsar, 17–18, 49

Nicholas, Mrs (Philip's nanny), 82

Nicholas, Princess of Greece, 102

Nicolson, Ben, 123

Nicolson, Sir Harold: on Victoria's sex life, 4; on royal attitude to non-royals, 6; on royal upbringing, 15–16; on George V's funeral, 51; and Edward's marriage, 55; dines at Buckingham Palace, 62; admires EQM, 69; and ER's Grenadiers Colonelcy, 99; and Lascelles' liking for Philip, 130; on Philip's appearance, 139; and George VI's illness, 145; on Lascelles, 244; on ER's Christmas speech, 262; and press intrusion, 263; and Philip's relations with press, 273; and Margaret's engagement, 291

Niven, David, 265

Nixon, Richard M., 340

Nkomo, Joshua, 382

Nkrumah, Kwame, 283, 297–9

Norfolk, Bernard Fitzalan-Howard, 16th Duke of, 65, 172, 180–1, 187, 231, 323, 350

Norfolk, Lavinia Mary, Duchess of, 186–7, 192

North Sea Conference, 460

Northern Ireland, 377

Norway, 89

Nottingham Cottage, Kensington Palace, 150, 153

Nyerere, Julius, 370, 384

Ogilvy, Angus, 301

Olav V, King of Norway, 414

Olga, Princess of Greece, then of Yugoslavia, 46, 124–5

Oliver, Alison, 338–9

Olympic Games, Melbourne (1956), 264, 270

Orr, James, 328

Osborne, John, 239, 241, 260

Osborne Naval College, 19

Oswald, Michael, 503–7

Owen, David, Baron, 374–5

Owen, Frank, 265

Paisley, Ian, 459

Pakistan, 296

palaces: management, 517–18

Palmer-Tomkinson family, 437

Panorama (BBC TV programme): 1995 Diana interview, 492, 530

Papua New Guinea, 378

Paris, 139–40, 275

Parker, Eileen, 265

Parker, Michael: Philip meets, 103; friendship with Philip, 112–13, 142; as Philip's Private Secretary, 138; cricketing, 147; in Malta, 158; and George VI's death, 165–6; at ER's Coronation, 189; on Philip's 1956 tour, 264; divorce and resignation, 265, 267; and Thursday Club, 266, 268–70; on Philip's role, 271; and Philip's relations with press, 273

Parker Bowles, Andrew, 341, 425, 429, 435, 456

Parker Bowles, Camilla: marriage, 341; relations with Charles, 400, 424–5, 429, 435, 438, 440–1, 454–6, 485, 489, 519; Diana's concern over, 440–1, 454, 456–7, 492; Charles gives bracelet to, 441; banned from Diana's wedding breakfast, 442; taped conversation with Charles made public, 485; advises Charles against TV interview, 488; in Dimbleby biography of Charles, 490; marriage breakdown and divorce, 490–1; public antipathy to, 529

Parker Bowles, Derek, 456

Parkinson, Norman, 394

Paul I, King of the Hellenes, 160, 301–2

Paul, Prince of Yugoslavia, 46, 69, 124–5

Paul, Sandra, 404

Peart, Fred, 322

Peat, Michael, 482, 515–18, 522

Peebles, Catherine ('Mispy'), 277–9, 336, 445

People, The (newspaper), 204

Philby, Kim, 266, 308, 312

Philip, Prince, Duke of Edinburgh: first meets ER, 80, 84–5; genealogy and background, 81–2, 116–17; education, 83–4; naval career, 84, 103, 136, 155–6, 159–60; ER's devotion to, 102–3; as prospective husband, 103–4; returns from Far East at war's end, 110–11; character and manner, 111–15, 117, 147–8, 272–3, 337; romances, 112; life-style and position, 113–14; opposition to, as suitor, 114–16, 121; engagement, 116–17, 121; naturalisation and name, 120–1; wedding, 121, 123–4, 127–30; official allowance, 124; awarded Garter and titles, 128, 178, 274–5; hostility to

press, 129, 141, 273; honeymoon, 130–1;
marriage relations, 133, 145, 156, 178–9,
264, 399–401, 448, 523; early married
homes, 134–6, 144–6, 157; appearance
and dress, 139, 147–8; sleeps naked, 139;
unwell on 1948 Paris trip, 140; and birth
of Charles, 141–2; home-making, 146;
sports and exercise, 147; food and drink,
148–9, 501, 511; thrift, 148; and domestic
organisation, 150, 156; supports and
assists ER, 156; in Malta, 156–9;
relations with Mountbatten, 156–7, 398;
polo-playing, 157; and birth of Anne,
159; visit to Rome, 160; 1950 visit to
Canada and USA, 162–4; speeches and
gaffes, 162; and George VI's death,
165–6; and ER's accession, 168;
entertains Duke of Windsor, 173;
position, role and duties on ER's
accession, 175–6, 178–9, 271–2, 174; on
family surname, 177–8; chairs
Coronation Committee, 181; at
Coronation, 187, 191; and
Margaret–Townsend romance, 203, 211;
on 1953/54 Commonwealth tour,
215–16, 219; helps ER with
speechmaking, 230; Palace modernisation
and innovations, 243, 261; intellectual
interests, 258; shooting, 258; 1956
Commonwealth tour, 264, 269–70, 275,
284; painting, 264; rumoured infidelities
and flirtations, 264–8, 275, 399–401; and
Thursday Club, 266–8; undemonstrative
nature, 268; sailing, 269; and
Mountbatten surname, 274, 285–6;
nominated Regent, 274; relations with
children, 275–80, 325–7, 490; and
Charles's education, 280–1, 327–8, 330,
332–3; 1959 visit to Canada and USA,
283; at Margaret's wedding, 292; and
Greek royal family, 302–3; 1965 visit to
Germany, 303–6; Barbara Castle on,
321; political views, 322; home life,
325–7; relations with Anne, 338; and TV
film of royal family, 353, 356–7, 359; on
cost of monarchy, 360–1; Civil List
allowance, 364–5; ER rebukes, 375;
views on EC, 377; offends Chinese, 388;
criticises Scargill, 389; relations with
Charles, 396, 491; in Ghana, 398; and

Duke of Windsor's funeral, 415; at
Balmoral, 419; and Charles's marriage
prospects, 426, 429; and Charles's
courtship of Diana, 436, 438; and
Fergusons, 449; and Edward's
resignation from Marines, 453–4;
ostracises Major Ferguson, 467; attitude
to Diana and Duchess of York, 474–5;
supports Charles, 475, 487; and Charles's
marriage breakdown, 477, 487; in
Argentina, 478; remains on Civil List,
480; religious observance, 499; and
alterations to Sandringham, 508; runs
Sandringham and Balmoral estates,
511–12; relations with staff, 519–20
Philipp, Prince, Landgrave of Hesse, 125,
309
Phillips, Captain Mark: marriage, 286,
393–5; Anne meets, 339, 341; riding,
339–41; honeymoon, 369; qualities,
393–4; marriage breakdown, 468–9
Phillips, Peter, 395
Piccadilly (No.145), 30, 36, 43
Pickering, Sir Edward, 182
Plaid Cymru (political party), 349
Player, Lesley, 468–70
Plunket family, 43
Plunket, Dorothé, Lady (*née* Lewis), 39,
247
Plunket, Patrick, 7th Baron, 247–8, 318,
351, 356, 380, 417–19, 429, 516
Plunket, Terence, 6th Baron ('Teddy'), 247
Poland: and outbreak of war, 86–7
Polesden Lacey (house), Surrey, 37
Ponsonby, Sir Frederick ('Fritz'), 12, 310
Ponsonby, Loelia, 15, 53
Pope-Hennessy, James, 57, 71, 172, 508–10
Porchester, Henry Molyneux Herbert,
Baron ('Porchy') *see* Carnarvon, 7th Earl
of
Porritt, Jonathon, 461
Portland, William Cavendish-Bentinck, 6th
Duke of, 67
Portugal, 275
Powell, Enoch, 317
Prasad, Rajendra, 295
Prempeh, Sir Osei (Agyeman III, King of
Ashanti), 298
Preston, Kiki Whitney, 46
Prince's Trust, 460, 488

Prince's Youth Business Trust, 460
Princess Elizabeth Land, Antarctica, 33
Private Eye (magazine), 402
Privy Council, 321–2
Profumo, John, 266, 307–8, 313
Public Estates, 367
Pye, Miss (maid), 129

Radcliffe, Cyril, Baron, 221
Rainier, Prince of Monaco, 467
Ramphal, Sir Shridath ('Sonny'), 382–4
Ramsey, Michael, Archbishop of
    Canterbury, 333–4
Rayne (shoemaker), 251
Reagan, Nancy, 496
Reagan, Ronald, 386, 496
Reibnitz, Baron Günther Hubertus von,
    410
republicanism, 524–6
Reynaud, Paul, 90
Reynolds, Paul, 471
Rhèdey, Countess Claudine, 11
Rhodes, Zandra, 394
Rhodes James, Sir Robert, 452
Rhodesia *see* Zimbabwe
Rhys-Jones, Sophie, 453–4
Ribbentrop, Joachim von, 86
Rice-Davies, Mandy, 307
Richardson, Sir John, 316
Richelieu (French battleship), 118
Riddell, Sir John, 458, 462
Ridley, Nicholas, 460
Rio de Janeiro: 1991 meeting, 461
Rizzo, Frank, 374
Roberts, Sir Frank, 303–6
Rome, 160
Romsey, Norton Knatchbull, Lord, and
    Penelope, Lady, 437
Roosevelt, Eleanor, 79, 97–8, 100
Roosevelt, Franklin Delano, 78–9
Rose, Kenneth, 246, 411, 498
Rosebery, Archibald Philip Primrose, 5th
    Earl of, 21
Routledge, Paul, 389
Royal Family (TV film), 353–60, 392, 399,
    495
Royal Institute of British Architects, 460
Royal Lodge, Windsor Great Park, 36
Royal Marriages Act (1772), 202, 409, 527,
    531

Royal Naval College *see* Dartmouth: Royal
    Naval College
Royal Oak, HMS, 88–9
Royal Palaces (TV film), 353
Royal Titles Act (1953), 181, 215
Roycroft, David, 458
Runcie, Robert, Archbishop of Canterbury,
    442, 458–9, 498
Russell, Bertrand, 302
Russell, Georgiana, 426
Russell, Lord Rudolph, 328
Rutland, Henry John Brinsley Manners,
    8th Duke of, 20
Rutland, Kathleen, Duchess of, 77
Ryan, John Barry, and 'Nin', 516

Sackville-West, Vita, 123
St Aldwyn, Michael John Hicks Beach, 2nd
    Earl, 315
St Paul's Walden Bury, Hertfordshire, 20
Salisbury, James Gascoyne-Cecil, 4th
    Marquis of, 67, 114, 204
Salisbury, Robert Arthur James Gascoyne-
    Cecil, 5th Marquis of, 204, 209–11, 220,
    223–4, 235–8, 297
Salisbury, Robert Arthur Talbot Gascoyne-
    Cecil, 3rd Marquis of, 6–7
Salote, Queen of Tonga, 187, 215
Sandringham, Norfolk, 9, 51, 88–9, 477–8,
    508–12
Sandys, Diana (*née* Churchill), 93
Sandys, Duncan (*later* Baron Duncan-
    Sandys), 297, 307
Santa Cruz, Lucia, 335, 425, 462
Savile, Sir James ('Jimmy'), 462
Scapa Flow, 88
Scarbrough, Laurence Roger Lumley, 11th
    Earl of, 240, 248, 260–1, 308
Scargill, Arthur, 389
Schmidt, Helmut, 376
Scott, Sir Walter, 20
Seitz, Raymond G. H., 525
Sellers, Peter, 403
Sèvres, Treaty of (1956), 231, 233–4
Shah of Iran (Muhammed Reza Pahlevi),
    226
Shand, Major Bruce, 424
Shand Kydd, Frances (*formerly* Countess
    Spencer; Diana's mother), 431–2, 440
Shand Kydd, Peter, 431

Sharpeville massacre (1960), 296
Shea, Michael, 387–8, 435, 444
Sheffield, Davina, 426
Sheppard, Allen, 462
Shulman, Milton, 359
Sierra Leone, 299
Silver Jubilees: George V (1935), 48–9; ER (1977), 377–8
Simon, Robin, 500
Simpson, Ernest, 47
Simpson, Wallis *see* Windsor, Wallis, Duchess of
Sitwell, (Dame) Edith, 98, 170
Sitwell, (Sir) Osbert, 33, 63, 92, 98–9, 121, 169, 258
Smirke, Charlie, 258
Smith, Horace, 254
Smith, Ian, 381, 383
Smuts, Field Marshal Jan Christian, 118–19, 165
Snagge, John, 165
Snowdon, Antony Armstrong-Jones, 1st Earl of: Baron rejects, 270; courtship, engagement and marriage, 285–6, 289–93; background, 289; Paris visit cancelled, 300; helps plan Charles's investiture as Prince of Wales, 350; children, 401; marriage relations, 401–6; title, 401; honeymoon, 402; life-style, 402–3; separation and divorce, 406, 408; relations with ER, 408
Snowdon, Lucy, Countess of (*née* Lindsay-Hogg), 406
Soames, Christopher, Baron, 223, 411, 421, 435
Soames, Mary, Lady (*née* Churchill), 324
Soames, Nicholas, 435, 437
Sobell, Sir Michael, 503
Sophie, Princess of Greece (*later* of Hanover; then of Hesse; 'Aunt Tiny'), 82–3, 113, 142, 305
Soraya, Queen of Iran, 226
South Africa, 116–20, 143, 165, 296–7, 385–7
South Korea, 476–7
Spencer family, 430–1
Spencer, Charles, 9th Earl (*formerly* Viscount Althorp; Diana's brother), 432–3, 473

Spencer, Frances, Countess (Diana's mother) *see* Shand Kydd, Frances
Spencer, John, 8th Earl (Diana's father), 430–2, 434, 436, 442, 472
Spencer, Raine, Countess (*née* McCorquodale), 39, 432, 472–3
Spencer, Lady Sarah (Diana's sister), 430, 433–4, 441
Spender, (Sir) Stephen, 98
'Squidgygate', 476
Stamfordham, Arthur Bigge, Baron, 17–18, 244
Stanley, Venetia, 77
Stark, Koo, 448
Starkie, Allan, 530
Steel, Sir David, 387
Stevens, Jocelyn, 289, 291, 403
Stewart, Don, 265
Stoney, Benita, 452
Strachey, Lady Mary, 111
Strathmore, Claude George Bowes-Lyon, 14th Earl of (EQM's father), 20, 77
Strathmore, Nina Cecilia, Countess of (EQM's mother), 21, 23–4, 28, 76–7
Streatlam Castle, Co. Durham, 20
Stronach, Ken, 519
Sturt, Lois, 46
Suez War (1956), 230–5, 238
Sultan, Ramzi, 468
Sun (newspaper), 444, 454, 469, 472, 476, 481, 486
Sunday Telegraph (newspaper), 471
Sunday Times (newspaper), 386–7, 473, 479, 490
Sunninghill Park, 134–5, 451, 471
Sutherland, Graham, 226

Taylor, Elizabeth, 139
Tennant, Lady Anne (*née* Coke), 431
Tennant, Colin, 195, 206, 288, 402, 405, 408, 431
Tensing Norgai (Sherpa), 186
Thaarup, Aage, 251
Thatcher, (Sir) Denis, 380
Thatcher, Margaret, Baroness: and Blunt case, 313; background, 379; becomes PM, 379; relations with ER, 379–81, 386–91; and Rhodesia crisis, 381–3; at Lusaka Conference, 383–4; and Commonwealth affairs, 384–6, 388; and

Falklands War victory parade, 389; and
miners' strike, 389; and disasters, 390;
achievements, 391; on Charles's Middle
East plans, 460; loses office, 464;
reforms, 525
Theodora, Princess (*later* Margravine of
Baden; 'Dolla'; Philip's sister), 83, 177
Thin, Dr Jean, 411–12
Thomas, Clement Price, 162
Thomas, George (*later* Viscount
Tonypandy), 350–1
Thomas, Ian, 251
Thomas, James Purdon (Viscount
Cilcennin), 218
Thompson, Janet, 433
Thorpe, Jeremy, 306
Thursday Club, The, 265–6, 268–9
Tim Bell Associates, 471
Timbertop (Geelong High School),
Australia, 330–1
Time magazine, 264–5, 268, 302
Times, The (newspaper), 211, 389
Toerring-Jettenbach, Carl, Count, and
Princess Elizabeth, Countess zu, 46, 124
Toronto Star (newspaper), 371
Townend, Colonel (of Hill House school),
279
Townsend, Marie-Luce (*formerly* Jamagne),
290
Townsend, Michael, 203
Townsend, Group Captain Peter: on 1947
South Africa tour, 118–19; attends
theatre with royal family, 165; romance
with Margaret, 193–214, 239, 263, 287;
background, 197; divorce, 201; posted to
Brussels, 205–6; on Richard Colville,
246; engagement to Marie-Luce, 290;
admitted to royal household as divorcee,
499
Townsend, Rosemary (*née* Pawle; *later*
Marchioness of Camden), 196–8, 201
Tranby Croft scandal, 9
Treby, Leslie, 148
Tree, Ronald, 35
Trestrail, Commander Michael, 447
Trinity College *see* Cambridge
Trudeau, Pierre, 322, 378
Truman, Harry S., 161, 163–4, 172
Tryon, Charles Tryon, 2nd Baron, 248

Tryon, Dale Elizabeth, Lady, 442
Tweedsmuir, John Buchan, 1st Baron, 244

United States of America: royal visits to,
78–9, 162–4, 275, 283, 374–6; and Suez
War, 231, 235; and Vietnam War, 238;
and Volta project, 297, 300
Usher, Frank, 148
Ustinov, (Sir) Peter, 265–6, 270

V1 weapon, 105
Vacani, Miss (dancing teacher), 97
Valiant, HMS, 103
van der Post, Sir Laurens, 423–4, 443
Vanguard, HMS, 117–18, 120
Vassall case (1962), 306–7
Verwoerd, Hendrik Frensch, 297
Victoria and Albert (royal yacht), 217–19
Victoria, Crown Princess of Germany, 6, 10
Victoria, Princess (Edward VII's daughter),
13, 49
Victoria, Queen: reign and character, 4–7,
531; children, 8; approves of May of
Teck, 11–12; ER compared with, 28, 33,
98–9; lives at Buckingham Palace, 33; at
Balmoral, 73–4; ER's interest in, 96;
rapport with servants, 320
Vietnam War, 238
Viktoria Luise, Duchess of Brunswick, 302
Volta, Upper, 297, 300
Vyner family, 170

Wales (country): Charles in, 336; attitude to
Charles, 349–50
Wales, Diana, Princess of: character, 9,
432–3, 438–9, 450, 465; and stepmother
Raine, 39, 432, 473; courtship, 430,
435–6; family background, 430–33;
Charles first meets, 433–5; relations with
press, 434–6, 444, 456, 472, 486–7;
engagement, 436–7; in Buckingham
Palace, 439–40; interests, 439; relations
with ER and royal family, 439–40,
443–4, 455–6, 474, 485–6; concern over
Camilla Parker Bowles, 440–1, 454,
456–7, 492; personal problems, 440–1,
444–5, 451, 473, 492; wedding, 441–3;
pregnancies and children, 444–5, 454;
and Duchess of York, 450; marriage
relations, 454–5, 457, 464, 472–7, 524,

527; public adulation, 454, 472, 486; staff leaves, 454–5; 1985 visit to Italy, 458–9; and father's death and funeral, 472; relations with children, 472, 477–8; Morton's book on, 473–4; recorded conversations with Gilbey, 476, 485; visit to South Korea, 476–7; separation, 478, 483–4; as potential Queen, 484; announces withdrawal from public life, 486; publicity, 486–7; relations with Hewitt, 486, 492; 1995 *Panorama* interview, 492, 530; divorce, 492–3, 529; familiarity with staff, 518; loses HRH title, 529

Walesa, Lech, 496–8

Wallace, Anna, 426, 435

Wallace, Billy, 287

Walsh, Bernard, 265

Walsh, John, 142

Wanganui, New Zealand: Collegiate School, 452–3

Ward, Barbara, 300

Ward, Frances, 247

Ward, John, 245

Ward, Stephen, 265, 307

Warner, Jack, 99

Warren, John, 505

Washington, George, 527

Waverley, John Anderson, 1st Viscount, 236, 238

Way Ahead Group, 530

Weinstock, Arnold, Baron, 503

Weir, Sir John, 161

Welf, Prince of Hanover, 328

Wellesley, Lady Dorothy, 98

Wellesley, Lady Jane, 426

Wellesley, Lady Violet, 106

Wells, H. G., 17

Wernher, Myra, 43

West, Dame Rebecca, 483

West Ilsley racing stables, 503

Westminster, Statute of (1932), 54

Wheeler-Bennett, Sir John, 70, 115, 311, 344–5

Whistler, Rex, 106

Whitaker, James, 434–6, 470

White Lodge, Richmond Park, 26

Whitelaw, William, Viscount, 362

Whitlam, Gough, 371, 421

Whybrew, Paul, 446

Wigram, Clive, 47

Wilding, Michael, 139

Wilhelm II, Kaiser, 4, 10, 311

Wilhelmina, Queen of the Netherlands, 90

William I (the Conqueror), King, 94

William IV, King, 4

William, Prince, 445, 465, 472, 477–8, 487, 492, 530

Williams, Marcia (Baroness Falkender), 318

Willox, Miss (Palace dresser), 137, 143

Wills, Jean (*formerly* Elphinstone), 209, 259

Wills, John, 109, 259

Wilson, Blair Stewart, 475

Wilson, Sir Charles, 334

Wilson, Harold, Baron: ER catches out, 229; and Greek demo, 302; 1964 election victory, 318; relations with ER, 318–22, 334, 372–4; and Charles's investiture as Prince of Wales, 349; 1970 election defeat, 361; criticises Philip's comment on finances, 361; and 1975 Civil List increases, 368; wins 1974 election, 372–3; awarded Garter, 373; retirement, 373

Windlesham, David Hennessy, 3rd Baron, 353

Windlesham Moor (house), Surrey, 144, 146–8

Windsor (name), 17, 176, 178, 285

Windsor Castle: in war, 93–6, 99–100; 1992 fire damage, 94, 478–9, 481; described, 94; restoration, 482

Windsor, Edward, Duke of (*formerly* King Edward VIII; 'David'): Abdication, 2, 56–7; dress, 7; birth and upbringing, 14–16; nervous manner, 16; World War I service, 16, 44; post-World War I tours, 18; character, behaviour and personality, 19, 44; George VI idolises, 19–20; rumoured engagement to EQM, 23–4; at ER's christening, 28; Civil List allowance curtailed, 35; social life, 37; and Princesses' childhood, 43, 47; relations with Mrs Simpson, 43–5, 47–8; women friends, 43–4; relations with father, 44; friendship with brother George, 46; at George V's death, 50; accession, 51; at George V's funeral, 51; declares intention to marry Mrs Simpson, 54–6; dislikes Buckingham Palace, 59; and George VI's Coronation, 67;

deteriorating relations with George VI, 69–70; marriage, 69; finances and allowance, 70–1, 343, 347–8; and denial of Royal Highness title to Wallis, 71–2, 345; EQM's hostility to, 72–3; Nazi associations, 76, 79, 310, 343–4; US visit cancelled, 79; in World War II, 88–90; as Governor of Bahamas, 93; not invited to ER's wedding, 125; visits Queen Mary, 125; book serialised, 152, 154; at George VI's funeral, 173; French home, 174; not invited to ER's Coronation, 183–4; at Queen Mary's funeral, 183–4; isolation, 259; at Oxford, 336; ER seeks reconciliation with, 343, 346–7; visits to England, 345–6; burial wishes, 346–7; declines invitation to Charles's investiture, 348–9; Mountbatten on, 397; death and funeral, 411–14; will, 416; *A Family Album* (with Kinross), 345; *A King's Story*, 343, 345

Windsor, Wallis, Duchess of (*formerly* Simpson): relations with EQM, 22, 68–9; relations with Edward, 43–5, 47–8; and Edward's accession, 51–2; at Balmoral, 53; Edward's intention to marry, 54–5; petitions for divorce from Simpson, 54; and George VI's Coronation, 67; marriage, 69; denied Royal Highness title, 71–2, 345; extravagances, 71; in Crawfie's book, 153; hopes for reconciliation with royal family, 173; relations with Donoghue, 184; on royal isolation, 259; ER seeks reconciliation with, 343, 346–7; burial plans, 346; ER meets, 346–7; ER agrees allowance to, 347–8; and Edward's death and funeral, 412–15; jewellery and wealth, 415; death and funeral, 417; *The Heart Has Its Reasons*, 343

Winterhalter, Franz, 61

Woman's Own (magazine), 153–4
Woods, Rt Revd Robin, Dean of Windsor, 327, 331, 333–5
World in Action, A (TV programme), 479
Wright, Peter, 311
Wyatt, Lynn Sakowitz, 467
Wyatt, Steven, 467–9
Wyatville, Sir Jeffrey, 36

York Cottage, Sandringham, 14, 508
York House, St James's Palace, 43, 46
York, Prince Andrew, Duke of: born, 284, 290; character and interests, 325, 445, 450–1, 466; welcomes birth of Edward, 325; home life, 341–2; Civil List allowance abolished, 365; education and upbringing, 392, 445–6; serves in Falklands War, 445, 448; naval career, 446; romances, 448; meets Sarah, 449–50; wedding, 451; children, 466; marriage problems, 466–9, 476; separation, 469–71; at Ascot, 475; at Windsor Castle fire, 478; ER pays allowance to, 479; protests at Charles's portrayal of parents, 491; divorce, 529; sympathetically depicted, 530
York, Sarah, Duchess of (*née* Ferguson): meets Andrew, 449–50; character and behaviour, 450–2, 465, 468–70, 474; wedding, 451; books, 452, 529; children, 466, 471; marriage problems, 466–8, 470, 476; extra-marital relations, 467–9, 475–6; separation, 469–72, 474–5; divorce and loss of HRH title, 529; promotional tours, 530; *My Story*, 529
Young, Patsy, 107

Zambia, 382–3
Ziegler, Philip, 117, 345, 347
Zimbabwe (*formerly* Rhodesia): wins independence, 381–4